Hurley Wisconsin: Bedtime Stories

Vice: A Chronology 1942-1982

Published in the United States of America
In 2024
By Gregory J. Landretti

ISBN: 9798882641602

Imprint: Independently published

Dedication

This book is dedicated to Roger B. Johnson, Agent, (Retired)

Wisconsin Department of Revenue

Badge #2

Thank you for keeping the memories alive.

Acknowledgments

I WOULD LIKE TO EXPRESS GRATITUDE to those who helped me with this document. First, of course, is my old work colleague, Roger Johnson. His thoughtful dumpster diving preserved the photographic evidence shown on these pages and provided the motivation to capture the stories.

I want to thank the following for reviewing the original manuscript:
- Paul Sturgul for applying his remarkable memory, relaying family histories, anecdotes, and insights into the motivations for many characters.
- Jimmy Lombardo, who grew up on Silver Street across from the First and Last Chance Tavern, for providing a unique perspective of the "lower block."
- Barry Hautala for sharing insight through his Santini family history.

I am particularly grateful to Andy Abraham. Andy grew up on Silver Street and introduced me to several characters. He knew more about Silver Street than most. His mother was Nora, the operator of Nora's, which still operates today.

I want to express my gratitude for the following for providing candid interviews:
- John Roach Jr. for providing an insight into the motivations and behavior of his father.
- Marcia Lyon and Tony Lysczyk for visiting over coffee at 9 Silver Street.
- Rudi Delfonso for sharing his life experiences on Silver Street.

Thanks to Ernie Moore who tolerated my presence for many hours as I dug through dusty copies of the Iron County Miner. A special thanks to Kathy Byrns, who worked for 30 years in the Hurley City Clerk's office and compiled the historic record of taverns presented in the addenda.

Finally, I am grateful to Linda Paoli for her patient proofreading and her thoughtful encouragement.

Authors Note

THIS WRITING IS PERSONAL. My grandfather, Felippo Alleva, emigrating from Capestrano, Italy, in 1906. He built a house at 110 First Avenue North, just one hundred feet north of the lower blocks of Silver Street in Hurley. In 1929, he bought a tavern at 118 Silver Street, where Nora's Bar currently stands. The Felippo Alleva Saloon was also a pool hall. Two years earlier, in 1927, when Roger "Spike" Severini occupied the building, federal prohibition authorities padlocked the structure.

110 First Avenue--Today

Felippo Alleva wore a broad mustache, and invariably embraced a twisted Toscano between his lips. Customers would gather around a pot-bellied stove in the front of the store to tell stories about lumbering, mining, and the old country. Gossip about Silver Street was rich and colorful. One day a customer, waiting at the counter, asked for service. My grandfather was sitting at the stove and told him matter-of-factly, "You serva you self, if I getta up, I losa my seat."

Fire destroyed the building in 1933, and a reporter stated, "Aside from the loss to the building and contents, it was found that a slot machine was broken open and the money removed from it." After the fire, my grandfather abandoned the pool hall and worked for Marathon Paper until his death in 1944.

Fred Fontecchio Jr.,[1] a second cousin, ran the Club Fiesta in 1949 on the lower block of Silver Street. The tavern was infamous and was subject to raids for gambling and after-hours violations. His father, Fred Fontecchio Sr. was my grandmother's brother. Fred Sr., along with his wife Carmella, ran the Liberty Bell restaurant on 5th Avenue since the beginning of the century. The family operated this business for 95 years.

I grew up in Ironwood, Michigan, one block from the Montreal River – the border between Michigan and Wisconsin. It never occurred to me that Hurley was anything out of the ordinary. The names of the tavernkeepers were common in my household, and they were often family friends or acquaintances. In about 1964, my father brought home three slot machines, which he rescued from under a pile of hay in a dilapidated barn. He said I could have them if I cleaned them up. I brought them back to life, and for many years, my nephews and nieces had endless fun feeding nickels and dimes into the one-arm bandits while waiting for the wheels to chug and the coins to spill.

As a teen, I spent Saturday afternoons digging through scratched 45 rpm records in the back rooms of the Hurley saloons. The rooms smelled like stale beer and old smoke, but the records only cost a nickel. As an older teen, I frequented Nora's tavern to listen to rock and roll bands while watching Nora, always with a cigar in her mouth, working behind the bar. Since my grandfather's pool hall was at the same site 40 years prior, Noras's cigar was thematic.

The motivation for this book began in about 2000. While working at the Wisconsin Department of Revenue in Madison, an agent visited my office with a green scrapbook. His name was Roger Johnson. He was in the liquor enforcement division and held badge #2. He said he heard that I was from Hurley and thought I might be interested in the book. The book contained original mug shots from prostitution raids beginning in 1942 and these photographs provide the main thread of this document. He explained that when the agency moved to a new building, the book was tossed into a dumpster. Roger fished it out. I have dedicated this narrative to Roger for his recognition of the importance of Wisconsin's history and for sharing the photos with me.

Although others have written about Hurley, I felt that the subject needed a deeper review and along with the photographs, the history deserved to be preserved and shared. Thinking it would be a quick project, I scanned and cleaned the photographs and considered alternative layouts. Originally, I felt that the photos would tell their own story and I printed a picture book. I soon realized that without narrative, the photos were only a two dimensional representation of something. To fully appreciate the photos in context, a narrative would be required.

As with so many endeavors, the research took on a life of its own and evolved far beyond the original scope to include news stories, genealogy research, criminal investigations, and interviews. I spent hours perusing old newspapers at the *Iron County* Miner and reels of microfilm at the *Ironwood Daily Globe* and the Carnegie Library. The old Iron County courthouse became a second office as I dug through musty files and dusty court dockets. I interviewed eyewitnesses to sordid events on Silver Street as well as retired tavern owners on the lower block.

I was treated to a number of remarkable coincidences as I uncovered dusty records. For example, while reviewing court records, I opened a docket to a page showing a case where the judge fined my mother $6 for speeding on 2nd Avenue in 1960. I learned that in the 1970's, I lived a few blocks from John Roach, one of the main characters. In 1980, I sat in the courtroom during the trial of Alex Raineri. In 1999, I bought a home in Hurley from Sherman Hart, only to learn that he was the son of "Two-gun" Hart and the nephew of Al Capone.

Preface

THE SCRAPBOOK

THIS STORY IS ABOUT VICE RAIDS in the City of Hurley, the state of Wisconsin, and other related areas. It covers the 40 years between 1942 and 1982, and the stories are presented chronologically. It includes mug shots recorded by state and federal law enforcement agents, guidelines followed by these agents, and the details of each raid. The source of the photographs is an 8 ½ by 11 inch scrapbook. It has an olive-green cover, the word "scrap book" embossed with black ink, and silver duct tape supporting the binding – standard state issue for collecting evidence in 1942. The pages are brown and brittle. All the photographs were black and white and most likely taken with a No. 3 Folding Brownie or the like. Corner clips mark the spot of lost images. The photos were scanned, the dust spots removed, and the exposure was adjusted.

The scrapbook was accompanied by the State Operating Manual used by beverage agents. It consisted of a two-inch thick stack of mimeographed onionskin. The manual covered search and seizure regulations, the use of guns and teargas, investigative strategy, and terminology. Sections of the manual are presented in this document.

THE PRESENTATION

TWO MODELS WERE CONSIDERED FOR presenting the information. The first was to follow the example of Katherine Dunn's *Death Scenes – A Homicide Detectives Scrapbook* which is abrasive and brutal in showing the forensic death photos collected by Detective Jack Huddleston in Los Angeles. This presentation provides no storyline. Instead, it simply places the gore into the reader's mind's-eye.

Another option was to present the photographs with subtitles only, as did Michael Lesy with *Wisconsin Death Trip*, a journal of post-mortem photographs published in 1973. This book also lacks a storyline and rests upon the notion that people in the death state are somehow entertaining. I found it devoid of substance and absent context. Susan Sontag, in her book, *On Photography*, says the Lesy's book, "…is rousing, fashionably pessimistic polemic, and totally whimsical as history."[2] I disagree.

Unlike the books cited above, I found it impossible to leave the story behind because the photographs begged for narrative. *Hurley, Wisconsin: Bedtime Stories* is somewhat of a photo journal to the extent that photos were available and that sources were accurate.

THE MUG SHOTS

THE MUG SHOTS, RETRIEVED from government files, have never been presented to the public. State and federal agents took the photographs at the time of arrest, and it is important to acknowledge that a 'mug shot" does not imply guilt. Identifying the people in the photographs presented an agonizing struggle which I resolved by using the first name and surname initial. The names in the narrative, however, are presented as publicly available in the press. While generational distance may moot the concern for anonymity, I apologize for any discomfort or embarrassment to family members.

* * *

All the mug shots are black and white. They vary in size depending on the film used but most are about 3 x 5 inches or smaller. The photos were either glued, taped, or attached with corner clips. Some have been lost because of handling. The photos contribute to the story because of attributes such as style of clothing, demeanor, and facial expression. Some show disdain, others embarrassment, and some outright antagonism. Some of the women have tightly closed eyes which was intentional and done to hinder recognition. The photos are placed in the year in which they were taken and there is no direct relationship between the narrative and the adjacent photograph.

Example of Scrapbook Page
Actual Six 8 ½" x 11"

THE STORIES

HURLEY HAS A LONG HISTORY of lawlessness, but this narrative covers 1942 to 1982. While the focus is Hurley, stories from other areas are included to place the subject matter in context: Hurley did not have a monopoly on vice. Prostitution and its associated behavior had a broad footprint in Wisconsin and in nearby states. In Wisconsin, most of the raids occurred north of Highway 29 in Superior, Hurley, Wausau, Stevens Point, and Green Bay, as well as rural areas in Lincoln and Langlade Counties. Anecdotal accounts are from Sheboygan, La Crosse, Kenosha, Milwaukee, and Madison.

The front story is a chronological narrative illustrated with images – a photo journal style – of the men and women who traded sex for money. The back story is specific to Hurley and rests on the underlying constructs of sociology, geography, economics, and interpersonal relationships.

THE GEOGRAPHY

GEOGRAPHICALLY, HURLEY IS LOCATED in the northeast corner of Wisconsin. It rests at the intersection of the Gogebic Iron Range to the east and the Penokee Iron Range to the west. The entire ore deposit is 30 miles wide and stretches 80 miles across the shoulders of Wisconsin and Upper Michigan. Tough men worked the mines and the forests, and during the first half of the 20th Century, a gauntlet of strip joints, gambling parlors, and brothels – a total of 84 saloons – spread along Silver Street, with the two lower blocks just west of the Montreal River being the most infamous.

Madison, the state capital, housed the main law enforcement for liquor, gambling, and prostitution. Madison is 275 miles south of Hurley and for many years, access was via a two lane road. It was difficult for law enforcement to patrol the city and in many cases, allies saw them coming, and warned of impending raids.

The Montreal River, on Hurley's east side, was the border between Michigan and Wisconsin. It played an important part in the stories as simply driving across the river invoked federal laws covering interstate transportation.

THE DEMOGRAPHICS

A FEW THOUSAND SOULS wove the social fabric of the hard rock mining community. Their rugged character evolved from long days of arduous work cutting lumber in the thick forests and digging red ore from deep underground. Often, sons followed fathers into the mines, the forests, the markets, and the taverns. Marriage customs reflected cultural and religious norms. Eventually, mixed nationality and religion marriages became more common: Italians married Finns, Poles married Slavs, and Jews married Christians. As society became more mobile, children left for opportunities in larger cities and for more moderate climates.

The population of Hurley decreased about ten percent every ten years: from 3,375 in 1940 to 2,105 in 1980. The most significant decrease was in the 1960s, when the iron ore companies shuttered the mines. The demand for services decreased, and the number of taverns declined. From its inception in 1884 and well into the 1930s, Hurley was known for being tough. Its residents were dauntless, and more specifically, the tavern clientele was often raw and pugnacious.

THE ECONOMICS

L UMBER AND MINING were the main industries in the region. Lumber was transported by water and rail to the Fox River Valley for processing. This period is nicely covered in Edna Ferber's fictional account *Come and Get It*. Most other businesses on the iron range supported the people working in these industries.

As the industrial revolution swept over the country, cars replaced horses, electric bulbs replaced kerosene lanterns, and asphalt replaced dirt. In the late 1930's, news of a European war spread through the country, and the vulnerabilities to war production became apparent. America needed steel and Washington focused on iron ore. The country needed healthy workers – free from disease – so as not to interrupt the flow of ore to the steel mills in Cleveland, Pittsburgh, Youngstown, and Gary. The need for healthy workers motivated federal and state authorities to cooperate in raids on Hurley to mitigate venereal disease resulting from prostitution.

PROLOGUE

THE MOTIVATING THREAT

AFTER WORLD WAR I, THE UNITED STATES carefully monitored the politics in Europe. In 1933, they noted the Nazi regime's agenda to construct the 3rd Reich. The rise of fascism pinnacled in September 1939, when Hitler invaded Poland with a devastating offensive maneuver. Fear rippled through Europe. Two days later, France and England declared war on Germany. At the same time, President Franklin Roosevelt told Americans about the Nazi aggression but pledged adherence to the Neutrality Act passed in 1937. However, the U.K was in trouble and Roosevelt began advocating for the Lend-Lease program in late 1939 and early 1940. By September 1940, equipment began flowing to the United Kingdom. In December 1940 Roosevelt referred the United States as the "Arsenal of Democracy" in one of his radio fireside chats. This was a turning point, and the speech primed the war machine. The U.S. needed steel.

THE FEDERAL PERSPECTIVE

IN 1939, CONGRESS AMENDED the Venereal Disease Act of 1918 (VDA), bolstering state authority to deal with this public health issue. On December 7, 1940, Assistant Surgeon General Vonderlehr urged comprehensive reforms to control venereal disease in the military. The VDA was the most significant effort to prevent sexually transmitted diseases in history and it was administered by the United States Public Health Service. The federal government made every effort to illustrate the magnitude of the issue. For example, James Stewart, MD, the State Health Commissioner of Missouri, reported that of the first 1,070,000 men examined by the Selective Service, there were 83,000 cases of syphilis and gonorrhea. The Health Service referred to prostitutes and all "promiscuous" women as "reservoirs of infection." Nonetheless, the message was mixed, as wartime propaganda extolled the virtues of masculine sexuality and encouraged women to provide comfort at USO dances, to serve as military nurses, and to volunteer with the Red Cross.[3]

* * *

In January, Surgeon General Thomas Parran of the U.S. Army warned against increased dangers from prostitution. He posited that it was "one of our most expanded industries."[4] He also said that "venereal disease today is still the greatest cause of non-effectiveness in the army." Parran reported, "under the selective service act, physicians had found 47,000 men suffering from syphilis of every million examined."[5]

* * *

Prostitution has long been known to be a lucrative "business" requiring limited skill and no training. Some have described it as "doing what comes naturally, only with increased enthusiasm." Undoubtedly, specific types of prostitutes, such as streetwalkers and call girls, have existed throughout the ages. As early as 1910, concern was expressed about indentured sex slaves at the International Congress in Paris, referred to as "white slavery."[6] Specifically, this was a situation where predators would coerce young women into living accommodations that eventually carried an expectation of prostitution. Under threat from their keepers and with nowhere to go, they would become sex slaves in exchange for food and shelter. In some cases, pimps would provide drugs for addiction and control. In other cases, prostitutes turned to drugs as a coping strategy, and some addicts turned to prostitution for drug money. It was this confluence of vice that authorities sought to uproot and eliminate. During the 1940s in Wisconsin, law enforcement focused on in-house prostitutes (inmates) and their keepers.

* * *

In early 1941, Representative Andrew J. May from Kentucky, introduced legislation making vice activities near military bases a federal offense. Known as the May Act, it became law in July 1941 and created "moral zones" forbidding alcohol and prostitution around military training facilities. This forced prostitutes to flee to safer territories, like northern Wisconsin.[7] Apparently, Representative May was not exempt from vice. At age 72, a judge sent Andrew May to a federal prison in 1947 after being convicted of war bribes.[8]

* * *

As the United States entered World War II, legislative changes became more aggressive, and the anti-prostitution laws evolved into the Public Health Service Act of 1944.[9] The FBI informed local law enforcement officials that during WWI, social diseases ranked a close third behind battlefield casualties and influenza in loss of resources.

THE STATE PERSPECTIVE

THE DEFENSE DEPARTMENT KNEW the importance of industry on the south shore of Lake Superior. The resources were documented on August 3, 1942, by Rod Van Every, writing for the *Wisconsin State Journal*: "Within a radius of 47 miles of Hurley, 20,000 men are directly employed in war work at iron mines, a powder plant, foundry, paper mills, logging, electrical power utility, and on Great Lakes boats." He then itemized the employment as 6,500 employed in the iron ore mines in Gogebic County, Michigan; 1,900 working in mines in Wisconsin near Hurley; 600 at work in the DuPont Powder plant at Barksdale; 100 employed in a Hurley foundry; 150 workers in the Lake Superior District Power Company in Ashland; 200 men in the Penokee Veneer Company in Mellen; 200 workers in the Marathon Paper Company in Ashland; and thousands more in logging and lumbering activities for pulp, paper, and lumber mills "and still more" at iron ore docks at Ashland. He also referred to the 5,000 lake vessels put into the port annually.

President Roosevelt ordered the Department of Health, along with the FBI, to ensure the health of workers in these industries. The directive quickly spread from Washington to state and local government.[10]

* * *

In early 1942, Janet S. Burgoon, the regional supervisor of the Federal Social Protection Section, asked Wisconsin state officials for help. She wrote, "In order to deal adequately with this problem as a war measure, the policy of repression of prostitution must be adopted nationally." She said, "The Beverage and Cigarette Tax Division of the Wisconsin State Treasury Department is to be commended for the excellent work which they have done to date in bringing the state in line with this federal policy. However, it has come to our attention that there are flagrant violations in Hurley where it is alleged a substantial number of taverns operate openly as houses of prostitution. May this office call upon you for appropriate action in Hurley at an early date in as much as the taverns in the state of Wisconsin are under your jurisdiction?"[11] Federal authorities now held Hurley in the spotlight.

* * *

In January 1942, Wisconsin's Governor Heil invited Iron County Sheriff Sam Giovanoni and District Attorney[12] J. C. Raineri to meet with state officials in Wausau to discuss military defense plans.[13] It would soon become apparent that the governor's invitation was neither collaborative nor benevolent.

In addition to Hurley, the federal government wanted to eliminate prostitution near the Badger Ammunition Plant near Merrimac, about 25 miles northwest of Madison. *The Capital Times* described prostitution as a "very dangerous foe" and that it can be as "deadly in its effect as enemy artillery or poison." The writer described how families use trailers when working for military establishments and how prostitutes also use trailers to provide service. He stated, "The honesty and decency of the average trailer home and the average tavern become the camouflage of illegal activities."[14]

Dr. C. A. Harper, Wisconsin's chief health officer, suggested that mayors within a 25-mile radius of Merrimac (near the Badger Ammunition Plant) "give serious consideration to ways and means of 'prohibiting entirely and completely all phases of prostitution.'"[15]

* * *

In 1942, the *Taxation Department Enforcement Manual* stated, "Prostitution has existed in every country and in every age in the recorded history of man. *Webster's Dictionary* defines a prostitute as "A woman who offers herself indiscriminately to sexual intercourse for hire." Wisconsin statutes[16] expand the definition to include "any female who intentionally does any of the following: has or offers to have non-marital sexual intercourse for money; or is an inmate of a place of prostitution." The taxation manual noted a reduction in prostitution over the years saying, "The practice of prostitution in Wisconsin was formerly much more widespread than it is at present – at least as far as conventional 'houses of prostitution' are concerned."

The *Manual* also described conditions and locations where prostitution could be found. It stated, "Wherever there were large numbers of men and a shortage of women, prostitutional practices flourished. In the far north, Hurley, Hayward, and Superior were flooded with miners, loggers, and sailors. Lacrosse, Beloit, Green Bay, and Milwaukee, as bustling rail, and shipping centers, provided a steady stream of lonesome males well provided with money. There were always places in these areas where, for a price, these men were provided with willing women. Such conditions were generally accepted (or at least tolerated by the public at the time)." Although the *Manual* specifically mentioned Superior, Medford, Antigo, Milwaukee, Kenosha, and Hurley, Hurley would receive most of the attention.[17]

* * *

In October 1942, the federal government praised Wisconsin State Treasurer John Smith for "ridding Wisconsin defense areas of prostitutes." Smith was a teetotaler, described by a United Press (UP) reporter as "white-haired and bombastic." Encouraged by the support of the Fed, Smith suggested that "streetwalkers be forced into military units under the command of women officers." He went on to say, "This is the time for realism. Men can't control prostitution – won't control it. Women can. You can't get prostitutes to work in factories. If they wanted to work, they wouldn't be on the streets. But you can't leave them on the streets. We clean them out of one place, and they show up in another. It's just like a game of ring-around-the-rosy." [18]

Smith said that if prostitutes worked in factories, "they would be under the control of men and that wouldn't work out. You couldn't keep track of them at night."

The UP article implied that Wisconsin was free from prostitution. The writer said, "Smith rid Wisconsin taverns of women soon after he took office in 1938. When prostitutes followed war workers and soldiers into the state, he was asked by the federal government to clean them out. With his lieutenant, John W. Roach, chief of the beverage tax division, he swept down on the state's boom towns and drove out unattached women. Trailers were stopped at the state line and if owned by prostitutes, they were turned back."[19]

* * *

Despite denials of vice, the *Taxation Department Enforcement Manual* stated: "In Wisconsin there has been a steadily increasing awareness on the part of the public of the evils of prostitution. The public today generally agrees that where there is prostitution there inevitably follows venereal disease, moral degeneration, bribery by cash or favors, and general deterioration of law enforcement from the beat patrolman to the highest courts. Today, prostitution as a commercial venture has been eliminated from most areas, being confined chiefly to Hurley, Superior, Medford, Antigo, Milwaukee, and Kenosha – and even these places are not operating on a scale such as they did in the recent past. The investigators of the Beverage and Cigarette Tax Division have been one of the most effective weapons and controlling commercial prostitution."

* * *

During the early 20th Century, it was a commonly held belief the houses of ill repute helped "protect the wives and daughters of respectful persons." Later, in the 1950s, Representative Estes Kefauver from Tennessee led a federal investigation into organized crime and held hearings throughout the country. During the Kefauver investigation in Superior, Wisconsin, the committee heard from prominent citizens and elected officials, including the district attorney. While they acknowledged the existence of several "notorious" houses of prostitution, they denied any connections with syndicate crime, white slavery, or corruption of public authority.[20]

THE TENOR OF THE ENFORCEMENT AGENCY

T HE STATE TREASURER CREATED the Beverage Tax Division in 1933, and as the name suggested, its purpose was to enforce the tax levied on alcoholic beverages. In 1939, when the state also imposed a tax on cigarettes, the Treasurer's Office changed the name to the Division of Beverage and Cigarette Taxes. The *Taxation Department Enforcement Manual* guided agents in investigating, gathering evidence, arresting, and prosecuting violators. Further, it cataloged the local perspective toward vice within the state. For example, in some municipalities, local law enforcement was aware of prostitution, but few considered it a serious issue. The state manual described how the public tolerated prostitution and stated that many believed it was necessary to satisfy the needs of "rough, rugged men." The public health authorities and moral crusaders who argued that prostitution "spread venereal disease, moral degeneration, and bribery" were in the minority.

However, a powerful federal law hovered over prostitution purveyors like a wet wool blanket. The Mann Act, also known as the White-Slave Traffic Act of 1910, intended to "Further regulate interstate and foreign commerce by prohibiting the transportation therein for immoral purposes of women and girls, and for other purposes."[21] Most people in the country believed that transporting or enticing women into prostitution was morally reprehensible, and judges treated the violation severely.

THE MAN FOR THE JOB

WISCONSIN STATE TREASURER, John M. Smith, appointed John Roach, 39, the arduous task of taming Hurley in preparation for World War II. Roach was the chief of the Beverage Tax Division of the State Treasurer's Office and he found himself up against Hurley, the little city that summarily ignored directives from Madison. Roach was the man for the job. He was tough, street-smart, and knew the territory. In 1942, he travelled more work miles than any other state employee, mostly terrorizing tavern keepers and prostitutes.[22] Roach vowed to pressure Hurley into submission.

In 1939, Kenosha Assemblyman Matt G. Siebert, introduced legislation to limit the number of Class B tavern licenses in Wisconsin municipalities. Governor Heil signed the bill which became known at the Siebert Law. This set up a conflict that would resonate in Hurley for several years.

With an opening salvo in early 1942, Roach told Mayor Bonacci that Hurley violated the Siebert Law and ordered him to decrease the number of taverns from 84 to 78.[23] These six licenses would lead to threats, conflicts, arguments, and retaliations.

Smith and Roach met with 200 resort and tavern operators from Vilas and Iron Counties at Little Bohemia Resort in Manitowish Waters during the second week of May 1942.[24] Coincidently, just eight years before, in 1934, the FBI had a shootout with the John Dillinger Gang at the same location. That raid failed, and both John Dillinger and Lester Joseph Gillis "Baby Face Nelson" escaped.[25] Smith and Roach hoped for better results.

At the same time, Roach met with Hurley officials and tavernkeepers and expressed concern about the relationship between taverns, prostitution, and disease. Rather than asking for cooperation, he threatened to "personally prosecute" if they exceeded the tavern quota. He then met individually with Hurley's city clerk in Manitowish "away from influence." Roach scolded him for issuing 84 tavern licenses in 1941. He said that city officials would be subject to prosecution "on the charge of malfeasance" if they issued the same number in 1942. This threat spawned a two-month debate amongst council members about property ownership, the quality of establishments, and the integrity of tavernkeepers.

The underlying issues were livelihoods, friendships, loyalties, and tax revenue. Council members chafed at the idea of restricting the number of licenses. Some said they would comply with the law and respect the state mandate. Others said they would "take the chance on going to jail" because "the city needed the revenue." One council member quipped that he "wished he had gone fishing the day that he decided to run for office."[26] As the council waited for the official quota, they agreed to review each application individually "so that the 'undesirables' could be 'weeded out' at the same time."[27]

The economic conditions on the iron range were fragile, and taverns played an important part, especially in Hurley. The *Iron River Miner* reported, "The 'economic system' of the burg is tied up with taverns. The buildings occupied by these taverns could not be used for any other purpose. They are owned in many instances by the leaders in the community. Now comes a law that says the city council must reduce the number of its taverns to 78."

Because of the ferocity of the debate, several Hurley officials met with State Treasurer John Smith and Attorney General[28] John Martin in Madison. They left with the belief that the city could issue the "questionable six licenses" since they were in the approval process when the Siebert Law was passed. Without hesitation, the city council granted the pending licenses, bringing the total to 84 for 1942.[29]

When John Roach heard this news, he was furious and ordered the mayor to rescind the licenses immediately. Although the mayor explained his understanding, he promised to void the approvals, nonetheless. Before he could act, however, Roach sent agents to every tavern in Iron County, telling operators to "make their taverns more acceptable to the public or face closure by the health department." Although the agents worked the county for a week and focused on taverns in Hurley, nothing suggested that prostitution was an issue.

THE DISPOSITION OF PROSTITUTION IN 1942

IN JUNE 1942, JOHN ROACH began a campaign to close the reported 110 houses of prostitution in Wisconsin. In the middle of the month, Brown and Langlade Counties told him they were free of "all houses of prostitution operated in connection with taverns." Marathon County reported that they closed five establishments.[30]

On June 30, after a tour of northern Wisconsin, Roach reported, "The vast majority of the houses of prostitution which have been running in connection with taverns in Wisconsin have been cleaned out." He also said that "sheriffs of various counties had pledged '100 percent' cooperation with the Beverage Tax Department in the drive to rid the state of such houses." In addition to Marathon County, he said that Langlade, Portage, and Shawano counties had been "cleaned up" in the past few weeks. Roach was confident that he had the problem of prostitution in Wisconsin under control although he qualified his position, saying "while there might be a few isolated places where such houses are still run with taverns, his agents were on the watch and as soon as he received information about them, he would take immediate steps to arrest the occupants and close down the houses."[31]

At the end of July, journalist William T. Evjue praised Roach in *The Capital Times* for closing three houses of prostitution in Jefferson County, east of Madison. Roach told Evjue that an establishment run by Hollis M. Caves in the unincorporated community of Kroghville was "the hardest spot they have ever worked on."[32] In that case, Roach arrested two woman and the proprietor of a tavern.[33]

It was apparent that John Roach was unaware of the challenge he would face in Hurley.

THE DEFINITIONS

MANY DIFFERENT TERMS DESCRIBE the places where prostitutes do business. Some are defined explicitly by law, but euphemisms are common. The list of synonyms includes: whorehouse, house of ill repute, house of ill fame, house of evil repute, house of assignation, house of accommodation, house in the suburbs, house of civil reception, jag house, house of pleasure, house of profession, house of resort, house of sale, house of sin, house of tolerance, immoral house, jag house, joy house, knocking shop, ladies college, loose house, naught house, bawdy house, roadhouse, cathouse, bordello, brothel, house of prostitution, disorderly house, house of disorderly conduct, a den of iniquity, house of assignation, hothouse, parlor house, pushing academy, rap club, call house, cat house, common house, crib, and dollhouse. A collection of establishments is a red-light district, the tenderloin, or a prostitution quarter.

The colloquial terms for prostitutes include sex worker, call girl, hooker, streetwalker, woman of ill repute, lady of pleasure. Contextually related terms include courtesan, model, escort, masseuse, tom, woman on the game, hustler, tart, woman of the streets, lady of the night, scarlet woman, chippy, moll, harlot, trollop, and wench.

The male customers are referred to as a john, customer, trick, buddy, or date.

THE TERRITORY

SILVER STREET BEGINS at the Montreal River, the border between Michigan and Wisconsin, and ends five blocks to the west at Fifth Avenue. In 1942, it was lined with small shops, grocers, clothing stores, banks, and taverns…mostly taverns. The lower two blocks, from the river to Second Avenue was an infamous stretch lined by strip clubs and bars. Some taverns stretched a block north and south of Second Avenue. The characters were homeowners, merchants,

Silver Street Lower Blocks Looking West from Trestle circa 1945

11

bootleggers, bartenders, gamblers, tourists, dancers, performers, prostitutes, and drunks.

Italians frequented the north side of the block between First and Second Avenue, while Finns frequented the south side. This orientation was because of social preferences rather than temperment. The lower block between the Montreal River and First Avenue was the most notorious geography.

THE KEY PLAYERS

THE KEY PLAYERS IN THIS 40-year drama would be a handful of characters from Hurley and Madison. When benign, it would be like an athletic event with changes in offense and defense and alternating strategies. When malignant, it would be war, complete with tactical maneuvers, machine guns, tear gas, and barricades.

On the offense were state and local authorities including the Beverage Tax Division of the State Treasury Department, led by John Roach, Clyde Tutton, and David Prichard,[34] operating from the Wilson Street Office Building in Madison. At the local level, the offense included the Iron County Sheriff, the Iron County district attorney, and various judges including Iron County Court Judge Richard Trembath and Circuit Court Judge Lewis J. Charles.

The defense was ironically played by actual "offenders." They consisted of a group of Silver Street tavern owners referred to as the "usual suspect" or the "players," in this narrative. They include characters such as Jack "Jackpot" Gasbarri, William "Blackie" Matrella, Joe and Dominic Vita, Dominic Napoli, John Carli, and Fred Fontecchio.

Alex Raineri played both offense and defense.

The two most consistent and colorful characters were John Roach and Alex Raineri. Roach would span the period from 1942 through 1948 as a beverage agent, a tough enforcer, a military officer, and a liquor salesman. Raineri's tenure spanned the entire period from 1942 through 1982, holding the positions of police officer, private attorney, district attorney, state legislator, judge, and finally, federal prisoner.

SILVER STREET: CAST & CREW

MOST CHARACTERS IN THIS STORY have ancestors from Finland, Poland, and Italy. The Italians, however, predominated the tavern industry on Silver Street, and examining the panoply of characters and their genealogical attributions is illustrative. The main text describes the principal characters to cement their role in events. Descriptions of the minor characters are presented in the endnotes at their first occurrence in the narrative so as not to distract from the flow.

The Silver Street Italians originated from two predominant areas of Italy: Asiago and Capestrano. The Asiago Plateau, in the province of Veneto in Northern Italy, comprises seven towns. Surnames from the Asiago region included Carli, Brunello, Mosele, and Rodeghiero.

Capestrano, a small village with a population of 877, is in the Province of L'Aquila, Abruzzo, 70 miles east of Rome. Surnames from Capestrano included Fontecchio, Santini, Gasbarri, Colasacco, Di Ulio, DeRubeis, Gentile, Stella, and Alleva.

Sons with these surnames are carved in marble and granite in the Hurley cemetery. The daughters are there too, but often they rest under Finnish, English, or Polish surnames. We can do nothing for the dead but exhume the stories in their memory.

Note: Should you not be interested in this genealogy, you can skip directly to the chapter entitled 1942. However, be forewarned that you will miss much of the depth and richness of the stories that follow.

The Raineri's

The Father – Joseph Raineri, Sr.

Joseph Raineri, Sr. was born in Italy. He migrated to France and later to Buenos Aires, Argentina. He arrived in Hurley in 1898. In 1903, he married Theresa Galdabini of Hurley and lived in the Village of Gile, two miles west of Hurley, where they raised their children. Raineri operated a small grocery store in the village, but after suffering a third fire in 1911, he moved his business to the Lucia building at the corner of 3rd Avenue and Silver Street. Joseph and his wife had three children: Angeline, Joseph Jr., and Alexander.

Angeline would eventually graduate from St. Mary's College in Notre Dame and marry Harry Meier, who would become coroner for Iron County.

Joseph Jr. was born on July 1, 1908, and Alexander was born on September 17, 1918. Joseph Jr. and his younger brother Alex would be key players on the Silver Street stage over the next several decades.

Joseph Sr. ran unsuccessfully for county sheriff in 1920, 1925, and 1928. With his grocery store on the corner of Silver Street, vandals stole his car twice in 1924: once in August and then again in October. With the election loss in 1928, Joseph Sr. abandoned the political effort, but his experience influenced his sons. Joseph Jr. and Alex grew up in the crucible of Silver Street politics and quickly learned how the businesses operated.

During the early 1920s, Joseph Sr. built four brick buildings at 17, 19, 21 & 23 Silver Street and leased these buildings, on the south side of the lower block, to tavernkeepers employed in the business of liquor, gambling, and prostitution. He rented the property at 17 Silver Street to Ralph De Massi, 19 Silver Street to Hjalmer Matson, 21 to Hjalmer Sakonen, and 23 to Jerry Lawler.

On December 28, 1926, federal authorities conducted the largest illegal liquor raid on Hurley's Silver Street in several years. U.S. Marshalls served temporary injunctions on 29 establishments, and all were scheduled to be padlocked within 30 days. While Joseph Raineri, Sr. was contesting his last run for sheriff, he learned that his properties were listed in this raid. Padlocking would be a devastating blow to his income. Three days after learning about the injunctions, Judge Risjord ruled that Raineri lost the run for sheriff.

Joseph Raineri was not a quitter. In 1927, he sold his grocery business to the Hurley Meat and Grocery Company and began an automobile dealership. In early March 1927, Federal Judge Claude Luse heard the padlocking case against two buildings, 17 and 19 Silver Street, in the U.S. District Court in Superior. Raineri's attorney presented witnesses who testified that both buildings were under contract for sale. He explained that the only reason they were not sold was that the defendant's wife was ill and unable to attend the signing. By the end of the day, the judge only padlocked one tavern.

By this time, Hurley had already gained a national reputation for vice, and in a March 12 article, a United Press reporter referred to Hurley as "Tijuana of the North." Shortly after, Ray J. Nye, the federal prohibition director, commented, "There is just one way to clean up Hurley, and that is through the padlock."

The Older Son – Joseph C. Raineri (J. C.)

Joseph C. Raineri earned a degree from the University of Notre Dame in 1930, the last year that Knute Rockne coached the Fighting Irish. He earned a law degree from the University of Minnesota and passed the Wisconsin Bar exam in July 1932. To avoid confusion with his father's name, he used the "J. C." or "Jay." As a young lawyer practicing in Hurley, he followed his father's politics of the Republican Party. In 1932, he introduced John B. Chapple, a Republican candidate for U.S. Senate from Ashland, during a presentation at the Iron County Memorial Building.

In December 1932, J. C. tried his first case in Iron County. The court appointed him to represent Joe May, who shot Alfred Wisnewski through the hand at his shack near Sand Rock in the Town of Oma. The district attorney was R. C. Trembath (who would later become the Iron County judge). When Trembath asked May why he shot Wisnewski, he replied, "He beat me up so bad I didn't know what I was doing, and I was a little bit drunk." The judge sentenced May to four months in the county jail.

In November 1934, Trembath squared off against J. C. in the Iron County district attorney race. Raineri won by a margin of 200 votes out of 3,900.

Joseph Raineri would not live to see his sons apply the lessons he provided on the streets of Hurley. On November 21, 1935, while making firewood, he slipped under the wheels of a truck and was crushed. The Iron County authorities who investigated the accident were his son, District Attorney J. C. Raineri, and his son-in-law, Coroner Harry Meier, who was married to his daughter Angeline. Within two years of his father's death, the Hurley Chamber of Commerce Board of Directors accepted J. C. as a member.

In August 1937, District Attorney J. C. Raineri delivered a warrant for Hugo Di Ulio, the former Hurley City Clerk, for embezzling $1,500. Di Ulio absconded with the money and moved to Milwaukee, where he worked as a representative of brewery interests in Wisconsin. He was eventually found guilty and sentenced to 1 – 3 years at the state prison at Waupun.

J. C. never lost interest in politics and never wavered from his father's political philosophy. In 1939, he attended a "Young Republican" convention in Sheboygan. In 1940, he was appointed to the advisory committee for the campaigns of both Wendell L. Willkie, the presidential nominee and for Walter Goodland, the candidate for Lieutenant Governor

Because of a medical condition, J. C. moved to Scottsdale, Arizona, and passed the Bar Exam in 1953.[35] He practiced law as late as 1971. In 1967, the Arizona State Bar admitted his son Anthony. J. C. died in Scottsdale in August 1992 at the age of 84. J. C. practiced civil and criminal law during his career, was well-regarded, and enjoyed a reputation as a conscientious attorney.

The Younger Son – Alexander J. Raineri

Alexander J. Raineri was born on September 17, 1918, just two months before the end of World War I and ten years after Joseph Jr.

Alex attended Lincoln High School in Hurley and lettered in football and basketball with his classmate Richard Matrella. In November 1935, while in high school, Matrella served as chair of American Education Week, and Alex presented a talk on "The School and Social Change." His classmate Richard Trembath, (the son of Judge R. C. Trembath) gave a talk on "The School and Democracy."

In June 1936, Hurley shared the range basketball championship with neighboring Wakefield, Michigan. The speaker was Edward W. "Moose" Krause, who lettered in four sports at Notre Dame. Krause graduated in 1934, just a few years behind John Roach. At the time of the speech, Krause was coaching St. Mary's College at Winona and prophetically "drew parallels between the attitude of the successful man in business life declaring that men must battle for their opportunities in either case." As co-captains of the time, Alex Raineri and Dominic Santini accepted the trophy at the end of Krause's presentation. (Krause later became the head basketball coach at the University of Notre Dame from 1946 to 1951).

In the family tradition, J. C. drove his brother Alex to Notre Dame in September 1936. Alex remained at Notre Dame through 1937. In 1938, he studied law at DePaul University in Chicago but remained active in Hurley events. In 1939, Alex served on the Salvation Army annual fund drive committee. In 1942, at age 24, he held a temporary assignment as the undersheriff of Iron County. This temporary job set the stage for the introduction of adversaries. In his role as undersheriff, Alex would take orders from a state beverage agent named John Roach.[36]

In 1943, Alex married Doris Bertagnoli while attending DePaul University Law School.[37] Alex graduated from DePaul and passed the Wisconsin Bar Exam in July. In October 1943, he served in the Army at Fort Leonard Wood, Missouri, with a division of combat engineers. After discharge, Alex went into business under Raineri & Raineri with his older brother J. C.[38] The brothers occupied an office in the Paul Building on Silver Street in Hurley. In November, Alex won a seat in the Wisconsin Assembly representing Iron and Vilas Counties. The position had been vacated by Margaret Pinkley Varda, who served as the Progressive Party representative. The

Progressive Party dissolved in 1944, and rather than running for re-election, Varda joined the U.S. Army as a WAC with the rank of Private and served in Europe.[39]

In August 1944, Alex and his wife had a daughter. In addition to his other roles, he was now a father. Alex continued with his civic duty by serving as chairman for War Bond Sales in Iron County in November 1944, service for which he received the President Eisenhower Prayer Award.[40] In November 1944, he was re-elected to the Wisconsin Assembly, where the Republicans held 88 of the 100 seats. Further, they controlled the Senate with 27 of the 33 seats. Walter Goodland, a Republican, was elected governor. At the federal level, the La Follette's disbanded the Progressive party and ran Robert La Follette Jr. for re-election as a Republican. He was defeated in the primary for the United States Senate by the infamous Joe McCarthy, who, coincidentally, was from Grand Chute, near Appleton in John Roach's backyard.

Raineri's term in the Assembly ended in 1947. At this time, his brother J. C. vacated the position of District Attorney in Iron County for health reasons, and Alex won the race. He was sworn into office in January 1948. On January 14, in his first public appearance, he met with Sheriff John Shea, the Chief of Police, Judge Trembath, and Hurley tavernkeepers and warned them to stop serving liquor to minors.

Alex would continue to be a presence in the story of Hurley and eventually, through a twisted turn of events, would become its most infamous victim.

The Gasbarri's

The Father – James Gasbarri

James (Vincenzo) Gasbarri operated the Flame Tavern at 15 Silver Street and was first arrested in the summer of 1942 in the first John Roach raid. He was born on January 26, 1886, in Capestrano, Italy, and arrived at Hurley in 1913. His first wife, Elizabeth D'Angela died about 1920, leaving James with two sons: John J. (b. 1913) and Louis (b. 1918). In 1923, James married Marie Brighenti.[41] The 1940 census shows that James and Mary lived at 182 First Avenue, one block off Silver Street. Gasbarri was a miner and tavernkeeper. Mary died in 1957 at 73, and her obituary[42] showed that she had five children and four foster children, including John (Jack) and Louis Gasbarri. James Gasbarri died on May 24, 1963, at 77.[43] His obituary reported that he had two sons, Jack and Louis, both living in Hurley. Jack was commonly known as "Jackpot."

The Oldest Son – John (Jack) "Jackpot" J. Gasbarri

Jack Gasbarri was born in 1913 in Ironwood. The 1940 census shows Jack and his young brother Louis lived together at 9 Silver Street in Hurley. In 1942, Jack was associated with Jackpot's Flame Bar, the Club Carnival in 1963, and the Show bar in 1956. John (Jack) "Jackpot" Gasbarri died on November 24, 1975, at the age of 61. Jack's first wife was Lois aka Frenchy. His second wife was Cira, and they married in 1968.

The Younger Son – Louis P. Gasbarri

Louis was born on August 16, 1918, in Ironwood. The 1940 census shows his occupation as bartender and his residence as 9 Silver Street. He lived with a group of young people, including his

17

brother Jack and his Jacks wife, Lois. Louis married Adina Emily Augusta Klug in January 1942. Louis and Adina worked at the Red Feather in 1955 and the Cactus Bar in 1973. Louis died on June 18, 1998, at age 79, and Adina died in 2015 at 95.

The Vita's

The Father – Clemento Vita

Clemento Vita was born in 1879 in Italy and emigrated to the United States in 1905. His wife, Mary, who was 12 years younger, emigrated in 1913 with her son Joseph. Clement was employed at Port Chester, New York, where he worked as a gardener, construction worker, and factory worker. They moved to Hurley in 1920.[44] Except for Joseph, the other children were born in New York. By 1930, the family included: Joseph, 24; Dominico, 16; Anthony, 14; and Lena, 12. They moved to Hurley and lived at 307 Third Avenue North. Clement purchased 21 Silver Street and opened the Hi-Ho Bar. Clement Vita died July 7, 1976, at 97, in Hurley.

The Older Son – Joseph Vita

In 1942, Joe Vita, 36, operated the Hi-Ho at 21 Silver Street, likely in partnership with his father. Joe is at the center of numerous misadventures throughout this story. He died July 18, 1970, at age 64, in Hurley.

The Younger Son – Dominic (Domenic) Vita

In 1940, Dominic opened The Swing Club opposite the N. W. Depot in Hurley at 507 Granite Street.[45] The Swing Club, although not located on Silver Street., was usually included in the raids on Hurley. Dominic Vita died in July 1987 in Hurley.

The Carli's

John Battista Longo Carli was born on 1880 in Asiago, Vicenza, Italy. Orsolina Domenica Vescovi was born in 1881 in Asiago. They married in 1902 in Ironwood, Michigan, and had four children: Andrew Walter "Chink" in 1900; Arthur Anthony in 1915; Antoinette Jean in 1918; and Alfred Dominic in 1919. Orsolina died in 1936 at 34, and John Battista died in 1953 at 73.

The oldest son, Andrew Walter "Chink," plays a significant part in the story of Hurley.

The Father – Andrew Walter "Chink"

Andrew Walter "Chink" married Veronica "Verna" Louise Sekelsky in 1922 in Montreal, Wisconsin. Chink and Verna had two sons: John Stephen, born in 1922, and Arthur Walter, born in 1923. In 1930 the family lived at 107 Bonnie Street in Jessieville Location.

In 1930, taverns clustered around the intersection of Bonnie Street and West Street at the base of Jessieville hill. In 1933, Andrew "Chink" Carli worked as a beer retailer out of his home on Bonnie Street[46], referred to as the Andrew W. Carli beer garden.[47] In 1934, the Ironwood city commission listed a beer business to Andrew for 107 E. Bonnie Street and John A. Carli[48] at 111 E. Bonnie Street. Chink's business was known as the Gogebic Flying Club from 1935-1937 and was located at 107 Bonnie Street. John Carli's establishment was the Little Monte Carlo at 102 South West

Street.[49]

In 1939, Chink tried to convert the Gogebic Flying Club from a beer and wine bar to a tavern. However, the City of Ironwood denied the request until someone abandoned a license.[50] In late 1939, Carli wrote a letter to the city commission telling them that he purchased the tavern of Joseph Klimanek at 412 W. Silver Street in Hurley and that he wanted to transfer the business to 107 Bonnie in Ironwood. The commission chair replied, "I think there are ample taverns in Ironwood. I presume this man sold out because it wasn't a paying business. When they retire from the business for lack of support, I feel we should reduce the number."[51]

In October 1940, the Hurley City Council granted a bartender license to Chink's wife, Verna[52], and a week later, they gave her a tavern operator's license.[53] On May 16, 1940, the Hurley City Council issued Chink[54] a tavern license for 413 Silver Street. He named it Chink's Bar[55] In 1942, it was one of Hurley's 83 taverns. In July 1943, he received a Combination Class B Tavern license. In September 1943, Carli transferred his liquor license to 201 Silver Street at the corner of Silver Street and Second Avenue, a structure called the Old Office Building.[56] He named the business Carli's Bar.

Between 1946 and 1949, Chink opened the Bowery at 24 Silver Street, and by 1951, his family moved to 308 North Second Avenue. Andrew Walter "Chink" lived hard and died in 1954 at 52.

The Mother – Verna Carli

Verna Sekelsky was born in 1903 in Wisconsin to parents who emigrated from Yugoslavia. At age 19, she married Andrew Walter Carli. She helped Andrew and her son operate the business. Verna Sekelsky died in 1968 in St. Louis, Minnesota, at 65.

The Older Son – Arthur Walter Carli

Arthur Walter Carli was born in 1923 in Ironwood. In April 1943, he served in the Army with the 1276 Combat Engineers in Europe and was discharged in January 1946. Arthur worked for American Motors in Kenosha and as a security guard at the Golden Nugget in Reno, Nevada. He returned to Hurley and worked at the White Pine Copper mine. In 1967, the Iron County Law Enforcement Commission, chaired by Felix Patritto, hired Arthur A. Carli, 43, as chief deputy and Ronald F. Morzenti, 26, as deputy for the Iron County Sheriff's Department. Carli lived at 126 First Avenue North and Morzenti at Iron Belt Avenue in Montreal.[57] In November 1976, Arthur Carli was elected to the position of Iron County Sheriff. In 1992, President George Bush awarded the Presidential Unit Citation to his military unit. Arthur Walter Carli died at 81 in Grand Rapids, Minnesota.

The Younger Son – John Stephen Carli

John Stephen Carli[58] was born on September 11, 1922.[59] He served in the Navy from January 13, 1941, to January 26, 1942. John was tough and mercurial. He led a tumultuous life; most of his activity focused on Silver Street. John Stephen Carli died in 2001 at 79 and is buried at the Southern Arizona Veterans Memorial Cemetery in Sierra Vista, Arizona.

The Matrella's

The Father – Richard "Blackie" Matrella Sr.

Richard "Blackie" Matrella Sr. was born in Italy in 1878 and emigrated in 1903. He worked as a miner for the Cary Mine. According to the 1910 census, Richard was married to Mary Kietho[60] and had a son, William, born in 1908. The 1930 Census, Richard shows that he was a widower and, in addition to three daughters and William, he had three other sons: Fredy (b. 1904), Richard (b. 1916), and Leonard (b. 1912). Richard Sr. died of pulmonary tuberculosis in 1935 at the age of 57.[61]

The Older Son – William Matrella

In 1942 William Matrella operated the Ritz located at 17 Silver Street. In 1947, he ran the Showboat at 100 Silver Street, and in 1949, he ran the Club Chateau. Finally, in 1950, he operated the Blackhawk. William Matrella died in 1979 at the age of 71.

The Younger Son – Richard "Blackie" Matrella Jr.

In 1946 Richard Matrella and Armas Hill operated the Showboat. In 1947, Richard operated the Show Bar. In 1952 he operated the Club Francis. In 1953 he ran Mickey's Rendezvous at 22 Silver Street. In 1953 he also operated the Carnival. Finally, in 1957 Richard Matrella and Jack Gasbarri partnered in the operation of the Club Carnival. Richard Matrella Jr. died in 1989 at the age of 73.

The Capone's

Gabriel Capone and Teresa Capone (nee Raiola) were born near Naples in Salerno, Italy. Gabriel was a barber, and Teresa was a seamstress who immigrated to the United States in 1893. The Capones had eight children: (Richard James Hart) b. 1892; Vincenzo, Raffaele "Ralph" James, b. 1894; Salvatore "Frank", b. 1895; and Alphonso, 1899. The other brothers – Richard, Ralph, and Al – would play a part in Hurley's history.

The Older Son – Richard James Capone

It could be argued that Richard James Capone was the most interesting of the brothers. As a young man, he fled violence, primarily out of fear because of a fight when he pommeled an opponent. Richard moved west, changed his name to Hart, and after a career in law enforcement, Richard returned to the Midwest and reconciled with his brothers. He died of natural causes in 1952, and his connection to Northern Wisconsin is through his son, Sherman Hart.

The Second Older Son – Ralph "Bottles" Capone

Of the brothers, Ralph "Bottles" Capone's was the closest to the story of Hurley. After Ralph was released from prison in 1935, he moved to Mercer to live quietly in a house on a local lake. Despite his new demeanor, the authorities harassed Ralph for the rest of his life. Ralph died in Hurley in 1974.

The Third Older Son – Frank Capone

Frank was brutal, and historians claim that Frank ordered the deaths of 500 people during his time in organized crime.[62] Frank was killed in 1924 in a hail of bullets fired in a gunfight with Chicago police.

The Youngest Son – Al "Scarface" Capone

Al "Scarface" became the head of the mob in Chicago. He took advantage of prohibition and was a bootlegger. He operated the syndicate in Chicago using fear and violence to maintain control. His operation lasted seven years until, at 33, he went to prison for tax evasion. After his release from Alcatraz, Al spent time with his brother Ralph in Mercer and died of syphilis in Florida in 1947.

The Fontecchio's

The Father – Fred "Bernardino" Fontecchio

Fred "Bernardino" Fontecchio was born in 1890 in Capestrano, Italy. He emigrated to the United States in 1906 and traveled to Hurley, where he married Carmella D'Andrea in 1909. They had three children. Fred was born in 1910, Betty in 1911, and Patrick in 1914. Fred Sr. and his wife Carmella[63] ran the Liberty Bell restaurant on 5th Avenue in Hurley.

The Older Son – Alfred "Fred" Fontecchio Jr.

Fred Jr. ran the Club Fiesta, the Club Francis, and the Bowery Club. Fred Jr. died in 1989.

The Younger Son – Pasqual "Patrick" "Patsy" Fontecchio

Pat "Patsy" moved to Chicago and co-owned a Chicago nightclub called The Black Orchid, located at the corner of Rush and Ontario from 1949 to 1959. Eventually, he moved back to Hurley to help run the Liberty Bell with his sister Betty.

The Santini's

Nunzio Santini

Nunzio James Santini was born in 1892 in Capestrano Italy. He emigrated to the United States in 1909. According to the Census report, Santini was a miner in 1910 and a bartender in 1920. He owned and operated a hotel at 29 Silver Street in 1930. In 1936, Nunzio married Ruby Umolac from Elcor, Minnesota. They ran the Santini Hotel until he died in 1954.

Other Family Members

The Santini family emigrated from Capestrano, Province of L'Aquila, Abruzzo, Italy. Bernardino (Fred) Santini was the father of Dr. F. J. Santini, Mayor Paul Santini, Dominic Santini, and Mrs. Carl (Viola) Hautala. Fred was the brother of Louie and Nunzio (Jim) Santini. Paul Santini founded Rudy's Bar and Restaurant.

Cira Gasbarri

Cira was born in Cuba on August 3, 1935, and emigrated to Florida in about 1958. She arrived in Hurley in 1962 to dance at the Club Carnival and married Jack "Jackpot" Gasbarri in 1968. Little is known about Cira's family. The record shows that she had a niece, Angel Acebal, from Hollywood, California, who visited in 1978. Cira died on February 1, 1987, at 51. Cira plays a major role in the last part of this narrative.

Madeline Mary Kozup (Angelo, Capone, Morichetti)

Madeline was born in 1920 in Mellen. She married to Dan Angelo[64] and helped him run Mickey's Rendezvous. After he died in 1949, Madeline married Ralph Capone[65] and helped him run the Rex Bar in Mercer. After he died in 1974, she married Serafino "Suds" Morichetti[66] and ran Connie's Supper Club in Hurley. She served delicious food. At age 55, Madeline attended Gogebic Community College, earned an L. P. N., and later established a nursing laboratory and left a substantial endowment to the college. She died in 2017 at 96.

Marcia Lyon "Marcia Ruth Lyon" "Kay Martin"

Marcia R. Lyon was born to Marcus Lyon and Ida Barenthin on December 11, 1915, in Tampico, Illinois.[67] She was their first child and was raised on a farm near Tampico and attended schools in Dixon, Illinois, 30 miles to the northwest. Marcia attended school with Ronald Reagan, and both were on the debate team. She related to me that during one debate, she chose the subject of agriculture since she knew Reagan was raised in the city and she knew about farming. She won, of course. Marcia carried her friendly manner and ability to converse throughout her life. She worked various jobs after high school and somehow traveled to Hurley for work. During her time in Hurley, she was a barmaid, bartender, card dealer, tavern owner, prostitute, companion, and keeper of a house of ill fame. Marcia was no stranger to law enforcement. She died in 2018 in Hurley.

Domenico "Dominic" F. Napoli

Dominic, the son of Frangesco "Frank" and Elizabeth D'Agostino, was born in 1912 in Seattle. He was close friends with Fred A. Fontecchio, who he had listed as a contact on his military registration card in 1940. Dominic Napoli died in 1989.

Kathleen Mary Napoli

Kathleen Mary Campbell "Kay" was born in Ashland to James E. Campbell and Flora M. Bushey. Although there is no record of her marriage to Dominic, her obituary shows her "as a bartender at local establishments," and in 1943, she listed her name as Napoli. Kathleen married Paul Pozego in 1949 in Bessemer and remained married to Pozego until her death in 2002 at age 84.

Richard Cristopher Trembath

Christopher Trembath was born in 1864, and in 1890, he and his wife, Sophie (Kneebone), emigrated from Cornwall, England. Christopher worked as a miner, and the family lived in Montreal, Wisconsin. The Trembath's had four children: two boys and two girls. They named one of the boys, born January 3, 1895, Richard Cristopher.[68]

Richard attended Hurley High School, where he was a good student: bright, with an ardent desire to achieve. After graduating, he taught high school for four years. In November 1916, at age 22, he was elected as the Iron County Register of Deeds. He served as the register of deeds from 1917 to 1924. In 1918, he met Ida Forsman from Duluth, and they married in September, and Ed Gibbons was his best man.[69]

In May 1919, the couple lived on Silver Street and rubbed elbows with a mix of immigrants, including Sam, Rose, Moses, and Benney Gertz, from Poland; Mike Danch from Serbia; and the Verichs, from Italy.[70] That same year, Richard filed for the draft, and the record describes him as having blue eyes, light complexion, blonde hair, and standing 5'11-3/4". He listed his father, Richard Couch Trembath, as next of kin.[71]

From 1925 to 1927, while studying at the University of Wisconsin – Madison, he served in the Wisconsin Assembly as an Iron and Vilas Counties representative.[72] Richard earned his law degree in 1927 and returned to Hurley to serve as district attorney for Iron County and as a supervisor on the Iron County Board. He was an elder in the Hurley Presbyterian Church and a member and past master of the Hurley Masonic Lodge. Judge Richard C. Trembath was elected to four consecutive six-year terms as the Iron County judge from 1938 until 1960. He died at age 69 on March 17, 1964, and was buried in the Hurley cemetery.[73]

Judge Richard C. Trembath played a central role in the story of Hurley during the mid-20th Century. It is doubtful that any other person had a similar view of the scene. He knew all the players, their strengths, frailties, desires, and hopes. He applied impartial and equal justice despite the unique challenges offered by the offenders. Iron County was fortunate to have Judge Trembath sit on the bench during this turbulent period.

Armand Francis Cirilli

It would be an unforgivable omission to neglect Armand Cirilli. Without him, most of the stories, specifically the details, would be lost to history. Armand Francis Cirilli was born in 1908 in Eveleth, Minnesota, to Orazio Roger Cirilli from Luciano, Italy, and Concetta DiDomenica from Beffi Aquila, Italy.

He moved to Ironwood in 1921 and lived in "the flats" at the base of Silver Street on the Michigan side of the Montreal River. In 1923, his family moved to Hurley, where he graduated from Hurley High School in 1926. Armand attended the University of Wisconsin School of Journalism and earned a Bachelor of Arts degree in 1931. In 1939, he married Martha Siguard Puumala from Erwin Township in Michigan. During the war years, Cirilli served as a commanding officer of a gun crew on Liberty ships. Armand worked in newspapers for over 50 years, most notably as a reporter, writer, columnist, editor, and partner in the ownership of *The Montreal River Miner*. Cirilli, always passionate, quick-witted, and inquisitive, died in Hurley in 1992 at 84.

23

1942

Hurley: The Players

UKNOWN TO MOST, PRE-WAR HURLEY, specifically Silver Street, would host a dramatic skirmish. Representing the city were municipal officials, property owners, tavern operators, bartenders, bootleggers, keepers, prostitutes, and making all this possible, customers. Representing the opposition were the State of Wisconsin and the Federal Government. They were represented by veteran operatives of the Beverage Tax Division of the State Treasury Department, FBI agents from St. Paul[74], and State Health Department officials.

Madison: The Players

ALTHOUGH THE FBI, other federal agencies, sheriff deputies, and local police were often involved in raids, the state beverage agents in Madison held the most significant authority. State Treasurer Robert K. Henry created the Beverage and Cigarette Tax Division In 1934. At that time, its only responsibility was to collect state tax on liquor and beer. At various times, legislation changed, and the division absorbed new responsibilities, such as the Thomson Anti-Gambling law, laws relating to prostitution, and new laws relating to liquor, beer, and cigarettes. Motivated by the war machine, this was their time to shine.

John Wiley Roach

Special attention must be given to the key antagonist during the early stories in the book. John Wiley Roach was born in 1902 in Edgar, Wisconsin, 15 miles west of Wausau. His father was a timber scaler, and his mother was a teacher. His mother's maiden name was Wiley, from Scottish descent, and his father was Irish. His mother homeschooled John. When he was a teenager, the family moved to Appleton. Playing basketball for Appleton High School in 1921, Roach played guard and helped capture the state championship. Roach was impetuous, fast on his feet, and an excellent all-around athlete. The University of Wisconsin in Madison recruited Roach to play football, but instead, he enrolled at Notre Dame at age 20 in the fall of 1922. The 139-pound reserve halfback played with the famous "four horsemen" under Knute Rockne's Fighting Irish from 1923 to 1926. During the years that Roach played for Notre Dame, they compiled a record of 34-4-1. In 1925, Roach was "one of the best backs of the year, although only a junior."[75]

John Roach--Notre Dame

Roach's nickname was "Cactus" because he had a prickly and aggressive personality, both on and off the field. In 1924, during a game between Wisconsin and Notre Dame, the Badger defense mercilessly harassed

Roach throughout the match for selecting Notre Dame over Wisconsin. At one point, Roach outflanked Wisconsin's defenders, and as he passed the end zone for a touchdown, he thumbed his nose at the pursuing Badgers. Rockne was angry at his arrogance. He pulled him from the game and benched him for the rest of the season. The following year, Roach played in Notre Dame's only appearance at the Rose Bowl, where the Irish defeated the Cardinals of Stanford.

While attending Notre Dame, Roach served as constable of St. Joseph County, Indiana, and was a deputy sheriff there for three years. According to Notre Dame records, he attended the University from September 14, 1922, to March 11, 1927. Although he was working toward a law degree, for an unknown reason, he did not graduate.

In the fall of 1926, Roach played with the Chicago Cardinals in the NFL and then coached at De Paul University in Chicago. In January 1928, he opened the Roach Sport Shop on College Avenue in Appleton. In 1929, Roach served as president of the Appleton Fire and Police Commission and coached football at Lawrence College. In the same year, he ran unsuccessfully for Outagamie County sheriff. In December 1931, the sports store succumbed to the depression, and in 1932, he lost his second attempt for Outagamie County sheriff.

* * *

The end of prohibition in 1933 did little to dissuade moonshiners. Alcohol was now legal and tax stamps became revenue generators for the government. In 1934, State Treasurer Robert K. Henry hired Roach as the chief inspector for the State Treasury Department. Kelly instructed Roach to raid moonshine operations. Within a few months, Roach and his agents had over 180 convictions for moonshining in Rhinelander, Milwaukee, Kenosha, Stevens Point, Stoughton, and Fond du Lac. In the Fond du Lac raid, 11 agents stormed a distilling operation and shot a moonshiner as he tried to escape. In May 1934, the Sheboygan Press carried two main stories. One was about Texas Ranger Francis Hamer gunning down Bonnie Parker and Clyde Barrow in Louisiana. The other described John Roach's raids on five taverns in Sheboygan County. Roach and his team raided stills in Green Bay, Oshkosh, and Milwaukee, and in mid-November, he arrested a moonshine ring in Madison.[76]

The job was not without risks, and gunplay was always a hazard. In September 1934, Matt Schumacher, one of Roach's agents, was shot and killed during a liquor raid at a residence in Kenosha County. Roach captured Charles Melli, 20, the suspected shooter.[77] The case made headlines, and because of inconsistencies in the defendants' testimonies, the Wisconsin Supreme Court granted Melli a new trial. Nonetheless, he was convicted. Roach's willingness to take risks brought him nearly hero status within the state. On November 17, 1934, in the *Wisconsin State Journal*, Roundy Coughlin wrote, "This John Roach chief inspector for the state on liquor is one of the busiest fellows in the state. They tell me he will work all week without sleep if he has duties to perform. He is one go-getter this John Roach and everybody looks to him and they say he has no favorites. His men claim they never saw such faithful, hard fearless worker in their lives as Roach."[78]

Roach continued to pursue illegal liquor operations with major raids near Stevens Point, Middleton, and Madison in 1934. While raiding a barn in Brown Deer, agents flushed out the bootleggers with a volley of tear gas. In Milwaukee, Roach and his team arrested six men, and when he asked them who the owner was, each pointed at the other. Eventually, an 84-year-old man confessed to being the ringleader. The old man told Roach, "I only needed one more night to sell the rest of my liquor. You mighta' let me know you were coming."

In November 1936, the politically Progressive Sol Levitan was reelected to a sixth term as state treasurer after an absence of several years. He ousted Democrat Robert K. Henry, who had hired Roach, an ardent Democrat. Trouble was on the horizon. The December 3, 1936, *Wisconsin State Journal* reported, "Dismissal of the 'overwhelming majority' of the State Beverage Tax Division's 90 employees and their replacement by 'good' Progressives appeared definitely today to be the course of action to be pursued by the new administration." The new administration told the employees that they would be replaced two weeks after the January 6 inauguration. It was rumored that Roach "would be retired." Many Progressives had their eyes on the post-election victory spoils. The *State Journal* reported, "Virtually every progressive assemblyman and senator has been camping on their trail seeking jobs for their uncles, father-in-law's, and cousins on the wife's side." Governor Phillip La Follette knew he would have to deal with the problem when he took office in January. As the Beverage Tax Division was not under the civil service system, firing was straightforward and brutal.

In mid-January 1937, Roach had no option but to resign as chief inspector. In a farewell article published in the January 15 *Appleton Post-Crescent*, he graciously praised his fellow agents and wished the new administration continued success.

Roach went to work for the IRS, and for two years, he awaited a change in the leadership of Wisconsin. The wait was not in vain. At the end of January 1939, the Democrats regained legislative and appointive power. The new state treasurer, John M. Smith, appointed Roach as Chief of the State Beverage Tax Division with a staff of 75. While continuing to hunt moonshiners, the focus began to shift toward prostitution. In April 1939, in his first speech after his appointment, Roach promised to eradicate "the selling of liquor to minors, the permitting of minors to loiter around taverns, and the presence of 'come-on' girls in taverns." He said that the tavernkeeper was obliged to observe a "moral as well as civil code." Roach said that officials should keep the tavern industry clean of "places of ill-repute" and "drive out dives and other reprehensible places from their community."

Roach and his agents arrested bootleggers in Portage County, Milwaukee, and Rhinelander. His strict interpretation of the law and relentless pressure on his staff weakened his popularity. In mid-June 1939, *The Capital Times* criticized him for firing an employee for drinking confiscated liquor. Associates found Roach's reluctance to compromise as both self-righteous and overly zealous. These characteristics decreased his political capital, and the press quickly took up rumors of intra-agency bias.[79]

They accused Roach of setting "politically motivated" height and age requirements for beverage tax inspectors and investigators, charges which he denied. The press said that these qualifications "are merely manifestations of the underlying desire of the present administration to evade civil service and put jobs of this kind on the political pie counter." [80] In August, the *Times* continued to report that the Beverage Tax Division used a patronage plan to select new employees. At the end of August, Lt. Governor Goodland praised Roach's law enforcement accomplishments to counter this negative news. He again received praise from the press for his daring and successful raids.[81]

Roach had a gift to gab, and despite his aggressive attitude toward his work – or perhaps because of it – he made friends quickly. In addition to having a rich athletic history, Roach also had significant statutory power. During this period, he made friends with Attorney General John Martin and Earl Louis "Curly" Lambeau, the founder, a player, and the first coach of the Green Bay Packers. It was also helpful that Lt. Governor Goodland (who, in 1942, would become Governor) was educated at Lawrence University in Appleton. They shared experiences as ten years before, Roach had owned a sporting goods business in Appleton and then coached at Lawrence.

With his brusk manner and expectation of action, Roach often annoyed colleagues. In June 1940, August Frey and John Roach began a long-term feud. Frey worked in the Division of Departmental Research within the governor's office. He was direct, undiplomatic, and an ardent reformer. As an auditor, he controlled the purse strings for many government operations. One of his duties was to order beverage tax stamps for use by the treasurer's department. Roach procured these stamps from Frey and then issued them to liquor suppliers, who were required to place them on containers. Roach disputed with Frey about the type of stamp and claimed that supply was not keeping up with demand. This put Roach in a pinch between distillers and wholesalers who waited to do business while Roach waited for Frey to supply the stamps.

Roach complained that he had run out of stamps on three occasions during the past year and that Frey intentionally delayed the supply. At one point, the press reported, "Roach, who is accustomed to rough and ready tactics in dealing with bootleggers, was so angered by the fussy Frey that he spoke to him in language offensive to the latter's dignity." Frey was insulted by Roach's tenor, but Roach treated him like a gnat. Roach believed the actual work was done in the field, and Frey only managed a desk. Over the next year, Roach and Frey had an ongoing feud with the newspapers covering the spar blow by blow. At one point, Frey authored a report to get Roach fired and slipped it into the hands of legislators. The report bobbled around the capitol building for several months but failed to gain traction. Soon, the report, along with its author, faded into history.[82] With renewed energy, Roach reignited the mission to clean up the tavern industry in Wisconsin.

In early October 1940, Federal Judge Patrick T. Stone from Superior heard a case regarding a young man who died from excessive liquor consumption. The judge, finding the news disturbing, asked Roach to clean up "the northern Wisconsin situation."[83] Within a few days, Roach announced to United Press reporters the start of a statewide effort to prosecute tavernkeepers selling to minors. Roach acted quickly, and during the first week of October, he raided roadhouses in Marathon and Racine Counties.

* * *

In early 1941, the focus of the Beverage and Cigarette Tax Division began to change. Rumors spread that Governor Heil wanted to move the Division from the State Treasurer's Office to the Tax Commission. At this point, Roach's division had a staff of 72 employees. Although the proposal was still alive in late January, Roach offered no public comment. Instead, he focused the division's efforts on creating an index of every tavern in the state. The index listed the number of slot machines in each establishment and noted those with associated prostitution. This would become an important document in future interactions with both the federal government and the press.

Roach told reporters that although his division only had arrest authority for liquor law violations, he, and his agents "repeatedly have aided private citizens in cleaning up undesirable conditions where local authorities have been reluctant to enforce the law." In January 1941, the *Sheboygan Press* carried a United Press article stating, "There would be cleaner competition, fewer taverns, and a more healthy public attitude toward the tavern business if Roach's agency were given wide licensing and enforcement powers according to some influential tavern operators." In late January, after the index of Wisconsin taverns was complete, Roach said, "Arrests of many tavernkeepers in all parts of the state can be expected in the near future because of their failure to respect the Wisconsin statutes."

Roach had to carefully exercise arrest authority for specific activities under his jurisdiction. He told the press that taverns operating in a "disreputable manner" would be presented to local authorities for prosecution without liquor-related offenses. Roach's commitment to a clean Wisconsin was sincere, but an event in the winter of 1941 would place him in an uncomfortable position.

On the evening of January 20, at the fifth annual banquet of the Tavern League of Madison, Roach shared the podium at Hotel Lorraine with William Wendell Wachtel, president of Calvert Distillers Corporation in New York. Wachtel surprised the audience with a blistering attack on the press. The *State Journal* reported that Wachtel shouted, "If there are any editors in this audience, I say this to you, you squeal and squirm for fear you will have your freedom of the press muzzled, but you buzzards got it coming to you. You have no right to print such lies. You're digging your own graves, and here's one spot where you'd better clean up your business." Wachtel's hostility, carried by misplaced passion, was out of context in Wisconsin. The "lies" to which he referred were allegations made by the press in New York where they supported the Women's Christian Temperance Union and the Anti-Saloon League. During his trip from his New York office to Madison, Wachtel made the mistake of believing the attacks from the press were universal. He continued the rampage claiming that tavern men were considered "second rate citizens in the eyes of the public." As his speech progressed, Wachtel became aware of the perplexed faces in the audience. His tenor cooled, and he warned tavernkeepers against illicit activities such as "switching, refilling, bootlegging, and adulteration" of alcohol. Realizing his misstep, he summed up his comments by saying, "This does not apply in Wisconsin, because you do not have these abuses, and I might point out you will go far and wide before you will find as good a man for the head of the beverage division as John Roach."[84]

Roach continued to get support for his vigorous law enforcement, even from the Tavern League of Wisconsin. In mid-March 1941, the League sent a resolution to Governor Heil, Secretary of State Fred R. Zimmerman, and State Treasurer John Smith. They commended Roach as "an outstanding official who has intelligently, impartially, and courageously enforced the liquor and excise laws of the state in an upright and efficient manner."[85]

In early April 1941, *The Sheboygan Press* reported that Roach swore out complaints against 12 taverns for closing hour violations. Roach told reporters, "The violations of the 1:00 a.m. ban leads to increased highway accidents, increased crime and a lowering of community morals." In mid-April, Roach told the Barron County Tavern League that they must "eliminate the dumps and dives that disfigure the reputation of a community."[86] In July, he talked to the *State Journal* about the tavern limitation law stating, "There seems to be the most difficulty in the northern part of the state. We've had no complaints of irregularities in the Madison area."[87]

* * *

The Federal Revenue Act in 1941 levied a $50 tax on each slot machine. This resulted in federal interest in Roach's index cards – his database of Wisconsin's slot machines. The Fed wanted to enforce the new $50 tax to generate revenue, and although Roach's index was officially "secret" during its preparation, it was, in reality, well-publicized.

The press disliked the idea of secret records. William T. Evjue, a reporter for *The Capital Times*, published several unfavorable articles referring to Roach and his stash of secret information. In early October 1941, Evjue wrote, "It is announced that John Roach, the head of the beverage and tax department, has been keeping tabs on the slot machines operated in Wisconsin and it is stated that the beverage tax department will co-operate with the federal government in the collection of slot machine taxes. The beverage tax division has been building up a series of graphic maps on which are stuck red, white, and blue-headed pins indicating the number of machines operating in each community. Mr. Roach has taken the trouble to get complete data on the number of places in which the law is being violated. Apparently, Mr. Roach is willing to co-operate with the federal government in collecting taxes on illegal machines but unwilling to co-operate with Wisconsin authorities who are charged with the responsibility of suppressing these machines." In early October, Roach said he would open the files showing the number of slot machines at each tavern.[88]

This issue dissolved on December 7, 1941, when the Japanese attacked Pearl Harbor and thrust the United States into war in the Pacific. The Pearl Harbor attack energized John Roach to root out vice in Wisconsin. Over 150 law enforcement officers attended a civilian defense meeting at the Dane County courthouse two months after the attack on Pearl Harbor. Among the speakers were federal and state officials, including John Roach.

Hurley: The Taverns

MOST OF THE TAVERN ENTERPRISES on Silver Street were in a constant state of flux. Sometimes it was difficult for authorities to keep the suspects straight. For example, agents served a warrant on Joseph Copanese, who held the license for the Blackhawk tavern. They also arrested Johnny Califano,[89] who happened to be there, and charged him with selling liquor without a license, having gambling devices, and keeping a house of ill fame. The next day, the agents dropped the charges against Copanese when they learned that he was not the operator. Instead, they switched the charges to three bartenders.

Operators used the complexity of the tavern business to their advantage. The enterprise involved the real estate owner, the personal property owner, the lessee, the tavern operator, the holder of the liquor license, and the holder of the bartender license. Sometimes an individual owned the real estate, operated the business, and worked as the bartender. Occasionally, a relative, spouse, or trusted friend would hold the liquor license because the operator was ineligible. In some cases, a bartender might be attached to the "identity" of the tavern, such that the actual owner remained unknown. If there was a silent partner in the business, it was the property owner – the holder of title. Very seldom did they get any mention, either in court or in the press. Furthermore, the owners of the real estate were often major players in Hurley politics.

The following table shows the operators, addressed and tavern names on the lower block of Silver Street in August 1942.

Operator	Silver Street Address	Tavern Name
Clement Vita	7	The Marigold Tavern
Joe Ottenstror	9	Montana Joe's Bar
Joe McRaniels	13	The Lucky 13 Bar
Jonas Biller	14	Welcome Inn
Jack Gasbarri	15	The Flame Bar
Mildred Lane	16	Jean's Chateau
Kathleen Napoli	17	The Ritz
Joe McRaniels	18	White Front
Virgilio DaPra	19	The Wisconsin Club
Joe Vita	21	The Hi-Ho Bar
John Calligaro	23	The Red Feather
Ben Romanowski	25	Benny's Bar
John Califano & John Copanese	26	The Blackhawk Bar
Minnie Rae Bathas	100	Rae's Blackhawk Bar
Fred Fontecchio, Jr.	104	Club Fiesta
Filomena Santini	114	Rudy's Bar
Edna Shields	116	TryAngle Inn

Hurley: The Prostitutes

THE WOMEN CAME FROM PLACES like Detroit, Chicago, Minneapolis, Milwaukee, and Superior. Although some had been in Hurley for over five years, most were nomadic and continually sought better money and working conditions. Some women had been married several times and had children cared for by relatives. Nearly all the women lived upstairs from the tavern where they worked. Prostitution in Hurley was always associated with liquor and gambling. The girls were generally friends. In one case, a mother kept her young child with her upstairs, above the tavern, and the other women helped care for the child. Another admitted to having grown children who were living on their own. Some traveled by bus or train to visit family or boyfriends on days off.

The Capital Times reported that most women were "veterans" and "only a few were young and attractive." The reporter wrote, "While the younger girls were in their early twenties, the older ones were a battered lot, cynical and hard-bitten, tough and foul-mouthed, and sour on the world."

The women worked the "third shift," sleeping from early morning until noon, shopping and

Helen B., Mimi Ray B., Dorothy W., Dorothy B.
Arrested in Hurley 1942

visiting in the early afternoon, and then returning to work at 4:00 p.m. when evening customers began to cross the threshold. Conscious of their appearance and its effect on potential customers, they dressed in snug-fitting current fashions. When working at the bar, they would start a "friendship" by asking for a drink. Then they would try to entice a customer to pay for sex and, if needed, initiate a dance to encourage the solicitation. They worked on commission.

Although they had some independence, they were not free to select their customers. As "inmates" of the facility, they were responsible for working when they were on duty. Sometimes the bartender would nod toward a sloppy drunk, and the girl was expected to lure him upstairs despite his appearance, condition, or age. A reporter witnesses one such unsuccessful solicitation between a young miner and a prostitute, "She sidled up to him at the bar, talked half a minute and they both disappeared upstairs. Two minutes later, they came back down. The girl nodded to the bartender, who grabbed the miner by the seat of his pants and half-shoved, half-kicked him out the door. The girl called the young man a dirty bastard since he only had 60 cents. Once the young man went sailing into the street, she returned to her stool at the bar." [90]

Reasons that women become prostitutes vary, but prostitution is seldom a choice. Instead, it is often part of a cycle including prepubescent sexual abuse, poverty, drugs, and sex trafficking. However, the actual reasons remain elusive without candid admission by the women. The women in Hurley prostituted themselves to survive and embraced a particular type of toughness required to survive the lifestyle. With time, attributions can only be drawn from recorded accounts and, to some degree, the expressions on the faces in mug shots.

In 1963, the FBI reported that women were eight times more law-abiding than men. However, authorities arrested 500,000 women annually for various crimes. They said that drunkenness ranked first with 112,000 arrests. The other significant infractions included theft, disorderly conduct, prostitution, assault, and vagrancy. The report noted that 800 women in the U.S. are charged with murder annually, and 2,200 are arrested for illegally carrying weapons. Men, on the other hand, accounted for 4 million arrests, primarily for forgery and counterfeiting. The report addressed the flexibility of morals between generations due to societal changes but focused on sexual behavior. Components of varying behavior relating to women's morals included environment, education, economic position, and religion. Studies showed that broken homes and insufficient income to hold families together were highly correlated with prostitution.[91]

Hurley: The Customers

CUSTOMERS INCLUDED GAMBLERS, vacationers, seasonal sportsmen, loggers, miners, sailors, and others just seeking sexual adventure. Male customers where commonly referred to as "johns" or "tricks," Although customers included men from all classes and professions, their identity was not well known and not likely reported when discovered. The combination of liquor, gambling, and prostitution made Hurley a novelty.

During this period, Hurley was a curiosity, attracting visitors such as hunters and groups of men on "adventure expeditions." There is little information from which to specifically profile the customers in Hurley during the 1940s. Even though prostitution is demand-driven, the john was exempt from prosecution, and authorities focused on prosecuting the girls and their keepers. For example, other than the keepers of the houses, the court records from the 1942 raid on Hurley are void of customer prosecution.

In addition to the johns, gamblers made up a large segment of Silver Street customers. Few gambler arrests occurred during this period because the focus was on the tavernkeeper. *The Capital Times* described the gamblers as "tight-mouthed, surly individuals who sit for hours hunched over their dice, roulette, and card tables, saying only what was necessary to conduct their games." When a Madison reporter asked one gambler about his history, the man replied, "If you sat down here to play blackjack, you big-mouthed prick, play your cards, and if not, get the hell out."

Tavern keepers took gambling seriously as it was profitable. The bars offered dice, blackjack, roulette, poker, and punchboards. However, slot machines were the queen. The machine mesmerized with lights, wheels, bells, and the sound of coins banging down the chute. Charles Fey, an auto mechanic from San Francisco, invented the device in 1895. He witnessed the ever-increasing demand for his machine until he death in 1944. An event that would forever change the face of the slot machine occurred in 1907 when the arcade manufacturer Herbert Mills from Chicago assigned the traditional "lemons, plums, and cherries" to the spinning wheels. These were the machines in the Hurley taverns, and they paid off in pennies, nickels, and dimes.[92]

Hurley: The Keepers

THESE WERE NOT TYPICAL PIMPS or card sharks. These were business owners, husbands, fathers, mothers, caretakers, and counselors. These tavernkeepers were middle-aged, strong, and resolute. Most, but not all, were men. Many were from the area with families and relatives in Hurley. Jonas Biller, operator of Montana Joe's was 43, married, and had lived in Hurley for five years. Virgilio DaPra of the Wisconsin Club was 35 and single. Joe Vita of the Hi-Ho was 41. Jack Gasbarri of The Flame was 29, married, and lived in Hurley his entire life. Johnny Califano of the Blackhawk was 61, married, and lived in Hurley for 35 years. William Matrella was 35, married, and was a Hurley native.

There were several female operators like Minnie Rae Bathas, who was 35 and ran Rae's Blackhawk Bar. Edna Shields[93] was also 35 and operated the TryAngle Inn. Katherine Napoli was 25 and ran the Ritz with her partner. It was not unusual for the spouse of an operator to run the establishment while her husband was in the service or prison. For example, Napoli ran the Ritz while her husband served in the Army, enlisting just a month before the 1942 raid on Silver Street. She was arrested, tried, and found guilty. The judge asked her if she had anything to say before sentencing. Being a victim of circumstance, she responded, "All I want to say is that I hate to have this against me, this charge of operating a house of ill fame."

Madison: The Agents

THE STATE NEEDED AGENTS. No experience was necessary as John Roach created a training program at Fort Camp Douglas, 70 miles north of Madison. He recruited men between the ages of 24 and 49 with specific qualities. Previous employment was unimportant. For example, recruits included a schoolteacher, a mechanic, an attorney, a former city official, a roofing contractor, and an electrician. Although many were already expert sharpshooters, having served during World War I, they all received gunnery training. They also became proficient with machine guns, riot guns, rifles, shotguns, and pistols.

Agents of the Beverage and Cigarette Tax Division of the Wisconsin Treasury Department
Training at Fort McCoy ~circa 1942

Madison: Focus Change

ALTHOUGH THE PRIMARY DUTY of the State Treasury Department was to enforce liquor and cigarette laws, because of the threat of war, the focus turned toward prostitution. The army was setting up a glider training camp near Antigo in Langlade County and Roach used his index to set the stage. He informed the press that 110 of the 13,439 licensed taverns in the state were engaged in prostitution.

On Friday, June 12, 1942, Roach ordered the district attorney of Langlade County, to close five taverns and evict the prostitutes from the county or he would "close them all by Saturday night."[94] Roach's records would now pay dividends. In mid-June, armed with this evidence, the Federal Department of Justice agreed to help.[95]

Hurley: Can Prostitutes Swim?

IN EARLY JUNE 1942, a field agent briefed John Roach about a recent visit to Hurley. He told him of a drunken customer in a tavern on Hurley's lower block who, taunting his "prostitute friend," claimed that she could not swim. She argued that she could and ordered six steins of beer. She poured them along the bar, stripped off her clothes, and slid the entire length of the bar using a breaststroke to "prove her point." The agent also reported that while traveling into town, he picked up a nude woman on the outskirts of Hurley who was hitchhiking back to Silver Street. She told him, "Somehow, she had lost her clothes."[96]

Hurley: Roaches Raid of 1942 – Planning

THE DECEMBER 7, 1941 RAID on Pearl Harbor thrust the United States into war with Japan. The country needed men to dig ore and harvest lumber, and anything that might interfere with production needed to be eliminated – including venereal disease. This motivated a covert attack on the purveyors of vice in Hurley.

During June and July 1942, John Roach carefully planned what was reported as "a sweeping raid through Wisconsin's barbary coast city of Hurley." His team focused on the taverns on Silver Street associated with prostitution, and timing would be crucial. Roach dismissed a late-night raid because taverns crowded with loggers and miners might lead to resistance and chaos. He also dismissed a daytime raid because many girls would not be working. Instead, he decided to "get the most with the least resistance" and planned an early evening raid. The team included FBI agents from Superior, State Health Department officials, beverage tax agents, and, unofficially, the press from Madison and Milwaukee.

On Thursday, July 30, Roach's crew registered at a resort north of Minocqua. From this command post, they traveled to Hurley, collecting evidence on Thursday, Friday, and Saturday nights. As a precaution, Roach stayed at a smaller resort about a mile to the south using the name "John Brown," the same pseudonym used by Al Capone. An extraordinary coincidence was that on the same day as the raid, Capone was at his summer home in Mercer, just a few miles from the resort where Roach, his agents, and the FBI hid out when they planned the raid on Hurley.

Always conscious of the press, Roach invited several reporters to witness the raid and issued them a password for entry into their planning room. The agents registered at the resort as a Milwaukee bowling team celebrating a tournament championship. After the raid, resort staff noted that they were a "suspicious-looking outfit" that "slept late and wrote reports on typewriters all afternoon." They slept late because they drove to Hurley at midnight and returned at dawn. Despite their unusual activity, the agents maintained their cover throughout the operation. When strangers inquired, they skillfully led the discussion to the topic of bowling. The operation was tight and without even a minor leak – despite the inclusion of the reporters.[97]

Hurley: Roaches Raid of 1942 – Preparation

ON TUESDAY MORNING, AUGUST 4, John Roach and 14 agents arrived at the Iron County courthouse in different cars at ten-minute intervals with 101 blank warrants. Surprised by the visit, Judge Trembath worked for over two and a half hours signing the warrants and swearing officers in closed quarters. Because of Hurley's reputed "warning system," Roach even swore the judge to secrecy. Later, when a courthouse employee asked the judge what those men wanted, Judge Trembath, mute, walked away.

Nonetheless, by mid-afternoon, barmaids whispered rumors of an impending raid. Prudent operators removed slot machines, covered dice tables, and hid roulette wheels. Others, despite the rumor, did nothing. Rumors were common but tearing down an operation required significant effort. The bold operators knew that if the rumor proved false, they would suffer a loss of revenue.

Under normal circumstances, Silver Street knew well in advance about impending raids. When agents traveled north through Minocqua on their way to Hurley, confederates phoned the warning to Silver Street tavern operators. By the time the agents reached Mercer, 20 miles south of Hurley, Silver Street was in full retreat. During prohibition, the tavern operators loaded slot machines, gambling tables, and moonshine onto trucks and hid the goods in the woods until the agents abandoned the search in frustration. Agents knew the operators hid the contraband, but it was impossible to search thousands of acres of wooded hills and valleys, and the tight-lipped community whispered not a word.

John Roach knew about the alliance between Hurley tavern owners and those "down the line" along Highway 51. He knew Hurley was a web of relatives, colleagues, and friends – many had emigrated from the same regions of "the old country." Roach was shrewd, and this summer of 1942, he was careful to ensure this raid would be clandestine. In fact, District Attorney Joseph C. Raineri, County Sheriff Sam Giovanoni, and Chief of Police Albino Endrizzi would not learn of the raid until the following morning.[98]

* * *

On Tuesday, August 4, 1942, 48 agents arrived in 18 vehicles at the Town of Oma schoolhouse, 6 miles south of Hurley. They approached at timed intervals, parked in order, and switched off their headlights. A curious young boy peddled by the schoolhouse and watched the men gather in groups. The agents ignored him because they had found no telephone in his home earlier that day. Instead, they drank coffee from thermoses and smoked cigarettes as they awaited the arrival of Roach and his companion.

At mid-afternoon, John Roach and two agents rolled into Hurley and parked the black sedan near the Sheriff's office. With authority he had come to enjoy, Roach walked directly into the office of Sam Giovanoni, the Iron County Sheriff. Before Giovanoni could say anything, Roach said he "wanted to show him something" and insisted he accompany him. Giovanoni and Roach got into the

Town of Oma Schoolhouse – Today

back seat of the vehicle as the driver turned south on 2nd Avenue. The sheriff was apprehensive and unaccustomed to taking orders, but he knew Roach from previous encounters and was aware of his authority.

South Side of the Lower Block of Silver Street
From First Avenue to the East
2007

The driver headed up the hill leaving Hurley, past the cemetery, and south along Highway 51. At 6:30 p.m., Roach, the two agents, and the sheriff arrived at the Town of Oma schoolhouse and Giovanoni found himself in the center of the posse. As the sedan rolled to a stop, Roach calmly placed the warrants in the sheriff's lap. Giovanoni realized he had been kidnapped and was about to be ransomed for his authority. He slid out of the car, observed the swarm of agents, and then said straight away to Roach, "Well, you'll go ahead with the raid anyway, so I might as well do it." With that, sheriff Giovanoni deputized the agents.

By this time, the word was out. The Hurley Common Council had a regularly scheduled meeting that evening at 7:30 p.m. Although it ultimately had to be canceled for lack of a quorum, the attending alders openly discussed the warrants and the possible timing of the raid. Despite the certainty, most of the "merchants" on the lower blocks of Silver Street remained oblivious, reckless, or unaware.

At 9:15 p.m., the agents crushed their cigarettes, poured the remaining coffee from their cups, and piled into their cars. This was neither an evidence-collection foray nor a drill – they carried official identification, badges, pistols, Thompson machine guns, and tear gas. Then, at 9:30 p.m., Roach signaled the cavalcade to move toward Silver Street.[99]

Hurley: Roaches Raid of 1942 – Execution

IN ORDER OF ASSIGNMENT, the agents rolled into Hurley, navigated the busy intersection at Hwy 51 and Silver Street, and then proceeded to their designated targets. These were the places where they had gathered evidence over the weekend; the places where girls, customers, and operators would recognize their faces. Roach positioned agents with Thompson machine guns at strategic points on the two lower blocks as backups in case of trouble.

The day had been nearly 90 degrees, and a few people meandered the street in short sleeve shirts. The vehicle procession went unnoticed until the agents began pouring from the sedans. Squads of three to five men burst into front doors armed with pistols, tear gas, and blackjacks. Others covered the back doors. After entering, the agents locked the doors, flashed their badges, and gathered the keepers and inmates. Once identified, the squad leader read the warrants and made

37

the arrests. In one tavern where business had been bountiful, agents served 15 warrants. One team had 30 warrants to serve at different taverns and because of the number, they had a difficult time locating the designated violators.

The newspaper reporters were given free reign during the raid. In fact, they were so close to the action that they found themselves with involuntary assignments. At one tavern, agents instructed Rod Van Every of the *Wisconsin State Journal* to lock the rear door and to locate and seize two missing girls.

Ruth M., Mrs. J.C S, Mary M. M., Stella J. Arrested in Hurley 1942

When Every went upstairs, he found the young daughter of the proprietor, who was visiting. She requested that he be quiet so as not to wake her five-month-old-baby. In one tavern, an agent failed to find a girl and asked the bartender where she was. The man replied, "We got no rules here. Ruthie, she left two, three days ago."

A team burst into the Ritz bar and arrested Kathleen Napoli. At the Flame, they nabbed James Gasbarri and at the Lucky 13, they arrested Joseph McRaniels. Agents apprehended Joe Ottenstror at Montana Joe's. Virgilio DaPra was seized at the Wisconsin Club, and Joe Vita at the Hi-Ho. Agents charged into the Red Feather and apprehended John Calligaro. At Benny's Bar, they rounded up Ben Romanowski and then arrested Minnie Rae Bathas at Rae's Blackhawk Bar.

The agents ignored the gamblers and focused on the girls, none of whom were found "entertaining" customers – which was fortuitous for would-be clients. After identification and arrest, the agents allowed the girls to gather their coats, hats, and purses. By 10:15 p.m., 45 minutes after they had left the schoolhouse, the agents drove 18 cars filled with prostitutes and keepers to the Iron County jail on the north side of Hurley. A few gamblers watched as things unfolded. A reporter noted that at one tavern, "Three well-fed, well-dressed tourists from Chicago enjoyed the situation." Realizing they were not vulnerable; they relaxed and savored the action so they could relay the story back in Illinois.

As agents cleared each tavern, they locked the doors or stood guard at those places without locks. One female bartender, who was asked to lock the front door, told the agent, "I don't know where the key is. This place has never been locked." One by one, the neon lights flickered out as the lower two blocks of Silver Street succumbed to the quiet and darkness of the hot August evening.

Hurley: Book 'em, Alex

WHEN THEY ARRIVED AT THE Hurley jailhouse, Roach summoned Undersheriff Alex Raineri to the scene. Raineri was in bed, and responding to the crises in haste, he arrived at the jail barefooted. He spent the night booking prisoners under the agents' watchful eye and could not communicate outside the facility. His brother, District Attorney J. C. Raineri, did not learn of the raid until the following morning.

John B. C. Arrested in Hurley 1942

Eventually, over 50 prostitutes and keepers crowded the small jail accompanied by 18 agents. This evolved into a social event as the girls joked about their "evidence" visits with the agents. They managed to coerce 45 packages of cigarettes, toothbrushes, and nylon stockings from the officials.

State officials questioned 51 people Tuesday night, and FBI agents interrogated the tavernkeepers. Although one woman suffered an anxiety attack, most just joked with the 17 guarding agents. One young woman told an agent that she wished she had left town on the four o'clock bus but smiling, she said it really didn't matter because "I wanted to see you again, honey." Women teased the agents about getting a drink while waiting to be booked. A reporter asked one woman if this was her "first raid," and she said, "No, it isn't my first, but I hope it's my last."

As things calmed down, the girls and their keepers huddled in the crowded cells and waited their turn with the agents. During questioning, one of the tavern operators told an agent, "We got no control of the girls. What the girls do we don't care."

The newspaper reporters watched with amusement as the agents pathetically typed with two fingers. They volunteered to type out the arrest records when they could no longer bear the frustration. The agents, assisted by the reporters, worked for the next two days filling out warrants and complaints. Most of the charges against the women were for being inmates of "disorderly houses" and for "soliciting for purposes of prostitution." Agents cited the bartenders and tavern operators for gambling and remaining open after hours.

Ben R. Arrested in Hurley 1942

As the girls socialized in the uncomfortable confinement of the Hurley City jail, the chief health officer in Madison ordered the Venereal Disease Section of the State Board of Health to examine them for social diseases.

Within a few hours, a crowd of over 2,000 gathered between Silver Street and the jail creating a carnival-like atmosphere. Although most were simply curious, some hurled curses at the agents. An alert officer prevented a drunken young man from smashing a reporter's camera. Instead, the man reeled with pen and paper and began to record the license numbers from the state cars. When an agent asked him what he was doing, he muttered, "That's my business."

A neighborhood woman told a reporter, "You wouldn't find better families anywhere in the state than Hurley, it's just that element down on Silver Street that gives us a bad reputation."[100]

Hurley: No One Knew

REPORTERS ASSAILED MAYOR BONACCI as he arrived at city hall on Wednesday morning. He grumbled through the crowd toward his office, "I don't know anything about it . . . I have nothing to say . . . I have no statement to make . . . Too busy." At that, he slammed the door to his office behind him. When reporters asked Roach why he didn't contact the mayor or district attorney before the raid, he said there had been no reason to do so but added, tongue-in-cheek, that the sheriff had been very cooperative.

Although it is likely that many people in Hurley either knew about or sensed the impending raid, most tavern operators were surprised. Roach addressed the press and offered several reasons why the raid was successful. He noted that because raids had been common throughout the prohibition period and inaccurate rumors circulated, no one knew if the threat was substantive. He said that swiftness was an important consideration in that the operators did not have time to remove machines, and the girls did not have time to remove themselves when the rumor was confirmed. Roach speculated that the girls and their keepers might have believed that the agents would use the traditional method of "marked money." At one point, he admitted that Hurley would continue with prostitution despite this raid and that tavern owners would accept the consequences. Roach knew he would return to Hurley.

Mellen: Fifth Column Fire

WAR FEARS WERE GENUINE, and the state justified the raid on Hurley as a precaution. Coincidently, a fire just a few miles from Hurley occurred on August 5, 1942. The fire destroyed the Penokee Mill in Mellen, located about 26 miles southwest of Hurley and just beyond the Iron County line. The company had the largest slicer in the world and rolled logs to make veneer. The veneer was used for making military aircraft under a U.S. Government contract and the fire raised suspicion of fifth-column activities.

Although they had gone on strike the day before, the fire put 288 men out of work. The company president attributed the fire to a short circuit in the hog-fuel boiler, but the FBI investigated the scene because the mill was part of the

John C. Arrested in Hurley 1942

40

military infrastructure. The War Production Board found nothing suspicious and told the company president to rebuild without hesitation. The board prioritized new equipment, and the fire drew attention to the region as critical to the war effort. Throughout the day, the company president received calls from contractors and suppliers in Washington, Montreal, New York, and Buffalo, all offering help to get the mill back into production.

Hurley: Unorganized Crime

Unknown Arrested in Hurley 1942

THE AUGUST 6 *WISCONSIN STATE JOURNAL* carried an editorial about the Hurley raid, praising State Treasurer John M. Smith and John W. Roach for "the housecleaning of the stronghold of organized vice in Wisconsin." The piece focused on the corruption in Hurley, which had "flourished there openly for years." The editor commented, "More than 275 miles from the state capital, Hurley's dives have operated without molestation by state or local authorities."[101]

Authorities seldom suggested the activities in northern Wisconsin as part of organized crime. While many of the proprietors of taverns, especially in Hurley, were of similar national origins and primarily Italian, there was no evidence to indicate that they were "organized" in any way.

There was nothing like the Camorra, an open group of gamblers, racketeers, and pimps who populated the region around Naples, Italy. Nor was there any sign of the Mafia, which mostly ruled the larger cities like New York, Philadelphia, and Chicago. Nothing like La Mano Nera, or The Black Hand found in the old neighborhoods of New York and the environment in which Al Capone and his brothers grew up. The closest association was Chicago's "Outfit" because of the link with the Capone family. Hurley had nothing more than a loose confederation of tavern keepers who set up gaming tables and slot machines, refilled liquor bottles, and hired prostitutes. Other than the "early warning system," organization served no useful purpose.

John C. Arrested in Hurley 1942

Hurley: Property Connections Irk Roach

ROACH WAS RELENTLESS IN HIS investigation. In addition to interrogating the tavernkeepers and prostitutes, he examined the relationships between the licensees and property owners. The tax and deed records showed that the Wisconsin Club, the Red Feather, and Benny's Bar had been in probate since 1936 under the estate of Joseph Raineri, Sr. As it was, Raineri's widow would receive a third of the estate, and two sons (J. C. and Alex) and a daughter would inherit the balance. Roach knew that the brothers would benefit by owning these properties, but he also knew that the father's transactions did not implicate them, and a judge would dismiss any accusation of collusion. Roach's research also showed that Mayor Bonacci's father owned the real estate hosting the Welcome Inn, one of the offending taverns. While these relationships would serve no useful purpose in prosecution, Roach became aware of the Hurley web, which only fueled his determination for revocation and padlocking. [102]

Virgilio D. Arrested in Hurley 1942

Hurley: The News Spreads

IN ADDITION TO THE *IRONWOOD DAILY GLOBE*, the *Wisconsin State Journal*, and the *Milwaukee Journal*, the story of the 1942 raid was reprinted in journals such as the *Bismarck Tribune*, the *Brainerd Daily Dispatch*, and the *Sheboygan Press*. Although this raid did not compare to the vice in Chicago 20 years earlier, readers undoubtedly drew inferences.

Hurley: A Hellhole of Gambling and Vice

AFTER THE RAID, THE AUGUST 6, 1942, *Capital Times* wrote, "In more than 50 years of notoriety as a hellhole of gambling and vice, Hurley had a few turbulent years during prohibition, but even the great dry era failed to black out the Midwest's greatest red-light district." *State Journal* reporter Rod Van Every wrote, "Hurley refused to believe it, but the lid was on." He continued, "Hurley referred to the raid as just a "flash in the pan, but the city forgot that America is fighting a war, one of production, one which prostitution can help lose. Hurley forgot that the federal government had singled out its Silver Street for special attention as defeating the war effort." He described

Kathleen N. Arrested in Hurley 1942

42

his perceived arc of the city's life "From a Town of wine, women, and song, Hurley has been changing into a ghost town."

Hurley: A Breeding Place of Espionage, Sabotage, and Disease

AFTER THE RAID, ROACH SAID, "Some of these places have never closed at night. Well, this is one night they will be closed, and more surprises are in the air." He vowed to examine each girl's background "for espionage activity and white slavery."

Unknown Arrested in Hurley 1942

When Roach said that the activities in Hurley threatened "thousands of men employed in the biggest iron ore docks in the world," He was referring to the Great Lakes ports of Superior and Ashland, which lie west of Hurley, Wisconsin, at distances of 110 and 30 miles, respectively. He said that many of these defense workers "drive to Hurley for parties and relaxation," and he summed up his comments by declaring Hurley a "reservoir for prostitutes" and a safe place for girls who were hiding from federal authorities. The *Ironwood Daily Globe* reported, "At Madison, State Treasurer John Smith said military officials of the Sixth Service Command[103] had requested a cleanup in the Hurley area and had asked for state cooperation in controlling venereal disease throughout the state."

On August 3, 1942, Rod Van Every of the *Wisconsin State Journal*, authored an article entitled "Roundup Follows U.S. Plea to Purge War-Effort Areas." The story described the "smoothly synchronized" raid on Hurley's "bawdy houses" carried out

Betty W., Judy L., Babe B., Arlene L. Arrested in Hurley 1942

"without a hitch." He stated that State Treasurer John M. Smith ordered John Roach to conduct the raid after federal authorities asked Smith to clean out areas vital to the war, saying that prostitution was a "breeding place of espionage, sabotage, and disease."

During the August 4 raid, Agents searched every tavern for evidence of covert activity. They tossed rooms looking for ciphers, notes, or correspondence. *The Capital Times* quoted Roach, "There is great danger that such a place may be the seat of

43

fifth column activities. The dives in Hurley would provide an excellent place for espionage agents and other subversive elements to hide out and to obtain important information from war workers, soldiers, and others who may come to these places." Despite the thorough search of the taverns on Silver Street, there was no evidence of espionage or fifth-column activity. By default, Hurley received a clean "patriotic bill of health."

Nonetheless, Roach's attack on Hurley was relentless. Van Every went on to mention that Hurley was the only city in Wisconsin that refused to observe the 1939 tavern limitation law. He wrote, "The situation which our investigators found when they started to work in Hurley was unbelievable, beyond description, and a disgrace to Iron County and the State of Wisconsin."

Hurley: Basic Rules and Procedures

BEFORE THE AUGUST 4 RAID, agents surveilled the taverns in Hurley. They used the "Basic Rules and Procedures" defined in the State enforcement manual to gather evidence. The manual stated, "It is of prime importance to prove 'intent' (or knowledge) on the part of both the prostitute and of the keeper and 'by its very nature most investigations of prostitution skirt the edges of entrapment.'" It emphasized that the investigator must know what is required and "how far he can go to get the evidence he needs." When surveilling, the agents carried neither weapons nor identification and avoided arguments and drunks. Instead, they identified themselves as roofing salesmen and often introduced their partners as relatives.

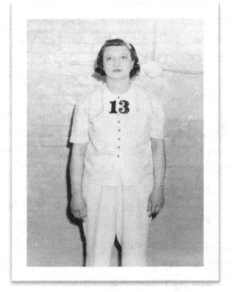

Rose L. Arrested in Hurley 1942

* * *

At 3:50 a.m. on July 31, 1942, two agents walked into the Ritz at 17 Silver Street, sat at the bar, and ordered Calvert's Reserve and water. Dominic Napoli operated the Ritz. Napoli had recently volunteered for military service, and his wife, Kathleen, managed the operation while he was away. However, at the time of the raid, she was visiting her husband, who was on leave out of state.

Two women, nestled at the opposite end of the bar, sized up the agents, and after a few minutes, a redheaded girl sauntered over, introduced herself as Tangerine, and asked if they would buy her a drink. An agent nodded yes, and she, in turn, nodded to Felix, the bartender who set up the glasses. The agent slid 75 cents across the bar.

Tangerine said she was 22 years old and from Detroit, and as she sipped the drink, she nudged against one of the agents asking him to join her upstairs. When he asked how much, she said, "two dollars." Then, side-stepping the proposal, he asked if she couldn't make more money in Detroit, and she responded that she couldn't work there anymore. The agent asked if they were the only girls in the tavern. She told him the boss had gone south to see her husband, who was in the army, and the other two girls had quit early since she was away.

The agent sidestepped the proposal for the second time and mentally noted a blackjack table and four slot machines. He took a turn at a roulette wheel, and after a few spins, he approached the other girl, about 20 years old, tall, and slender, with dark hair and a fair complexion. Then, as he pulled up a stool, she snuggled beside him and introduced herself as Peggy. As she talked to another agent, he leaned away and poured his drink into a small vial hidden in his jacket pocket. Peggy didn't notice the container, and when he turned toward the bar, she leaned over and asked him if he wanted to go upstairs for two dollars. The agents begged off and left the tavern.

Unknown Arrested in Hurley 1942

During their debriefing the next day, the agents drew a floor plan of the Ritz, marking the location of the bar, the roulette wheel, the blackjack table, and the slot machines. They talked about two girls who had not yet been approached and decided to gather more evidence and returned the next night. In addition to more women, they noted Kathleen Napoli working the bar.

Cedric Parker, a reporter for *The Capital Times* wrote, "Just before 3:00 a.m., as they settled at the bar, three girls approached: Peggy from the previous night, a girl named Bonny, and an unnamed blond who was tall, slender, and about 26 years old. The agents ordered Old McBreyer whiskeys, the reporter ordered a Virginia Dare, Peggy had a Canadian Club, and Bonny and the blond had Kesslers.

One of the agents asked the blond if they had been busy. She candidly told him that two girls had left the previous Saturday because business was poor. She was talkative and told him that she had been "in the business" for two years and had worked in Davenport, Ottumwa, and various places in Illinois. She said she came to Hurley after being forced out of Davenport and that she had been working and living at the Ritz for the last two months. She said her boss was back in town and pointed out Kathleen Napoli, working the dice table across from the bar. The agent described Napoli as "a tall and slender brunette about 35 years old." Finally, the blonde invited one of the agents upstairs to "have a party." He asked how much the party would cost, and she replied, "two dollars." At 3:10 a.m., the lead agent told the girls that they would return after getting something to eat.

Felix P. Arrested in Hurley 1942

45

Hurley: Embedded Reporters

PARKER DRAFTED THE STORY IN his head as the events unfolded. He noted that they arrived on Silver Street after midnight to minimize their drinking and to watch for closing hour violations. He listened as the agents obscured their identities by posing as colleagues in the oil business. Parker stated, "When we arrived in Hurley Saturday night, the town was roaring. Neon lights

blazed the length of Silver Street. Jukeboxes blared from every door mingled with shouts and laughter. Drunken lumberjacks stumbled out of taverns – sometimes propelled by a bartender. Dirty, unshaven men slumped in doorways and sprawled on the curbs."

Parker described how he and agents "Art and Joe" entered a tavern they had missed the night before. The older agent, a man of about 50, bought a round of drinks and talked to the operator about fishing. There were no girls in the

Ruth A., Patricia D., Judy B., Rita B. Arrested in Hurley 1942

bar, and as the bartender began to close, the senior agent asked if he had "any women in the place." Wiping the bar, he told them that he did not operate "that kind of business" and added, "There are plenty of them in town if you want them."

Striking out, they tried another tavern. As they entered, three girls approached them. A brunette, who Parker described as "almost pretty," asked an agent, "How about a drink for us, buddy?" He ordered a round. Parker described one of the girls as a "heavy-jowled woman about 40 years old" and another as a "grotesquely painted creature of indefinite age." The bartender poured the girls' drinks from different bottles than the men's. It was part of the routine for the girls to drink diluted liquor or colored water. After the second drink, one of the girls "tickled Joe on the back of his neck" and asked, "Why don't you come upstairs with me, buddy?" He tried to change the subject, but the girl "nearly pulled him off the barstool and toward the staircase." Then, gripping the bar, he asked, "How do I know what kind of girl you are?" Without hesitation, she told him she paid $3.00 a week for medical examinations, while another girl interrupted and volunteered the news that the doctor examined her just yesterday.

The girl named Bonny asked for a nickel for the jukebox, but before she got a response, Sue grabbed a dime from Joe's change and slid it into the machine; she punched the numbers for Harry James "Sleepy Lagoon." As the trumpet trailed off, the agents retreated from the tavern and in the shadow of their car, they recorded the girls names, the tavern's layout, and the conversation's narrative as evidence of "solicitation."

Further down the street, they sidestepped a man of about 60 with bloody lips, a bruised face, and a black eye. Parker reported that he was "swaying blindly" and that "he was a lumberjack – you can tell by the smell – even in open air." The man mumbled that he had been rolled and had no place to sleep. When an agent asked him who beat him up, he slurred, "I'm no squealer, but I'll get 'em." The drunk staggered east toward the Montreal River and faded in the shadow of the Chicago and Northwestern trestle. As he disappeared, another man exited the door of a nearby tavern and teetered on the lip of the stairway. Parker reported, "Afraid to attempt the descent, he flopped down on the top step, his feet sprawled across the doorway and passed out." Within a few minutes, the bartender came out and "kicked the lumberjack's legs out of the way and returned to the reeking tavern."

Louis C. Arrested in Hurley 1942

For three nights, the agents worked in teams of two and three, gathering evidence of prostitution in 15 taverns. Rod Van Every wrote, "The street is a riot of colors from dozens of neon lights – curbs are jammed with cars – drunks stagger from door to door – girls solicit openly – gambling flourishes. This is the infamous Silver Street on Saturday night." Van Every said that for 40 years, Hurley was a "wide-open town where the law is a forgotten book." He went on to say, "Two nights we spent with state beverage tax investigators prowling around just two blocks of this infamous street where commercialized vice, gambling, and degradation are the usual thing" and "where the girls wore evening gowns and spun roulette wheels." He described one woman as "somewhere about 40, bleary-eyed with bewildering henna hair."

Compared to other Wisconsin municipalities, Hurley provided more "journalistic" opportunities for colorful prose. Van Every laced his article with a surreal description of Hurley. He exclaimed, "In some of the lesser places, broken down lumberjacks, most of them 50 to 65 years old, lay in drunken stupors on benches along the walls." He described Silver Street as having the same vigor as Bourbon Street during Mardi Gras, "every joint was rocking and rolling with the blast of jukeboxes. The girls played them with the customers' nickels. Coins from the same sources were wheedled for the slot machines."

Hurley: The Last Place Left

IN A CONTINUING SERIES OF ARTICLES, Madison reporters described the prostitutes as "virtual prisoners." For example, they noted that many knew nothing of the local community, and in one case, one girl was unaware of her proximity to Lake Superior, 20 miles to the north. The women came from various places, but mainly from the Midwest. One girl said she left Detroit because federal authorities began patrolling the military camps and threatened women with a five-year jail sentence for soliciting. She told a reporter that Hurley was "the last place left." When questioned by the FBI about possible "white slavery," most girls said they were in Hurley by their own choice and that they "felt safe" in the city.

Hurley: Results from the Medical Tests

ON AUGUST 7, DISTRICT ATTORNEY J. C. Raineri requested that Judge Risjord of Ashland serve as a special prosecutor for the cases resulting from the Hurley raids. On that same day, the health examiners reported that all the tests for syphilis were negative, although three cases were "suspicious." The examiners identified two girls receiving treatment for venereal disease at the time of arrest. Raineri asked the judge to send the girls to the women's prison at Taycheedah until they recovered.

Dorothy M., Ester H., Shirley G., Joan D. Arrested in Hurley 1942

Hurley: The Mayor Goes on Vacation

TWO DAYS AFTER THE RAID, Roach announced that he was considering criminal charges against the mayor, the city clerk, the city attorney, and several council members for violating state law by issuing 84 liquor licenses. In a letter to the Hurley officials, Roach "suggested" that they comply with the tavern limitation law "otherwise, there might be the possibility of prosecution for malfeasance and neglect of duty." Quoting the statute, he noted that the penalty could be "imprisonment in the county jail for not more than one year, or in the state prison, not more than five years, or by fine not exceeding $500."

The city clerk responded in a letter explaining that the city council approved 78 licenses when the law went into effect. He said the council would have approved six additional applications had they not adjourned their meeting early. Further, he said the city received legal advice that the 84 licenses complied with the law. He wrote, "Until we receive legal advice to the contrary, we shall continue to grant 84 licenses." Explaining that the city carried a heavy relief load and that economic conditions in the area were poor, the clerk said that the additional $1,500 from the six additional licenses "would be a godsend."

Roach sent a terse response stating that rather than simply being "approved," the licenses must have been "granted, issued, or in force" when the law took effect. In the letter, he again warned of the possible consequences of non-compliance. After this communication salvo, the mayor and the city attorney told Roach that his boss, State Treasurer John Smith, and Attorney General John Martin had previously given them a verbal opinion that the 84 licenses were legal.

Roach was shocked by this news and most certainly marched into Smith's office without knocking. After wrestling with Smith and Attorney General Martin, he responded to the Hurley clerk that the opinion was not binding because it was neither in writing nor had his division been informed. He was furious and reiterated his threats about prosecuting of local officials who do not "act against law violators."

After a heated interagency discussion in mid-August, Treasurer John Smith told *The Capital Times* that he sent a letter to Hurley's mayor stating that the tavern quota should be 78, contrary to what the Hurley officials believed.

P. Smith Arrested in Hurley 1942

* * *

On August 13, Mayor Bonacci abandoned the argument about the tavern quota. He declared seven liquor licenses invalid and refunded each applicant the $200 license fee. He told Roach that all seven were declared void because they were issued in a block. This reduced the number of licenses from 83 to 76 and allowed two additional licenses to reach the limit of 78. There was no shortage of demand, and seven applicants immediately filed requests for the remaining two permits. Mayor Bonacci, under constant bombardment, announced he was taking a vacation. He told the council members that he would "probably return in time for the September 1 meeting." However, he appointed a council member as the mayor pro tem and instructed him not to call a meeting unless notified by phone. With that, he gave the mayor pro tem a telephone number and left town.

After hearing about the mayor's vacation, Roach told the clerk to keep the seven "illegal" taverns closed until the next council meeting. He threatened the council with arrest if they issued additional licenses before the mayor returned. Given the threats, the council did not discuss the two licenses until September 1. Despite his vacation, the mayor could not escape the controversy.

After discussing the tavern quota with Roach and the Attorney General, State Treasurer Smith clarified his decision in a letter to the Hurley city clerk. He wrote, "Your representatives will clearly remember my position was that you had exceeded your number of licenses and must reduce them to 78. I only promised to wait two or three days to get your facts on which to ask for an opinion from Attorney John Martin."[104]

The Hurley representatives must have heard what they wanted to hear. They had returned to Hurley believing that 84 taverns were acceptable and there was no need to submit "additional facts." On September 1, the mayor had not yet returned from his vacation but authorized the mayor pro tem to hold a council meeting. During a closed session, the council had a protracted discussion of the remaining two Class B liquor licenses.[105] The council issued one to Anna Maki, the other to James Francis.[106]

Hurley: Arraignments and Charges

IN THE MIDDLE OF THE QUOTA DISPUTE, on August 7 and 8, Judge Trembath arraigned the prisoners in a courtroom overflowing with state agents, reporters, defendants, and the curious. The state charged most girls "as prostitutes and inmates of houses of ill fame." They charged the tavern operators with three primary offenses, including violating the hours law, operating gambling equipment, and operating houses of ill fame. After the arraignments, the judge set court dates for September.

Before returning to Madison, John Roach met with the mayor, the sheriff, and the police chief to reiterate his position on the tavern law and the harboring of prostitutes. Despite the reality of the previous week, the police chief unabashedly asked Roach about the possibility of allowing taverns to sell liquor after one o'clock. Roach bristled at the comment and stated, "No tavern in the state was allowed that privilege." When Roach returned to Madison, he told reporters about his meeting with the city officials and promised to "keep prostitution out of Hurley."

Gust D. Arrested in Hurley 1942

Hurley: Licentiousness and Vice

THE MADISON AND MILWAUKEE newspapers engaged in a nonstop rampage of the raid. At the same time, the little *Montreal River Miner* tried to fend off the heavy blows against the city. The editors of the Madison papers sent copies to Hurley city officials with front-page pictures of the girls posing in front of the county jail, one with a young woman thumbing her nose at the photographer.

In retaliation, Armand Cirilli insulted Cedric Parker, *The Capital Times* reporter and photographer, stating that he was an admitted Communist who must have "passed up a course at the University in Madison on the ethics of journalism." Cirilli wrote, "Or else he must have been all hopped up before he visited the taverns with Roach's men. Cirilli aimed the second barrel at Van Every of the *Wisconsin State Journal* writing "Even if some of the stuff they wrote was true, it exceeded the bounds of good taste." An example of the pointed journalism to which the Cirilli referred was the August 6, 1942, *Journal* article that began, "Hurley, the sodden, unabashed and arrogant whore of Wisconsin cities, is again in the limelight as the forces of law once more descend upon this historic nest of licentiousness and vice."

The David versus Goliath battle continued. The *Miner* criticized Roach and asked how "harboring reporters and taking them with the agents on the trips through the taverns is any necessary corollary of a vice raid." Cirilli accused Roach of "looking for headlines when he took a flock of reporters with him." Despite Cirilli's reproach, the editor reported that many in Hurley felt that "the line was allowed to go too wide open" and that "we had it coming."

The bantering continued. On August 9, *The Capital Times* poked fun at a recently published brochure from the Iron County Advertising Association. The brochure stated, "As in the days past, people will come to Hurley 'for fun.' Its tavern district is a rendezvous for the gayer tourists. Many drive from miles away to get a look at Hurley. Many chuckle as they count the taverns

Clement V., Pearl C., Bernard S. Arrested in Hurley 1942

that line Silver Street. The miners, who bring iron ore from over 2,200 feet below the earth's surface, are for the most part solid family men. The lumberjacks are still pretty much of the transient variety. They still come to Hurley for a 'good time.' You will see them sitting in front of taverns that cater to their trade."

Hurley was under the thumb of John Roach and the Department of Taxation, and the press hammered the city. The animosity toward outsiders escalated because of the relentless criticism.

Hurley: Roach's Near Death Experience

REVENUE AGENTS, DOCTORS, TAVERNKEEPERS, lawyers, and prostitutes crowded the courthouse waiting for the hearings to begin. Witnesses and curiosity seekers sat upright in the wooden pews. The women dressed in their best attire, and the men held their hats in their laps. Roach stood by the door and watched the proceedings, eager to draw first blood. The courtroom was spotless, with everything freshly polished. Many glanced at Roach in disdain, but given his demeanor, it mattered little. Unknown to Roach, the biggest threat in the room was the custodian. *The Montreal River Miner* reported that when Roach dropped his cigarette on the newly waxed floor and then crushed it with his heel, anyone who knew the custodian "agreed that this was good cause for mayhem."

Hurley: The Sentences

ON SEPTEMBER 23, 1942, THE COUNTY COURT judge, based on a motion from the state, dismissed three charges against Bernard Santini, of Rae's Blackhawk at 100 Silver Street, and placed them against Minnie Rae Bathas. She pled *nolo contendere* to the closing hour and gambling charges but waived the preliminary hearing for operating a house of ill fame. Others followed the same strategy, agreeing to waive preliminary hearings and pleading guilty to prostitution charges. This would allow sentencing at the county level, which might be more lenient.

The strategy worked. The county judge fined eight operators $250 each and suspended six-month jail sentences upon payment of the fines.[107] While the fine sounds trivial, $250 in 1942 equates to $5,000 today.

Mildred L. Arrested in Hurley 1942

Wisconsin: Activity in Other Areas

IT IS IMPORTANT TO ACKNOWLEDGE that Roach did not single out Hurley during 1942. Earlier, in June, he said, "There is no reason why 110 taverns out of 13,439 should be permitted to bring disrepute upon the tavern industry of the state." Roach ordered the Langlade County district attorney to close five houses of prostitution by the following Saturday night and warned that if the DA did not comply, he would "take action." That same night, Roach delivered similar messages to county officials and tavernkeepers in Brown, Kewaunee, Door, Marinette, Oconto, and Shawano Counties.[108] Authorities from Brown and Langlade Counties assured Roach that "all houses of prostitution operated in connection with taverns in those counties had been closed."

* * *

Also in June, the Dane County district attorney began a John Doe probe in Madison to review over 100 taverns. The circuit judge issued a subpoena to get information from Roach, but he was out of town. In his absence, the judge and the district attorney questioned Harold Craney, a chief investigating officer who worked for Roach.

* * *

In late July, Roach and his crew raided the Rustic Rathskeller west of Wausau on Highway 29 and arrested Anna De Vogelaere as a keeper and two women as prostitutes. Then they raided the Willow Inn in Clark County, two miles from Abbotsford, and arrested Arnold F. Lieders as a keeper and two women as inmates.[109]

* * *

In late August, after the Hurley raid, Roach and his team raided the Hi-Ho[110] and the Pastime Club, both near Green Bay and both suspected of prostitution. Agents arrested seven women along with the tavernkeepers. They arrested Emma La Duke, keeper of the Pastime Club, but could not find Eva Kitson of the Hi-Ho Club. Roach said these raids resulted from a complaint from the war department because several servicemen had "contracted venereal diseases at the taverns."[111]

* * *

Oneida County rests between Rhinelander and Minocqua. Roach busted three brothels in Crescent, Newbold, and Pine Lake townships. On September 4, agents raided Oneida County and arrested Lena Rapier of Lena's Farmhouse on Highway 47 northwest of Rhinelander. Lena's Farmhouse was different from Hurley's taverns as the "Farmhouse" was a brothel. They also arrested Elizabeth Seraphine of Seraphine's tavern on Highway 17 north of Rhinelander.

Langlade County sits between Wausau and Rhinelander, and Antigo is the county seat. In

Langlade County, they pinched Marge Agostine, owner of Marge's Tavern, and Ella Bleckschmidt of the Whitehouse Tavern. Agents charged them with selling liquor after 1 a.m. and operating houses of ill fame. The judge released most defendants within a day after they paid fines and court costs. The women arrested for soliciting pled guilty, but the judge postponed sentencing until receipt of syphilis test results.[112] The White House tavern would survive this raid, and Ela Bleckschmidt would be newsworthy until 1982.[113]

Diane C., Kathleen M., Sally O., Peggy O. Arrested in Hurley 1942

Madison: A Letter from Eliot Ness

AFTER THE END OF PROHIBITION in 1933, Eliot Ness worked several jobs, including as an alcohol tax agent in Ohio, Kentucky, and Tennessee, as Safety Director of Cleveland, and as Director of the Social Protection Division of the U.S. Federal Security Agency. In this last position, his mission was to eliminate venereal disease, which he referred to as "Military Saboteur Number 1." In 1942, Ness authored a book entitled *What About Girls?* which was published in 1943 by the YMCA's Armed Services Department, warning of the dangers of venereal disease. At this time, Ness did not know that his nemesis, Al Capone, would die of syphilis just three years later.

In early September 1942, Ness wrote a letter to John Roach and his boss, Treasurer John Smith. Ness wrote, "You are to be particularly commended on the excellent work which you have recently done in closing the houses of prostitution which were operating in the taverns of Hurley, Wisconsin." The letter was high praise for Roach, and it fueled his enthusiasm to pursue Hurley's rogue operators.

Hurley: Not Part of a Reform Movement

ROACH'S RENEWED VIGOR did not go unnoticed, and many wondered if he was being too righteous. The *Wisconsin State Journal* called the raid on Hurley a "morals raid" in which John Roach "closed down Hurley's Silver Street's houses of prostitution."

On September 6, the *Journal* reported that agents raided 33 taverns in 11 counties since mid-June, arresting 81 prostitutes. Roach said that he would "Continue to eliminate prostitution where it is in any manner connected to the tavern industry." He reassured the public that this effort should not be considered a "reform movement" but rather a "consideration for public health and the welfare of the national defense." He praised the FBI and the State Board of Health, which cooperated in the raids, and said that the legitimate tavern associations told him they supported "the campaign." Although this was a statewide initiative, 42% of the prostitution arrests were in Hurley.[114]

Madison: Roach Gets Recognition

NEWS OF WISCONSIN'S EFFORTS to eliminate prostitution spread across the country, and John Roach was in the limelight. In September, the National Tax Association selected Roach as the chair of its conference in Nashville. The Association focused on bringing leaders to the forefront and for John Roach to be recognized by peers on the national stage was a significant achievement.

Hurley: The Case of Rocco Legato

ROCCO "AL" LEGATO WAS A SHADY character with a sordid history. Legato had a record as a white-slaver from 1933 and he spent time at federal prisons in both Chillicothe, Missouri and Leavenworth, Kansas.[115] In 1935 at age 26, along with an accomplice, the FBI arrested him for holding a 22-year-old St. Paul girl prisoner in Kankakee, Illinois.[116] In 1942, he and Loretta Legato were fined as being inmates of a disorderly house in the Town of Spencer near Wausau.[117]

On September 13, 1942, Legato drove Mae Collins from St. Paul to Duluth to meet Jack Gasbarri. If Collins met his approval, Gasbarri would hire her to work at his tavern, Jackpot's Flame in Hurley. She did, and Gasbarri took her to Hurley. This seemingly benign event would prove disastrous for everyone involved in May the following year.

* * *

In March 1943, after the FBI cracked one of the largest white slave rings in Midwest history, Legato was behind bars in the Ramsey County jail in St. Paul. He had been indicted by a federal grand jury for transporting a woman from St. Paul to Deadwood S.D. for prostitution.[118]

* * *

On May 2, 1943, Thomas Madden, the deputy U.S. Marshall from Superior, arrested Gasbarri at the Flame tavern for violating the Mann Act. Gasbarri pled not guilty, and the judge scheduled the trial for the following week in Federal court in Duluth.

The Mann Act, also known as the White-Slave Traffic Act of 1910, made it unlawful to transport a woman across a state line for immoral purposes. The FBI charged Gasbarri with transporting Mae Collins from Duluth to Hurley in September 1942 for the purpose of prostitution.[119] On May 12, Gasbarri pled guilty to the "white slavery" charge, and a federal court judge sentenced him to 2½ years in federal prison along with a fine of $1,000 ($20,000 today).

* * *

Rocco Legato, who transported Mae Collins to Duluth, pled guilty as a co-conspirator. However, a St. Paul Federal Court previously sentenced Legato to five years on a separate Mann Act violation, and the Duluth Court allowed his two-year sentence to be served concurrently.[120] After this sentence, the record shows that Legato got a fine for speeding in 1952 but failed to appear in court. Rocco Legato died in 1969 at the age of 60 in St. Paul.[121]

Hurley: The Me Kaivata Auttaa (We Need Help) Situation

As fall approached, the Hurley City Council faced continued and varied complications. During their October 6 meeting, they debated the request to transfer a liquor license from the Ironwood House to the Club Chateau. The proprietor's wife presented a letter of authorization from her husband, who was overseas in the army. The council expressed concern that the "flagrant" transfer of licenses might create a "rent war," and they moved cautiously with the request. Fortuitously, they found a reason to table the discussion when they realized that the operator wrote the letter in Finnish, and they needed a translator to ensure rent authenticity.[122]

Hurley: The Case of the Missing Sheriff and the Disappearing Women

AFTER THE AUGUST ARRESTS were settled, Silver Street returned to normal until mid-December. Roach knew that the penalties were trivial and suspected that Hurley was open for business. He planned to raid the lower blocks on the evening of December 13 and spent the afternoon with the judge preparing 27 warrants. However, the inability to find the sheriff to deputize the agents thwarted his plans. The raid would have to wait until the following evening, and Roach anticipated a bust without the element of surprise. On Monday, December 14, a somber John Roach, and his crew of agents scoured the lower blocks of Silver Street, serving 12 of the 27 warrants. As anticipated, several tavern operators and most of the girls were absent.

Roach was furious. He held 18 vacant warrants for the missing girls and growled at one bartender, "The girls won't get away next time. There won't be any slip-ups then." Roach believed the tavernkeepers warned the girls during the six hours it took to find the sheriff. To salvage the effort, he arrested Jack Gasbarri of Jackpot's Flame, Joe Vita of the Hi-Ho, and bartenders of five other taverns on various counts.

A frustrated Roach handed the warrants for the missing targets to the sheriff and instructed him to serve them when they returned. He threatened that if they didn't show up, he would "take other means."

Two of the keepers had good reasons for being absent. Roach was going to charge them with possessing gambling devices, keeping houses of ill fame, selling liquor after-hours, and obstructing the view of the interior of their taverns. Another operator was going to be charged with possessing gambling devices, keeping a house of ill fame, and not having a tavern license. The following Monday, the judge arraigned James Shields,[123] the operator of both the TryAngle Inn and the Ritz, for being an inmate of a house of ill fame and for failure to have an operator's license.[124]

Madison: Closing Time

IN LATE DECEMBER, the Wisconsin legislature debated the closing hour law for Wisconsin taverns. The current law prohibited the sale of liquor after 1:00 a.m. statewide but did not require establishments to close at that time. Further, Milwaukee enjoyed a later time for serving liquor. Local ordinances governed the closing time, and statewide practices were not uniform. Roach announced that he would support legislation establishing a uniform and statewide tavern closing law.

Tavern closing time was a thorny and pervasive issue which continued for decades. It would be debated, defiled, and deliberated by tavern owners, the press, local governments, and the legislature. There was no substantive resolution. The envy of Milwaukee's extended closing time annoyed the rest of the state. Hurley, and probably many other areas, responded to Milwaukee's privilege by violating the law and accepting prosecution, resulting in fines. Later, these closing-hour incidents would haunt the taverns of Hurley as the state counted them as "offenses," regardless of their triviality.

1943

Hurley: Young Women Wanted by the FBI

IN EARLY 1943, in a curious twist, the FBI ran a help wanted ad in the *Montreal River Miner* stating, "Women between the ages of 18 and 40 are needed for clerical work by the FBI for employment in Washington D.C. No previous clerical experience is necessary. Starting salary is $1,440 per year." Curiously, just six months earlier, the FBI was in Hurley arresting women who fit that same profile.[125]

Hurley: Pleading Guilty, But Not for Prostitution

THE DECEMBER RAID CAUSED several tavern operators to plead guilty in January. Jack Gasbarri, Kathleen Napoli, and Joe Vita, operators of the Flame, the Ritz, and the Hi-Ho, respectively, pled guilty to possessing gambling devices, obstructing the view of their taverns, and selling liquor after-hours. Waiving their hearings on the house of ill-fame charge, they were bound over to county court.

The law required that the windows on the street side of taverns be unobstructed so that police could determine if they closed on time. After 1 a.m., the police directed their spotlight at the windows of the taverns. The operators made money after 1 a.m. and used curtains or boxes to block the windows. Obscuring windows was a common offense and carried a minor citation, reimbursed by serving a few more drinks after-hours.

In the third week of January, the state dismissed the four charges against Kathleen Napoli because she was not on the premises at the time of the raid, and a warrant was never served. Further, the tavern was in the name of her husband Dominic, who, as previously mentioned, was in the Army at the time.[126]

As January progressed, William Matrella pled guilty to operating a house of ill-fame at the Ritz. Edna Shields, the proprietor of the TryAngle Inn, pled guilty for having gambling devices, selling liquor after-hours, and obstructing the view inside her tavern. Jack Gasbarri, the Flame operator, waived a preliminary hearing for operating a house of prostitution and was bound to the court on a $500 bond. The judge rescheduled the case against Louis Gasbarri (Jack's brother) for serving liquor without a bartender's license and being an inmate of a house of ill fame.

Madison: Roach Out and Tutton In

IN LATE JANUARY 1943, Roach enlisted as a captain in the army, and the state granted him a leave of absence.[127] The agency appointed his assistant, Clyde Samuel Tutton, 36, as acting chief of the Beverage Tax Division. Soon after his appointment, Tutton told the press, "Sale of liquor to minors and traffic in prostitution in connection with taverns will continue to be vigorously prosecuted. I advise all members of the industry and liquor retail trade not to anticipate any relaxation in the prosecution and administration of Wisconsin liquor, beer, and cigarette laws. You may be assured that the policy of cooperation with all legitimate tavernkeepers will be followed."[128]

Tutton promised to follow in the footsteps of John Roach, footsteps that would eventually collide after the war.

Hurley: The Turbulent Case of Stanley Serbin

STANLEY SERBIN WAS BORN in Calumet, Michigan, in 1909 and moved to Ironwood in 1915 at the age of six. When he was 28, in July 1935, the Hurley City Council issued him an operator's license, and the following year, he opened a tavern at First Avenue and Silver Street.

On the morning of May 21, 1936, Serbin was shooting cans with a .22 caliber rifle in the alley behind his tavern. Stephen Trochim,[129] 27, and a group of friends approached Serbin. Trochim joked about his accuracy and stretched his arm, hat in hand, challenging Serbin to shoot it. Serbin aimed and sent the bullet through Trochim's hand rather than his hat.[130] Trochim was horrified as the bullet tore through two fingers. A doctor treated Trochim at Runstrom's Hospital in Ironwood. Serbin assured police that it was a "playful stunt with an empty gun." Trochim, on the other hand, refused to talk to anyone about the incident.[131]

* * *

In September 1937, police arrested Serbin for "drunken or reckless" driving.[132] Then, in November, Lois Bannor and Eugene Frith assaulted Serbin after a quarrel. The police arrested the couple, and the judge charged Bannor with improper noise and disturbance. Frith, unable to pay the $10 fine, spent ten days in the county jail.[133]

* * *

In late 1938, Mr. N. G. Wilson, likely an attorney from Milwaukee, posted a notice in the *Ironwood Daily Globe*. It read, "Suitable compensation will be paid for information as to the whereabouts of Stanley Serbin, formerly of Hurley, Wisconsin, or for the whereabouts of a 1937 Buick Club Sedan Serial No. 3201632, License No. 692-048, Wisconsin."[134] At some point, Serbin must have returned the car as it was sold at auction February 16.[135]

* * *

On August 2, 1939, Police Chief Albino Endrizzi arrested Serbin and Frank Caruso for fighting. Caruso pled guilty, and Judge Trembath found Serbin guilty. He fined them $5 each.[136] In August 1939, the Hurley City Council licensing committee stated, "We, your license committee, beg to report that we have examined the following applications and recommended the granting of the same." [137] With that declaration, the council granted Serbin a Class B beer and liquor license.[138]

* * *

Serbin's business failed to gain traction as on November 22, 1939, Hurley Police arrested him for vagrancy. A frustrated Judge Trembath simply told Serbin "to get out of town." Serbin failed to take the order seriously, and on December 14, police arrested him for being drunk again and charged him with being a "habitual criminal." Unable to post a $500 bond, Serbin resided in Sheriff Sam Giovanoni's jail.[139] At trial, Judge Trembath gave Serbin a 50-day sentence, which he offered to suspend if Serbin would vacate Iron County. He refused to leave, and in December 1939, Trembath forced the issue, ordering Sheriff Giovanoni to bring Stanley Serbin to Waupun to serve a term from one to two years.[140]

* * *

After Waupun, Serbin returned to Hurley. On February 2, 1943, he enticed Cira Gasbarri of the Flame Bar and Jean Hunter, a prostitute, into a "free-for-all" brawl. Things got out of hand when Hunter, Jacqueline Evans, and Ruth Malone – all prostitutes – joined the fray. Two women attacked Officer Steve Rajkovich[141] when he tried to break up the fight. When he regained control, he arrested them for resisting arrest and for assault and battery. The judge ordered Hunter to 15 days in the county jail and suspended the 90-day sentences of Evans and Malone, providing they leave town. Police arrested Serbin on a repeater charge as well as assault and battery. On February 9, after being out for only a brief period, Judge Trembath sentenced Serbin to 1–3 years in the state prison at Waupun,[142] and back he went.

After his second term in prison and knowing that Hurley was trouble for him, he returned anyway. He became infatuated with Ida Bushaw, 48, a waitress at the Red Feather Tavern in Hurley. In the autumn of 1949, Serbin, now 41, broke into her home in Ironwood. Serbin threatened her with a knife, but she talked him down, and he agreed to leave.

Nonetheless, Serbin obsessed about Bushaw, and on December 1, he entered the Red Feather Tavern on Silver Street, wanting to talk to her. She was afraid and tried to avoid him, but he caught up with her and pinned her to the back of the bar. Then he pulled a large kitchen knife from his jacket and slashed her across the abdomen, arm, chest, and hand as she struggled. Louis Gasbarri, the proprietor, wrestled the knife from Serbin and called the police. When Bushaw arrived at the Grandview Hospital, the doctor gave her a 50-50 chance of survival. The judge set bail at $2,500. District Attorney Alex Raineri reported that Serbin admitted to the crime. In January 1950, with Bushaw recovering, Serbin pleaded guilty to "assault with intent to murder," and Judge Risjord sentenced him to 1–7 years at Waupun. Busha recovered in the hospital until mid-December when she was released.[143]

*   *   *

On January 29, 1955, after spending two weeks in the Grand View Hospital in Ironwood, the turbulent life of Stanley Serbin, 48, ended.[144] The obituary did not identify the cause of death.

Madison: Tutton Pontificates

IN APRIL 1943, Clyde Tutton told tavern owners, "The future livelihood of the tavern industry in Wisconsin depends upon its 100 percent compliance to the code of conduct which prohibits selling liquor to minors, allowing prostitution in connection with taverns, and selling liquor to a person who has overindulged." Referring to local officials, Tutton commented, "By their revocation or refusal to grant licenses to known violators they can clean up that small 5 percent of the retail trade that persists in flouting the Wisconsin laws." He also repeated Roach's warning, "The state of Wisconsin retains the right to immediate action on the sale of liquor to minors or prostitution in connection with the tavern. In the case of a sale after-hours, we shall notify the local authorities. In the event they neglect to conform to the Wisconsin statutes after the warning, arrests will be made."[145]

Although the agents patrolled the entire state, Tutton – like Roach before him – kept an eye on Hurley, and Hurley lay low on the horizon. However, a sustained low profile was not in Hurley's nature.

Hurley: Vagrancy at the Hi-Ho

HURLEY ATTEMPTED A SUPERFICIAL response to the warning by arresting a woman at the Hi-Ho for vagrancy in late April 1943. The judge sentenced her to 90 days in the county jail as this was her second offense. This minor infraction at the Hi-Ho prefaced a more severe violation, eventually carrying a far more serious penalty for one Hurley tavernkeeper.

Hurley: A "Uniform" Tavern Closing Law

BY MID-JUNE, HURLEY COUNCIL MEMBERS were relieved because they received only 69 liquor applications, nine fewer than allowed. This would mitigate the threats from the Beverage Tax Division.

At the same time, state lawmakers passed the Squires Bill, which set a uniform closing time of 1 a.m. for all Wisconsin municipalities except Milwaukee. Recognizing many shift workers, they set the Milwaukee time at 2:00 a.m.[146] Tutton again pledged to strictly enforce closing laws and offered anonymity to anyone who turned in bootleggers. He made no excuse that this was, among other things, an economic issue. He said, "The sale of illegal liquor deprives each town, city, or village of tax money."

Tutton appealed for public help, saying, "It is of the interest of everyone to report his suspicions, and the fact that rumors may be unsubstantiated has no bearing on the subject as it is necessary that proper investigation is conducted before any prosecution can be instigated." Tutton was unabashedly appealing to the public to ensure that the state collected all tax revenue. There is no evidence to indicate that anyone was reported, at least for this reason.

Hurley: A Raineri Recess

IN OCTOBER 1943, Iron County District Attorney J. C. Raineri entered the U.S. Naval Reserve as a lieutenant. James E. Flandrena, a 15-year Iron County Judge, was appointed acting district attorney during his absence. With J. C.'s absence and Alex's return to school, Hurley was absent from the Raineri brothers – for a while.[147]

Hurley: State Agents Sweep Lower Blocks

THINGS WERE QUIET ON SILVER STREET during the summer of 1943, and tavern owners became complacent. Hunters gravitated to Hurley during deer season, and the Beverage Tax Division embarked on their own three-day hunting season in mid-October. Senior Agent Harold Craney of the Wisconsin Beverage Tax Division made a routine visit to Hurley. Agents arrested the keepers of 17 taverns on the lower blocks of Silver Street including Dan Angelo, Virgil DaPra, Fred Fontecchio, Jr., Joseph McRaniels, James Gasbarri, William Matrella, and Dominic Vita, to name a few.

This pack would become the "usual suspects" while others would fade into history. They owned taverns with colorful names like Jean's Chateau, the White Front, the Flame Bar, the Ritz, and the TryAngle Inn.

In court, most pled guilty to obstructing the view into their taverns and operating after-hours. In what would become a tired threat, Agent Craney warned, "If on any future regular check-up on taverns in Hurley any improper operation is shown, it may be necessary for Clyde S. Tutton, chief of the Beverage Tax Division, to request the cooperative assistance of other state agencies and the federal authorities to correct conditions."[148]

Hurley: Ironwood Cop Runs Amuck

AS IF IT WASN'T BAD ENOUGH that Hurley was under the thumb of State and Federal authorities, it was subject to an unusual event involving a Michigan law enforcement officer. Although those involved tried to cover it up, the gritty little *Montreal River Miner,* always keeping an ear to the ground, reported the event in November.

At 7 a.m. on November 1, 1943, after several hours of drinking at a Silver Street tavern, a uniformed and quite drunk Ironwood police officer began challenging people about their patriotism. In a fit of hubris, he chased the bartender of the Santini Hotel into the alley and then harassed people along Silver Street as he wobbled westerly. Within a few blocks, he entered the Gus Lewis Café and staggered up to the owner. Lewis was startled as the drunk cop shoved his revolver into his stomach and asked if he was an American. Lewis instinctively pronounced his allegiance. Satisfied, the cop targeted a waitress and continued the interrogation. Terror-stricken, she managed to profess loyalty. Unable to find someone to shoot for not being an American and having run out of staff, he approached a customer sitting in a booth eating his breakfast. The customer exclaimed that he, too, was an American despite a mouth full of toast. The cop, baffled and angry, sneered at the customer and said, "I am going to shoot you anyway."

As he cocked the hammer of his revolver, Lewis hollered "duck," and the gun belched a .38 caliber round, barely missing the customer. The bullet tore a hole through the corner of the booth, passed through the partition wall, and burned through the bartender's coat hanging on the opposite side of the wall. Lewis called the Ironwood police chief, and a Michigan squad car raced across the Montreal River into Wisconsin. The chief holstered the revolver, cuffed his officer, and carted him back across the state line. The *Montreal River Miner* stated, "The policeman, in deference to his family we omit his name...."[149] In apparent deference to the neighboring city, no charges were filed. There is no record of whether the bartender's coat hole was repaired, if Lewis charged the customer for his breakfast, or if the waitress returned to work.

Madison: People Need a Drink

IN MID-NOVEMBER 1943, Clyde Tutton reported a "definite shortage" of whiskey in Wisconsin. The liquor industry blamed speculators for "hoarding large stocks" and alleged they "cleared the way for the return of bootlegging." The Alcohol Beverage Control Association said that the liquor shortage was caused by the "conversion of distilleries to the production of industrial alcohol and an increase of between 200 and 300 percent in consumer demand for distilled spirits." In response to the shortages, the federal government surveyed law enforcement agencies and found that bootlegging was returning at a "modest scale minus the sawed-off shotguns and gangsters of the prohibition era."[150]

Hurley: The Victrola Violation

TAVERN OPERATORS, PARTICULARLY those operating on the law's edge, felt harassed by fickle authorities. The following event in mid-December 1943 illustrates the point.

Fred Fontechio, Jr. played Christmas music on a Victrola at the Club Fiesta on the lower block of Silver Street. While patrolling, the Hurley police chief entered the tavern and heard the music. For an unknown reason, a city ordinance forbade "the playing of music by a Victrola, piano, or any other similar instrument in the part of a tavern where liquor is sold."[151] Since taverns on the lower block of Silver Street generated bucketloads of money, Fontecchio, grumbling as he did, pled guilty in Iron County Court and paid the $25 fine.

Hurley: The Colliers Magazine Incident

HENRY FRANCIS BROWN WAS A Seventh-Day Adventist from Lansing, Michigan. He was also the secretary of the American Temperance Society. In November 1943, he gave presentations on "America's Fifth Column" at the Bessemer Veterans Memorial building and the Ironwood Memorial Building. The billing stated, "For more than 17 years the speaker has made a study of the problem of liquor, traveling in 40 different countries on four continents. Just recently he completed studies at Yale University on the scientific aspects of alcohol."

Colliers magazine editorialized using Brown's observations in their December 25, 1943, issue. They wrote, "We haven't been in Hurley, Wisconsin, but Mr. Henry Francis Brown of the American Temperance of the Seventh Day Adventists in Lansing, Michigan, writes to notify us that Hurley 'is known far and wide as the wettest town on the map.'" The article quotes Brown, "Hurley's population is less than 3,000. I counted sixty-five taverns in its five blocks of Main Street. On one block, there are nine taverns side by side, and they look across the street at nine taverns side by side – eighteen in one block. It's a story that ought to be told to the nation." *Collier's* stated, "Well, we've told it. We shall now sit back in our chair and wait for explanations from Hurley, and we hope that they will include what else Hurley does in its spare time, if any."

An infuriated Armand Cirilli, the editor of the *Montreal River Miner*, published a response on December 23. Cirilli wrote, "Well, here is our answer. To begin with, we don't attempt to apologize or explain away our taverns. We could point out, however, that Hurley is in the center of an iron ore range with a population of over 30,000 people. That is the center of the last remnants of the logging industry and that Hurley is the oasis, as it were, for approximately 100,000 people. Because of publicity, such as above, some enterprising men have capitalized on it and made two blocks of our city the "playground" of the North."

Cirilli was incensed and hammered the keys of his typewriter, quite likely wearing the ribbon threadbare. "We confine ourselves, however, to *Collier's* attempted wisecrack of 'what else Hurley does in its spare time. If any.' To begin with, the people of Hurley are busy in the war effort. Its men labor 3,000 feet below the surface of the earth to turn out its share of the 80,000,000 tons of precious iron every year for the vital steel of our nation. They are busy in the lumber camps sawing logs and cutting pulpwood to meet the critical demands for wood products.

He wrote about the quality of education, the modern sports facilities, and the success of high school graduates. He wrote about Hurley's participation in war efforts and social enterprises including war bond purchases and activity in the Women's Club, the American Legion, the Legion Auxiliary, the Chamber of Commerce, the Red Cross, and at least a dozen fraternal organizations. He noted that 400 men had left home to risk their lives fighting against fascism. He summed up the article, "In fact, the people of Hurley are so busy doing the better and worthwhile things in life that we don't have the time and are too patriotic in these trying times to go driving around to distant cities to count the taverns on their city streets."[152]

Stung, neither *Collier's* nor Henry Francis Brown extended the courtesy of a response.

Florence Co: John Carollo and the Saga of Spread Eagle

THERE IS NO ONE PLACE to put this story since it ranges from 1934 to 1968. The setting is Florence County in northern Wisconsin and has a thread to Hurley. There is one main actor, two competitors, a couple of judges, federal prisoners, a disbarred attorney, and a gaggle of prostitutes. With that introduction, it might as well be placed here, in 1943.

* * *

John Carollo, Jr. – Part 1

Florence County is mostly forested, with no cities or villages and only eight townships. One of the townships is Spread Eagle which has a cluster of homes on the south side of a chain of lakes. The Town of Spread Eagle borders Upper Michigan and is 60 miles south of Marquette. For most of his life, John Carollo, Jr.[153] lived in Spread Eagle.

In 1934, after serving a term at the Marquette Branch Prison, local authorities denied Carollo a tavern license in upper Michigan, so he moved across the state line to Spread Eagle. There, despite not having the one-year residency requirement, he made a deal with a Florence County official to purchase a tavern and a liquor license.[154]

* * *

In January 1936, U.S. District Judge Fred M. Raymond, in Marquette, impaneled a grand jury to "improve conditions in the Upper Peninsula."[155] The jury was investigating illegal liquor production and wanted testimony from Carollo and his sister Theresa. Not wanting to testify, they hired Attorney Ray Derham,[156] from Iron Mountain, Michigan, to help. Derham knew little about Carollo and simply reviewed the grand jury subpoena. He told Carollo that neither he nor his sister needed to comply with the order. He advised that it was illegal because the name of the issuing officer had been typed rather than hand written. Relying on this technicality had two results. The first was a minor issue: Carollo was held in contempt for not appearing at the grand jury.[157] The second was devastating.

After learning about the advice that Derham gave Carollo, Judge Raymond was furious and ordered Derham's name to be "stricken from the roll of attorneys in the western federal court district for one year." The judge disbarred Derham on the spot. Derham was shocked and admitted that he failed to review Carollo's background. Further, he was embarrassed as he had recently completed a 2-year term in the Michigan state senate, and this tarnished his reputation.

* * *

The connection to Hurley is Mike Flannery, one of John Carollo's competitors in Spread Eagle, and the story is worth a side trip.

On May 29, 1939, Florence County Sheriff Ode N. Christensen and 12 officers raided disorderly houses owned by Ray "Mike" Flannery, Alphonse Fontecchio, and John Carollo. The police arrested a total of eight, and with a swift response, a circuit court judge from Marinette padlocked the buildings.

Ray "Mike" Flannery

Flannery claimed he was "virtually driven out of the tavern business in Florence County." [158] He traveled to Hurley, and on June 28, 1939, when the city council examined the applicants for liquor licenses, they held Flannery's application "for further investigation."[159]

The Hurley City Council withheld the Flannery application because the padlock proceedings in Spread Eagle were still under consideration. In addition to Flannery, Fontecchio and Carollo were out on bail. On July 11, 1939, the Hurley City Council "unanimously accepted the license committee's report, with one rejection, that of Mike Flannery. The meeting minutes read, "Mike Flannery's application was ordered held for further investigation after it was brought out that the man has an unsavory reputation."[160] The *Montreal River Miner* reported, "the application of Mike Flannery for a retail liquor license was held over until an investigation of a charge against him at Spread Eagle can be made."[161] Flannery's application stayed on the agenda for the next week.

At the end of July, a judge padlocked the taverns owned by Flannery (Star Inn), Carollo (Carollo's Hill Top), and Fontecchio (Pine Tree Inn) for one year.[162] So, after Carollo's joint in Spread Eagle was padlocked, the Hurley City Council, finally granted Flannery a Class B beer and liquor license on August 1.[163] Then, on August 4, Flannery was issued a Hurley tavern license[164] because the Florence County District Attorney dismissed all charges when the defendants paid fines.[165] Flannery persevered, and Witcoff along with the Hurley City Council, offered him a new opportunity in Hurley.

John Carollo, Jr. – Part 2

Meanwhile, John Carollo opened a new brothel in Spread Eagle, and operated until August 1942 when, based upon a grand jury investigation, he was arrested for violating the Mann Act. The judge set the bail at $2,000.[166] In early 1943, Carollo was charged with transporting Eunice Case, a prostitute, from Spread Eagle to Marinette, Wisconsin, via Iron Mountain, Michigan. Carollo's attorney argued that the travel through Michigan "was only incidental since it was on the route." The prosecutor produced two witnesses who had worked for Carollo: Clyde Haines and Lee Stanley. Both had to be transported from a Wisconsin state prison to testify at the trial.

It was learned that after Carollo dropped off Eunice Case aka The Platinum Blonde, she, along with Haines and Stanley, robbed Anne's tavern at gunpoint near Manitowoc. This Mann Act entanglement motivated the judge to sentence John Carollo to two years in federal prison. Carollo was temporarily released on a $1,000 bail bond.[167] Never wanting to miss an opportunity, he used the time to transport a prostitute from Gilbert, Minnesota, to Spread Eagle. He didn't get far as the police were watching him. They arrested and charged him with another violation of the Mann Act.[168] About the same time, a judge sentenced Eunice Case to 3–6 years at Taycheedah for the holdup (she held the gun.)[169] Clyde Haines got concurrent terms of 1–5 and 3–8 years at Waupun.

In October 1943, Haines asked Governor Goodland to make him eligible for parole so he could join the army. However, Goodland summarily denied the request because of Haines nine previous arrests, three of which were felonies, and separate probation and parole violations.[170]

* * *

In February 1963, Beverage Tax agents along with the Florence County District Attorney, arrested John Carollo, now 50, just before midnight for operating a house of ill fame. He was apprehended at a home in Spread Eagle along with Patricia Miller, 23, and Michele Benson, 26. He was released on a $3,500 bond.[171] In early June, Carollo paid a $1,500 fine and the women paid $250 and $25, respectively.

* * *

In mid-February 1965, state agent Fred Schleisinger of Milwaukee visited the Highway Inn, a roadhouse in Spread Eagle. Michelle Benson, 28, from St. Louis, invited him to engage in sex. Schleisinger promptly arrested her for solicitation along with Lois Berry, 43, the keeper of the house.

With this arrest, the Town of Spread Eagle rose from the ashes of the 1939–1950 prostitution raids. Attorney Robert Kennedy from Rhinelander defended the women. He was, interestingly, also the district attorney from neighboring Forest County. During a March 30 preliminary hearing, Kennedy moved to suppress the evidence against the women, arguing that it was illegally obtained. They both pled not guilty, provided bail bonds, and waited for trial.[172]

At the hearing in April, a Florence County judge denied the motion for suppression. In mid-March 1966, both women pled *nolo contendre*. The judge fined Berry $600 and Benson $400 and ordered the women to stay out of the area or he would put them in jail. Attorney Walter Dalla Gramma initiated a padlocking action on the Highway Inn.[173] This was just another bump in the road for Michelle Benson.

* * *

In mid-September 1968, state agents arrested Carollo again for keeping a house of ill fame in at the Green Garage in Spread Eagle. They also nabbed Michelle Benson, 30, of Spread Eagle and Penny Marcus, 23 of Milwaukee for soliciting.[174] This was Benson's third arrest for prostitution. In court, the judge fined John Carollo $1,750 along with a suspended three-year prison sentence and two years of probation. Benson was fined $500 but instead of the promise of prison, she was ordered to leave the state. Penny Marcus paid a $200 fine and got sent back to Milwaukee.[175]

After a long run in the prostitution business, Carollo faded from the record in 1968.

1944

Hurley: Joe Vita Gets a Gift

IN MARCH 1944, AGENT H. K. JOHNSON arrested Joe Vita, 39, of the Hi-Ho, and 28-year-old Hazel Calligaro[176]of the Red Feather Inn, after a federal grand jury in St. Paul indicted them for violating the Mann Act. On May 12, they pled guilty before Judge Robert C. Bell in federal court in Duluth. The judge released both on $5,000 bail and scheduled sentencing for the end of the court term.

In May, both Calligaro and Vita changed their pleas to guilty. Vita pled guilty to one count and the government dismissed five others. In June, United States Marshals delivered Joe Vita, along with five others to Leavenworth Federal Prison for violating the Mann Act.[177] Calligaro pled guilty on two counts while another was dismissed.[178]

The FBI considered the Hurley defendants are part of a white slave ring "who activities spread over five states," and they referred to Vita and Calligaro as the two "who handled the vice syndicate's affairs at Hurley." It would be wrong to trivialize the characterization given the statistics presented in the *Minneapolis Daily Times*, "Principle defendants to be sentenced are: Mrs. Andrew J. (Indian Sadie) Anderson, 63, notorious madame in Superior, Wis.' Willie Foreman, 39, Duluth, who the FBI said was guilty of more than 100 separate violations of the White Slave Traffic Act in 1943 alone, and Gene Hill, Duluth, a main spring in the interstate traffic between Duluth and Superior."[179]

In May 1944, Judge Bell sentenced Hazel Calligaro to two years in federal prison and five years of probation. Joe Vita got 3½ years and a $500 fine.[180] Upon release from prison, the Hurley City Council granted Vita a tavern license for the Hi-Ho at 21 Silver Street in June 1947.[181]

* * *

In early June, Alex J. Raineri filed papers to run as a Republican for the State Assembly representing Iron and Vilas Counties. In November, he won the seat vacated by the Progressive Margaret Varda.

Hurley: Eau Claire Ministers Demand a Clean Up of Hurley

IN EARLY 1944, THERE WAS A NATIONWIDE push to eliminate slot machines. Most of the pressure was on areas near military bases where officials believed that the mechanical bandits were robbing soldiers. Others believed that it was a moral issue reflecting poorly on local communities. Although there were issues in the southeastern counties in Wisconsin, most of the controversy centered in St. Croix and Clark Counties, near Eau Claire. A hearing in Madison resulted in the resignation of Robert A. Forsythe, the district attorney in St. Croix County, and a request for the removal of the Sheriffs of both St. Croix and Clark Counties was considered but tabled by Governor Goodland.

Reverend Raymond E. Ewing, pastor of Robert's Congregation Church, near Eau Claire, and five other local ministers spearheaded the petition. The ministers argued that since the presence of illegal slot machines was well known, the district attorneys and sheriffs should search the taverns and seize the equipment. However, the county officials said their role was to respond to complaints rather than raid taverns looking for violators.

The St. Croix and Clark County complaints looped Hurley into the issue, and the ministers demanded that Goodland clean up the northern city, which they felt to be an embarrassment to the State. Goodland complied and told Hurley Sheriff John Gersich and District Attorney J. C. Raineri to "clean up" the city or he would remove them "from office upon a substantiated complaint." The governor's threat was made public in Iron County, and when the sheriff visited each tavern, he found that they had already "complied" rather than face an inevitable brutal raid.

During this period, there were over 500 machines in Iron County "with one or more in constant operation in every tavern." The *Montreal River Miner* stated, "Just how long this 'taboo' on slot machines in Iron County will remain in effect is questionable, but it may be stated with at least some assurance that it will last as long as Gov. Goodland remains in office."[182]

Hurley: Raineri and Raineri

IN AUGUST 1944, the Raineri brothers, Joseph and Alex, formed the law firm of Raineri and Raineri and set up an office in the Paul Building on Silver Street in Hurley. Both had studied at Notre Dame, but Joseph graduated from the University of Minnesota and Alex from DePaul University in Chicago.[183]

Hurley: The Hardly Worth the Time Raid

GOVERNOR GOODLAND DID NOT TRUST Hurley, and on September 18, 1944, agents ravaged Iron County, raiding 48 taverns. After 1 a.m., they stormed the taverns in Hurley, Montreal, Pence, Iron Belt, and Mercer. Under threat of being removed from office, the sheriff delivered complaints prepared by state agents.[184]

The *Wisconsin State Journal* reported, "Although past raids there have been conducted primarily to stamp out houses of prostitution run in connection with taverns, those arrested Tuesday were charged only with minor violations."

In Madison, Tutton tallied the most recent Iron County arrests and reported 157 since August 1942. In what was now a tired cliché, he said that he "expected the tavernkeepers of Hurley to operate their taverns in compliance with the statutory requirements." He also repeated the familiar threat to "ask the assistance of other agencies and federal authorities" if Hurley doesn't comply with the law.

This raid netted a wide cast of characters from all over Iron County. The list was so long that the *Wisconsin State Journal* set it in a six-point font. Agents focused on Silver Street, including Jackpot's Flame bar, the Club Fiesta, the Lucky 13, the Red Feather, and the Swing Club. They arrested the usual suspects, including Andrew Carli, James Gasbarri, Fred Fontechio, Jr., Joe McRainels, Louis Gasbarri, Dominic Vita, and John Califano.

The charges against most county taverns were minor, and operators paid small fines for selling alcohol after hours and operating a tavern without a license. The judge dismissed three cases for lack of evidence.[185]

Mercer: The Case of Ralph Capone

MOST STORIES OF RALPH CAPONE focus on the early years when he was associated with his brothers and the Chicago syndicate known as the "Outfit." This story, however, picks up after Ralph served time in prison and is specific to his relationship with northern Wisconsin. Ralph Capone endured this history, and the tension between him and the authorities never waned. Instead, his character emerges from events and relationships as they intersect with local personalities.

*　*　*

Hurley was not exempt from the notoriety of major crime in Chicago. In April 1944, authorities searched the area around Mercer in search of Al Capone's brother, Matt, 35, wanted for the murder of James Larkin, a 52-year-old gambler and former horse trainer. Larkin was shot through the head in Capone's Cicero tavern, The Hall of Fame, and his body was deposited in a west-side alley. The Chicago Press pestered local Sheriff John Gersich and the *Iron County Miner* about the search for Matt.[186]

In mid-December 1944, Henry J. McCormick, a staff writer for the *Wisconsin State Journal,* wrote a series about Ralph Capone. He speculated how the war's end might affect tourism in northern Wisconsin. He focused on the criminal influence and specifically mentioned Ralph Capone, who, at this time, had retired near Mercer – 25 miles south of Hurley. In the first article, McCormick mused if Ralph Capone might "attempt to bring prostitution into the Mercer area." Ralph had operated several speakeasies and nightclubs with his brother Al in Chicago during the 1920s, and this reputation followed him like a grey ghost. Most notably, he operated the Cotton Club of Cicero, which the Chicago Crime Commission characterized as a "'whoopee' spot where liquor flowed freely, and it served as a rendezvous for those interested in nightlife." Ralph also operated an infamous brothel in Forest View called The Stockade.

In the first article on December 14, McCormick reported that Al Capone was no longer affiliated with the Chicago syndicate. He noted a dramatic change in Capone's personality and attributed it to the pressures of prison or mental deterioration from a physical ailment.[187] He referred to him as "loquacious" and very different from his feared reputation as a loathsome gangster. McCormick reported that Capone spent summers at his brother's home on Big Martha Lake near Mercer.

McCormick reasoned that Capone's ability to encourage business overshadowed any fear of their presence in the region. McCormick said Al and Ralph abandoned a criminal lifestyle after prison. While this may have been true for Al and Ralph, younger brother Matt was still on the run for the killing of James Larkin. McCormick said that Matt was "cooling off" while that case settled down."[188]

In the second article of December 15, McCormick wrote about the local perception of the Capone brothers. At this time, Ralph ran Beaver Lodge and was about to manage Billy's Bar in Mercer. McCormick praised the businesses as "high quality, operating efficiently, and clean." He wrote that these "legitimate" qualities made the Capone operations different from the taverns in Hurley.

McCormick reported that Ralph was eager to put his reputation behind him. He wrote, "Ralph doesn't want public opinion against him – one of the reasons he gives so freely to any and every charity hereabouts – and bringing in prostitution to this particular area would be highly unpopular with the large number of people who own summer residences in this section and send their families here for the summer."

McCormick was both easy on the Capones and critical of local authorities for enforcing gaming laws, specifically slot machines. He wrote, "There would seem to be no reason why 'the law' in northern Wisconsin should enforce the ban against gambling devices inasmuch as it's been thoroughly ignored for years and is being ignored today."

McCormick reported little concern about Chicago gangland influence in the area. He wrote, "For one thing, your private operator in northern Wisconsin doesn't scare easy, and don't ever think there wouldn't be trouble if Ralph Capone or his henchmen tried to 'muscle in.' Trouble in the wide-open country where high-powered rifles are owned by almost everybody is different kind of trouble than the Chicago kind where it's mostly close work." He summarized, "It's just a matter of good business. Murder, extortion, and muscling-in simply are not good business in the present case."[189]

McCormick's third article on December 17 was a summary of the history of Al Capone, biographical, and only one column long. He talked about Capone's start with Brooklyn's Five Points gang, his transition to Chicago under Johnny Torrio, and "Big Jim" Colosimo. He reported about the Capone's "notorious" Four Deuces Club located at 2222 South Wabash in Chicago and how Colosimo was murdered on the floor of the lounge. He discussed the St. Valentine's Day massacre and Capone's eventual truce with Bugsy Moran. He ended the piece by describing the seriousness of Al's mental state and that the FBI was still watching his behavior. [190]

McCormick's fourth and last article in the series described how businesses in the Manitowish area were concerned about how outside "wartime profiteers" could build large establishments, compete with local resorts, and survive down seasons.

Here, McCormick was as generous toward Manitowish as he was caustic toward Hurley, stating, "In general, northern Wisconsin presents the situation of little or no enforcement against gambling because public opinion favors a free rein. The same goes for bars staying open after hours. It's good business, the general public believes, to let such things go because they help attract tourists." He noted that Manitowish could develop year-round entertainment. Yet, when referring to the area 30 miles to the north, like his predecessors, he ranted against Hurley stating, "Oh yes, and then there's Hurley, that much-publicized sin spot right on the Wisconsin-Michigan border. Actually, Hurley presents sin in a most unattractive setting. It lacks the color and showmanship of other recognized sin spots at Butte, Reno, and Las Vegas. Hurley is a collection of low, smelly, law-breaking dives that obey regulations only when it's absolutely necessary. Anyone who's been there will vouch for that, and yet nice people will make the trip there in the summer to get a glimpse of the goings-on."

McCormick saw a dual opportunity in Manitowish. It could attract high-end clientele, assuming Capone didn't tarnish its reputation, while also allowing the "respectable crowd" to witness the low, smelly, law-breaking dives in Hurley.

McCormick's comments cut deep. He stated, "I had been told that Hurley had changed a lot. The change has been more apparent than real. More of the vice is concealed than formerly was the case, and they don't stay open until all hours as they once did. The same law-defying conditions are there, however, even if they are more concealed."

Referring to Manitowish, he said, "They want no trek of the Hurley honky-tonk down into this nearby section. Resort operators – and that goes for Ralph Capone as well as the others – know that people will go on an occasional slumming expedition but that they won't spend their vacations in that kind of an atmosphere." McCormick reported as though he had firsthand knowledge.

He went on to complement Emil Wanetka of Little Bohemia. He said that Wanetka was "one of the smartest operators in the section" because he made a "rich haul the summer after FBI men had cornered John Dillinger and his infamous gang" at the resort. McCormick reported that Wanetka put a few "extra" bullet holes in the wall to add to the attraction of the criminal resort. Unknown to most, John Roach and his state-owned .38 revolver deposited some of those holes.[191] McCormick continued to discuss Wanetka's business acumen, "The final touch was when Emil Wanetka hired John Dillinger's father to work at his resort after his son had been cut down by FBI men coming out of a Chicago theater."

Compared to the thrashing McCormick gave Hurley, he went soft on the notorious gunfight at Little Bohemia, saying, "The tourists ate it up. Now, do you think many vacationers wouldn't get a little shiver of pleasure as seeing in the flesh the notorious Brothers Capone?"[192]

Perhaps McCormick would have been more generous to Hurley had the little city embraced more notorious, violent, or gun-slinging criminals.

1945

Madison: Alex Raineri v. The Woman's Christian Temperance Union

IN JANUARY 1945, Alex Raineri was sworn in as a member of the State of Wisconsin Assembly in Madison. It didn't take him long to act on behalf of the tavern owners – a powerful part of his constituent base.[193] His actions as a legislator would mark him as a target for John Roach. Raineri quickly supported a bill that would allow taverns statewide to have the same closing hours as Milwaukee's 2 a.m. on weekdays and 3:30 a.m. on Saturdays. As a member of the Excise and Fees Committee, he fiercely supported the proposal. The *Wisconsin State Journal* reported, "Wisconsin wet and dry forces, traditional opponents, fought a furious but no-decision contest." The Woman's Christian Temperance Union appeared at the hearing and argued that the bill "would contribute to war plant absenteeism, use up and waste war-needed manpower and materials, and breed 'moral and social destruction.'" The nays prevailed as the bill failed to make it out of committee.[194]

Madison: Inception of the Thomson Law

IN MID-JANUARY, Governor Goodland moved to strengthen the enforcement of anti-gambling laws. In a speech to the legislature, he chided local officials saying, "Some county officials have been lax in curbing the slot machine and have accepted bribes for permitting them to operate."[195]

Goodland wanted to outlaw gambling and Vernon Thomson, a Richland Center legislator, introduced a bill connecting gambling to liquor licenses. If a tavern had a gambling machine, the local authorities could revoke the liquor license for one year. The "Thomson Bill" authorized the State Treasury Department to "summarily seize and destroy all personal property used or kept in violation" of gambling laws. The bill was robust as treasury agents could immediately revoke liquor licenses after a hearing with the violator and noticing the municipality. The violator could appeal to the circuit court with the appeal time added to the revocation period.[196]

Hearing of the proposal, Hurley city officials ordered taverns to cease gambling. Facing the risk of a raid and the loss of a liquor license, most tavern operators complied. The *Montreal River Miner* reported, "Slot machines are conspicuous by their absence again in Hurley and the county and just why we do not know. City officials ordered the machines out of Hurley on Tuesday and ordered all forms of gambling stopped pronto."[197] Losing slot machines was one thing, but the liquor license was the golden goose, and the risk was too high for most operators.

The disappearance of gambling equipment coincided with the absence of state raids. However, it didn't take long for the lull to collapse. Without threat from raids, the machines, tables, and dice came out of hiding from the confines of Dago Valley Road and other locales to find their way back into the taverns. They emerged from camps in the woods, cellars, and under haystacks in barns.[198]

In mid-February, Alex Raineri, a member of the Assembly Judiciary Committee, voted against the Thomson Bill resulting in an acrimonious debate on the floor of the Assembly. A vote of 57 to 37 defeated a motion to postpone it indefinitely. Raineri wanted the state beverage tax officials to be deputized before they could enforce the bill. This proposal was equally defeated. The Thomson anti-gambling bill passed the Assembly by 56 to 38 in what the *Wisconsin State Journal* termed the

"70 minutes of the bitterest debate of the 1945 session."[199]

Back at home in Hurley, in March, Alex Raineri was named director of the Seventh War Bond drive in Iron County.[200]

After spending time with his constituents, Raineri's animosity toward the bureaucratic authorities in Madison increased. A conflict between Raineri and Roach was inevitable now that the Thomson Bill was gaining momentum.

Madison: Introduction of the Thomson Bill

ALTHOUGH THE WISCONSIN ASSEMBLY engrossed the Thomson Bill in early March, it would have difficulty moving forward. As the bill went through committees, it grew heavy as assembly members added drug stores, barbershops, restaurants, and any other business licensed by the state to the list of potential violators. Eventually, the bill moved out of an optimistic Assembly with a 59-38 vote. When it reached the Senate, members became concerned that the amendments were onerous and would not withstand a constitutional challenge. As such, they wanted to add a "severability" clause, and the bill fermented in the senate.[201]

Madison: Spring Raids in Hurley and Elsewhere

FINALLY, A RAID DESCENDED upon Hurley like a spring storm in early May. State agents laid siege to taverns for selling liquor and allowing minors to "loiter about their places of business." They arrested the operator and eight minors at Brackett's Tavern in Pence and the Avalon in Hurley.

In mid-June, the Hurley City Council approved the quota of 78 liquor licenses.[202] The Thomson anti-gambling law was now close to being signed. The law had morphed, and now State Treasury Agents would be required to cooperate with local officials. State agents had the authority to seize "slot machines, numbers jars, roulette wheels, and similar mechanical gambling devices." After the seizure, the agents would need to inform the district attorney. To motivate the district attorneys to act, they would have to bring an action within ten days or report directly to the governor.

A reporter from Madison wrote, "Yet the boys and girls who like to pull the levers on the slot machines may be assured that within a few weeks, those play-things will be scarce indeed." The press reported that the new law would give "tremendous new power and responsibility" to Clyde Tutton, acting chief of the State Beverage Tax Division, and parenthetically commented, "Roach would have liked his new job."[203] This slamming of the legislative gavel ensured the conflict between Raineri and the Beverage Tax Division.

Hurley: Hurley, Hayward, and Hell

HURLEY'S REPUTATION AS A sin city was well-established in the latter part of the 19th century when mining drove the demand for lumber, and raising hell was a way of life.

However, on June 1, 1945, Hurley was subjected to a hellish broadside from *Esquire Magazine,* which renewed the phrase "Hurley, Hayward, and Hell." E. E. Roberts attributed the epigram to a brakeman on the old Milwaukee and Northern Railroad in the late 1800s when directing the riders to the north country of Wisconsin. The brakeman prefaced the phrase by hollering, "All Aboard, for Hurley, Hayward, and Hell!" Roberts wrote that these three places were "The toughest places anywhere, and the first two a little tougher than the third."

Comparing Hurley to hell consumed a few paragraphs but to make his point Roberts ended the commentary with a story about a lumberjack who, after a week in Hurley, was asked by his boss what he thought about the place. The lumberjack, who must have had a head for business, replied, "Well, if I owned Hurley and Hell, I guess I'd live in Hell and rent out Hurley."

Roberts dedicated a good deal of print to Hayward as well. Most stories were about heavy drinkers, the Hayward Fire Department, and John Dietz, a pioneer who terrorized that part of the state. He described how Hayward evolved to a tourist economy saying, "Yes, Hayward gradually got 'civilized,' but Hurley never wholly did."

With the scent of nostalgia, Roberts jabbed at the 78 taverns in Hurley: "The home folks claim that the town couldn't support four taverns on its own thirst." He talked about the aroma of pasties wafting from Daoust's bakery, the heat of the saunas, sunken caves traversing old mine shafts, and the murder of Lottie Morgan – an axe to the head in 1890, one block off Silver Street.

Roberts ended his article by describing a scene from the basement of the old Burton Hotel. He narrates, "There is an odd hollow sound from the echoing depths of the building. We listen fearfully. Finally, there heaves into view a 'strange, legless, fingerless wreck' of a man. As this pitiable hulk makes its way across the lobby, pushing a broom before it, the face turns to us and the lips move, but no sound comes. The half-man disappears into the darkness. Someone explains he is an old Finnish lumberjack who got drunk one night and fell asleep in the snow and froze off his legs and fingers and has never been able to speak since – a fitting caretake for a ghost hotel."[204]

Madison: The Thomson Bill Gets Implemented

The Thomson Bill created quite a stir. It had been controversial, continuously debated, and modified without interruption.[205] Rumors of heavy lobbying to defeat the bill – up to $100,000 – spread throughout the capital. Despite the chaos, Governor Goodland signed the anti-gaming law on June 29, 1945.[206] Clyde Tutton was frustrated as the state could no longer act unilaterally. Instead, the law required that any discovery of gambling be reported to the district attorney. The district attorney was then obligated to prosecute the tavernkeeper. As with the current law, if there was failure to act, the governor could remove the district attorney from office.

After signing the law, the legislature petitioned a Dane County circuit judge to hold a grand jury to investigate the lobbying. The entire legislature, all 133 members, would be subpoenaed to testify.[207] The en masse subpoena intended to focus on a few legislators without singling them out in public.[208] On July 9, eight Senators, two Assemblymen, and William T. Evjue, (the editor of the Capital Times), were called to testify.[209] However, there is nothing to indicate that this hearing produced any indictments.

Tutton met with his agents on the day the law took effect to determine an enforcement strategy.[210] The following day, he said that his division would check all 71 counties for slot machines, roulette wheels, punchboards, number jars, pinball machines, and baseball pools. He said the "review" would be "enforced impartially throughout the State of Wisconsin" and his agents would look for all devices that paid out with things such as chips or free games.[211]

Wisconsin: The Dragnet

R EPORTER JOHN WYNGAARD[212] described 39-year-old Clyde Tutton's demeanor as "Sober-spirited, big and earnest and transparently honest, Tutton undertook his new job with some trepidation. For it is a big one. The eyes of the whole state are upon him."[213]

He and his agents struck on July 4. He told reporters, "In two days there won't be any machines operating in Wisconsin."[214] Agents cast a wide net and descended upon Jefferson, Dodge, Ozaukee, Sheboygan, Fond du Lac, Kenosha, Lincoln, Iron, and Oneida counties. In Iron County, they seized two dice tables, a bing table, and 85 packages of unstamped cigarettes at the Club Fiesta, now operated by James Francis, Fred Fontecchio, and Steve Trochim. They found a dice table and roulette equipment in the basement of Mickey's Bar and Café operated by Dan Angelo. They found dice tables, punchboards, horse race machines, and a blackjack table at other county taverns.[215] Tutton methodically notified District Attorney J. C. Raineri of every arrest. Near the end of July, Raineri issued warrants to the tavernkeepers.[216]

Because the Thomson law didn't cover blackjack, dice, and roulette, the judge heard four of the cases as civil actions under Wisconsin's general gambling law and processed them within ten days, fining each defendant $10 and then suspending the fines. Although he criticized the state for bringing "half cases" before the court, he ordered the sheriff to destroy the gambling equipment in front of witnesses. In a rare tobacco violation, the judge fined Fontecchio $10 for having the unlicensed cigarettes at the Club Fiesta.[217]

Meanwhile, Tutton tried to clarify the duties of his agents regarding the equipment covered under the new anti-gambling law. He argued that illegal gambling devices, subject to seizure, included "slot machines, ticket jars, pinball games with payoffs or free plays, bingo, punch boards, baseball, football and lottery tickets or any numbers tickets, raffle tickets such as drawing for an auto or other objects of value." He excluded card and dice games if played for treats and "skeeball and similar games of skill, including ray gun, or pinball machines that do not have payoffs."[218] It proved a challenge to classify gambling machines, and the debate continued.

Madison: A Popular Comic Book Investigator

W HILE TUTTON'S RAIDS WERE COMPREHENSIVE, the $10 fines and dismissed cases equated to a failed investigation. *The Wisconsin State Journal* characterized Tutton's raid as "dull and fruitless." To add insult, they published an article comparing Tutton with Kerry Drake, a popular comic book investigator.

When comparing Tutton to Drake, the *Journal* wrote, "They're both enlisted on the same side of right and justice against the nefarious slot machine racket, Chief Tutton on the front page and Mr. Drake on the back in the very serious portions of our comic section, and either one could be quite a help to the other. So far, they're both doing equally well, although it would seem that such a highly-placed and of course comparably paid public servant as Chief Tutton could make things a little more interesting for a color-hungry citizenry licking its chops over the prospect of a good juicy vice

74

ring at the hamburger grinder."

The *Journal* continued to mock, "Chief Tutton, who began with a fine flare in the romantic northland, of late, has been reduced to hauling in some almost boring candy punchboards, two penny peanut prizes, and free-play pinballs – and all operated by people cursed with the most ordinary sounding names."

The *Journal* goaded Tutton to find more colorful targets, "Can't our Mr. Tutton find us at least one little Roulette? Life is getting awfully dull in dear old Wisconsin with only Andersons and McCormicks and Smiths and Jones for salt and pepper and no Roulette for the paprika shaker. It's a good thing we've still got comic strips."[219] The *State Journal* criticized with a typewriter, bravely mocking with keys banging against the rubber platen. It was different in the field and Tutton was furious and embarrassed.

Wisconsin: Tutton Goes on the Offensive

IN EARLY AUGUST, Tutton and team busted 12 taverns in five counties including Clark, La Crosse, Marinette, Marquette, and Waushara. Using the new Thomson law, his agents confiscated 33 gambling devices including 13 slot machines. Most of the machines played nickels and dimes and the taverns included The Lucky Twelve, the Log Cabin, the BBB Tavern, and the Y Club. Since the law was enacted, the Beverage Tax Division had netted 1,093 gambling devices.[220]

Hurley: 21,000 Cigarettes Go Up in Smoke

WHILE TUTTON'S AGENTS RAIDED counties for slot machines, the trouble in Hurley shifted to the tracks. In early August, the sheriff and a Chicago and Northwestern Railway investigator reported the theft of 21,000 cigarettes from a freight car in the Hurley railyard. The *Montreal River Miner* reported, "Neither clues nor ashes were left behind."[221]

Hurley: The Cases Dissolve

TUTTON PUSHED HARD, and in mid-August, his crew seized 36 gambling machines in Crawford, Buffalo, Portage, Taylor, and Waupaca Counties.[222] At the same time, the Iron County Court processed the cases from the July raid in Hurley. District Attorney J. C. Raineri presented each case to Circuit Judge Alvin Risjord. However, Raineri framed each as an overreach of legislative intent. The judge agreed, issued small fines, and dismissed other cases for lack of evidence. District attorneys and sheriffs from other counties watched the events so they could plan for their upcoming cases. The *Montreal River Miner* reported that the activity in the court "must be a great disappointment to somebody" but went on to say, "The Thomson law has its desired results, however, and that must be conceded. The purpose of the law was to drive slot machines out of the state. It is safe to make the prediction that there are no slot machines in the state, and at least none in Iron County."[223]

Hurley: A Barmaid Snubs a Cop

THE LEGAL CLOSING TIME OF 1 A.M. meant little in Hurley. In mid-August, a few minutes after 1 a.m., a Hurley police officer, after receiving complaints, asked the bartender of the Club Chateau to close the tavern and turn down the music. The bright but defiant barmaid simply said, "No," and the cop retreated. After additional complaints, he returned at 2:20 a.m., and without comment, cited her for being open after hours. The operator paid the $50 fine without objection.[224]

Hurley: V-J Day

THE JAPANESE SURRENDERED ON August 15, 1945, and the news reached Hurley via radio. The *Montreal River Miner* reported, "Within 15 minutes crowds began to gather on Silver Street. Cars went zooming up and down the main street with horns sounding; traffic regulations were momentarily ignored."

The mood was crazy, and several young men lit a huge pile of cardboard boxes on fire in the middle of 4th Avenue and Silver Street. The *Miner* said, "People love a fire, and there the crowd gathered. By eight o'clock pretty nearly all of Hurley, Ironwood and the surrounding towns passed through famed Hurley's Silver Street to see 'what's happening.'"

There was hysteria, and at 8 p.m., the mayor and sheriff ordered all taverns to close for safety. When learning that the taverns were going to close, people rushed the doors to get a last drink or a bottle to take home. The *Miner* continued, "Although many taverns closed on orders, others 'closed' the front door only and entrance could be made by the rear. Officials winked at this interpretation of closing."[225] Of course.

Madison: The Big Fight About the Thomson Law

IN CHIPPEWA COUNTY, County Judge Orin Larrabee declared the Thomson anti-gaming law unconstitutional in late October 1945. In response, Attorney General John Martin warned operators not to put their gambling machines "back in view." Martin was uncompromising and ordered the Chippewa County District Attorney to appeal the judge's decision to the Supreme Court. Martin said, "The law would be enforced until the Supreme Court ruled otherwise" and that state agents "would continue to inspect and confiscate." Hedging, he commented, "Even if the Supreme Court should rule the law unconstitutional, the operators could not get back any of the 1,200 gambling devices which they have seized since the law went into effect in July."

Judge Larrabee felt that the Thomson law violated a defendant's right to plead and prevented county officials from administering their statutory duties. He called the law "vague and uncertain."[226]

On January 11, 1946, the Wisconsin Supreme Court reversed Larrabee's action and ruled that the Thomson Law was constitutional. This was a bitter fight over several months. This was a crucial decision as agents had already confiscated over 5,000 slot machines since the bill was enacted.[227] Tutton and his team were elated as they had been operating under the premise of success and the work was validated.

Madison: There Is No Letup, And There Won't Be a Letup

IN MID-SEPTEMBER, after seizing 17 gambling machines in a tavern near Marshfield, Tutton announced that slot machines "were eliminated from Wisconsin as far as the general public is concerned." He said, "I definitely don't think there are any slot machines in the state. If there are any, they are not in the open." He continued, "There is no letup, and there won't be a letup." A recent raid of a Bakersville tavern in the Town of Lincoln in Wood County netted two 5-cent machines and brought the count to 1,214 machines seized under the Thomson law.

The *Eau Claire Leader-Telegram* praised Tutton, saying that he "has turned a good job and the Republican legislators and governor who gave him the tools in the Thomson law to accomplish it, may take a whopping measure of pride."

The article continued, "There will always be those who will attempt to have it repealed. Some of this will come from the well-meaning and sincerely unsuspicious who simply crave freedom in all forms for the sake of the principle, even if they and their neighbors get burned."

After the "well-meaning" reference, the *Journal* attacked its opponents: "But most of it will come from the racketeers who have now been deprived of their steadiest and most lucrative source of income in the upper reaches of Wisconsin – the same crooks who sent their conscienceless lobbyists down here last session to plead with tears as big as meatballs rolling down their barroom tanned cheeks that, 'we don't need no Thomson law!'" [228]

Hurley: The Story of Badman Jackie Kahl – The One-Man Crime Wave

JOHN RAYMOND KAHL JR. "Jackie" was born on June 24, 1921, in Klemme, Iowa. When he was eight years old, he robbed a dentist's office in Boone, 80 miles south of Klemme. In 1938, at 17 years old, Kahl was arrested for mail theft and was jailed in Ramsey County Jail. Using a tablespoon, he escaped by loosening the bricks and bars. Kahl shimmied down a 65-foot pipe using a rope made from bedsheets.[229] He was captured and sent to the federal prison in Sandstone, Minnesota, where he served as an orderly. After release, Kahl worked as an orderly for a brief period at St. Barnabas hospital. In these two settings, he developed his craft of thievery by posing as a doctor. The board paroled him when he was 21, and he quickly assumed the alias of "Dr. John A. Anderson." He met Norma G. Dahl of Albert Lea in a bar in Minneapolis. They traveled to Kansas City, where they were married. In August, he stole a car in Boone, Iowa where he entered Miller hospital posing as a doctor. There, he pirated $1,000 from the clothing in the doctor's lounge.

He then changed his identity and traveled under the alias of "Dr. Fred Anderson" and met Louise Mayaski, 19, from Steven's Point.[230] They married, making Mayaski his second wife in a few months. For three months in 1945, they roamed Minnesota and Wisconsin stealing cars and robbing gambling houses, netting $14,000 in the Duluth area. At an earlier date, Kahl lost "a couple of thousand dollars" gambling in Hurley, and now he wanted to recover his loss.

In early September 1945, police hunted for "Badman Jackie Kahl" in St. Paul and referred to him as a "one-man crime wave." Three months after being paroled, police stopped him as he exited his car. He made a "feeble attempt" to reach for his .38 pistol, but police restrained him. He later told the police, "If I'd seen you first, you'd be dead by now." When arrested, He was driving a stolen car with two license plates. Police charged him with auto theft, grand larceny, bigamy, and violation of the Dryer act, which made auto theft a federal crime.

He told the police that he intended to rob a gambling tavern in Hurley but admitted the risk when he said, "I stood a chance of getting hell shot out of me." He admitted to the police that he selected easy targets because "they couldn't holler!" The Hurley press responded, "The Badman was safe there. It is only the normal, law-abiding, tax–paying public – the ones without guns and stolen cars and hot cash – at whom these places dare to holler. Now, let 'em yell."[231]

*   *   *

Jackie Kahl Jr. continued his criminal behavior. He violated postal laws, escaped from prison, committed conspiracy to cause escape, had parole violations, and committed mass violence crimes. In January 1952, he began serving a sentence at the U.S. Penitentiary at Alcatraz. His case file contained 2,500 pages. [232] With the closure of Alcatraz, the government transferred Kahl to Leavenworth in Kansas. In July 1958, Kahl escaped from Leavenworth but was quickly apprehended.

*   *   *

In 2010, Kahl's granddaughter, Dawn Shields, won a photography award for an album, entitled "Legacy." A few years prior, she discovered the history of her grandfather. Shields traveled to Alcatraz and photographed the 'life' of her grandfather, who was known to her as "Papa Jack." The album described Kahl's seven prison breaks and eleven suicide attempts.[233]Despite his daring adventures, he considered the lower blocks of Hurley to be most dangerous.

Little is known about his life after prison, although we know that he was eventually married and had children and grandchildren. Jackie Kahl died in Jefferson City, Missouri, on February 25, 1996, quite likely by suicide, as indicated by the note in "Legacy."

Madison: Esoteric Bombast Inked in Madison

IN AUGUST 1945, Aldric Revell of Madison's *Capital Times* wrote a full column article about the change in tenor of the "up north" taverns and the effectiveness of agents in eliminating slot machines from the state. He wrote, "The Thomson anti-gambling law has resulted in a new sartorial style for northern Wisconsin tavernkeepers, and resort owners' customary habiliments are now sackcloth and ashes, with a boutonniere of invective."

He described how all the gambling devices had been removed from the state and how upset the tavern operators were. He ended the biting piece, "In years to come they will also discover that tourists don't come to Wisconsin for the gambling, despite what some resort owners would have us believe. After a while, the boys might even take off their sackcloth and ashes and walk around like normal people once again."[234]

Madison: Roach In and Tutton Out

IN MID-1945, ROACH RETURNED from military duty with a chest full of medals and several commendations. He assumed his old position in state service.

The Capital Times reported, "After duty in Salt Lake City, he volunteered for South Pacific service and participated in five battles and two invasions, receiving several citations. When the Army secured the Philippines, Roach became provost marshal of Manila and reorganized that city's police department."

He witnessed the Japanese atrocities on the Filipinos. While stationed in Manila, two of his special investigators were murdered and Roach hunted down the culprits. He exercised the same vigor as when in Wisconsin and found the perpetrators who murdered 15 local officials, he brought down Manila's corrupt mayor, eliminated the city's black market, drained all illegal liquor, stopped criminal trafficking, and jailed 19 individuals who threatened his life. Roach continued to do his homework. During the prosecution of a criminal, the main witness was kidnapped to prevent him from testifying. Nonetheless, the evidence was so thorough, seven of the defendants changed their pleas from "not guilty" to "guilty." *The Capital Times* wrote, "The Manila authorities were so impressed by Roach's knowledge and ability with police work, they asked him to reorganize the entire police department."[235]

Upon his return, he faced a more personal conflict. He was entitled to his old position, which Clyde Tutton currently held, but the decision to reinstate Roach was up to the State Treasurer, John Smith.

To complicate matters, Smith had promoted Tutton to a permanent position in June 1944 so that his pay would reflect his duties. Tutton would lose the authority he believed he had earned, along with a pay reduction. One journalist said, "Apparently, Tutton did not relish the prospect of being moved down the official ladder upon the return of Roach and decided to leave state government instead.[236] Unhappy with the inevitable loss of the position, Tutton, a CPA, accepted an executive position with the Wisconsin Liquor Company in Milwaukee.

Between the time that Tutton resigned, and Roach returned, Smith asked F. J. Mattingly to serve as the supervisor of investigations.[237] After a 33-month leave of absence, Major John W. Roach resumed his $4,000-a-year position as chief of the Treasury Department's Beverage Tax Division in late October.[238]

The Madison press praised Tutton as an effective leader upon his departure. *The Capital Times* wrote, "Mr. Tutton has won the admiration of thousands of people in Wisconsin for the fine job he performed in ridding Wisconsin of the slot machine racket after the passage of the Thomson anti-gambling law."[239]

In 1949, the *Waukesha Daily Freeman* referred to Tutton as "A man of dignity and probity" when identifying him as the manager and lobbyist of the Wisconsin Wine and Spirits Institute.[240] Tutton gave up the position in 1955. In 1961, he left the liquor industry and became a lobbyist for Petroleum Retailers of Milwaukee. Tutton countered all the criticism leveled at him in August via honor and fortitude. Clyde S. Tutton died in Milwaukee on March 1, 1981, at 75.

1946

Hurley: Taverns Crowd Out Other Business

O N JANUARY 9, 1946, the Hurley City Council tackled the issue of zoning . An alderman proposed that "At least one block in Hurley to be free of taverns." He argued that "There was not enough buildings at present for other business to start and pointed out that at least four or five people wanted to go into business but could not find 'suitable buildings.'"[241] There is no record of a zoning change.

Hurley: Roach's Raiders Flank Hurley from the East

F OR SEVERAL WEEKS, Governor Goodland received complaints "that prostitution and gambling again were thriving" in Hurley and that "servicemen and discharged war veterans were the principal victims." The *Wisconsin State Journal* reported, "According to information reaching the executive office, veterans were losing their discharge pay, and war bonds at gambling and a few had been 'rolled' – their money taken away from them – after they had drunk too much in the all-night saloons."

Roach planned to address these allegations. In the *Wisconsin State Journal*, Rex Karney wrote that this would be "the first step in a new state campaign to make Wisconsin's notorious 'sin city' toe the line."[242]

John Roach advanced like a bull with renewed vigor and vengeance toward Hurley. It had been four years since his last attack on the saloons on Silver Street, and little had changed. If he could tame Manila, certainly, he could deal with Hurley.

During the week of January 10, 1946, Roach sent a crew to recon Hurley's Silver Street and surrounding areas in Iron County, including Mercer and Oma. During the afternoon of Thursday, January 17, 14 agents, along with the obligatory reporters, met in Wausau. They left at staggered times to rendezvous at the North-Western depot in Ironwood.[243] At 11 p.m., it was 12 degrees, and low-slung clouds rolled off Lake Superior from the north toward the neon lights of Hurley. Five black sedans, loaded with agents, reporters, tear gas, and guns, motored down the Aurora Street hill through the flats and slowly coasted to a stop on the lower block of Silver Street.

The Club Fiesta was the most polished operation, boasting four bars and a five-piece orchestra. Roach and three agents slipped out of the lead vehicle and bull-dozed their way into the tavern. As if on cue, a five-piece dance band was playing the Harry James hit "Who's Sorry Now." The agents found two girls working at the bar and told them to get their coats for a trip to the Iron County jail. One of the girls said, "I can't go without my stockings on. Any of you boys want to go upstairs while I put them on?" A weary woman patron told the agents, "It's about time this joint got knocked off." When agents entered the back room of the tavern, they found James Francis, a co-owner of The Fiesta, shooting craps with a group of men. When he realized that a raid was taking place, he shouted at the agents, "Shut the whole ------ place up. I got 65 people on the payroll and if you want to make this a ghost town keep this up." One of the players told the agents, "I didn't spend three years in a foxhole to be shoved around by a bunch of you ------- guys." Serafino

Marchetti, the campaign manager for Representative Alvin O'Konski, was in the craps game and complained to the agents that he wished they had arrived 20 minutes earlier before he began losing. Another player told the agents that he had returned from the war a month ago, and this was the first night his wife let him out.

Simultaneously, other agents advanced to the second block and raided the White Front tavern, arresting two women for prostitution. They netted the same at the TryAngle Tavern. By 11 p.m., Roach rounded up 19 people at the county jail.

At the TryAngle, ten WWII veterans, all wearing army discharge buttons, sat at the bar. As the agents showed their badges, the men exited the smoky tavern onto Silver Street and away from the trouble. War abroad was one thing, but trouble at home was another.

Along Silver Street, they arrested James Francis and Steve Trochim at the Club Fiesta, Jack Califano at the Blackhawk tavern, Stephan Allen of Steve and Kay's tavern, Nunzio Santini of the Santini Hotel, James Klemich of Jimmie's, and Richard Matrella and Armas Hill[244] of the Showboat.

As the word of the raid spread through Hurley, neon lights flickered off at 1:00 a.m. – two to three hours before "normal" closing time. The agents visited nearly 80 taverns and ordered the operators to remove any window blinds within 24 hours. Finding all the Hurley taverns closed, the reporters went to Ironwood, where the closing time was 2:30 a.m., which was said to be "strictly enforced." An Ironwood police officer told them, "I'm glad to see Hurley cleaned up – those drunks keep coming over here all the time and cause us trouble." The contrast was striking. Ironwood had a population of 15,000 with 21 taverns compared to Hurley, with a population of 3,500 with 78 taverns.[245] The influx of serious, and legal, drinkers flowed across the state line like a brisk west wind at 1 a.m.

In his usual colloquial language, Aldric Revell wrote in *The Capital Times*, "Spurred by complaints that discharged veterans were being fleeced of their mustering out pay by operators of honky-tonks and sin spots, a squad of 14 agents…staged a quickie raid on three gambling houses and two houses of prostitution here Thursday night." He referred to Hurley as a "honky tonk Babylon of the north wood," and "the city where sin is an indestructible hydra-headed serpent."[246] Revell filled two columns with neon adjectives and carnival nouns.

Oddly, Governor Goodland told Iron County officials that he did not order the raid, but he said that if he were "being blamed for the raid he would shoulder the blame."[247]

* * *

At the end of January, dressed in their courtroom finest, they paraded through the Iron County Courthouse: Lois Gasbarri, Richard Matrella, Joseph McRainels, James Shields, and Margaret Pricket.[248] The judge hurried through the minor charges of violating hours but was more thoughtful about gambling and prostitution-related offenses. Most of the defendants paid fines ranging from $25 to $250. One defendant forfeited his bail bond by skipping town, not wanting to face the judge.[249] Of particular interest to Roach was Don Angelo, who ran Mickey's Bar and Café. Angelo was a multiple offender, and his conviction could lead to Roach's goal: revocation of liquor licensure.[250]

Madison: Purple Prose from Revell's Typewriter

ON JANUARY 23, REVELL poured additional purple prose onto the pages of *The Capital Times*. He described his ride with the Roach crew, "While you good people were snug in your beds last Thursday night around midnight, I was flitting in and out of drafty houses of ill fame in Hurley, with my warm brown eyes at the hoydens of the demi-monde." Being on a literary roll, he quipped, "This brochure might well be entitled 'My Life and Times in a Bordello.'" The article read like pulp fiction, as he continued, "In that manner, I handled myself with precision and eclat, despite the flotsam and jetsam that was around. One of the jetsam had on a sweater, too."

Even academics in Madison must have had to look up his words. He referred to Roach as the "squad leader" and reported that Roach instructed him to "watch the front door at one unlucky tavern." Revell inserted himself as a character in the drama, "Acting like George Raft, I coldly stared down the 12 individuals in the bar one after the other, with the knowledge that if anyone had dared make the slightest move, I would have been out the front door ahead of them and well on my way to Wausau." With his renewed comfort behind the typewriter in Madison, Revell reported that the "squad leader" asked him to go upstairs and watch a prostitute gather her belongings before being carted off to jail. Revell thought the best of it and exclaimed, "I ain't protected by civil service." Nor was he deputized, despite his likely desire.

After booking all those arrested, the agents and reporters retired to the St. Jame's Hotel in Ironwood. The reporters banged away on typewriters until early morning. A tired and irritated John Roach searched several hotel floors along the alley the following day. Revell asked him what he was doing. Roach exclaimed, "Some lug was playing a pinball machine until 4 a.m. this morning, and I couldn't get to sleep. I knew it was a pinball machine because it had that clicking sound when the balls hit the pins. Revell fessed up that it was the typewriters.[251]

Hurley: Raineri v. Roach

BOTH JOHN ROACH AND ALEX RAINERI received orders from the governor. Although Roach was a Democrat, he had a good working relationship with Governor Goodland, a Republican. Raineri was also a Republican, but he and the Governor had opposing positions toward the tavern industry. Given these twisted politics, Roach maintained a stronger bond with Goodland.

Raineri bristled at the idea of being under Roach's thumb, but he had no choice. He unabashedly supported the operators on Silver Street as they were a mainstay of his constituency. This is where he grew up and these were his people.

Always the intelligent aggressor, Roach was using the Thomson Law to shut down the Hurley taverns. The law allowed for the revocation of a tavern license if there were two offenses, which was a new tool. Tavernkeepers who had a previous conviction became aware of the State's strategy and they began to plead not guilty, hoping for a trial and a lighter sentence.

Madison: Summoned to Madison

ON JANUARY 21, THE DAY AFTER the raid, Governor Goodland summoned Iron County District Attorney Joseph Raineri, Iron County Sheriff John Gersich, and two defendants – James

Aspinwall and Serafino Marchetti – to Madison. Goodland told them, "The lid on vice, gambling, and tavern law violations will remain clamped down on Hurley." The Governor told Raineri that the State Attorney General would help if necessary. Raineri reported that the authorities removed all slot machines from the county since the Thomson law took effect. However, he also admitted leniency on closing-hours violations because "it was difficult to obtain convictions." The sheriff told the Governor that he only had one assistant, "who worked about 16 hours a day." Raineri promised to bring charges against future hours violators.[252]

Since there was no apparent input from either Aspinwall or Marchetti, the only conceivable purpose of their attendance was to witness. The Governor likely wanted them to spread the seriousness of his intent to fellow operators.

Just to emphasize the point, on January 25, Goodland followed up the meeting with a letter to District Attorney J. C. Raineri stating that he would hold him and the sheriff responsible for tavern law enforcement.[253]

Hurley: Down The Gaudy Avenue of Sin

THE *WISCONSIN STATE JOURNAL* MOCKED Hurley's efforts to enforce the Thomson Law. The columnist reported, "Hurley hasn't been much different, except that Hurley, citizen and official alike, didn't even bother to look the other way. They looked right square at it . . . and so what?"

The *Journal* enquired, "So what came last week when John Roach and his tough boys from Madison swept down the gaudy avenue of sin, clapped some of Hurley's highly regarded citizens and their female employees into the hoosegow, and announced that an old law was going to close up some of the two-time offenders for good."

The article connected the Raineri brothers saying, "Again, let there be no surprise that Assemblyman Alex Raineri, a state lawmaker who has taken certain oaths and obligations, thereupon warned Mr. Roach he was 'going to take care of him' and his agents, between threats complaining bitterly that Mr. Roach has used 'poor judgment in not warning Mr. Raineri's constituents that the raiders were on their way and that the law was as it says in the books. That, of course, would be funny . . . if it came from anybody but a state lawmaker, and the brother of Hurley's district attorney, who, presumably, knows the law even if those who help make it don't. It's still not surprising. It's just Hurley."[254]

Hurley: Not a Split Decision

ON TUESDAY, JANUARY 29, in Iron County Court, Assistant Attorney General Earl Sacshe represented the State Attorney General's office. Sacshe, District Attorney J. C. Raineri, and Beverage Tax Attorney Arthur Fadness huddled in the courthouse for four hours discussing strategy. They found that careful reading of the Thomson Law required multiple offenses *in the same year*. There would be no shuttering of Mickey's Bar and Café since Don Angelo's offenses were in different years.[255] John Roach was in the courtroom but not at the strategy meeting. When Fadness told him about the legal interpretation, his enthusiasm deflated.

At this time, elected legislative positions were not full-time jobs. Assemblymen and senators held private jobs in their respective districts. While Assemblyman Alex Raineri represented Iron County, he also operated a private law practice in Hurley. His brother, J. C., served as Iron County District Attorney since 1934. This created an awkward situation in court. Alex represented the defendants, while J. C. prosecuted the same.[256] However, the situation would get more awkward as John Roach confronted Alex Raineri.

Alex entered a plea of *nolo contendere* for Dan Angelo, owner of Mickey's, for his second offense, and Judge Trembath fined Angelo $50. After the judge levied the fine, Raineri coldly asked Roach, "Is this case closed now?" Ready for confrontation, Roach snapped, "No, it's not closed. This man has a record of previous offenses, and the statutes provide that his license shall be surrendered." Judge Trembath ordered both men into his chambers.

After the strategy meeting, Roach had consulted with Fadness who found more information. In chambers, Roach pulled the ace from his sleeve and introduced an obscure law requiring the forfeiture of a liquor license after multiple offenses – not necessarily in the same year as with the Thomson Law. Raineri was furious. He was caught off guard by a man he despised. Back on his heels, Raineri appealed to emotion. He told Trembath that rigorous enforcement of minor offenses would "take the bread and butter jobs" from Hurley residents and use of this law "threatens the very existence of Hurley's thriving saloon business."

Raineri shouted at Roach, "You guys didn't use any judgment! These people don't know the law, which never has been used before. You should have given them some warning first that they were in danger of losing their licenses." Roach said it would have been "ridiculous" to warn the violators that he planned to raid their establishments. Knowing he had the upper hand, Roach fired another shot at Raineri, using the tavern owners as proxies. He argued, "It's certainly not my fault that these fellows don't know the law. In the first place, most of these men have been in business for a long time and certainly should know the regulations that apply to taverns." Raineri took the wrong approach when he appealed to sensitivity saying, "Some of these people just took over their places and are trying to make a living."

Roach was relentless and fired back, "The guys who are second and third and fourth offenders aren't newcomers, and you know it. They're old-timers who have been violating the law for years and trying to get away with it." Raineri lost any momentum that he might have had and circled back, again accusing Roach of using "poor judgment," and repeated that Roach should have warned the tavernkeepers that revocation of their licenses might result from continued violations. Raineri should have retreated, but instead, he accused Roach of not being "the smartest guy in the world, who should sit as judge and jury on these people who are trying to make a living." Roach squared off and attacked Raineri's part-time job, "Nuts! You guys in the legislature write the laws, and you, for instance, certainly should know what's in the books. All I do is enforce the laws and in this case the governor has ordered me to enforce them to the limit. And I'm going to do it." Attorney Raineri took the bait and responded, now as Assemblyman Raineri, "You'll hear plenty about this next session. There will be plenty of calls of the house. I don't think you're fit to administer this law if you don't use better judgment than this." Roach knew he won. It was not a split decision and he flatly responded, "That's your opinion."[257]

Hurley: Judge Trembath Earns His Pay

ON TUESDAY, JANUARY 29, and Wednesday, January 30, most defendants pled *nolo contendere* before County Judge Trembath. *Nolo contendere* literally means "no contest." In legal terms, it means that the defendant does not accept or deny responsibility for the charges but agrees to accept punishment. The defendants used this plea because it couldn't be used as an admission of guilt if a civil case followed the criminal trial.[258]

District Attorney J. C. Raineri, stressed from the numerous charges, warned the girls that if they were arrested again for the same violation, he would "place a repeater act charge against them, sending them to the state prison if found guilty." With conviction and intent, he announced, "We mean to stamp out prostitution in Hurley." While in town for the trials, three state agents revisited the taverns on Silver Street, warning the operators not to obstruct their windows with "curtains, blinds, or screens."[259]

Trembath went through an exhausting litany of charges, dismissing cases, recording bond forfeitures, fining for hours violations, admonishing prostitution, sentencing then suspending jail time, and ordering gambling machines destroyed.[260] Matrella pled guilty to operating a gambling house and was fined $150. The judge fined Louis Gasbarri, the operator of the Red Feather, $50. For some reason, Armos Hill appeared with a large white dog before the judge and proclaimed that he was innocent of running a gambling operation at the Club Fiesta. Apparently, the dog had no effect as Judge Trembath fined him $50.[261]

After leaving the military, John Roach suffered a significant defeat with his first major raid. He knew that Hurley got the best of him despite his successes during the war, his effort in Manila, and his military adulations.

At this time, the effect of the Thomson law was debatable. Records showed that 195 tavernkeepers had at least two convictions against them but continued to run their businesses. Twenty-eight were in Iron County, 20 in La Crosse County, and 17 in Brown County.

Madison: Roach Gets More Adulation

DESPITE HIS EXPERIENCE in Hurley, in early March, the Spirits Club of Wisconsin in Milwaukee made Roach an honorary life member and appointed him head of the newly formed Alcohol Beverage Council – an organization created to promote good relations with the liquor industry.[262]

Hurley: Everybody Gets Reelected

DR. M. J. BONACCI PRACTICED MEDICINE at 317 Silver Street. In the spring of 1946, he was re-elected by a 32-vote margin to his seventh term as mayor of Hurley, narrowly defeating grocer Dante Barnabo.[263] In June, Alex Raineri announced his candidacy for reelection to the state assembly, and his brother J. C. ran unopposed for Iron County district attorney.

The November elections gave Alex Raineri a second term in the state assembly and his brother J. C. another term as district attorney. Although Governor Goodland beat his opponent, he failed to carry Iron County by nearly a two-to-one margin.

The political footprint in Hurley was poised to remain stable, and the state knew the chance for reform was slim. Despite the odds and with the fortitude he was noted for, Roach and his team schemed to tame the city.

Hurley: Waiting for Fireworks

THE DEMAND FOR TAVERN LICENSES remained strong. At the June 12 meeting, the Hurley City Council held a two-hour closed session to discuss how to deal with 90 tavern applications. The *Montreal River Miner* reported, "For the first time in a decade, the council chamber was crowded with spectators – jam-packed is the word. Expecting 'fireworks' or some sort of rising out of the clamor for licenses." However, when the council convened in open session, they granted only 72 of the possible 78 licenses and postponed debate on the remaining 12. The *Miner* reported, "The spectators were disappointed as the action was passed without discussion and without dissent." The fireworks would not occur until the following Wednesday, when the council issued the remaining licenses.[264]

On June 18, the city council considered the remaining 12 liquor licenses. After debate, the council issued only six. Licenses for the Showboat and the Club Fiesta were at the forefront. Four owners and three attorneys, representing the respective taverns, were at the meeting, and entanglement was inevitable. The *Montreal River Miner* reported, "The climax, after hearing the cases stated by both sides, was a series of motions, motions to amend, a threatened veto by the mayor, a request for a secret ballot – the withdrawal of the original motion and quick passage of a motion to table the entire matter until June 27th."[265] Even a knowledgeable student of Robert's Rules of Order would find it challenging to unravel the proceedings, and the skirmish ended in a stalemate.

For the first time in 13 years, the mayor vetoed the council's decision to grant licenses to Richard Matrella and Fred Fontecchio for The Showboat and the Club Fiesta. However, within a week, the mayor withdrew his veto, and the council granted the last two liquor licenses to Fontecchio and Matrella.[266]

Langlade County: The Continuing Saga of White and Red

THERE WERE TWO BROTHELS in Antigo: The White House tavern and the Red Star. John Roach raided both on the evening of July 13, 1946, and arrested Anne Martin as the keeper of the White House and Ella Ottman as the keeper of the Red Star.[267] Between the two brothels, Roach netted four prostitutes. The story of these two facilities is a saga extending from 1942 to 1982 with episodes noted in this narrative.

Hurley: A Better Chocolate Soda

IN AUGUST 1946, TWO Minnesota reporters visited Hurley looking to revive the old "Hurley, Hayward, and Hell" theme. Disappointed, they returned to St. Paul and filed a story saying, "Hurley's fame in the future would be because it could turn out a better chocolate soda than any other city."

The St. Paul reporters should have stuck around. On a cool evening in late September, Iron County Sheriff John Gersich and Hurley Police Chief Albino Endrizzi teamed up and raided the lower block of Silver Street nabbing the operators of the Club Fiesta, the Down Beat, the Showboat, and Mickey's café. In a couple of days, Dominic Napoli, Emil Rova, John Carli, and Richard Whip, to name a few, paid $100 fines for gambling violations. Ever optimistic, Cirilli wrote, "Hurley has now become a normal Wisconsin city and intends to remain so. That our local officials have resolved to keep our house in order is praiseworthy and deserving of compliments and cooperation."[268]

Madison: Lynch Him First, then Tar and Feather Him Later

ROACH AND HIS CREW thought Hurley was tough until they tried to close the "games of chance" at the Germantown fireman's picnic in August, where the effort created a riot. *The Eau Claire Leader* reported, "He was forced to withdraw when an angry crowd gathered around with cries of 'lynch him' and 'tar and feather him.'" When Roach asked two sheriff deputies to help him, they refused.[269] Roach might have felt safer in Manila.

Momentum was building against the Thomson Law, and Governor Goodland was in a tight three-way race in the August 13 primary election. An editorial in the August 1, 1946, *Wisconsin State Journal* said, "It is extremely doubtful if recent activities of the state beverage division have been helpful to the Goodland campaign." The article reiterated the purpose of the law, which was to eliminate commercialized gambling. It noted, "But recently, beverage tax inspectors and Chief John Roach, in particular, have taken a crack at fraternal picnics, church festivals, and other events where 'social' bingo and other types of gambling were sponsored. That type of cleanup is not particularly popular with the average citizen."[270]

By expanding his authority, Roach diluted his influence, and it's difficult to imagine how he drifted from the original intent of the Thomson Law. Many felt that the raids were overzealous and demonstrated unusually bad judgment.

Madison: Presentation to the Lion's Club

IN SEPTEMBER, ROACH delivered a presentation to the Lions Club in Madison. Despite the recent criticism of his actions, he told the audience, "We shall continue to carry out our duties…If the enforcement of the law is not desired on the part of the citizens of our state, it is up to them to have the law repealed." He challenged the recent criticism in the press, "Too often, the enforcement officers are put on trial rather than those who are actually violating the law."[271]

1947

Madison: Roach Writes for Detective Magazine

IN JANUARY 1947, *Detective Magazine* published a story entitled "When P. I.'s (Philippine Island's) Black market Turned to Murder" by John Roach.[272]

* * *

The Army might have fully funded roach in Manila. However, at this time in Wisconsin, Roach complained that his staff of 17 investigators was insufficient, and he needed $139,000 for eight additional investigators and two chemists. The chemists would help refine his liquor investigations.[273]

Hurley: Three Pledges

CONCERNED ABOUT FUTURE RAIDS, local law enforcement canvassed taverns in Iron and Vilas Counties, looking for gambling and prostitution. On Wednesday, January 8, local officials arrested nine tavern owners, including Fred Fontechio Jr., Richard Matrella, John Carli, and James Francis. In those days, justice was quick; they all pled guilty and paid fines the following day.[274] District Attorney J. C. Raineri made the same threadbare assertion, promising to clean up Hurley.

The *Iron County News* reported that Raineri said, "It is our absolute intent and purpose to see to it that such conditions will no longer prevail and continue to exist in Hurley."[275]

On the same day, the *Ironwood Daily Globe* reported that Raineri suggested "an exhaustive investigation relating to any and all women . . . frequenting taverns as barmaids or in a like capacity who do not have operator's licenses." He further suggested that the Sheriff "arrest them as vagrants or place such other charges as may be necessary against them to the end that any and all women in this category be arrested or ordered to leave the county."

The following day, Raineri said, "It is our absolute intent and purpose to see to it that such conditions will no longer prevail and continue to exist in the city of Hurley." [276] After so many repetitions, the inane promise "to clean up Hurley" must have made readers eye's glaze over.

Hurley: Never-Ending Hours

IN EARLY FEBRUARY, state agent Henry Robertson cited eight taverns in Hurley for remaining open after hours. The group included Lois Gasbarri, Louis Gasbarri, Richard Matrella, and Dan Angelo.[277] One can only imagine that customers who remained after hours were those who had well-established patterns on bar stools and no desire to drive to Ironwood.

Hurley: The Burton Hotel Burns

THE BURTON HOTEL STOOD PROUDLY on the southwest corner of 5th Avenue and Copper Street in Hurley. John Burton constructed the building in 1886, featuring 100 rooms and a 216-foot promenade porch. It had a rich history, hosting mining executives, lumber barons, and old Finnish ghosts. Authors Edna Ferber in her novel "Come and Get It"[278] and E. E. Roberts, in his *Esquire* article "Hurley, Hayward, and Hell," both used the hotel as a setting. On Sunday, February 2, 1947, the Burton Hotel burned to the ground.[279] This was another site that would cease to contribute to the essence of Hurley.

Madison, Hurley: Governor Goodland Dies

IN FEBRUARY 1947, JOHN ROACH announced that he was considering running for congress representing the 2nd district of Wisconsin. Two weeks later, however, he abandoned the effort for "personal reasons."[280] In Mid-March, Roach's ally in the fight against gambling and prostitution, Governor Walter Goodland, died at the age of 84 of a heart attack.[281]

Meanwhile, in northern Wisconsin, the Iron County Republican committee appointed Assemblyman Alex Raineri as chairman.[282]

Hurley: Obey The Law or Get Out

IN EARLY MAY, 68 HURLEY TAVERNS petitioned the city council to reduce the license from $400 to $200. Sixty residents filed a counter-petition asking the council to "stand firm" because the taverns consumed more than their fair share of municipal resources. Reverend Chester L. Harries, the pastor of the Hurley Presbyterian Church, submitted a third petition showing the tax impact of the taverns. He collected 142 signatures asking the city council to increase the license fee. Harries argued that the taverns cost the city additional money in police protection. In addition to the fiscal impact, the reverend complained about minors loitering in taverns, gambling, and the refusal of operators to close on time. The impassioned clergyman said, "Why can't the tavernkeepers be law-abiding. It's time to shout, 'obey the law or get out.'"[283] After hearing the arguments, the city council left the fee at $400.

Hurley: Modest Allegiance

EARLY SATURDAY MORNING OF MAY 31, the team of Sheriff John Gersich and Police Chief Albino again probed the dens on the lower block with pen and paper. Within a few days, Judge Trembath read the citations and fined 13 of the usual suspects $35 each for hours violations. The disreputable group included Dominic Vita, Louis Gasbarri, Dan Angelo, Fred Fontecchio Jr., Richard Matrella, and Lois Gasbarri.

This soft raid likely symbolized vigilance and modest allegiance to Madison. Although annoyed, the players likely recovered the $35 by the following evening.[284]

Hurley: Summer Chump Change

D ESPITE DISTRICT ATTORNEY RAINERI'S repeated declaration to keep Hurley clean, John Roach was unconvinced and saw through the facade. Over the weekend of June 14 and 15, Roach confiscated roulette, dice, and blackjack tables from the Club Fiesta and the Showboat. Judge Trembath fined Fontecchio and Matrella $150 each ($2,000 today). Given the income from gambling, this was chump change they paid the fines from a roll of bills. Dominic Napoli, James Francis, John Carli, and Biagio Disalle paid $40 each. Before the state men rolled south along Highway 51, their antagonists had ordered new equipment.[285]

Hurley: Trouble at the Down Beat – the Flash of a Blade

A T 10 P.M. ON SATURDAY, JULY 26, Tony Stella, an elderly carpenter from Hurley, harassed customers and spilled drinks at the Down Beat Tavern at 121 Silver Street. Rocco Brighenti, a bartender, "escorted" Stella out of the bar and told him to stay out. Stella wandered around Silver Street but returned to the Down Beat and pestered another patron. This time, Raymond Dudra, 29, the tavern operator, grabbed Stella's wrist with one hand and the back of his neck with the other. As Dudra pushed him through the door and onto the sidewalk, he noticed "the quick flash of a blade" and felt pain in his chest. While still holding Stella, Dudra stuttered, "take it out." Stella broke off the attack and shuffled down Silver Street and Dudra stumbled back into the tavern and yelled, "I've been stabbed." The police caught up with Stella half a block away. When they questioned him about the stabbing, he said he didn't remember it.[286]

The blade pierced Dudra's upper abdomen and left a two-and-a-half-inch puncture. He was taken to the hospital in serious condition but eventually recovered.

At the hearing, Dudra testified that he did not see Stella holding a knife and recalled only the flash of the blade. The only weapon police found on Stella was a five-inch folding knife in his rear right pocket. Although the blade was dirty, it showed no blood or signs of moisture.[287]

The judge set a hearing for August but postponed it because Dudra relapsed from the injury and had to travel to the Wisconsin General Hospital in Madison for surgery.[288]

J. C. Raineri prosecuted Stella for intent to do great bodily harm during the trial on Tuesday, December 2. After a day and a half of continuous objections, both parties rested. Judge G. N. Risjord instructed the 12-person jury to "determine if the intent to do bodily harm was in Stella's mind." Regarding Stella's intoxication, the judge told jury members that they "could find Stella incapable of forming a felonious intent." After 40 minutes, the jury returned a verdict of "simple assault," and the judge sentenced him to nine months of hard labor in the county jail.[289]

While Dudra eventually recovered from his injury and returned to the Down Beat, one cannot help but wonder if Stella ever expressed gratitude to the judge and jury.

Madison: The Get Roach Plot

B Y NOW, ROACH WAS A WELL-KNOWN character on the iron range. As such, the July 16, 1947, *Ironwood Daily Globe* carried an AP story headlined, "GOP 'Get Roach' Plot is Charged." Roach worked under the elected State Treasurer John M. Smith, who operated by the book, a philosophy shared by Roach. The Republicans in the legislature (including Alex Raineri) wanted Roach to be under the direct control of Governor Rennebohm and the legislature. The Republican assembly members battled over a bill that would move Roach's division from the State Treasurer's Office to the Department of Taxation. Assemblyman Beggs from Madison said that the motive for moving Roach was to get him to quit because he witnessed a group of Republican lawmakers gambling at a roadhouse.

The situation was rich in irony. Roach had been escorting a reporter through the roadhouse showing him that the Thomson Bill eliminated gambling. During the tour, they ran into a pack of Republicans gambling and their secret exposed. Nonetheless they denied that this was a motive for moving Roach's division and argued that the division "could function more efficiently under that tax department as it reports to the governor."

The Senate passed the bill on June 18, but it was defeated in the assembly on July 11. The next day however, they reintroduced it, and it passed with a vote of 48 to 47.[290]

Roach was now concerned about the Governor splitting up the division. In a presentation to the Cudahy Kiwanis Club later in July, Roach said, "The unfair thing about the bill is section 34, which permits the commissioner of taxation to take over the division in 'whole or in part.' This is a slap in the face for many persons who have given their best years to the state, including some 43 veterans among the 50 male employees of the division."[291]

Hurley: The Usual Suspects Pay the Usual Fines

ON AUGUST 9, STATE AGENTS hammered Hurley arresting five operators of five joints. They nabbed the operators of the Showboat, the Club Francis, and the Club Fiesta. Two weeks later, on August 26, the operators paid fines of $300 to "get back to business."[292]

Madison: Roach's Boss, John Smith Dies

ON AUGUST 17, STATE TREASURER John Smith, the man who hired John Roach and who served as his boss for Roach's entire career, died of a heart attack in Madison. *The Capital Times* wrote that "He often got into arguments with other constitutional officers because he refused to cut the corners on any law affecting his office and followed the letter and spirit of the law to the extreme." He and Roach were cut from the same cloth, and with the death of Smith, the legislative proposal to move Roach's division lost support. Nonetheless, Roach would still have a new boss.

During the first week in September, Governor Oscar Rennebohm appointed John Sonderegger, 32, of the Rennebohm Drug Company as a temporary replacement for John Smith.[293] The Beverage Tax Division, absent an elected treasurer, was under the governor's direct control.

Vilas County: Trouble in Vacation Land

IN LATE AUGUST, RUMORS SPREAD about commercial gambling in "northeastern Wisconsin" and, around the capitol building, legislators whispered that the "north was opening up again." Hearing about it, Governor Rennebohm assured the legislature that "The laws will be enforced."

John Wyngaard, in his syndicated column "Under the Capitol Dome," traveled north to discover for himself. He discovered gambling in Vilas County, saving him the trip to Hurley. A Milwaukee reporter validated the information a month later and Wyngaard quoted him, "A number of places were conducting gambling games, with only a semblance of secrecy and discretion."[294] All of the places were in rural areas: the Plantation, just north of Woodruff, the Jack o'Lantern, just east of Eagle River, the Club DeNoyer, west of Eagle River at the intersection of 51 and 70; and the Tia Juana Club, north of Eagle River on Highway 45.[295] Some hosted a race wire so patrons could bet on their favorite horse. Others hosted roulette, dice, craps, and blackjack. It was tourist time, and the establishments enjoyed the additional income before the end of the season.[296]

On August 23, the *Rhinelander Daily News* referred to the *Journal's* work and headlined a piece entitled "Where's John Roach, hard-boiled enforcement chief of the Wisconsin Beverage and Cigarette Division?"[297]

Most believed Governor Rennebohm was nearly as tough on vice as former Governor Goodland. The *Oshkosh Daily Northwestern* reported, "The racket boys know that a resort can lose its tavern license if it is found with slot machines. So, the 'slots' are out. But anyone can easily find an opportunity to play the roulette wheel, toss the dice, engage in 'blackjack,' and also lay their money on the racing nags, at some of the so-called respectable resorts." It continued, "They can get into the 'clubrooms,' marked for 'members only,' without the slightest question. That is how conditions have changed since Gov. Goodland has passed on."[298] The elimination of slot machines didn't have any effect on the demand for gambling. Previous reports arguing that tourists were more interested in scenery than gambling could well be disputed.

Hurley: The D.A. Plays an Ace from His Sleeve

ROACH SENT HIS AGENTS to Minocqua and Eagle River where they found nothing. Roach told the Associated Press, "The employees far outnumbered the customers throughout the entire area."[299] Since he was already in the area, he continued north on Highway 51 to persecute Hurley. There, he targeted the Club Fiesta and the Showboat. On August 26, his crew arrested five men in these two taverns, including John Carli and James Francis. Although he had warrants, he couldn't find Donald Napoli or Richard Matrella. Even though the agents confiscated and destroyed blackjack and dice tables, the taverns remained open after-hours. At 2:20 a.m., on the same evening, Roach found "them selling beer and liquor right and left." The best he could do was add a charge for operating after-hours. The next day, when Roach tried to deliver the warrants to Napoli and Matrella, bartenders told him they were "out of town."

* * *

As with previous attempts, this effort to revoke licenses failed. On September 3, District Attorney J. C. Raineri said he would not proceed with revocations against Napoli or Matrella because the equipment seized did not fall under the Thomson Act. Roach was flummoxed until Raineri presented a letter from Assistant Attorney General Willard A. Platz, whom he had met several days before. Roach read the words carefully, "Dear Mr. Raineri, Your conclusion that the equipment found in Matrella's place known as the Showboat in Hurley, does not come within the provisions of the Thomson Act is correct and your decision not to commence revocation proceedings on the basis thereof is hereby approved." Raineri played an ace from his sleeve and courteously promised to send a copy to Roach. Roach was spitting mad, and, without a word, he left Hurley empty-handed and furious.[300] On September 12, with the state agents in court, Judge Trembath fined Matrella $100 for the gambling equipment.[301]

Hurley: He Punched the Baker

IN EARLY SEPTEMBER, CITY COUNCIL member Lyman Daoust voted against granting a liquor license to Matt Bertolini.[302] Nonetheless, the motion passed. Then Daoust resigned, saying he had recently moved from the ward he had represented. Within a few days, Bertolini entered Daoust's Pasty Shop. After arguing, Bertolini leaned over the counter of freshly baked pasties, grabbed Daoust by the collar with one hand, and punched him in the head with the other. Doust filed charges in Iron County Court, and Judge Trembath fined Bertolini $20 for assault and battery.[303] [304]

Hurley: The Heat's On

HURLEY'S LEGAL VICTORIES came at a cost. Local officials were weary of the lower block, Madison's pressure, and John Roach's persecution. At the end of October, Iron County Sheriff John Shea, Hurley Chief of Police Albino Endrizzi, and District Attorney J. C. Raineri summoned the usual suspects. They told them to behave and warned that "the heats on" and "this is the end." The gang nodded agreeably, left the meeting, then thumbed their noses.[305]

With Hurley sizzling on the back burner, Roach and crew followed leads in Waukesha, Milwaukee, and Kenosha at the governor's request.

In November, the governor announced that John Sonderegger, temporarily appointed in 1947, would continue to serve as state treasurer "until the department gets reorganized" and until "modern methods and modern equipment" are placed within the treasury department.[306]

Hurley: Deaf Ears and a November Raid

THE OCTOBER WARNING FELL ON DEAF EARS as on November 1, 14 state agents raided the lower block again, targeting the Club Fiesta, Club Francis, and the Showboat. Roach arrested Dominic Napoli, William Matrella, and five dealers for operating blackjack, craps, and dice games.

Silver Street was competitive, as with most economies, and the early-warning system was sometimes selective depending on quarrels and feuds. A reporter wrote, "Other clubs in town known to have a 'table or two' had plenty of time to get rid of them before the state men got around to visit them."[307] Sometimes, news of an impending raid was not shared with the small operators allied with the flagrant, and they got caught in the same net.

Brown County: A Gunfight at Joyces Lunch

IN EARLY NOVEMBER 1947, Kay Vaughn operated a disorderly house called Joyce's Lunch in the Town of Lawrence, Brown County. A little after midnight, four men from Oshkosh entered the joint, one being Leslie Clark, 28 of Milton. Clark got began arguing with two men already at the there – Ervin Galst, 32, and the bouncer, William Farley. Somehow a gunfight began, and Clark took a round to his right thigh and Farley was shot in his foot. Police could not sort the melee because of different stories, so for the time being, they charged Kay Vaughn as the keeper, two women and prostitutes, and Galst as an inmate.[308]

When the dust settled in mid-November, the judge sentenced Kay Vaughn to one year at Taycheedah after she pled guilty to keeping a house of ill fame and the prostitutes received hefty fines. Irving Galst got 10 days in jail as a previous offender.[309] On December 8, a judge sentenced William Farley to 90 days.[310]

No one ever figured out who fired the guns, but "Joyce's Lunch" took the fall and was shuttered and sold.

Madison: John Roach Eyes Job

IN EARLY DECEMBER, JOHN ROACH reported that not a "single illicit still" had been confiscated during 1947, and later that month, he announced that the Wisconsin Wine and Spirits Institute offered him the position of executive manager.[311]

It is common for industries to recruit government employees who have enforced laws relating to those industries. These government employees are fluent in the statutes, administrative rules, court cases, and procedures. Further, they are generally not paid well for their effort. These individuals are prime candidates for industries that value these characteristics. In addition, these companies can lure candidates with substantial salaries. Roach's knowledge and experience enforcing liquor laws made him a top candidate for employment in the liquor industry. This wasn't unique. His former colleague, Clyde Tutton (after being nudged out of State service by Roach), worked for the Wisconsin Wholesale Liquor Company.

Roach had several offers, one from the Wisconsin Wine and Spirits Institute. This would be a good fit for Roach as he was amiable, knowledgeable, and had a lot of contacts. These characteristics appealed to the Institute as they represented liquor wholesalers and lobbied for favorable legislation.

John Wyngaard[312], in the *La Crosse Tribune*, published an impassioned plea for the governor to consider the pay of civil servants and used Roach as the example. He said that unless the State recognized the contribution of dedicated people like Roach, they would lose these people to private industry and cited the loss of Clyde Tutton.[313] Over a few weeks, Roach leveraged the Institute offer to increase his pay with the State. In January 1948, Roach turned down the offer from the Wisconsin Wine and Spirits Institute based on a promise of a $50 per month raise.[314]

Members of the Institute were upset because they thought they had a firm agreement. Within a brief period, and much to Roach's dismay, they hired Clyde Tutton for the position.[315]

At the end of January, the Wisconsin State Emergency Board delayed Roach's salary increase in late January, saying they would adjust all state salaries by March 1. Roach was irked because he had abandoned the position of general manager for the Wisconsin Wine and Spirits Institute in early January, a position which would have increased his income substantially. This delay would nag him through the summer of 1948.

∞

1948

Hurley: Another Fine Mess

THIS STORY IS NOT ATYPICAL of the activity on Silver Street and is an example of the involving ownership, licensure, operation, and employment.

The confusion arose when the council approved the transfer of the licenses of both the Club Fiesta and Club Francis from Domenic Napoli first to James Napoli then to James Francis.[316] This muddled mess cast doubt on who owned what. The incestuous mix of owners, operators, and bartenders made it impossible for Roach to track the license trail. Since there is nothing more in the record about these transfers, Roach probably just gave up.

Rita W. Arrested at Red Star Inn
Antigo 1948

Hurley: A Personal Best

THE STATE REPORTED THAT of the 267 liquor law violations during 1947, Iron County held the record with 32. *The Iron County News* referred to the record as an "undesirable distinction." Milwaukee County came in second, with 30 arrests. For comparison, Milwaukee County, with a population of 864,000, had one arrest per 28,800 people, whereas Iron County, with a population of 8,700, had one arrest per 272 people. Iron County had one hundred times more liquor violations per capita than Milwaukee. [317]

Brown County: Publicity-Seeking Madison Snoopers

AFTER SEVERAL DAYS OF SURVEILLANCE in early February ended with a raid on 13 night spots in Brown County. There were citations for violating the hours law and for serving minors. Only the Hi-Ho Club was nabbed for prostitution. The operator, Eve Kitson, was arrested along with two prostitutes and the bartender.[318]

This was Kitson's third arrest since 1942. When arrested, she told the state agent, "I'm not going to jail. I am paying for protection, and I am going to get it."[319]

The defense attorney and amicus lawyers were furious because they believed Roach was picking on Brown County while southern Wisconsin operated untouched. Even the District Attorney, Norman Basten, was upset with Roach, attacked Roach in court, and accused him of being overzealous.

Roach told the judge that "Brown County was one of the

Carol A. Arrested at the Red Star Inn
Antigo 1948

worst in the state as far as tavern law violations were concerned." He criticized both the district attorney and the sheriff for being lax. The defense attorney told the judge, "Mr. Roach had better clean up his own backyard before reproaching Mr. Basten."[320]

During the trial, the defense attorney asked Jerry Clifford, a prominent local Democrat, to provide a character statement for District Attorney Basten. Clifford said Basten was "absolutely square, and has been conducting a good, sensible administration." He continued, "State agents make more over a glass of beer in Brown County than they do over a murder in Milwaukee." He summed up his comments by slamming Roach, saying he was "sick and tired of those publicity-seeking Madison snoopers."[321]

These Brown County officials held together, but who Kitson was paying for protection was never discussed.

Madison: John Roach Pushes Back

THE PRESS, LOCAL AUTHORITIES, AND VIOLATORS tossed insults at John Roach. He was particularly annoyed that the Brown County officials should criticize his actions rather than prosecute the defendants.

Roach had enough and charged like a bull out of the gate. At an April meeting with northern Wisconsin law enforcement officers in Antigo, he said, "Lawmakers who pass laws and then criticize those who enforce them are hypocrites." He continued, "A lazy official is a termite in his organization and community. Officials who hold their jobs for personal gain and continually alibi can be put in the category of buck-passing officials and are a detriment to the community they represent."[322]

Susan G. Arrested at the Red Star Inn
Antigo 1948

Roach issued a formal statement telling local officials to "use greater care in examining applicants for liquor licenses in order to eliminate undesirable operators from the tavern business." He urged local government to "investigate thoroughly the character of the individual" applying for licensure.[323]

Hurley: Strength Under Adversity

IN SEPTEMBER 1944, A MINER NAMED Dante Barnabo, 34, worked deep underground at the Montreal Mine, west of Hurley. At 9 a.m. on Saturday, September 8, Barnabo, Thomas Belanger, and Peter Brackett were taking a break when a slab fell from the ceiling. The chunk of ore brushed Brackett, killed Belanger, and buried Barnabo under the rubble. Coworkers dug him out and sent him to the surface, but the slab broke his back and crushed his legs, and the mining company called a specialist from Milwaukee to perform surgery.[324]

Barnabo would spend the rest of his life in a wheelchair. Not to be without work, in March 1945, he purchased a grocery store at 300 Maple Street in Hurley.[325] In April 1948, four years after the accident, grocer Dante Barnabo, now 38, ended Dr. Bonacci's 14-year tenure as mayor of

Hurley. As with many of his predecessors, the new mayor promised strict enforcement of gambling, closing hours, and selling liquor to minors.[326]

Hurley: The Story of Felix Patritto

FELIX PATRITTO[327] HAD BEEN in trouble since his teens. In February 1925, the 16-year-old robbed Mike Perl's confectionery store.[328] In September of the same year, police nabbed Patritto and Clarence LaFave while robbing Joseph Raineri's meat market. Patritto escaped, but within a few days, Duluth police arrested him when they spotted him "wandering around the streets in Duluth."[329]

* * *

In October 1925, LaFave was released on Probation by Judge Risjord with the understanding that he would join the Army. The judge released Patritto (on probation when arrested) on a $500 bail bond pending a trial.[330] In January 1926, Patritto was sentenced from one to three years in the reformatory at Green Bay for violating probation and attempted robbery of the Raineri meat market.[331] There is little in the record about what he did in the ensuing years. However, in 1938, he ran for first ward alderman but lost.[332] Although he was tenacious, he lost again in 1940.[333] In August of that year, at a city council meeting, he objected to the issuance of three individuals who applied for liquor licenses in Hurley, arguing that they were not residents.[334]

* * *

In July 1941, Patritto applied for a tavern operator's license.[335] Later that month, the mayor appointed a committee of three to review the applicants and gave them the authority to reject undesirables. The committee rejected two applicants but issued a license to Patritto.[336] In 1942, he ran again for alderman of the first ward but was defeated again.[337] In May 1942, the city appointed Patritto as a volunteer fireman.[338] Things changed dramatically in August 1942 when John Roach arrested Patritto and 51 others. Patritto pled *nolo contendre* for being an inmate of a house of ill fame and paid a fine.[339] Despite being arrested the week before, on August 11, the Hurley City Council granted Patritto a bartender license.

* * *

Patritto's trajectory changed on May 4, 1943, when the Hurley City Council, under wartime emergency, appointed him to serve on the Hurley police force.[340]

In October 1944, three convicts escaped from a prison camp near Lake Tomahawk. Their "short period of freedom staged a crime wave that included stealing an automobile, committing burglary in Ironwood, and robbing two lumberjacks after threatening them with a revolver." The undersheriff, John Shea, and officer Patritto nabbed the trio on October 1, 1944. The judge sent the perpetrators to the State Prison at Waupun for 1–3 years.[341]

* * *

After five years as an officer, in May 1948, Mayor Barnabo moved Patritto into city hall as police and fire steward."[342] In July, the *Iron County Miner* reported that Patritto was an "enthusiastic assistant coach of his son's baseball team 'when he is not putting out fires.'"[343] In April 1949, Patritto served with the Hurley Eagles Auxiliary.[344] In July 1953, the school district hired Patritto as the janitor of the Lincoln Building.[345] After 18 years and four attempts, in April

1956, Felix Patritto was elected to the board of supervisors for the first ward in Hurley.[346] In June of that year, a committee headed by Patritto, Paul Santini, and John Siebert assembled a group of ten Hurley organizations to plan a summer recreation program for children in Hurley. The *Iron County Miner* reported, "Patritto said that a long-range program is visualized with recreation facilities for both summer and winter to be provided."[347] As chair of the committee, Patritto helped appoint William Zell as Hurley's new recreation director and had Alphonse Riccelli help in the effort. The committee wanted a recreation leader for the girls, and Patritto led the effort. He then scheduled a meeting with representatives of a dozen civic, fraternal, veterans, and industrial organizations and asked for help.[348]

* * *

In an ironic twist, in July 1956, Patritto, as a city council member, granted a liquor license to his old boss, Dante Barnabo, for Porky's bar at 327 Silver Street.[349] In November 1963, the VFW named Patritto "Man of the Year," and the Boy Scouts asked him to chair the finance committee for their fund drive.[350]

Stories of redemption are rare in these pages. While Felix Patritto wasn't perfect, his story hits all the notes including tenacity, perseverance, and fortitude.

Hurley: Who's on First

IN MAY 1948, THE HURLEY CITY COUNCIL helped shuffle tavern licenses: John Califano moved from 26 to 102 Silver Street and Matt Bertolini slid from 24 to 26 Silver Street.[351] Although these transfers were business-related, to the casual observer, it might have looked like the license holders were trying to obfuscate ownership. While that was not the case, it did have that collateral benefit.

Hurley: Mayday!!! A Raid on the Lady's Room

DESPITE THE NEW MAYOR'S EFFORT, on May 1, John Roach and 28 agents surprised Silver Street with an evening raid. They stormed the Bank Club, the Congress Bar, and the Down Beat Club and arrested the operators. When agents noticed a scurry of activity near the ladies' room in the Congress bar, they busted through the door and found several men trying to shove slot machines up a hidden stairway.

Although Roach said he was looking for minors, his agents focused on gambling equipment. Roach nabbed an assortment of violators, including James Lawless,[352] William Matrella, and Joseph Moselle. The Congress bar yielded a "Las Vegas haul," including a roulette wheel, a craps table, a blackjack table, and three slot machines. Other places were empty of both gambling machines and prostitutes. Roach was disappointed but then angry when he learned someone tipped off the denizens except for a few operators.[353] The defendants and three state agents appeared in court at the end of May.

State agents joined Sheriff John Shea at the county jail to ensure the destruction of the gambling equipment. Roach promised revocation of the licenses of the Down Beat and the Congress. District Attorney J. C. Raineri faithfully filed the papers with Judge G. N. Risjord in circuit court for revocation under the Thomson Act.[354]

In early June, Risjord revoked the licenses of James Lawless of the Congress Bar and Joseph Moselle of the Down Beat. Both surrendered their liquor licenses, and on July 7, the judge issued restraining injunctions. However, Hurley being Hurley, the next night, the city council granted licenses to the wives of Lawless and Moselle.[355] In July, the city council issued all 78 tavern licenses to eager operators. Being faithful to history and despite revocation, the doors of the Congress and the Down Beat never stopped swinging.[356]

Madison: The End of an Era

IN LATE JULY, THERE WERE RUMORS again that John Roach would resign because of pay disputes with the State Treasury Department. State Treasurer John Sonderegger said, "Roach told me last week that he had several offers under consideration but assured me he would let me know immediately if he decided to leave."[357]

In mid-August, John Roach resigned as Chief of the Wisconsin Beverage Tax Division. On September 15, his new employer would be Calvert Distillers Corporation and his salary would be $10,000 per year ($131,000 today). He was going to be Calvert's public relations adviser and work out of their New York headquarters.[358]

This marked the end of a period never to be repeated in the Wisconsin's history. Roach worked for the State for only 15 years, from 1933 to 1948, with two intermissions: a two-year stint for the IRS and three years in the Army.[359] Roach's years as a beverage agent were replete with successes and failures and highlighted by passion and adventure.

John Roach was resolute, independent, and demanding. He believed in the mission and expected loyalty from his agents. He was street-smart and enjoyed the respect of his superiors including governors and members of the Wisconsin legislature. His presence would be missed.[360]

Hurley: The Squadron Raid

AS WITH HIS PREDECESSORS, Governor Rennebohm was informed of blatant gambling in northern Wisconsin. In the summer of 1948, after raiding the Jack O' Lantern at Eagle River and finding gambling equipment, the governor, and State Treasurer John Sonderegger "decided to leave agents in northern Wisconsin for the remainder of the resort season." Although Roach was now out of the picture, Fred Mattingly, one of his agents, spearheaded the effort.

On August 27, the *Iron County News* stated, "A squadron of Wisconsin beverage agents swooped down on the Showboat, the Club Francis, and an unlicensed building behind the Club Fiesta at about 11:30 Saturday night."[361] They arrested Fred Fontecchio, Jr., Leo Mallick, Nicolas Casanova, and Brazio Di Salle. They arrested Eddie Itsof for gambling in a hut near the alley behind the Club Fiesta. Agents reported that the "games were in full tilt" at Itsof's place.[362] They confiscated blackjack tables, roulette wheels, dice tables, and slot machines. In court, the fines ranged from $75 for dealers to $300 for Fontecchio and Casanova for operating a "gambling den."

Agent Mattingly reported this as the seventh raid on the Club Fiesta in the last five years and the fourth on the Showboat. In addition, agents raided both twice in the previous year.[363]

Hurley: The *Rhinelander Daily News* Offers a Suggestion

AN EDITORIAL IN THE SEPTEMBER 8 edition of the *Rhinelander Daily News* said, "Hurley is the lone community in the state where the Thomson anti-gaming law is being openly violated. One establishment there has been raided four times in five years. The raid in which six Hurley men were arrested and fined a total of $1,375 will be no more productive than other raids, so far as stopping gambling is concerned until the Governor steps into the picture." The article went on to point out the governor's options such as calling "in the district attorney and sheriff and demanding that they enforce the law."[364]

To suggest that the Governor demand the district attorney and sheriff enforce the law meant that the *Rhinelander Daily News* had not been keeping up with their reading.

Appleton: Another City Denounces Hurley…and Gambling

IN EARLY SEPTEMBER, THE EDITOR of the *Appleton Post-Crescent* published a denunciation of Hurley, "Hurley is far enough from Appleton so that its influence is negligible here. But no place in the country is sufficiently far away from us to neglect to observe the wicked influence upon thousands of people made by professional gambling.

"It needs to be said over and over again that gambling is a sport or a biting piece of viciousness depending upon whether the game is natural, that is one arising between friends for the fun of if it or an abnormal that is one where the customers or victims are rounded up by spoilers or good looking women and the game is not run for fun but for business.

"There were six pleas of guilty to running these gambling joints at Hurley recently. Admissions of this sort speak for themselves. Roulette wheels, craps games, blackjack tables were among the fancy dishes served up to those on a hectic pursuit of gold where there is no gold.

"Professional gambling invariably invites the criminal element but even if it didn't, it should be smothered for making yaps out of people by inoculating them with a fever for which there is neither sulfa nor penicillin."[365]

Madison: David Pritchard Replaces John Roach

In October 1948, Governor Rennebohm reassigned John Sonderegger as the insurance commissioner and appointed Clyde Johnston as a temporary treasurer until the November election. [366] More importantly, he appointed David H. Pritchard, 60, a 14-year veteran and former auditor, to fill John Roach's position as director of the beverage and cigarette tax division.[367] Prichard was now in charge of the enforcement division of the Wisconsin Beverage Tax Department, and his chief aids were Fred Mattingly and Arthur Fadness, two members of Roach's squad.

Hurley: Raineri Replaces Raineri

IN NOVEMBER, AFTER THREE TERMS in the Wisconsin Assembly representing Iron and Vilas counties, Alex Raineri retired from the legislature. He immediately ran for District Attorney, a position his brother recently vacated. He won by a slim margin of 106 votes out of 4,010. In the November 5, *Montreal River Miner*, Raineri wrote, "I wish to take this means of offering my most humble thanks to the voters of Iron County for electing me to the office of the district attorney on Tuesday. I promise to conduct the office intelligently, impartially and will give you an honest administration." Alex was sincere but his brother J. C. had been a respected district attorney for 14 years, and he would be a tough act to follow.[368]

Hurley: Cirilli Divines a Raid

CEDRIC PARKER SNOOPED AROUND HURLEY and slid into Armand Cirilli's *Iron River Miner* office. Parker was trying to dig up dirt on Congressman Alvin E. O'Konski, the U.S. Representative from Hurley.

Cirilli, ever clever with words, twisted a tale about Parker. He wrote, "The Madison newspaperman enjoys bending an elbow now and then. He visited our local 'gin mills.' Boasting a prolific typewriter and a vivid imagination, we shall be very surprised if a little piece on our town does not appear in *The Capital Times* very soon."[369]

On December 11, Agent David Prichard gave Cedric Parker something to write about. Pritchard's team of nine agents raided three taverns in Hurley and two near Wausau. In Hurley, the Club Fiesta and the Showboat got clipped – as usual. Agnes Perlberg[370] now ran the gambling operation at the rear of the Club Fiesta – it was called "The Barn." Agents pinched her for having five slot machines, cards, and poker tables. In the front of the Club Fiesta, they arrested Fred Fontecchio, Jr. and Jean Winters for operating a "26" table. Over at the Showboat, agents arrested Richard Matrella, Bud Howell,[371] and Brazio Di Salle at the Showboat, for operating a craps game and a blackjack table.[372]

Cirilli was right. The product of Parker's "prolific" typewriter began with the December 26 issue of *The Capital Times*. It would be a series about gambling in Hurley, and the first article featured two pictures of the lower block, one by day and one by night. Parker described the December 11 raid, "Through what appears to be a highly effective 'tip-off' service, they knew 12 days before the raid occurred that two state agents had been gathering evidence of gambling in Hurley and that a raid could be expected at any time."

Parker said that five different tavern operators told him about the pending raid. He said that one evening, well before the raid, he approached a blackjack table at The Showboat, and when the dealer asked about his business, he told him that he was a "salesman for photographic supplies." The dealer speculated, "Reason I asked was I thought you might be a state man. There's been a couple of them in town, working the street, and I thought maybe you might be another one." The dealer told Parker that when Hurley gets press, it helps business. He asked him why they would stay open if they knew a raid was impending. The dealer told him, "Because we'll probably make enough to pay all the fines if we go on operating until the raid comes off. If we closed up the gambling and waited for the raid, there wouldn't be any percentage in that. We can expect just so many raids, ever so often, and that's that. Might as well make hay while we can. We talked it all over and that's what Dick thinks – he's my boss." The dealer was referring to Richard Matrella, the operator of The Showboat.

Parker got a similar story at the Club Fiesta from "Freddie," who treated him with suspicion. "Freddie" turned out to be Fred Fontecchio, the tavern operator. He told Parker, "There'll be another raid one of these days, and I expect I'll see you along with the boys when they come." Fred was a veteran, and gambling at the Club Fiesta continued without hesitation.

Parker visited another tavern where the operator had covered the gambling tables with oilcloth. He asked if he could play blackjack or poker. The operator told him, "Not here tonight, Bub. You can go down to the Fiesta or the Showboat – I understand they're operating yet, but I've closed down the tables for a while." Parker asked why and the man replied, "Because the heat's on temporarily. I got snagged in the last raid, and I'm laying low for a few days until this one blows over."[373]

Hurley: Cirilli Pokes at Parker

A T THE END OF DECEMBER, Armand Cirilli returned fire at Parker, writing, "Amply qualified to make the rounds in Hurley taverns, Cedric Parker reports that he spent three days – and nights, in this city." In response to Parker describing a card dealer as "loquacious," Cirilli said, "All you have to say is 'hello' to Cedric Parker and you have been interviewed." Cirilli was merciless: "The article is most amusing to those who are acquainted with the situation and people in Hurley. Parker puts fancy words in the mouth of a blackjack dealer who probably has trouble saying, 'you make me very funny.' The folks at the Club Francis deny saying anything to the Madison newspaper editor." Cirilli said everyone knew that a raid was due and said, "Well, even the people up here in the sanctimonious 300 block could have told Parker that a raid was expected."[374]

Hurley: August Derleth Writes About Hurley

D ECEMBER MADE UP FOR THE calm and quiet of the latter part of 1948. The *Milwaukee Sentinel* wanted to sell papers and since they were running a story about Hurley, they placed an ad in the December 10 *Iron River Miner*. The *Sentinel* pitched a feature by the prolific writer August Derleth. Derleth periodically wrote a column entitled "History Passed This Way" for the Sunday edition of the *Sentinel*. The ad claimed that the story would "Recapture the colorful years of the history of Hurley." It said, "It brings you the story of more than 100 inspiring years of your community's progress. You'll treasure it for years."

Although Derleth was an inspired and thoughtful writer, Armand Cirilli was not impressed. After the article was published, he wrote, "Folks from this area were calling at the newsstands on Monday trying to get their money back for the *Milwaukee Sentinel* which they purchased on Sunday, which alleged it would carry a stirring story on Hurley and its glamourous history. Apparently, the Hurleyites expected something startling, but most of the readers were obviously disappointed." Regarding Derleth, Cirilli wrote, "He didn't beat his brains out doing research on this 'exclusive story of Hurley.'"

Actually, Derleth wrote a historically accurate description of Hurley's history. However, Cirilli said it was "dull" and didn't compare with the tales of Hurley "that came out of the Milwaukee newspapers during the days of prohibition. In those days, the *Milwaukee Sentinel* told of drunks and lewd women trudging from one tavern to the other on snowshoes. The Montreal River floated away bodies each morning after the 'swampers' cleaned up the saloons." After writing about Derleth's mundane description of Hurley, Cirilli quipped, "We suspect that August Derleth has never seen our much-maligned little community."[375]

1949

Hurley: Early Risers Steal Panuccis

IN HURLEY, WHILE GAMBLERS worked the tables and prostitutes the beds, Bruno and Fortunato Rodeghiero baked bread in the back room of their bakery at the corner of Silver Street and 2nd Avenue. Between 2 a.m. and 4 a.m., bakery thieves slipped through the unlocked front door and absconded with $27 in cash and two dozen panuccis – Italian bread buns.[376] The bakers didn't realize the theft until the milkman arrived at 5 a.m.,[377] about the same time the tavern clientele were going to Gus Lewis Café for breakfast, perhaps a $27 breakfast with their own bread.

Hurley: Julius Barto's "Suicide"

IT WOULD BE UNFAIR to characterize the relationship between Ironwood and Hurley as tense. A more accurate description would be that Ironwood tolerated Hurley while believing itself morally superior. Hurley, in all truth, was rife with vice, while Ironwood, by comparison, was lily-white. This brings us to a most unusual story. At 9:15 p.m., on January 7, 1949, a passerby found the body of Julius Barto, 44, from Montreal, on the shoulder of US-2 near Bessemer. Barto had eight stab wounds in the "region of his heart." After examining the body, William Jennings, the coroner of Gogebic County in Michigan, ruled the death a suicide.[378]

During the evening of January 7, the temperature dropped to 7 degrees F.[379] Assuming Mr. Barto wore a heavy jacket, which would have been typical for the weather, the coroner implied that he drove a knife through his parka several times to inflict a fatal wound. The *Iron County News* reported that "a large knife was found in the dead man's hand." It went on to say that Barto "…was last seen in Hurley, where it was reported he was in good spirits and that he had not been drinking."[380] The record reports Barto's most serious charge was for DUI in 1926.[381] At the time of his death, Barto was employed as a saw filer at a lumber camp near Rockland, Michigan.

Something nefarious happened, and it is reasonable to believe it happened in Hurley. An excellent way to avoid an investigation at that time would be to dump the evidence in Michigan.

Madison: The Transfer of a Division

A THREE-MONTH BATTLE BEGAN in January about the bureaucratic placement of the Beverage and Cigarette Tax Division. Governor Rennebohm wanted to move the Division from the State Treasurer's Office to the Department of Taxation to help insulate the enforcement of state liquor and gambling laws. The move would offer more stability as the elected Treasurer only served a two-year term while the Department of Taxation provided a six-year term under the governor.

The three-month debate included political infighting, legislative maneuvering, and employee appeals. Ultimately, the Governor got his way and signed a bill which transferred the Beverage and Cigarette Tax Division from the Treasurer's Office to the Tax Department, effective April 1.[382]

Madison: John Roach Predicts Hurley to Win

BILL ASPINWALL WAS FROM HURLEY. After graduating from UW-Madison, worked for the University of Wisconsin Athletic Department in Madison from 1932 to 1972. During this time, he served as the first full-time account and business manager. For many years he had the additional duty as ticket manager.

In March 1949, the Hurley Midgets competed for the state high school basketball title. During the final game, Aspinwall sat next to John Roach. La Crosse Logan was up by nine points, and Aspinwall was despondent. Roach said to Aspinwall, "Why are you looking so sad, Bill?" Aspinwall told Roach to look at the scoreboard and "You can figure it out yourself." Roach quipped, "Don't worry, the Midgets will win. Those guys at Hurley never quit. I know."[383]

Hurley won the state championship by scoring the final basket in the last 40 seconds of play, beating La Crosse Logan 37-36. Roach was right, he knew Hurley.

Hurley: The Arthur Burgoyne and Marguerite Cole Incident

ARTHUR G. BURGOYNE GREW UP in Harrisburg, Pennsylvania. In 1938, at age 24, he was arrested for robbing a bathhouse in Pittsburgh. The judge put him on probation for ten years. In 1944, while serving in the army in North Africa, a military court found him guilty of being absent without leave, disposing of government property, and wrongfully using a government vehicle. The Army sentenced him to 15 years in federal prison. He was paroled after four years and On May 2, 1949, Arthur Burgoyne, 33, and his girlfriend Marguerite Cole, 26, traveled from Chicago to Hurley looking for work.[384]

Within a few days, Hurley police arrested Marguerite Cole for being drunk and disorderly. When they took her into custody, she "went on a rampage" and destroyed furniture and fixtures in the Iron County jail. When she got out of jail, she worked as a server at Mattie's Bar, operated by Matt Bertolini and located on the lower block of Silver Street. Burgoyne took a job at a photographic shop in Ironwood. Bertolini let the couple live upstairs of the tavern.

After Cole worked at Mattie's for about a week, she told her boyfriend that Bertolini encouraged her to work as a prostitute. Burgoyne was enraged and confronted Bertolini, who denied the accusation. To mend the issue, Bertolini said he would pay for Cole's transportation back to Chicago.

On the morning of May 12, after several days of no payment, a frustrated Arthur Burgoyne confronted Bertolini about the money at 12:30 a.m. in Mattie's Bar. The argument escalated to shouts, and when Bertolini told the couple to move their stuff out, Burgoyne pulled a .22-caliber revolver from his jacket. Pointing the gun at Bertolini, he demanded the travel money. Bertolini told him to get out, and Burgoyne shot him twice.[385] One bullet shattered the bone in Bertolini's right arm and lodged behind his shoulder blade. The other bullet tore through his upper left arm. A third shot went wide. When Bertolini's wife tried to call the police, the enraged Burgoyne exclaimed, "I killed Mattie and I'll kill you too." The .22 belched a round missing her by inches and lodged in the wall next to the phone. At that point, Cole attacked Mrs. Bertolini and wrestled her to the floor to prevent her from calling the police. Burgoyne then forced her to open the cash register.

Grabbing $45, he and Cole ran out the back door just as two customers came in the front. [386]

Burgoyne and Cole traveled east to Bessemer, where they found a ride to Mercer. They intended to take the train from Minocqua to points south, but before they could make their getaway, the Iron County Sheriff rounded them up.[387]

Over the next several days, arguments, charges, countercharges, and eventually, warrants were issued against everyone involved in the incident. When Burgoyne admitted shooting Bertolini, the new district attorney, Alex Raineri, charged him with "assault, regardless of life" and charged Cole with aiding and abetting. Unable to post the $3,000 bond, they resided in the Iron County jail until the trial.[388] Sheriff Shea charged Burgoyne with attacking Bertolini "in a manner evincing a depraved mind regardless of human life without any premeditated design to effect the death of the person assaulted."[389]

Cole's testimony cast a wide net, and the judge issued warrants for Richard and William Matrella for gambling and supporting a disorderly house. The sheriff charged Bertolini with operating a house of prostitution and "inducing a woman to practice prostitution." At trial, the Matrella brothers pled guilty in county court, but the judge waited for the doctor to discharge Bertolini before calling him to appear.

In mid-May, the circuit court judge sentenced Burgoyne to 1–7 years at the Wisconsin state prison in Waupun and Cole 1–3 years at the Wisconsin Industrial Home for Women in Taycheedah. From the hospital, Bertolini pled guilty in Iron County Court, and the judge fined him $75 for operating a disorderly house.

The May 20, 1949, *Montreal River Miner* published a sidebar about the affair. "One of the fellows who assisted in bringing the shooting victim to a hospital was an Ironwood man who had been ordered out of the city. What was he doing in town? There are too many 'characters' drifting into town. We have enough of the home-grown variety without 'importing' them and permitting these people to take root here."[390]

* * *

In January 1950, Marguerite Cole escaped from Taycheedah with another inmate but was quickly apprehended at a roadblock, and the judge added six months to her sentence.[391] The Wisconsin Department of Public Welfare granted Arthur Burgoyne parole in November 1950, and he moved back to his home state of Pennsylvania. Governor Walter J. Kohler, Jr., commuted his prison sentence on January 31, 1952.[392]

After their "Bonnie and Clyde" moment, both Burgoyne and Cole disappear from the record.

Hurley: Marguerite Cole Takes Revenge

AS A RESULT OF THE BERTOLINI SHOOTING, local officials raided Silver Street taverns on the evenings of May 12, 13, and 14. In total, they arrested the six operators. They charged each of them for violating the hours law and one for gambling. The judge issued a warrant for William Matrella of the Chateau bar, accusing him of pandering. A warrant was issued for Matt Bertolini, based on the complaint from Marguerite Cole, for operating a house of prostitution.

This raid was not without gunfire. Three men wanted some late-night liquor in one of the taverns after 1 a.m. They knocked so hard that they broke the window on the door. Ironically, a cop, who was in the tavern, saw them run to their car. As they raced along Silver Street, he fired a warning shot, but they ignored it. Scrambling into his squad car, he tore after them toward Mercer. There, the trail went cold.[393]

As a result of the raid, the judge fined Matrella $75 for "contributing to the support of a disorderly house." Others, including Richard and William Matrella, and Fred Fontecchio, Jr., were fined $70 for gambling violations. With a final twist, Marguerite Cole testified that in addition to the other gambling charges, Matrella ran a bingo table at the Showboat, which resulted in an additional $75 fine.[394]

Hurley: The First Raid of 1949 and the Group of 77

DAVID PRITCHARD AND HIS AGENTS were relentless. At 10 p.m. on Sunday, May 22, beverage agents scoured the Club Fiesta, the Club Francis, and the Showboat. There was no warning, and these were clean arrests early in the evening. Familiar with the routine, neither Fontecchio nor Matrella displayed much emotion.

Both paid $400 fines for "setting up, keeping, and managing craps tables." Even though the money was good, the fines were getting steeper and having to replace gambling equipment was increasing the cost of operation.[395] The big threat, however, was revocation, and these taverns walked a fine line.

In mid-June, the state petitioned the court to revoke the licenses of the three taverns. Although the defendants had 20 days to dispute the charges, the issue was moot as the licenses expired on June 30. The city council – i.e., the co-conspirators – granted new licenses to different operators for the same taverns. They granted a license to Thomas Baribeau for the Club Fiesta, Eugene DeCarlo for the Club Francis, and Doris Grant for the Showboat.[396] The process was smooth and efficient, and to say it wasn't deliberate, would be naive.

In July 1949, the Hurley City Council issued 77 Class B Combination liquor licenses along with a pile of bartender's licenses. The list took ten inches of print in the *Montreal River Miner*. Although neither Fred Fontecchio nor Richard Matrella was listed, their proxies blended in with the group of 77.

Madison: Prichard Dispels Rumors

RUMORS FLOATED AROUND MADISON that the Division of Beverage and Cigarette Taxes would not enforce the Thomson anti-gambling law during the summer tourist season. Prichard dispelled the rumor in a speech to the Wisconsin District Attorneys Association in early June telling them that he hired four new investigators to help enforce the Law in a "systematic manner." Prichard also admonished local licensing agencies for failure to "eliminate chronic violators" of liquor and gambling laws.

He said that if the local government fails to take the issue seriously, the state may take over the licensing authority, as is done in 24 states. He said that although his division's main work was collecting taxes on liquor, beer, and cigarettes, the gambling laws "attract the most attention."[397]

Hurley: The Second Raid of 1949

A S SUMMER EMERGED in northern Wisconsin, Prichard's undercover agents gathered evidence from Vilas and Iron Counties. Weeks of investigation led to the second raid of 1949. The neon lights of the lower block reflected off wet asphalt on the evening of July 10 as Fred Mattingly and 21 agents descended upon Hurley looking for the usual suspects, associates, and hangers-on.

They arrested 14 people: ten for violating gaming laws, two for operating houses of ill fame, and two for prostitution. They arrested Joseph Moselle at The Down Beat and James Shields at the TryAngle Inn for operating houses of ill fame. Agents apprehended Doris Grant at the Showboat, Thomas Baribeau at the Club Francis, and Eugene DeCarlo at the Club Fiesta for blackjack and bingo. In a brick house behind the Showboat, agents nabbed Armas Hill for operating a roulette table – the first gambling arrest in a residence. Agents also arrested Walter Mazerka for gambling at the Rex Hotel in Mercer and James Shalecki for selling whisky and possessing slot machines in his house in Vilas County.[398]

Judge Trembath's courtroom was "packed with victims of the raid, state agents, and curiosity seekers." Some paid fines of $300 to $400, while others pled not guilty, hoping for a favorable outcome in court.[399]

Since the previous raid occurred in May, this raid was unexpected. With Fontecchio and Matrella out of the game, Baribeau and DeCarlo at the Club Francis and the Club Fiesta felt the sting.

Hurley: The Third Raid of 1949

P RICHARD AND FOUR AGENTS traveled to Hurley on August 9 to testify in court for the previous raid. Since Prichard's strategy was to tame the sin city with relentless attacks, he visited Silver Street since he was already there. Doris Grant made another appearance at the Showboat, and not surprisingly, they arrested Thomas Baribeau at the Club Francis and Eugene De Carlo at the Club Fiesta for gambling. The net also covered other employees working the equipment at these taverns.[400]

Armand Cirilli wrote, "Four state agents were in town for a hearing in a case in the county court of Wednesday morning, so they decided to make a raid on several of the 'old reliable' taverns on Tuesday night to pass the time."

Hurley: The Very Short Trial of Patsy Jewel Johnson Miller

A FTER THE IMPROMPTU RAID of August 9, agents Schauer, Fadness, and Waterworth testified in the case against Jewel Johnson, aka Patsy Jewel Johnson Miller, resulting from the July 10 raid. During the trial, an agent told District Attorney Alex Raineri that Jewel solicited him at the Down Beat, and the defense countered that the agent entrapped the girl by asking for sex. In her defense, the girl described herself as a war widow and innocent of the charge, and the jury of two men and three women deliberated for 30 minutes and declared her not guilty.[401]

Hurley: The Fourth Raid of 1949

THE BANNER HEADLINE in the *Wisconsin State Journal* on August 22 wasn't a sudden coup in a foreign government or a Nobel scientific breakthrough. Instead, it proclaimed, "Gambling Still Flourishes at Hurley." Staff writer Phil Drotning, after a ride-along with state agents, wrote, "Despite Wisconsin's Thomson anti-gaming act and repeated raids by beverage tax division agents, Hurley hasn't changed one bit – gambling is king and liquor its queen." He described the failure of raids on two notorious "gambling, liquor, and 'girlie joints.'" One "joint" was the Bank Club, formerly the Hurley National Bank. The clickety-clack of his typewriter must have been intense as he described the Bank Club, "Instead of receiving and disbursing dollars and cents it merely receives them, and disburses such alien commodities as Old Forester, Gordon's gin, and a thousand other varieties of whiskey, gin, beer, and wine." Naturally, the usual suspects got early ink, "The city's major financial transactions now seem to be handled in other local institutions, known variously as the Club Fiesta, The Show Boat, The Club Francis, and The Bowery."

* * *

Drotning got good mileage at the expense of the Bank Club. He railed, "The customers are different too. They don't come into mumble apologies about their last overdraft. Instead, they stand around muttering 'hit me' or 'eighter from Decatur.'" In contrast to the bombast in the introduction, he ended it with a thud, "Hurley hasn't changed a bit."

* * *

Drotning said that he asked a barmaid at the Club Fiesta how things were going. She told him that business would be better if "Those state guys didn't raid us every so often" and, "Those fines cost money and they always take all the equipment. They got a roulette wheel this year that cost 6,000 bucks." She was talkative and said, "Yeah, and those wheels are hard to get. You can't just go out and buy them. We haven't even got one now, but we may again in a couple of weeks. Whenever there's a story in the papers that they got a wheel from us, someone who has one hidden away usually comes around and offers to sell us one."

The Madison reporters should have been grateful to Hurley for allowing them to use action verbs and colorful adjectives and to explore up north idioms. Generally, their stories about Hurley were as close to fiction as they could get while on the payroll.

Fred Fontecchio got a lot of ink. Drotning wrote, "Then a short fellow with curly, graying hair, a cane, and a limp walked in and went to an office at the rear of the barroom. The girl said, "'That's Freddy, our little boss,' the girl whispered, 'I mean our big boss.'" Fontecchio's office in the Club Fiesta explains his relationship with Eugene DeCarlo, the license holder. The money was great, and Fontecchio hired DeCarlo to hold the license while he was the silent partner behind the bar.

That night, Fontecchio sat at the bar, smoking a cigarette, and watched the front door while dealers set up the craps and blackjack tables in the back of the room. Then, after he left for the dining room, two uniformed cops happened in, sat in a booth, and ordered coffee. By now, gamblers enthusiastically tossed white dice across green felt. One of the cops carried his coffee into the gambling room, greeted a few people, then returned to his booth, where a waitress topped off his cup. Drotning described the scene and said, "The craps game didn't even slow down." At 9:30 p.m., the Club Fiesta was so crowded that the dancing girls couldn't get to the dressing room, so they changed costumes on stage. Fontecchio continued to monitor the front door.

* * *

Drotning left the Club Fiesta, went into the Showboat, sat at a table, and ordered a drink. Comparing the MC to the one at Club Fiesta, he remarked, "Same jokes, different girls." While Drotning was checking for surgical scars on the dancers, there was a hubbub at the front door, and someone shouted, "Lock the door! The hostess, strategically located, slammed, and locked the door. She hollered through the glass, "We're all filled up, I can't let you in." The entrance was jammed on the inside as some customers tried to leave. She was steadfast and resolute: the men were temporarily imprisoned in a tavern with nude women.

Meanwhile, toward the back of the club, a series of well-rehearsed maneuvers converted the gambling area into open space. Dealers quickly covered the blackjack and craps tables, which now sat quiet and abandoned. Employees disassembled equipment with practiced hands, and it disappeared into the ether. The craps tables racks stood silent and obscure against the sidewall. The gamblers understood the threat and now focused on the floorshow. With the sleight of hand over, the hostess unlocked the front door. Annoyed, the two guys waiting at the door complained, saying they couldn't find any gambling at the Club Fiesta and wanted in. The hostess read the situation perfectly and admitted the agents.

Drotning, noticing the skittishness of the hostess at the Showboat knew that the game was afoot. He rushed back to the Club Fiesta. There, he watched Fontecchio slowly limp around the joint with a satisfied grin as the two agents "looked around, back in the office, back of the bar, and in the men's room." Drotning wrote, "The whole episode, in both establishments, had taken hardly five minutes. Despite the tumult, the floor shows hadn't stopped," and he "doubted that one customer in 10 knew that they had just witnessed a gambling raid." Someone noticed the flurry and asked Fontecchio what had happened. He whispered, "We just got raided. We got away fast." A customer sitting near the craps table commented, "I never saw so much action in 30 seconds in my life."

Anticipating the raid, Fontecchio tried a new strategy. Agents – and customers – typically used the tavern's front and back doors. This night, Fontecchio posted signs on the back door directing customers to the front. He then locked the door because it entered the gambling room. Then, as the raid began, the agent at the back door was stuck and wasted valuable time rounding the building. This time was needed to transform the gambling room, which was done post haste with precision. John Carli, the owner of The Bowery and Fontecchio's friend, arrived to check on him. When he asked how things went, "Freddy smiled and nodded."[402] Drotning ended his article, "That's Hurley on a Saturday night."

Hurley: Gambling Law an Annoyance

THE NEXT DAY, the *Waukesha Daily Freeman* carried a story, "Still at the Head of the List is Hurley." The article stated, "At the head of the list stands Hurley where the Thomson anti-gaming law is regarded as nothing more or less than an annoyance." The *Freeman* reproduced the story about the Club Fiesta and proclaimed that "an alarm had been given in plenty of time to put the gambling tables away and clear the stage. Within five minutes after the agents had left, the

110

scene changed again to the way the Club Fiesta and other dives along the main street are operated every night during the height of the summer tourist season."[403]

Hurley: Hurley Gamblers Bide Their Time

THE AUGUST 23, 1949 EDITION of the *Wisconsin State Journal* published a front-page banner headline: "Hurley Gamblers Bide Their Time." Even the neon lacked enthusiasm as the usual suspects promoted stripping in the absence of gambling. They felt the sting of the raid in their pocketbooks and, for the time being, averted the risk of arrest.

Drotning wrote that the only excitement in the Club Fiesta was when a stripper's skirt fell off. He said she was embarrassed, went back to the dressing room, fixed the skirt, and then returned and "took it off on purpose." However, it was gambling, not stripping, that generated profit. Drotning quoted a local "They're trying to operate a small-time joint on a big-time basis. They can't hire all those strippers and entertainers and meet a big payroll without some gambling revenue." The summer raids pinched their income, and the usual suspects were low on cash and worried. Drotning speculated that "at least four out of five of Iron County residents are opposed to gambling. It continues to exist because of non-existent local enforcement and because some of the leading citizens – not tavern-keepers – are economically involved."

Drotning interviewed residents and asked them about solutions to Silver Street gambling. They suggested larger fines, on-site state agents, and the arrest of patrons. Regarding enforcement, he wrote, "Most Hurley people agree that only state beverage tax agents can keep gambling down in Hurley. The police don't try to stop it, and the county sheriff hasn't got the time to stop it." Drotning ended the article by citing the incestual relationship between the taverns and local authorities. He wrote that "Hurley police don't bother to enforce gambling laws" and that "Some members of the force tend bar in joints during their off-duty hours."[404]

Hurley: "Under the Dome" Editorial

NOT ONLY DID DROTNING pen the headline story in the August 23 *Wisconsin State Journal*, he also got the byline for the "Under the Dome" column entitled, "Reform? Hurley Never Heard of It!" He opened the column, "We came up here because of repeated reports of gambling in Hurley, to satisfy ourselves that state beverage tax agents are really trying to control gambling in the state." The column rehashed his previous observations but with fewer adjectives.

He noted that Hurley was a persistent trouble spot in Wisconsin, and he referred to the "Hurley, Hayward, and Hell" cliché saying, "Hayward is all cleaned up these days, and we hear less about hell every year, but Hurley is still going strong."[405]

* * *

Phillip T. Drotning was a prolific writer, humanitarian, and historian. He was born on the 4th of July 1920 in Deerfield, Wisconsin, just east of Madison. After graduating from UW-Madison in 1941, he served as a Marine until 1943. Then he worked as a journalist for the *Wisconsin State Journal* and the *Milwaukee Journal* and as executive secretary to Governors Oscar Rennebohm and Walter J. Kohler Jr.[406] In 1965, he worked for Standard Oil. Phillip Drotning had a dozen books to his credit. He retired in 1985 and died in 1993.[407]

Hurley: A Journalistic Love Fest

ARMAND CIRILLI USED the September 2, 1949, *Iron River Miner* to comment about Drotning's investigative reporting in the *Wisconsin State Journal*. Referring to the headlines in the Journal, Cirilli commented that "It must have been a dull day in Madison." Referring to two stories about Hurley, He continued, "Although the stories were well done and factual for the most part, they were certainly blown up and featured beyond their importance."

Cirilli was no stranger to prose and sparred, "Drotning made some significant observations for a fellow who was in town only a couple of days. He talked to a few people and learned some stuff that we've known all the time." Then, Cirilli did the unthinkable. He complimented Drotning's writing, "Although the Madison reporter does let his imagination take over in a couple of spots, most of his dope is factual and his observations are good and sound." Then Cirilli took it to the next level, saying that "Drotning's articles, plus a recently inspired zeal by the state agents to clean up Hurley, will spell the end of gambling here."[408]

It was a journalistic love fest and the *Journal* responded to Cirilli's compliment. They wrote, "With singular devotion to civic duty, a Hurley, Wis., newspaper cites its own town's sins on the front page this week, and magnanimously gives The *Wisconsin State Journal* credit for public service which it accepts with pardonable pride."[409]

Now, the relationship morphed into a moderated tennis match between old friends rather than the typical pinball and tilt dialogue. Cirilli responded, "Actually, we've done little, if anything, to 'clean up Hurley.' Frankly, we have not been too zealous in those efforts." He explained the economic motive for gaming, and, despite his criticisms, he admitted that some operators were "boyhood chums." He said the *Miner* did not attach emotion to its reporting as their business was "to print the news."

Cirilli referred to "some influential men" who thought that gambling would improve tourism. Instead, they found that its associated evils outweighed its benefits. He continued, "There are too many in this racket who are no good. They make trouble for the taverns. They make trouble for the town" and that there "are many things that happen down the street that doesn't get into print. Most of them are traceable to the evils – and the men – associated with gambling and worse."[410] This makes one want to learn the identity of the influential men and the unreported stories. Unfortunately, this type of information rarely gets ink.

Hurley: Holiday Magazine – A Take on Wisconsin History

MARK SCHORER WAS BORN IN Sauk City in 1908. He earned a master's degree at Harvard and a Ph.D. in English at the University of Wisconsin–Madison in 1936. Despite his educational prowess, he described himself as a "persisting hayseed." The undeniable fact is that he was an exceptional writer. In the July issue of *Holiday Magazine*, Schorer authored a 16-page article about Wisconsin, its cultural contributions, its industrial evolution, and its philosophical underpinnings.

In the opening sentence, Schorer describes a way to think about Wisconsin's historical essence. "In Wisconsin, history always seems very near; it is so much a part of daily life that it is never quite remarkable. It has not yet been entombed in monuments, and thus it cannot be resurrected because it has not been buried. It is not something that you come and look at casually; it is something that you live. History is like a green shade in which the little towns of Wisconsin slumber."

Supporting the narrative with photographs, Schorer transports the reader around the state, stopping at small-town destinations just long enough to give thumbnail sketches of their heritage. Schorer didn't shy away from controversial history. He traveled north, adjacent to the St. Croix River, and modified the threadbare cliché. He wrote, "There are whole communities which, even when they will it, cannot shake off their inheritance. It was proverbial among lumbermen seventy-five years ago that the four toughest places in the world were Cumberland, Hayward, Hurley, and Hell, and that the first three were tougher than the last. Cumberland has managed to reform its lumber-camp morality." This was the inevitable preface for a visit to Hurley.

Schorer continued, "Hurley has had a harder time. A phenomenal boom town in the 1880's, it developed a nearly allegorical reputation for viciousness. Edna Ferber's novel *Come and Get It* pictures authentically the rowdy drunkenness and robbery and murder which systematically went on in Hurley's innumerable wooden saloons. When the lumber market collapsed, the population of Hurley shrank, but not its reputation. Prohibition gave it occasion to reassert its historic rowdy role, and throughout the 20's and into the 30's, with over half a hundred speakeasies, it became a haven of gangsters and rumrunners – the one wholly wide-open town in Wisconsin."[411]

Schorer continued, "Hurley is exceptional, yet not wholly so. Most of these northern towns have something stark about them, even something rather brutal. They were the products and the victims of the lumber interests, an enterprise too ruthless to allow for geniality or social grace."[412]

Armand Cirilli didn't have much to say. He mostly quoted the sections of the article that referred to Hurley and Little Bohemia. He made a slight comment that Schorer failed to mention the vein of iron upon which Hurley was built. Cirilli's reticence might have indicated that he admired the writing.

Hurley: Local Law Enforcement Adopts a New Strategy

LOCAL AUTHORITIES adopted a new strategy: harassment. In early September, the District Attorney Alex Raineri sent a letter to the Iron County sheriff and the Hurley police chief telling them that gambling violators "will be prosecuted to the fullest if arrested." The chief responded, "Gambling in Hurley is down, and it will stay down."[413] There had been four raids since the first of January. The folks on Silver Street did not anticipate another two by the end of the year.

Hurley: Heads Might Roll

IN THE FIRST WEEK OF SEPTEMBER, Agent Arthur Fadness served a summons for license revocation to Eugene DeCarlo of the Club Fiesta, Thomas Baribeau of the Club Francis, and Doris Grant of the Showboat. They had 30 days to appear in circuit court to defend their position; if they failed, the judge could either suspend for 90 days or revoke.[414]

Hurley: The Fifth Raid of 1949

IN WOOL TROUSERS AND JACKETS with collars turned up, young state agents surveilled Silver Street's taverns during the last weekend of September. They were trained to blend in while noting the action of bartenders, dancers, and gamblers. They documented their observations in their notebooks when safely back in their vehicles. A few days later, on Wednesday, September 28, four agents armed with 32 warrants, and no courtesy, delivered the paperwork to somber operators of the Club Chateau, the Down Beat Club, the Club Francis, the Club Fiesta, the Congress, and the Bowery. Part of the cast included Eugene DeCarlo, Thomas Baribeau, Louis Gasbarri, Andrew Carli, William Matrella, and Dominic Vita.

Judge Trembath fined most for hours violations. Two women got nicked for prostitution, Joe Vita for operating a house of ill fame, and Eugene DeCarlo for a gambling violation. The building in the alley behind the Fiesta must have been a money-maker as it always had a blackjack table, a roulette wheel, and a craps table, making it an easy and consistent target. Another roulette wheel would soon be in tatters. Prichard had the confidence of a man vindicated, and he commented that the raid was "one of the most successful in rounding up liquor law violators."

Either the early warning system used in the old days had failed, or agents found a workaround. This time, they appeared from the ether with the power of paper rather than machine guns.

In court, Trembath fined the 14 operators, including the Swing Club, the Bank Club, the Hi-Ho, the Flame, and the Red Feather, for violating the closing hour law. Joe Vita and two prostitutes at the Hi-Ho paid $45 each, and the judge ordered the women to leave Hurley.[415]

Hurley: Suspensions Ordered

THE SHELL GAME used in July – switching licenses at renewal – would not be repeated. In late October, the governor ordered Circuit Judge G. N. Risjord to revoke the licenses of the Club Fiesta, the Club Francis, and the Showboat. It could have been "game over," but the usual suspects kept up their shenanigans.

The confusion resulted because the operators of both the Club Fiesta and the Club Francis had surrendered their licenses to the Hurley City Council a few days before the trial. As such, there was nothing to revoke. Then, the city council issued new licenses to Ray Anderson for Club Fiesta and Pascoe Pezzetti for Club Francis. The players were smug and thought they beat the system.

Unmoved, Risjord suspended the new licenses for 90 days, causing the defense attorney to appeal to the Wisconsin Supreme Court. Nothing was clear at this point, and Agent Fadness and District Attorney Alex Raineri discussed the situation at Risjord's bench. The judge concluded that he could not move forward under an appeal to the Supreme Court, so he delayed all suspensions.

The judge now needed to unravel who held which license for which tavern. The *Miner* stated, "Conjectures were made on whether the two taverns issued new licenses were now operating on the old permits or by the new licensees." After review, and based upon the recommendation of Agent Fadness, the judge changed his original order of revocation to a 90-day suspension of the three taverns. Fadness was irate because he wanted revocation and the tavern operators snuck through a loophole. He promised that the legislature would fix it during the next session."[416]

Hurley: The Sixth and Final Raid of 1949

O N DECEMBER 12, AFTER A WEEK of surveilling Iron County, state agents raided 19 taverns, including the Club Francis, the Bowery, the Club Fiesta, Mickey's Rendezvous, the Swing Club, the Bank Club, the Hi-Ho Club, the Red Feather, The Ritz, and the Club Chateau.[417] Most of the arrests were for hours violations. Some of the operators suffered multiple arrests during 1949, and the judge would visit these charges.

In January 1950, 19 taverns headed for either suspension or revocation. Armand Cirilli wrote, "Whether you are for or against these tavernkeepers, it is not a pretty picture. We have had some terribly turbulent tavern troubles in the past, but this is probably the worst." He continued, "For most of them this matter of license revocation is something they don't entirely deserve. They are the victims of a bad situation." He wrote about the 1949 raids and the reason for the state's "zeal" in the effort. Regarding the vigilance of the state, he said that Agent Fadness "was reported to be living in Hurley" and that "A wit-about-town suggested running him for alderman of the first ward."[418]

The law required at least two convictions to begin revocation. In the third week of January 1950, the state dismissed seven cases with only one violation, including the Club Fiesta, the Club Francis, and the Rendezvous. The others remained on the docket.

The defendant's attorney, J. C. Raineri, objected to revocations because the violation count extended back to 1942, before the enactment of the Thomson Law. He argued that violations before the law's enactment should not count toward the total. Further, he posited "that it was not the intent of the legislature that the law should be retroactive and labeled the present proceedings ex post facto charges." He continued, "some of the violations cited occurred on premises other than the one for which the current license is held." Some defendants were elated by the argument as they believed that revocation was inevitable.[419]

While the judge might have been conflicted about revocation, he wasn't shy about suspension. He slammed Doris Grant of the Showboat with a 90-day suspension and 5 to 30 days for the others. As opposed to padlocking – like during the days of prohibition – suspensions allowed the businesses to remain open to sell soft drinks and food. The *Montreal River Miner* reported, "Hurley is a law-abiding town at the moment. Gambling has been 'down' for several months. The taverns who have been known to 'stretch' the 1 o'clock closing law are locking the doors pronto and on the dot. Although the suspensions are hitting some taverns in the pocket, they came at a time when 'there is practically no business anyhow.'"[420]

While revocation and padlocking were the norm in "the old days," this was the first time in Hurley's history that a judge used suspensions.

Hurley: Christmas Eve Mystery Fight

O N CHRISTMAS EVE 1949, William Johnson, 60, got into a fight at the L & M Bar at 109 Silver Street. The bartender separated the men and led Johnson, drunk and unstable, to a booth where he fell asleep. In less than an hour, Johnson woke up. He tripped from the booth onto the floor, bleeding from a severe cut to his chin. The police chief arrived and asked Johnson to identify his adversary. Johnson "couldn't recognize the guy, didn't know who it was, and said he "would like to forget about it."[421] A doctor stitched up Johnson's chin and sent him home to celebrate the Holiday.

1950

Hurley: Stiffer Penalties

IRON COUNTY GREETED the new decade with a series of trials resulting from raids in December 1949. After the attorney for the defendants condemned the "sneak raids," the testimony devolved into a war of words along with acquittals for Silver Street taverns. Rumors were that agents "pulled out purportedly to appear at trials elsewhere in the state." Defense attorneys criticized the state for being overzealous with obstruction offenses that they didn't enforce outside Iron County. Others complained that "the better taverns are paying for the 'major sins' of a few and that the tavern industry should keep its own house in order." State enforcement authorities were under attack, and retreat was impossible.[422]

Even the press ridiculed the state's methods. For example, the *Montreal River Miner* reported, "The entire Gogebic range is chuckling over testimony given by a state man telling of going into one of the Hurley taverns – buying a drink of Old Thompson, keeping it in his mouth and then spitting it into a bottle when he got outside. Just what and how they expected to prove anything from this evidence had people on both sides of the river guessing."

Agents arrested 19 Hurley tavernkeepers in the December 12 raid, with most offenses for being open after hours. Because they believed that the state wanted to revoke their licenses, the 19 asked for jury trials when they appeared in court. They preferred to be tried by a jury of their peers who would be sympathetic to losing a local business. After juries acquitted the first two defendants, the state, recognizing the pattern, called a recess and left Iron County for duties elsewhere. They returned a few weeks later and asked the judge to dismiss the remaining 17 warrants. The move was intentional, and the state decided to focus on revocations rather than on hours violations. Instead, they filed a revocation or suspension complaint against 11 of the 19 tavern owners in county court.[423]

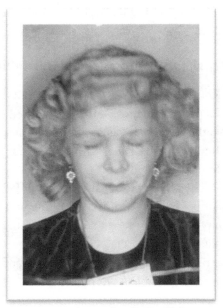

Pat J. Arrested at Hi Ho Club
Hurley 1950

On January 22, Judge Trembath dropped the charges on three taverns. He suspended six others for 12 to 15 days. The licenses of William Matrella of the Chateau Club and Joe Vita of the Hi-Ho tavern were suspended for 30 days.[424] Without alcohol, all taverns strictly observed the hours law as sitting at the bar drinking soda until 2 a.m. was not appealing.

Hurley: A Quiet but Focused Raid

ON AN EVENING IN FEBRUARY, State agents drove north on an icy Highway 51. Arriving in Hurley, they headed straight toward the Hi-Ho and the Blackhawk, both on the lower block of Silver Street. At the Hi-Ho, they arrested Joe Vita and three prostitutes. They nabbed James Quigley,[425] four prostitutes, and a bartender at the Blackhawk.

In county court, Judge Trembath fined each woman $50 and told them to leave Iron County. As operators, the judge fined Vita and Quigley $250 each and sentenced them to six months in the Iron County Jail, then suspended the sentences upon payment of the fines and court costs.[426]

The 1949 raids were exhausting, but the first raid of 1950 was simply boring. The March 10 issue of the *Montreal River Miner* reported, "A downstate newspaper, writing about the most recent raid on Hurley taverns says, 'It's the same old story – but a new chapter.' The way the state agents have been acting, 'another chapter' could be written any minute. Our saloon reporter saw a couple of them peeking through the Venetian blinds on the 400 block."[427]

Hurley: DeRubeis Beats Barnabo

IN APRIL 1950, PETER J. DERUBEIS defeated incumbent Dante Barnabo. DeRubeis worked for the Pickands Mather Company as a mining engineer. This was his third attempt at the office, with two earlier runs against Dr. Bonacci.

The recent suspensions and the February raid dampened the spirit for gambling and prostitution. The mayor-elect said – as did all incoming mayors before – that "The exotic dancers, also known as 'strippers' are 'all through' in the Hurley night clubs and that the operators have already been warned." [428]

Edna K. Arrested at Big Ednas Superior 1950

Hurley: Iron County Gets New *Miner*

IN APRIL, THE *Montreal River Miner* and the *Iron County News* merged to create the *Iron County Miner*. The *Montreal River Miner* began in 1885 and eventually incorporated the *La Nostra Terra*, the *Gogebic Iron Spirit*, the *Gogebic Iron Tribune,* and the *Iron County Republican*.[429]

Hurley: This Sure Comes at a Bad Time

THE COLD FEBRUARY RAID yielded poor profit for state agents. Their next attempt was in May. For a week at the end of May 1950, agents Fadness, Hoffman, Hablewitz, and Chryst meandered through the streets of Hurley in the early morning, behaving like restless tourists. Adjusting their guns under their jackets, they casually entered the taverns of Silver Street. Once inside, they reconnoitered the space, walked to the bar, and ordered a drink. They talked to one another, not script-like, but with the familiarity of men with a history. They began their rounds after midnight to avoid over-drinking while impersonating customers who frequented Hurley in the early summer. On these nights, they took mental notes of activity and exchanged glances with women who leaned on the bar with their elbows and rested a shiny shoe on the footrail, comfortable in the surrounding. Since this was their first raid, the more experienced agents split the new guys between them. They proceeded from tavern to tavern until they covered 27 joints on Silver Street.

Before the evening was over, they gathered enough evidence to issue warrants on a gaggle of tavernkeepers and prostitutes on Thursday. They nabbed a long list of operators including the Four-Ever Amber, the Swing Club, Betty's, Johnny's, the Club Fiesta, the Showboat, the Blackhawk, Nora's, the TryAngle, the Hi-Ho, Smokey's, Mickey's Rendezvous, the Club Royal, the Club Francis, Sloppy Joe's, the Chicken-in-the-Basket, the Bowery, the Avalon, the Range Bar, the Red Feather, the Downbeat Club, the Ritz, the California House, and the Duck Inn, all for violating the hours law.

At the Hi-Ho club, agents arrested the operator, Joe Vita, for running a house of ill fame along with a prostitute named Pat Johnson. They charged Andrew Carli of the Bowery for "knowingly suffer and permit to be set up and operate a gambling device," which was a long description of having a blackjack table. They also arrested Joan Anderson for running a gambling device at the Bowery.

One tavern keeper said, "This sure comes at a bad time. We've just got through putting down $400 to the city for a new license." Further, newly appointed Mayor DeRubeis was distressed because the operators "had been warned" right after his election in April. Naivety was a rite of passage for new mayors.

Lorraine H. Arrested at Big Edna's
Superior 1950

A new generation of agents began replacing those who took part in the raids of the early 1940s, and the *Iron County Miner* reported that they "hardly look the part of enforcement officers" and that "they looked like a couple of 'youngsters' out looking over the town."[430]

*   *   *

During the middle of June 1950, the Hurley tavernkeepers, busted earlier in the month, trotted into Iron County Court. When the dust settled, the sheriff served 30 warrants, and most pled not guilty. However, as they approached the judge, one after another changed their plea to guilty and paid fines.

The usual suspects fell in line. Andrew Carli of the Bowery paid fines for violating the hours law and for gambling on the premises. Joan Anderson paid a fine for running a blackjack table at the Bowery and paid a $250 fine. Pasco Pezzetti, the license holder for the Club Francis, paid a $50 fine for a closing-hours violation. Joseph Vita, the operator of the Hi-Ho, paid a $50 fine on a closing hour charge but was bound to the circuit court for operating a house of ill fame. Pat Johnson, arrested for prostitution at the Hi-Ho, failed to appear and forfeited her $25 bail bond. All the other defendants were fined $40–$50 for closing hour violations.[431]

Later in the month, Joseph Vita of the Hi-Ho pled guilty for operating a house of ill fame, and the judge suspended a six-month jail term upon payment of a $250 fine.[432] Dominic Vita, of the Swing Club, pled guilty to a closing hour charge and paid a $50 fine. As in the past, there were so many arrests that court cases, fines, and sentencing often overlapped.

Hurley: The Short Case of Frank Boho

O N MAY 8, A WOMAN FILED A "statutory offense" complaint against Frank Boho of Boho's at 9 Silver Street.[433] The police chief took Boho into custody but released him when he posted a $1,000 bail bond. On June 5, District Attorney Alex Raineri and Boho waited for the complainant in Iron County Court. When she did not appear, Raineri learned she had left town. As such, he motioned for dismissal, and Judge Trembath agreed. On the same day, Boho applied for a Class B Tavern license.[434] Shortly after that, Raineri sent a letter to the city council recommending that it refuse to grant the license."[435] The motive was unclear, although Raineri could have believed that Boho intimidated the witness and "encouraged" her to leave.

Helen M. Arrested at Big Edna's
Superior 1950

As of June 9, 75 Hurley tavernkeepers filed for Class B liquor licenses with the Hurley City Council, and an additional two were expected before the June 14 meeting.[436] With a not so subtle sleight-of-hand, on June 13, Mrs. Frances Boho applied for a liquor license. The city council granted the license the following day.[437]

Hurley: A Barrel of Ink

T HE JUNE 16, 1950, edition of the *Iron County Miner* used a barrel of ink to write about liquor-related issues in Iron County. The front page offered three articles. The first headline read, "State Official Promises Law Enforcement." The second headline read, "Words, Charges Hurled at city council Meeting." The third headline read, "Tavernkeepers Pay Fines." Then, on page five, Armand Cirilli wrote about how Leo Negrini, the chief of police, promised to "hold the line" on the one o'clock tavern closing time. Cirilli reported that when Negrini told this to some "tavern folks," he got some "dirty looks." Cirilli ended his column, "You've heard the expression, "Hurley, Hayward & Hell." We don't know about hell, since none of our friends have been able to communicate from that place, but it can be reported that in Hayward it is mighty tough to buy a drink after 1 o'clock." The *Miner* used the last of its ink on page six

Mabel M. Arrested at Big Edna's
Superior 1950

to itemize the application of liquor licenses by Peter DeFranco, Mrs. Dominic Vita, William Aijala, William Matrella, and Mrs. Frances E. Boho.

Hurley: Perhaps the National Guard

Donna Jean M. Arrested at Big Edna's Superior 1950

IN THE MIDDLE OF JUNE, Judge Trembath hosted agent David Pritchard, agent Fred Mattingly, Mayor Peter DeRubeis, and Chief of Police Leo Negrini in Iron County Court. Pritchard replaced John Roach as head of the enforcement division of the State Beverage Tax Department in October 1948. However, he kept a much quieter profile than Roach, and this was a rare appearance in Iron County. Pritchard spoke plainly and reported that he intended to keep a "watch on Hurley" with four agents constantly patrolling the area. The state agents expressed concern about an "occupant of a Hurley tavern 'who got tough'" with them. Pritchard said they "won't take that kind of stuff even if it means bringing the national guard here to keep order." The Hurley officials promised their cooperation, saying, "gambling is virtually extinct in Hurley."[438]

Hurley: The Case of Blackie Matrella

Jane R. Arrested at St. Paul Rooms Superior 1950

THE PENOKEE AND GOGEBIC IRON RANGES employed thousands of miners, and the moonshine business was lucrative. In 1922, two years after the advent of prohibition, local police raided the little village of Cary, just west of Hurley. They arrested Battista Paris, a repeat offender. However, having no family, he failed to show up in court and left the country.[439] Police also arrested Richard Sr. "Blackie" Matrella for "shipping a keg of moonshine by streetcar from Cary to Bessemer." Unable to pay the fine, Matrella served a stiff sentence of four months in the Marquette prison.[440] Richard Sr. had two sons: William (the eldest) and Richard Junior. In 1927, traffic officer Meno Bartaluzzi tried to arrest William for a confrontation in a Cary store. When his brother Richard came to his aid, William roughed up the cop. Bartaluzzi regained control and arrested both for resisting. Bartaluzzi was furious, and after cuffing William, he kicked him so severely that he needed surgery and a two-week hospital stay.

In Iron County Court on May 10, 1927, the judge released Richard but found William guilty of resisting an officer.[441] That same month, Richard filed a $10,000 suit against Sheriff Kalliommaa and Officer Bartaluzzi.[442] In January 1928, the judge dismissed the case.[443] Later that year, in August, Police Chief George Rubatt, raided the Cary location and arrested Richard Matrella Sr. and three others for moonshining. The judge fined Matrella $200 ($3,500 today). He left the courthouse to get the money but never returned.

Ruth M. Arrested at St. Paul Rooms
Superior 1950

When the police caught up with him, they learned he didn't have $200, so the judge sent him to the Iron County jail for 60 days. Seven years later, in 1935, Richard Matrella Sr. died of tuberculosis at age 57.[444] His son William inherited little more than his father's nickname, "Blackie."

* * *

In 1930 and 1932, William ran unsuccessfully for alderman of the sixth ward.[445] In 1937, the Hurley City Council appointed him as a fire steward.[446] At the same meeting, the council appointed J. C. Raineri as city attorney.

* * *

Blackie knew money and over the years, he acquired ownership in several Silver Street taverns, including the Club Chateau, the Blackhawk, and Mickey's Rendezvous. However, these acquisitions fueled a dispute between Matrella and newly elected Mayor Peter DeRubeis. In April 1950, after running on a platform to cleanse Silver Street, DeRubeis balked at Matrella's application for multiple tavern licenses.

Matrella already held a license for the Rendezvous, and on June 14, he requested a license for the Blackhawk. This infuriated DeRubeis, who said he would veto a license for the Blackhawk if the council approved it. Matrella preferred the Blackhawk and told the council to "Take back the Rendezvous, but I'm not going to hand you the Blackhawk." DeRubeis, full of authority, replied, "And I'm not too sure you'll get that one either." So, the council, eager to move along, rescinded the license for the Rendezvous as Matrella asked. With five days to veto the Blackhawk, DeRubeis considered retaliation.

Carroll O. Arrested at St. Paul Rooms
Superior 1950

Matrella fumed and said he was being "squeezed out" because the mayor favored friends. He said that if DeRubeis vetoed the license for the Blackhawk, he would continue to rent it so that the mayors' friends could not get "their hands on it." Matrella seethed and confronted the mayor saying, "It's a very low-down trick and nobody but you, Mr. DeRubeis, could do it." Then he pointed at DeRubeis and yelled, "You're not the mayor of Hurley; Marks[447] and Tony Trolla are the mayors."

Matrella went over the line. DeRubeis told Police Chief Leo Negrini to evict Matrella from the council chambers. Matrella regained his composure and replied, "You don't have to throw me out. I'll go." On his way out, he heard the mayor say that he was going to file charges against him. Matrella mocked from the corridor, "I hope you do."

DeRubeis told the council that he would not let someone like Matrella "put the rap on me." Reiterating his post-election pledge, "Hurley tavernkeepers are going to have to operate right if they are going to operate at all" and referred to Matrella's comments as "false" and "malicious." Regarding the rescinded license for the Rendezvous, DeRubeis said, "We don't want that kind of money," and the episode left the Club Chateau and the Rendezvous absent licenses.[448]

Harriet N. Arrested at the St. Paul Rooms Superior 1950

At the special June 21 meeting, the Hurley City Council discussed other tavern licenses. They approved a bartender's license for Frank Reardon of the Rendezvous, among others. Despite the mayor's rancor, the council approved Matrella's license for the Blackhawk. DeRubeis was irate and vetoed the action. The city council abandoned DeRubeis and overruled the veto 9-1.

DeRubeis lost control, stood up, and lectured the council, "You fellows are going to take the responsibility. That man came here and insulted us. You have accepted that insult. I won't. God help you. I have stood and will stand on my convictions. Nobody is going to push me around."

The council went on to grant 55 liquor licenses. Recognizing the reality of Silver Street, one council member remarked, "In some cases, we are just legalizing prostitution."

At the same meeting, the council granted a bartender's license to Frank Reardon for Mickey's Rendezvous, the tavern that Matrella abandoned. The intent was unclear, but it appeared that Reardon got issued a license for a job that he did not have.[449] The Case of Blackie Matrella continues in 1952.

Helen C. Arrested at the St. Paul Rooms Superior 1950

Hurley: Cirilli Sums Up the Situation

IT IS IMPOSSIBLE TO PARAPHRASE Armand Cirilli's summation of the transition in Hurley. At the end of June 1950, he reflected on the current situation, "For about a year now the state has been pecking away at Hurley. At first, they were after gambling. There is virtually no gambling here now . . . so the state is checking for the closing hour law. For many years, the state made periodic raids in Hurley. In between raids, they ignored Hurley . . . except that some of the boys came to town for fun. But it is almost a year now that the state has been playing for keeps. Why?

June D. Arrested at the St. Paul Rooms
Superior 1950

"Why? Because they made up their mind to clean up Hurley. Why? Because there is a big file in the office in Madison of letters from Hurley citizens…and tavernkeepers which make complaints…or squeal, on this or that tavern, or person, or condition. A state official said this week that 'you would be surprised at the letters in my office.' Then, too, state officials resented the brazen attitude of tavernkeepers who were raided, let us say, for gambling and then stayed open until wee hours, showing no respect for the state men. The agents are admittedly sore about the 'not guilty' pleas and jury trials. These are some of the reasons for the 'zeal' to 'clean up Hurley.'

"Today Hurley is a law-abiding city. Last Saturday night Silver Street was dark at 1 o'clock. Folks had to go over to Ironwood to continue their revelry…and drinking. Never thought it would ever come to that. Over these many years, the Hurley taverns would get the 2 o'clock flow from Ironwood. Now the Ironwood taverns get the customers who are still thirsty after Hurley closes up.

"They tell us there is some feudin' down the street over tavern buildings and alleged effort to pressure tavernkeepers into buying liquor at certain places. Some of the stories rate interesting listening."[450]

Personal anecdotes are far more interesting that what is published in the press. However, it is difficult to confirm stories without more than one witness and then, with two sides to the story, things can become incomprehensibly complex in a hurry. Because of a life time of connections, Cirilli's language often nudges up against the word on the street and without his insight, the feelings and color of Silver Street would be lost.

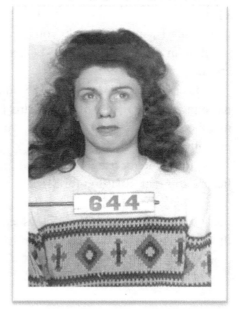

Jerry K. Arrested Blondies Evergreen
Langlade County 1950

Hurley: Soykenen v. Hill

LAURI SOYKENEN, 32, AND CHARLES HILL, 56, were former loggers from Mercer. At 11 a.m. on July 29, the two men drank their way through Hurley, meandering into the Magic Bar at 102 Silver Street. Having already consumed a large quantity of liquor, they began arguing about some unknown topic. William Aijala, the operator, ordered them out of the tavern. Their argument escalated on the sidewalk, and a witness said that Hill "whipped out his pocket knife" and sliced Soykenen's belly, face, hands, and neck. Soykenen staggered along Silver Street, leaving a trail of blood. Arriving at the V-Café at 8 Silver Street near the trestle, he collapsed, his intestines protruding from the wound to his stomach. In serious condition, an ambulance rushed him to the Runstorm Hospital in Ironwood. By the time the police arrived, Hill had disappeared.[451] [452]

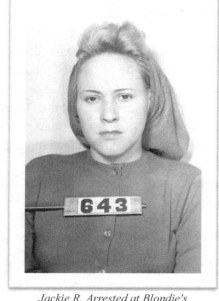

Jackie R. Arrested at Blondie's Evergreen Langlade County 1950

* * *

Police arrested Charles "Kalle" Hill two weeks later, on August 12, in Ironwood. After waiving extradition, he appeared in Judge Risjord's court on August 16. Hill had been working in logging camps but was not currently employed, so the court recorded him as a transient. He pled not guilty. Unable to post the $1,000 bail bond, he remained in the Iron County jail.[453]

* * *

On September 18, Hill pled guilty to the stabbing of Lauri Soykenen, and Judge Risjord sentenced him to 1–3 years in the state prison at Waupun.[454]

Superior: A Summer Raid on the North End

HOWARD'S BAY RESTS at the confluence of the St. Louis River and Lake Superior. Here, the city of Superior angles at the northwest point of Wisconsin under the watchful eye of Duluth. The city's north end is a triangle of land jutting into the bay with eight large slips cut into the landscape like crooked teeth. Teamsters load and unload freight, and a shipyard occupies the east end of the bay. During the first half of the 20th Century, sailors hobnobbed in the dark streets around the docks and visited the brothels on Superior's north end. In 1950, North Third Street, John Avenue, Ogden Avenue, and Tower Avenue hosted merchant marines looking for temporary love in multi-story single-family houses. These houses held families years before, but by 1950, nefarious entrepreneurs partitioned each upstairs into small rooms just big enough for a bed and washstand.[455]

In mid-August 1950, 14 state tax agents, along with the Douglas County sheriff, raided brothels at 1124 North Third Street, 314 John Avenue, 1608 North Third Street, and 504 ½ Tower Avenue.

They nabbed 24 women for prostitution. Unlike Hurley, these were not taverns, and sailors waited in lobbies and parlors, reading newspapers and magazines while waiting for their favorite girl.

Authorities arrested three women as keepers, 11 as solicitors, and ten as inmates of disorderly houses. The arrest records showed that the women came from 11 different states.

Later in the month, when the Douglas County sheriff tried to deliver 17 arrest warrants at four brothels, the women had skipped town to avoid appearing in court.[456]

In mid-September, agents arrested eight men for gambling at 601 Ogden, 612 Ogden, and 330 Tower Street in Superior.[457]

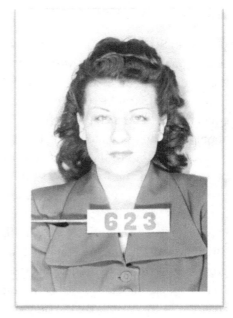

Rita L. Blondies Evergreen Inn
Langlade County 1950

Hurley: Differences Between Superior and Hurley

SUPERIOR AND HURLEY BOOKEND NORTHERN Wisconsin: Superior on the west, Hurley on the east. Although Hurley had more taverns, Superior matched Hurley in prostitution. There were several significant differences between the two cities. First was the clientele. The customers in Superior were mostly Great Lake sailors, while Hurley's customers were loggers, miners, and tourists. Second, Superior bawdyhouses were actual houses, while in Hurley, the upstairs of clubs and taverns served as brothels. Third, the keepers in Superior were mostly women, while in Hurley, they were primarily men. Finally, the geography was different. Superior's red-light district was off the main street and hidden in the shadows of ore docks. Hurley's red-light district, on the other hand, was the main street, glowing with neon.

Mercer: Ralph "Bottles" Capone Summoned

ON THE EVENING OF SEPTEMBER 25, 1950, a Chicago mobster followed William Drury, a former police lieutenant, to his home. After Drury backed his Cadillac sedan into his garage, the killer pumped four shotgun slugs through the windshield into Drury's face.[458] Four hours later, gangsters gunned downed Attorney Marvin J. Bas on a Chicago side street.[459] Drury and Bas had something in common. Both were scheduled to testify about organized criminal activity to the Special Committee on Organized Crime in Interstate Commerce in Chicago.

Senator Estes Kefauver from Tennessee chaired the committee. The only person from the midwest on the committee was Senator Alexander Wiley, from Chippewa Falls, Wisconsin, and he wanted to focus on Chicago because of the murder of Drury. Wiley said that "The slaying of Lieut. Drury has terrorized every potential witness and has made the task of the crime investigation committee infinitely more difficult. However, the committee will work twice as hard now that the underworld has challenged congress." Wiley implored Kefauver to ask President Truman "to order the FBI to probe into the Drury slaying."

126

Virgil Peterson was an FBI agent for 12 years. For seven years he managed the FBI offices in Milwaukee, St. Louis, and Boston. Beginning in 1942, he was the Operating Director of the Chicago Crime Commission. Peterson testified that the Capone syndicate was "flourishing with underworld links in many parts of the nation" and that "the syndicate had formed alliances with powerful gang leaders including Ralph Capone and 20 others."[460]

For over a month during the summer of 1950, Deputy U.S. Marshall Thomas Madden searched for Ralph Capone, who he considered a suspect in Drury's murder. On September 20, he found him at his brother Al's summer home on Big Martha Lake near Mercer. Madden

Club Carnival Silver Street
~circa 1950

interrupted Ralph Capone while he entertained guests. He slapped a subpoena in his hand, ordering him to appear before the senate crime committee led by Kefauver in Chicago. Wiley and Kefauver docketed Capone as the first person to testify at the secret Chicago hearing.[461] In 1950, an Associated Press writer described Ralph Capone as "one of the overlords of the national syndicate which controls gambling, vice, and other rackets."[462]

Capone testified but the outcome of the committee was tainted. Historian Michael Woodiwiss, wrote in the June 1987 journal *History Today*, "The Kefauver Committee manipulated its evidence to fit a nebulous conspiracy theory focusing on the Mafia. The Committee made no appreciable impact against crime in the 1950's and seriously impeded any other approach to the problem of organized crime."[463]

Hurley: The Buddy Howell Incident

THROUGHOUT THE SUMMER and into the fall, Mayor DeRubeis sulked because the city council overrode his veto to prevent granting a liquor license to Blackie Matrella. However, DeRubeis would be somewhat vindicated in October.

On October 6, 1950, a police officer found Edward Schneider sitting on the curb in front of the Club Chateau with blood on his face. He told the cop that Buddy Howell, the operator of the Club Chateau, hit him. However, the fight actually began in the Flame, and then Schneider walked to the Chateau and sat on the curb. Based on Schneider's story, the officer confronted Howell in the Chateau where Howell denied the assault. Wanting to avoid a problem, Howell invited Schneider into his tavern for "a cup of coffee." As the police officer walked away, Schneider came crashing out the front door. Howell told the cop that when Schneider entered the tavern, he attacked him.

The officer asked two girls standing at the bar about the fight. One said she didn't know anything about it, and the other told the cop that it was none of his business. The cop, by this time, patience exhausted, carted both women off to jail.[464] After booking them for vagrancy, he "chased them out of town." The following day, he arrested Buddy Howell. That evening, the mayor scolded council members, saying they "should be more particular to whom they give licenses." He said the only reason he did not oppose Howell's license was because he did not want a repeat of the incident where the council vetoed his opposition to the license of the Blackhawk.

The judge fined Howell $10 for assault and $25 for allowing "indecent conduct, fighting, quarreling and disturbances in his place of business." Shortly after that, to the satisfaction of the mayor, a council member filed a petition to revoke Howell's license, stating that he "maintains and keeps a disorderly, riotous, indecent, and improper house."[465]

In late October, for the first time in the history of Hurley, the city council revoked a tavern license. For the time being, Buddie Howell and the Club Chateau were out of business. DeRubeis was pleased that he made some progress toward ridding Hurley of "so-called exotic dancers." The pressure continued. During the third week of October, police arrested a dancer, Patsy Miller, for "immoral behavior." The judge fined her $35 and ordered her to "get out of town within six hours."[466]

Hurley: Alex Raineri Gets Defeated as D. A.

In early November 1950, George D. Sullivan, a local attorney, defeated Alex Raineri for the position of district attorney by a wide margin (2,360–1607). Raineri had held the position since 1949, a period of one term, whereas his brother J.C. had held the position for 14 years.

Hurley: The Devastating Winter of 1950

THE CHARACTER OF HURLEY would change forever beginning on Thanksgiving 1950. On November 23, it was nine degrees below zero, and a north wind howled at 25 miles per hour, pegging windchills at 30 degrees below zero. Everybody huddled inside.

The old Bonino building, also called the Board of Trade building, sat on the corner of Silver Street and First Avenue. It was two stories, had a wood frame, and a brick veneer exterior wall. Four tenants occupied the building: the Showboat, the Club Fiesta, the Club Fiesta Grill, and the Magic Bar.

Shortly before noon, a spark ignited a fire in the Showboat, and within a few minutes, the entire building was aflame. Then, as heat weakened the mortar in the frozen outer walls, they collapsed onto Silver Street, injuring some firefighters. The water used to extinguish the flames quickly turned to ice. Despite the efforts from the Hurley, Ironwood, Montreal, and Bessemer fire departments, there was little left by day's end.

In addition to their businesses, several people lost their dwellings, including Fred Fontecchio, Jr., who had moved his family to the second floor the day before. Others were William Aijala of the Magic bar, Richard Matrella of the Showboat, and Doris Grant of the Club Fiesta Grill. Several girls also lost their upstairs apartments, and the fire destroyed "The Sky Room," a supper club and dance hall above the Club Fiesta.[467]

Other buildings damaged on the lower block of Silver Street were the Club Francis, the Kentucky Liquor House, the Kentucky Club bar, Sloppy Joe's bar, the Town tavern, Santini's Hotel and Bar, and the Spa tavern. Just across First Avenue from the blaze, Club Francis took the brunt of collateral heat, smoke, and water damage.[468]

It was a total loss. Fred Santini and Teresa Gentile lost the building, Tony Trolla lost the fixtures in the Club Fiesta Grill, and the operators, their families, and the girls lost their belongings and homes. The *Iron County Miner* reported that "Only the west wall of the Hurley building stands intact, with portions of other walls protruding from a rubble-filled basement in what was once the gayest corner in the city's tavern district."[469] The Town Tavern, just west of the Bonino building, escaped the blaze primarily because of the north wind, a heavy sidewall, and the fire department's work.

*   *   *

Two days later, on November 27, Ironwood had its worst fire in over 60 years. Along with several local fire departments, the Hurley Fire Department fought the blaze that engulfed the Glassner block. The fire consumed the Coffee Shop restaurant, Stern and Field, Hamacheck's Rexall Drug Store, McClellan's Variety Store, the Gilbert Beauty Shop, some apartments, a law firm, and an art studio.[470] Investors would rebuild the structures in Ironwood, whereas the land under the old Bonino building would remain charred and vacant.

*   *   *

The hellish assault on Silver Street was not over. On December 1, 1950, just before noon, the chimney in Sloppy Joe's tavern glowed red, and the wood siding burst into flame. Because a worker reported a chimney fire, the fire department tried to use water from the truck only to discover a malfunctioning pump. By the time the Ironwood fire department arrived, the fire had enveloped parts of the Spa tavern and the adjacent Kentucky Liquor House. The firefighters doused both facilities with water for two hours. At 3 p.m., they examined "the building from attic to basement and 'found not even a spark.'"[471]

However, at 3:45 p.m., Police Chief Leo Negrini examined the scene again and smelled smoke. He reported the smoke to the fire station and then found "a fire that could have been put out with a pail of water." He asked a passerby to hoist a hose to the second-floor window. When he opened the window to get the hose, the stairway burst into flames. Negrini acted fast, dashing through the flare-up, down the steps, and onto Silver Street. In a short time, the fire burned hot, consuming the second floor of the building.[472] Tony Trolla lost the building, and Jonas Biller, the operator of Sloppy Joe's, lost his business. The fires of 1950 dampened the spirits of Silver Street merchants, radically reduced the number of taverns, and sent customers to the remaining establishments.

1951

Lincoln County: No Stranger to Agents

BLONDIE'S EVERGREEN, AKA BLONDIE'S PLACE, was a roadhouse in the Town of Bradley in Lincoln County. Its notoriety was widespread, and being 30 miles south of Minocqua, it was conveniently within reach of tourists. State agents raided Blondies in 1942, 1943, 1946, 1947, and 1950. In nearly every case, a woman operated the joint. Agents arrested May June Skelly in both 1943 and 1947. In 1949, they arrested Rita Wayne as the keeper. By 1949, agents arrested a total of nine women as inmates.[473] In December 1950, agents nabbed Joseph Callahan as the owner, Jackie Reed as the proprietor, and Jerry King, an inmate. in January 1951, Circuit Judge Gerald J. Boileau of Wausau shuttered the facility.[474]

Sheboygan County: The Intersection between Politics and Prostitution

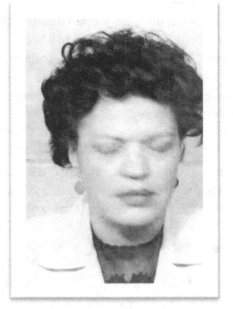

Antoinette B. Arrested at the South House Langlade County 1951

GOVERNOR WALTER J. KOHLER JR. was born in 1904 on the Kohler estate near Sheboygan, where his family built the plumbing business. Kohler attended Phillips Academy and then graduated from Yale when he was 25. That year, his father, Walter J. Kohler Sr., was elected governor of Wisconsin. Kohler Jr. began a career with the company formed by his grandfather and was known as a man of integrity. Wisconsin elected him as governor for three terms, from 1951 to 1957.[475] The village of Kohler, established in 1912, was a planned community much like Greendale in 1936, only more elaborate.[476]

It is almost certain that Kohler knew about the goings-on in Sheboygan County since the factory played a vital role in its economy and employed several thousand employees, mostly men. Although he was, like his father, a man of character, it is likely that he turned a blind eye to the private lives in the community. This would change, however, as Wisconsin chose him as their 33rd governor in 1951, when he carried 59 of the 71 counties.

The same month he took office, civic groups from Sheboygan complained to the state attorney general about open prostitution in the county. Kohler was probably embarrassed to get this report from those in his backyard. He

Betty B. Arrested at the South House Langlade County 1951

130

targeted the issue, and on January 26, 1951, he unleashed 24 state agents led by Fred Mattingly and David Pritchard to Sheboygan. Along with D.A. John G. Buchen and Sheriff Harold B. Kroll, the agents led a team of 24 in a simultaneous raid of six roadhouses in Sheboygan County. They netted 26 women from the Tin Roof, the Green Bungalow, the Club Royal, the Greenhouse, the Casino, and The Farm. The Tin Roof, Green Bungalow, and Club Royal were all near Plymouth, the Casino and The Farm were just outside Sheboygan, and the Greenhouse was in Sheboygan proper. [477]

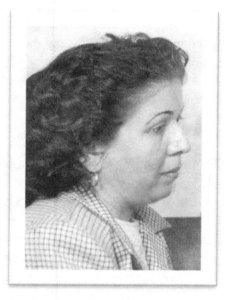

*   *   *

On February 1, Circuit Court Judge Henry A. Detling fined 21 inmates $25 each. On February 15, 1951, a municipal judge fined several women for aiding and abetting prostitution, including Hattie Cook, Myrtle Bodenstab, Vera Bertram, Alma Dean, and Margareta Sulivan.[478]

Rose Marie S. Arrested at the South House Langlade County 1951

*   *   *

Based on the January raids, on March 30, 1951, Sheboygan District Attorney John Buchen worked to padlock five Sheboygan County roadhouses, close them for one year, and require the sale of all personal property.[479]

Mercer: Ralph Capone Vis-à-vis Matt Capone

ARMAND CIRILLI WEIGHED IN about Ralph Capone despite the feds' relentless attack to nail Capone for tax evasion. Cirilli wrote, "Ralph has been making his home in Mercer for more than several years . . . minding his own business as far as his residence in Mercer is concerned." Ralph was generous and friendly, and well-liked by the people of Mercer. However, the people of both Mercer and Hurley felt differently about his brother Matt.

Matt had visited Hurley the previous year and Armand Cirilli wrote, "In a short stay here, he made a nuisance of himself...he tried to 'muscle in' on several businesses." Cirilli went on to say, "Everybody was afraid of him. Eventually, he got in trouble in some sort of scraps and had to be ordered out of town."

Cirilli continued, "He came back two weeks ago. Carrying a gun in his hip pocket, he visited a couple of places and tried to put the 'bum' on the owners 'for a

Louis G. Arrested at The South House Langlade County 1951

131

thousand bucks,' so the story goes. Finally, the sheriff got wind of this hoodlum and ordered him out of Hurley. He stayed in Mercer for a day, but they put the 'bum's rush' on him out there too. Later the Chicago papers carried a story about him being picked up for "disorderly conduct,' but the charge was dismissed for 'lack of evidence.'"[480]

Hurley: Just a Good Tavern Brawl at the Bowery

THIS STORY DESCRIBES A BIG MESS, and even level-headed Judge Trembath agreed. Donald T. Recore, 27, a World War II veteran, occupied a bar stool at the Bowery Tavern on Silver Street on April 8. In the early morning hours, Joe Pietrocatelli, 32, the bartender served Recore a lot of whisky. Recore was cantankerous and after getting into an argument with Pietrocatelli, he left the tavern. A confusing fight ensued, and the police tried to unravel the story. Recore said that Pietrocatelli followed him and "started fighting." Recore said that John and Arthur Carli came out of the tavern, and after breaking up the fight, Arthur Carli chased him across the street and "wanted to fight over there." Recore said he ran to his car, got in, and locked the doors.

Pat G. Arrested at The South House Langlade County 1951

Recore then said Pietrocatelli arrived and broke the car window. Then, both Pietrocatelli and John Carli "got in the car and 'started pounding' him." He said he pushed them out and drove to the sheriff's office but "unable to arouse anyone there," he drove home.

Things got even more confusing in court. District Attorney George S. Sullivan argued with J. C. Raineri because Raineri was the city attorney but was representing the defendants as a private lawyer. Sullivan said that it was unethical that he served in both roles, and they bantered until Trembath interrupted saying stating, "the matter was not for the court to rule on."

Besides Recore, the only other witness was John Morris, a city cop, who said that John Carli called the police at 4:40 a.m. and reported a fight outside the Bowery. When Morris arrived, John and Arthur Carli stood, hands in pockets, alone, as Recore and Pietrocatelli had vanished.

When Raineri finally questioned Recore, he admitted "that Arthur Carli had not struck him and denied that he had kicked Pietrocatelli. J. C. Raineri representing the defendants,

Wilma S. Arrested at The Blackhawk Tavern Antigo 1951

132

called for dismissal, saying the "evidence didn't show any injury except a bump on the head and asserted that there must be a 'grievous bodily injury' for a charge of assault with intent to do great bodily harm."[481]

Judge Trembath was upset about the lack of detail and dismissed the assault charges against Joe Pietrocatelli and the Carli brothers. He noted that "no evidence had been presented to show who started the fight, call it 'just a good tavern brawl. I can't spend any more time on it.'"

A few days later, the judge – probably sending a subtle message – fined Arthur Carli for violating the hours law.[482]

Hurley: John Carli and the Taxi Beating

YOUNG PENNY LIND WORKED for John Carli at the Bowery for several weeks in the spring of 1951. On May 21, as Carli and Lind rode along Silver Street in the back of a taxi, Carli became furious, and his infamous temper erupted. He severely beat Ms. Lind, bruising her eye and cutting her lip. She escaped from the taxi and walked to

Monica "Billie" S. Arrested at the South House Antigo 1951

the jail to report the beating. Sheriff William Thomas picked up Carli and locked him in jail. After a while, "the woman said she did not want to press charges against her employer," and the sheriff cited both for disorderly conduct.[483] In June, the case was postponed indefinitely.[484]

Hurley: The Raids of 1951

HURLEY WAS QUIET, unassuming, and monotonous during the first half of 1951. Either there was no vice during that period, or agents were busy elsewhere. The first possibility was ridiculous – the second, probable. Things had to change; inaction would damage Hurley's reputation. The Upper Peninsula American Legion convention was a catalyst in the third week of June. Up to 5,000 Legionnaires would descend on the motels and the Elks Club in Ironwood.[485]

Not to miss an opportunity, on the weekend of June 23, Arthur Fadness and his beverage agents slid into Hurley and nabbed a dozen violators. The *Iron County Miner* reported, "The agents 'worked' the town during the past weekend while the tavern district was enjoying a slight 'boom' due to the Upper Peninsula American Legion convention in Ironwood."

June K. Arrested at The South House Langlade County 1951

133

* * *

Agents arrested Agatino DiGiorgio, Arthur Abraham, John Rajkovich,[486] and Joe Vita for keeping disorderly houses. They collared Louis Gasbarri of the Red Feather and Penny Lind at the Bowery for gambling and pinched two women at Nora's and two at the Ritz for solicitation. Agents confiscated several slot machines despite them having been cleaned out of Wisconsin years ago.

* * *

By August 1, the judge had heard all the cases except for two women arrested for prostitution at the Ritz who failed to appear in court.[487]

* * *

On July 15, before the hearing and court cases resulting from the June 23 raids, Police Chief Leo Negrini, armed with warrants issued by D. A. Sullivan, raided the lower blocks of Silver Street again. He served warrants on Agatino DiGiorgio[488] of the Ritz, Julius Mattei[489] of the Club Chateau, and Lois Gasbarri[490] of the Jackpot's Flame Tavern, all for after-hours violations.

Alice B. Arrested at The Blackhawk Tavern Antigo 1951

When handed the warrant, Julius Mattei, having had enough, gave Police Chief Negrini a tongue-lashing, earning him another warrant. At the city council meeting on July 18, Negrini encouraged the city council to revoke Mattei's tavern license. He told the council that Mattei used "foul and abusive language" and then resisted arrest. Mattei got all wound up again and yelled at Negrini, which started a verbal brawl between the mayor, police chief, Mattei, and council members. The *Iron County Miner* could only describe it as "Unprecedented in the history of the council."[491]

Hurley: Just to See the Wheels Go Round

I N JULY, THE CASES WENT to court, and Agent Fadness testified that the slot machines paid off in "nickels and free plays." However, the tavern owners argued that the machines "never pay off and never give free plays" and were "for amusement only." The machines were in court as evidence. The defense attorney challenged the agents to play the machines and supplied the necessary nickels. The agents plugged the machines and pulled the levers, but not a single coin fell down the chute. The state surmised that the operators triggered the machine's "totalizer devices" (preventing the machines from paying) during the 18 hours between the arrest and the time of confiscation. District

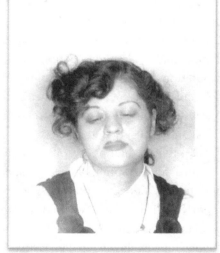

Doris A. Arrested at The Tin Roof Sheboygan County 1951

134

Attorney George D. Sullivan pointed out the foolishness in the belief that gamblers played the machines "just to see the wheels go 'round.'"

Sullivan told the judge that there were "quite a number of machines in town" and the defendants testified they had recently purchased the machines from "Kid Paul or Powell."[492] Paul or Powell was nowhere to be found and the judge warned the defendants "to get the machines out of their premises" or that "in the future they would be confiscated and destroyed."

Langlade County: The South House Raid

ON THE EVENING OF September 13, 1951, state agents and the county sheriff raided The South House in Langlade County near Antigo and arrested four women aged 22 to 36. The county judge fined each girl $100 and June King, 33, the keeper, $400.[493]

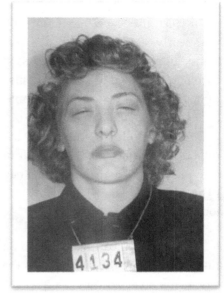

Joyce L. Arrested at The Tin Roof
Sheboygan County 1951

Mercer: Ralph Capone – A Short Story

In 1930, a Federal Judge sentenced Ralph Capone to three years at Leavenworth for evading taxes from 1922 to 1928. In addition to the prison term, he fined Capone $10,000. At that time, Capone owed $5,662 in taxes. This amount would grow dramatically over the years with penalties and interest.

* * *

The 1950 Senate Crime Investigation Committee cast a wide net over the Midwest, primarily because of the Capone reputation and because Senator Alexander Wiley from Chippewa falls was on the committee. Ralph testified at the Special Committee Chicago in 1950 but this committee yielded few results.

* * *

The reports that Ralph was now head of the syndicate concerned Chicago and Madison authorities. Further, the fact that authorities in Madison failed to stop vice in northern Wisconsin led to the belief that the syndicate might invade the region. However, the people of Iron and Vilas Counties lived with the knowledge that a certain amount of vice was inevitable, part of the economy, and woven into the social fabric. Rather than taking the word of the authorities "down south," the communities judged Ralph Capone on his behavior.

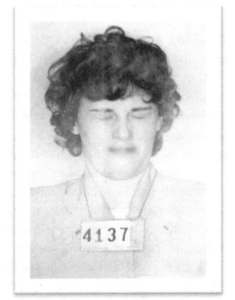

Ruth P. Arrested at The Tin Roof
Sheboygan County 1951

135

In 1951, the federal government said Ralph Capone owed nearly $97,000 in taxes.[494] At that time, Capone claimed total assets of $26,000. Assistant U.S. Attorney Lawrence J. wanted to know why his brother James Capone held the title to Ralph's home on Big Martha Lake near Mercer, which he believed to be elaborate. A June 1952 Associated Press article stated, "Ralph Capone, brother of "Scarface Al" Capone, former Chicago gang leader, has taken up residence at a new lodge on the shore of Big Martha Lake."[495] In reality, the lodge was little more than a cabin.

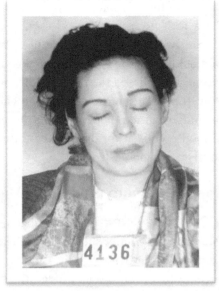

Shirley S. Arrested at The Tin Roof
Sheboygan County 1951

* * *

Before the hearing, Ralph said that his brother James held title to the property. At the time, very few knew that he had a brother James. This, too, would become a revelation. It turned out that James had gone missing for 33 years. After the fight in which Al received his scar, James tossed a gang member through a plate glass window and believed that he had killed him. In fear of retribution, James jumped a train headed west, stopped at Homer, Nebraska, and adopted a new name – Richard James Hart. He made Homer his home and, ironically, became a law enforcement officer, breaking up illegal liquor operations during prohibition. He dressed like his cowboy hero and became known as Two-Gun Hart[496]. Fox Television interviewed the sons of Hart for "A Current Affair" in 1990, and[497] Turner Network Television produced a movie entitled "The Lost Capone" in the same year.[498]

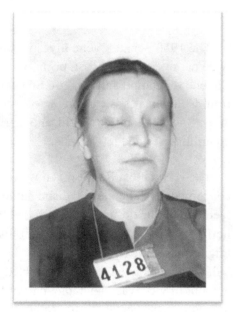

Vera B. Arrested at The Tin Roof
Sheboygan County 1951

Hart married and raised a family of five children but about 1951, he was nearly blind and broke. In desperation, he asked his brother Ralph for help. James' son Sherman accompanied him to Mercer as a guest, and Ralph provided Sherman with a job as a bartender at Billy's Bar.

It was not common knowledge that Ralph and Al had a brother and a nephew, and the Chicago press reported this news as a "fantastic disclosure." However, it was far from news in Mercer as the relationship between Ralph, James, and Sherman was commonly known.

Cedrick Parker, an editor at *The Capital Times,* drafted a four-part story about Ralph in September. Two photographs splashed across the front page and accompanied the first edition. A five-inch block photograph showed James Capone, 63, (James Vincenzo Capone, aka Two-Gun Hart) with his wife talking to a reporter in Chicago at the train station. James wore a broad tie and a cowboy hat and carried a cane. A larger photograph of the Rex motel and Billy's bar in Mercer sat adjacent. The caption noted that Sherman Hart, the nephew of Al and Ralph, now managed the facility. [499]

*   *   *

In addition to the property on Big Martha Lake, the U.S. attorney wanted to know about the business at the Rex Hotel/Billy's bar. Ralph had just resigned as manager of the facility in June, and the property was sold at auction on September 1. The new owner appointed Sherman, who had served as a bartender, as manager.[500] Ralph managed the establishment for a salary of $3,300 a year before it sold. Walter Liebner and his wife Viola owned two-thirds of the property, and Larry Fell of Minocqua, the other third. Viola Liebner purchased the title at the auction.

Margo D. Arrested at The Casino Sheboygan County 1951

Ralph told Parker that he never owned property in Wisconsin and maintained his Illinois residency throughout. He earned income in Wisconsin, paid income taxes in Wisconsin, and purchased an out-of-state fishing license in Wisconsin. He earned $20,000 a year from his business in Cook County, Illinois – Suburban Cigarette Company, where he operated 300 machines. He told Parker that he didn't like newspaper publicity, but because his name was Capone, they wouldn't leave him alone. He said, "The name Capone will live a thousand years, and I never can live it down. All I want is to be forgotten and to try to live like a human being should live, like you would like to live." Capone told Parker that his mother provided the money for Al's home on Lake Martha. He said that using money from his mother, he took care of Al as he was "pretty sick" after his release from prison.[501]

Parker interviewed Viola Liebner. She told him that she and her husband were neighbors at Martha Lake, and her husband Walter used to fish with Ralph. She said that when they purchased Billy's Bar,[502] they asked him to manage it since he knew about business. Liebner had nothing but good things to say about Ralph Capone, including his admirable work ethic. When Parker asked her if she thought he had abandoned the rackets, she said, "Of Course, you know that Ralph could have stayed in Chicago and made millions if he had wanted to be crooked. If he is what some people say he

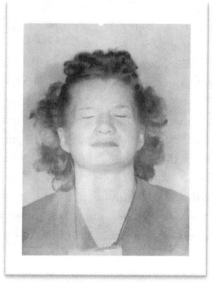

Jean M. Arrested at the Casino Sheboygan County 1951

137

is, why would he come way up here to this place?"[503]

M. E. Brandt, the clerk of the Town of Mercer, told Parker that he had known Capone for ten years and said, "Ralph Capone has always been a gentleman and a straight-shooter in this community." He continued that he had been to his home on Lake Martha and described it as "unpretentious, nothing elaborate, not even the furniture."

Parker interviewed several people in the Mercer area, including a restaurant owner, a gas station owner, a food locker operator, and a professional woman. None expressed a bad comment about Ralph Capone.[504] In the continuing investigation, the government summoned several Iron County residents, primarily craftsmen who worked on Capone's home, to appear in Chicago.[505]

* * *

Finally, in late November 1952, a federal judge dismissed the tax fraud charges against Capone. He also said that from now on, the taxation department transactions should be at "arm's-length" with him.[506]

* * *

Louisa M. Arrested at The Club Royale
Sheboygan County 1951

However, Capone's tax troubles did not end. In March 1955, the government levied a $12,300 tax judgment against him for unpaid taxes from 1922 through 1925.[507] Including interest and penalties, the amount totaled $23,555. Capone sent a check for $446.31 as the final payment in February 1958. After he made the payment, the Feds didn't let up. They now told Ralph to pay taxes owed on income earned from 1926-1928, which amounted to $87,000 but with interest and penalties, it totaled $120,000 ($1.3 million today).[508]

* * *

Whenever Capone went to Milwaukee, police detectives followed him. In July 1958, Capone, and Joseph Krasno – a former gambler and current owner of a Milwaukee tavern – complained to detective Captain Charles Nowakowski of the Milwaukee police department about the constant harassment. Nowakowski said that if he didn't want the police to follow him, he should "stay out of Milwaukee." Adding an insult, Nowakowski suggested, "Capone pose for a new picture for the Milwaukee police rogues gallery since the photo in the files was outdated."[509]

* * *

In February 1959, an Associated Press reporter wrote that the chief counsel of the Senate Rackets Investigation Committee – Robert F. Kennedy – the was looking for

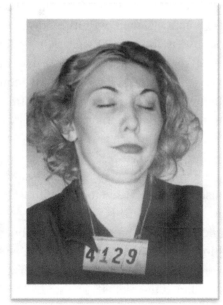

Ilene D. Arrested at The Casino
Sheboygan County 1951

138

Capone. He wrote that they tried to find Sam "Mooney" Giancana and Ralph Capone to deliver a subpoena. Kennedy claimed that Giancana was "the chief gunman for the successors to the old Capone mob." The committee believed the couple colluded with labor union officials to get amusement machine operators to pay protection money. The committee wanted testimony to validate their belief that "the hoodlums resorted to acid-throwing and ax-wielding raids to even murder."[510]

In May 1959, U.S. Marshall, Ray H. Schoonover, searched for Ralph Capone. Schoonover talked about a current problem he had with Ralph Capone. The Senate Rackets Investigating Committee wanted Capone to testify. However, news of the subpoena reached Capone before it reached the county sheriff, and Capone disappeared. Schoonover said, "My deputy, Tom Madden, in Superior, could have got him. Tom has been a deputy for 20 years and knew where Capone was. They must have thought that we didn't have a deputy up in that area."[511]

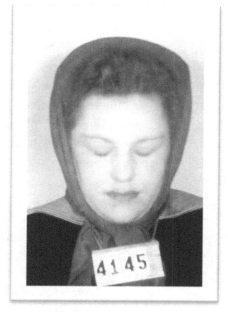

Anna W. Arrested at The Club Royale
Sheboygan County 1951

*   *   *

The same month, Armand Cirilli wrote, "The *Chicago Daily News* has now placed itself in the same category as the *Milwaukee Journal*. When circulation drops, just write a sensational story, tie in the name Hurley, and give it both barrels."

The August 31, *Chicago Daily News* published a story claiming that Ralph Capone was the "Crime boss of Hurley" and described him as the headmaster of a vice school of B-girls. Cirilli noted that "The story is so fantastic that it doesn't even carry the name of the writer responsible for this garbage." Cirilli then quoted the highlights from the Chicago newspaper.

"How the crime syndicate runs a finishing school for honky-tonk B-girls in Wisconsin will be told to the federal grand jury after Labor Day. Ralph "Bottles" Capone, the young brother of the late Scarface Al Capone, is the finishing school 'head-master,' says the U.S. attorney's office... Ralph Capone is the crime boss of Hurley, Wis., a country cousin of Calumet City, according to Robert Tieken, U.S. attorney.

"Once it was a miner's and lumberman's town. Today, Hurley's Silver St. is lined with honky-tonks. In these dives, girls from the Midwest and Canada are taught 'mooching and dipping.' Then they are sent out to populate dives throughout the Midwest. Some of the girls were

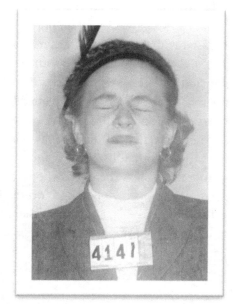

Gayle R. Arrested at The Club Royale
Sheboygan County 1951

139

booked through a Toronto theatrical agency, say prosecutors, and then sent to Hurley on promises they would get a chance to dance. 'Sorry, the jobs are all filled up,' the girls are told at Hurley.

"The girls usually don't have the bus fare home. The agent who was going to do so much for them offers to let them move temporarily into his place. It's suggested they can pick up 'pocket money' by drinking with honky-tonk club customers, including 'sportsmen' up for hunting and fishing.

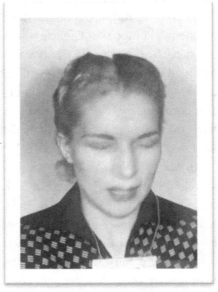

Jerry M. Arrested at The Casino Sheboygan County 1951

"After a few days or weeks, they're told some big spenders wouldn't miss a few dollars if a girl picked up his change or even his wallet. This 'jackrolling' works well on drunks. 'Classes' in dressing rooms backstage at several clubs, U.S. investigators were told, feature an experienced woman pickpocket who teaches new girls the 'swiftdip' removal of a man's wallet. Having gone this far, it's suggested to girls they 'go for the big money – all the way' and become prostitutes. Many girls said they refused only to wake up one morning to find they'll been slipped a 'Mickey Finn' – doped drink. Others said they were beaten."

Cirilli condemned the article and noted that Ralph Capone had never lived in Hurley, had not been in Hurley for over three years, and suggested that the *Chicago Daily News* writer had been "hitting the pipe."[512]

*   *   *

From when he became head of the syndicate until his death in 1947, government authorities and the press were obsessed with Al Capone, the syndicate, and its associates. They authorities hounded the former members of Capone's gang and the press spilled stories across the front pages of America's newspapers accompanied by photos of bullet holes, blood, and dead bodies.

After prison, there was no way that Al's brother Ralph could live a normal life in Chicago, despite having a legitimate business there. His choice for normalcy was Mercer, Wisconsin, "up north," off the beaten path, and nestled in the woods. No matter where he went, he carried the curse of the Capone reputation: a name that, over the years, had been drilled into the public mind and synonymous with murders, extortion, and illegal liquor.

*   *   *

Cedric Parker once asked Ralph if he ever considered changing his name. He said that he had thought about it but

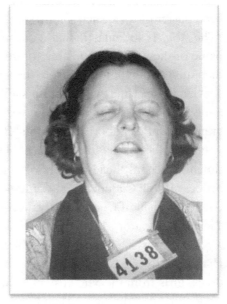

Myrtle B. Arrested at The Farm Sheboygan County 1951

140

wouldn't out of respect for his mother, who he cared for until her death in 1952.[513]

*　　*　　*

In February 1963, agents from the U.S. Treasury Department raided Ralph Capone's cigarette vending company on Ogden Avenue in Brookfield, Illinois. They seized 238 machines, three safes, and all other personal property. As evidence of the prolonged prosecution of the name, one of the prosecutors said, "When it comes to a Capone, we never give up." While the seized property was valued at $60,000, it only reduced Capone's debt by $16,237, leaving a balance owed at $207,057.[514]

*　　*　　*

In 1963, George F. Mueller and Son's ran a vending company that distributed coin-operated machines in Cook County. They operated out of Blue Island, Illinois, a small city on the south side of Chicago. Mueller bought 70 of Capone's cigarette machines which had been confiscated by the Fed.

On March 18, 1963, someone blew out the garage doors of the Mueller building with a stick of dynamite.[515] Local, state, and federal authorities failed to find any leads or apprehend any suspects. Even Attorney General Robert Kennedy expressed concern about this bombing and promised to visit Chicago to discuss the incident.[516] The event further branded the Capone name regardless of the perpetrator or the motive.

*Katherine K. Arrested at The Farm
Sheboygan County 1951*

*　　*　　*

In November 1965, Ralph Capone and his attorney met with an IRS attorney from Washington who wanted Capone's delinquent taxes for the period 1926 to 1928. With penalties and interest, the figure was $223,000 ($2.2 million today).[517] Although not in prison, Ralph Capone would never be free from the clutches of the federal government.

After living in Mercer for 31 years, Ralph Capone, 81, died in Hurley on November 22, 1974. If Capone was involved in any way with illegal activity over that period, there was no evidence to show it. Instead, he lived a modest life, as demonstrated by his housing, job, acquaintances, and friends. Unfortunately, the only way Ralph Capone beat the curse of his name was death, and, ironically, he spent his last days at the Sky View Rest home in Hurley and died two blocks south of Silver Street's lower block.

Hurley: A Beating with a Window Pole

RETURNING TO 1951, it was quiet during the late fall in Hurley: no liquor seizures, gambling busts, or disorderly roadhouse raids. The worst incident occurred on October 22 when Joseph McRainels, of Lucky 13 attacked and beat his bartender, Matt Vidovich, with a window pole. The reason for the beating was unknown but Judge Trembath fined McRainels $35. McRainels subsequently fired Vidovich.

141

Sheboygan County: Governor Kohler Continues

THROUGHOUT THE SUMMER OF 1951, Sheboygan County District Attorney Buchen noticed brothels reopening in Sheboygan County. In the fall, he asked Governor Kohler and Attorney General Vernon Thomson to hit them again.

On December 6, agents collected evidence of prostitution while, at the same time, Governor Kohler spoke at the Wisconsin sheriff's association convention in Sheboygan. He told them, "Wisconsin would continue to be hostile to organized crime, vice, and corruption."[518] This was his home turf, and he was serious.

At 10:30 p.m., on December 13, David Prichard and Fred Mattingly rallied 21 state agents. Concerned about a tip-off, the Attorney General withheld the raid information from the sheriff until the night before. Despite this slight, Sheriff Kroll eventually added seven deputies to the team. [519]

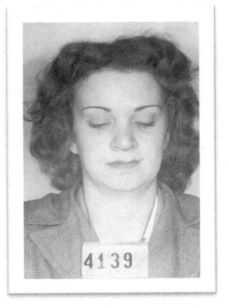

Jean D. Arrested at The Farm
Sheboygan County 1951

Over the years, the only place allowing embedded reporters was Hurley, but now, they tagged along in the governor's home county. Prichard notified the Milwaukee newspapers, and reporters huddled at the county jail waiting for the parade of defendants.

In a coordinated operation, the agents dispersed, raiding four disorderly houses referred to by the press as "hot spots." Armed with search warrants, they hit the Greenhouse in Sheboygan, The Farm on Highway 141, and the Casino just south of Sheboygan. Near Plymouth, they raided the Club Royale, the Green Bungalow, and the Tin Roof.[520] Although the raid netted 19 women, "no patrons were placed under arrest." Their surveillance was incomplete as they found the Greenhouse and the Green Bungalow closed for business.

The Sheboygan press reported, "The jail quarters were a bedlam until after 2 a.m." Deputies photographed and fingerprinted each girl while trustees deployed additional bedding and mattresses "to accommodate the unexpected visitors." The district attorney identified four women as previous violators earlier in the year despite three having changed their names.[521]

* * *

In February 1952, a municipal court judge fined Hattie Cook of the Green House $300 for aiding and abetting prostitution. Circuit Judge Henry A. Detling issued fines of $300 to $350 to the operators including Myrtle Bodenstab of the Farm, Vera Bertram of the Casino, Alma Dean of the Bungalow, and Margareta Sullivan of the Tin Roof. The judge also fined 22 prostitutes $25 each.[522]

A Milwaukee federal judge slapped a $20,617 tax lien against the Casino in Sheboygan, operated by Vera Bertram. The lien covered 1937 through 1950, and Bertram was out on bail, but the news worsened when she stood before Judge Henry Detling in April.[523]

* * *

Judge Detling of the Fourth Judicial District faced a hefty workload in April 1952. There were

13 criminal cases, 59 court cases, and 53 jury cases for the spring term. The first action on the docket was the state's case against the owners of the Club Royal, The Casino, The Farm, and the Tin Roof.

On April 21, Detling slapped a hefty fine against several women. He fined Ann Joiner of the Club Royale, Myrtle Bodenstab of the Farm, and Vera Bertram, of the Casino $1,000 each for operating brothels and contempt. Because the brothel keepers continuously ignored court orders, in May, Judge Detling warned that if prostitution continued, he would send the offender to jail for contempt. State authorities signed affidavits supporting the judge's position.

On May 24, 1951, Judge Detling ordered five of the taverns closed as disorderly houses stating that they were used "for purposes of lewdness, prostitution, and assignation." District Attorney Buchen said this action was "the biggest step taken thus far to lick the problem of prostitution in the county."

Marie R. Arrested at the Club Royale
Sheboygan County 1951

143

1952

Hurley: Catch-As-Catch-Can

AN APPROPRIATE OPENING FOR 1952 was Armand Cirilli's wit, "A. T. Fadness and his minions don't like it when local tavern keepers plead not guilty after they are arrested. So, before the trials are even held, they come back again. And catch them again."[524] And that explains how dockets became strangely entangled throughout the years.

Hurley: The Mr. & Mrs. Reeves Incident

RAYMOND REEVES AND his young wife, Wanda, traveled due north in the winter of 1951, destined for Hurley. A dust-covered Mississippi plate with white numbers across a blue field hung conspicuously against the white snow of Iron County.

Although not a great musician, Ray convinced Blackie Matrella that he could entertain the clients of Mickey's Rendezvous on Silver Street. His wife, Wanda, was street-smart, charming, and aggressive. James Francis hired her as a bartender at the Club Francis.

The Reeves settled in by cruising the streets of Ironwood, Hurley, and Ashland, noting the locations of shops, alleys, and traffic patterns. The Ironwood police, provincial yet cautious, noticed the blue Mississippi plates and learned that Reeves was working on Silver Street.

The mines were operating, there was discretionary income, and shoppers perused well-stocked shelves anticipating Christmas. The Reeves mingled with the crowd, shopping for clothing and jewelry. They often found what they liked, and in Ashland, Ray absconded with two men's suits from Penney's and another from Lew Anderson's Men's Store. In Hurley, he swiped a man's topcoat, shirt, and jacket from Paul's Store.

In Ironwood, his wife stole three pairs of panties, nine sweaters, and three blouses from Kresge's and a woman's suit and dress from O'Donnell's Style Shop. Ray netted two pairs of trousers from Men's Wear and a man's suit from Stern & Field. And for accessories, the couple picked up several pairs of earrings from Albert's Jewelry store.

The jig was up when Wanda got nabbed for trying to steal clothing from Penney's in Ashland. Ashland police tracked similar thefts to Ironwood, so they called the Ironwood police "to report that a girl with a southern accent was suspected of stealing." The Ironwood police pulled their notes about the Silver Street entertainers with the Mississippi car.

When the Ironwood cops notified the Hurley police, things began to unravel. The manager of Mickey's

Helen L. Arrested at John Carollo's Hilltop Town of Florence 1952

Rendezvous told the cops that he seized Reeves' guitar because he violated his performing contract. Unbeknownst to their employers, the Reeves had packed and were ready to leave town. In an unexplained twist, James Francis carted Reeves to Mayor DeRubies's house. There, Reeves admitted to the thefts. DeRubeis phoned Chief Negrini and asked him to bring some handcuffs for Reeves.

After the police found the stolen merchandise stowed in the back seat of Reeves' car, "A steady stream of merchants called at the jail to identify articles."[525]

On January 12, the municipal court judge in Ironwood fined the Reeves for theft and concealment of stolen property and sent them packing. The Reeves were lucky as others were treated worse for doing less. It is likely that authorities and store owners were just pleased to see them gone.

Hurley: A Fresh Batch of Agents

O N THE EVENINGS OF January 11, 12, and 13, a dozen new agents, fashionably dressed, collected evidence along Silver Street. These new agents offered fresh faces to young prostitutes in the Hi-Ho, the Ritz, the Blackhawk, and the Club Chateau.[526]

On January 27, state agents, Sheriff William Thomas and District Attorney George Sullivan arrested Julius Mattei and James Quigley, the owner and bartender, respectively, of the Club Chateau. Then they visited the Blackhawk, but Blackie Matrella was out of town, so they arrested the bartender, John Califano. Along with two prostitutes, they all posted bail.[527]

On February 5, Agent Fadness told the judge that some of the violators had 32 convictions since 1942, and they asked for padlocking. The operators of Nora's, the Blackhawk, the Hi-Ho, and the Club Chateau pled *nolo contendere* to running disorderly roadhouses and paid fines. All six girls arrested for prostitution skipped town and forfeited bonds.[528]

Philis H. Arrested at John Carollo's Hilltop Town of Florence 1952

Joyce J. Arrested at John Carollo's Hilltop Town of Florence 1952

Hurley: The Usual Suspects Get Burned

AT 1 A.M. ON MARCH 28, 1952, an oil heater malfunctioned and started a fire in a building on the north side of the lower block of Silver Street. The Hurley, Ironwood, and Montreal fire departments responded but found the hydrant on the corner of Silver Street and First Avenue inoperable. They shifted to the hydrant at First Avenue and Copper and ran a line to the Montreal River, a block east. These delays allowed the fire to establish, and by 6 a.m., the fire destroyed the French Casino at 14 Silver Street and the Club Chateau at 16 Silver Street and damaged the Allies tavern at 12 Silver Street and the White Front tavern at 18 Silver Street. Respectively, the fire put Gust DiUlio, Julius Mattei,[529] Buddy Howell, and Joe McRaineil out of business.[530]

This fire vacated most of the buildings left standing after the 1950 fire on the north side of the lower block.[531] Armand Cirilli

John Carollo's Hilltop
Town of Florence 1952

squarely summed up the condition, "Hurley fires are tragic because the buildings are never reconstructed as they do in other cities. If a building goes down in Hurley, it is the end. Our heritage there is at best a billboard. That is a bad sign. It means that this city is stagnant. Under the status quo our city can only go backward. Is it too much to hope that maybe something can be done to turn the wheels in the other direction?"[532] As usual, Cirilli was poignant and well spoken.

Hurley: Grand Jury Puts Finger on Hurley

DURING THE WEEK OF APRIL 20, 1952, a federal grand jury in Madison began investigating organized crime in western Wisconsin. Shortly after the grand jury convened, the needle swung toward Hurley. The jury heard from Iron County sheriff William Thomas and District Attorney George D. Sullivan about possible organized crime connections to gambling, narcotics, and prostitution in the Hurley area. The grand jury concluded that "prostitution is an established and profitable business in Hurley, Superior, and one or two isolated locations."[533]

The *Iron County Miner* headlined the article: "Grand Jury Puts Finger on Hurley." Meanwhile, Circuit Court Judge Lewis J. Charles deliberated the possibility of padlocking four taverns as a "nuisance." The *Iron County Miner* reported, "After several postponements, the judge was to hear the cases against the Blackhawk tavern, the Hi-Ho, Nora's and The Ritz, the operators and the landlords."[534]

In the first week of May 1952, Judge Charles postponed the padlocking hearing until May 15 based on a request from the defendant's attorney. The attorney argued, "that the complaint does not state facts sufficient to constitute a cause of action." District Attorney Sullivan filed complaints against the four taverns for having facilities that provided "lewdness, assignation, and prostitution." He requested that the court find the taverns as nuisances and that the tavernkeepers "be perpetually enjoined from continuing, maintaining or permitted such nuisances." He asked the court to close the taverns for one year.[535]

*Lora. R. Arrested at the
Wigwam Tavern
Washington County 1952*

Hurley: Blackie Matrella Goes to College

On May 2, 1952, Blackie Matrella drove a prostitute from Hurley to Lafayette, Indiana, while agents tracked the trip. In late-July 1954 the FBI arrested Matrella on charges of white slavery under the Mann Act. A U.S. Court Commissioner set bail at $3,500 and sent Matrella to the Ashland County jail. Alex Raineri, Matrella's attorney, worked to help raise bail money. In the meantime, the woman returned to Hurley and worked as a barmaid.[536] On January 27, 1955, Federal Judge Patrick Stone sentenced Blackie Matrella to 18 months in a federal prison.[537]

Hurley: Taverns Hit a New Low

In 1942, HURLEY HAD 85 taverns before the quota changed to 78. This created conflict between tavernkeepers, municipal officials, police, and state agents. By 1952, the license requests had tumbled to 60, with at least six taverns lost to fires in 1950 and 1951.[538] All of the taverns lost to fire over the years played front and center in Hurley's story. In 1952, many rested as bare gravel without a hint of life. With their demise went thousands of stories, forever lost to history.

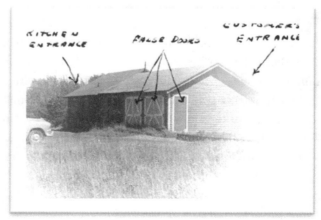

*John Carollo's Hilltop
Town of Florence 1952*

Hurley: Injunction to Padlock

Jean P. Arrested at the Rathskeller Inn
Wausau 1952

DURING THE SECOND WEEK OF JULY, Judge Charles ordered an injunction to padlock Nora's Bar, the Hi-Ho Bar, and the Blackhawk tavern. The district attorney urged Judge Charles to "Declare the Taverns nuisances and that the defendants 'be perpetually enjoined from continuing, maintaining or permitting such nuisances.'"

Between the time of arrest and the injunction, Nora's, on the second block, had become Frenchy's, although Nora Abraham still owned the building. Clement Vita owned the building at 21 Silver Street, where Joe Vita operated the Hi-Ho. Frank Copanese owned the building at 26 Silver Street, where Blackie Matrella operated the Blackhawk.

Of the three taverns facing padlocking action, only Nora's posted the $500 bond necessary to prevent closing. While the bond prevented padlocking, the judge filed an injunction forbidding the use of the building "for purposes of lewdness, assignation, and prostitution." If Nora violated the injunction, she would forfeit the bond, and the judge would fine her for contempt. The operators of the Hi-Ho and the Blackhawk did not post bond.[539]

At the end of July, the operator of "Frenchy's" moved on, and the building stood vacant. While the tavern was empty, Nora Abraham operated a small grocery store on 2nd Avenue on the north side of Hurley. The operators of the Hi-Ho and the Blackhawk eventually posted bonds that restrained the padlocking proceedings. As with the cases in Sheboygan County, if the operators violated the injunction forbidding "lewdness, assignation, and prostitution within the year, they would forfeit the bonds and be held in contempt of court.[540]

Hurley: The Raids of 1952

Marylin D. Arrested at the
Wigwam Tavern
Washington County 1952

THE YEAR WAS EXCEPTIONALLY QUIET, with only two raids: one in August and one in November. Despite the limited effort, the raids would prove highly productive. At 1 a.m. on Monday, August 11, state agents, along with the Iron County Sheriff, arrested John Kalasardo[541] of the Band Box and Julius Mattei of the Club Chateau. For the first time in this writing, they arrested three prostitutes in a Hurley residence. John Kalasardo, new to Hurley, wanted to upscale his operation. He purchased and remodeled the house behind the Band Box on the Northside of Silver Street. The *Iron County Miner* referred to it as a "plush parlor."[542]

After Mattei's original Club Chateau, located at 16 Silver Street, burned in 1951, he opened another tavern with the same

148

name at 121 Silver Street. Here, the sheriff arrested two women for soliciting. Everyone provided bail bonds.[543]

In late August, Hurley police arrested Louise Dall of the Blue Note Club, James Gasbarri of Jackpot's Flame, and Richard Matrella of the Club Francis, all for remaining open after-hours. They pled guilty and paid fines.[544]

* * *

Example FBI Arrest Record
Fingerprints on Second Page Not Shown

The deer season in Wisconsin was prime hunting time for state agents on Silver Street. Adventurous men traveled from all points south, including Chicago. The new agents donned red plaid and Kromers and blended in with tourists, milling about on the lower blocks. On the evenings of November 23 and 24, 1952, they arrested John Carli and Joan Anderson at the Bowery for

149

operating gambling equipment along with Andrew Carli for refilling liquor bottles. They arrested Lois Gasbarri of Frenchy's and Julius Mattei of Club Chateau for keeping houses of ill fame and Carole Roberts for being an inmate. They nabbed Richard Matrella at the Club Francis and Doris Grant at Mickey's Rendezvous[545] for operating gambling tables.[546]

During the December 16 preliminary hearing, Judge Trembath dismissed the prostitution charges against Julius Mattei because the state "failed to submit sufficient evidence to link Mattei with any solicitation." While Mattei skirted the ill-fame charge, the jury returned a guilty verdict for operating gambling equipment.[547]

The state was miffed because Mattei slid by the prostitution arrest, so they retaliated with trivial allegations, including the failure to "scratch or mutilate Wisconsin stamps from empty bottles and failing to destroy or break bottles after they had been emptied of their original contents." Mattei, angry and vindictive, responded by appealing the gambling conviction.[548]

Judge Trembath ordered Lois Gasbarri bound over for a jury trial for keeping a house of ill fame. Gasbarri recoiled at the reality of facing a jury, and in early February 1953, she pled guilty in front of Judge Trembath in Iron County Court. The judge sentenced her to four months in the county jail but suspended the sentence pending a $400 fine.[549]

* * *

During the two raids in 1952, agents arrested four for keeping a house of ill fame, five for gambling, three for soliciting, three for hours violations, and two inmates. The prostitution arrests were the big fish and were most likely to pave the path to revocation.

Hurley: The Julius Mattei Stalking Incident

MAYOR DERUBEIS AND CHIEF OF POLICE NEGRINI were tough on the lower blocks and made enemies on both sides of the strip. DeRubeis had loud, notable, and well-documented arguments with Blackie Matrella in the summer of 1950, with Buddy Howell in October 1950, and with Julius Mattei in July 1951. Mattei took matters to another level in September 1952.

Someone, at one-hour intervals, called the homes of the mayor and the police chief from 11 p.m. to 4 a.m. The next night, September 12, DeRubeis and Negrini noticed Julius Mattei following them as they drove around Iron and Gogebic Counties. The next day, Negrini arrested Matei, charging him with stalking and disorderly conduct.

In Iron County Court, Mattei said that he couldn't have made the calls because he was at the Mount Zion Inn in Ironwood during the early hours of September 11 with Biago DiSalle and Buddy Howell. However, an employee of the tavern, James Chiolino,[550] testified that he showed Mattei the telephone location. DiSalle testified that Mattei periodically used the phone and that "he had heard the conversations." No one testified in Mattei's defense.

After deliberating for 55 minutes, a jury of four men and two women found Mattei not guilty of disorderly conduct.[551] Given the evidence, it is difficult to speculate about the verdict.

150

Hurley: Possession and Use of Narcotics

L OCAL AUTHORITIES RELENTLESSLY prowled Silver Street during the summer. On August 29, the sheriff arrested two nightclub entertainers at Club Francis (now located at 28 Silver Street) for the possession and use of narcotics. In September, the judge sentenced them to 60 days in the Iron County jail.[552]

Later that month, the judge fined the operator of the Club Chateau for keeping a house of ill fame and suspended the nine-month jail sentences for two women providing they leave Iron County by 7 o'clock "that evening and never return."[553]

Hurley: A Frightening Combination – Frenchy and a .38

O N OCTOBER 28, RICHARD SALO, 22, from north Ironwood, sat at the bar in Frenchy's on the second block of Silver Street. He was liquored up, muddled, and insulted "a couple of working girls." Thinking that they had ganged up on him, he left the tavern but soon realized he had forgotten his hat and glasses. He returned to the tavern and stumbled toward Lois Gasbarri, who stood at the end of the bar. She was apprehensive and told him to stop. He lingered for a moment then advanced a few feet. Gasbarri grabbed a .38 revolver from behind the bar and shot him in the ankle. Chief Negrini arrested Gasbarri and stuck her in the Iron County Jail until she posted a $1,000 bond.[554]

Gene P. Arrested at the Rathskeller Inn Wausau 1952

* * *

In late November 1952, Gasbarri was bound over to the circuit court for assault with intent to do great bodily harm.[555] In the interim, in early February 1953, she pled guilty in Iron County Court for being the keeper of a house of ill fame. Although given a 4-month jail term, the judge suspended the sentence.

* * *

However, on February 27, 1953, Gasbarri faced a ten-person jury in the court of Judge Lewis J. Charles for shooting Salo in the ankle. Attorney Charles Santini argued that Gasbarri shot in self-defense and "did not intend to do great bodily harm" and that "she was not the aggressor."

After deliberating for several hours, the jury foreman told the judge that "they absolutely could not agree." The judge excused the jury and moved the case to the following term.[556]

* * *

On May 28, 1953, the court retried Lois Gasbarri for the October shooting at Frenchy's. The ten-person jury convicted her of simple assault, and the judge sentenced her to four months in the county jail.[557]

1953

Hurley: The Case of Madero Dawson

MADERO DAWSON, 38, worked as a railroad dining car waiter – and drug dealer – in Chicago. Jeanne Carter, 24, and Denise Courtney, 21, danced at the Backstage Show Club on the north side of Chicago.[558] After meeting Dawson in a Calumet City bar in 1952, the girls traveled to Hurley. Both being hardcore addicts, they quickly needed more heroin. Since their regular dealer in Chicago had been arrested, they contacted Dawson who airmailed 31 grains of heroin to Hurley.

* * *

In August 1952, police arrested Courtney and Carter at the Swing Club on a drug charge. In September, the Iron County judge sentenced both girls to 60 days in the Iron County jail. The next month, authorities arrested Dawson.[559]

In January 1953, a federal grand jury in Madison indicted Dawson for selling the heroin to the girls.[560]

* * *

Mona M. Arrested 504-½ Tower Avenue Superior 1953

In June 1953, at federal court in Madison, Dawson was charged with "selling heroin, mailing it, and on one conspiracy account."[561] Federal authorities wanted to make the case and send a strong message about the use of heroin. On June 9, they heard testimony from Chief of Police Leo Negrini, Iron County District Attorney George Sullivan, Iron County Sheriff William Thomas, Milton Cayer, an employee of the Hurley post office, and Gordon Kasten, manager of the Western Union office in Ironwood along with the two women already sentenced on the narcotics charge.[562]

Courtney testified that she "had been using dope since she was a teenager" and that the habit escalated to four times a day.[563]

* * *

In September, the Federal Court Judge at Wausau sentenced the two women to one year in a federal narcotics hospital in Lexington, Kentucky.[564]

* * *

In June, the *Capital Times* reported, Dawson was found guilty after "two pretty Hurley dancing girls" testified Tuesday that they had arranged with a "Dawney" Dawson to have dope mailed to them from Chicago.[565] In August 1953, a federal jury found Madero Dawson guilty. Federal court Judge Patrick T. Stone fined him $500 and sentenced him to three years in Federal prison.[566]

Madison: State Agent Can't Raid Brothels

In 1952, the Wisconsin Supreme Court ruled that "no public employee was entitled to workmen's compensation unless that employ was injured performing duties specified under the law." As such, if an agent were injured in a brothel raid, he would not be entitled to workman's compensation.[567]

In January 1953, in response to the decision, the State Tax Department announced that the Beverage Tax Division agents would stop raiding brothels because the law was not specific to prostitution. However, they would be covered under workman's compensation if the prosecution was associated with liquor and gambling violations.

Midwest: The Mann Act – Casting a Wide Net

THE MANN ACT, ALSO KNOWN AS the White-Slave Traffic Act of 1910, made it unlawful to transport a woman across a state line for immoral purposes. Although there were hundreds of violations of the Mann Act in the early 1950s, most of the stories were in Texas, California, and Wisconsin.

On January 21, 1953, a federal grand jury investigated a "white slavery ring" in the mid-west, specifically in Wisconsin, Illinois, North Dakota, South Dakota, and Minnesota. The Fed assigned the case to assistant U.S. Attorney Alex Dim, who worked in Minneapolis and Duluth. [568]

Bessie Rye T. Arrested at 504 ½ Tower Avenue Superior 1953

On January 23, the grand jury indicted three men, ages 32, 23, and 30, for inducing women to travel across state lines for prostitution. The cases included transporting a woman from Minneapolis to Sioux Falls, another for transporting a woman from Houston to Minneapolis, and the third for transporting two women from Minneapolis to La Crosse.[569] The grand jury indicted 15 men and women in the white slave ring.[570]

Hurley: Trouble at the Bowery

ON JANUARY 30, 1953, POLICE CHIEF LEO NEGRINI went into the Bowery tavern to collect a March of Dimes container. John Carli, the operator, began to "abuse him" and call him names, followed by a "brief" altercation. Negrini left the tavern and got a warrant for Carli's arrest. He and Officer John Barto returned to the tavern and arrested Carli. Negrini charged him with resisting an officer, disorderly conduct, and being a repeat offender for gambling and assault. At about the same time, Carli started a fight with John Krenzel, a customer from Ironwood, and Negrini charged Carli with a fourth count of assault and battery.[571]

On the morning of February 20, John Carli pled guilty to resisting an officer, disorderly conduct, assault, and battery in front of Judge Trembath in county court. The judge sentenced Carli to 60 days in the county jail for each offense, allowing Carli to serve them concurrently. Then he ordered a stay during which time Carli was to sell his personal property and stock before March 14, when he would begin his jail term. (His father, Andrew, owned the real estate). Trembath dismissed the "repeat offender" offense because "there were insufficient convictions on state charges against Carli to substantiate the charge."[572]

Hurley: Gambling Operator Temporarily Skips Town

O N THE EVENING OF February 24, state agents raided the Super Bar, operated by James Francis. They confiscated three slot machines and a craps table.

State agents arrested John Rajkovich the previous November for operating a gambling machine at the Club Francis. After the arrest, Rajkovich skipped town. When he returned, he operated the Casino tavern, where, in late February, the sheriff caught up with him for the previous gambling arrest.[573]

In March, James Francis of Jimmie's Super Bar, and John Rajkovich, proprietor of the Club Casino, pled guilty in county court, and Judge Trembath fined each.[574]

* * *

The same evening, a fire destroyed the building rented by Nora Abraham as a grocery on 2nd Avenue. She previously owned Nora's tavern on Silver Street.

Hurley: Odds and Ends

I N MID-MARCH, THE Hurley City Council continued to fiddle allowing Julius Mattei to transfer a tavern license from the Club Chateau site to that of the Club Blue Note on the corner of First Avenue and Silver Street.[575]

Hurley: The Raids of 1953

O N APRIL 26, HURLEY POLICE cited Ambrose Orsoni[576] of the Four-Ever Amber Bar, Doris Grant of Mickey's Rendezvous, and James Lawless, of the Congress bar, for violating the closing law. Although they were ordered to appear in county court, they brushed it off as a suggestion. They were persuaded, however, after the police delivered warrants. When the appeared in court, each contributed $50 to the county general fund.[577]

Patricia S. Arrested at 504-½ Tower Avenue Superior 1953

* * *

It was seemingly impossible for Hurley tavern keepers to abide by the hours law. In early May, Hurley police arrested four tavern keepers on hours violations. For example, On May 12, 1953, Hurley Police walked into Mickey's Rendezvous at 22 Silver Street at 3:40 a.m. and arrested Doris Grant for operating after-hours. This was the second time in two weeks that police nabbed Grant for the same offense. In both cases, Richard Matrella appeared in court on her behalf and paid the fines.[578]

* * *

On May 23 and 24, state agents fanned out across Iron County and nabbed the operators of nine taverns, including Julius Mattei, for operating without a license as it had been revoked. They also arrested two bartenders at the Chateau, including Mrs. Patrick Judge. The state also arrested John

Kalasardo of the Band Box, James Gasbarri of Jack Pot's Flame, and Doris Grant of Mickey's Rendezvous.[579]

* * *

Agents returned in less than a month. On June 18, they raided 25 Iron County taverns, mostly for being open after hours. In addition to an hours violation, agents arrested Dominic Vita, of the Swing Club, for having a "numbers jar."

Also cited for hours violations were the operators of the Bank Club, the French Casino, the Band Box, Jack Pot's Flame bar, Mickey's Rendezvous, the TryAngle Inn, the Red Feather, the Bowery, and the Club Francis. This menagerie included an updated list of usual suspects, including Margaret Prickett, James Gasbarri, Doris Grant, Louis Gasbarri, Andrew Carli, James Shields, and Richard Matrella.

Except for one violator, Judge Trembath fined everyone $35. On the charges of gambling and staying open after hours, he fined Dominic Vita $135.[580]

* * *

Rose R. Arrested at 504- ½ Tower Avenue Superior 1953

State agents stepped up enforcement in northern Wisconsin during the summer. From July 31 through August 2, newly appointed beverage agents stormed Vilas, Iron, and Price counties. They nabbed 35 suspects, including the same group as in early July.[581] Most of the citations were for violating the hours law and were ineffective in the short run. The tavernkeepers appeared in court, paid small fines, then returned to work the "night shift." However, these hours violations were important as they laid the foundation for building a case for revocation and subsequent padlocking.

* * *

During tavern hunting season in November, state beverage and tax agents made their usual rounds, concentrating on the lower two blocks of Silver Street. They hit five taverns and delivered 16 warrants. The state action against the Flame Bar was a mess. They could not arrest James Gasbarri for operating a house of ill fame and for operating after-hours because he was out of town. Instead, they arrested the bartender and a prostitute.

At the French Casino, agents arrested the operator John Rajkovich for keeping a house of ill fame, operating a craps game, and selling liquor after hours. They also arrested a bartender and a prostitute at the French Casino. At the Hi-Ho, they arrested the operator Joe Vita for keeping a house of ill fame along with two prostitutes including Betty Martin. At the Blackhawk, agents arrested Adele Petri[582] for keeping a house of ill fame, a prostitute for soliciting, and for being open after hours. Agents arrested the operator James Gasbarri at the Flame Bar for keeping a house of ill fame and for being open after hours. They also nabbed three women at the Flame for soliciting. Jack Gasbarri and co-owner Richard Matrella at the Carnival Bar got collared for operating a craps game.[583]

* * *

155

On December 11 in county court, James Gasbarri and Adele Petrie pled guilty to operating disorderly roadhouses,[584] and Judge Trembath fined each $400. He fined Jack Gasbarri for setting up, keeping, and using a gambling device at the Club Carnival and for an after-hours violation. Richard Matrella paid fines for "betting money upon a game played by himself and others" using a craps table. After determining that there was insufficient evidence, Trembath dropped the soliciting charge against Betty Martin of the Hi-Ho, which led to dismissing the case against Joseph Vita for operating a house of prostitution. The prostitutes either received minor fines or dismissals.[585] The most serious penalty was the suspension of Joseph Vita's tavern license for 90 days.[586]

The Wisconsin Beverage and Tax Department kept their promise of continued pressure on Hurley. In a rare "focused raid" on December 14, state agents arrested Vincent Calvi for operating a "beano"[587] game at a tavern on Silver Street. Judge Trembath fined Calvi $100.[588]

Hurley: The Patrick Judge Incident

IN APRIL 1953, HURLEY POLICE surveilled Patrick Judge, 26, suspecting that he was transporting prostitutes from Milwaukee. In March, the parents of a 17-year-old Cudahy girl reported her missing, and police issued a statewide bulletin.

During the second week of April, Dolores Nelson got into a fight with some other girls and jumped out of a second-story window of Frenchy's and tumbled onto Silver Street.[589] Hurley police officer Hugo Bellardinelli was at the scene and carted Nelson off to jail, where the chief of police asked her about the leap. To his surprise, Nelson told him about her relationship with Patrick Judge.

She told the sheriff that she met Judge in Milwaukee, and he "talked her into coming to Hurley," promising her a "lucrative job." She said she was "disappointed" when she could not find work in either Hurley or Ironwood. She also said that she and Judge had grown close and had a sexual relationship.

Rose Marie B. Arrested at 1619- ½ N. 5th Street Superior 1953

Superior police collared Judge within a few days of the Hurley police bulletin. On April 9, Sheriff William Thomas transported Judge from Superior to Hurley to be prosecuted for having sex with, and abusing, a child under 18 years old.[590]

* * *

On April 24, Patrick Judge sat for a hearing before Judge Trembath. Undersheriff Eino Nevala testified about the girl's age, and Dr. John Pierpont discussed the defendant's condition. Nelson confused the issue by changing the date she had sex with Judge. Despite the confusion, Trembath cut to the chase and declared that the defendant did "unlawfully and carnally know and abuse a female child under 18 years of age."[591]

The charge was serious, and Trembath ordered him over to Iron County Circuit Court for trial.

He set the bail at $2,500, forcing Judge to spend the interim at the Iron County Jail. On May 12, Judge's attorney filed a petition for a writ of habeas corpus with Douglas County Judge Carl H. Daley in Superior to reduce the bail amount. Daley summarily denied both.[592]

* * *

On May 20, 1953, Patrick Judge filed an affidavit of prejudice against Iron County. Judge Charles transferred the case to the Douglas County Circuit Court in Superior.[593] Patrick Judge may have married his young companion, Dolores Nelson during this period. In late May, state agents raided Hurley and arrested "Mrs. Patrick Judge" for tending bar at the Club Chateau without a license."[594] On June 30, she pled guilty, and the judge fined her $250.[595]

Since Patrick Judge was in the Iron County Jail and Dolores Judge was out of a job, she was now homeless. She hung around the streets of Hurley, and inevitably, the police arrested her for vagrancy and put her in the Iron County jail – in a different cell than husband. Judge Trembath sentenced her to 30 days and ordered her out of Hurley upon release. After a few days, she appealed the sentence, somehow posted a $100 bail bond, and requested a jury trial in county court.[596]

Barbara M. Arrested at Roadside Lunch/White House Tavern Stevens Point 1953

* * *

Meanwhile, Patrick Judge stood trial on September 8 in Douglas County Court in Superior."[597] The trial took two days, and on September 10, after 42 minutes of deliberation, the jury returned a guilty verdict. On September 25, Judge Carl Daley sentenced Patrick Judge, 26, to 1–3 years at the state prison in Waupun. However, the defense attorney motioned to set aside the verdict until he could prepare a supreme court appeal.[598] Judge Daley granted a one-year stay, and Patrick Judge was released on a $1,500 cash bond.

* * *

In December, Mrs. June Judge (aka Mrs. Patrick Judge and Delores Nelson)[599], was scheduled to appear in circuit court to appeal her conviction for vagrancy in county court. However, she failed to appear, and it was reported that she was "outside of Iron County at the moment."[600] June Judge again failed to appear at the circuit court on December 15. Judge Charles learned that she "has been out of the city for some time," and he ordered the case back to county court.[601]

Helen J. Arrested at the Ritz Bar Hurley 1953

* * *

At the end of Patrick Judge's one-year stay, his attorneys had done nothing to appeal his case to the Supreme Court, and Iron County D. A. Sullivan notified

Judge Daley in Superior. Daley authorized the Sheriff to apprehend Judge, who had lived as a free man in Milwaukee for the past year. Although he had returned to Hurley in late September, he failed to report to the Sheriff. On October 8, 1954, Sheriff William Thomas apprehended Patrick Judge, now 27, ushered him into the Iron County jail, and then escorted him into the state prison lobby at Waupun.[602]

After these events, both Patrick Judge and Mrs. Patrick Judge disappear from the records, along with the reason for the fight that caused Dolores Nelson to jump from the second-story window of Frenchy's.[603]

Hurley: Clean as a Hound's Tooth

I N LATE APRIL, CIRILLI played the optimist. The *Iron County Miner* reported that Hurley was "clean as a hound's tooth these days and a very law-abiding city" and that "The 1 o'clock closing of taverns is reported to be strictly enforced and that all 'undesirable characters' have left town."

Mayor DeRubeis told tavernkeepers that there would be no more "winking" at the closing law. Cirilli wrote, "At 1 o'clock on Sunday morning 'you couldn't buy a drink in Hurley,' it is claimed." Satisfied with this new normal in Hurley, DeRubeis pledged, "the heat will stay on."[604]

The story to date has shown emphatically that the words of mayors, district attorneys, police chiefs, and state agents meant little to the fundamental nature of Silver Street. Although the promises, threats, and reassurances may have been sincere, the efforts were constantly thwarted by the local constituency.

Kathryn S. Arrested at Roadside Lunch/White House Tavern Stevens Point 1953

Hurley: Two Revocations

O N APRIL 14, 1953, Chief of Police Leo Negrini complained to the Hurley City Council that Frenchy's bar and the Club Chateau operated in a "disorderly, riotous, indecent and improper manner." Mayor DeRubeis was furious and ordered Negrini to summon Lois Gasbarri and Julius Mattei to explain why the city council should not revoke their tavern licenses.[605]

* * *

At the April 21 meeting, Attorney Charles Santini represented the tavernkeepers. The city recalled Lois Gasbarri's shooting of Richard Salo in the ankle and the girl leaping out of the second-floor window of Frenchy's.

Santini argued that since Gasbarri had not yet been convicted, the evidence was not valid. Regarding the window incident, Santini began to argue there was no proof, but the witnessing officer, Hugo Bellardinelli, testified to the opposite.

The mayor commented that Patrick Judge stayed at Julius Mattei's Club Chateau "for three or four days and that he had sex with underaged Delores Nelson at the tavern."[606] Santini tried to

158

argue that the reason for the revocation action against Mattei was "malicious intent." Further, he said that since Mattei moved his license from 121 Silver Street to 101 Silver Street, he committed no offense. (The 121 address is where Patrick Judge offended the young runaway.) DeRubeis explained that "the charge is against the individual and not a specific location." Mattei, characteristically impetuous, asked if any other revocations were being considered and told DeRubeis to name them.

Santini ruffled the hearing as he tried to muscle it like a trial with continuous objections to evidence and procedure. DeRubeis was decisive, and soon, both tavernkeepers were temporarily out of business. The city council revoked Gasbarri's license with a vote of 11-1 and Mattei's license with a vote of 7-5. During the hearing, the fourth ward alderman wanted to add the Bowery to the list, but DeRubeis refocused the hearing on Frenchy's and the Club Chateau. At the end of the meeting, DeRubeis instructed Chief Negrini to "pick up those licenses. That's my order." When Santini threatened to appeal, DeRubeis countered by saying, "there is no appeal."[607]

*   *   *

Despite his certainty, on April 29, the sheriff served notices of appeal from Santini and Mattei to the mayor. DeRubeis announced that he asked the state for help, and they agreed. City Attorney Alex Raineri was miffed and called the appeal "unorthodox." He said it was similar to a legal procedure such as "appealing from county to circuit court," adding, "which certainly is not the case here."[608]

On June 4, Circuit Court Judge Charles dismissed the appeal because "the petition failed to allege jurisdictional defects." Judge Charles did grant a writ of certiorari requiring the city clerk to turn over council records regarding the revocation.[609]

*   *   *

However, on June 26, Judge Charles dismissed the writ filed by Santini and Mattei on a technicality. Because Santini served a *copy* of the writ rather than the original,

Jean R. Arrested 504 ½ Tower Avenue Superior 1953

the clerk refused to comply arguing that the writ was not legal. Hurley City Attorney Alex Raineri then filed the dismissal motion because "Mattei's attorney has not served a legal order on the city clerk."[610]

Hurley: Cirilli Weighs In

O N APRIL 24, ARMAND CIRILLI commented about the effect of state agents inability to engage in prostitution raids because of the loss of workmen's compensation. He said, "Since that time, prostitution has 'blossomed' in its full evil bloom all over Wisconsin." He summarized, "The places that were closed up by the state, or doing a 'quiet' business, are going 'full steam.' That may account for the 17-year-old girl episode now in the courts here."[611]

159

Hurley: Hurley Says We Need State Agents to Prosecute Prostitution

A T THE END OF April 1953, the Iron County D. A. petitioned the legislature to encourage state agents to arrest prostitutes. He told the Assembly Judiciary Committee that "prostitution has increased upstate since the agents stopped raids." He said that if help is not provided, the state will have "a year and a half of the worst lawlessness in Wisconsin since prohibition." He and State Assemblyman Arne Wicklund[612] testified that "prostitution can't be wiped out by local authorities because they 'can't get the evidence.'" [613]

Agent Mattingly told the committee that he heard from "practically every portion of the state that prostitution is increasing." Mattingly expressed genuine concern but explained the limitations caused by the workmen's compensation issue. It wasn't that he did not want to do it, it was that he was unable. He said, "We are not asking for the job, gentlemen; it is unpleasant." [614]

Hurley: A Rare Rejection

D URING THE MID-MAY meeting, the Hurley City Council did a rare thing by rejecting a tavern license. Marian Kruger applied for a license for 121 Silver Street, but the council rejected her request and refused to give a reason, but the quiet talk under the table was that the license "was for someone else." [615]

Hurley: Cirilli Bemoans the Loss of Talent in Hurley

O N MAY 22, ARMAND CIRILLI compared Hurley to Las Vegas. He described how the owners of the Las Vegas establishments were able to support major talent because of gambling revenue. Cirilli stated, "We had the same thing in Hurley on a smaller scale. The clubs here boasted some expensive shows a few years back. The club owners did not pay for these shows on the revenue from "shortie" beers. It was the gambling tables that supplied the dollars. When the state stepped in to stop gambling, the owners were hard-pressed to pay for the talent. It was pretty rough going after that. It is too tough scratching right now for the clubs that provide floor shows."[616] Cirilli's intent was not clear although the charitable interpretation would be that he was simply stating facts, rather than lamenting the loss of gambling.

Hurley: A Civil Meeting with Civil Servants

A FTER THE COUNTY-WIDE RAID IN LATE MAY, D. H. Prichard, head of Wisconsin's Beverage Tax Division, Fred Mattingly, Chief Of The Enforcement Division, and Hurley Mayor DeRubeis addressed 60 Iron County tavernkeepers. They talked about enforcement of the 1 a.m. closing law. The article in the *Iron County Miner* reported, "Several of the 'victims' of the weekend raids were in the audience and the meeting, and the questions were put in a 'friendly' way."[617]

Superior: A Cop Violates the Mann Act

R UDOLF C. MAST, 31, was a police officer in Superior. In April 1952, Mast traveled to Minneapolis for an appointment at the Veterans Administration hospital. One evening, he visited the Saddle Bar in a seedy area of Hennepin Avenue. The bar offered live entertainment, competing with other Minneapolis sex joints like Moby Dick's and the Pink Poodle.

At the Saddle, Mast met Darlene Morrison, 17, and Phyllis Bennett, 19. Bennett approached him and asked if he wanted "to go to bed with her for $20." He laughed at her, thinking she "looked like a typical bum." He suggested she go to Superior, get a job scrubbing floors at Sally's Hill rooms, and stay at the Androy Hotel. The girls traveled to Superior and met Mast at the Androy on Tower Avenue. However, Mast had become aware of an ongoing Mann Act dragnet and told them that "the town is hot" and that they needed to leave immediately.

Ida B. Arrested 504 ½ Tower Avenue Superior 1953

In early September 1953, after a grand jury indicted Mast on two counts of violating the Mann Act, the Superior Police Department suspended him. At trial, Mast didn't deny the suggestion about working at Sally's Room, but he said he did not know that Sally's was a brothel. Regardless, the prosecution charged forward, asserting that after befriending the girls and learning that they were looking for work, Mast told them that he could help them get jobs as prostitutes in a brothel operated by Sally Dalbo near the wharves. Most damning, he told them that he would use his authority as a cop to ensure their safety.[618]

The Federal prosecutor called two FBI agents, and a dozen witnesses including employees of the Androy hotel. In early October, a jury found Mast guilty, and the judge sentenced him to 18 months in prison.[619]

Hurley: The Anthony Orsoni Incident

ON JUNE 14, 1953, ANTHONY ORSONI of Montreal had too much to drink while on a sojourn to Silver Street. He became unruly while on the lower block, and a tavern operator called the police. In a rage, Orsoni would have none of it and bashed the arm of one of the officers and bit the other's finger. They managed to wrestle him down and then lock him up. The officers visited a doctor for their injuries. Orsoni's alcohol-related bashing and biting cost him $50 plus $23.50 in court costs.[620]

Hurley: And the Beat Goes On

AS OF JULY 1, 1953, the Hurley City Council granted an additional 18 tavern licenses bringing the total to 62. Also, they approved seven new bartender's licenses.[621] Conspicuously missing were applications from The Swing Club, The Super Bar, the Spa, the Club Chateau, the Turf Exchange, and Frenchy's.[622] Nonetheless, given the number of new bartender licenses, Silver Street must have had an insatiable thirst in the summer of 1953.

Madison: Agents v. Prostitutes

G OVERNOR KOHLER HEARD the testimony offered to the Assembly Judiciary Committee about state agents' risks when prosecuting prostitution, and he didn't like it. In early July 1953, he signed a bill that "Required Wisconsin beverage tax Department agents to enforce laws against prostitution."[623]

The timing of the new law coincided with Dr. Alfred Kinsey's report entitled *Sexual Behavior in the Human Female*. Kinsey concluded that "85 percent of women and 95 percent of men could be jailed for their sex acts by strict interpretation of laws" and "Many people, perhaps, fortunately, have no conception that everyday sexual activities may, in actuality, be contrary to law."[624] At this point, Wisconsin would have been satisfied by stopping the upper one percent of so-called "everyday sexual activity."

Northern Wisconsin: 93 Tavernkeepers and 36 Inmates in 26 Days

S TATE AGENTS HAD a short break from raiding brothels from November 1952 through July 1953, waiting for a new law which would resolve the workmen's compensation issue. Now, the agents were back in force, working to tamp down the proliferation of prostitution. In late August, David Prichard told *The Capital Times* that his division had been raiding northern Wisconsin with no help from local authorities. The agents arrested 93 tavernkeepers and 36 inmates in 26 days. Without the help of local authorities, state agents raided four brothels and arrested 25 people in Superior within a week.

Toni E. Arrested at 1601 N.3rd Street Superior 1953

Some objected to the state not notifying local authorities before the raid, so Prichard clarified the protocol, saying that the state only notifies local authorities if the complaints come from them. He said that if citizens complain, the state bypasses the local level.

He hinted at mistrust of local authorities, citing Hurley as an example of being subject to constant state raids and subsequent arrests but few license suspensions by municipal government. Although prostitution gets most of the headlines, Prichard said it was "a relatively minor part" of their work. He emphatically said he would enforce liquor laws and prosecute "red-light districts." Finally, he said, "I want those people to know that the heat is on."[625]

Superior: The Red-Light District of Superior

O N THURSDAY, AUGUST 20, state agents and Sheriff Anthony Jenda raided four brothels in Superior and arrested 21 women. They hit Superior's well-known joints hiding in plain site on

162

Tower Avenue, John Avenue, and North 3rd Street. These buildings were multiple-room residences clustered in a "red district" just south of Howards Bay on Lake Superior, only a block from where the freighters moored after long trips across the Great Lakes. A municipal judge and the district attorney charged 18 women as inmates and four as keepers. Refusing to face the consequences, the judge issued bench warrants for 17 women who failed to appear in court.

Vilas County: The *News-Review* & *The Capital Times* Duke It Out

VILAS COUNTY WAS ANNOYED with the state for raiding taverns for violating closing hours. Dan Satran, the editor of the *Vilas County News-Review* in Eagle River, refused to print the names of those arrested. He said that he was "sick and tired of seeing the state men hound our reporters and Northwoods tavern owners without too much good reason." Satran called the closing time for taverns in the north unfair, using Milwaukee's privilege of being open "until 2:30 every night of the week and 3:30 a. m. on Saturday evenings" as an example. Satran railed against the efforts of law enforcement saying, "The state would be better off tackling bootlegging in Wisconsin, the minor's drinking problem, downstate gambling, and vice (which does exist) than raiding North Wood places. Raiding 35 places in Vilas and Iron counties is nothing for anyone to crow about."[626]

Fannie S. Arrested 504-½ Tower Avenue Superior 1953

Cirilli published Satran's full editorial in the *Iron County Miner*, and wrote, "Bet the *Milwaukee Journal* won't reprint that."[627] True to Cirilli's prediction the *Milwaukee Journal* didn't reprint the editorial. However, the *Capital Times* didn't shy away from the challenge. Further, it pounced on Satran unapologetically with a blistering broadside.

On August 28, the *Times* wrote, "Editor Satran has apparently adopted a new reapportionment law in which he, instead of the Legislature, is to be the judge of what is a good law and what is a bad one. He takes the position that if he considers a law to be a bad one it should not be enforced." The editor mocked northern Wisconsin by saying that the area wanted to "dominate the legislature by making acres, rather than people the basis of representation."

That was clever but the *Times* didn't stop there. It launched a more direct attack saying, "The writer then focuses on the desire of the northlands of Wisconsin to encourage crime, "For years, slot machines and other gambling rackets flourished in the area in violation of the law. Local law enforcement officials and local newspapers ignored the lawlessness even though gangster elements were invading the state. The racketeers made a clean-up, the newspapers got more advertising, and the local law enforcement officials came in on the graft."

The *Times* article was imbued with hostility and bordered on spite as the evidence did not support their accusations. In fact, far more wealth had been accumulated in Madison and Milwaukee via graft than in northern Wisconsin. It is difficult to point to any one individual who made a bundle with slot machines or roulette tables in Wausau, Hayward, Superior, or Hurley. The value of housing up north has always paled compared to that in Wisconsin's metropolitan areas. In Wisconsin, wealth has always been east of the line from Madison to Green Bay. Over the years, if anyone got rich in northern Wisconsin, it was the iron and lumber barons from New York, Milwaukee, and the Fox River Valley.

The *Times* article said, "The situation was finally cleaned up when the late Gov. Goodland put through the present anti-gambling law. But the North has not changed, as Editor Satran demonstrates. The newspapers are still for lawlessness."[628]

Notably, the author of this piece wisely remained anonymous since he failed to provide evidence for his conjecture. What happened can best be offered by metaphor. Two editors of small northland newspapers went musky fishing, as if on Gile Flowage. Satran baited the line and Cirilli cast the lure. They missed the *Milwaukee Journal* but hooked, played, and netted the *Capital Times*.

The hoopla surrounding the war of words escalated.

Betty K. Arrested 504-½ Tower Avenue
Superior 1953

The *Merrill Daily Herald* and the *Park Falls Herald* fell in with the up-north contingent. As usual, Cirilli had some choice words for Madison's *Capital Times*. He wrote, "Like a great deal of the thinking of *The Capital Times* it is warped by other considerations and prejudices. This time the paper ties in the 'areacrat' charge in an attack on the Vilas County newspaper. Why doesn't the *Capital Times* say anything about the preference shown Milwaukee in tavern hours?"[629]

Langlade County: The White House of Antigo – Again

ELA E. BLECKSCHMIDT, NOW 50, continued to operate the White House tavern in Antigo. Demand for services in the area had grown over the years, and Ela added staff. On August 13, 1953, agents arrested five women for prostitution at the White House. The judge fined Bleckschmidt $500 as the keeper and suspended a six-month jail sentence.

Hurley: A Suspicious Fire at the Club Carnival

DURING THE EARLY morning of Wednesday, September 9, a "suspicious looking" fire damaged the subfloor and the walls at the new Club Carnival on the lower block of Silver Street. The fire department found small fires in nine different places and the lingering smell of gasoline. The operator was in Chicago at the time of the fire lining up entertainment for the grand opening.[630] Authorities found the fire similar to other recent arson attempts in Hurley. The fire marshal investigated but found nothing suspicious.[631]

Hurley: A *Milwaukee Journal* Scoop

IN LATE SEPTEMBER 1953, the *Iron County Miner* reported, "The *Milwaukee Journal* scooped us all on a story about 11 Hurley area tavernkeepers facing revocation of licenses. Everyone was wondering where the *Journal* got the story. It had a Hurley dateline and District Attorney George Sullivan was quoted at length. However, Sullivan denied giving the *Journal* any information."

Some tavern owners were trying to find the source of the story since it exaggerated the violations. They eventually learned that the culprit was the Wisconsin Beverage Division in Madison. Because the writer quoted D. A. Sullivan, the *Journal* attached a Hurley Dateline, but the *Iron County Miner* found the cite dubious.[632] Although the facts of the entire affair became muddled, it evoked a firestorm of editorials.

The *Marinette Eagle-Star* weighed in, "One of the defendants has a record of 12 convictions for sale of liquor after-hours, two for gambling and seven for prostitution. The others have from three to 11 convictions. None of them can be said to be of good character, as the law specifies an applicant for a tavern license shall be. On the contrary, most of them are notoriously bad and should have had their license removed. The Hurley City Council should have acted a long time ago to put these people out of the tavern business."[633]

Jerry D. Arrested at Roadside Lunch/White House Tavern Stevens Point 1953

Hurley: More Editorial Banter

WALTER "SHAKES" JANSON, a former editor of the *Marinette Eagle-Star*, weighed in on the revocation of the 11 Hurley taverns. He wrote that the local authorities in Hurley were not cooperative when trying to solve the tavern problem and that the city council shouldn't renew the license of repeat offenders. He said, "A good example is offered by the City of Hurley where the city council apparently takes little cognizance of the lack of character of applicants for liquor licenses."[634]

This was legitimate criticism. On more than one occasion, the city council would meet shortly after a Silver Street raid and grant new licenses to those arrested. Council members favored friends while simultaneously filling the city coffers with license fees.

Armand Cirilli complained about the imbalance between the hours violations and the revocation penalty. He pointed out that closing hour violations occurred throughout the state. He wrote, "In Milwaukee, the taverns can remain open until the wee hours with the sanction of the law. We don't appreciate the zeal of the state agents in this respect."[635]

The *Vilas County News-Review* supported its ally in Hurley, "Obviously the state men are becoming a little 'heady' with editorial backing from a number of down-state newspapers and are out like Don Quixote when they are trying to ride down and root out of business operators who are offending no worse than hundreds of taverns in counties downstate." The paper referred to the "downstate" newspapers as having a "holier than thou" attitude and criticizing the *News-Review* as being "in cahoots with lawless 'criminals' up-state." They then charged, "Brother, was the pot calling the kettle black."[636] This journalist's civil war pitted the north against the south in "America's Dairyland."

In a mid-October front-page editorial, *The Milwaukee Journal* proposed that "the state agents ought to look around the state a little bit more instead of spending all their time in the north country." Cirilli chimed in, "Instead of placing such a great emphasis on 'after-hours' they might take a better look at widespread selling of liquor to minors and at prostitution…all over the state."[637]

Hurley: Another Heroin Charge

O N THE EVENING OF September 27, 1953, authorities served a federal warrant to Kenneth Frederickson, a piano player in a tavern on the lower block of Silver Street.[638] The Iron County Sheriff drove the Chicago man to the Douglas County jail in Superior to await a hearing before Federal Court Commissioner Charles Bishop. Frederickson faced a charge of receiving, concealing, buying, and selling heroin.[639] Not being able to cover the $1,000 bail, he sat in the Douglas County jail. This was the second narcotics event in 1953; the other was in January with *The Case of Madero Dawson*.

Mildred Z. Arrested at 314 John Street
Superior 1953

Hurley: The Ugly Face of Revocation

B Y THE THIRD WEEK OF OCTOBER, Iron County District Attorney George Sullivan, at the request of the State Beverage Tax Division, delivered revocation complaints to ten Hurley tavern owners, including Margaret Prickett of Margaret's, John Rajkovich of the French Casino, James Gasbarri of Jackpot's Flame, John Kalasardo of the Band Box, Louis Gasbarri of the Red Feather, Joseph Vita of the Hi-Ho bar, and Richard Matrella of Mickey's Rendezvous.[640]

On December 7, Circuit Court Judge Charles suspended the liquor licenses of eight Hurley taverns for periods ranging from 45 to 75 days with the longest for Richard Matrella of Mickey's Rendezvous. To name a few, John Kalasardo of the Band Box, John Rajkovich of the French Casino, and George Reardon[641] received the shortest suspensions.

Joseph Vita's attorney, Warren Foster, postponed the case to write briefs challenging the constitutionality of the suspension law."[642] The judge postponed the case against John Rajkovich of the French Casino until January 1954.[643]

During the second week of December 1953, Matrella, James Gasbarri, Louis Gasbarri, and Margaret Prickett posted bonds to appeal to the Wisconsin Supreme Court. It was business as usual until the Supreme Court ruled on the appeals.[644]

Hurley: Pushed Around by State

THE LEAGUE OF WISCONSIN MUNICIPALITIES held its annual meeting in Madison in October 1953. The Madison newspapers took advantage of interviewing Mayor DeRubeis during his visit. DeRubeis expressed concern about "undue and unwarranted emphasis on Hurley" regarding the closing hour issue. Even the editor of *The Capital Times*, William Evjue, remarked that he "was 'impressed' with the mayor's views." The event lasted for several days, and during the conference, DeRubeis lunched with David Prichard, director of the Beverage Tax Division. They talked at length about the tavern situation in Hurley.[645]

DeRubeis told *The Capital Times*, "Hurley and northern Wisconsin generally are being 'pushed around' by the State Beverage Tax Division in its enforcement of the 1 a.m. tavern closing hour law." DeRubeis commanded respect, and the *Times* listened when he said, "Beverage tax agents like to come into Hurley and make a grandstand play." He shifted the focus and said he could find situations in Milwaukee similar to Hurley. Milwaukee's closing hours continued to annoy the entire state, most particularly northern Wisconsin. As in the past, Milwaukee got special legislative attention because of the factory three-shift schedule. DeRubeis argued that Iron County miners worked three shifts also and should be entitled to the same privilege. DeRubeis acknowledged that Hurley was not singled out as he recognized that agents arrested 600 tavernkeepers for violating closing hours during the year.[646]

Hurley: An October Beating at the Club Carnival

AROUND BAR TIME ON THE MORNING of October 16, 1953, Kenneth Aho, 23, a college student from Wakefield, was drinking at the Club Carnival with friends. The group was boisterous, and Richard Matrella, the operator, encouraged them to leave. They stumbled out the door and meandered along Silver Street. Matrella caught up to Aho on the corner of Silver Street and Second Avenue, fractured his skull with his fist, and left him unconscious on the sidewalk.[647]

Aho spent three days at the Grand View hospital and then filed an assault and battery complaint. District Attorney Sullivan served the warrant to Matrella for "intent to do great bodily harm." Judge Trembath summoned Matrella to Iron County Court on October 27. Aho dropped the case at the arraignment when Matrella agreed to pay all the doctor and hospital bills.[648]

This seemingly unprovoked attack definitely had an unreported motivation.

Hurley: Two More October Beatings

ON MONDAY MORNING, OCTOBER 26, John Carli, the operator of the Bowery, beat up Clarence Leavitt from Saxon. Leavitt filed charges, and Carli pled not guilty to assault and battery in Iron County Court, which incidentally, was the case heard directly after Matrella's. Carli pled *nolo contendre,* and Judge Trembath fined him $15. Then, Trembath dismissed Carli's countersuit against Leavitt for assault and battery.

John Carli was not having a good day. After the Leavitt case ended, he sat through a jury trial where he faced three "traffic-related" counts: exceeding the speed limit, passing a car on a curve, and reckless driving. The trial lasted all day, and in this case, Carli took the beating. It took the jury 25 minutes to return a guilty verdict on all counts.[649] Carli requested a change of venue, but during the third week of November, Judge Lewis J. Charles denied the request and set a court date for December.[650] In mid-December 1954, Judge Charles fined Carli $50 plus $91.50 in court costs.[651]

Hurley: Under Mercer's Eye

IN EARLY NOVEMBER, the Mercer police department received a letter from a Tomahawk woman asking them to keep an eye on Hurley. The woman wrote, "Police Dept, Mercer, Wis. Dear Sir: I want you to watch Hurley and keep it in order. I don't want disorderly houses going on as they are no good to anyone only bring disgrace to every family that lives there, or any town that have them. A week ago Sunday drove thru up there. You have pretty places and towns. I really hope that stay that way." [sic] The Mercer police department sent the letter to Cirilli and said, "I sort of always figured that Mercer should be the protector of the good citizens of Hurley. I see that we will have to increase our police department."[652]

Hurley: The *Milwaukee Journal* Photographs the Neon

ALSO IN EARLY NOVEMBER, a reporter and a photographer from the *Milwaukee Journal* visited Hurley to survey the state of events. They printed a six-column picture showing the neon on the lower block of Silver Street. Armand Cirilli responded, "It is a periodic thing this business of writing up Hurley." Criticizing the *Journal*, he said that the reporter could not find much to write about, "so to earn his gas money, he resurrected some of the stuff from 30 years ago." Cirilli, with his usual wit, wrote, "For a while, we thought he was going to revive the one of 'bodies floating down the Montreal River.'" Cirilli walked back his mini-essay, writing, "Maybe we 'earned' this latest story on Hurley. There have been some strange goings-on in those first two blocks these past few months."[653] Cirilli had his thumb on the pulse of the lower blocks. He knew the characters but, unfortunately, he couldn't print everything he heard although sometimes he nudged toward rumor. Nonetheless, one cannot help wondering what adventures those untold stories held.

* * *

In early December, Armand Cirilli reflected on the motive for the visit from the *Milwaukee Journal* reporter. He commented about how down-state is fixated on the lower two blocks, and Hurley residents don't understand why other areas of town are neither visited nor discussed. Cirilli wrote, "As we have said before, what happens in those first two blocks 'screams so loud' they cannot hear what we have to say about the rest of our town."[654] An apt observation indeed.

168

Hurley: Judge Trembath & Freemasonry

O N MONDAY, DECEMBER 7, 1953, Judge R. C. Trembath was reelected as the "Worshipful Master of the Hurley Masonic Lodge."[655] It is reasonable to believe that all the secrets within Freemasonry would be necessary to survive the daily docket of Silver Street cases.

Hurley: Hurley Takes the Gold

O N DECEMBER 19, 1953, David Prichard reported 57 closures in Wisconsin – most for gambling or prostitution – filed by the State Beverage Tax Division since 1949. Hurley was the winner with 34 of the 57. The runner-up was Florence County with six, and Brown, Chippewa, and Langlade shared the bronze with two apiece. Prichard said that "53 taverns had been closed temporarily or their owner put out of business since his agents began cracking down under a revocation and suspension law in June 1949." During this period, they dismissed only four cases.

Hurley had 15 taverns with three or more convictions, and "one operator registered his 15th violation recently." In addition to gambling and prostitution, violations included being open after-hours, sales to minors, sales to "habitual drunkards," and loitering. Prichard suggested a law to require the initial tavern application to be cleared by the beverage tax division.[656] The entire state tavern industry bristled by this idea, and it was dropped from Prichard's agenda.

1954

Hurley: Don't Mess with Hurley Women

IN A BOLD BUT FOOLHARDY move, on the evening of January 5, 1954, state agents raided 301 Silver Street, where grey-haired women fingered colored chips and focused on multiple bingo cards. When a state agent cuffed the caller, Clyde Singleton, the women abandoned their cards, pushed back their chairs, and stormed the agents. They were hostile and demanded they be left alone, claiming it was their only entertainment in the dead of winter. The merciless agents told them to "find other means of entertainment."[657]

Cirilli wrote, "There's nothing like the wrath of a little old lady and the state agents who broke up the beano game on Tuesday night had a lot of little old ladies on their neck and some of them weren't so little. The good ladies who get their leisure from a card and a bundle of corn were pretty mad and the state minions got told off plenty."[658] Regardless of the severity of the offense, the state applied the "constant pressure" promised by Pritchard. To many in Wisconsin, this felt like death by a thousand cuts. A few days later, Judge Trembath fined Singleton $100 ($1,100 today) for the gambling infraction.

Hurley: A Hard Act to Follow

AT 9:45 P.M. ON A BRITTLE COLD Monday in January, Georgia Newman danced for tips in a Hurley tavern. As best she could, the 41-year-old slithered, stripped, and sipped a lot of whiskey while performing. Then, after a few less-than-stellar sets, she responded to crude jeers by incorporating a loaded revolver into her act. The alcohol-related gesture of pointing the gun at the audience put her in lock-up. Judge Trembath confiscated the gun and gave her the choice of a $20 fine or 75 days in jail for being armed while drunk and then added 30 days for being drunk and disorderly. She couldn't catch a break and without the gun or the $20, she went to jail. When she got out, she hopped a bus home to Terre Haute and, hopefully, pursued a different line of work.[659]

Hurley: The Beatings will Continue

THE SAME JANUARY DAY that Georgia Newman was brandishing her revolver, Alex Bulkowski from Ironwood mugged Peter DeCarlo from Hurley on Silver Street. DeCarlo claimed the Bulkowski stole $20 and valuable papers. Trembath set bail at $1,000 but, unable to provide the bond, Bulkowski took up residence in the Iron County Jail until trial. On February 16, Bulkowski filed an affidavit of prejudice against Judge Trembath, and acting Judge James E. Flandrena reduced the bail to $250. Despite the reduction, Bulkowski could not provide the bond and returned to the county jail.[660] The case went flat when, in mid-May 1954, Iron County Circuit Court Judge Lewis J. Charles dismissed the case against Bulkowski when Peter DeCarlo failed to show up for the hearing.[661] Presumably, the papers were not that valuable.

Hurley: What's in a Name

IN MARCH, A MILWAUKEE newspaper criticized the simplicity of tavern names. Cirilli wrote, "A Milwaukee columnist recently commented on the lack of imagination of tavern and night club owners in naming their establishments, with most of them simply tagged as "Joe's Place." or "Art's Place." The writer said that the English were much more imaginative in this regard. The Milwaukee scribe may have cause to lament the situation in the beer city. In Hurley, it is different. For one thing, the bountiful supply of inns in this city must necessarily inspire a greater variety. Here in Hurley, we have some pretty fancy-named places. We have the Swing club, the Club Carnival, the Holiday Inn, and the Band Box. Some years ago, a sign painter talked one old Finn owner into calling his place "The Rendezvous." The poor fellow couldn't say it with a mouthful. On the lighter side, we have the "Four-Ever Amber Bar." Then there's Chicken in the Basket, Connie's Drumstick, the Ritz, Hi-Ho Bar, and some other fancy-named places which at the moment escape us. Truly the Hurley gin mills must perforce have a variety of names."[662] Perforce means "by necessity." Sometimes tavern names are easier to pronounce than adverbs used by journalists.

Hurley: A Circulating Pump

HURLEY HAD A DISTINCTIVE DYNAMIC. As soon as girls were ordered out of town, more arrived to occupy the same joints. Most likely, the beds never cooled. The demand for liquor and prostitutes appeared – and likely was – insatiable. The Hurley City Council granted 61 tavern and 23 bartender licenses in July.[663] The rest of the spring and summer, police continued to pound the beat, arresting tavernkeepers for previously ignored infractions, such as serving minors and selling firecrackers.

Hurley: The Raids of 1954

THERE WERE THREE primary raids in 1954: April 4, May 1, and July 31. The few raids were starkly juxtaposed against the severity of the offenses. Overall, agents arrested eight as keepers, 12 for solicitation, 14 as inmates, and 21 for operating after hours. Six individuals were multi-offenders. Bernard Patritto[664] of Frenchy's, James Gasbarri of the Flame, and John Rajkovich of the French Casino, were each arrested twice as keepers. Lois Gasbarri of Frenchy's and Martha Smith of the Flame were each arrested twice for being inmates and for solicitation.

The raids focused on specific activities. For example, the April and July raids targeted prostitution, whereas the May raid targeted hours violations. The May raid accounted for all 21 after-hours arrests in the year. The offenders with multiple arrests included the Blackhawk with nine, the French Casino with eight, Jackpot's Flame with nine, Frenchy's with seven, and the Club Holiday with three.[665]

* * *

In one incident, Hurley police arrested two women at Mickey's Rendezvous for "lewd and lascivious" behavior and acting as "common drunkards." In early July, the women got a slice of justice as Trembath sentenced each to 90 days in the county jail unless they left town by 5 p.m.[666] Although not specified, they likely left.

171

* * *

In August, tavernkeepers marched into Judge Trembath's court, paying fines, pleading guilty, pleading not guilty, changing their pleas, asking for jury trials, begging for mercy, thumbing their noses, blaming the state, and so on. James Gasbarri, John Rajkovich, and Bernard Patritto all pled guilty to operating houses of ill fame and were assigned to county court. Five tavernkeepers pled guilty to remaining open after-hours and paid fines. Five women admitted guilt for soliciting, and Trembath fined each $115. Those that pled guilty to being inmates paid fines of $50.[667]

In mid-August, Armand Cirilli went straight to the point when he wrote, "The state men made quite a 'haul' on their last visit to Hurley, and it seems to us that at least some of the nightspots in town were 'asking for it.' There is no use going into the sordid details, but it's the truth."[668]

Hurley: The Case of Mr. and Mrs. Tully & Associates

DURING THE SUMMER of 1954, Marie Florence Tully, 31, lived with her husband, Max E. Tully, 36, in an "Ironwood motor court." Max would usually drive his wife to Hurley to work at the French Casino, but sometimes, his friend, Pete Piazza, would drive her. The route took the couple across the Montreal River into Wisconsin to the French Casino on Silver Street. At the French Casino, Mrs. Tully bartended, worked as a B-girl (drink solicitor), and a prostitute. It is possible that Piazza, being new to the city, didn't understand the significance of the commute.

* * *

On June 8, 1954, the FBI asked a naval intelligence officer, Bernard H. Stacey, to surveil the French Casino. As Stacey sat at the bar sipping a beer, he glanced at Marie Florence "Rusty" Tully playing cards with a bartender. She caught his eye and approached him from behind the bar. She first asked if he would buy her a drink and then, leaning over the bar, she asked him "if he wanted a girl." He replied that he was not in a hurry. When Stacey began to leave, he "received another solicitation." He knew that her husband, Max, was in the bar, but he couldn't tell if Max had heard the enquiry. Although light as a feather and barely a whisper, that simple encounter led to an FBI arrest and subsequent prosecution.[669]

* * *

In the first week of December 1954, Federal Judge Patrick T. Stone convened a 17-member federal grand jury to investigate the transporting of girls into Hurley across state lines.[670] The judge specifically mentioned Calumet City, Indiana. The court subpoenaed several residents, a tavernkeeper, and a woman bartender from Hurley to appear at Madison.[671, 672]

* * *

In mid-December, U.S. Marshal Thomas F. Madden, arrested William Matrella, James Shields, Pete Piazza, and Donald Harris for inducing women into prostitution. In addition to the "inducement" charge, Matrella was accused of transporting a woman from Hurley, Wisconsin to Ironwood, Michigan where she took a plane to Indiana. Because Piazza drove his wife from Ironwood to Hurley to work at the French Casino on Silver Street, the FBI charged Piazza with transporting a woman across state lines for immoral purposes, a violation of the Mann Act. Police transported Matrella and Piazza to the Ashland County jail, where the judge set the bail at $3,500 each.

172

The FBI charged James Shields with "enticing an Illinois girl to come to Hurley for immoral purposes." She traveled from Danville, Illinois to live in Hurley as a prostitute. They wanted to charge Donald Harris of Springfield with two counts of transporting girls from Peoria and Calumet City to Hurley, but he had left town after being ordered to do so. By following the judge's order, Harris was a free man - temporarily.

In late-December, Matrella, Piazza, and Shields appeared before Federal Judge Stone in Wausau on charges of violating the Mann act. Each pled not guilty, and the judge required $3,500 each in bond before releasing all three.[673]

Pete Piazza, 42, pled not guilty,[674] and in April, Alex Raineri convinced the judge that when driving Marie Tully, "he simply went along for the ride." Judge Stone dismissed the charges against Piazza because of insufficient evidence.[675] Piazza dodged a bullet.

Max Tully was not so lucky, despite his wife's testimony that she was not a prostitute, the jury found him guilty of two counts of violating the Mann Act at trial on April 15, 1955, in Wausau. Judge Stone sentenced Tully to 2½ years in federal prison.[676]

* * *

In June 1955, a federal judge in Milwaukee "denied a plea for leniency" and sentenced James C. Shield, 52, to 18 months in prison.[677]

* * *

In October, police caught up with Donald Harris, 35, who they now said was from Gary, Indiana. On October 20, 1955, A 12-person jury heard the arguments in the case in federal court in Superior in the presence of Judge Stone. Harris was on trial for transporting a woman in November 1953, from Peoria to Hurley and in March 1954, from Calumet, Illinois, to Hurley for prostitution. The woman was his wife, Rube "Carmen" Harris. She testified, however, that she stole her husband's car in Illinois and drove it to Hurley. She said, "she visited an establishment in Hurley 'for a few drinks' and was arrested as an inmate of a house of prostitution during a raid." She denied that her husband traveled with her. The story was too thin, and the jury found Donald Harris guilty of violating the Mann Act. Harris's attorney said he would appeal the decision.[678] The appeal didn't get any traction and in early November 1955, Judge Stone sentenced Donald Harris to 2 ½ years in federal prison.[679]

Hurley: Free Press Spins a Tale

IN JULY, KEN MCCORMICK, a *Detroit Free Press* staff reporter, visited Hurley and wrote an article in the Sunday Magazine section. The introduction described Hurley as "practically on the outskirts of Ironwood" and "possibly the only place in the world where the croupier welcomes nickel roulette bets." McCormick had a way with words. He wrote, "It's called the poor man's Monte Carlo and a piker's Las Vegas. Anything goes. A bar patron, while sipping a drink, can watch a craps game, a poker game and a stripteaser, all without turning his head."

McCormick said that a bartender at the Club Carnival told him it cost $750 a week for a "big name" performer and that "Obviously, we can't pay the nut with this kind of business. Following his eyes, you saw what apparently is the answer: girl 'entertainers.'" McCormick estimated that there were 200 "girl entertainers" in Hurley and the condition "just growed" as "Early lumberjacks and miners set a pattern that hasn't been disturbed.

McCormick continued, "The places stay open as long as there is one droopy-eyed customer around" and referring to the cops he wrote, "Hurley has a police force, but policemen are seldom in the spots – except occasionally when one wants a cup of coffee."

He talked to a dealer who showed him how he could hold an ace and simultaneously deal from the deck. The dealer said he didn't cheat the locals, but when a "wise guy" visits the table, "I barge in and then, boom! I let them have it!"

McCormick implied that Michigan helped prosecute Hurley's vice. He wrote, "Among the reasons that Michigan authorities can't take a 'live and let live' attitude to the community in the sister state is that the operators haven't been too particular about the age of the 'entertainers' they import.'" When asked about the operators, one 'regular' customer told McCormick, "Nothing much scares these characters except one thing – they don't want to get into no jam with them G-guys."[680]

Armond Cirilli found the article so ludicrous that he reprinted it in full in the *Iron County Miner* and added his critique. He said McCormick "is supposed to be some shakes of a writer in the Detroit area. We are surprised to hear that because the article is almost irrelevant, 90% irresponsible, and 100% ridiculous. His sympathy with the Michigan authorities who can't do anything about what goes on over the 'border' is strictly a laugh. His claim that there are 200 'entertainers' in Hurley (the quotes are his) is more than an excess of newspaper license. It is a fantastic lie, and he knows it."

The following week, Cirilli said that the Detroit article "caused quite a sensation in Iron County and over in Ironwood." He continued, "The *Miner* sold like hotcakes" and that those that read the piece were "pretty mad" and that the Ironwood residents said that McCormick "should confine his talents to his hometown."[681]

Despite McCormick's assertions, there is no evidence to suggest Michigan had the slightest interest in curbing Hurley's vice. This type of sensationalism was not uncommon when big-city writers visited Hurley. Its reputation always preceded a visit, and while often disappointed to see less than two blocks of taverns, the correspondents felt compelled to exaggerate the experience with flashy adjectives and assertions. Cirilli said it best when de described "the incredulous article as 'fantastic, juvenile, and amateurish.'"

Hurley: What Could Possibly Go Wrong?

ON SUNDAY, SEPTEMBER 5, AT 2:50 a.m., a police officer returning from Cary noticed two men brawling on the second block of Silver Street. He hurriedly exited his car and separated the men. He methodically took names and wrote citations. Only then did he return to the location where his car used to be. Embarrassed, he called the station for a ride.

Rudolph Perhalla, 20, and Joseph Ravanelli, 23, watched the police officer break up the fight, but they were unable resist temptation as the officer left the keys in the cruiser's ignition. Their ride ended 45 minutes later in Bessemer, Michigan, about eight miles to the east. From there, they rode in the back seat of another police car, back along the same route to the Hurley police station. Judge Trembath did not find the incident amusing and bound them over for trial in Iron County Court.[682]

Perhalla appeared in court the following week. Trembath dismissed the theft charge after Perhalla agreed to plead guilty to disorderly conduct. After finding the young man $100, he suspended the fine and placed him on probation for nearly a year. The case ended after Trembath ordered Perhalla to pay $2 for a missing flashlight.[683] There is no record of what happened to his accomplice.

Hurley: Still No Angel

IN NOVEMBER 1954, Lewis C. Reimann published a book entitled *Hurley: Still No Angel*. The press release stated that the book "is the first complete story of the community which grew up on pine and iron ore and which still retained its lawlessness and vice through prohibition days with their raids, hijacking and bootlegging." The advertisement for the book said, "See Hurley Before You Die" is still a lure to suckers who flock there to witness the shoddy bars, the lurid nightclub shows and the undercover gambling, to say nothing of the habits of the vice joints."

Armand Cirilli addressed Reimann's book and Edna Ferber's work *Come and Get It* which used Hurley as the setting. He wrote, "Very few people bothered to read 'Come and Get It.' Probably fewer will bother to read Reimann's book.[684]

* * *

In February 1955, Reimann, a resident of Ann Arbor, wrote a letter to Armand Cirilli complaining about how Cirilli bashed his book. Reimann wrote, "Your recent comment on "Hurley – Still No Angel" was sent to me: I can well understand why you do not like the book and use up space in your paper to say so. If you did make a favorable comment about it, would it not lose advertising space from the taverns and from the whiskey distributors? The 'conglomeration of nothing' as you call it is made up of reports on the continued lawlessness from the Wisconsin Beverage and Cigarette Tax Division. The 88 arrests and fines against the taverns for illegal sales to minors, gambling, and prostitution during the year preceding August 1954, are not fabrications but come from the law enforcement agency set up by the Wisconsin legislature." Reimann referred to quotations he used from Edna Ferber's book and the Milwaukee newspapers.

He summarized his letter, "No amount of whitewash on your part will change the facts which stare people in the face when they visit your shoddy night clubs and taverns or read of arrests for sales to minors, gambling and prostitution."[685]

The self-righteous tone of Reimann's letter received a swift rebuke from Cirilli in a ten-inch column. Cirilli wrote, "Lewis C. Reimann, the fellow who authored the book, "Hurley – Still No Angel," is mad at us. We've panned his book a couple of times and he doesn't like it. We still insist that the book is a conglomeration of nothing, poorly put together. This is the universal opinion of everyone with whom we have talked to, who has read the book. The only reference to the *Iron County Miner* in the book is that although we do not condone what goes on in Hurley, we go along with it. That may be true, but the proof he offers in the book on it is plain stupid. He cited the fact that we printed a story anent some man being elected president of the Heilemann Brewing Co. He ran the picture of an ad that we ran for Sunnybrook whiskey. The first two citations are stupid, and they indicate that he knows nothing about running a newspaper. Matt Secor is not a member of *The Miner* staff and never has been. In his closing sentence in the letter, he says: 'I know a newspaper has to have advertising support to live. But, what a price to pay for a clean conscience.' Phooey! We don't get $100 a year in revenue from the taverns here. Sometimes our conscience does bother us anent our city – but not for the reasons Reimann would believe."[686]

Given Cirilli's breadth of knowledge and street-smart demeanor, it might have been a good idea for Reimann to have asked him to review a draft of his document before publishing it.

Reimann must have held a grudge against Cirilli's taunts. In May 1955, he wrote a letter to the *Iron County Miner* saying that "his next book on Hurley won't be as mild as the first one." Cirilli wrote, "Guess that Lewis is still mad at us for some of the things we said about the book."[687] Reimann must have had second thoughts as there was no second book.

Hurley: The Range Beverage Robbery

DURING THE SECOND WEEK OF November, three eighth graders entered the Range Beverage Company on Silver Street through an unlocked door. They pocketed $133 in cash, several bottles of whiskey and wine, a wristwatch, and a cigarette lighter.[688] The police identified the young thieves and two additional accomplices within a few days. Just before appearing in court, four of the boys skipped town. They were on the lam with no firm plan and police rounded them up in Carlton, Minnesota, southwest of Duluth. Confronting a penalty worse than jail, the Iron County Sheriff carted them home to face their parents.[689]

Hurley: The Mayhem Case of John S. Carli

THIS STORY NEEDS TO BE TOLD IN ONE CHUNK. Presenting it in sections would introduce unnecessary complexity and make it difficult to follow. It covers the four-year period from 1954 to 1958 and follows the tumultuous activity of one of Silver Street's most tenacious, impetuous, and violent players.

In the evening of December 17, 1954, John Garber, the owner of the Gateway Inn in Land O' Lakes in Vilas County, traveled to Hurley to talk to a member of the band performing at the Bowery on Silver Street. While Garber stood at the end of the bar waiting for the set to end, John Carli, the manager of the Bowery, along with Alfred Carli, his uncle, attacked Garber and beat him severely.[690]

The men punched Garber in the eye, smashed their fists into his torso, and John Carli pinned him to the floor and bit off part of his ear. Bartender Edward Harris leaped into the fray and separated the men. The next day, John and Alfred Carli, along with Ed Harris, were charged with assault and appeared before Judge Trembath in county court. They all pled not guilty, and the judge released them on bond.[691]

* * *

On January 5, 1955, Edward Harris, John Garber, Police Chief Leo Negrini, and John Carli testified in front of Judge Trembath. The bartender, Edward Harris, told the judge that he saw both John and Alfred Carli beat Garber. Harris testified and signed a statement that his only involvement was breaking up the fight. Harris had been in jail since January 3 and, concerned about the ramifications of his testimony, he asked the judge if he could stay there. Trembath dismissed the assault charge against Harris.[692] Ed Harris, a native of La Grange, Georgia, might have headed south since he disappears from the record.

John Garber's testimony was explicit. He told the judge that Alfred Carli pinned him to the tavern floor while John Carli "chewed off part of his right ear." Even for Judge Trembath, who had heard a lot during his tenure, this must have been appalling. Without delay, he immediately bound Carli to the circuit court for assault with intent to do great bodily harm.[693] After this hearing, John S. Carli moved to Milwaukee.

* * *

On February 11, 1955, John Garber filed a $161,000 suit in Iron County Court against Carli. Garber complained that he "suffered severe mental pain and anguish and great indignities and humiliation and will be permanently disfigured."[694]

* * *

Also in February, Hurley's mayor consulted an attorney about suing the *Milwaukee Sentinel* for publishing a story about "syndicate" operations in the city. The author of the article was John S. Carli who wrote it in likely retribution for the revocation of the Bowery license in 1954. Carli told the *Sentinel* that the revocation "was a conspiracy on the part of the syndicate because he wouldn't join." He then petitioned Judge Stone saying, "Certain conditions in Hurley required the attention of the federal government," and added that he was referring to prostitution.

Shortly after that, Carli said he had changed his mind because many Hurley people, mostly "businessmen," had asked him to drop the issue. He said, "To catch a handful of culprits, I would have to hurt a lot of innocent people, I have decided against asking for a grand jury investigation of syndicate operations in Hurley."

The mayor responded that he was "never afraid" of an investigation and said, "I was so sick and tired of hearing charges and claims that I almost welcomed the grand jury investigation. It would have been good to clear the air once and for all."[695]

* * *

On March 11, 1955, John Carli filed a counterclaim against John Garber in Iron County Court. The suit asked for $456,000 because he "suffered mental and physical pain . . . and great indignity and humiliation." Carli claimed that Garber assaulted him, and that Garber lied to the Chief of Police. He complained about having to pay legal fees of $2,500 and that he suffered a current income loss of $1,000 "and anticipation of a loss in the future of income totaling $250,000."[696]

* * *

In May, 1955, Judge Charles dismissed the assault charge against Alfred Carli due to a technicality, but the district attorney filed a more serious mayhem charge against John.[697] As a result of the biting incident, the judge recharged Alfred, this time with being "privy[698] to the intent to disfigure by biting off an ear.[699] In simple terms, the judge did not think that Alfred Carli knew that his nephew was going to bite off the ear of John Garber.

* * *

On June 1, 1955, Judge Trembath held preliminary hearings in the "mayhem cases" against John and Alfred Carli. On June 24, he changed the charge against Alfred Carli from "intent to disfigure" to assault and battery. Alfred pled guilty, and the judge fined him $50. Detached and pragmatic, Trembath ordered John Carli, 33, to the circuit court for trial.[700]

* * *

The trial opened ten months later on March 14, 1956, and Judge Carl H. Daley of Superior presided in Iron County Court. Carli could have chosen either a jury or a bench trial. He chose a bench trial because it was quicker and minimized damaging information in front of a jury. On the other hand, with a bench trial, the judge would follow the rules precisely without objection and determine the verdict without debate. With a bench trial, there may be an inclination to convict as the position is elected, all the witnesses faced the judge directly, and the judge yields a verdict.

Carli's attorney, Joseph E. Tierney of Milwaukee, said that he would prove that there was a conspiracy by Hurley city officials against his client. Resort owner John Garber delivered exhausting testimony requiring the entire morning.[701] The next day, Joun Carli contradicted Garber's testimony and denied that he had actively participated in the beating. Judge Charles gave the district attorney ten days to file a brief for Carli's attorney to respond.[702]

* * *

On June 26, 1956, the judge reduced John Carli's charge from "mayhem" to "assault" and sentenced him to a one-year term at Waupun. Carli's attorney said he would seek a ruling from the Wisconsin Supreme Court. As such, Judge Charles granted a 60-day stay of execution, giving Carli time to appeal.[703]

* * *

In July, Carli's attorney asked Judge Daley for "a dismissal of the conviction and sentence and/or cutting of the sentence." He told Daley that he "didn't give proper weight to the defendant's witnesses."[704]

* * *

This infuriated Judge Daley, and on August 7, 1956, he denied the appeal saying that the defendant's attorney was trying to accuse the chief of police, the mayor, and the district attorney of wrongdoing. He admonished Carli and told him that he was the person on trial, not the municipal authorities."[705] The judge used the power of the gavel to pin Carli to the floor of the courtroom, and his attorney nearly tapped out.

* * *

However, the Supreme Court "Hail Mary pass" was still in play. On May 2, 1957, Carli, now 34, was preparing to appeal the Iron County Circuit Court conviction to the Wisconsin Supreme Court.[706] Carli's attorney would attack the preconditions of the bench trial. His brief argued that his client was denied his right to a speedy trial and "that there was not sufficient evidence to warrant conviction."[707]

* * *

On November 8, 1957, all seven Wisconsin Supreme Court justices presided at the appeal hearing of John S. Carli.[708] After listening to the arguments and reading the briefs, on December 3, 1957, the Wisconsin Supreme Court ruled that John Carli "must serve a year in State Prison at Waupun for biting off half the ear of John Garber, Manager of Kings Gateway Hotel at Land O'Lakes. Justice Thomas E. Fairchild argued that "the ear-biting could not have been justified as self-defense, even if the court believed Garber had struck the first blow." He said, "We are satisfied that the extent of the injury is sufficient to constitute great bodily harm and that there is ample evidence that the injury was intentionally inflicted."[709]

* * *

On December 26, 1957, John Carli, tenacious and impertinent, filed for a rehearing with the Wisconsin Supreme Court.[710] The Supreme Court was not amused, and the appeal flopped. On June 25, 1958, Iron County Sheriff Eino Nevala escorted John S. Carli to the Wisconsin State Prison at Waupun to serve his one-year sentence.[711]

Ironically, Carli was initially sentenced on June 26, 1956. If he had served his term then, he would have been out of prison a year before he actually went in. Despite the numerous articles and descriptions of this ordeal, the reason for the original altercation was never explained. It is as if the underlying cause of the fight evaporated, and the reaction became a reality.

Hurley: Cirilli Says Enough is Enough

AT THIS TIME, IT IS NECESSARY to rewind to the end of 1954, at which time moral turmoil was on the rise in Hurley. Many were outraged over the grand jury hearings, the FBI raids, the Mann Act violations, the beatings, and the severed ear. On December 24, 1954, Armand Cirilli published a column entitled "Time for Action!" He wrote, "Most Hurley people, in almost all walks of life, for one reason or another, have been willing to look the other way at some of the things that go on 'down the line' in this city. However, at least at this moment, there are quite a few citizens who are aroused over some of the things that have happened and some of the reports concerning the taverns and clubs in that area.

"The stories anent a few of the places down there are pretty sordid. They are pretty awful. Even some of our more 'broadminded' citizens, even those who are willing to accept these places and the conditions that they abet, in the 'acrimony' of our city, now are frankly shocked.

"The way things have been going these past few months, it's hard to ignore them. It's got to a point where we can no longer shrug off these conditions. The responsibility to do something about them, however, rests even heavier on our city and county officials."[712]Cirilli was spot on. 1955 had been a rough year. Unfortunately, it would take a while for the fallout to dissipate.

Hurley: The Unraveling of the Bowery

THE BEATING OF JOHN GARBER at the Bowery on December 17, 1954, triggered two events that moved along parallel tracks. The first was the prosecution of John Carli and his Uncle Alfred; the second was the revocation proceedings against the tavern license of the Bowery.

Mayor DeRubeis persevered during his term, suffering defeats and humiliation at the hands of both the city council and the keepers on Silver Street. But he never abandoned the effort, and Christmas Eve would not hinder his pursuit. Instead, he called a special meeting of the Hurley City Council for 1:30 p.m. on December 24 to urge the aldermen to revoke the license of the Bowery at 101-103 Silver Street.[713][714]

John Carli's mother, Verna Carli, held the tavern license. Her son John, 32, was the operator. The mayor directed City Attorney Alex Raineri to draft the complaint and have Police Chief Leo Negrini sign it. The language alleged that Verna Carli "does keep or maintain a riotous, indecent and improper house" and focused directly on the fight.

Verna and Arthur Carli attended the meeting to argue against revocation. The discussion turned into a melee with accusations, charges, and insults flying across the room. Subjects and objects intersected, and topics veered off course. Aldermen argued about the source of authority and the distribution of enforcement. One alderman accused the mayor of discrimination when enforcing the law. Another exclaimed that the police should be "out of politics."

Verna Carli sat quiet and reserved, watching the frenzy. After the men exhausted their virility and the mayor ended the meeting, she asked DeRubeis why the reasons for the complaint had not been discussed. The mayor, flustered from the goings-on, stammered that "they will be brought out at the hearing."[715] The relentless warrior, DeRubeis scheduled the meeting for New Year's Eve, the following Friday.[716]

* * *

On December 31, 1954, 25 people crowded the city hall to hear the discussion of the revocation of the Bowery license held by Verna Carli. The original complaint – running a disorderly, riotous, indecent, and improper house – was amended to include that John Carli "did then and there unlawfully and feloniously bite and maim the person of one John Garber." The council wrestled with John Carli's role with the Bowery, and it was eventually established that he was the tavern's manager. After a 15-minute closed session, ten aldermen returned a unanimous vote to revoke the license for the Bowery. Upon adjournment, DeRubeis ordered Police Chief Negrini and two of his officers to confiscate the license of the tavern. They drove directly to the tavern and, finding the door bolted, returned to the station empty-handed.

Robert J. Beaudry, a West Allis attorney, represented Verna Carli. As promised, right after the meeting, he filed a writ of certiorari with Judge Charles in Ashland requesting a review of the revocation procedure. The judge granted the writ and slammed on the brakes. He issued an ex-parte restraining order preventing the seizure of any licenses from Mrs. Carli.[717] Further, the order put the burden on the city to show why they should not be restrained from taking the licenses and why they should not be restrained from interfering with the "peaceful and lawful operation of the tavern, pending the hearing of the writ of certiorari." The order required the city to respond within 14 days.

The reaction was swift. Mayor DeRubeis, Police Chief Negrini, and City Attorney Alex Raineri traveled to Ashland to ask Judge Charles to reconsider the order. The Judge refused. He told the mayor that he would have to wait until the January 11 hearing. The mayor, frustrated and disappointed, told Judge Charles that "the license will be taken off the wall sooner or later."[718]

* * *

At the hearing on January 11, 1955, Judge Charles ruled in favor of the city. He said that Verna Carli's writ of certiorari had no merit, and as such, he quashed the restraining order. The judge ruled that the procedures followed by the Hurley City Council were lawful. As a backup strategy, Attorney Beaudry asked that Mrs. Carli be allowed to operate the tavern while preparing an appeal to the Supreme Court. Judge Charles swiftly denied the request.[719]

* * *

On March 18, 1955, Verna Carli's lawyer, Robert Beaudry, and City Attorney Alex Raineri asked that the Wisconsin supreme court dismiss the proceedings for revocation, pointing out that foreclosure action had begun, John Carli was leaving Hurley, and that he could not make the payments. Raineri told the mayor that the license "would revert back to the city for disposition."[720] During the third week of March, the Wisconsin Supreme Court dismissed Verna Carli's appeal to stay open. Once the order was delivered to Mrs. Carli, the police removed the Bowery's license from the wall.[721]

*   *   *

The skirmish was not over. In April 1955, the Hurley City Council denied the Bowery license to John Smith. In addition, Fred Fontecchio, Jr. asked to transfer the license for the Club Fiesta, currently held by his father, Fred Fontecchio, Sr. However, Fred Senior did not sign the application, and Police Chief Leo Negrini told the council that Fred Sr. "is not willing that the permit be transferred."[722]

*   *   *

In March, Dorothy Jean Smith, a resident of Mercer, applied for a tavern license for the Bowery. For an unknown reason, her effort was thwarted in March 1955 when her application for a tavern license was summarily "tabled for further study."[723] In June 1955, the Hurley City Council approved a transfer of the Club Fiesta license to the site of the Bowery. Fred Fontecchio sought the transfer, but Mayor DeRubeis objected because he had fought hard to rid Silver Street of the Bowery. The mayor refused to refer to the tavern as "John Carli's Bowery, so Fontecchio named it "Freddie's Bowery."[724] After a short intermission, Fontecchio turned the license back to the city.

*   *   *

Finally, in March 1956, the council granted a tavern license to Smith (Mrs. Alvin Lewis) for the Bowery at 101 Silver Street. [725] This was not without conflict as, when the mayor conceded his opposition, Supervisor Baldovin accused him of "political expediency" since an election was on the horizon in a few weeks. DeRubeis said that politics was not the question, but "money is the factor here," arguing that it better to have the building occupied. Baldovin countered by saying that the Bowery license had been rejected many times and the "reasons for the rejection still exist." The motion to grant the license passed on a 5-4 vote, and the Bowery was back in business.[726]

1955

Hurley: The Raids of 1955

AFTER A YEAR OF HORRIFIC fist fights, ear-chewing, Mann Act violations, and literary battles, Silver Street braced for the new year. The frigid winds of January slowed the traffic on Silver Street and things remained quiet through Valentine's Day, breathing hope of an early Spring in northern Wisconsin. Bartenders listened to benign complaints from barstool customers. Keepers searched for new talent to entertain the boys of summer, and Mayor DeRubeis contemplated the fall election, and state agents planned their summer vacation in Hurley.

* * *

Paul L. Arrested at Blondie's Evergreen in Lincoln County 1955

Given the previous two years, even a rusty clairvoyant could predict that 1955 would be brutal. The Iron County Sherrif initiated the first salvo on February 19, netting ten for hours violations and putting three female vagrants into the hoosegow. Later that day, using a judgment torn from a western novel, Trembath ordered three vagrants out of town by 6 P.M.[727]

* * *

The state waited for the weather to improve and launched raids on March 12, June 24, July 7, July 19, August 26, and October 22. By November, agents of the Tax Department made 71 arrests during seven raids. The state made 13 arrests for keeping prostitutes, 14 for soliciting, six as inmates, 35 for staying open after hours, two for refilling bottles, and one for gambling.[728] A few notable keepers caught for prostitution included Lois Gasbarri of Frenchy's, Joe Vita of the Hi-Ho, and James Gasbarri of Jackpot's Flame.[729]

* * *

Dorothy M. Arrested at Blondie's Evergreen in Lincoln County 1955

When the state stormed Silver Street on March 12 with 18 agents, tavern operators should have understood their resolve. Despite knowing that agents roamed the streets for several days before the raid, it was business as usual instead of vigilance. This would be a costly mistake.

Fadness drove his agents like a man possessed. By early July, weary agents drove long hours between Madison and

Hurley. Fadness didn't care. He wanted to break the "sin city of the north." His agents signed up for the effort, and he expected them to be faithful to the task. Arriving in Hurley, they organized their paperwork, pinned their badges, holstered their guns, and went to work. Fadness pushed them through the summer and into autumn. He was determined to make the case, and despite the frustrations and risk, the boys met the challenge.

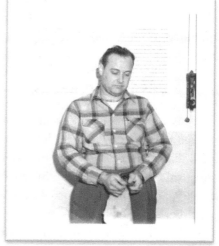

Joseph M. C. Arrested at Blondie's Evergreen in Lincoln County 1955

* * *

In December 1953, Armand Cirilli joked about Fadness setting up an office in Hurley. Now, in August 1955, after four productive raids, Cirilli wrote, "It was suggested here in a facetious vein a couple of years ago that Mr. Fadness might acquire legal settlement in Hurley, and we could run him for alderman of the first ward.[730]This is 'truer' than ever at the moment. The boys down the street are now calling him Art. Real chummy, you know."[731] Cirilli didn't know that these attitudes would pivot after the subsequent three raids.

* * *

By the end of August, state agents invaded the two lower blocks of Silver Street, and early on August 26, they arrested several tavernkeepers. As with previous campaigns, the arrests overlapped with court dates and sentences of earlier arrests. As the charges piled up, agent Fadness drafted summons and complaints to revoke the licenses of 12 tavern operators,[732] including Lois Gasbarri from the Holiday Inn, Gilbert Boatz of the Club Carnival, and Teresa Kalasardo from the Band Box.

Except for Guido Fontecchio, those arrested for hours violations pled guilty and paid fines. Fontecchio stalled, asking for a jury trial. The jury called his bluff, and the judge tossed him into the Iron County jail since he couldn't pay the fine.[733] In hindsight, this was terrible strategy.

Hurley: The Edward Kay Incident

EDWARD KAY OPERATED Kay's Sportsman's Bar in Bessemer, six miles east of Hurley in Michigan. On March 19, 1955, Kay was on a busman's holiday, drinking at the French Casino on Silver Street. There, he taunted the owner, John Rajkovich. Having exceeded the breaking point, Rajkovich pulled a knife from behind the bar and slashed at Kay. Kay recoiled from the attack, stumbled out of the tavern, and checked himself into the hospital. It took a dozen stitches to "prevent permanent injury."

At the end of April, Kay filed a $37,350 suit against Rajkovich, to which Rajkovich filed a counterclaim.[734]

Catherine W. Arrested at the French Casino in Hurley 1955

183

Although the record is void about the outcome of the suit and countersuit, Kay got clipped the following year for using Silver Street tactics at his bar in Bessemer. In June 1956, a Michigan judge fined him $300, and the Michigan Liquor Commission suspended his license for 60 days for "adulterated or misbranded liquor" and "use of labels on containers which do not represent contents." [735]

Hurley: The Sulo Hellen Scuffle

Susan G. Arrested at the French Casino in Hurley 1955

IN ANOTHER FIGHT about the same time, Richard Matrella tangled with Sulo Hellen at the Club Carnival. Hellen claimed that Matrella assaulted him and sued for $102,000. Matrella said that he hit Hellen in self-defense.[736] In early June 1955, an Iron County jury found Matrella not guilty after deliberating for four hours.[737] Hellen was furious at the loss and filed complaints against Richard Matrella, Jack Gasbarri, James Gasbarri, James Quigly, and John Kalasardo, claiming "that their places are nuisances and charging them with lewdness, assignation and prostitution." Earlier, when John Carli was under fire and threatened to request a grand jury investigation, this is the same group of tavern owners that he referred to as a "syndicate" in Hurley. These "places of nuisance" included the Miniature House, the Club Carnival, the Flame Bar, the Blackhawk Tavern, and the Band Box.[738]

In August, after appeal and new trial, the jury in the court of Judge Lewis J. Charles, found Matrella not guilty and ignored his $500 counterclaim.[739]

Town of Kimball: Arthur Brunello & Dago Valley Road

Lois G. Arrested at Frenchie's Holiday Inn in Hurley 1955

Arthur BRUNELLO, 43,[740] lived on Dago Valley Road[741] in the Town of Kimball just west of Hurley. Brunello supported his wife Tekla, his aged mother, and their 12-year-old son by working 70 hours a week as a farmhand. Living in a wooded area, Brunello had the cover he needed to have a second job: operating a 35-gallon moonshine still. He might have supplied moonshine to his brother August who operated the Bank Club. Refilling bottles provided tax-free intoxication.

Maybe agents followed the scent of fermenting yeast, although it is more likely that someone snitched under threat from the state. On May 6, 1955, Wisconsin Beverage Agents busted his operation with axes and guns. Judge Trembath released him on a $500 bond and transferred the case to the circuit court for trial.[742] In mid-May, Brunello pled guilty in front of Judge Lewis J. Charles. Brunello was devastated when Lewis sentenced him to 1–2 ½ years in state prison. However, much to Brunello's relief, Lewis stayed the sentence and placed Brunello on probation instead.[743] Judge Lewis likely considered Brunello's family situation, the absence of a record, and the harshness of the legal penalty for moonshining when he opted for probation rather than prison. It is also likely that Brunello stopped making moonshine.

Hurley: State Begins to Dismantle the "Syndicate"

I N LATE JUNE, at the request of the Wisconsin Beverage Tax Division, District Attorney George Sullivan filed complaints in Iron County Court to focus on repeat offenders and the group that John Carli referred to as the "syndicate." These included John Rajkovich's French Casino, Clement Vita's Hi-Ho Bar, Joe and Clement Vita's Riverside Bar, Clement Vita's Doll House Tavern, James Francis's Frenchy's Bar, Malt Bertolini's Flame Bar, and James Gasbarri's Blackhawk Bar.[744] Of these seven, the Vita's operated three, all located on the lower two blocks of Silver Street.

Pee Wee F. Arrested at Frenchie's Holiday Inn Hurley 1955

Hurley: Padlock Request and Closure Responses

A S A RESULT OF THE RECENT RAIDS to date, the state asked circuit court Judge to padlock several Silver Street taverns because their operations "resulted in lewdness, prostitution, and a menace to public morals." On August 17, Judge Charles closed the French Casino, the Hi-Ho, the Riverside, and the Blackhawk. Because the judge ruled that the lawyer representing three taverns was incompetent, he withheld judgment for the Doll House, Frenchy's, and the Flame.[745] Judge Charles would hear these cases in early November.

Scotty O. Arrested at the French Casino in Hurley 1955

Hurley: Follow the Money

T HE *IRON COUNTY MINER* REPORTED that 90% of the money collected in tavern-related arrests goes to the state, whereas the remaining 10% stays in the county. From

Gail D. Arrested at Frenchie's Holiday Inn in Hurley 1955

January 1954 through June 1955, these fines totaled $8,000 ($92,000 today).[746] Given the presence of state authorities in Hurley during these two years, the state probably earned its keep.

The amount of time that state agents spent in Hurley was well-known, and when Armand Cirilli learned that they made an after-hour arrest in Oneida County in September, he quipped, "We were

185

surprised to learn that the state agents were making arrests in other places. How do they find time from their duties in Hurley?"[747]

Hurley: Cirilli Weighs in Again

A rMAND CIRILLI OFFERED a slice of humor in the middle of the relentless pressure on Silver Street during 1955. He wrote, "Milwaukee must have a million cops. There's one on every corner. The nation's finest, they say. Milwaukee may have the best cops in the country – but they have the crummiest nightclubs."[748]

Langlade County: The Disturbing Case of the Gypsy Inn

D ESPITE PREVIOUS CONVICTIONS for prostitution, the town board granted June "Jerry" Netzel, 34, and Wilma "Toni" Therrien, 44, a tavern license for the Gypsy Inn south of Antigo. The women lived near Antigo for eight years and were notable for bartending in their kimonos. Their friendship, sometimes tempestuous, endured several job changes and multiple arrests.

On November 7, 1955, while working in the kitchen at the Gypsy, they argued about a man from nearby Tigerton. The situation exploded when Netzel attacked with a blackjack. Therien retaliated with a chef's knife stabbing Netzel eight times in the chest.[749] In April 1956, in Langlade County court, Therrien argued self-defense. The jury, unconvinced, returned a guilty verdict of third-degree manslaughter. Judge Andrew W. Parnell sentenced Wilma Therrien to 2–4 years at Taycheedah.[750] Netzel was buried in an unmarked grave in Antigo.

Rose M. Arrested at Jack Pot's Flame Bar in Hurley 1955

Hurley: Court Cases, Fines, and Padlocks

I T WAS A DARK NOVEMBER FOR Silver Street when Judge Charles heard 19 cases in Iron County Circuit Court. On November 3, 1955, Lewis heard charges against Silver Street taverns for prostitution, liquor, and hours violations. Judge Charles, fed up with the procession of defendants, said that anyone disagreeing with his decisions would have to appeal directly to the Supreme Court.

The *Iron County Miner* headlined, "20% of Hurley Taverns Face Closing." The article opened, "Silver Street has received one of the 'roughest' blows since the days of prohibition as the result of action in Iron County Circuit Court, which could padlock six taverns and close some

Hjalmer H. Arrested at Jack Pot's Flame Bar in Hurley 1955

186

eight others on license suspension orders." It was a mess of epic proportion for Silver Street, the intersection of the tavern operator's belligerence and state authority. Defendants considered appeals to the Wisconsin Supreme Court, ignoring lower court action.

Andrew H. Arrested at The Blackhawk Tavern Hurley 1955

Six taverns faced padlocking while eight others faced being shuttered. The fall-out was broad and severe. For example, even though the Doll House and the Riverside had already closed, the judge ordered them padlocked and suspended their licenses.

Judge Charles revoked the licenses of the Hi-Hat, the Bowery, and the Club Francis. He suspended the licenses for periods from 20 to 60 days for the French Casino, the Club Carnival, Frenchy's, the Flame, the Blackhawk, the Band Box, Connie's Drumstick and Margaret's. However, because Frenchy's ownership changed and he was no longer in business, he dismissed the padlocking charge against the tavern.

Anticipating disaster, several taverns abandoned their licenses including the Club Carnival, the Band Box, and Connie's. Others posted bonds and awaited hearings.[751] When the Riverside and the French Casino failed to post bond, the judge padlocked each for a year. Judge Charles ordered six places padlocked, and eight more faced license suspensions.

Although the judge ordered Naomi Willard's Connie's Drumstick and Margaret Prickett Margaret's Bar padlocked, both businesses closed on October 28, so padlocking was moot. On November 8, Judge Charles padlocked the Riverside Tavern and the French Casino, both for a one-year period. [752]

Connie M. Arrested at Jack Pot's Flame Bar in Hurley 1955

* * *

On November 25, Andrew Rodeghiero, the operator of Smokey's pled guilty, and Judge Trembath fined him $300 for operating a house of ill fame. Just before padlocking, John Rajkovich, the of the French Casino, changed his plea to guilty and paid $100 on an hours charge.[753]

* * *

On November 28, Andrew Holappa[754] of the Blackhawk and Hjalmer Harris[755] of the Flame offered to plead guilty rather than face trial in circuit court. Judge Trembath granted the requests and fined each $500.[756]

* * *

On December 6, Gilbert Boatz of the Club Carnival, and Teresa Kalasardo of the Band Box, who had received a 60- and 45-day suspension on an hours charge, appealed to the Wisconsin Supreme Court. They argued that agent Fadness did not have "proper authority to start the

187

suspension actions." During the appeal, the state argued the law gives "any beverage tax investigator authority to make such complaints, without specific instructions from the state tax commissioner."[757] That was definitive, and the appeal stalled.

Adele P. Arrested at Arrested at The Blackhawk Tavern Hurley 1955

* * *

During the December 13 Hurley City Council meeting, Hjalmer Harris made a simple request. He asked to transfer his license from the Flame to the Club Francis. Typically, this would not have been an issue, except that the judge had suspended Harris's license until December 27. The city chambers became an unlikely venue for a dog fight. The council was conflicted and moved the issue like a hot brick. One alderman argued that the council should deny the request. Another said that Harris "didn't know what he was doing" and that if arrested again, he would go to jail, and "the council would be guilty, too." Someone expressed concern about the liability. Another said, "He already has a license. If he wanted to break the law, he could do it in his present location." Ultimately, tradition overcame reason, and they granted the license transfer with a close vote.[758]

* * *

Despite the Supreme Court granting a temporary stay, on January 3, 1956, Teresa Kalasardo closed the Band Box for the 45-day suspension, and Gilbert Boatz closed the Club Carnival as a result of the 60-day suspension.[759]

Martha S. Arrested at Arrested at The Blackhawk Tavern Hurley 1955

* * *

1955 was tough for Silver Street. Operators hoped that the state's lust for justice was satiated, and that Madison would leave them alone. However, any optimism was foreshadowed by recent events, and tavern operators huddled at back tables, drinking coffee, and sharing stories about the 1955 raids.

1956

Madison: DeRubeis Out, Giovanoni In

IN MID-1955, MAYOR DERUBEIS got into a spat with the *Iron County Miner* over the property assessment of the Cary Mine. The Pickands, Mather Company owned the mine where DeRubeis was a mining engineer. The controversy was over assessing all property – including the Cary mine – at full market value, a practice that DeRubeis opposed. In a reckless maneuver, DeRubeis used the *Ironwood Daily Globe* to express his opinion. Armand Cirilli pounced, "Mayor DeRubeis must be made to appreciate that there is freedom of the press in this country. He can't scare us. If he is re-elected mayor, we'll support him if he is right – but we'll oppose him if he is wrong. The *Iron County Miner* wants to see the big and small get the same break. If the mayor will get out and make a good campaign and quit threatening people, stores, and institutions, he'll have a better chance of getting reelected."

Hurley voters took notice and on April 6, Sam Giovanoni, a hardware merchant on Silver Street, defeated Peter DeRubeis by a margin of 118 votes. Rather than an epic shift in policy, Giovanoni doubled down on domesticating the lower block. Upon taking office, he told the new city administration that their mission was to "run our own town" and future events would demonstrate his resolve.

Hurley: The Raids of 1956

THE PLAYERS OF SILVER STREET, hoping for a more "agreeable" new year, were surely disappointed. In 1956, authorities arrested 65 perpetrators during 15 raids from January through September. Of the 15, the state conducted four, while the Hurley police conducted 11. While technically a raid, some only netted a few violators and hardly earned the term. However, five police raids during the summer yielded 25 arrests, all for violating the closing hours law.

On the other hand, the state conducted four raids: three early in the year and one in September. During these raids, they uncovered 30 violations. In addition to 13 arrests for violating the closing hour law, police arrested two for gambling, two as inmates, seven for soliciting, and three for keeping a house of prostitution.

* * *

Despite inherent tension between state and local officials, the pattern of arrests appeared to be strategic – and perhaps cooperative –with the Hurley police citing hours violators and the state doing the heavy lifting with gambling and prostitution. In the fall, the state followed evidence protocol and provided legal prosecution. If the friction between state and local authorities had not been published, they could have been perceived as partners.

* * *

By the end of the year, some tavern operators fared worse than others. Gilbert Boatz, of the Club Carnival, suffered seven arrests for violating the closing hour law. Teresa Kalasardo of the Band Box, and Hjalmer Harris of the Club Francis, had five arrests each for hour's violations. Naomi Willard of Connie's Drumstick and Andrew Orsoni of Four-Ever Amber got clipped for

189

running gambling equipment. However, the big losers were the keepers, including James Quigley at the Miniature House, Lois Gasbarri at Frenchy's Holiday Inn, and Margaret Pickett of Margaret's. In these three taverns, agents arrested seven girls for prostitution.[760]

Town of Kimball: Idele's Hideout

ON FEBRUARY 8, 1956, in what could hardly be considered a raid, state agents visited *one* tavern and arrested Idele Bowers of Idele's Hideout, Town of Kimball, for selling beer to minors. In late February, Judge Trembath fined Bowers $250 in Iron County Court. The agents likely stopped at Idele's Hideout while in town for a court appearance. Local youth fabricated fake I.D. cards and boldly presented them at Idele's for a nickel shorty.

Hurley: The Demise of the Dancing Duo

THE DANCING COUPLE OF Carmen Rivera and Pedro Guzman performed at the Show Bar for several weeks in the summer of 1956. On the humid night – both outside and inside – of July 16, Police Chief Geach arrested the couple for "indecent and immoral conduct." While the judge fined the dancers $25 each, Jack Gasbarri, operator of the Show Bar, escaped prosecution.[761] The fact that they performed for "several weeks" *before* being arrested raised eyebrows.

Madison: No Special Drives Against Taverns

IN MARCH, A CHICAGO tavern trade publication accused Wisconsin agents of being overzealous.[762] They wrote, "Wisconsin's taverns are gradually being turned into solemn mortuaries as a result of over-zealous state and local enforcement officials who suddenly regard the suppression of all form of amusement in taverns as their most important and most urgent duty." They continued, "Tavernkeepers are resentful of a 'reform wave which is taking all of the pleasure out of public drinking places.'"

David Prichard denied the assertion, "The sentiment expressed is directly contrary to what I feel is the true sentiment of Wisconsin tavern operators. There has been no special drive made at this time against taverns by their department or by local officials."[763] In general, he was probably accurate. However, Hurley was an exception, and it would be easy to argue that a "special drive" had been underway for about 60 years.

Hurley: Distasteful and Disgraceful

THE STATE RAIDS IN JANUARY, February, and March 1956 annoyed both Mayor Giovanoni and Armand Cirilli. On May 8, Giovanoni told the city council, "We are going to see if we can't enforce the law. We don't want the state agents 'living' in our city anymore. It's our baby and we'll see if we can't do something about it." Riding on a wave of enthusiasm, one council member asked if the police could "stop the playing of jukeboxes on Sunday morning when people are going to church. At least we can observe Sunday morning in that respect." He also suggested that "certain signs and pictures on the lower block should be removed." He didn't have to say neon nudes or seductive posters: it was implied.

* * *

On May 11, Cirilli delivered an impassioned criticism of the Beverage and Cigarette Tax Division and argued that local control was preferable. He wrote, "The new administration has announced that it will enforce the tavern laws. That seems to meet with the favor of almost everyone ... even those who don't want to see a "graveyard" made of Silver Street. In fact, the state agents had pretty well already made a "graveyard" of our tavern section. The constant invasion of our city by the state agents was distasteful and disgraceful."[764]

In mid-1956, tavern merchants in Hurley were under constant surveillance because of the density of taverns and the concern of such things as tax stamps, liquor quality, and intoxication. Under perfect conditions, a tavern could be visited by an agent who could recognize an infraction. However, during this time, authorities overstepped the boundary.

Merrill: The Other Side of the Coin

On June 21, 1956, at the League of Wisconsin Municipalities conference in Merrill, Prichard responded to Cirilli's comments. He told the audience that *some municipalities* freely issue licenses to repeat offenders who "sell to minors, to intoxicated persons, and who harbor prostitutes." A curious individual asked him to identify the culprits. Prichard didn't miss a beat and answered "Joseph Vita, John Rajkovich, Lois Gasbarri, Steve Trochim, and Gilbert Boatz, all from Hurley."

Prichard was pessimistic and said that he "doubted if the 505 arrests made by his division in 1955 had 'accomplished anything of a permanent nature,'" and said, "At best, these arrests have only prevented a bad situation from getting worse."[765]

Hurley: The Chosen 54

On Saturday, June 23, 1956, the Hurley City Council granted 54 tavern licenses.[766] Regarding David Prichard's comments, Armand Cirilli quipped, "Well, genial Dave isn't going to be happy when he sees the list of those who got licenses last Saturday from the Hurley council."[767] This cadre of violators withstood the onslaught of the first half of 1956, and the city council rewarded them with fresh tavern licenses. Cirilli was right. David Prichard was not happy.

Among the chosen 54 were Joe Vita, Nora Abraham, Matthew Bertolini, August Brunello, John Kalasardo, James Lawless, Serafino Morichetti, Ambrose Orsoni, Margaret Prickett, and James B. Quigley. To add insult, the council issued bartender licenses to repeat offenders, including Adele Petri, Joseph Vita, and Ellen Vitich.[768]

Hurley: An Olive Branch Gone Bad

On September 5, D. H. Prichard felt compelled to pen a letter to Hurley stating the obvious, "Law violations by Hurley tavern operators could be improved, if not entirely eliminated, if the licensing board of the city would use the authority granted to them by law and refuse to renew the license of those operators who consistently and flagrantly violate the law."

He postured with an olive branch to nudge the council by praising city officials for making a

191

sincere effort to "eliminate the bad elements now operating taverns on Silver Street." Finally, Prichard appealed to ideals. He told them they did not have to grant renewal to anyone "not of good moral character nor a person who has habitual been a petty law offender."[769] To demonstrate the degree of failure of the suggestion, in 1957, the Hurley City Council approved six additional licenses – *two for repeat offenders.*

Hurley: Senator Estes Kefauver Doesn't Inhale

ON SEPTEMBER 25, SENATOR ESTES KEFAUVER ran for vice president on the ticket with Democrat Adlai Stevenson. Kefauver used a loudspeaker to address a crowd of 1,000 in front of the St. James Hotel in Ironwood. Kefauver traveled with an entourage of 54, along with 22 reporters. After the speech, his 15-car motorcade traveled across the Montreal River and through the valley of "girlie joints" before heading to the airport. Neither Kefauver nor the accompanying press whispered a word about the so-called horrors of Silver Street. Nothing could interfere with capturing votes.[770]

Hurley: Ten Days in October

ON OCT 16, THE HURLEY CITY COUNCIL granted a tavern license to James R. Vitich. Although council members argued that Vitich was not a Wisconsin resident, the permit was passed on a split vote. This would be the beginning of a long and tumultuous relationship.

At the same meeting, the council issued a tavern license to Anton DiGeorgio for the French Casino. Ten days later, the sheriff arrested DiGeorgio for remaining open after hours, and the judge fined him $100. It is unlikely that the fine was included in the pro forma financial statement.

Madison: Men Without Mustaches Wanted

IN MID-OCTOBER 1956, the State Bureau of Personnel posted an ad for new hires. David Prichard and Fred Mattingly searched for fresh agents, specifically men between the ages of 21 and 30. They said they would join "the closest thing the state has to the FBI – the Beverage and Cigarette Tax Division of the Tax Department." The conditions of employment differed from other businesses. They wanted men without mustaches who were not "playboys." They wanted men who were neither "too good looking," nor did they have to be "six-footers with broad shoulders."

They pointed out that the men would spend most of their time in bars, work every weekend, travel the entire state, and carry guns during 20-25 raids per year. The notice described the covert process of gathering evidence. It stated that agents must earn the trust of the bartender to avoid suspicion, as part of the job was to pour a sample of alcohol into a hidden vial. It's unclear how much evidence they could gather since their allotted expense was 35 cents a night.[771]

Armand Cirilli noticed this ad in September and wrote, "The state bureau of personnel is looking for young men who are willing to drink, dance and flirt!! Relax, though, for they're only needed as beverage and cigarette tax investigators to help tighten the enforcement of laws protecting minors. Sounds like interesting work and pay goes all the way up to $384 per month,[772]

PLUS EXPENSES! And the kicker is – you can sleep mornings! *Now, if a Hurley guy got one of those jobs, he could live at home.*[773]

Minneapolis: Hurley Workers Drunk All the Time

IN NOVEMBER, TRYGE M. AGER and Robert T. Smith, writers for the *Minneapolis Tribune*, published a three-part story much like the 1953 series in the *Milwaukee Journal*. The article waded through the old stories of *Hurley, Hayward, and Hell*, Edna Ferber's *Come and Get It*, and the gruesome tale of Lottie Morgan. The only exaggeration was when Ager and Smith took liberty with the geography stating that "Big Time gangsters, such as the Capones and John Dillinger, built palatial homes around Hurley."

The article described Police Chief Henry Geach, 43, "He doesn't carry a gun or blackjack. He carries a pair of handcuffs and a conviction that he can clean up Hurley" and "has the owners of Silvers Street's cabarets and saloons worried." Ager and Smith interviewed Mayor Giovanoni and quoted him, "If you had money to invest in a business and walked down Silver Street, you'd keep right on going. You wouldn't want to settle here, and you'd be afraid your employees would be drunk all the time."

Geach told the reporters that despite having four officers, they couldn't gather evidence of prostitution because they were too well known. Geach said, "You used to be able to charge them with vagrancy, but now the law reads that if each has a dollar in her purse, she is not a vagrant."

The writers quoted Judge Trembath, "Silver Street has never been accused of corrupting the youth of Hurley. They stay away from there. We have a rigidly enforced $250 fine for allowing minors in the taverns." They followed up with quotes from Reverend Chester L. Harries, the pastor of Hurley's First Presbyterian Church, "When I came to Hurley, everything was rough and ready. A tavern was either a place of prostitution or not. The glitter, the gay lights, the floor shows all came much later." He said that "certain mortgage interests" helped buildings remain open for their profit, and the "Silver Street situation is so inbred in the minds of many people that they are convinced the community cannot exist without the taverns."[774]

Tryge and Smith wrote about the demographics and economics of Silver Street, "Of Hurley's 3,000 residents, 1,061 are employed in mining and live like people in any small town." They said that a tavern owner told them, "If Silver Street had to depend on Hurley residents, it would close down 58 of the 60 saloons."

It was difficult to criticize the article. Usually, Cirilli, like a bulldog, would have taken on the big city newspaper, but he demurred because the writers focused on Hurley's intent to improve using lawful policing protocol.[775]

Hurley: Frenchy's Flying Gun Incident

ON NOVEMBER 29, Roger Arenson, 31, a Milwaukee roofing and siding salesman, got into a fight with a "girl employee" on the second floor of Frenchy's on Silver Street. During the argument, Arenson threw a pistol through the window, narrowly missing Camillo Bolt, a city employee, who was shoveling snow off the sidewalk. Bolt retrieved the gun from the street, and soon afterward, Sheriff Nevala retrieved the gun from Bolt. The sheriff reported that the gun was new and never fired. Meanwhile, Arenson accepted residence at the Iron County jail.[776]

The next day, Iron County Sheriff Eino Nevala released Arenson from custody, and he paid a $40 fine and headed back to Milwaukee, where life was safer. Unfortunately, the details of the second-floor squabble have been lost to history.[777]

Hurley: No Known Relatives

The last twelve months were full of controversy, angst, and hope for renewal. At the end of December, the state agents, the sheriff deputies, the police, the city council, the tavern owners, the bartenders, and the prostitutes settled into holiday peace.

Although the typical, mundane, and ordinary routine of tavern customers never made the press, this is how most of the year was spent. This silent majority wanted little more than to socialize over a drink, complain, tell stories, toss dice, and enjoy the taste of tobacco.

The *Iron County Miner* published a poignant tale in late December, "John Borini, about 68 years old, a retired woodsman, dropped dead Wednesday night while crossing the street in the 100 block of Silver Street here. He had lived in a tavern rooming house in Hurley for nine years. However, he had been a woodsman in the Hurley area since he was a youth. He was born in Russia. There are no known relatives."[778] And so, both the life of John Borini, and the events of 1956, ended with an inaudible whisper.

1957

Hurley: The Raids of 1957

IN AN UNUSUAL year for policing immoral and wicked behavior in Hurley, state agents hit Silver Street in two raids: one in March, the other in July. There were 25 arrests for all the customary crimes during the year. Hours violations topped the list with a paltry nine. Five women got arrested for prostitution, and two for being inmates. There were three gambling charges, three arrests for keeping a house of prostitution, one for obstructing the windows after hours, and two for serving minors.

The keeper arrests included a newcomer, James Vitich, of the Club Chateau, and a veteran, Lois Gasbarri of Frenchy's. However, in mid-year Fred Jenkins purchased Frenchy's and concerned about tradition, he too got arrested. The final keeper arrest went to Margaret Pricket, who at the time of the raid, was out of town. Agents eventually caught up with her along with a summons for

Eva R. W. Arrested at the Friendly Tavern Taylor County 1957

keeping a house of prostitution at Margaret's. The group that faced gambling charges included Joan Jakubiak of the Club Chateau, John Rajkovich of the French Casino, and Serafino Morichetti of Connie's Drumstick. John Kalasardo faced charges for obstruction.

* * *

On June 21, in the middle of arrest, warrants, summons, hearings, and fines, a special meeting of the Hurley City Council honored tradition and granted tavern licenses to the usual operators, including Richard Matrella, Margaret Prickett, Serafino Marchetti, and John Kalasardo.

* * *

All other arrests and citations occurred sporadically throughout the year, conducted by the Iron County Sheriff, Eino Nevala, or the Hurley Chief of Police, Henry Geach. They included Mercer and Iron Belt taverns, and James Francis was collared in the Town of Oma.[779] As the year rolled on, everybody paid fines except for three women who skipped town.[780]

* * *

On August 9, a six-person jury found John Rajkovich not guilty of dealing at a blackjack game.[781] On August 16, after deliberating for an hour, a jury of five men and one

Diane M. Arrested at the Friendly Tavern Taylor County 1957

woman returned a guilty verdict against Pat Holliday for soliciting at Margaret's Bar, which cost her $200.[782]

* * *

In the fall, the sheriff arrested Albert Koski of the Spruce Haven Bar on Highway 51 in the Town of Carey. The Hurley police arrested Annabelle Whitford of the First and Last Chance tavern at 6 Silver Street for serving minors.[783] This is noteworthy since it is the only violation against the First and Last Chance during the period covered by this writing. The name of the tavern is revealing. The building was in the flood plain and squeezed on a sliver of land between the old Milwaukee and Northern Railroad trestle on the west and the Montreal River on the east. It was, indeed, the "first and last chance" to get a drink – depending on if you were arriving at or leaving from Hurley, along Silver Street.

Jean C. Arrested at Ma Baileys Woodruff 1957

Hurley: Warrants for Revocations

IN MID-APRIL, STATE AGENT FADNESS signed revocation warrants against the Club Francis, the Club Carnival, Connie's Drumstick, and Steve Allen's Bar.[784] At the end of May 1957, Judge Charles suspended their licenses "for the remainder of the year." The license year ended on July 1, so, in effect, the taverns closed for one month. Steve Allen had enough and permanently closed the doors. In late July, Serafino Morichetti of Connie's Drumstick changed his plea to guilty and paid fines for an hours violation and gambling. Likewise, John Kalasardo changed his plea to guilty and paid fines for both an hours violation and obstruction.

Richard Matrella and Jack Gasbarri were partners in the operation of the Club Carnival. At the time of suspension, Gasbarri held the license. At the June 18 meeting, the Hurley City Council granted a tavern license to his partner, Richard Matrella. However, the permit was only good for two weeks should he decide to open. The license request was controversial, and a few aldermen argued it was illegal. Requesting a legal opinion, City Attorney James Flandrena said that "he was satisfied that a license could be legally granted."[785]

Now, Matrella and Gasbarri held the liquor license. On July 5, Hurley police arrested Richard Matrella at the Club Carnival for selling liquor after the legal closing time. The $125 fine[786] was trivial compared to the threat of closing the operation.

Betty M. Arrested at Ma Baileys Woodruff 1957

With a going concern and 30 employees, Jack Gasbarri did not want to close the Club Carnival.

196

He arrived at court with counsel who argued that agent Fadness did not have the authority to issue the warrant since the law squarely placed that authority with the director of the Wisconsin Tax Department.[787] In mid-September, Gasbarri pled guilty to the hours charge and paid a fine.[788] The Club Carnival remained open.

Langlade County: The Disturbing Case of the Gypsy Inn

In January 1957, Langlade County Sheriff John Gray told a *Capital Times* reporter, "I feel certain that prostitution is operating in at least two taverns near Antigo. But I have no evidence to back up my opinion. And it is impossible for me or my officers to get any evidence because we are too well known." Gray thought the state should investigate the situation."

David Prichard reported that in addition to Langlade County, the worst in the state include Superior and Hurley. He said the division tried to gather evidence in the county but lacked resources. Prichard said that if the local authorities couldn't get evidence because of insufficient resources, "they can harass the places in other ways. They can always bring 'vagrancy' charges and make it tough."[789]

James R. V. Arrested at the Chateau Bar Hurley 1957

Madison: Who Was Fred Zimmerman?

FRED R. ZIMMERMAN, BORN IN 1880, navigated Wisconsin state government throughout his life. He was an assemblyman in 1909, secretary of state in 1923, governor in 1927, beverage tax commissioner in 1936, and secretary of state, again in 1939. As evidenced by his history, Zimmerman was exceptionally popular with voters and made numerous friends over the years, one of them being Ma Bailey.[790]

Town of Woodruff: The Case of "Ma" Bailey

THE STORY OF MARGARET "MA" BAILEY BEGINS in 1942. In July, state agents raided a suspected disorderly house run by Margaret "Ma" Bailey, 54.[791] The agents searched all the rooms but found nothing.

* * *

On August 13, 1943, undercover agents revisited Bailey's house. This time, they collected evidence of prostitution and arrested Bailey. District Attorney Donald C. O'Melia prosecuted her In Oneida County court at Rhinelander, where Bailey pled guilty, and the judge fined her $400. The judge fined her two employees and then

Lynn J. Arrested at Frenchy's Hurley 1957

ordered them "out of the county."[792] In early 1944, agents revisited Bailey's place but came up empty-handed, but later that year, they swung back around and nabbed Bailey along with a 33-year-old employee. The judge fined Bailey $600.[793]

* * *

Five years later, on April 6, 1949, Fred Mattingly caught Ma Bailey, now 62, operating a disorderly house. The D.A. proposed a $1,000 fine, but Judge H. F. Steele reduced it to $800 with a 90-day jail term if not paid. After paying a fine, her employee returned to Milwaukee[794]

* * *

On August 1, 1951, Attorney General Vernon Thomson asked Prichard to investigate Ma Bailey "after getting a complaint from a neighbor in the area." Prichard complied, and after the raid and arrest of Bailey, now 63, things got weird.

The judge required a hefty $1,000 bail bond. Bailey didn't have the money, so L. G. Neuville, a real estate salesman from Minocqua, posted the bond for her release. Neuville then wrote a letter to Fred Zimmerman, the Secretary of State, telling him that Mrs. Bailey was seriously ill and that state agents misrepresented themselves when they raided her facility. Neuville felt an "injustice was done" and that Attorney General Vernon Thomson and the Beverage Tax Division were "just trying to get the headlines." In August, Zimmerman, now 71, asked A. G. Thomson to "close his eyes and drop the prosecution."

Louise J. Arrested at Frenchy's Hurley 1957

Zimmerman said he met with Bailey on August 16 while in Woodruff on other business. He told Thomson, "She must be 80 years old and in bad physical shape. I feel devilish sorry for her because I know she is a real old lady, and in pitiful shape." Thomson was furious. He asked, "Why should a state official take an interest in this case when there are thousands of old people in the state more meritorious of help?" Thomson was so disturbed that he sent a letter to the Oneida County District Attorney encouraging "vigorous prosecution" of the case and offered help.[795]

When Zimmerman called the Beverage and Cigarette Tax Division, Prichard told him that Bailey had three previous convictions for prostitution between 1943 and 1949, that she was actually 64 years old, and that since 1943, she had paid $1,800 in fines for running the joint. Unmoved, Zimmerman asked Prichard to forget about Bailey. Prichard, unintimidated, told Zimmerman that "his agents would not forget to appear in Rhinelander when needed in court."[796]

Things got dicier when Attorney General Thomson revealed that the wife of State Treasurer Warren Smith expressed interest in the case. When contacted, Dena Smith said she had "obtained addresses of the agents who staged the raid." She said that she got the names as a "courtesy" but that her husband had "no interest in the incident." Although this fork in the road met a dead end, it fueled the intrigue about Ma Bailey.

The news of the imbroglio reached Governor Kohler. On August 30, he said although he did not intend to investigate Zimmerman's intercession on the part of Ma Bailey, he found it "highly improper" and that "it is the business of every elected official to enforce the law."[797]

Upon learning of Zimmerman's efforts, "Silver-haired Mrs. Margaret 'Ma' Bailey shook her head over the news. She said, "I'm sorry for old Fred. I hate to see him get into trouble on my account. Fred and I have known each other for years. I saw him earlier this summer, but it wasn't in this case. I don't know anything about Fred's politics." When asked how long she knew Zimmerman, she said, "Almost as long as I've been in this country, and I came here 27 years ago."

Patricia H. Arrested at Margaret's Bar Hurley 1957

The *Rhinelander Daily News* quoted a local resident, "Ma has known a lot of big men in her time, and old Fred Zimmerman has been dropping in this town for many years." Also, "Ma has a heart of gold. There is many a man in this town she has helped financially. And there's many an old person, who has been given refuge at Ma's place. No, leave Ma Bailey alone. She's all right." The only person the reporter could find with any criticism was Bailey's neighbor, who expressed concern about land value.[798]

Bailey built a new house in 1946 on old Highway 47, two miles east of Woodruff, "secluded amidst evergreens." The *Rhinelander Daily News* wrote, "A stranger would miss the entrance unless properly informed, for the narrow driveway is unmarked. 'Ma' Bailey's house is a handsome brick-red structure."

A reporter visited the residence and wrote, "Though 'Ma' opened the door, has a brisk walk, and speaks swiftly with the sureness of a smart woman, it is easy to believe the reports of her illness that delayed her court appearance. Her skin is pasty and the lines of her face deep."

She showed the reporter the dining room and said, "My friends (the three women booked as inmates of a disorderly house), and I were

Ma Bailey's House Woodruff

merely playing cards when the agents stepped in. Then they waited two hours, but naturally, no one came to my home."

She said she hired a Madison attorney because the local attorneys would only persuade her to plead guilty, but she emphatically claimed, "I am not guilty."[799]

* * *

On September 17, 1951, Bailey's attorney, Martin Morrissey of Madison, carried a handful of newspaper clippings to Oneida County court and told Judge Boileau that he did not think Bailey could get a fair trial in the county and requested a change of venue. The judge denied the request but issued a continuance as two doctors testified to Bailey's poor health.[800]

* * *

In early October 1951, Miles McMillin, writer for Madison's *Capital Times*, took his turn with the event. He wrote, "It seems that everyone around the capital was shocked by Zim's conduct. It now appears that this was a case of somewhat delayed and decidedly misplaced shock. Mrs. Bailey, it turns out, has been operating her establishment up in Oneida county for at least ten years right under the noses of several Republican district attorneys and she has never been bothered. In that period there have been no local law enforcement officials who have called on Mrs. Bailey in an official capacity. Whatever non-professional visits were paid her by the law enforcement people came from the beverage tax division in Madison."

McMillin referred to his work colleague at the *Times* saying, "Aldric Revell, who sits to my right and slightly behind me in the office as well as in political thinking, called Dist. Atty. Forest W. Rodd in Rhinelander" and asked him several questions about Bailey. Rodd told Revell that

"She's been here around 20 years" and that he had never received any complaints about her in the three years that he had been the district attorney. Rodd said that he had heard rumors about her but that "you don't prosecute on rumors."

McMillin probably had many conversations with Cedric Revell about his adventures in northern Wisconsin as he wrote, "It is all very reminiscent of the slot machine days up north. There was a state law against slot machines then, but you couldn't hear the loons on the lakes over the jangling symphony of those one-armed bandits. For some reason, the sheriffs and district attorneys in the area couldn't hear the whirr of those wheels on which rode the prayers of the suckers. Walking into some of the local bistros, the law enforcement officers had to have the finesse

Mary Ann S. Arrested at Mary Ann's Clipper Inn Brown County in 1957

of a Harland Carl[801] to keep from bumping into slot machines, but they never saw them. They always said they heard 'rumors' that there were some in operation, but they were always across the line in some other county."[802]

* * *

On December 14, 1951, while still serving as the Secretary of State, Fred R. Zimmerman, 74, died in Milwaukee, and the Governor appointed his wife, Deana, to finish his term.

* * *

Six years later, on May 27, 1957, two state agents of the State Beverage Tax Division appeared at Baily's residence. Ma Bailey had a security system. She circulated special cards to her customers who, in turn, would share the cards with friends wanting to use her facility. The customer would present the card at Bailey's door before she allowed entry. The agents procured a couple of the special cards and now, presented them to 70-year-old Ma Bailey. She carefully inspected the cards before letting them in. After she was satisfied, two girls led the men to separate bedrooms. The agents arrested Jean Collins, 26, of Eau Claire, and Betty Morgan, 32, of Milwaukee, for prostitution. Although the women declared their occupations as a waitress and a saleslady, the sheriff booked them for solicitation for purposes of prostitution. They booked Ma Bailey as the keeper of a house of ill fame.

At court, both the district attorney and the defendant's attorney asked the judge to reduce the charge against the two young women to misdemeanors. Judge George Richards disagreed and denied the request. The judge set Bailey's bond at $1,000 and $300 for each woman.[803] Bailey would have to stand trial in the court of Circuit Judge Gerald J. Boileau. Boileau was born in Woodruff, but the court was in Wausau. In the autumn of 1957, Bailey's attorney filed an affidavit of prejudice against Boileau.

The affidavit was accepted. On December 3, 1957, the now 71-year-old "Ma" Bailey appeared before Judge Charles in circuit court in Ashland for keeping a house of prostitution. Bailey told the judge that she had lived in Woodruff for 33 years and admitted to having two previous convictions. She explained that she "had not been engaged in keeping a place of ill fame continuously" and that she had "not operated a tavern for some time."

Although the judge doubted her sincerity, he considered her age and health and her promise to close her business. He sentenced her to one year of probation and told her that if she violated the condition, she would serve a year at the woman's prison at Taycheedah. Judge Charles fined Bailey $500 and her employee Jean Collins $200. The other woman, Betty Morgan, skipped town and forfeited her bail.[804]

The case of Ma Bailey advances a successful business model not instructed at the university level. First, political contacts are critical. Second, a small staff is easier to manage. Third, operating from home reduces overhead costs. Fourth, a foolproof security system is essential. Finally, live long enough to get mercy from the court if you get nabbed. Regarding Margaret "Ma Bailey," well, she retired.

Margaret "Ma" B. Arrested at Ma Baileys Woodruff 1957

Brown County: The Case of the Clipper Inn

CONSIDERING THE MUNDANE outcome of this story, it has an excessive number of moving parts, including the Brown County Sheriff, a traffic cop, a keeper of a bawdy house, an associated prostitute, an assistant attorney general, a Brown County supervisor, the Brown County district attorney, a gaggle of judges, the Governor, an FBI agent, state beverage agents, a bevy of attorneys, and a flock of newspaper reporters.

* * *

In 1950, Mary Ann Sanderson operated a one-room brothel at her cottage at Bay Beach in the

Town of Preble near Green Bay. In June, the sheriff arrested Sanderson for being a keeper of a house of ill fame along with Winona Mae "Bobby" Murphy as a solicitor. The judge fined Murphy $100 and sent her on her way.[805] While there is no record of any penalty to Sanderson, there is solid evidence that she continued with her occupation.

* * *

In August 1956, Sanderson, now 47, opened the Clipper Inn on the south side of Green Bay in the Town of Bellevue. The Clipper Inn was a small facility consisting of a barroom and bedroom and, consistent with her business model, she only had one employee.

* * *

From 1952–1956, Artley M. Skenandore was the constable for the Town of Hobart, and the chief of the Brown County civil defense auxiliary police. In the early spring of 1957, Skenandore befriended Mary Ann Sanderson and frequented The Clipper Inn. He told Sanderson that he was going to run for sheriff in the fall. Sanderson, eager to have an ally in law enforcement, gave Skenandore campaign donations along with gifts, liquor, and the "use of her employee." Sanderson thought that, in return, she was protected from prosecution but in mid-March 1957, three state agents raided the Clipper Inn. They arrested Sanderson as proprietor and Ann Baird, 28, for prostitution.[806]

In June, Municipal Judge Donald W. Gleason fined each woman $650. After the raid, Sanderson decided to quit the business. She listed the building for sale and relinquished the tavern license.[807]

In November 1957, Skenandore was elected as Sheriff of Brown County.[808]

Meanwhile, Sanderson steamed about losing her business and struck back at what she perceived as an injustice. In February 1958, she filed a sworn affidavit saying that she expected protection from Skenandore in return for the gifts, which she carefully itemized. She claimed that Skenandore knew about the March raid but didn't tell her.

Sanderson's affidavit swept through the Brown County Board and Francis Leanna, chairman of the Town of Scott and a member of the Brown County Board of Supervisors, asked the governor to remove Skenandore from office. That is when a bunch of attorneys, judges, the A.G., the D.A., the FBI, and the Governor came into the picture. After a long and arduous investigation, the Governor first chided, then exonerated Skenandore. The reporters mopped up the rest of the story.[809] The May 19, 1958, *Capital Times* published a nearly full-page article describing the investigation of Skenandore. Despite the potential of a sordid crime story, the article reads as boring as dry toast.

1958

Hurley: Cirilli Resigns from the *Iron County Miner*

ON JANUARY 1, 1958, ARMAND CIRILLI resigned as the editor of the *Iron County Miner*. Cirilli took the position of Iron County welfare director after Nancy Caruso resigned from the position.[810] Although he left as editor, he continued to write his column "About People and Things." Cirilli would continue to contribute to the *Miner* over the next several years.

Hurley: The Raids of 1958

THE IRON COUNTY SHERIFF and Hurley police arrested five tavern owners in 1958 for violating closing hours, including Richard Matrella of the Club Carnival and Andrew Orsoni of the Four-Ever Amber. As a warm-up for hunting season, on November 7, agents pinched James Quigley of the Miniature House as a keeper and two women for soliciting.

* * *

From the inception of time, veteran agents told fresh recruits, "You can't call yourself a Beverage Tax Agent unless you worked Hurley during deer season." New agents were eager to endure this rite of passage, thereby earning the privilege of passing the adage on to their disciples. The annual prostitute hunt occurred on the weekends of November 11 and November 22. During these two raids, they arrested seven saloon operators for keeping houses of ill fame. Agatino DiGiorgio of the Ritz got nicked twice. Five other regulars got nabbed as keepers, including Richard Matrella of the Club Carnival, Margaret Pricket of Margaret's, Adele Petri of the Show Bar and Club 26, James Quigley of the Blackhawk, and William Soucie of Kay's. Employees were not exempt; agents arrested ten women for soliciting and five as inmates. Most offenders pled guilty and paid fines.[811]

Hurley: Lois Gasbarri Gets Lucky

IN JUNE 1958, A MILWAUKEE judge placed Lois Gasbarri, the operator of Frenchy's, on probation for five years for a case that had been pending in circuit court for more than a year. She had pled guilty to being the keeper of a house of prostitution in Iron County Court. The Milwaukee judge initially sentenced her to two years at the Wisconsin State Prison for women at Necedah but stayed the sentence in favor of probation. However, he stipulated that if she were "convicted of violating any state laws or engages in the operation of a house of prostitution during the next five years," she would have to serve the sentence.[812]

Hatley: Agent Fadness Dies

IN SEPTEMBER 1958, ARTHUR FADNESS, 61, a 25-year veteran of the State Beverage Tax Division, who had led state raids against Hurley for many years, died of a heart attack while conducting a raid against St. Florian's Catholic church picnic at Hatley, Wisconsin.[813] Fadness was dedicated and efficient, and played a significant role in the story of Hurley from 1942 until his death.

Hurley: An Alcohol-Related Interstate Crime

JOHN SHELKY, 18, AND JAMES WALLIS, 30, drank their way along Silver Street until early in the morning on October 20, 1958. After the taverns closed, the team went on an alcohol-related window-breaking spree. They methodically smashed the front windows of the taverns where they had been drinking, including the Flame, the Hi-Ho, the Speedway, and the Club Carnival. Neither yet satisfied nor sober, they busted the windows of the Erspamer Lumber Company, Valsuano's store in Gile, the WJMS transmitting site in the Town of Carey, Giovanoni's hardware store, the National Tea store in Ironwood, Marco Gotta's bar in Gile, and Louis Gasbarri's vehicle, parked on Silver Street.

After police arrested Shelky, he told them he and his friend had been drinking at Tony's Flame bar, the Hi-Ho, the Speedway, and the Club Carnival. The police promptly arrested these tavern owners for serving a minor. On October 21, the owners pled not guilty to the charge.[814]

Having been on the lam for several days, Wallis finally turned himself in as Shelky's accomplice. In court on October 28, Judge Trembath ordered Wallis to pay for the damage and Shelky to "pay a portion of the cost if he obtains work." Trembath placed both men on probation, and Shelky looked for a job.[815]

1959

Hurley: The Never Ending Case of John Carli

ON JUNE 25, 1958, JOHN S. CARLI entered the Wisconsin State Prison at Waupun to serve a one-year sentence. Carli's attorney petitioned Governor Thomson for clemency. After a hearing, the governor's pardon lawyer recommended commutation.

* * *

In the first week of January 1959, Wisconsin Governor Vernon W. Thomson commuted Carli's sentence.[816] Despite being sentenced to "not less than one year in state prison, Carli was out after six months. Carli was tough, tempestuous, and now hostile after spending time in prison. He sought retribution for the perceived wrongs levied against him in Hurley

* * *

On April 3, Carli appealed to the city council for damages when police arrested him at Finnegan's Rainbow Bar on Silver Street in 1958. He alleged that police officers John Geach and Ted Erspamer assaulted him "without any cause or reason whatsoever…with such force and violence causing him to be thrown against a stove, table and chairs and other objects in an about the place." He said the cops beat him "with their hands, fists, knees and 'billy clubs.'" Carli said the injuries "required medical and hospital care and that he suffered a loss of wages."[817] Covering all the bases, Carli also claimed that officers violated his civil rights.

After reviewing the allegations, Hurley City Attorney James Flandrena recommended dismissal, and the council so voted.[818]

* * *

In May, Carli filed a civil action in federal court, and a U.S. marshal served a summons to Matt Connors, Hurley City Clerk, and Chief of Police Henry Geach.[819] In June, Hurley hired a law firm from Merrill to help Flandrena defend the city.[820]

* * *

On August 11, 1959, Federal Judge Patrick T. Stone heard the case in Wausau. Stone, indifferent yet earnest, dismissed the suit, denying federal jurisdiction and "failure to state a claim upon which relief could be granted in federal court."[821]

* * *

Carli was resolute and combustible, and his pitbull reputation preceded him. In early September 1959, he filed a $50,000 suit for the same offense in Iron County Circuit Court sans the civil rights charge. This time, the Iron County sheriff served summons to Connors and Geach.

* * *

The judge scheduled the case for June 27, 1960. Carli's attorney requested a postponement because his client, now living in Zephyr Cove, Nevada, was "physically unable to come to Hurley for the trial." In response, the city's attorney and the police arranged for a physician to examine Carli in Reno. After the examination, the doctor told the judge that Carli was able to attend the trial in Hurley.[822] As such, the judge denied the motion for a medical stay, and on June 27, 1960, when Carli failed to show up on the first day of the trial, his attorney moved for voluntary dismissal of the suit. Judge Charles, in Iron County Circuit Court, granted the motion and "allowed the city $50 for attorney fees and also fees for two witnesses."[823]

* * *

At 2 a.m. on September 2, 1960, John Carli visited the Hurley police department. When he refused to leave, Chief Geach "took him by the arm and 'escorted' him out of the room." Carli claimed that Geach "without warning, grabbed him and shoved him out of the room." Witnesses disagreed on a common explanation; some agreed with Geach, some with Carli. Carli complained to the city, and each, through their attorneys, filed briefs.

* * *

On September 15, the Hurley Police Commission conducted a hearing.[824] On November 8, they dismissed Carli's allegations saying that there was "no justification" in the complaint and that "police officers have the right to ask or, if necessary, to force anyone to leave the police station who is not there for the conduct of official business."[825]

* * *

In late October, John "Butch" Carli applied for a liquor license in Hurley despite declaring his home as being Lake Tahoe, Nevada. Despite all the trouble, angst, and rancor caused by Carli, on November 9, 1960, by a vote of 6-5, the Hurley City Council granted him a Class B Combination Liquor License for the Ritz at 17 Silver Street.[826] If the Hurley City Council lacked any quality, it was not consistency. In fact, the council granted the same license for Carli in 1961.[827] However, something happened between 1961 and 1962 that changed the perspective of the city council as on July 20, 1962, the Hurley City Council voted 10–1 to *reject* the application of a Class B combination liquor license for John Carli for 17 Silver Street.[828] Although it was a solid rejection, there was nothing in the record that would offer an explanation. This was the last entry in the record for John S. "Butch" Carli. It is likely that he spent the rest of his life in Arizona, which is the site of his burial in 2001.

Hurley: The Raids of 1959

THERE WERE MINOR infractions for operating after-hours from January through July. However, the rest of the year was not as smooth as, during that period, the state racked up seven arrests: four for keeping houses of ill fame.

* * *

On November 19, state agents arrested two girls for soliciting at the Brass Rail at 108 Silver Street. On November 23, they nabbed Agnes Perlberg of Aggies, and Agatino DiGiorgio, of the Ritz Bar, both for keeping houses of prostitution. The four prostitutes at Aggies and two at the Brass Rail, pled guilty and paid fines.[829]

* * *

At the end of November, state agents arrested Agatino DiGiorgio of Blondie's Ritz Bar and James Quigley of the Hi-Hat as keepers. They also cited three tavern owners for remaining open after hours, including John Kalasardo of the Band Box, Richard Matrella of the Club Carnival, and Adele Petri of the Show. All pled guilty; all paid fines.[830]

Hurley: They Stole the Wrong Car

IN EARLY JULY 1959, two Ironwood teens, 15 and 16, appeared in Iron County Juvenile Court for stealing a car from Iron Street in Hurley. They abandoned the vehicle at Antigo and hitched a ride to Springfield, Illinois. That was the end of their adventure as Springfield cops rounded them up. After an overnight in the hoosegow, Hurley police carted them home. Judge Trembath wanted to hear the case but had to recuse himself. He was, nonetheless, happy to get his car back.[831]

Peoria: The Sad Case of Christina Jester

CRISTINA JEAN JESTER was born on January 16, 1937, in Tower Hill, Illinois, a small village 50 miles southeast of Springfield. Her parents divorced when she was seven, and her mother remarried in 1954. Her stepfather described her as troubled, and the impetuous 15-year-old married, gave birth to three daughters, then divorced. Jester suffered through two more marriages, both ending in divorce

In July 1959, now 22, Cristina – also known as Marcia Antrim Jester, Marcia Jean Jester, and Christina Antrim – performed in Hurley as a dancer. There, she met Floyd Calligaro, 44, who operated Medo's Speedway at 115 Silver Street. Infatuated with the young woman, Calligaro proposed marriage in July 1959.[832] They moved to Milwaukee, but after four months, the relationship cooled, and Calligaro returned to Ironwood. Jester, now Marcia Calligaro, looked for work in Peoria.

On Friday, December 18, 1959, she entertained at a "striptease emporium" called the Combo Club. After her set, she argued with her boss, and he fired her. The next day, she called Floyd and begged him to get her out of Peoria. Despite her dispute with her boss, she returned to the Combo Club, and he let her perform. Afterward, she flirted with an ex-con named Elmer "Bucky" Smith, 27. They went to the Slipper Club and talked until 4:30 a.m. at which time Smith left.[833] Calligaro turned her attention to another customer described by a waitress as a "red-faced, middle-aged man" named Benson. Shortly thereafter, they left the Slipper Club. [834]

Within 90 minutes, someone fired three .38 caliber bullets into her chest at point-blank range.[835] The next day, a driver noticed her body on a rural road a few miles north of Peoria. She was still dressed in her dancing outfit.[836]

Authorities cleared Floyd Calligaro using a lie detector on Monday, December 21, in Springfield. On January 20, 1960, Woodford County held a coroner's jury and finding nothing, and the case went cold.[837]

1960

Hurley: The Winding Down of An Era

RICHARD C. TREMBATH, 64, WAS ELECTED as Iron County Judge in 1938. After serving for 22 years, he retired on January 31, 1960.

Trembath was born in Iron County. After graduating from Hurley high school, he taught in Kimball township for four years. Then he served four terms as the Iron County register of deeds, and in 1924, he was elected to represent Iron and Vilas counties for two terms as a member of the Wisconsin legislature. During this period, he earned a law degree from the University of Wisconsin, graduating in 1927. He returned to Hurley in 1930 and opened a law practice. Shortly after, he was elected as district attorney. After serving two terms, he resumed his law practice until 1938, when he was elected to the bench. Trembath served the public for 41 years,

His public service was admirable, his willingness to serve Iron County was praiseworthy, but his fortitude for enduring Silver Street was commendable.

Governor Gaylord Nelson appointed Iron County District Attorney George D. Sullivan, as his replacement.[838]

* * *

Thousands of stories were lost on March 17, 1964, when Richard C. Trembath, 69, died at the Grand View Hospital and was buried in the Hurley cemetery.

Hurley: The Raids of 1960

THE PATTERN OF ENFORCEMENT on Silver Street changed in 1960, with agents focusing on different taverns at different times. The state concentrated on serious violations while the sheriff covered underage drinking and hour's violations. The state effort began in April and ended in November. While it is difficult to speculate about the pattern, it appeared as cooperative strategy.

Agents of the Tax Department arrested 30 individuals during the year for keeping prostitutes, soliciting, housing inmates, and refilling liquor bottles. Agents charged five as keepers, including Agnes Perlberg of Aggies and Anton Lysczyk[839] of Kay's. The city council issued Ann Montonati a liquor license for the Hi-Ho in June,[840] and by November, agents charged her for keeping a house of prostitution.

In a rare case, agents arrested Agnes Perlberg in both July and August, for having a house of ill fame and for refilling liquor bottles.[841] Judge Sullivan fined her $150 for the refilling charge, and each of the two prostitutes, paid $125 for soliciting.[842] In September, Perlberg waived a preliminary hearing on the keeper charge and waited for trial in circuit court. One month later, she surrendered her liquor license to the city clerk without explanation[843] and paid two $500 fines for the two charges of keeping a house of prostitution.[844]

Ann Montonati pled guilty to keeping a house of prostitution in December. Judge George D. Sullivan fined her $500. After sentencing her to one year at the Wisconsin Industrial School for Women at Taycheedah, he stayed the sentence and put her on probation instead.[845]

Of the five charged with keeping houses of prostitution, the state focused on the team of Anton Lysczyk and Kay Martin, the operators of Kay's Bar. The charge against Lysczyk case went to court, and in October 1961, Lysczyk pled guilty in Iron County Court and paid a $500 fine.[846]

1961

Hurley: The Raids of 1961

IT WAS A PECULIAR YEAR with hit-or-miss attention from state agents, a few arrests for hours violations, the arrest of a keeper and a prostitute, and a guilty plea. In mid-March, agents arrested the notorious "gang of all-nighters," including Naomi Morichetti of Connie's, John Giovanoni of the Fiesta, Richard Matrella of the Club Carnival, Adele Petri of the Show Bar, Rudolph Santini of Rudy's, and Albert Allen of Allen's.[847] Over the next several weeks, each pled guilty and paid a fine.

* * *

State agents raided the TryAngle Inn at 116 Silver Street on August 12. They arrested James C. Shields, the operator, and Carol Pelletti, an inmate of a house of prostitution. The next day, Pelletti paid a $50 fine.[848]

* * *

On September 3, state agents hit the lower block arresting Theresa Kalasardo of the Band Box, Adele Petri of the Show Bar, and Jack Gasbarri of the Club Carnival. The trio visited Judge George Sullivan in Iron County Court, paid fines, then went back to work.

Hurley: Alex Raineri Announces Candidacy for County Judge

IN EARLY FEBRUARY, Iron County District Attorney, Alex Raineri, 42, announced his candidacy for Iron County judge, a position currently held by George Sullivan. By this time, Raineri had served four years in the Wisconsin Assembly and two years as district attorney for Iron County.[849]

Hurley: Raineri Campaigns at the Expense of Joan and the Dutchess

ON FEBRUARY 18, 1961, Judge Charles suspended the licenses for Joan Jakubiak of Joan's Bar for 90 days and Nora Davis of the Dutchess for 30 days for keeping houses of ill fame.

District Attorney Alex Raineri was now on the campaign trail and pontification was in order. He condemned the actions of Silver Street taverns saying, "It has come to my attention that there are other taverns in Hurley that are operating in a manner equally as bad or even worse than this. Also, in the past, by some unwritten rule, Silver Street was out of bounds for the Sheriff's Department, but that is no longer the rule, and the sheriff is going to visit Silver Street as soon as it comes to our attention that any of these taverns are violating the law."

Raineri continued, "We are going to make a thorough check of all places reportedly operating indecent or disorderly houses. The city administration has been advised of the intentions of this office and has agreed to give its full cooperation."[850] Over the next 20 years, this pledge would unravel and lead to Raineri's undoing.

Hurley: A Campaign Bid for Moral Integrity

I N MID-MARCH, a few weeks before the election, District Attorney Alex Raineri continued to assert his moral integrity. Because of recent state raids, he told tavern owners to close on time and he warned that the Hurley police would enforce the law.

Every tavern owner complied except for Richard Matrella, the operator of the Club Carnival, who was promptly arrested. This was the perfect foil for Raineri's campaign. Leaning on the virtue of equity, Raineri carefully framed his comment and said, "I cannot, in all fairness to the tavern operators in the city, permit one bar to remain open and order the rest to close."[851] After paying the fine, Matrella stayed open after hours to recover the cost.

Hurley: Sullivan Routs Raineri

D ESPITE A CAMPAIGN to eliminate underage drinking and closing hours, on Tuesday, April 4, 1961, Alex Raineri lost by a landslide to incumbent Judge George Sullivan of Gile, 2,542 to 881. Sullivan had served as county judge since February 1, 1960, succeeding Trembath and appointed by the Governor. This victory assured Sullivan six more years on the bench and prohibited Raineri's advancement.[852] Exact reasons for the loss are unknown but one of them could have been Raineri's association with Silver Street innkeepers and, perhaps, a general lack of trust.

Hurley: The Band Box Gets Buttoned Up

I N LATE-MAY 1961, STATE AND INTERNAL REVENUE agents arrested John Kalasardo of the Band Box, for tax delinquency. Kalasardo owed $44,000 in back taxes based upon the 20 percent entertainment tax law. The FBI sealed the cash register in late May and tagged the personal property. The next day, they removed the beer and liquor, the bar, bar stools, and other fixtures. Then they padlocked the tavern and turned the liquor license over to the city clerk.[853]

One month later, the Hurley city council granted a liquor license for the Band Box to Theresa Kalasardo – and that is how the game was played.[854]

Hurley: The Violent Case of Sylvia Cole

I N 1960, POLICE IN Brooklyn, New York, issued a detainer warrant against Lillian Loretta Barber, 23, for robbery, grand theft, and assault. Later that year, Barber changed her name to Sylvia Cole and evaded authorities by traveling from New York to Milwaukee, then to Hurley.

In 1961, she worked as a barmaid at the Hi-Hat Tavern on Silver Street, operated by Thomas Chiolino. Cole had been dating a local resident, Ronald L. Lundgren, for a month. On the evening of Saturday, June 11, she spent time with Lundgren in her apartment. Then, promising to return, Lundgren left to watch a boxing match on TV at his mother's house, where he lived. When he didn't return, Cole imagined that he was with another woman. Angry and tempestuous, she roamed Silver Street looking for him while drinking along the way. Eventually, she hired a taxi and ordered the driver to the Hi-Hat. She retrieved a .38 caliber revolver from behind the bar, returned to the taxi, and directed the driver to Lundgren's home, telling him to wait. At 5 a.m. Lundgren's mother answered the door and told Cole that he was upstairs asleep. Cole pushed her aside, ascended the staircase, and fired a bullet through Lundgren's heart while he slept. Mrs. Lundgren and her daughter followed close behind. As they wrestled with Cole, she fired two more rounds, both going astray.

After subduing Cole, Mrs. Lundgren ran to the street and told the taxi driver what happened. The driver came upon Officer Albert Stella on Silver Street. When Stella arrived at the home, he found Cole lying over Lundgren's body, surrounded by a pool of blood.

District Attorney Alex Raineri prosecuted Sylvia Cole before Judge Charles in Ashland at the end of June. She was charged with first-degree murder and refusing an attorney, she pled not guilty. The judge ordered her held without bond.

* * *

In mid-September, Cole revealed her real name as Lillian Loretta Barber, and that she was married to a man named Bowen and had three young boys who lived with his mother in North Carolina. At a September 14 preliminary hearing, over the defense attorney's objection, Police Chief Henry Geach read a nine-page confession statement, signed by Barber, into the record. At this point, she accepted counsel.

* * *

Judge Charles presided over the trial, which began on October 30 in Iron County Circuit Court. In his summary argument, District Attorney Raineri read the confession statement into the record. Despite the defense attorney's objection, Judge Charles allowed the statement to be entered as evidence.

Mrs. Lundgren testified that she wrestled the gun from Barber with the help of her daughter. Officer Stella said that when he arrived at the scene, Barber was lying across Lundgren's body and crying, said, "I didn't mean to do it." [855]

Although Raineri had asked for a life sentence for first-degree murder, the jury of 11 men and one woman returned a guilty verdict of second-degree murder after deliberating for an hour. On November 3, the Iron County Sheriff transported Lillian Loretta Barber to the Wisconsin Home for Woman State Prison at Taycheedah to begin serving 5–25 years for the murder of Ronald Lundgren. [856]

* * *

On May 26, 1962, Barber and a companion, Alice Grignon, escaped from Taycheedah. [857] Authorities apprehended them the next day and escorted them back to prison. A judge added two years to Barber's sentence. On August 2, 1962, the parole board denied her request for parole. However, at that time, a member of the parole board told Raineri about the New York warrant for Barber. In late January 1966, Barber waived extradition, and authorities transported her to New York for prosecution. [858]

After that date, the world was a safer place, as Lillian Loretta Barber faded from the record.

Wilder, Kentucky: The Two Sides of "Big Jim" Harris

THE CITY OF WILDER is located in northern Kentucky, just south and across the Ohio River from Cincinnati. Wilder is a spit of land five miles long and a mile wide and is intersected, north to south, by Licking Pike. During the 1940s and 1950s, Wilder was a caldron for vice and home to infamous dens, including Club 19, the Hi-De-Ho, Club Manana, and the Latin Quarter.

* * *

In 1940, James E. Harris, 27, began working for the city of Wilder. For 15 years, Harris held two jobs in the small town. During the day, he served as marshal. At night, he operated a tavern replete with gambling and prostitution. It was a scheme that the Mafia would have envied. Harris protected his own business using his municipal paycheck, persecuted the competition using his police authority, and siphoned cash from a bevy of his prostitutes.

Harris worked with a trusted crew, including a cousin, Dwight Penick, and a friend, Raymond Haggard. Penick, a motorcycle club member, was the muscle, and Haggard had the business sense to run the operation. The crew operated the 19 Club on Licking Pike, a three-story house, with a tavern and restaurant downstairs, and apartments upstairs. The apartments provided housing for prostitutes.

Sometimes Harris did simultaneous duty. For example, in mid-October 1948, Miles "Jock" Austin, 33, got shot in the ankle while dealing dice at Club 19, and Harris brought Austin to the hospital. The press, eager to learn the details and location of the shooting, tried to contact Harris but they couldn't find him. They called his house, and his wife said he wasn't home.[859] The next day, now reporting as Marshal Harris, said that Austin received the wound when the gun accidentally discharged when he was selling it.[860]

* * *

Another example occurred the following year. In November 1949, George Hoer fired four shots at his former girlfriend, who lived on the third floor of Club 19. Wilder arrested the man and carted him off to jail.[861] Police held Hoer on a $10,000 bond, but unable to pay, he remained in jail. During the arraignment, Hoer asked to be released to try to seek warrants against the Club 19, claiming they ran a "bust-out gambling operation and a disorderly house." Hoer didn't get out, and the county attorney let the allegation slip.[862]

* * *

And so it went until the autumn of 1949 when a combination of events threatened the marshal's hustle. Olly Tryling ran a gypsy cab, and other drivers funneled select customers to him if they wanted a "specific type" of entertainment. Tryling would deliver the customer to Club 19 and then collect 40% of the money that the dealers could steal.

At the end of November 1949, Tryling drove Paul Smithson to Club 19 in Wilder. He sensed the young man's enthusiasm and looked forward to a payoff. Tryling didn't know that Smithson had just robbed the bank where he worked and had $7,000 in his pocket. Smithson thought he would make a tidy profit playing cards and refill the till before anyone noticed. This would prove to be a fool's errand as the dealer took $4,000 of the hot money. When the bookkeeping was done, Raymond Haggard, the moneyman for Club 19, paid the taxi driver his $1,640 cut.[863]

After a reporter learned that Marshal Harris held the deed for Club 19, all hell broke loose. Harris's nemesis, Campbell County Attorney Wesley Bowen, sunk his teeth into Harris's operation. In May 1950, Bowen prepared warrants against the operator and employees. The charges included handling and confederating to commit a felony, gambling, and prostitution. Bowen wanted to padlock the front door.[864]

"Big Jim" Harris was arrested in early June 1950 and charged with pandering, operating a disorderly house, gambling, and confederating to commit a felony. The case dragged on while Harris conducted his daily business of arresting crooks and giving speeding tickets. In late July, a Campbell County Grand Jury indicted Harris on 11 counts of pandering, conspiracy, and gaming.

A jury convicted Harris of operating a disorderly house, and the judge sentenced him to one year in prison. However, Harris appealed and was acquitted because the bank cashier refused to testify "after having been brought into the court on three different occasions from the federal prison."[865]

* * *

This catch-and-release game continued for several years, and when Club 19 closed, Harris reopened it as the Hi-De-Ho with his accomplices. In the early-1950s, at the same time that Marshal Harris raided his competitors such as the Club Manana and the Latin Quarter, gangster Harris raked in $700 a night from the prostitutes at the Hi-Dee-Ho.

* * *

The "real" law caught up with Marshal James Harris in February 1956. Authorities escorted the "vice-lord of Wilder" to LaGrange reformatory, a medium-level prison, to serve a three-year term.[866] Harris was a model prisoner, and in mid-May 1958, he was released and placed on parole.[867] Despite this unpleasant experience, Harris remained on the seedy side of the street. He managed the Bongo Club and its successor, the Stardust Club, located in Monmouth, Kentucky until state beverage agents busted the Stardust in early 1959.[868]

* * *

When the Stardust closed, Harris moved to Hurley. Harris probably met Richard Matrella via the exotic dancing circuit. It also could have been that he knew Hurley would provide work and a haven from hostile authorities. It is likely that Harris worked for Richard Matrella at the Club Carnival based on arrest records and Matrella's work in Newport, Kentucky.

* * *

In August 1961, Campbell County, Kentucky, empaneled a grand jury to investigate evidence of gambling and prostitution. The incident that motivated the grand jury was a charge by Hattie Jackson, a prostitute who claimed that two high-ranking state officials received payoffs from prostitution. James Harris traveled from Hurley and testified that he made payoffs to "several officials in the Newport area several years ago" and that "It involved many thousands of dollars over a period of years." Harris said, "They (the syndicate) would rather have Newport going than Las Vegas – that's how big this thing is." Harris noted that Newport is the center of the largest gambling layoff betting[869] in the country, and 'over the (dice) tables you can bet more than twice what you can in Vegas.'" At the time of his testimony, Harris had already been living in Hurley, where he helped operate two nightclubs. The grand jury eventually returned 59 indictments, mostly for gambling.[870]

In mid-November 1961, another grand jury was called in Campbell County, Kentucky. Seven Newport ministers initiated the jury with "misfeasance and nonfeasance" complaints against the state's attorney general, William Wise. The grand jury wanted to hear from James Harris and summoned him to appear. A warrant was issued for his arrest when Harris didn't show up.[871]

On November 19, 1961, Iron County Sheriff Jerry Thomas arrested Harris on a contempt warrant. The warrant charged that Harris failed to appear before a grand jury in Newport on

November 17. He faced the Iron County Judge, who released him on a $500 bond. At that time, the judge noted that although Harris had been in Wisconsin for about three years, he had no arrest record.[872]

On November 24, 1961, Harris told Iron County Judge George Sullivan that he tried to get to Kentucky to testify in front of the grand jury, but a snowstorm prevented air travel. He also told the judge that later, he talked to a Campbell County prosecutor who said he did not have to appear. Judge Sullivan had initially declared Harris "technically guilty" of contempt and fined him $25. However, after learning that the Campbell County authorities never notified Hurley that the grand jury had dissolved, he suspended the sentence.[873]

Jim Linduff has another take on the events in Wilder in his book *When Vice Was King: A History of Northern Kentucky Gambling, 1920-1970*,[874] Linduff writes, "The Hi-De-Ho in Wilder was purchased by "Big Jim" Harris in 1940. Gambling and prostitution were the club's standard fares. Harris, who had previously opened the Stark Club in Newport, determined that his joint in Wilder was easier to operate and that local officials were more tolerant primarily because he was at the time the marshal of Wilder! The place became notorious as a bust-out gambling operation, and the whore's rooms were wired so customers could be blackmailed with photos and audiotapes.

In 1950, the joint was renamed the 19 Club in a failed attempt to disguise the operation. The Cleveland Syndicate, concerned by the loss of gambling business at the Latin Quarter nearby, and worried that a blackmail scheme would cast a bad light on their clubs, convinced the Kentucky State Police to raid the Hi-De-Ho in 1951, effectively shutting down the club. After a long trial, Harris was sentenced to three years of jail time in 1955. Harris would return to run several strip clubs later, but it was a great example of Northern Kentucky justice that he continued to be the Marshall throughout his early brushes with the law."

* * *

Hurley would have provided a haven for Jim Harris if he had paid his taxes. Given his history, however, the federal government looked over his shoulder. By 1964, Harris moved back to Kentucky, and in early July, authorities arrested him in his old stomping ground, Campbell County. He agreed to return to Wisconsin to face three counts of failure to file income tax returns from 1959-1961 while operating Hurley taverns. To his disadvantage, he faced U.S. Attorney Edmund A. Nix in Eau Claire.[875] Nix, an aggressive prosecutor, summoned Harris to face a federal judge in Eau Claire on August 26, 1964. The judge fined Harris $150 on two counts, put him on probation for the third, and ordered him to pay taxes and penalties.[876] Harris complied.

* * *

In July 1972, local police and the Campbell County deputy sheriff raided several taverns in Newport Kentucky. They arrested Charles E. Tuttle of the Cherry Pit, James E. Harris, operator of the Jai Alai Club, Wilfred M. Rodgers of the Body Shop, Gallie Eisner of the Pink Pussycat, Vance Raleigh of the Brass Mule, and Richard Matrella, operator of the Galaxy Club. All faced fines of $100 for obstructing their windows. This was an expensive raid for a minor offense and the mayor offered an obligatory promise saying that "Gambling and other forms of vice in Newport will be eliminated."[877] The notable point, of course, is that Richard Matrella now operated a tavern in Kentucky along with his colleague, James Harris. Harris continued to operate the Jai Alai nightclub through 1980.[878]

1962

Hurley: Margaret Pricket's Story

O N NOVEMBER 14, 1958, Margaret Pricket, the proprietor of Margaret's Bar at 18 Silver Street, was arrested for keeping a house of ill fame.

* * *

On August 10, 1959, based on a technicality – a late and incomplete transcript – a judge dismissed the charge. State agents were miffed and a few hours later, they rearrested her for the same November offense. This time, there would be no technicalities.[879] On November 1, 1960, the state amended the charge to disorderly conduct. After the hearing in Iron County Circuit Court, she paid a $100 fine.[880]

* * *

On March 2, 1962, while Pricket enjoyed the warmth of Florida, her tavern at 18 Silver Street went up in flames.[881] Pricket owned the building and operated the business, and this fire left another vacant lot on the lower block. Four years later, the Hurley City Council denied Margaret Pricket's application for a liquor license for the Hotel Bar at 9 Silver Street.[882]Presumably, Margaret Pricket retired.

Hurley: Held in Bondage in Hurley

I N JUNE 1962, U.S. IMMIGRATION agent Glen F. Rice testified at the Senate Rackets Subcommittee in Washington. He stated that "a Montreal booking agency recruited Canadian girls for clubs in Wisconsin and in the Chicago area where 'immoral activities' are carried out." He told the committee that there was a conspiracy between "officials of the American Guild of Variety Artists, a woman known as Billie Brown, and an 'organized crime element.'"

Billie Brown ran a booking agency In Montreal called the Paramount Entertainment Bureau. She lured naïve girls with stardom through newspaper ads stating, "Show girls wanted for night club and entertainment work – no experience necessary." Rice claimed that after Brown created a dependency, she led the girls into prostitution.

Agent Rice told the committee that Brown "sent 11 Canadian girls between 15-17 years of age to work at the Band Box in Hurley, Wis., a honky tonk operated for fishermen and hunters by members of the Chicago crime syndicate." Under oath, Rice testified, "They were held in literal bondage while in Hurley. Hoodlum guards watched both the front and back doors to prevent their escape from forced training as strip-teasers and prostitutes." Rice said that in one case, in the middle of winter, some girls tried to escape but their car got stuck in the snow and shortly afterward, they were "transferred" to the Riptide Club in Calumet City, Illinois.

Agent Rice said when the women arrived in Calumet City, they were forced to live with Samual "Snozz" Holzman, co-owner of the Riptide. Holzman was called to testify. Philip Warden, a reporter for the *Chicago Tribune*, wrote that, "fat, perspiring, hook-nosed Samual "Snozz" Holzman, a convicted white slaver…would neither confirm nor deny charges that he forced young girls into prostitution and confiscated most of their fees.[883]

216

Several women testified about forced prostitution. Joan Gainsley said that she was a dancer and B-girl at the 21 Club in Calumet City. Although management tried to force her into prostitution, she said that neither she nor others had been threatened or beaten. Gainsley also testified that while she worked at the Band Box in Hurley, ten percent of her income went to her booking agent, but nothing was deducted for social security

Corinne Suzette Stein, a performer from Pittsburgh, complained to her union – the AFL-CIO American Guild of Variety Artists (AGVA) – that while her working conditions were "lurid and obscene," she was never coerced into prostitution.[884]

* * *

On June 19, District Attorney Alex Raineri said Rice's allegations were probably true. Gordon Corry, chief of the enforcement branch of the State Beverage Tax Division, let the Band Box (and perhaps his enforcement agency) off the hook when he said, "the Band Box 'strictly speaking, is an entertainment place – with floor shows – and not a house of prostitution."[885] Raineri complained that tavern operators used the AGVA contracts to show that the dancers were legitimate entertainers, thereby making prosecution difficult.

* * *

On June 21, State Attorney General John W. Reynolds announced that "the state is going to crack down on Hurley, the Northern Wisconsin community figuring in national vice news." He was emphatic and said, "The state is going to move in with all its powers. It's about time we clamped down on Hurley. It's long overdue." He said that the first step in the process would be to send investigators.[886] Madison's *Capital Times* criticized Reynolds for "telegraphing a punch." They argued that if the state had all the power they claimed, "Where has the attorney general been?"[887] Coincidentally, that same day and shortly before Reynolds statement, agents arrested four prostitutes on Silver Street. [888]

Hurley: The Scourge of The Lower Blocks

HURLEY BURST ONTO THE national stage propelled by the sensational proclamation of the sexual bondage of teenagers. Madison considered Hurley's behavior reprehensible. John Gronouski, head of the Wisconsin Tax Commission, summoned a group "to work together to help rid Hurley of unsavory conditions existing in nightclubs and taverns operating in the lower two blocks of Silver Street."

The assistant state attorney general, employees of the Beverage and Cigarette Tax Division, the county judge, the editor of the *Iron County Miner*, the mayor, a councilman, a schoolteacher, the police chief, the county sheriff, and the city attorney crowded into a meeting room in Madison.

Gronouski focused on the two lower blocks of Silver Street, and Police Chief Henry Geach narrowed it further, saying that "the city has 40 to 45 good taverns and four to six that are continual troublemakers," calling them "crumb-bum" taverns. He noted that the solicitation of drinks by B-girls is one of Hurley's major tavern problems and the "unlimited and uncontrolled issuance of tavern licenses in past years." Francis Secor, the editor of the *Iron County Miner*, commented about the girl who claimed to have been held in bondage at a Hurley tavern. He said she should be "hauled back here and made to prove her statements." He continued, "Our problem here is those

217

girls running around the taverns half-dressed, not being held in bondage by armed guards."

Mayor Giovanoni, a little off-track, commented that property values would have to be increased by $3.5 million to replace the entire $27,000 it receives in license fees should the taverns be closed. Judge Sullivan responded that eliminating "the six or seven trouble spots would amount to a relatively small loss." Gronouski implied the obvious: "with about 50 taverns for Hurley's 3,000 residents, some operators who cannot make a living on legitimate operation might resort to illegitimate areas to survive."

Gronouski suggested an ordinance like Milwaukee's, prohibiting dancers and waitresses from sitting with customers. A city council member, eager to advance, said he would introduce the ordinance at the next council meeting on July 10. However, both the mayor and the city attorney balked at the idea. The mayor would not commit, and the city attorney flatly opposed the idea. City Attorney Flandrena argued that it would be impossible to enforce and that it would be considered a "civic action" carrying little weight. He suggested that state law would be taken more seriously and said, "It is better not to have an ordinance than to have one you can't enforce." Gronouski was miffed by the tepid response and emphasized that experienced authorities developed the Milwaukee ordinance. Police Chief Geach, annoyed because the council often ignored his recommendations for denying licenses, told Gronouski that he would enforce the ordinance should it pass.[889]

* * *

During the city council meeting on July 10, Alderman Robert Olson proposed a motion to pass an ordinance written by the Wisconsin Tax Department. The council was mute. Olson made the motion a second time, and no one responded. The motion for an ordinance to regulate the behavior of B-girls died for lack of a second. The *Iron County Miner* reported that the council's silence showed "their obvious protest and rebellion against being ramrodded by the state into accepting a document drawn up by the Wisconsin Tax Department and state attorney general's staff."

Gronouski fumed. His most earnest attempts at diplomacy were met with disdain and contempt. He had previously commented that Hurley was the only town in Wisconsin with a B-girl problem outside of Milwaukee. Because of the council's inaction, he promised to marshal all available state resources to end the scourge of Silver Street's lower blocks.[890]

* * *

The July 16, 1962, *Capitol Times* presented a two-inch bold capitalized headline: "State Maps Hurley Drive – Move Slated to Halt Vice." Gronouski did not trust Mayor Giovanoni nor anyone in any authority in Hurley. As evidence, he promised to move ahead with plans to assault the city. He said, "I will continue preparations for a broad, department-wide program to eliminate the element in Hurley which is giving Hurley and the state of Wisconsin a most unsavory reputation."

Mayor Giovanoni wrote to Gronouski and said that any tavernkeeper arrested and convicted of any violation serious would be subject to suspension or revocation. He finished the letter with a near apology, "I am not writing this letter to soften you up, but I will do everything in my power to follow up my suggestions.'"[891]

* * *

On July 18, the Hurley City Council adopted a resolution "aimed at wiping out all illegal operations connected with the tavern business." The council unanimously passed a measure whereby the court would provide a certified copy of the arrest and conviction of anyone holding a liquor license. The council would then "consider additional punishment." City Attorney James E. Flandrena described the measure as "adhering to the American principle " by allowing the city council to determine if violations were "willful or accidental." The previous ordinance, offered by the state, failed to get any traction and Flandrena called it "unAmerican" because "it superseded state law and took away the right of appeal."

The mayor told the council that the time had come to take tavern law enforcement "seriously," and he promised John Gronouski he would "undertake a vigorous campaign to eliminate the elements giving Hurley a bad name and that he intended to "lay down the law." The threadbare intent reappeared. Mayor Giovanoni told the council that it was time "to take tavern law enforcement 'seriously.'"

After all the bluster and patriotic hubris toward the proposed ordinance, the council passed it unanimously. Although not certain it would make much of a difference, Giovanoni wrote to Gronouski saying that he was going to meet with the sheriff, the district attorney, the city attorney, and the chief of police and together, they would "lay down the law" and used tools at his command, "some of them implements that have been available for years but 'have never been used before.'"[892]

Hurley: Standing Up for Sin

AFTER THE HURLEY CITY COUNCIL denied the ordinance proposed by the Wisconsin Tax Department on July 10, the July 12 edition of *Chicago's American* replied with a story entitled "Standing Up for Sin." They said, "The city council of Hurley, Wisconsin took up the question of sin this week, and decided in favor of it. Hurley (pop. 2,673) is the wide-open town on the Upper Michigan border which played a stellar role in recent Senate testimony about B-girls and white slavery, and which has acquired a big-league reputation as a sin town. Anyway, a proposed anti-vice ordinance banning B-girls came up at the council meeting Tuesday. It wasn't exactly voted down; it just died. Nobody even seconded the resolution to adopt it. One reason given was that the ordinance would 'give too much power to the police force.'

In our experience, politicians usually find a few words to say in praise of reform and civic virtue, even when voting against it. Hurley's city fathers may add frankness to other qualities for which their town is renowned."[893]

Hurley: Police Chief Moves to Shut Down Three Taverns

IN AUGUST AT MADISON, State Beverage and Cigarette Tax Division enforcement chief Gordon H. Corry reported that revocation and padlock actions had begun on three Hurley taverns and four licensees. In cooperation, Hurley Police Chief Henry Geach organized and served the complaints. The padlock proceedings were against Kay's Bar, the Four Aces, and the Hi-Ho, although the Four Aces and the Hi-Ho had been closed since the previous spring. The license revocations were against Joseph Vita of the Hi-Ho, Adele Petri of the Show Bar, Theresa Kalasardo of the Band Box, and Jack Gasbarri of the Club Carnival. The complaints listed multiple offenses against each tavernkeeper and were filed in Iron County Court.[894]

* * *

At a special court hearing on October 17, Judge Sullivan ruled on prostitution convictions for the four taverns. First, he denied motions for new trials, and second, he ordered the padlocking for Kay's Bar, the Four Aces Bar, and the Hi-Ho for one year. Vita posted a $5,000 bond, allowing him to keep 22 Silver Street open for the year. Marcia Lyons and Anton Lysczyk had purchased 7-9 Silver Street from Joseph Vita, the site of Kay's Bar and the Four Aces. They posted a $2,500 surety bond allowing them to keep the tavern open for the year.

* * *

On October 31, Judge Sullivan suspended the liquor licenses of Vita, Kalasardo, Petri, and Gasbarri. However, he issued a stay of execution because of an appeal. When the appeal time ran out in November, Sullivan issued 90-day suspensions of the licenses for the Hi-Ho, the Band Box, the Show Bar, and the Club Carnival. Bundled in the same article as the suspensions and padlocking, Patricia Jean Struzyzski and Janet Sprester were arraigned on charges of soliciting at Joan's Bar at 19 Silver Street.[895]

Hurley: Lois Gasbarri Skirts Prison

IN SEPTEMBER 1962, A MINNEAPOLIS grand jury indicted Lois Gasbarri, now 49, and Lawrence O'Brien, 25, from Minneapolis, for transporting a woman from Minneapolis to Hurley for purposes of prostitution on two separate occasions. On May 22, 1962, with help from O'Brien, Gasbarri transported a woman from Minneapolis to Hurley by car. Then, Gasbarri transported a woman from Minneapolis to Hurley by bus on June 11, 1962. These cases of white slavery were scheduled for U.S. District Court at Minneapolis before Judge Gunnar H. Nordbye.[896]

Both Gasbarri and O'Brien were convicted at Minneapolis Federal Court on October 22, 1962.[897] On November, the judge sentenced O'Brien to five years in a federal prison. On the other hand, Gasbarri was acquitted of the one count of white slavery and returned to Hurley.[898]

1963

Hurley: Another Affidavit of Prejudice

IN NOVEMBER, STATE AGENTS ARRESTED JULIUS Mattei, proprietor of the Ritz, for running a house of prostitution and pandering. In January 1963, Mattei filed an affidavit of prejudice against Iron County Judge George Sullivan. Judge Bjork of Phillips reviewed the issue and summarily dismissed the case for lack of evidence.[899]

Superior: Still Up and Running

IN JANUARY 1953, a judge fined Irene Bell, 47, Lillian D. Crocker, 33, and Mildred Dalba, 44, for keeping houses of prostitution in Superior. He suspended six-month jail sentences in exchange for $500 from each. A fourth woman Rye Taylor, 65, missed the court date as she was in the hospital.[900] Although there is no reference, it is likely that Taylor healed, then paid both her doctor fee and her court fine. At this point, we must fast forward ten years.

* * *

In 1963, Irene Bell, now 57, was still in the business of prostitution. During the second week of December, two men stormed into her apartment, tied two "boarders" to a bed, sliced Bell's leg with a knife, and smacked her in the head with the butt of a gun. The men ransacked and looted the apartment, making off with $2,100 in cash and rare coins.[901] The crime went unsolved, and considering that there is no record of further prosecution for prostitution, Irene Bell may have retired.

Hurley: Police Chief Geach Leaves Hurley

HENRY GEACH WAS A patrolman from 1937 to 1943 and served as the Hurley Police Chief since May 1, 1956. His sincerity and fortitude must have significantly influenced Commissioner Gronouski as in January, after resigning from his job in Hurley, Gronouski hired him to work in Madison.[902]

Hurley: A Death at the Show Bar

JENE E. MOEHRL, 24, FROM MEMPHIS, rented a second-floor room with his wife, entertainer Mary Paulette, at the Show Bar at 28 Silver Street. On the evening of March 18, 1963, Moehrl fell asleep while smoking, and his cigarette ignited the mattress. John Gentile, the first fire-fighter on the scene, rushed into the burning room, carried Moehrl out to the street, and administered artificial respiration. However, Moehrl was beyond recovery. Eldon Fremming of the state fire marshal's office in Park Falls investigated the incident and verified the cause of the fire. Gentile was hospitalized with smoke inhalation. Although the fire severely damaged the tavern, it was repaired and reopened.[903] In late April, Gentile received a commendation for his effort to save Moehrl and a letter of thanks from Moehrl's parents[904]

Hurley: The Raids of 1963

A T THE END OF MARCH, state agents arrested Lynette Taylor, Lois Gasbarri, and Dorothy Klosno on charges of soliciting for purposes of prostitution at Club 13.[905]

* * *

In mid-June, state agents arrested Lois Gasbarri (again) and two associates for soliciting at Club 13. They nabbed Jack Gasbarri at the Club Carnival, Andrew Orsoni of the Four-Ever Amber Tap, Serafino and Naomi Morichetti of Connie's Drumstick, and a few others for violating the hours law.[906]

Walworth County: Hurley of the South

I N AUGUST 1963, STATE AGENTS visited Lake Geneva and Delevan and arrested 13 people for gambling, liquor, and prostitution. Madison's *Capital Times* wrote, "Walworth County, that old citadel of Republican respectability, is having it pretensions punctured by state law officials." The writer said that "For a long time Lake Geneva has been called the 'Hurley of the south.'"[907] The only reference to this comparison was in this article. It's difficult to imagine that the upscale area of Lake Geneva resembled Hurley in any respect.

Ironwood: Raid Envy

I N THE EARLY EVENING OF Wednesday, September 11, 1963, the Ironwood Police raided the nefarious operations of DeMassi's Teen Center, Bob's Dairy Bar, Subway Recreation (a pool hall with pinball machines), and a facility called Teen-Town. Besides pinball machines, these facilities sold ice cream, pizza, and in the case of Teen Town, a coin shop with pinball machines. In a Hurley-like raid, the Department of Public Safety, the Department of Public Works, and the Gogebic County prosecuting Attorney raided fourteen establishments. The *Ironwood Daily Globe* reported that the authorities entered three of the four teen centers simultaneously but "hit the fourth establishment, the Subway Recreation, minutes later."

The Gogebic County prosecutor reported, "No resistance was offered." The well-coordinated raid produced seventeen pinball machines, which paid off in "free games." The prosecutor said these devices violated city and state law and they were "liable to seizure and destruction without violation of constitutional provisions." These agent wannabes "planned to destroy the machines without delay."

As Ironwood's Keystone Cops wrestled pinball machines from Teen-town, an Ironwood youth played taps on his bugle on Aurora Street. Three defendants paid a $100 fine instead of serving 60 days in the county jail.[908] In this case of raid-envy, the Silver Street crowd laughed their shot glasses right off the bar.

Hurley: The End of the Mining Era

O N OCTOBER 19, 1963, the Montreal mine sent its last load of ore west toward Ashland on the Soo Line. At its peak, in 1929, it employed 800 people on the Penokee Range. The Montreal nine opened in 1886 and ran continuously through 1963 – a period of 77 years. At one time, it was the largest producer of underground iron ore. This was just one in a series of economic blows to Wisconsin's iron range, and closing the Montreal mine, after yielding 45 million tons of ore, foreshadowed the end of that industry in the area.[909]

Hurley: Another Breakfast and Gun Story

R ECALL THAT IN NOVEMBER OF 1943 an intoxicated Ironwood cop shot up the Gus Lewis Café on Silver Street. This story is not the same but is similar enough to recall the previous event. On Thursday, October 17, Martin E. Korhonen, 51, drank himself goofy from late evening to 6 a.m. at the Club Carnival. About the time most people were preparing breakfast, Korhonen, in an alcohol-induced stupor, pulled a loaded semiauto pistol from his jacket, pointed it at a young woman, and threatened to shoot her. The bartender wrestled him to the ground. The *Iron County Miner* wrote that in addition to pulling the gun, "He also had to pull more than $250 from his wallet to stay out of Iron County Jail," and, of course, he donated his semiauto to the Hurley police department.[910]

1964

Wisconsin: Madison's *Capital Times* Rails Against Gambling

IN APRIL, MADISON'S *CAPITAL TIMES* COVERED half its editorial page condemning proposals to introduce pari-mutual horse racing to Wisconsin and they probed the motives of the proponents. The Speaker of the Assembly, Paul Alfonsi of Minocqua, said that the *Capital Times* was the only newspaper in the state that opposed gambling. The *Times* shot back, saying it "is proud of the distinction and ashamed that the rest of the press is neglecting its responsibility." The *Times* article continued, "we know that gambling brings with it the hoodlums of the gambling syndicates. There are bribery and corruption, and good government goes out the window."

Three members of the Wisconsin Assembly – Paul Alfonsi, George Borg, and Michael Barron – introduced gambling bills in 1963 and again in 1964. This was an unusual alliance. Alfonsi grew up in Pence, nine miles west of Hurley, and represented Iron, Vilas, and Oneida Counties. The *Times* wrote, "Alfonsi represents the district that includes Hurley, which is noted for its gambling and prostitution. Borg represents a district that includes Lake Geneva. The Lake Geneva area is noted for its gambling. Last year state agents made prostitution raids in Lake Geneva and nearby areas." Barron represented Milwaukee and would later serve as a circuit court judge and a member of the Wisconsin Supreme Court.[911]

The *Times* quoted Wisconsin's first governor, Nelson Dewey, who said, "Gambling is a history of crime, corruption, demoralization of moral and ethical standards, and a lower standard of living for everyone." They ended the editorial with a quote from another Dewey; this time, it was the former Governor Tom Dewey of New York. The governor relentlessly fought against the Mafia and successfully prosecuted Charles "Lucky" Luciano on charges of forced prostitution in 1936. He also nailed Waxey Gordon and Dutch Schultz. Governor Tom Dewey said, "The entire history of legalized gambling shows that it has brought nothing but poverty, crime and corruption, demoralization of moral and ethical standards and ultimately a lower standard of living and misery for all the people."[912]

Amidst rumors of bribes in Milwaukee by "wealthy Milwaukeeans and Chicago sports-enthusiasts," the horse racing bill died in the Assembly by a vote of 57–31.[913]

Hurley: The Bowery Burns to the Ground

ON MAY 21, 1964, A FIRE DESTROYED the old Bowery building and two other buildings on the southwest corner of the intersection of Silver Street and First Avenue across from the White Way Hotel. The fire was hot, and flames shot 50 feet into the air. Firefighters saved the adjacent L & M Bar at 109 Silver Street, but heat, water, and smoke damaged the Santini Hotel, located across First Avenue.[914]

Madison: The Solution is Hidden Under the Dome

ON MAY 29, AN ASSOCIATED PRESS reporter wrote, "A number of Hurley nightspots – hit in a state crackdown last winter – reportedly are back mixing prostitution with their liquor business." He quoted Tax Commissioner George Corning, "I think you could say the situation in Hurley is going from bad to worse." Frustrated with the state's lack of authority, Corning said, "Until we get some effective control, it will be difficult if not impossible for us to curb this activity in Hurley. Local municipalities had control over local licenses, and he said that 39 operators had recently filed applications in Hurley including some 'known criminal records or are on behalf of persons with records.'" He continued, "There is no question but that officials of Hurley could act if they wanted to correct the abuses and further is no question but that the federal government could take positive action."[915]

These thoughts had been expressed so often that even the casual reader of daily news must have skipped to the cartoon page. One of the reasons for the repetition was that the individuals in charge of prosecution – governors, agency heads, division administrators – changed during election cycles and each, in turn, thought their effort to be novel.

As with all previous attempts, Corning complained about a lack of cooperation, saying that his department had received "negative cooperation" from Hurley authorities. The AP reporter wrote, "Corning said that in the last ten years, beverage and cigarette tax division officers have made more than 1,000 arrests in Hurley. 'But charges of solicitation are reduced to lesser charges with resulting minor fines."[916]

Corning recognized the history but placed the blame at the local level. Despite his condemnation, he did not say that Hurley authorities violated the law. The sheriff, the police, the district attorney, and the city council exercised the authority entitled them under criminal and municipal law. No one acknowledged that the solution to the problem was under the capitol dome in Madison. Each legislative session was an opportunity to either introduce new legislation or hone existing laws, but other than the Thomson Law in 1945, the legislative docket was absent any meaningful effort.[917]

Having said all this, there was no law against favoritism, political maneuvering, minimal sentencing, foot-dragging, and lack of enthusiasm, and to be certain, Hurley was guilty of all of these.

Hurley: Mattei Fined for Failure to Pay Taxes

IN JUNE, JULIUS MATTEI, 35, of the Ritz, pled *nolo contendre* to avoiding income taxes from 1957 through 1960. On June 12, a district court judge fined Mattei $1,200, placed him on probation for a year, and ordered him to pay the back taxes and penalties.[918]

Iron County: Gambling with Moonshine

THE PRODUCTION OF ALCOHOL for consumption can introduce heavy metals or methanol. Heavy metal poisoning occurs when metals like lead or cadmium accumulate in the body, preventing organs from functioning. Methanol is a common contaminant in moonshine. If not removed during

225

processing, it can damage the optic nerve and lead to blindness or death. These are legitimate concerns for regulating the production of consumable alcohol. However, the overriding factor for liquor law is money.

According to the Urban Institute, "Alcohol taxes are sometimes called a corrective or "sin tax" because, unlike a general sales tax, the tax is levied in part to discourage the consumption of alcohol because the choice to use it has costs both to the consumer and the general public (such as increased health care costs). State and local governments tax cigarettes, and have begun taxing marijuana and soda, in a similar way."[919]

In 2024, the Wisconsin tax on liquor is $3.25 per gallon, which is paid for by vendors. The Federal alcohol excise tax on distilled spirits is $13.50 per proof gallon.[920] In 2020, Wisconsin collected $73.8 million from taxes on beer, wine, hard cider, and liquor.[921] Tax evasion is the primary reason liquor laws are so vigorously enforced.

* * *

In late June 1964, state agents descended on a residence located at 706 Cary Road and arrested Laura Peite for making and selling liquor without a permit. Judge Sullivan sentenced Peite to 1–10 years in the Wisconsin Industrial School for Women at Taycheedah." This was a pretty stiff sentence as the State was serious about losing tax revenue. Peite must have heaved a sigh of relief when Sullivan stayed the prison sentence and placed her on probation for one year instead. She did suffer, nonetheless, the loss of $1,000 to the court.[922]

Hurley: Lois Gasbarri Clicks the Heels of Her Magic Slippers

IN JULY 1964, THE HURLEY CITY COUNCIL approved 13 of the 14 bartender licenses on its agenda. The 14th was that of Lois Gasbarri who was singled out by councilman Italo Bensoni. The State Beverage and Cigarette Division had previously sent a letter to Mayor Paul Santini telling him that a state law prohibited the licensing of habitual offenders and convicted felons. The letter identified Gasbarri as having 12 convictions as a keeper and inmate of a house of prostitution and as having spent time at the state prison at Taycheedah in 1957. In customary Hurley fashion, the council vote was split 3-3. Mayor Paul Santini cast the tie-breaking vote "which authorized the granting of the license." [923]

Hurley: Kay's Set on Fire

ON JULY 22, 1964, someone threw a "firebomb" against the side of Kay's at 9 Silver Street at 3:30 in the morning. Firefighters put out the fire, and an investigation by the state fire marshal led to a dead end.[924] Residents speculated that the bomber could have been a dissatisfied customer.

Hurley: The Raids of 1964

IN A RENEWED EFFORT to clean up Hurley, state agents raided the lower block and arrested a dozen denizens. They charged Jack Gasbarri, of the Show Boat and the Club Carnival, with 13 counts of remaining open after-hours, selling liquor after-hours, and selling cigarettes without a license. They arrested Theresa Kalasardo, of the Band Box, on six counts of being open and selling after-hours. They arrested Joseph Vita, of the Hi-Ho, and John Soffa, of Shorty and Mary's, for keeping houses of prostitution. Anton Lysczyk was charged with using violent and abusive language, indecent conduct, and threatening to shoot State Agent Richard Breed at the Hi-Ho.[925]

Members of the city council were frustrated and angry. At the August meeting, one council member wanted to know why the local police had not made the arrests asking, "Are the tavern owners running the city, or are the councilmen who the people duly elect?" Another blamed the police commissions and said that if they were unwilling to act, "They should resign in favor of some citizen who is willing to do something about the problem." Councilman Prospero said, "It is unrealistic for the council to grant tavern licenses to habitual violators and then expect the police department to uphold the law" and that the city council "cannot escape the responsibility of the violations found in Hurley."[926] Prospero had voted against issuing Lois Gasbarri a bartenders license in July.

* * *

In early September, state agents arrested Irene Leuffgen of Billy's Bar, and Monroe Lambertti of Monty's Corner Inn in Mercer, for staying open after hours. With the inevitable certainty of precision clockwork, they arrested Lois Gasbarri for keeping a place of prostitution at 23 Silver Street.[927]

In mid-November, an Iron County Court judge dismissed the keeper charges against Anton Lysczyk and Lois Gasbarri. Gasbarri's lucky streak didn't miss a beat.[928]

* * *

During the second week of November 1964, the State Attorney General heard rumors that dancers would travel to Hurley for prostitution during hunting season. The girls would earn 25 cents for pushing a $1.74 drink and get a $5.00 commission for a $25 prostitution fee.

Tax Commissioner George Corning took a break from hunting "up north" and visited Silver Street. He was surprised to find only a single agent assigned to the lower block while the clubs ran "wide open." Corning was distraught, and he left Hurley to regroup. A single agent faced two problems: the agent would be easily recognizable, and the workload was overwhelming. Corning changed out his hunting gear and assembled a formidable team to blitz Silver Street on the second weekend of deer season.

* * *

On November 23, 1964, Tax Commissioner Corning, Attorney General Walter Cole, Assistant Attorney General Roy Dalton, investigators from the FBI, and agents of the Wisconsin Cigarette and Beverage Tax descended upon the three taverns on the lower block. They wasted no time arresting 25 "exotic dancers," some from Chicago Il. and Macon, GA., who were "imported into Hurley for the deer season and were soliciting drinks and prostitution in three Hurley night clubs."

They collared Jack Gasbarri of the Show Bar and the Club Carnival, and Teresa Kalasardo of the Band Box. The next night, Hurley Mayor Paul Santini ordered a total "crackdown on vice in Hurley." He told the Fire and Police Commission "to enforce all liquor laws, anti-prostitution laws, and state statutes and city ordinances in 'regard to any form of misconduct and tavern violations.'"[929]

* * *

On November 24, Iron County Judge Arne H. Wicklund produced restraining orders and closed the Show Bar, the Club Carnival, and the Band Box because of "lewdness, assignation, and prostitution."

* * *

Police Chief Niilo Maenpaa was furious about the state interfering with his department duties and said, "Without the state, we had no trouble. The city police department is understaffed: we're all underpaid. Get that straight, will you? What am I going to do, camp on the doorsteps of those places all night?"

District Attorney Raineri was also miffed. He said that what bothered him was not the warrants or the charges but that the arrests were made before he issued the warrants. Raineri told Corning, "I am sick and tired of getting back reports that your department is not satisfied with the way I handle our cases. So, I'm going to let you have your department handle these yourself." Corning replied, "I have never said one thing wrong about the way you handle these cases. And yet you constantly have been critical of me and the department."[930]

Following the raid, circuit court Judge Charles revoked three tavern licenses and suspended the Band Box license for 30 days. To the dismay of the state, the orders would take effect ten days after issuance, thereby allowing the taverns to operate for the rest of the deer hunting season.

Hurley: State Promises to Clean Up Hurley

TAX COMMISSIONER GEORGE CORNING tried desperately to motivate Hurley to police itself. He bemoaned that this small city of 2,700 consumed a large share of state resources. Like many of his predecessors, in early September, he vowed "to have licenses revoked" and promised to initiate court action "to force Hurley tavernkeepers with a criminal record out of business." He upped the ante by threatening action against city council members who approved licenses for "ineligible applicants," but he stopped short of identifying the specific actions. Corning said, "We have exhausted all of our efforts to remedy the situation up there by other means, so we have no alternative."[931]

Iron County: Judge Sullivan Dies; Wicklund Appointed

ON OCTOBER 25, 1964, Iron County Judge George D. Sullivan died at 49. Sullivan served as Iron County judge since February 1, 1960. Former Governor Gaylord Nelson appointed Sullivan to fill the position left when Judge Trembath retired. Sullivan was from Montreal and graduated from Hurley High School in 1933. He attended Gogebic Community College for two years, then earned a Bachelor of Arts from the University of Wisconsin at Madison. He then taught high school in Hurley for eight years and returned to the University of Wisconsin to earn a law degree in 1948.[932]

* * *

Governor John W. Reynolds appointed Arne H. Wicklund of Gile, in November 1964, as the Iron County judge. Wicklund would serve at the pleasure of the Governor until the election in April 1965. Wicklund had been the Hurley High School correspondent for the *Montreal River Miner*. He entered the University of Wisconsin at Madison and earned a Bachelor of Arts in Economics in

228

1947 and a law degree in 1950. Like his predecessors, he served in the state assembly for Iron and Vilas counties.[933]

Hurley: Council Approvals Advance Then Recede

DURING THE SUMMER OF 1964, State Tax Commissioner George Corning warned the city council that several tavern applicants were not eligible for licensure because they had criminal records. With a confident thumb to the nose, the council granted the licenses anyway. Corning was furious and filed a complaint in Iron County Court for the revocation of the license held by Marcia Lyon. Marcia Lyon – also known as Marcia Ruth Lyon and Kay Martin – ran Kay's at 7 Silver Street. She had previously been convicted for operating a brothel, prostitution, soliciting, and pandering.[934] Corning pressed Circuit Court Judge Charles of Ashland and on September 25, the judge revoked Lyon's tavern license for one year.[935] Later, on October 20, Judge Lewis revoked the license of James C. Shields of the TryAngle Inn. [936]

Hurley: Revocations Will Continue

IN LATE NOVEMBER, Judge Charles declared four taverns in Hurley public nuisances. He suspended the license of Teresa Kalasardo of the Band Box for 30 days, revoked the licenses of Jack Gasbarri of the Club Carnival and the Show Boat, and suspended the license of Joseph Vita of the Hi-Ho for a year.[937]

Hurley: An Open Appeal

IN THE AFTERMATH of the hunting season raid, the *Iron County Miner* appealed to the citizens of Hurley to deal with the situation on Silver Street. On November 27, they wrote, "The time is long overdue for the decent people of Hurley to get together to demand that the last remnants of vice and indecency be chased out of our city. We can no longer take the attitude that 'leave it alone and it will die by itself.' We can no longer take consolation in the fact that other cities in Wisconsin have the same thing and that decent people from Hurley have been solicited right in front of Milwaukee's principal hotel.

"There are at least several reasons why the City Officials will have to take steps to clean up the last, sick vestige of a Hurley that was. In the first place, it is the thing to do. We cannot any longer argue that it is part of our economy – and that closing those few joints will add more empty buildings. We are trying to get new industry. Some people are working day and night towards that end. No business is going to come to Hurley when we give "yellow journalism" the opportunity to run eight-column headlines across the front page. Sure, we are angry with these newspapers. We are angry with State agents. Some of the people who are writing us up and arresting the tavernkeepers and girls down the street are an icky ilk. (But that is not a factor.) By allowing what is down the street we allow them to come to our city and give us a bad name. Decent people in Hurley cannot any longer ignore the lower end. The city officials can no longer look at it as a "necessary" economic evil. It has to be wiped out. It has to be wiped out for our economic and social welfare. It's just plain no good for anybody.

229

"Our City 'survived' the closing of the Montreal mine, the lay-off of hundreds of miners. It appears that we are on our way back. We can't make it all the way back if we tolerate the yoke around our neck which is the few joints in the first block. We must not wait for fellows the like of George Corning to do it. We have good people in our community who must demand that our local officials do the job. The only way to do it is to refuse licenses for these places.

"Let's make it impossible for the metropolitan press to write us up adversely. Let us eliminate the shame that all decent people felt this week. We must do it. The time is now."[938]

Hurley: A Phoenix in Hurley

IN EARLY DECEMBER, Mayor Santini held a closed meeting with the city attorney, the acting police chief, and members of the police commission. He ordered the police "to strictly enforce all laws dealing with the operation of taverns." He also suggested that the police ordinance "be amended to give the mayor more supervision over the police department."[939] Once again, Hurley tried to rise from the ashes to get tough on vice.

1965

Hurley: Almost a Cold Case

IN EARLY MARCH, Oliver "Peeps" Piippo, 46, argued with Ronald Kivi, 47, at 2:30 a.m. at the Band Box on Silver Street, operated by John Kalasardo. Although witness accounts varied, Piippo "either fell or was knocked down, his head striking the steps to the stage." Piippo was unconscious and Kivi, unable to revive him, called for a taxi to deliver Piippo to his home. Observing Piippo's condition, the taxi driver took him to the police station instead. The police shunted the taxi and Piippo to the hospital, where he was pronounced dead on arrival.[940]

* * *

When questioned by District Attorney Alex Raineri, Kivi offered three versions of the incident. Dissatisfied with all explanations, Raineri charged Kivi with "homicide by reckless conduct," and he was arraigned in front of Judge Arne Wicklund on March 12. Wicklund set the bail at $1,500, but unable to pay, Kivi sat in the Iron County Jail.[941]

* * *

At Iron County Court on March 17, Judge Wicklund said that a preliminary hearing failed to show probable cause and that there was "insufficient evidence to constitute homicide by reckless conduct." Wicklund advised Raineri to come forward if new evidence arose and ordered Kivi free from jail.[942] That was almost the end of the story.

* * *

John Kalasardo, the operator of the Band Box where Piippo died, retired to Florida, and passed away in 1980. After Kalasardo died and 16 years after Piippo's death, on February 21, 1981, a witness to the killing told an FBI agent what actually happened. With the promise of anonymity, the witness said the truth could be told since John Kalasardo was now dead. He said Kalasardo hit Piippo on the head with a blackjack, killing him instantly. The FBI informed Iron County District Attorney Paul Sturgul, who took the man's testimony. Sturgul said, "The development in the case 16 years ago after the apparent homicide occurred has closed the case."[943]

Hurley: The Embarrassing Raid of 1965

ON SUNDAY, MARCH 28, state agents arrested Henry Kimball and Lois Gasbarri of Club 13 for keeping a house of ill fame along with two prostitutes from Milwaukee. In a highly unusual arrest, agents nabbed Ernest Opp of Skeeview, Illinois, for patronizing a house of prostitution. Likely embarrassed, Opp failed to appear in court and forfeited his $82 bail bond.[944] In June, the case against Kimball was dismissed but the judge fined Gasbarri $100 on a vice charge.[945]

Hurley: A Grocer Purchases the Finn Block

THE SOUTH SIDE OF the second block of Silver Street lay in tatters with burned-out lots and a few old wood and brick taverns. In early May, a local grocer bought the entire strip. The *Iron County Miner* reported, "The is the south side of this 'famous' thoroughfare, which during most of the years since Hurley was born, back about 1884, has harbored 10 or more saloons, taverns, or night clubs. In June, the razing operations will start on what remains of the once-famous Hurley block. It has a colorful history, dating back to when this was a colorful town. The second block on the south side was known for many years as the block with the 'Finn saloons.' It was the location of saloons operated by people of Finnish descent and catered exclusively to the rough, hardworking, and hard-drinking Finn lumberjack. These were colorful people. There were other taverns on the block, but it was known as the 'Finn block.' On the east corner, there was the New Central. If you could talk to the old-timers, you can do a column just on that building. Dating back to before the turn of the century, it has quite a past. The building which now houses the Congress, also has an interesting history. There is the Montreal House, which part of it now houses Sig's.

"Anyhow, it was a block of drinking places...nothing but saloons, and other taverns and at least several night clubs. Hurley people never walked on that side of the street. Back in the days when you walked to Ironwood, you always crossed over to the north side of the street. It was just automatic. You didn't walk on the other side...although actually, there were almost as many taverns on the north side.

"So, suddenly, bang! A big supermarket and maybe some other related businesses are moving into the Finn block, in the heart of what was once a famous saloon district."[946]

The Erspamer family would move their grocery store from 5th Avenue. The new single-story steel building with a large asphalt parking lot changed the character of Silver Street dramatically. The taverns now occupied part of the second block's north side and the first block's south side. The geography had been pinched by state agents, fire, and demolition. The glory days of the lower blocks were gone, dissipated like vapor off a sauna rock. Now, the street was hot in another way as the FBI tightened the net.

Hurley: Same Addresses, Different Names

Despite the numerous appeals, threats, and promises, it was business as usual at the June Hurley City Council meeting. The council issued tavern licenses to Charles Chandler at 9 Silver Street, Anthony Iafolla at 6 Silver Street, Teresa Kalasardo at 22 Silver Street, Ellen Vitich at 19 Silver Street, and Henry Kimball at 13 Silver Street.[947]

Milwaukee: Medo and a Question of Judgement

AFTER THE DEATH OF Cristina Jean Jester in 1959, Floyd "Medo" Calligaro moved back to Milwaukee and teamed up with Russel F. Jaeger, 58, to run a gaming operation. It didn't go as planned. On August 28, 1965, FBI agents arrested Calligaro and Jaeger for "accepting bets without paying the $50 occupational wagering tax." Although it didn't affect the penalty, they ran their gambling scheme in an apartment across the street from the police headquarters in what could be considered a terrible location.[948]

Hurley: A Murder on the Lower Block

IN OCTOBER 1965, HENRY KIMBALL, 25, operated Club 13 on the lower block of Silver Street. James R. Vitich, 40, operated the French Casino at 19 Silver Street.

At 6:45 a.m., Susan Kalla was waiting on tables at the Club Carnival. She noticed Henry Kimball and James Vitich arguing over the glass partition that separated the bar from the restaurant. At 11:10 a.m., Vitich and Kimball left the Club Carnival and walked across Silver Street toward Club 13 with Vitich in the lead. Because of an earlier injury, Vitich had limited use of his right arm. As the argument escalated, Kimball threatened to pull Vitich's arm off. At the centerline of Silver Street, between the French Casino and the Club Carnival, the men squared off, and Vitich warned Kimball not to come any closer. Kimball threatened Vitich and began removing his jacket to fight. Vitich feeling threatened, pulled a .41 caliber revolver from under his sweater, and fired three shots at Kimball.[949] One bullet passed through the window of the Club Carnival, another embedded in the wall, and the third passed through Kimball's chest, killing him instantly. Vitich, pistol in hand, meandered toward the French Casino[950] and then back to the Club Carnival. There, he sat in a booth. When Susan Kalla, the waitress, approached him, he told her that "if Kimball got up off the street, he would shoot him again."

When Chief of Police Albert Stella arrived at the scene, he found Kimball's body lying in a pool of blood in the center of Silver Street. Vitich walked toward Stella and said, "I shot him." Stella told Vitich to wait in the car while he called an ambulance to remove Kimball's body.[951]

District Attorney Alex Raineri charged Vitich with first-degree murder in Iron County Court. Judge Arne H. Wicklund declared Vitich indigent, appointed an attorney, and set bail at $50,000. In November, Vitich pled not guilty of first-degree murder.[952]

On December 7, Vitich's attorney told the judge that he couldn't find any witnesses and requested that the trial be moved out of Iron County."[953] Judge Lewis J. Charles presided over the trial in Ashland on December 13 and 14. Vitich faced a jury of seven women and five men.

Vitich told the jury that Kimball "threatened to tear off his crippled right arm" and advanced toward him as both men crossed Silver Street. He testified that when he fired the fatal bullet, "Kimball was in a crouched position as if he was going to spring at him." Vitich also claimed that Kimball threatened him with a gun, and he fired two warning shots before the fatal shot, but a second gun was never found.[954]

On December 16, James Vitich got lucky. Although District Attorney Raineri charged him with first-degree murder, after two and one-half hours, the jury returned a verdict of manslaughter. Judge Charles sentenced him to ten years in the Wisconsin State Prison at Waupun.[955]

Although the actual amount of time served is unknown, it was less than ten years. On February 14, 1972, Hurley police arrested him for speeding, and in May 1972, the judge fined him $150 for having refilled liquor containers when he managed 19 Silver Street.

Bessemer: The Last Mine Collapses around a Failing Economy

ON NOVEMBER 26, 1965, the Pickands, Mather Company announced that the last mine on the range – the Peterson mine at Bessemer – would close in February 1966. Pickens said that the depleted ore body would put 220 persons out of work.[956] This cudgel smacked against the last large employer on the Gogebic and Penokee range. Iron ore was dead, and families were about to become fragmented, disoriented, and displaced as they searched for new employment. As the deep shafts and long drifts filled with water, other forces closed in on Silver Street.

233

Hurley: The Case of Lyon and Lysczyk

THE OLD MILWAUKEE AND NORTHERN RAILROAD trestle overlooks Silver Street just west of the Montreal River. Next to the trestle on the south side of the street, a dusty alley separates the elevated rail from the first building – 7 Silver Street. The building housed many taverns over the years, including Idele Bower's "The Dells" and Josie Marin's "Jodie's Bar." From February to July 1958, Andrew Holappa owned the building, and the business was known as Kay's bar. For the next year, William Soucie held the title, and the business was the "Lucky 7." In July 1959, Anton "Tony" Lysczyk owned the facility, and the name reverted to Kay's Bar when Tony Lysczyk, 44, and Marcia Lyon, 49, became business partners. In March 1963, the title transferred to Marcia "Kay" Lyon,[957] and it continued to be known as Kay's Bar, sometimes referred to as Kay's Rooms. Swapping of names and transfer of ownership on Silver Street was not unusual. What was unusual was the attention Kay's would get in the 1960s from United States Attorney Edmund A. Nix.

* * *

In July 1961, Nix successfully prosecuted James Harris on a tax evasion charge and now focused on Lyon and Lysczyk. During 1964 and 1965, Lyons and Lysczyk employed four women at Kay's Rooms: Frances Vitello, 23, and Carol "Carman" Dixon, 24, both from St. Louis; Alice Payne, from Poplar Bluff, MO, and Mary Joan "Gigi" Taylor, 36, from Milwaukee.

* * *

After hearing about Kay's Rooms in 1964, Alice Payne called Lyon and asked if she needed help. Payne traveled to Hurley, worked for ten days, then returned to Missouri. In 1965, she learned that the FBI was looking for her and, needing a hiding place, she chose Kay's. The tavern was well-known, and Alice Payne was popular. A customer asked to have Payne join him in Wausau. Lyon paid for the flight from the Ironwood airport to Wausau for an evening visit. Upon return, Payne split the $100 fee with Lyon and Lysczyk.

* * *

In February 1965, Carol Dixon, 24, traveled by train from St. Louis. When she arrived at Green Bay, she called Kay and, speaking in code, told her when "the package would arrive" to ensure transportation from the train station.[958]

* * *

During the summer of 1965, FBI agent Matthew Crehan and a partner worked the lower block, assembling a list of prostitutes as they meandered from joint to joint. Crehan entered Kay's as a customer and asked "Gigi" about what was happening in Hurley. Gigi told him that there were taverns, strip shows, and women. When he asked where to find a woman, she said he was in the right place. He had enough evidence at that point but continued the ruse and eventually used price as a reason to leave. Crehan gave the list to U.S. District Attorney Edmund Nix. Nix delivered the information to the state attorney general's office and to District Attorney Alex Raineri and waited. When he realized that neither would act, regardless of the damning evidence, he advanced.

Nix demanded further investigation using the 1961 Travel Act.[959] This relatively new federal criminal statute prohibited the use of U.S. mail or interstate or foreign travel for the purpose of engaging in certain specified criminal acts, including prostitution. Nix had what he needed, and his complaint resulted in a federal grand jury investigation in November 1965."

234

When this news hit Hurley, Silver Street was replete with rumors of tapped telephones. To make matters worse, FBI agents roamed the street during the fall of 1965, looking for narcotics, gambling, and prostitution.[960]

* * *

Notice of the grand jury splashed across the front page of Madison's *Capital Times* in mid-November. Nix said the jury would "study complaints of racketeering in Hurley and possible operation by a national crime syndicate." He subpoenaed 20 Hurley residents to appear at Madison for the jury investigation, including a former Hurley mayor, the district attorney, the chief of police, the Iron County sheriff, and at least one council member. A specific inquiry was to discover evidence of interstate transportation for racketeering, narcotics, prostitution, or white slavery.[961]

This investigation was unprecedented. Instead of city police, county sheriff, or state agents, the FBI infiltrated Hurley with contempt. It was hunting season, and they used Roach's costume trick of donning Kromers and plaid jackets. They scrutinized every doorway along the lower block of Silver Street, but it was no secret that Nix had Kay's Rooms squarely in the crosshairs.

Although the names of the grand jury witnesses were confidential, Laurie Van Dyke, a reporter for the *Milwaukee Sentinel,* cornered the Ironwood airport manager in the federal building in Madison. She was eager to tell a tale and related to Van Dyke that the airport manager kept notes of "suspected prostitutes arriving in Ironwood," claiming that he knew they were prostitutes because "there's a mark about them."

Agents had surveilled the airport during the early fall, along with the bus depot and the train station in Ironwood. Van Dyke rousted another witness who told her that the girls used to be "free-lance," but now they were paid off by the tavern owner, and the money went to the syndicate. The witness said, "This is big stuff. You're really going to get some big stories out of this before it's over." Either the witness exaggerated, or Van Dyke leaned heavily on the keyboard as these charges dissolved when witnesses testified that the problem on Silver Street was relatively benign and relegated to a few "entertainment" businesses. The grand jury investigation resulted in the arrest of a "syndicate of *one* – Kay's Bar."

Armand Cirilli, Hurley's literary defender, described Van Dyke, "Our generation has had its troubles with the *Milwaukee Journal* and the *Milwaukee Sentinel.* It seems like the distinguished *Journal* and its lesser member of the family take turns 'working us over.' Lately, it has been the *Sentinel*, who assigns a tall, almost shapely gal, by the name of Lauri van Dyke to report on our sins. But, even Lauri, who is quite a Reporter, was not able to come up with very much on the grand jury investigation of Hurley."[962]

The Madison newspapers were eager to pick the carcass of Hurley's lower block. The bold capitalized headlines of the December 2 issue of *The Capital Times* announced that "Action Is Near" regarding the grand jury investigation.[963] However, the article was shallow, brief, and a disappointing prelude to what happened.

* * *

Several people were indicted by the grand jury in early December 1965. Nix leveled charges of using interstate mail, telephone, and telegraph facilities in the operation of Kay's and, more specifically, against Marcia Lyon, Anton Lysczyk, and three employees. The charges had possible penalties of a $10,000 fine and five years in prison. During the first week of December, The FBI nabbed Mary Joan "Gigi" Taylor, 36, in Milwaukee.[964] Nix charged Lyon for "using a telephone to induce another woman to travel across state lines" to work in a brothel. This related to hiring Alice Payne while she was in St. Louis. Nix also charged Lyon and Lysczyk with conspiracy to violate federal law.[965]

* * *

In mid-December, FBI agents arrested Lyon and Lysczyk and delivered them to the Ashland County jail. They pled not guilty, posted bail of $3,500 each, and returned to Hurley. Authorities could not serve a warrant to Alice Payne, aka Paula Payne, of St. Louis, as she had disappeared.

After the action by the Federal Government, the Wisconsin authorities realized that their failure to act appeared as apathy. Wisconsin Deputy Attorney General John H. Bowers insisted that his office was "vitally concerned and interested in this situation." However, the offer was too little and too late, and Nix summarily dismissed it.

* * *

On November 29, 1966, U.S. Attorney Nix prosecuted Marcia Lyon and Anton Lysczyk in Federal District Court in front of Federal Judge James Doyle in Madison. In his opening statement, Nix vehemently advanced his reason for intervention saying, "The Federal government had the right to step into what otherwise might be a state case where there was a complete breakdown of local law enforcement." During the court proceedings, Judge Doyle affirmed, "If local law enforcement officers continue to fail or refuse to take effective action, the federal authorities may be expected to act again and again."

* * *

Madison Attorney Darrell MacIntyre defended Lyon and Lysczyk and persuaded the judge to drop two charges against the couple for lack of evidence. During testimony, Lyon described herself as a "cook and bedmaker," and Lysczyk said he was a "bartender and maintenance man." They concurred to be partners for income tax purposes, and Lyon testified that she "received one-half of the earnings of prostitutes working at Kay's Rooms" but denied charges of interstate travel.

* * *

On December 1, 1966, after deliberating for two hours, the jury found Lyon and Lysczyk guilty of two counts of conspiring to use and using interstate transportation to promote prostitution. Doyle released each on a $3,500 bail bond.[966]

* * *

The June 20, 1967, edition of the *Wisconsin State Journal* reported that from 1959 to 1965, Kay's Rooms had over 2,800 customers. During the court case, Doyle described the customers as "more criminal than many – perhaps most – of the defendants upon whom I frequently impose sentence. The hundreds, perhaps thousands, of men who patronized this place must have been either cruel or pathetic, or perhaps both. The quality they must have shared is an utter lack of self-respect. One who represents himself does not use others as these men used these women."

Doyle used his court to demonize prostitution and said it was an "assault upon the dignity of the human spirit." He stated that the prostitutes were "victims of a system to which the label of slavery is accurately attached. In dealing with these two defendants, we deal not with issues of sexual freedom among consenting adults but with sordid commercial exploitation of human beings."

Nix portrayed a local conspiracy to promote prostitution by describing the conditions before the

236

Travel Act. First, he asserted that the Hurley City Council could have closed these businesses by not issuing liquor licenses. Second, he argued that the Hurley city police made little effort to enforce the law. Finally, he said that most convictions under Iron County District Attorney Alex Raineri resulted in small fines. Everyone got a black eye from the prosecution.

Judge Doyle sentenced Lyon and Lysczyk to three years in federal prison and fined each $2,600. Nix told the press, "The conviction was a significant step forward in restoring law and order in the northern Wisconsin community. Local law enforcement officials were either unable or unwilling to take effective action to combat open and flagrant violations of Wisconsin liquor and prostitution laws. We hope that this successful prosecution will provide encouragement to the overwhelming majority of decent citizens of Hurley who earnestly seek diligent and effective law enforcement in their community." [967] Anton Lysczyk pled guilty, while Marcia Lyon appealed her case.

Madison: Side Note – The Attorney

Madison Attorney Darrel MacIntyre defended Lyon and Lysczyk. In terms of flamboyance and disposition, MacIntyre was the perfect match for defending keepers of a house of ill repute. MacIntyre was notoriously "loud and arrogant." Doug Moe, a writer for *The Capital Times,* said that MacIntyre "did not believe in negative publicity and that "Any day that his name was in the paper was a good day."[968] MacIntyre was fiery in court and had several run-ins with judges. Not only was MacIntyre a legal spectacle, but he also ran a loose business practice.

In 1966, a year after Kay's trial but before Lyons appellate hearing, MacIntyre pled *nolo contendre* to tax evasion charges, and U.S. Supreme Court Judge Doyle sentenced him to prison. After all the appeals and requests, MacIntyre served three months in Sandstone Federal Prison in 1967.[969] A little over a year later, on November 5, 1968, Tony Lysczyk began serving his term at the same prison.[970]

Prison didn't slow MacIntyre. Instead, he worked in the library, prepared for the Marcia Lyon case in his cell, and drummed up business in the yard. He left Sandstone not only prepared for Lyon's appellate case but with a new client in tow. This was a character who occupied front-page stories nationwide – Billy Sol Estes.

Sol Estes, a Texas businessman and natural criminal, created a fake mortgage business to sell imaginary ammonia tanks to Texas farmers. He became wealthy and schemed to defraud the federal government of cotton quota funds. In 1962, Sol Estes bribed Department of Agriculture officials for grain storage contracts. President John F. Kennedy heard about his dealings and ordered the FBI to investigate. A jury declared Sol Estes guilty in 1963, and a federal judge sentenced him to 24 years in prison at Sandstone, Minnesota.[971] In addition to being the site of a federal prison, the small city of Sandstone served as a hub of entrepreneurship and a centerpiece of coincidence for players embroiled in vice.

Hurley: The Case of Lyon and Lysczyk – cont'd

MacIntyre, with his law license reinstated, appealed Lyon's conviction. In June 1968, the U.S. Seventh Court of Appeals in Chicago reversed the conviction and ordered a retrial in the Western District Court. After hearing testimony, the three-person court agreed that Lyon had been denied her "right of confrontation" during her June 1967 trial.[972]

* * *

Lyon, now 52, was retried in March 1969 in federal court in Milwaukee. The jury found her guilty, and the judge sentenced her to one year in prison and fined her $2,000. Nix reported that "the conviction and sentencing complete the federal government's first effort to bring law enforcement to Hurley.'" He hammered state and local authorities and said that they "are apparently unwilling to take effective action to combat these open and flagrant violations."[973] Lyon spent from April to December in the Federal Prison Camp at Alderson, West Virginia.[974]

* * *

During an interview with Lyon and Lysczyk in September 2007, Lyon told me that Jackpot Gasbarri and Dick Matrella of the Club Carnival sent Officer Bert Stella into her place to complain that she had too much business. She said that, for a while, she paid Gasbarri and Matrella to funnel the money to District Attorney Alex Raineri, who initially took the money but later "went against it." Eventually, she became tired of the payments and decided to "try it on her own." At that point, Gasbarri and Matrella offered her up to the FBI. Lysczyk claimed that Raineri made payments to a state agent and Nix.[975] Other than the statements from Lyon and Lysczyk, there is nothing in the record to support these allegations.

* * *

Lysczyk was only a helper at Kay's, but he enjoyed taunting state authorities. In 1962 and 1963, he covered his Doberman with a blanket with the words 'state agent' emblazoned on the sides and paraded it along Silver Street. Anton was from Bessemer, where his father was a cabinetmaker, but he lived in Hurley most of his life and was a faithful companion to Lyon. In 1969, the judge summoned Lysczyk from Sandstone Prison to testify at her trial, but he refused to cooperate, citing the 5th Amendment. Annoyed, the judge added six months to his 3-year sentence.

* * *

Marcia Lyon spent the rest of her life with Tony Lysczyk at 7-9 Silver Street. She followed sports and played the lottery. Marcia was friendly, talkative, and energetic. She prided herself on being a good employer and caring for her employees.[976] She spent the end of her life at Villa Maria Nursing home in Hurley, just a few blocks south of the old courthouse. Marcia "Kay" Lyon died on September 16, 2018.

Hurley: Club Carnival Goes Legit

AFTER EDMUND NIX CHECKED off Kay's, he turned his attention to the other side of Silver Street. The Club Carnival at 14-16 had seen its share of trouble, including gambling, prostitution, and shootings. Rather than crossing swords with Nix, in late 1965, Jack Gasbarri closed the Show Boat, the Band Box, and the Club Carnival converting the latter into a supper club. He abandoned exotic dancing saying, "Hurley area people have always stated that the range needed a dine and dance place. Now we have given the Gogebic range that spot." He advertised: "Fine food and dancing complete with a dance band from Denver." It appeared as though Silver Street was finally clean. The *Iron County Miner* stated with certainty that there were "no exotic dancers in Hurley."[977]

Hurley: Hoopla and the Threads of a Conspiracy

WITH THE HOOPLA OF THE grand jury over, promises of rooting out corruption fell flat. After Lyon and Lysczyk went to prison and Jackpot went straight, Nix had nothing left. In December 1965, the *Iron County Miner* weighed in on this notion and wrote the grand jury's epitaph entitled "Grand Jury Over; What now?"

The *Miner* wrote, "The 'grand jury investigation of Hurley' is over. Why was it called? What was it intended to accomplish? Four arrests were made, all related to one alleged house of prostitution. What about the newspaper charges of gambling and narcotics? Was the so-called grand jury probe necessary to make these arrests? Perhaps it was essential to place certain evidence on record before making these arrests. But we can't understand the need for the array of witnesses which included a former mayor, who's "evidence" was never taken, an alderman-supervisor, and at least three city and county enforcement officers. We can't seem to tie it all up together."[978]

The observer has to wonder about the motivation of the grand jury, the hype, and the threats when only one establishment was busted. Could Lyon's assertions of a conspiracy have been true? The question as to why the Show Boat, the Band Box, and Club Carnival avoided both persecution and prosecution still lingers.

Kay Lyon's belief of a conspiracy was probably right. The facts are that the Federal government empaneled a 23-member grand jury to take testimony from 20 witnesses under oath in Madison to grab one offender from a small building near a dusty alley by the railroad tracks in Hurley. The next act was about to begin.

1966

Hurley: Just the Croupier, the Blackjack Dealer, and the Bookmaker

THE 1964 INTEREST IN legalizing gambling returned in 1966 as part of Shawano native Peter Abdella's campaign platform for the Wisconsin Assembly.[979] However, the news was poorly received by large resort operators. Tony Wise, the operator of Telemark resort near Cable, said, "I'm basically against legalized gambling. There are so darned many unsavory things connected with it. The big Chicago boys always get associated with it and we want to keep this type of trash out."

Wise had been instrumental in removing Hayward from "Hurley, Hayward, and Hell." He cited Hurley as an "example of a community which clung to prostitution and gambling. It's obvious they got no help from it." On the other hand, many smaller establishments favored legalized gambling, specifically "state-inspected slot machines, with a substantial portion of the income earmarked as tax revenue."

Abdella also suggested a pari-mutuel racetrack between Eagle River, Rhinelander, and Minocqua. Russ Holperin, the operator of the Eagle River supermarket, said, "Gambling only attracts the leeches in our society." In a letter to a local newspaper, Holperin wrote, "I remember well a time when Wisconsin did have gambling. The first night in town, a father or mother got in a hot game, and blew all their vacation money and the next day the family had to return home. So, were we any ahead? Did the butcher, the baker, and the candlestick maker get any of the vacation money? You bet not – just the croupier, the blackjack dealer, and the bookmaker." Harvey J. Kandler, the pastor of the Congregational church "rapped gambling as rigged, selfish and parasitic."[980]

Abdella failed to win a seat in the Wisconsin Assembly.

Madison: Organized Crime Verified in Wisconsin

Legalized gambling machines would have to wait until 1999, when Act 9, the Biennial Budget Act, "decriminalized the possession and operation of five for fewer video gambling machines" in taverns. The reality of the situation is that gambling machines are illegal in Wisconsin. However, if a purveyor has five or less, the law is not enforced.[981]

The State of Wisconsin Legislative Reference Bureau, in Informational Bulletin 12-2, November 2012, writes the following, "Wisconsin Act 9, the biennial budget act, decriminalized the possession and operation of five or fewer video gambling machines in an establishment licensed to serve alcohol beverages for consumption on the premises, such as a tavern or restaurant. It reduced the penalty from a felony to a $500 civil forfeiture per machine and also removed the threat that an establishment could have its alcohol beverage license revoked solely because of having five or few machines. Mere possession of any gaming machine remains illegal, and the machines are subject to seizure, but tavern video gambling was *de facto* legalized"[982]

Despite years of turmoil and moral indignation, in 1999, the Wisconsin legislature abandoned former principles while holding tightly to the reigns of enforcement to generate tax revenue.

Machines flooded taverns throughout the state, including Hurley *and* Madison. Gamblers now sit in darkened rooms, inserting hard-earned cash to watch the wheels spin on computer controlled devices. The State of Wisconsin – the silent croupier – shamelessly rakes in the profit.

In fact, the State of Wisconsin currently runs the largest gaming operation in the state with the State Lottery. Since 1988, the Wisconsin Lottery has generated more than $19.1 billion in total revenue.[983] The odds are astronomical being 1:240,000 for each ticket ranging from $1 to $10.

A 2017 study by The Pew Charitable Trusts, found that "the poorest households spend a disproportionate share of their income on lotteries." The study reported that the bottom 20% of income earners in the US spent 7.9% of their disposable income on lottery tickets, compared to just 0.9% for the top 20%.[984] Ironically, the administration of the State Lottery resides within the Wisconsin Department of Revenue, the same agency that harassed and persecuted the operators on Silver Street for over half a century for having nickel slot machines.

Hurley: City Council Warned Not to Approve Licenses

IN FEBRUARY 1966, Attorney General Bronson La Follette concentrated on Hurley. With the case against Kay's cemented, the State focused on four other taverns. In June 1965, E. O. Jones, the director of the Department of Taxation, sent a letter to Mayor Paul Santini and all board members identifying "the convictions against certain license applicants on June 22." He told the city that "the state would bring action against the operators if the council granted the licenses."[985] The letter revealed that by 1965, Louis Gasbarri had accumulated 13 state convictions, including nine for violating hours laws, two for being an inmate of a roadhouse, one for gambling, and one for selling liquor without a license. La Follette pointed out that on his 1965 application, Gasbarri claimed that he had never been convicted of violating any law.

The Band Box, now operated by Teresa Kalasardo, showed 23 previous convictions. However, it had already been declared a public nuisance, and padlocking was underway. The Liberty Bell Chalet, operated by Pat Fontecchio and Betty Lehocky, had two after-hours violations in 1964 and 1965 and gambling convictions from 1947-1949. The complaint against Naomi Morichetti of Connie's Drumstick was based upon hours violations from 1961 through 1964. However, the city council believed the evidence against the facilities to be weak. They ignored La Follette's warning and approved the licenses without debate.[986]

1967

Milwaukee: Hurley Takes Some Heat

IN EARLY MAY 1967, Milwaukee and state officials discussed organized crime in Wisconsin at the *Milwaukee Sentinel's* annual Forum for Progress. Charles Wilson, head of the state crime lab, said, "organized crime is centered in Chicago as it was in the 1930s but has moved north into Wisconsin." Wilson cited the 1963 unsolved Milwaukee gangland-style slaying of Kenosha jukebox vendor Anthony Biernat and recent "vice operations" in Hurley. His reference to Hurley was likely the federal prosecution of Kay's, implying that it was "organized crime."[987]

Madison: Reorganization of Criminal Investigations for Prostitution

IN CHAPTER 75, THE REORGANIZATION ACT OF 1967, the Wisconsin Legislature moved the Department of Justice under the direction of the Attorney General. The State Crime lab, the arson investigation program, and the criminal investigatory functions of the Beverage and Tax Division were consolidated and, along with the intelligence functions of the Attorney General's office, formed the Division of Criminal Investigation. Chapter 141, Laws of 1969, increased the responsibilities of the Division to include enforcement of laws related to dangerous drugs and narcotics, organized crime, and prostitution.[988]

The Department of Taxation was created in 1939 but had predecessors going back to 1868. Chapter 75 renamed the Department of Taxation to the Department of Revenue in 1967 when James R. Morgan was Secretary. The Department was no longer involved with prostitution raids but kept some cigarette and liquor enforcement authority.[989] In hindsight, the enforcement of drug dealing, organized crime, and prostitution should have been under the purview of the Department of Justice.

Madison: Convictions Tumble from Kay's Trial

TESTIMONY FROM THE Lyon trial revealed collateral infractions. In August 1967, the grand jury indicted William Miller, 29, of Chicago Heights, Illinois, for transporting a prostitute from Chicago to Superior in 1962. The jury also indicted Thomas L. Kane, 29, from Spring Grove, Illinois, for transporting Patricia Burnside from Chicago to Hurley in 1965.[990]

Edmund Nix prosecuted Kane in United States Court in Madison in January 1968. The jury found Kane guilty and on March 7, Judge James E. Doyle sentenced Kane to 18 months in federal prison.[991]

Despite limited success, Nix had was applauded by Madison's *Capital Times*. They noted that the recent cases had resulted in a total of 5½ years in prison for the perpetrators and that this "far exceeds all of the penalties for all the arrests made in Hurley since the town was founded."[992]

* * *

Of course, at that time, it was difficult search records, so the *Capital Times* deserves some slack. In reality, the length of sentences far exceeded the 5½ years under U.S. Attorney Nix. The record shows the following penalties from 1942 to 1967 for prostitution-related offenses directly related to

Hurley. In 1942, Jack Gasbarri was sentenced to 2 years and Rocco Legato to 5 years. In 1955, Blackie Matrella went to a federal prison for 1½ years. In 1953, Patrick Judge was sentenced to 1–3 years. In 1955 Max E. Tully was sentenced to 2½ years, James C. Shield to 1½ years, and Donald Harris to 2½ years. In 1962, Lawrence O'Brien got 5 years. These approximate 23 years of prison time not including the convictions from the Kay's Rooms incident.

1968

Wisconsin: Help Wanted

WITH ITS NEW AUTHORITY, the Department of Justice needed additional help to boost enforcement. They placed an ad in the *Wisconsin State Journal* offering a pay of $540 per month ($4,700 today) with raises to $785 ($6,800 today)." The responsibilities were laid out: "Work for the Wisconsin Department of Justice as an investigator enforcing compliance with laws covering alcoholic beverages, gambling, prostitution, and cigarettes." At this time, when higher education was more available, they required "a college degree or four year's pertinent work experience."[993]

Milwaukee: A Grand Jury on a Budget

IN JANUARY 1968, the Department of Justice set up a sting operation in Milwaukee. They rented an apartment on the east side and enlisted a state agent to act as a broker. The agent interviewed women for a "mythical" brothel in Waukegan, Illinois. Seven women signed up and after getting a $50 advance, they readied for the trip. During his interviews, the women told the agent that they had worked as prostitutes in "Hurley, Antigo, Milwaukee, and other Wisconsin cities" and disclosed the names of men associated with prostitution and narcotics. The sting produced overwhelming evidence, and agents promptly arrested several men and women for narcotic violations and raided a roadhouse in Antigo.[994] Despite not gathering evidence under oath, this was far less expensive than empaneling a grand jury.

Madison: An Embarrassing Slip of the Tongue

DAVID CARLEY, THE FORMER Democratic National spokesperson, served as the master of ceremonies on the Democratic campaign trail in October 1968. He boasted about Attorney General Bronson LaFollette, the party candidate for governor, saying that LaFollette "favored more vigorous prostitution."[995] Silver Street might have been temporarily enthused but there is a significant difference between "prostitution" and "prosecution." The audience had a belly laugh at Carley's expense.

1969

Madison: The Warren Report

IN MAY 1969, Wisconsin Attorney General Robert W. Warren concluded that Wisconsin had organized crime groups. The *Warren Report*[996] said that brothers Frank and Peter Balistreri oversaw the "family" syndicate in Milwaukee since 1961. Warren listed the Balistreri illegal activity of "La Cosa Nostra" as "B-girl" operations, gambling, interference with lawful commerce, prostitution, and loan sharking."

Warren said that Racine, Kenosha, and Walworth County were "centers of operations" for the Chicago and Rockford organizations and that "Hurley had a national reputation for prostitution and gambling and that the city was part of the prostitution circuit."

Warren wanted federal assistance under a new federal crime control law[997] and to broaden the jurisdiction of the Criminal Investigation Division. He also wanted to increase penalties for mob-type crimes, to permit forfeiture of

Armand Cirilli Editor, Iron County Miner
Hurley, Wisconsin 1969

vehicles used for the illegal transportation of drugs, narcotics, or gambling devices, to create a way to protect witnesses and jurors, and to allow the attorney general along with district attorneys to seek grand jury investigation of crimes between counties.[998]

Wisconsin Dells: The Stag Party

JULIUS MATTEI APPEARED IN 1951-1953 for arrests on hours violations, keeping a brothel, disorderly conduct, and selling liquor without a license. After running out of luck in Hurley, Mattei moved to Wisconsin Dells, but the move didn't change his luck. On Oct. 2, 1968, Mattei pled *nolo contendre* for failing to pay federal income taxes for 1962 through 1965.

* * *

At midnight, on January 27, 1969, a squad of state agents intervened in a March of Dimes stag party in a poorly conceived raid at Behnke's Supper Club near Baraboo in Sauk County. They found themselves in a crowd of 500 people, including Sauk County lawyers, judges, law enforcement officials, go-go dancers, and Green Bay Packer linebacker Ray Nitschke. Despite the size of the crowd and the notoriety of the guests, the agents confiscated gambling devices and pornographic movies.

They arrested Ronald Flock, the owner of Behnke's, and Julius Mattei, 41, as the event organizers. The *Janesville Gazette* described Mattei as "an unsavory character from Hurley with a long police record for gambling and operating houses of prostitution." [999]

* * *

245

The state dropped the gambling charges against Mattei and Flock in early March and hinted at political favoritism. The *Gazette* wrote, "On March 3, Sauk County District Attorney William Johnson dropped the charge against Mattei, who is an associate and relative of Assembly Republican Floor Leader Paul Alfonsi, a powerful leader of the state Republican party." When asked about the charges, Johnson told a Madison reporter, "Sometimes it isn't beneficial to reveal to the public why a charge is dropped."

Iron County Miner Business Sign
1969

The Sauk County District Attorney said that there was insufficient evidence to convict Mattei and the raid was under a cloud of entrapment. The *Gazette* asked, "Why is 'entrapment' such a major factor in this case when most other vice arrests are made under almost identical circumstances? When a plainclothes vice squad policeman goes with a prostitute to her room and gives her money, is this not entrapment? When an undercover police informer buys narcotics from a pusher, is this not entrapment?

The *Gazette* then exposed the heart of the issue saying, "Apparently in Wisconsin, it depends on who gets entrapped. And in the stag party case, it looks as if the police entrapped somebody who might be politically embarrassing to people in high places."[1000]

Instead of penalizing the men who played the gambling machines, authorities launched a John Doe probe into Julius Mattei's business. The *Capitol Times* referred to Mattei as "a long-time hoodlum with a record of offenses including gambling, illegal tavern operation, and operating houses of prostitution." They also said that Assemblyman Alfonsi and Mattei had frequently been seen together in Hurley, Minocqua, and Eagle River and that state agents claimed that Mattei was related to Alfonsi "although none could pinpoint the specific relationship."

They reported that "Alfonsi, majority leader in the Assembly, was convicted in 1966 of accepting a bribe to promote legislation. However, the State Supreme Court reversed the decision, and after a second jury trial, he was found not guilty.[1001]

* * *

Meanwhile, Mattei's attorney, John Bowers, asked the judge to consider probation rather than jail time. Bowers told the judge that Mattei was "a product of the environment in which he lived prior to 1962" and said, "Mattei is a man of 'limited education and limited intelligence.'" Bowers argued that Mattei, since leaving Hurley, wanted "to build a new life in a lawful manner, and he had been engaged in a program of constructive rehabilitation."

Regarding the arrest at the March of Dimes stag party, Bowers told the court that Mattei recently "found himself caught in a situation which resulted in a tremendous onslaught of publicity and caused him pain at a time that he was trying to escape from the world of his past. Anyone experiencing being exposed in that manner is bound to suffer."

Judge Doyle was so enraged by the plea that he sentenced Mattei before the federal attorney, John O. Olson, had a chance to argue. Realizing his misstep, he apologized to Olson and let him talk. After Olson finished, Doyle calmly sentenced Mattei to jail for 60 days for failing to file the income tax returns.[1002]

Hurley: Vitich, Blackie, and Frenchy Get Indicted

ON JULY 2, 1969, A FEDERAL GRAND JURY IN Madison indicted Ellen M. Vitich, 49, John "Blackie" Ravenelli, 39, and Lois L. "Frenchy" Gasbarri for charges of interstate traffic in prostitution.[1003] More specifically, the grand jury indicted Ravenelli on charges of "conspiring to use interstate facilities for prostitution; traveling in interstate commerce for prostitution, and using the telephone in interstate commerce for prostitution."

* * *

In November, U.S. Attorney John O. Olson described Ravenelli as "a central figure and, as such, is representative of all that is evil in Hurley." He implored enforcement officials to address the vice in northern Wisconsin. Olson focused on Hurley, saying, "Hurley has been and remains the single symbol of the cancer of commercial vice in this district. In my lifetime, there have been attempts – almost too numerous to recall – to clean up Hurley. Those attempts have resulted in arrests and convictions. Yet Hurley remains only slightly less wide open than it was during lumberjack days." Olson continued, "A knowledgeable person can still find whatever he desires in Hurley."[1004] Olson's attack on Hurley came at the same time as U.S. District Judge James E. Doyle sentenced Ravenelli to 18 months in prison.

* * *

Eight months later, in July 1970, Olson cut a deal with John Ravenelli. Ravenelli would receive immunity from further prosecution if he described how he and Ellen Vitich operated a prostitution house in Hurley.[1005] At Vitich's trial, it was revealed that Miss Crystal Nemitz of Berwyn, Illinois was "induced to travel interstate for the unlawful purposes of prostitution." The evidence was a telephone call between Hurley and Berwyn.[1006]

* * *

On July 16, 1970, a Milwaukee Federal Judge dismissed two charges against Ellen Vitich. Then, after five hours of deliberation, the jury failed to reach a verdict on the remaining charges. Ellen Vitich, now acquitted, returned to Hurley.[1007]

* * *

The charge against Lois Gasbarri was because she had moved to Ironwood. When she commuted to work at the Club 13 in Hurley, she crossed the state line.[1008] There is no record about the disposition of the charges against Gasbarri, but it would not stretch credulity to believe that they were dismissed.

Columbus, Ohio: Deducting the Cost of Groceries

DESPITE THE FOCUS on northern Wisconsin, an exception must be made for the unusual – and depending on your perspective – the entertaining. In the fall of 1969, the Columbus vice squad received 30 complaints about prostitution in a residential neighborhood.

Detectives David Verne and John Hawk visited the suspected house. A 69-year-old woman met them at the door. They greeted her politely, and she, in turn, told them to return in 30 minutes.

When they returned, they found a grocery list pinned to the door with a note saying that the cost of the grocery items would be deducted from her fee.

Verne and Hawk obliged and went shopping. When they returned, they handed her the groceries and promptly arrested her on three charges of prostitution.

Hawk said the woman looked "20 years younger than she was." She told the agents that she thought prostitution was "illegal only at night and that she practiced prostitution to supplement her old age pension." Hawk said, "It's the oddest arrest I've ever gotten."[1009]

1970

Wisconsin Dells: Retractions and Suits

To SENSATIONALIZE THE CHARGES against Julius Mattei during the raid of the stag party in 1969, both the *Janesville Gazette* and *The Capital Times* took excessive liberty. They called Mattei an "unsavory character" and a "hoodlum." They itemized his list of past offenses being gambling, illegal tavern operations, keeping houses of prostitution, and failing to file income taxes. A huge mess ensued when Mattei called them out, and both newspapers published multiple retractions in January 1970.[1010,1011]

* * *

The apology was not enough. In April 1971, a furious Julius Mattei filed multiple lawsuits. He filed a $1 million civil lawsuit against the *Janesville Daily Gazette* where he said that the editorial referring to him as an "unsavory character" was "false, malicious, and defamatory." He sued *The Capital Times* editor and publisher Miles McMillin for defamation for a 1969 broadcast over WKTY in La Crosse, a station owned by Lee and Associates. He filed a $500,000 suit against William F. Huffman Radio for the same broadcast on WFHR.

Both lawsuits referred to the same program in the "Hello Wisconsin" segment. Mattei claimed libel for a portion of the broadcast that stated, "The people of Sauk County were shocked when District Attorney A. William Johnson, and appointee of Governor Warren Knowles, dismissed the gambling charges against Julius Mattei, a hoodlum with a long record of arrests on prostitution, gambling, liquor, and income tax charges."

Mattei didn't stop with WKTY and WFHR. His lawyer rounded up another 12 stations in Wisconsin and Minnesota who aired the program.[1012] When the dust settled, Mattei had filed suit against 16 radio stations in the region. Finally, he filed a $1 million suit in Rock County Circuit Court against the Gazette Printing Company.[1013]

* * *

In August 1971, the police chief of Lake Delton, Paul W. Anderson, signed an affidavit saying Julius Mattei had a "good and exemplary character." The following week, a reporter asked Anderson if he intended to swear that Mattei had an "exemplary" character. The police chief said, "Is that what the affidavit says? No comment. Talk to my lawyer."

Lee and Associates came at Mattei will all guns blazing. They asked the court for a summary judgement showing Mattei's arrest and conviction record for possessing slot machines, keeping of a house of ill fame, operating and using a craps table, selling intoxicating liquor without a license, selling fermented malt beverages without a license, disorderly conduct, willfully failing to file U.S. income tax returns for the period of 1962–1965, and failing to file State of Wisconsin income tax returns for the period of 1957–1960. [1014]

* * *

A volley of charges and counter-charges continued until May 30, 1973, when a judge dismissed the $1 million defamation suit against WKTY. The agreement said the suit "is to be dismissed on its merits."[1015] In June, Mattei dropped his suit against *The Capital Times* in a stipulation for dismissal.[1016] In hindsight, if the journalist had exercised due diligence with the initial reporting, Mattei's record would have been exposed, the broadcast would have been accurate, and all of the tribulation could have been avoided.

Winnipeg: Happily Married Prostitutes

WHILE 1970 WAS A SLOW YEAR for vice in the United States, sociology professors were researching prostitution north of the border. Professor William Morrison, head of the Sociology department of the University of Winnipeg, used a $2,500 grant to study prostitution and to "cover office expenses and pay prostitutes for interviews." Morrison reported that "more than 50 prostitutes he interviewed said they were happily married, and many had families. Some said that their husbands were aware but didn't mind because it generated "more money to support the family.'"

Morrison's study focused on women who worked by appointment and reference versus the "less-selective streetwalker." He reported, "These girls honestly believe they are doing a service to society...and their clients are usually happily married upper-middle-class types who think they cannot get sexual satisfaction with their wives." He also said, "Business is usually conducted from the home during the day, although some are transacted in hotel or motel rooms selected by the clients." Morrison argued that he thought prostitution should be legal in Canada.[1017]

From an academic perspective, the study raises questions about the declaration of the null hypothesis, the randomness of the sample, the inclusion of flawed data, or a biased researcher. On the other hand, the conclusions could be valid, but unique to Canada.

1971

Hurley: A Short Period of Intense Fires

THE CLUB CARNIVAL, CONSTRUCTED IN 1958 at 14 Silver Street, witnessed a panoply of vice over 13 years. At 1:40 a.m. on Sunday, March 7, 1971, a fire spread quickly through the building. Firefighters found the nearest hydrant frozen and pumped water from the Montreal River, one-half block to the east. The blaze continued all night and leveled the structure. The business, operated by Jack Gasbarri and Richard Matrella, was now in ashes, and this section of Hurley's infamous "lower block" lay bare.[1018]

* * *

On the evening of Friday, May 14, 1971, a fire started in the front of the Cactus bar at 26 Silver Street, gutted the first floor, spread to the second floor, and blasted through the roof. High winds moved the fire to the rear of the building, where it jumped to the second floor of the Outhouse Bar at 24 Silver Street.

Because of the heat, firefighters sprayed water at the Show Bar at 28 Silver Street to prevent it from igniting. The adjacent Band Box suffered water and smoke damage. The fire marshal could not determine the cause, and the blaze left two additional holes on the north side of the lower block of Silver Street.[1019]

* * *

Richard Matrella knew Marshal James Harris as far back as 1961, and Matrella became familiar with the rackets in northern Kentucky, specifically Newport. Sometime in the late 1960s, in addition to the Club Carnival in Hurley, Matrella owned and operated the Galaxy Club in Newport. The area was under heavy pressure from authorities who wanted to clean up the vice associated with local nightclubs. In March 1970, a fire tore through the Galaxy Club. The *New York Times* reported, "The damage was estimated at $100,000 and arson was suspected by its owner, Richard Matrella. The club remained closed after the fire."[1020] Between 1970 and 1976, six "nightclubs" in the Newport area were damaged or consumed by fire, including the Beverly Hills Supper Club, which killed 158 people in May 1977.

* * *

At 2 a.m. on February 26, 1973, a fire started on the upper floor of the Band Box at 22 Silver Street. Two women woke up coughing in thick smoke. They rushed down the stairs and onto Silver Street with little clothing in below-zero temperatures. Fire crews from Ironwood and Hurley fought the fire, but the wood building, built in 1890, was tinder dry and consumed in a few minutes. The cause remained unknown.[1021]

* * *

On May 4, 1973, while James and Ellen Vitich attended a pre-trial hearing in Madison, the Club 13 burned down and took the French Casino with it. While unfortunate, this is an apropos lead-in to the next story

Hurley: The Malevolent Tale of the Club 13

THOMAS CHIOLINO, 38, OPERATED the Mama Belle Vista Supper Club two miles west of Minocqua on Highway 70. He was also the president of 19 Silver, Inc., which controlled two adjacent taverns in Hurley: The Club 13 and the French Casino, at 13 and 19 Silver Street. The husband-and-wife team of James and Ellen Vitich ran the businesses at these locations and employed Elvera Lincoln, 42, as a bartender at Club 13.

* * *

Ever since Edmund Nix nabbed Marcia Lyon and Anton Lysczyk at Kaye's, the Federal Government monitored the remaining operations, and during 1971, they focused on the Club 13, a few doors west of Kays. U.S. Attorney John O. Olson kept a low profile, but his agents dug into records and scurried around Hurley collecting evidence.

Toward the end of November 1971, Olson felt confident that he had enough evidence on the operators of the Club 13, and he dropped the net by summoning a grand jury in Madison. Olson handed subpoenas to the FBI for delivery to six women to appear before the grand jury in Madison to determine if any federal laws had been broken.[1022]

* * *

The Vitich's were rightfully scared. They saw what happened to Lyon and Lysczyk and knew they might go to prison if the facts came out. Since their employees had been summoned to testify at the grand jury, they used Thomas Chiolino as the heavy. On November 20, Chiolino called all the girls into the kitchen of the Club 13 and told them, "Anyone who causes Jim Vitich to go to jail will end up in a box six feet underground."[1023] The threat worked. Although all the girls – Marie Sukup, 23, Elvira Lincoln, 42, Carol Ann Purpora, 24, Cindy Porath, 18, Judy Harrison, 22, Judith Carter, 21, and Lenore Rembalski, 20 – testified to being prostitutes, none claimed a relationship with Vitich. The girls that made up this "kitchen crew" were petrified by Chiolino's threat.

This simple yet frightening event in the Club 13 kitchen would lead prosecutors down the path to conviction. With the grand jury securely sequestered, no news left the courtroom during the hearings of January 1972. However, Olson knew that he needed to discover an employer-employee relationship between the women and the Vitich's. The break came as the testimonies of the young women failed to match, and their stories littered the trail with lies, fabrications, and falsehoods. Olson knew he had enough information to tease out the truth in court. On February 23, 1972, FBI agents arrested all the women for perjury.[1024]

* * *

The trial began on July 26, 1972, in Madison, and U.S. District Judge Samuel M. Rosenstein presided. The U.S. Attorney questioned Lenore Rembalski about lying to the grand jury. The judge ordered District Attorney Alex Raineri and Thomas Chiolino to "bring all documents, records, and books in their possession pertaining to 19 Silver, Inc., the corporation that operated the Club 13 and the French Casino."[1025]

* * *

On August 2, 1972, Marie Sukup provided shocking testimony. She said that she had been fired twice. Once for refusing to have sex with a Hurley police officer for free. The second for objecting to "having sexual relations with a Milwaukee County judge at a discounted price." The courtroom

252

was stunned and silent. Later, the *Waukesha Freeman* was direct, profound, and witty when they published a headline stating that the "Judge Was a Cheapskate."[1026]

Sukup admitted to being a prostitute but said that she did not share her fees. When her attorney objected, the prosecutor explained, "he was attempting to show that an employer-employee relationship existed between James and Ellen Vitich, the operators of Club 13, and Marie Sukup.[1027]

*　*　*

Olson needed to get the girls to admit a relationship with the Vitich's and he used the pressure of the perjury charge to pick apart their stories.

Although Sukup was terrified by Chiolino's threat, her roommate, Judy Harrison, had no such inhibition. Sukup had told Harrison about the encounter with the Milwaukee judge and Harrison repeated what she heard. She said that the judge told Sukup that he "was entitled to special privileges" and that he had struck Sukup during an argument. Harrison said that Vitich fired Sukup for the incident but then rehired her. Harrison also testified that Sukup had sex with a customer in their shared room. She described the role of Ellen Vitich as bartender and solicitor, and James Vitich set the price and deducted the cost of rent from the fee.

Olson did not ask for the judge's name, but George E. Alderson, the executive director of the Wisconsin Judicial Commission, sat in the courtroom and stewed. He wanted a name to attach to a violation of the code of ethics for judges. A reporter recognized him and inquired if he was "assigned to listen to the case." Alderson said that he was "observing it because of 'curiosity.'" Curiosity was an accurate term, as it was curious that the state prosecuted a prostitute while a masochistic freeloading judge remained on the bench.

Harrison also testified about the cop demanding free sex. She said that Sukup argued with James Vitich, and he told her that she was "jeopardizing the business." Harrison said the cop wanted to retaliate by "running Sukup out of town." Her refusal to work for free earned her the title of the "No Discount Prostitute," a term used thereafter by the press.

Harrison laid it out for the jury. She told them that the minimum fee at the club was $15, but there was always a negotiation for more. The girls split the money with the Vitich's, who deducted $5 per day for their rooms for the "days that they actually earned any money." Ellen Vitich took the stand and testified that she and Sukup had sex with a male customer in a room they shared.[1028] Olson had his connection.

*　*　*

The following day, three FBI agents testified they had visited the Club 13 and the French Casino in November during the Michigan dear season. They saw girls disappearing with men into the backroom from time to time. A parade of witnesses followed, including FBI agents, the grand jury attorney, and Thomas Chiolino.

*　*　*

One of the witnesses at the trial was Alex J. Raineri. At this time, Raineri served as the Iron County District Attorney, the Hurley City Attorney, and a private practice attorney. Raineri said that, based upon the request of James Vitich, he drew up the incorporation papers for 19 Silver Street Inc. that included Club 13 and the French Casino. Raineri also said that he prepared income tax returns, W-2s, and liquor license applications based on information provided by Vitich.

253

Olson asked Raineri if he was "familiar" with the operation of Club 13, and he said that he "knew the location." When Olson asked Raineri who operated the place, Raineri replied, "I don't know, I don't hang around there."[1029]

* * *

Earlier, Olson promised to name the Hurley policeman and the Milwaukee judge and leveraged this knowledge to encourage Sukup to change her plea, but he already had the connection that he needed, and the government rested its case. The cop and the judge remained anonymous. Sukup, now facing sentencing on the perjury charge, headed back to Milwaukee.

* * *

Four days later, Marie Sukup appeared in Milwaukee Court for violating probation. Agents arrested her and 21 others in a gambling raid in Milwaukee. The $25 fine for gambling was the least of her problems.[1030]

* * *

On August 16, Judge Rosenstein sentenced Marie Sukup and Lenore Rembalski to one year in prison and three years on probation for perjury, then suspended sentence in favor of probation. The judge ordered Sukup to "avoid prostitution, other illegal activity, and not to return to Hurley for any purpose."[1031]

Judge Rosenstein told them that they deserved another chance and said, "Most important of all is that you stay away from parasites of our society who are looking for women like you to make life easier for them." He also said that the court was "concerned with conditions at Hurley which obviously casts a stench on Wisconsin that ought not to be allowed." Casting a broader net, he said, "There are other Hurleys in other states that also ought to be eradicated."[1032]

* * *

While Sukup was being sentenced, another grand jury hearing was underway, and every other girl gave up the goods on the Vitich's. At this point, the girls feared additional prosecution more than Chiolino's threat.

After the girls testified, the Feds hit the ground running. On August 17, armed with sealed indictments, they invaded the Club 13. They scoured the building and found bugging equipment in second-floor bedrooms. They seized $5,800 in cash, canceled checks, and corporate records. Finally, they confiscated a tape recorder with a conversation between a girl and her client, and they rounded up three guns, two of which were loaded and ready.

The meeting in the kitchen of Club 13 during the previous November had caught up with the Vitich's. Agents arrested James, his wife Ellen and Thomas Chiolino. They charged Ellen with illegal activities in interstate commerce. They charged James Vitich and Chiolino with conspiring to cause witnesses to lie before a federal grand jury. Vitich was charged with a second count which accused him of coaching prospective witnesses to lie. U.S. Magistrate Patrick Crooks in Wausau released the three on bail.[1033] On August 24, 1972, James Vitich, Ellen Vitich, and Thomas Chiolino, pled not guilty to all the charges.[1034]

* * *

The grand jury remained open and vital. On October 2, 1972, the jury called four Hurley police officers to testify, and summoned Mayor Paul Santini, Police Chief Leo Negrini, and former chief Albert Stella.[1035]

* * *

On November 1, Negrini and Stella testified. The subpoena issued to Mayor Paul Santini was quashed because he told the court that being confined to a wheelchair made it difficult for him to travel. Olson was determined and said that he would send another subpoena for Santini.[1036] As testimony was given, stories unraveled, and prosecutors burned through legal pads.

* * *

On November 7, 1972, Judge James E. Doyle recited the indictments to the panel before selecting jurors in the case against the Vitich's and Chiolino. He stressed the "kitchen" incident to ensure jurors understood the seriousness of the charges. He also emphasized that Vitich coached the girls on what to tell the grand jury.[1037]

* * *

On November 8, Judy Harrison, one of the women from the Club 13, testified that Vitich coached her. She told the court, "Everything was pretty rounded out on what we were going to say." Leaving little to chance, Chiolino made them practice their testimony in the kitchen of the Club 13 at different times, some sessions attended by James Vitich. Harrison testified that Vitich ensured them they could plead the Fifth Amendment if they were asked any questions other than their names, ages, or addresses. Harrison said the group agreed to answer "important" questions by reciting "I don't remember."

Harrison did not hold back with her testimony. She told the jury that she "had worked in Hurley on several occasions in the past two years" and that "She was first driven from Milwaukee to that city by Vitich." She described how the business worked and that "the girls took men customers to one of four bedrooms above the Club 13. The customers first were checked out by Vitich's wife, who tended the bar." She continued, "If Mrs. Vitich thought the customer was 'all right,' the girls were allowed to approach and solicit him in the barroom. The women were told to write down the amount of money they received on a slip of paper, and at the end of each night, Mrs. Vitich collected the slips and the money and split the cash equally with the girls after taking out $5 a day for their room and board." Harrison also said Vitich instructed her and another girl to "pack your clothes for an overnight date." He then drove them to Minocqua, where each received $300 for their services.[1038]

* * *

After deliberating for three hours on November 10, 1972, the jury found James Vitich and Thomas Chiolino guilty of conspiring to commit perjury. U.S. Federal Court Judge James E. Doyle freed the two on bail, but they faced steep penalties.[1039]

* * *

U.S. Attorney John O. Olson kept the heat on – possibly the most intense investigation in Hurley's history. The strategy of patiently picking off establishments one at a time, while resource consumptive, produced results. It should be acknowledged however, that prison sentences, license revocations, and fires, had reduced the number of suspects. In early December 1972, Olson was uncompromising and hunted for more information. He subpoenaed all the members of the Hurley City Council, including Laurence Lewis, Felix Patritto, John H. Gulan, John K. Soffa, Jr. and Joseph Alleva. He also subpoenaed the Iron County sheriff, and Deputy Lt. Ronald Morzenti. Finally, he issued six Jane Doe subpoenas for women employees of the Show Bar and the Band

255

Box.[1040]

Fear penetrated the lower block of Silver Street. This was the first time the city council members were ordered to testify at a grand jury. They knew they approved liquor licenses for convicted violators, and now they had to answer questions in federal court.

* * *

In February 1973, an FBI agent queried District Attorney Alex Raineri about the whereabouts of James and Ellen Vitich. Raineri, volunteering too much information, said that he saw them "in the casino room of the Flamingo Hotel in Las Vegas on January 18." This violated their probation order.[1041]

* * *

Two months later, on April 14, 1973, the Vitich's were on trial; the second for James Vitich in a year. In November 1972, a jury found him guilty of conspiring to cause others to commit perjury. Now, he faced a violation of the International Travel Act of 1961, a federal law prohibiting interstate or foreign travel, or the U.S. mail, for certain unlawful activities.

The government focused on "dirty linen," literally. The linen used for prostitution activity at the Club 13 was transported to Duluth, Minnesota, for laundering. As a result, the Fed charged the Vitich's with using interstate commerce to conduct illegal activities.

The defense attorney first tried to have this charge dismissed, only to be thwarted by U.S. District Judge James E. Doyle. The attorney argued that the Travel Act was not applicable because they could have laundered their own sheets and, therefore, the "travel" was "merely incidental to the alleged offense."

However, Doyle cited a case where a ticker tape machine, while not essential, was needed only to facilitate illegal gambling. He said that the laundry service, like the ticker tape machine, facilitated the prostitution activity.[1042]

* * *

James and Ellen Vitich traveled to Madison on May 4, 1973, to appear at a pre-trial hearing. When they arrived, a Dane County marshal cited them for contempt for violating probation in February when Alex Raineri reported that he saw them in Las Vegas.[1043]

The Vitich's were not having a good day. That evening, at 10:30 p.m., the bartender at the Club 13 noticed smoke coming from the false ceiling of the second floor. The fire spread up the stairway to the French Casino and quickly engulfed the two facilities. Several buildings suffered smoke damage including Dottie's Diner, the former Hi-Ho tavern, and Shorty and Mary's. Although three firemen fell from a ladder that buckled, and one suffered smoke inhalation, none were seriously hurt. The Hurley Fire Chief, Angelo Maffesanti, speculated that faulty wires caused the blaze.[1044] Although insured, the Vitich's would return to a smoldering lot on Silver Street.

* * *

On Thursday, May 17, 1973, James Vitich, charged with interstate transportation for prostitution, abruptly changed his plea to guilty. However, he faced another charge of causing others to commit perjury before the grand jury, for which he would be tried separately.[1045]

* * *

At trial, Ellen Vitich argued that her name appeared nowhere in the business papers of either the French Casino or the Club 13 and that she was only a salaried employee. Despite her defense, on

256

Friday, May 18, the jury found her guilty of using interstate commerce for purposes related to prostitution.[1046]

*   *   *

James and Ellen Vitich faced Federal Judge James Doyle for sentencing on July 12, 1973. The Vitich's attorney argued against imprisonment, saying, "Prostitution is condoned by the people of Hurley and neither local nor state officials have ever done anything about it." Judge Doyle, unmoved, sentenced Ellen Vitich to one year and James Vitich to four years in federal prison.[1047]

*   *   *

Two weeks later, Judge Doyle sentenced Thomas Chiolino to six months in prison along with a $3,000 fine and two years of probation. The sentence was stayed to September 28 after Chiolino's attorney said this was the busiest season for his supper club in Minocqua.[1048] However, on August 23, Thomas Chiolino turned himself into the marshal's office in Madison for delivery to a federal prison.[1049]

*   *   *

Olson wasn't finished. On August 23, 1973, the federal grand jury indicted Rose Chesley, 46, for perjury. At the arraignment in September, Chesley pled not guilty, and Doyle set the trial for November.[1050] A jury found her guilty in early 1974. At a pre-trial sentencing hearing in August 1974, the judge learned that Chesley had five children and lived part time in Hurley and part time in Rockford, Illinois, with her family. Empathetically, Judge Rosenstein placed Rose Ann Chesley on probation for two years.[1051]

Milwaukee: The Tragic Case of Marie Sukup

TWO YEARS PASSED, and Marie Sukup, now 21, was stressed and afraid. The "no discount" prostitute ruminated about Chiolino's death threat. After lying to the jury, she was prosecuted for perjury and changed her plea to guilty. Then she was arrested in Milwaukee for a gambling violation while on probation. On March 4, 1973, Marie Sukup, 22, took an overdose of tranquilizers and was found dead in a north-side Milwaukee apartment.[1052]

1972

Madison: Madison Reassures Itself of Its Self-Righteousness

IN LATE 1971, THE IRON COUNTY MINER jabbed at the capital city. Responding in January 1972, the *Wisconsin State Journal* boasted about the inherent goodness of Madison.

They wrote, "Lest the rest of the state becomes overly apprehensive, we want to assure all in Wisconsin that Madison has not become a 'sin city.'" They admitted, however, "Madison's reputation as a clean and decent place to live suffered when taverns featuring nude shows moved into the city." The editorial brazenly faulted Hurley for the influx of nude dancing in Madison when it stated, "When a Hurley newspaper characterized the capital city of Wisconsin as worse than the upstate sin town in its heyday, the usual riff-raff associated with this low-grade 'entertainment' moved in."

The *Journal* turned from coy optimism to reassurance stating, "We'd like to assure all citizens that our university is quiet and studious, our schools are buzzing with activity, our churches are well-occupied if not filled, our stores are being patronized without harassment, our industry is humming as well as it can."[1053]

One way to consider Madison's "goodness" is by reviewing the crime statistics from 1972. According to the Madison Police Department, there were 60,900 calls for services and 676 convictions for crimes including murder, rape, robbery, aggravated assault, and larceny.[1054] If every person in Hurley called the police once per year, it would take about 30 years to equal the Police calls in Madison during 1972.

Another way to describe Madison's "goodness" is to consider the next story, although it takes a strong stomach.

Madison: The Crime Story of Danilo Zabala "Chico" Artez

During the summer of 1971, Danilo Zabala "Chico" Artez, 36, rented a house near Lake Kegonsa, ten miles southeast of Madison. Artez, the son of a minister, had earned a degree in journalism from the University of Minnesota. Artez was smart but unscrupulous. He observed the money being made in Madison with the advent of using massage parlors and saunas for prostitution. While in Minneapolis, Artez and accomplices kidnapped several women, transported them to Madison, imprisoned them, and forced them to work as prostitutes. Artez rented two places for prostitution: Kathi's Sauna in Monona and an apartment on Main Street in Madison, just five blocks south of the capital square.

Rumors of the enterprise spread throughout the area and the Monona and Minneapolis police provided tips to state authorities. In late 1971, A grand jury was impaneled to examine the evidence. The floodgates opened on January 18, 1972, when the grand jury reported its findings. District Attorney Gerald C. Nichol and Attorney General Robert Warren issued warrants for four men and two women for 38 violations in both Wisconsin and Minnesota. State agents, a district attorney investigator, and Dane County sheriff's deputies executed the warrants. Because this was an interstate operation, the indictments would be a mix of state and federal charges. The state charges would first be heard in circuit court whereas the federal charges – Mann Act violations – would be heard in federal court in Madison.

The grand jury produced evidence that "at least 20 women, ranging in age from 17 to 21, were kidnaped or enticed from Minneapolis to Madison where they were sexually tortured, beaten, and forced into prostitution and acts of sexual perversion." They reported that the women were imprisoned in a house near Lake Kegonsa, a few miles to the south.

Authorities charged Artez with 15 vice counts. Although he was armed, police arrested him in Milwaukee without incident. They also arrested Kathleen Gayle Ghinter aka Kathi Artez, Richard G. "Tex" Simpson, Marvin Smith Jr, Ruth Riebe, and Alfred Jackson.

Attorney General Robert Warren compared the arrangement, specifically the living arrangement, to the "Manson Family." Warren said, "We have to recognize that Madison, Wis. has achieved the dubious reputation for being a place where almost anything goes. This has a role to play in attracting this type of activity. The 'permissive' and 'libertine' attitudes allow nude go-go bars to give rise to 'this kind of event or ring.'"[1055]

Danilo Z. "Chico" Artez – Part 1

On January 19, 1972, three defendants faced state charges in circuit court. Danilo Artez was charged with 15 counts of kidnaping, false imprisonment, sexual perversion, battery, soliciting prostitutes, and keeping a place of prostitution. The judge set his bail at $50,000. Ruth Riebe, 22, was charged with three counts of soliciting prostitutes and the judge set her bail at $6,000. Richard G. Simpson, 24, was charged with false imprisonment, obstructing an officer, endangering safety by conduct regardless of life, and sexual perversion, and his bail was set at $20,000. As none were able to post bail, they took up residence in the Dane County jail.

Two members of the ring – Kathleen Ghinter and Alfred F. Jackson – were on the run. Ghinter faced charges of kidnaping, soliciting prostitutes, and battery. Jackson, 18, faced charges of having sexual intercourse with a child. The indictment stated that Ghinter, Artez, and others conspired to "teach and train the women on how to perform and engage in acts of prostitution." When two Minneapolis women wanted to leave the Monona parlor, Richard Simpson beat and tortured them. When one girl objected to her treatment, she was beaten and burned with a soldering iron. The indictment also alleged that the defendants forced a 15-year old into prostitution.[1056] By January 21, Police had apprehended both Ghinter and Jackson.

* * *

On the same day in U.S. District Court, Artez pled not guilty to nine federal counts. Judge James E. Doyle set bail at $10,000 although that bail was moot as Artez was already in Dane County jail for failure to raise the $50,000 bail on state charges.[1057]

* * *

By January 27, Ruth Riebe was freed on $3,000 bail and worked to reopen the business at Kathi's. However, things got dicey when it was learned that "many prominent persons from the Madison area as well as from out of town" had patronized Kathi's Sauna.[1058]

* * *

After two months in the county jail, on March 22, Artez was released on a reduced bail of $20,000 despite being declared a flight risk by the prosecutor. As a condition of bail, Artez had to report to the Dane County district attorney every week, remain in Dane County, with the exception of periodic trips to Milwaukee.[1059] Riebe was about to stand trial and her testimony threatened Artez.

Artez met her at the Brass Monkey tavern on Stoughton Road. After several drinks, he offered to drive her home, but he took her to his apartment instead. There, he assaulted her. He punched her in the face, his fist causing a laceration below the eye. Then he choked her and smashed her head against the floor. The injuries required stiches to her face and head.[1060] After reporting the incident to the police, her trial was postponed, and the Wisconsin Department of Justice issued a warrant for Artez.[1061]

* * *

Despite the court order to stay in Madison, on March 25, Artez spent the weekend with a 17-year-old girl in a Minneapolis hotel.[1062] On March 29, Artez surrendered to authorities. Because of the assault on Ruth Riebe and the trip to Minneapolis, he was sent back to the Dane County jail.

* * *

On April 1, Circuit Court Judge Richard W. Bardwell went soft on Artez. Bardwell said that "he did not think the charges against Artez were very serious." He said, "We've got a lot of unsolved crimes in Madison that are a lot more serious. That bothers me more." He went on to say, "nobody was apparently killed, nobody was apparently hospitalized." Assistant Attorney General David Mebane balked at Bardwell's comment saying, "The victims thought some of these crimes were serious, judge. Two people were almost killed. We almost had two murders here. Does this court condone that type of action?" Barwell continued to minimize the offense telling Mebane, "I just said there were a lot of unsolved murders that maybe you could be spending your time thinking about those." The only consequence was an additional $5,000 tacked onto Artez's bail figure.[1063]

* * *

On April 7, Kathleen Ghinter 23, from Little Falls, Minnesota, changed her plea to no contest on two conspiracy counts in U.S. District court. She also planned to change her plea in circuit court on six counts resulting from the Dane County grand jury. The plea agreement allowed her to sign for the bail, both state and federal. Further, several of the federal offenses would be dismissed. She agreed to testify against the other defendants and the state promised to hold her in protective custody. Ghinter made the deal because of her deep involvement in the business. She and Artez rented the building that housed Kathi's Sauna, she managed the facility, and she admitted to assaulting one of the girls to "prove herself."[1064]

* * *

On April 13, Ruth Riebe, a native of Hutchinson, Minnesota, changed her plea to no contest and agreed to cooperate with the state. As part of the plea agreement, the judge placed her on probation for two years. Alfred Jackson, now 18, changed his plea to no contest and the judge placed him on probation for three years.[1065]

* * *

The trial of Danilo Z. "Chico" Artez opened on June 6, 1972. In his opening statement to the jury, the district attorney said that this was "one of the most bizarre and saddest stories he ever heard. Artez stood trial for 15 vice counts and the prosecution introduced an account book and a soldering iron seized at the house near Lake Kegonsa.[1066]

Sherry Miller Kincaid, 19, testified that she was tortured "because she had 'disrespected my man and disrespected the family.'" She said that "my man" referred to Artez and that "It more or less meant that he owned me." Ortez ordered her torture and Simpson carried out the sentence. Kincade testified, "First he hit me in the stomach and knocked me against the wall." Then Simpson "ordered her to remove her clothes and he hit her again with his fist" She was then gagged and "tied in a 'spreadeagle position on the bed.'" Simson said he would teach her "to show disrespect for our family and our man." He pounded her stomach and warned her that if she screamed, he would kill her. Kincade told the jury that "He asked me whether I preferred to be hit in the stomach 10 times with his fist or kicked with his boot." She said that she would prefer being hit "so he hit me 10 times in the stomach and kicked me anyway." The torture continued when Simpson stuck a soldering iron in her nose, "yanking it back and forth until her nose bled." She said that he did the same thing to other parts of her body, but she didn't go a doctor out of fear.[1067] After the beating, Kincade complained to Artez and showed him the bruises. Artez replied, "You're lucky, I told him to kill you."[1068]

Kincade testified that she had been taken to Madison from Minneapolis to be a masseuse at Kathi's but instead, she was "forced to live in Artez's house on Lake Kegonsa as part of his 'family.'" She told the jury that Artez took turns sleeping with the girls.

Cheryl Dugas, 18, testified that she was taken from Minneapolis with the promise of being a go-go dancer in Madison. She said that she escaped from the house and took a bus back to Minneapolis. One of the women testified that Artez claimed that he was married to "many women."

Sheila Duffy, 18, testified that Marvin Smith took her to Madison from Minneapolis. She said that she got one paycheck from the "sauna," but Artez made her give the money back. Being afraid of Artez, she said that she agreed to sex "every night for the first several weeks" that she was at the house.

Vennie Rainey, 21, had a 3-year-old son and no history of prostitution. Artez had her come to Madison to become a go-go dancer. Instead, he made her work at Kathi's Sauna. After a while, "he and his employes taught her how to treat men and collect money from them." She engaged in prostitution via Kathi's Sauna and lived at the "cottage" where Artez beat her. She told the jury that she "was afraid to leave Artez because he had threatened to have her, her son, and other members of her family killed if she tried to leave."

* * *

On June 8 it was Ruth Riebe's turn to testify for the state according to her plea agreement. She didn't hold back and told the jury that she "typed a list of tricks." The list was entered as evidence, labeled as an exhibit, but had not yet been introduced. She told the jury that her prostitution was either at Kathi's sauna, in the apartment on Main Street, or in "various hotels and motels." She testified that Richard Simpson "was allowed to beat her after she argued with one of the members of the 'family.'"[1069]

* * *

Kathleen Ghinter was the "Kathi" in Kathi's Sauna. Emerging from protective custody, she took the stand on June 9 as a witness for the state as she, also, had a plea agreement. She said that she dated Artez in 1970 and that he behaved like a "perfect gentleman." Not long after Artez moved in with her, he set her up with a "trick." She glared at Artez in the court room and said, "I knew

261

nothing about going to bed with any tricks." She testified that Artez forced her to solicit door-to-door at a Minneapolis motel. Her testimony was damning as she flatly stated, "I was so ashamed that he had dragged me down so bad, I had no other choice. He'll use your mind until you're no longer capable of using it yourself. You don't laugh, you don't cry for fear of getting beat up."

Her testimony darkened as she said that Artez forced her to dress him, undress him, and give him a bath. She said that if she crossed him in any way, he would burn her hair or her legs with cigarettes. She continued, ""He lowers you" and then told the jury that he forced her to pose nearly nude and then sent the photograph to her mother "so that her mother would not want to have any contact with her." She described a suicide attempt from an overdose of sleeping pills to escape the clutches of Artez. She looked directly at him and said, "I thought I'd rather die than live with Chico Artez in that hell, in that damn prison that you made."[1070]

* * *

In a strange twist, on June 10, Judge Bardwell dismissed two counts against Artez leaving 13. He said that there was not enough evidence to show that Artez kidnapped 17-year-old Cheryl Douglas. Bardwell also dismissed that charge that Artez solicited prostitutes. The same day, Richard Simpson took the Fifth Amendment after he was asked about beating any of the girls.[1071]

* * *

On June 22, 1972, the jury returned a guilty verdict for Danilo "Chico" Artez on 11 of the remaining 13 charges. The maximum penalty for the offense was 35 ½ years and a fine of $16,800. The district attorney requested a 30-year sentence. Judge Bardwell again shocked the prosecutor by sentencing Artez to ten years at Waupun along with a fine of $3,000. Artez would be eligible for parole in three years.

Bardwell doubled down on his leniency by shifting much of the blame to Madison. He said, "The indictment of Artez 'in a sense has been an indictment of the City of Madison. Maybe it will cause a rude awakening of the County Board and City Council that sex should not be allowed to run rampant in the city.'" In a surprising show of unity, both the defense attorney and the prosecuting attorney were stunned by the sentence.[1072] Within a few days, Artez was delivered to the state prison a Waupun. However, he still faced the federal charges for violating the Mann Act and Judge Barwell would not be there to help him.

* * *

In June, Madison found itself in the spotlight as a "sin city" and, arguably, a more politically fraught sin city than Hurley ever was. Alderman Eugene Parks said, "the press has implied that nude dancing has attracted 'riff-raff' who have operated houses of prostitution catering to lawyers, bankers, restaurant owners, politicians, and policemen – the same element now clamoring for moral decency." He continued, "nude dancing can lead to rampant prostitution only if law enforcement agencies allow it."[1073] Judge Bardwell commented, "Just why Dane County and Madison authorities do not crack down on obscene dancing remains a mystery." Bardwell was opposed to the need for a grand jury to act against "so-called go-go joints." He said, "communities which attempt to regulate against obscenity by withholding liquor licenses are "taking the long-way round to do something simple.'"[1074] It is difficult to understand the motive of Judge Bardwell as he simultaneously condemned authority and indulged a criminal.

* * *

In October, Danilo Zabala "Chico" Artez appeared in U.S. District Court with a plea deal. If he pled guilty on one of the ten counts against him, U.S. Attorney John O. Olson would request dismissal of the remaining nine counts at the sentencing hearing. Artez seemed contrite and told the judge that he would like to get back to Waupun as soon as possible because he was "handling psychological evaluations at the prison, and there was no one else there to do the job."[1075] Artez, a master of deceit, did not fool Olson.

* * *

On November 1, U.S. District Judge James E. Doyle sentenced Artez to five years in prison on the charge of conspiracy for interstate commerce for prostitution. The term would be served concurrently with his state sentence of ten years. Before sentencing, Artez told the judge that "he had come to Madison two years ago to operate a sauna legitimately. He claimed that he was unable to keep female help because of advances made by men." He went on to say that "he recruited prostitutes from Minneapolis and told them he didn't care what they did as long as they acted on their own hours." He concluded by saying that he got rid of the prostitutes because "he found that he didn't need them because he had developed a cosmetics business that promised to be profitable." After Artez finished, U.S. Attorney Olson remarked that this was "one of the finest performances I have ever seen in a courtroom." Doyle simply said that he was not impressed and Danilo Zabala "Chico" Artez was carted off to prison.[1076]

* * *

Richard G. "Tex" Simpson – Part 1

The focus shifted to 25-year-old Richard G. "Tex" Simpson. On November 9, 1972, he entered a crowded courtroom "in high cowboy boots, a leather jacket, a shaved head and a goatee mustache." He faced two counts of false imprisonment, two counts of endangering safety by conduct regardless of life, one count of sexual perversion, and one count of obstructing justice. The trial had two parts. The first was to determine if Simpson was guilty of the charges. The second was to determine if he was mentally ill when the crimes took place.

Kathleen Ghinter, the first witness, offered a blistering testimony. She said that Simpson had bragged to her that he "could torture a girl for 24 hours straight and lot leave a mark on her." Ghinter testified that Artez sold a girl to Simpson for a quarter so that he could punish her. After the 25-cent exchange, Artez told Simpson, "Now she's yours." The prosecutor said that Simpson was the enforcer and prevented girls from leaving the family. Ghinter said that the girls could escape but they were "so brainwashed with fear that they didn't."[1077]

Vennie Rainey testified that being at the parlor and at the Lake Kegonsa house was like being in a "concentration camp" with Simpson being "like a prison guard." She testified that Simpson said "he was going to keep me there for a while then bury me." She also described how Simpson tortured another girl from Minneapolis with a soldering iron because "she had disrespected the family."[1078] On November 10, after deliberating for an hour, the jury found Richard Simpson guilty. With the verdict delivered, the next part of the trial was to determine if Simpson was mentally ill when the crimes took place.

In a packed courtroom, it took the entire morning for Simpson to describe his life. Simpson told the jury that he had once beat up a ten-year-old girl, watched a young man rape a girl, and that he had homosexual and incestuous sex. He confessed that he never had "traditional" intercourse because he didn't want to get a girl pregnant.

He recited several incidents from his childhood. He told the jury that when he was in sixth grade, his mother forced him to wear dress pants to a square dance when all the other kids wore jeans. When he came home, the pants were dirty, and his mother beat him for "about 10 to 15 minutes." He said that at a family get together, he was drinking a glass of milk with his little finger extended. His mother thought the action was vulgar and nearly broke his finger.

He told the jury that when he was 12 years old his mother beat him often for perceived offenses. He said that she forced him to have oral sex with "many of her friends and herself as well." He said that his mother "whipped him nearly every day" after school. He said that during his childhood, she would leave for extended periods before returning. He said that he knew that she was a prostitute. When he was 15 years old, his mother died after taking "six bottles of sleeping pills." Simpson said that made him mad and that, "I was waiting for the day when I would be big enough to revenge her for what she did to me." The following year, his father, who he was close to, died in an industrial accident.

He talked about several head injuries from motorcycle accidents and that he "committed himself several times to hospitals for mental trouble." His attorney asked for an example and Simpson said, "It's like you and I are talking right now and the next minute I have my hands around your throat." Tom Hibbard of *The Capital Times* described his testimony "to be alternately sadistic and puritanical as he unfolded the tale of his unhappy life."[1079]

Dr. Joseph Brown, the defense psychiatrist testified that Simpson had told him that he had "worked over" 19 to 20 prostitutes "in the hope that by working them over, they would learn how terrible prostitution was and get out." Brown said that Simpson "was chronic schizophrenic and was unable to 'conform his conduct to the requirement of the law. Simpson only vaguely perceives the wrongness of his behavior.'"[1080]

The maximum sentence that Simpson faced was 20 years. However, on November 17, Judge Bardwell postponed his sentencing. He said that the Wisconsin Supreme Court "has strongly urged a pre-sentence investigation in all serious criminal cases." Although he referred to Simpson's behavior as "reprehensible," he said that "It would be unfair to the state, court, and defendant not to order one." Nobody objected.[1081] After the investigation, the jury found him to be sane, and therefore, guilty as charged.

*   *   *

Meanwhile, on November 28, Federal Judge Doyle placed Kathleen Ghinter on probation for two years. The relief was short-lived as Circuit Judge Bardwell refused probation on the state charges until he could review the pre-sentencing report. Bardwell rebuked Ghinter when she burst into tears. He said, "You don't realize the breaks you've already gotten. You're not helping yourself by your show of emotion." When her attorney told the judge that the federal government had arranged both a job and an educational program for Ghinter, Bardwell said that she should "not have presumed that she would receive probation…when she pleaded no contest." Her attorney replied that she had already spent 70 days in jail, but the judge was unmoved.[1082]

However, a couple of days later, Ghinter reappeared before Judge Bardwell. He had read the pre-sentencing report and told Ghinter that he would not interfere with her "federal educational program" and he put her on probation for three years. She cried again, but this time, Bardwell took her hand, and he wished her luck.[1083] Kathleen Ghinter went on to earn an associate degree in administrative support, then married and settled into life.

*　*　*

On December 19, 1972, Judge Bardwell held the sentencing hearing for Richard Simpson. As with other testimony from Simpson, this took an odd turn. There was something in Simpson that wanted to get out, to be recognized, to be controlled, and to reconcile his history. He begged the court to give him the maximum term of 20 years. He said, "It's going to be an improvement on the way I've lived. I'll get heat, I'll get good food and clean linens for the first time in my life." He went on, "I don't mind prison, I welcome it. You could put me away for the rest of my life and I wouldn't care." He concluded his statement by pleading with Bardwell, "You're an officer of the public. It's your job to give me what I want. I want the maximum." Bardwell was shocked as he had never heard anyone ask for the maximum. Taken aback, he explained that "he had to judge him on what the evidence showed, and on the basis of the pre-sentence report which the court ordered." The judge concluded by referencing a report from the probation officer which said that Simpson "eschewed sex, money and liquor." Bardwell said, "In a society that we have today somebody might say to the average person, 'What else is there?'" Judge Bardwell sentenced Richard Simpson to nine years in prison.[1084] Simpson was the last of the original group of six indicted by the Dane County Grand Jury regarding Kathi's Sauna.

Richard G. "Tex" Simpson – Part 2

Don Wells operated several taverns in Madison in the early 1970s including the Brass Rail, Mr. Peepers, the Peppermint Lounge, and a strip joint called Diamond Don's. In June of 1974, Don Wells had an epiphany. Soon afterward, he founded the Upper Room Christian Fellowship Ministry. Reverend Richard Pritchard was the pastor of Heritage Congregational Church and was Madison's leading opponent of the sex-for-sale business. Pritchard worked with Wells through the Fellowship Ministry to reform prostitutes.[1085]

During his time in prison, Richard "Tex" Simpson also had an epiphany. After serving his time, he moved to Madison on January 6, 1981. There, he joined the Heritage Congregational Church and worked with the Upper Room Christian Fellowship Ministry.

*　*　*

In March of 1982, he sat for a chilling interview with Mike Miller of *The Capital Times*. He told Miller that "I tortured women for a living. My first six years in prison I figured out 200 methods of torture I could use on human beings. I wanted to experiment with them when I got out." In terms of keeping the prostitutes in line, he said, "I was brutal. There is no defense for what I did. I didn't enjoy doing it, but I enjoyed being good at it." He told Miller that "I am working now in an organization trying to help women get out of prostitution."

Simpson gave a presentation to a citizen's group at Madison East High School on March 24, 1982, about current crime in the area. He told the audience that while in prison, he watched "hours of religious shows on television" and said that "I am not the same person I was then. I am a

265

Christian." He said he first began watching religious programs because "they all had some foxy ladies on them." This led to his listening to the message, and he was converted. He recalled an instruction from Kathleen Ghinter telling him to discipline one of the girls. He said, "She was supposed to be tortured off and on again for 72 hours in the garage. I remember just like it was yesterday." He went on to say, "The beating was called off after about eight minutes because Chico was looking in the window and it made him sick. He came in and said that's enough."

He discussed the operation of "Kathi's Sauna" and said, "not all of the women who worked as masseuses also worked as hookers. In fact, we had a lot of decent girls who gave straight massages and nothing else." Simpson described an incident that ended the career of one of the masseuses. He related, "I remember once – we had these really dark rooms with only red light bulbs – a girl was back there and the guy she was with kept trying to talk her into doing something sexual. She kept saying no. He kept insisting she do something to him, and when he turned over, she got a look at him and discovered it was her priest. She was no good to us after that. Every time she would get with a guy, she would see that face of her priest."

When asked about the infamous "list" of clients, Simpson said, "It really didn't have names in it. It had nicknames, and a brief description of who each person was." When asked who they were, he responded that "there were senators, businessmen, councilmen, FBI agents, judges, out-of-state governors, and reporters." Someone asked if any were from Madison. Simpson said, "I am not saying where they are from but that most – but not all – were from out of town."

He commented that only about one-third of the operation at Kathi's got arrested. Simpson told the audience that, on several occasions, he turned down parole opportunities because he wanted to "serve the entire term of his sentence." One reason he gave for avoiding parole was concern that he might hook up with Artez. Simpson said that after he became a Christian in 1978, he "he turned down all of his prison 'good time' so that he would do his duty and serve his full sentence."[1086]

*   *   *

Four years later, in February of 1986, 40 people marched along State Street in Madison to protest against the State Street Adult Amusement Arcade. Simpson was there. He told the group who he was and said, "A few of you are too young to remember my case" and then said that he was a born-again Christian and his faith "rescued him from a life ruined by pornography."[1087]

*   *   *

Richard G. Simpson died on July 31, 2010, in Madison. When he was first arrested on June 19, 1972, he gave his address as the Veterans Administration Hospital. His military service was never mentioned in the trial, in his years in prison, or during his life afterward. His obituary stated that he was a "very active member of the Chinese Christian Church for over 20 years." He was buried at the Southern Wisconsin Veterans Memorial Cemetery in Union Grove, Wisconsin.

His gravestone is inscribed as follows: Richard G. Simpson, PFC, U.S. Army, Vietnam, February 28, 1947 – July 31, 2010. Below the date, it states, "Beloved Servant of Christ Jesus Defender of the Weak and Humble." Richard Simpson's story is a classic tale of suffering and redemption.

*   *   *

In June of 1972, Judge Bardwell sentenced Danilo Z. "Chico" Artez to ten years in prison with eligibility for parole in three years. While in prison, he wrote short stories and novels and organized a Jaycee chapter.

In 1975, Chico Artez fell in love with an Appleton woman while in the Fox Lake Corrections Institute. He was so enthralled that he sent a formal wedding invitation to Circuit Court Judge Richard W. Bardwell. The press did not report whether Bardwell attended or provided a gift. The humor was not lost on *The Capital Times,* as they wrote, "No mention is made of where the couple expects to go on their honeymoon."[1088] Judge Bardwell gave Artez a late gift when, in March of 1976, he reduced his term by 141 days to credit the time that he spent in jail before conviction.[1089] He was paroled later that year.

*   *   *

The FBI along with the Wisconsin Department of Justice conducted a five-month investigation of prostitution in 1977. In November of 1978, FBI agents arrested Danilo Z. "Chico" Artez, now 42, in Minneapolis on federal charges of transporting 15-year-olds between Minnesota and Wisconsin. There was no reform and Artez was up to his old tricks.

He faced four counts of violating the Mann Act, each carrying a possible 10 years and $10,000 fine. In a search of his apartment in Rochester, they found "prostitution paraphernalia" and a list of names along with photographs, presumably for purposes of blackmail.[1090] At the end of November, Artez waived extradition based on an indictment by a U.S. District grand jury in Madison.[1091] On December 1, he was released on a $15,000 surety bond in Minneapolis and ordered to appear in Madison within ten days.[1092]

*   *   *

On December 9, 1978, a St. Paul grand jury returned 22 indictments against six people relating to a four-state juvenile prostitution ring operating out of Rochester. Artez was the ring leader but five others were also charged including George Clark, Vicki Ann Sherman, Marquetta Hays, Paul Boyd, and Wilbert Ratcliff aka Jimmy Taylor.[1093] Chico Artez was in the center of it again.

*   *   *

On January 3, 1979, the U.S. Attorney learned that the charges in Minnesota, where the prostitution ring was based, were more severe than in Wisconsin. He asked Judge Doyle to dismiss the indictment against Artez and let him face a Minnesota judge.[1094]

*   *   *

Since Artez had no remorse, the Minneapolis court heard the same old story. A 13-year-old girl testified that Artez recruited her as a go-go dancer but then beat her when she would not have sex with him. Eventually, one of Artez's women employes convinced the young girl to become a prostitute.[1095] The testimonies from the young witnesses where nearly identical to those in 1972. The only differences were the names, the ages, and the enforcer. After "Tex" Simpson took an alternative path, Artez hired George T. Clark. He was an imposing figure at 6'11" and 350 pounds.

An FBI agent testified that Artez married Sally Jo Turnbaugh so that, as his wife, would not be able to testify against him. Turnbaugh was likely his prison wife. The plan didn't work since the FBI showed that Artez "had been married three times since 1968 but never divorced."[1096]

On March 30, 1979, a jury returned a guilty verdict on eight counts against Artez, now 43, in a U.S. District Court in Minneapolis. Only seven women testified out of a possible 25. The prosecution only called those that they needed as the others were too frightened to testify.[1097]

* * *

On June 2, 1979, in Minneapolis, Judge Henry MacLaughlin referred to the crimes as "shocking, heinous and despicable." He then sentenced Danilo Artez to 15 years in a federal penitentiary.[1098]

* * *

After his release in 1995, Artez lived in Minnesota. Six years later, he moved to Green Bay where, in June 2001, he created a business called, "Friends of Homeless Women and Children." The business was a front that he used to lure young women into prostitution. He registered the business location being a vacant lot in St. Paul.

* * *

On October 29, 2003, he recorded the same organization in Green Bay with an address being an apartment on Janice Avenue.[1099] Later that month, he was arrested and charged with two felony counts for working with children and for failing to register as a sex offender.[1100]

* * *

In June 2004, Artez, now 68, was charged with a felony for "being a child sex offender working with children."[1101] He was convicted for letting teenage girls drink, use drugs and have sex in his apartment and told them "It was fine as long as the police weren't involved."[1102] In mid-August, a Brown County judge sentenced Artez to four years in prison and eight years of supervision and registered him as a sex offender.

* * *

There was no apparent epiphany for Danilo Zabala "Chico" Artez. Perhaps he was destined to be tormented by the same devils for the rest of his life.

1973

Hurley: Old, Dilapidated, and Unfit

ON MAY 16, the Hurley City Council agreed to clean up the burned-out buildings on the lower block of Silver Street, including Louis Gasbarri's Cactus Bar, the old Outhouse Bar, Theresa Kalasardo's Band Box, and Richard Matrella's Club Carnival. The council wanted them either removed or repaired and authorized City Attorney Alex Raineri to file a complaint against the owners of the buildings identified as "old, dilapidated, dangerous, unsafe, unsanitary, or otherwise unfit for human occupancy."[1103]

Milwaukee: Lawyer Arraigned as Pimp

ATTORNEY RONALD PACHEFSKY, 43, operated a law practice on Wisconsin Avenue in downtown Milwaukee between June of 1971 and August of 1973. Pachefsky also operated a side hustle pimping out his receptionists in the adjacent office. He told his receptionists that if they wanted to make extra money, they should go into the adjoining office and wait. Pachefsky would have a client pay $10 to have sex with his receptionist. One woman testified that she had ten or twelve encounters and got $10 for each. Three other women testified that they also took advantage of the extra pay, although one demanded $25. Pachefsky, representing a woman during her divorce, offered to reduce her $125 bill by $10 every time she "performed a sex act."[1104] In August of 1976, Pachefsky pled no contest and abandoned his law license.[1105]

Milwaukee: The Forlorn Case of Connie Purpora

CAROL PURPORA, AKA CONNIE PURPORA, now 24, was one of the women threatened by Thomas Chiolino in the kitchen of the Club 13 in 1971. While awaiting sentencing on the perjury charge, Purpora moved into a friend's apartment in Milwaukee.

At this time, U.S. Attorney John O. Olson was investigating the relationship between Hurley and Milwaukee and moved to convene a grand jury investigation. Carol Purpora agreed to participate. The court appointed Madison attorney, Kevin Lyons, to represent Purpora. However, on October 1, 1973, before she could testify, someone drove a knife into her heart. Lyons asked the FBI to investigate.[1106]

Both the Milwaukee Police and the Medical Examiner ruled the death as suicide.[1107] Lyons was suspicious and wrote to Milwaukee District Attorney E. Michael McCann[1108] asking for an inquest. Lyons cited relevant facts leading to his suspicion saying, "Among these circumstances, according to the FBI, are the facts that no fingerprints were found on the knife which fatally wounded Miss Purpora in the heart and the fact that she died on the day that she had determined to become a witness for the federal government in a pending grand jury probe of rackets and prostitution in Milwaukee County." Lyons said that he believed Purpora's death was "either self-murder (suicide) or homicide (murder)."

* * *

There is no indication that an investigation was ever conducted, and the case went cold.

269

However, suicide by knife to the heart is exceptionally rare and difficult. An attempt to do so would probably require holding the knife and falling against an object, such as the floor. In such a case, fingerprints would be all over the weapon. There were no fingerprints on the knife in Purpora's death. It was probably murder and the absence of an investigation is suspicious. Certainly, the Milwaukee police could have considered motive, opportunity, and means to narrow the search.

Milwaukee: The Ferris Jewell Connection

UNITED STATES ATTORNEY JOHN OLSON held the federal grand jury in Milwaukee in mid-November. One indictment was for Farris Jewel, 39, of Milwaukee. During the investigation, Jewell told the FBI that he was unaware of Purpora's whereabouts. As a result of the grand jury, he was charged with transporting women across state lines for prostitution and for concealing and providing a home for Carol Purpora, knowing she was a fugitive.

* * *

Farris Jewel was an unsavory character. Three years earlier, in June 1970, Jewell, referred to as "the Bear" or "The Running Bear," was involved in a shooting death in Madison. Helen Reichert, 22, was originally from Madison but lived at the Milwaukee YWCA at this time. She knew Jewell and needed a ride from Milwaukee to Madison for a babysitting job. Jewell and Odell White, 33, drove her from Milwaukee to Madison. While traveling on Packers Avenue, they became entangled in a road rage incident with Robert Borchardt, 31, a Madison construction worker. After an ongoing argument and a series of cut-offs, both vehicles stopped at a traffic light on the corner of Commercial and Packers Avenue. White decided he would confront Borchardt. Jewell handed him a .32 caliber semi-automatic from the glove box of his blue 1968 Lincoln Continental.[1109] White walked over to Borchardt, reached through the open window, and fired a round into Borchardt's head, killing him instantly. Borchardt's green Pontiac rolled forward and came to rest against a fence at Oscar Mayer's factory.[1110]

* * *

Jewell testified in court on a promise of immunity and was released.[1111] During the trial, White tried to convince the jury that "he went to punch Borchardt but forgot that he had a gun in his hand." Unconvinced, they found White guilty, and the judge sentenced him to life for first-degree murder. On appeal, the Wisconsin Supreme court upheld the lower court ruling, and White went to learn hard labor at the State Prison at Waupun.[1112]

* * *

In 1973, Farris Jewel appealed a conviction for the interstate transportation of women between Milwaukee and Chicago for prostitution. The record described how Jewel threatened Susan Hunter "if she did not become his 'woman.'" Jewel forced Hunter into prostitution, and she worked in Hurley for him in October 1972. Both Susan Hunter and Carol Purpora said that at one time, they lived in a building owned by Jewel. However, Hunter refused to reveal her current address because she was afraid of him.[1113] There is no record of the outcome of Jewel's conviction for violating the Mann Act in 1973.

* * *

Farris Jewel was the connection between Hurley and Milwaukee when he employed Susan

Hunter to work in Hurley in 1972. One can only wonder if any of the other young women who worked on Silver Street had silent partners outside of Hurley.

* * *

Farris Jewel "The Bear," died in Milwaukee in June 2013 at age 79.

1974

Madison: The Cold Case of Misty Hayes

IT WAS A NIPPY 53 DEGREES on March 7, 1974, in Lexington Park, Maryland. Nonetheless, Eunice Winget, aka Misty Hayes, 32, removed all her clothes except her high black leather boots. With her black leather purse slung over her shoulder, she directed traffic at what the press described as "a very busy intersection." One man became distracted and ran his car across a churchyard, tearing up the lawn.

The Lexington Park police arrested Mrs. Winget but failing to appear in court, she forfeited her $250 bond, and the judge issued a bench warrant for her arrest. She was apprehended, paid the fine, and contributed $10 to help repair the church lawn.[1114] However distant, Misty Hayes is connected to Hurley and her story is presented in the next episode.

Madison: Prostitution, Debauchery, And Other Immoral Acts

BEFORE THE CLUB CARNIVAL burned in 1971, Richard Matrella, at age 56, moved to Newport, Kentucky, a place introduced to him by James Harris. There, he managed two "nightspots," including the Galaxy Club. In early November 1973, Matrella and Oscar "Leon" Snow traveled to Wisconsin to face charges of white slavery. When the offense occurred, Matrella had been part owner of the Club Carnival.

Snow had been convicted in Cincinnati in federal court for transporting women from Kentucky to Tennessee for prostitution. Matrella had been convicted in Kentucky for pandering.[1115] Although both were out of custody awaiting appeals, they faced charges in Madison.

On April 3, 1974, Matrella faced four counts of transporting women from Kentucky to Hurley to work at the Show Bar before its demise. U.S. Attorney John Olson charged him with transporting women across state lines "to engage in 'prostitution, debauchery, and other immoral acts' in Hurley." Misty Hayes had worked for Matrella and Olson called her to testify.

Hayes explained that sexual "favors" were based on the price of champagne. She told the jury that the women at the Show Bar earned up to $140 a week plus a 50-cent commission on drinks. They earned a $6 commission on a $33 bottle of champagne and $12 on a $55 bottle. The $55 champagne included sexual intercourse. Hayes testified that she worked at the Show Bar on three occasions, and "Jackpot" eventually fired her for "selling 'tricks' off the premises."

As evidence of interstate transportation of women, Olson told the jury that Matrella purchased an airline ticket for one woman, bus tickets for two others, and drove a fourth in his Cadillac. The defense attorney argued that the girls "volunteered" to go to Hurley because rates were higher and "the cost of transportation was refunded to Matrella from the money they made in Hurley." Misty Hayes added intrigue when she testified that she worked at a strip joint called the Fuzz Club in Newport Kentucky, operated by a police sergeant.

Hayes testified that Richard Matrella purchased an airline ticket for her to travel from Cincinnati to Duluth where Richard's brother William met her at the airport and drove her to Hurley. Hayes said that when she tried to board the plane, the crew refused to let her board the plane because of her "scanty costume." After explaining that it was the same outfit she wore on the street, the crew let her on the plane.

Olson called others to the stand. Through some process of magical thinking, on cross-examination, several of the girls testified that they did not consider themselves prostitutes and that "if they could satisfy customers buying 'bottles' without giving then sexual favors they would do so." Olson pressed a witness, "In your opinion, were any sexual favors given on the premises of the Show Bar without the purchase of a bottle?" The defense attorney objected saying that the woman was not qualified as an expert witness because she did not consider herself a prostitute but rather, an exotic dancer. Olson replied that, given her previous testimony, she should qualify as an expert. The judge agreed, and the girl answered, "No."

The government wanted to connect Jack Gasbarri with the ownership of the Show Bar, but Gasbarri refused to answer any questions, taking the Fifth Amendment instead.[1116] The business of the Show Bar was a tangled arrangement, but Olson teased out the facts: Louis Gasbarri (Jack's brother) held title, Adina Gasbarri (Louis's wife) held the liquor license, and Richard Matrella owned the fixtures.

* * *

On April 3, 1974, after deliberating for an hour, the jury found Richard Matrella guilty for bringing women from out of state to the Show Bar in Hurley. The judge released him on a $10,000 signature bond and told him not to leave Wisconsin, Ohio, or Kentucky.[1117] One week later, his co-conspirator, Hank Snow, faced the same charges.[1118]

* * *

On June 21, Judge Doyle sentenced Oscar L. F. "Hank" Snow to four years and Richard Matrella to two years in federal prison. Gratified, his mission complete, U.S. Attorney John O. Olson resigned his post and entered private practice.[1119]

Madison: Federal Judge Rosenstein Takes It on the Chin

UNITED STATES FEDERAL JUDGE Samuel M. Rosenstein from Miami filled in when Judge James Doyle vacationed in the early 1970s. In July 1974, Rosenstein heard the perjury case against Rose Chesley aka Rose Taylor, a waitress at the Show Bar in Hurley. Chesley told the judge that she waitressed at the Show Bar on Silver Street, lived in both Hurley and Rockford, and that she had five children. The jury found Chesley guilty of perjury, and Rosenstein placed her on probation for two years.[1120]

Rosenstein was deeply affected by the testimony and railed against state and local law enforcement, and the people in the Hurley for permitting these criminal activities. After hearing the testimony of young women, he said, "I am convinced that a state of practical involuntary servitude exists at Hurley. That's polite language for slavery and slavery is an ugly word in anyone's language."[1121] He said that he thought there was "something wrong with the licensing agents," and he said couldn't understand why the women would risk jail to protect the operators.[1122]

Rosenstein got hammered for his criticism with most correspondence unsigned. He apologized, saying he "did not mean to criticize the entire Hurley community, but only officials who permit unsavory conditions there." His comments cut deep, and his apology fell on deaf ears.

On July 30, *The Capital Times* dramatized Rosenstein's remarks when they wrote, "Among the seemingly eternal verities that distinguish northern Wisconsin are its pines, its lakes, its mosquitoes, and the whores of Hurley. We swat the mosquitoes, admire the lakes and pines, and ignore the whores."

The *Times* concluded, "Judge Rosenstein ought to save his breath. The only time law enforcement agencies get upset about prostitution on Hurley's Silver Street is around election time. The agents swoop down then on a few bars, arrest a few women, and then relax until another election comes up."[1123]

However, the next day, July 31, their tone changed. Miles McMillin of Madison's *Capital Times* wrote, "Ordinarily, anyone who has words of derogation about Hurley and its whores gets a resounding skyrocket from these quarters. And it would be something less than the truth to say that we did not get a charge out of Federal Judge Samuel Rosenstein's shot at Hurley the other day." McMillin continued, "However, Judge Rosenstein is from Miami, and I suggest to him that the chief difference between Miami and Hurley, aside from the climate, is the fact that Hurley's whores are far less numerous than Miami's and work for much lower fees."[1124]

Hurley: Sodom, Gomorrah, and Rosenstein

IN THE FIRST WEEK OF AUGUST, Madison's *Capital Times* published an article by Armand Cirilli where he scolded Rosenstein. Cirilli recalled a recent sermon where God told Abraham that "he would spare Sodom even if there were only 10 good people in it." Cirilli said, "Not so a man named Judge Samuel Rosenstein of Miami. Lord over his bench at Madison, he was as thoughtless as our Lord was charitable; he was as ill-informed as our Lord was kind."

Cirilli may have gone part-time, but his literary prowess had not lost its edge. He wrote, "Judge Rosenstein called Hurley a den of iniquity from a court in the federal building at Madison – a city where nudity takes place during the cocktail hour; where high school girls take their clothes off on a stage during 'amateur night;' where you can walk into a 'studio' and take pictures of nude women until 2 a.m.; where strange things take place in sauna parlors."

Cirilli added perspective: "But Hurley at the present time has one marginal strip joint where it is reported that there is a champagne routine which has been known to culminate in an offer of prostitution. That is our sin."[1125]

Cirilli got in the last word, and most wondrous, it came wrapped in Madison's *Capital Times*.

1975

Town of Newbold: The Boom Bay Bar

T HE BOOM BAY BAR WAS in the Town of Newbold, on Highway 47 near Rhinelander. It had
been in business since at least 1950 with little trouble. Things took a turn in January 1973
when an agent for the Wisconsin Department of Justice arrested Barbara Maclin, 19, aka Barbie
Doll, for solicitation. She offered to have sex with the agent for $25 and then went to his hotel
room in Rhinelander, where she got pinched. Barbie Doll was not cooperative and resisted. It was
an awkward arrest as the agent had to handcuff her in order to dress her before carting her off to
jail.[1126]

On January 14, 1975, there was a dust-up about the dancers at the Boom Bay. The *Rhinelander
Daily News* wrote, "A rural Rhinelander night spot's off-again, on-again bout with local officials
and citizens concerning nude entertainment, is nearing a decisive point." Local citizens expressed
concern about prostitution and what the *Daily News* referred to as "topless and bottomless
dancers."[1127] Presumably, the term "nude dancing" was not yet in vogue. In March 1976, keeper
charges against the operator, Kenneth Hart, were dropped.[1128]

The Boom Bay Bar continued to offer "topless and bottomless dancers," and the rumor of
prostitution lingered. In 1986, Randy Barber, the operator, said, "dancers who perform while
wearing little more than shoes and bracelets drop by for a week or two on a circuit that includes
Green Bay, Appleton, Milwaukee, and Minneapolis." His wife reported that "some dancers may
offer to have sex with customers, but we don't condone it."[1129]

In July 1994, authorities revoked the license of the Boom Bay Bar after 25 years of business.
The revocation resulted after the stepson of the owner let a 15-year-old runaway dance in the
nude.[1130]

Milwaukee: So Many Policemen!

I N EARLY FEBRUARY 1975, a Milwaukee police officer was about to get married, and his fellow
officers wanted to host a stag party with the obligatory nude dancer. Another officer, wanting to
get good talent at a low price, confronted a prostitute and threatened arrest unless she agreed to
perform at the party. It was the obvious solution since the girl was a skilled dancer and coercion
minimized the cost.

They got more than they bargained for as she both danced nude *and* offered sexual favors to all
40 officers. In an alcohol-related incident, the guest of honor "danced nude on a platform with a
nude woman." After the party, the cops passed the hat and gave the 21-year-old $103 for her
services.

It is challenging to keep such events private, and it ended badly when an investigator arrested
the girl. He asked her to identify those with whom she was intimate. She said, "I can't recall the
number; there were so many. Although she went to trial, the officer who coerced the young woman
failed to appear, and the judge dropped the charges.[1131] On March 12, after a parade of 31
witnesses at trial, Robert R. Starker, the guest-of-honor of the party, paid $175 after pleading guilty

for lewd and lascivious conduct at his own bachelor party.[1132]

On July 17, 1975, Milwaukee Judge Donald Steinmetz exonerated the arresting officers as he said that "it was coincidence that they did not appear for the woman's trial," which was scheduled the day after the party. Not all was forgiven, however, as Starker got fired, four cops resigned, 34 were suspended, and five warrants were issued.[1133]

Given the hoopla, one cannot help but wonder about how Starker's fiancé received this news.

Madison: Governor Patrick Lucey Intervenes

PATRICK J. LUCEY SERVED AS Governor of Wisconsin in 1975. He was aware of the problems of prostitution in Hurley. However, Hurley was fighting with the Wisconsin Department of Natural Resources in February about a solid waste disposal plan. Late in the process, the DNR fined the City of Hurley $8,000. Part of the problem was slow action on the part of DNR. Governor Lucey was unhappy with the DNR and said, "It was part of a pattern of agency foot-dragging in time after time would 'study, re-study, procrastinate, and postpone' decisions and not take action." Lucey intervened and said, "it was a pretty heavy penalty for a community that had lost its two major industries."

At a press conference, John Wyngaard, chief of the *Appleton Post-Crescent's* Madison bureau, asked Lucey, "What was the other major industry?" After a short hesitation, quick-witted Lucey replied, "Uh . . . mining."[1134]

Hurley: Cirilli Hammers Madison

IN 1975, MADISON WAS RIFE with exotic dancing, escort services, and prostitution. Topless restaurants, such as the Dangle, offered lunch within a block of the Capitol building. At 5:00 p.m., commuters passed prostitutes who hovered around street corners. Occasionally, a female officer, dressed as a prostitute, would nab an unexpecting customer. For the most part, however, it was a free for all.

The local newspapers ran ads for Do-It-Yourself nude photography on East Johnson Street, Whiskey A-Go-Go on the beltline, The Rising Sun Counseling Clinic for adults on West Main, and the Geisha House on East Washington Avenue. Nude dancing and its associated wickedness blanketed the Capital City, and so-called escort services offered sexual massages in the metro Madison Area. In April 1976, Police Lt. Ted Balistreri, head of the Dane County Metro Narcotics Squad, said that as many as 42 escort services operated in the area on January 1, 1976.[1135]

Armand Cirilli, tenacious and righteously irritable, would not abandon a chance to needle Madison. He wrote a piece for the *Iron County Miner,* which the *Wisconsin State Journal* courageously published on November 10, 1975. Cirilli noted the advertisements for sex on the Journal's entertainment page and called Madison the "new" Hurley. He wrote, "it's about time Hurley in Iron County lost the title of Wisconsin's "No. 1 Sin City" and that he could not think of a more "worthier successor than the state capital of Madison." He continued, "If Madison is any seat of culture, that page soils the image. On it is found a curious offering of food, flesh, X-rated Heaven, Erotic Dreams, and a general potpourri of pornography."

"There is an ad showing a well-endowed topless gal who will dance in the nude starting at 4:30

in the afternoon . . . there are three ads for massage parlors right on top of each other which proclaim, '15 beautiful playmates to serve you in stereophonic elegance.'"

Cirilli admitted that Hurley has long been considered a "capital city" for some of life's more illicit pleasures, especially around hunting season" but "Hurley pales by comparison to the enticements of Madison as revealed in the advertisements."[1136]

He was right in his assessment, as the zeitgeist of the 1960s evolved into a crude and overt exhibition of sexuality that enveloped large cities. In Wisconsin, as authorities hammered at smaller cities such as Hurley, La Crosse, and Kenosha, the real show emerged under the watchful eye of legislators within a block of the capitol dome.

Milwaukee: Sid Caeser Gets Special Attention

ON OCTOBER 25, A TWO-MONTH John Doe probe investigated organized crime in Milwaukee County. Authorities issued prostitution-related charges against Anthony Pipito, 38, Angelo Fazio, 59, Joseph B. Basile, 35, Leroy Bell, 48, Richard McCormick, 37, and Craig Kuper, 23. Authorities charged Pipito with three counts of soliciting prostitutes and one charge of extortion. They charged Fazio and Basile with three counts of soliciting women to work as prostitutes. They charged Bell for soliciting juveniles to serve as prostitutes. They charged Kuper with pandering.[1137]

Comedian Sid Caesar performed several times during 1975 in Milwaukee. When Caesar got lonely, he asked Anthony Pipito to provide some company. When Pipito was to stand trial in January of 1976, the district attorney cut a deal with Caesar. In exchange for freedom from prosecution, he agreed to testify against Pipito. Caesar testified that Pipito provided girls on three occasions during 1975. On the third request, Pipito sent a girl who had sex with Caesar and charged him $200 plus a $20 cab fare. The next day, Caesar told Pipito, "That's kind of a stiff price, $220. Pipito later returned the money to Caesar. His two future engagements with prostitutes were fee-free. A prostitute testified that Caesar smoked marijuana and while she performed a sex act with him – true to form – he was "laughing constantly."[1138]

On January 15, 1976, the jury returned a guilty verdict against Anthony Pipito, now 39, for soliciting a prostitute for Caesar.[1139]

Hurley: Jackpot Gasbarri Dies

IN 1975, JOHN "JACKPOT" GASBARRI owned the Show Bar and the White Way Motel, both on Silver Street. Jackpot died on November 24 at the age of 61. Gasbarri was a member of the remaining confederation of strip joint operators in Hurley. He was also a veteran of many raids and unapologetically tangled with city, state, and federal authorities. Pallbearers at the funeral included Robert Palmquist, James Vitich, Thomas Chiolino, Jerel Gasbarri, Judge Alex Raineri, and Agatino DiGiorgio.

1976

Madison: The Loss of a Legend

AFTER DISCHARGE FROM THE ARMY in November 1945, John Roach returned to his old position displacing Clyde Tutton, who had assumed his duties during Roach's military tour.

In August 1948, Roach resigned as chief of the Wisconsin Beverage Tax Division and worked as a public relations adviser for the New York headquarters of Calvert Distillers Corporation. Roach held this position for over a decade and traveled within each state every two years. After his employment with Calvert, Roach moved back to Madison and made two unsuccessful runs for the city council. Beginning with his military tour, Roach started drinking heavily, and after two heart-related hospital visits in March 1976, he died at his home in Madison on Sunday, May 16, 1976, at 73.

Two weeks later, Tom Butler, a reporter for the *Wisconsin State Journal,* wrote a tribute to Roach. He said, "His death ended a colorful career that included football, law, soldiering, business, and government service. He accomplished more in each profession than most people do in a lifetime."[1140]

That was John Roach: tough, arrogant, poignant, likable, smart, and accomplished. He was the ultimate antagonist during the vice raids of northern Wisconsin.

Wisconsin: Natural Laws and Individual Sovereignty

David E. Brown, 44, ran for city council in Eau Claire in the spring of 1976. However, the previous December, police had arrested him for soliciting a prostitute. The charges were subsequently changed to two counts of pandering to which the candidate pled no contest. He stated, that if elected, he would "be a guardian of your natural laws and ensure that your individual sovereignty is respected."[1141] Brown was subsequently sentenced to concurrent 90-day jail terms, lost the election, and was unable to guard his constituents natural laws or individual sovereignty.[1142]

* * *

In March, DOJ agents arrested four prostitutes at Gigi's Pussy Cat Lounge and the Tom Cat Show Lounge in Oshkosh. The women were from Oshkosh, Milwaukee, Chicago, and Tampa.[1143] The home locations of the prostitutes were far less interesting than the names of the taverns.

Madison: I Want My Money Back

IN EARLY SEPTEMBER, Adelia Schoville, 28, a prostitute working for a Madison escort service sued police officer Daniel Miller. Miller, an undercover cop, approached Schoville for sex services and he paid her $60. She made him sign a "contract" stating that he was not a cop. He signed the contract, arrested her, and took the money back. She felt he violated the contract and sued him in small claims court for the $60.[1144] For the record, Miller did not get any service for the $60, which might have rendered the contract invalid. However, the outcome is not on record.

∞

1977

Madison: The Case of Escort Services

A T THE BEGINNING OF 1976, the Metro Narcotics and Vice Squad reported 42 escort services operating in Dane County. Many, if not all, provided sexual massages. By May of 1977, a series of investigations and stings knocked the number down to about a dozen who continued to advertise in Madison's newspapers. In 1976, police arrested 21 women for prostitution and nine men for pandering. Madison passed an ordinance in April of 1975 prohibiting "commercial sexual gratification" and many arrests were for violation of this ordinance. [1145]

* * *

On February 24, 1977, a Metro Vice Squad detective made an appointment through Ultimate Escort Service. Michelle Cerro, 19, met the officer and, without any negotiation, told him "Anything for $100." Even though he didn't pay, he got what he wanted: an arrest. Another detective made an appointment with Grace E. Gerber, 36, from Heavenly Escort Service. For whatever reason, perhaps depreciation, she only charged $45. The police arrested Vernon H. Bullis, 36, "when he was caught collecting a percentage of the money after he had driven Ms. Gerber to the motel.[1146] In June 1977, Bullis got nailed again. This time for arranging "an undercover policeman to have intercourse with a woman he employed through Golden Girl Escorts."[1147]

* * *

Near the end of May 1977, police arrested Richard F. Fletcher, 50, for operating Your Pleasure Escort service aka prostitutes available. At about the same time, Michelle Cerro, now 20, got nabbed for the second time in five weeks. Fletcher said in his court complaint, "I've been in the business the longest in Madison so I must be doing something right." A woman receptionist told police 'That "she had made about 100 escort calls, at least half of them involving sex for money, in a year and a half."[1148]

* * *

During the middle of April, police arrested Robert Turner, 25, for pimping his wife Donna Doll Turner, 19, out of the Hollywood Escort Service. From the Your Choice Escort Service, they arrested 25-year-old Beverly Kay Autry. Prostitutes were everywhere and came in all ages. A detective arrested Renee Martha Munoz, 18, working out of the peculiarly named New Birth Escort Service.[1149]

* * *

On May 19, Police arrested Homer B. Parker, 31, along with his escort, from Sophisticated Lady Escorts. In a plea deal, the prosecutor promised immunity to the escort if she would testify against Parker who allegedly threatened her with a gun. The district attorney closed his argument by saying "justice is convicting Homer Parker for soliciting prostitutes." Parker's attorney told the jury in closing, "Hell hath no fury like a woman scorned" and characterized the woman as having a "fantasy of violence." The argument must have been persuasive as Paker was exonerated.[1150]

New York: Prostitution is Addictive

IN EARLY MAY 1977, Drs. Samuel S. Janus and Barbara E. Bess of New York Medical College presented their findings at Toronto's American Psychiatric Association meeting. Their research showed that prostitution was an addiction rather than an option. They said that "Prostitutes commonly claim they are selling their bodies as a means of accumulating funds to open a business or maintain their families and that they always are planning to return to respectability. When they do renounce the practice, it is usually because of suffering a severe beating, facing the threat of their children being taken away, or a long jail sentence."

Although a small sample, 22 women said they abandoned prostitution altogether and 18 said that they returned to the practice after an average of 4 years. Janus and Bess said that the rate of recidivism exceeded that of narcotic addiction. They identified several reasons prostitution was "irresistible" including "excitement, courtship with danger, ability to outwit a client and beat the law." They told the audience, "To prostitutes, other prostitutes appear more exciting than ordinary women and sharing stories about johns and their escapades give them a vicarious thrill."[1151]

Madison: Clothing Optional in Taverns

AT THE END OF MAY 1977, Madison was in the same position as Hurley years before. Reverend Richard Pritchard met with Mayor Paul Soglin and demanded that he shut down the Dangle, a nude dancing tavern near the Capitol building. Soglin told Pritchard, "I'm not about to go out and try to close the Dangle or any other nude dancing places." [1152]

After the meeting, Pritchard showed reporters the city ordinance that read, "nude entertainment 'shall constitute grounds for revocation' of a retail Class B liquor license." Later, Soglin said that he would enforce the ordinance only "if it is mandatory that nude dancing establishments be shut down."

City Attorney O'Brien said that he "does not recall any test cases of the ordinance that calls for entertainers and employees in taverns to be wearing clothes at all times." Then, in a quote nearly copied from Hurley's dialogue, Police Lt. Ted Balistreri said that he does "not see the necessity for us going out and arresting" tavern owners for violating the ordinance. The ordinance is available for use by the city council to revoke licenses." Ironically, the same words were usually directed toward Hurley by state officials from Madison.[1153]

Madison: Madison Prostitutes Are Amateurs

LITTLE WAS BEING DONE to advance the cases in Dane County Court. City Attorney Larry O'Brien explained that the reason the cases were not moving forward was that the court was overwhelmed. As such, after two years, many massage parlors continued to operate. Metro Lt. Ted Balistreri said that the police "had limited goals in enforcing the sex laws and do not expect to eliminate prostitution. We are responsible for keeping tabs on such operations to keep syndicated crime out of Madison, make sure juveniles are not involved, and prevent women from being forced into prostitution." Balistreri went on to say that because of the prosecution, "The people who were in it just to make a quick buck got out." District Attorney James Doyle, Jr. said that if a woman agreed to testify against her pimp, the charges against her would be dropped although this is often a difficult choice for a prostitute because of "fear and loyalty." He went on to say that "Most Madison prostitutes are amateurs, sometimes students or former students and husband-and-wife teams."[1154]

Most of the explanations, arguments, and excuses were echoes reverberating from a time long ago in Hurley. The behavior, rationale, and the characters were the same; only the location was different.

1978

La Crosse: Prostitution is Everywhere

WESTERN WISCONSIN HAS ONLY a few large cities: Superior to the north, Eau Claire in the center, and La Crosse to the south. Each of these cities were subject to vice raids over the years. Like other areas, prostitution was usually bundled with liquor in taverns. In the 1970s, the venue changed and such places as saunas, massage parlors, and escort services became the preferrable model. This eliminated the need for licenses for taverns, liquor, and bartenders. These businesses were not limited to the large cities such as Madison and Milwaukee.

In January, La Crosse detectives, along with state agents, arrested six women and two men at Carol's Sauna, VIP Rap Parlor, and Models Unlimited. In a rare case, the men were charged with patronizing a house of prostitution, a misdemeanor. Two of the women arrested had also been arrested with six others the previous October with a raid on Carol's Sauna, Lolita's, and Rhonda's Rap.[1155]

Appleton: Trouble on John Roach's Home Turf

IN FEBRUARY, TWO MILWAUKEE women were arrested by a Wisconsin DOJ agent in Appleton for prostitution. The women approached the agent in a local tavern and offered intercourse for $50. The agent went to a motel with the women where they increased the price to $100 for intercourse "and other sexual favors." At the motel, one woman exposed her breast to the agent while the other fondled his leg near his ankle, uncomfortably close to the badge that he had tucked into his sock. Realizing that he had enough evidence, he retrieved the badge and arrested the women. One of the women was fined $250 in Outagamie County Court along with 60-days in jail for carrying a .25 caliber pistol in her purse. This was the first prostitution arrest in Outagamie County in ten years.[1156]

Kenosha: The Tragic Case of Candy Lee Jones

WHILE HURLEY HAD ITS SHARE of vice incidents over the years, none compared to what happened at the other end of the state in Kenosha during the late 1970's. This story follows five characters over several years citing their interaction with prostitution, fighting, lying, murder, and larceny.

* * *

At 2:18 a.m. on December 5, 1977, Albert "Lee" Gooch, 27, and Nathaniel "Hollywood" Johnson, 27, saw 14-year-old Candy Lee Jones standing on the corner of 65th Street and 15th Avenue in Kenosha. They swung over to the curb and beckoned her to the car. As she approached, Johnson extended his arm, pistol in hand, and shot her twice in the chest. Jones staggered onto the sidewalk and fell against the entrance to Freeman's Record Store. Edna Freeman heard the shots and the thud against the entry. She found Jones bleeding and as she comforted the girl, Jones said "Please don't let them shoot me again." Candy Lee Jones then died on the sidewalk in a pool of blood.

* * *

Nineteen-year-old Timothy Green said he witnessed the shooting. He said he was sitting on his porch rolling joints when he saw Nathaniel Johnson shoot Candy Jones. Green said he was afraid and went to his stepfather's house, crawled through the basement window, and hid until morning, at which time he told his stepfather what had happened. Green had previous interactions with the shooters. When he began to receive threats, he sent his wife and child out of state. However, the police held Green as a material witness. At the time, Green was also in trouble as he faced burglary charges. Police arrested Nathaniel Johnson and after Green testified at the preliminary hearing, authorities dropped the burglary charges, and paid his expenses to move out of state.

* * *

Albert "Lee" Gooch, 27, and his younger brother Archie "Tito" Gooch, 20, had been in court in late December on charges of raping two Racine girls, ages 15 and 17. The girls told police that the Gooch brothers tried to coerce them into prostitution at gunpoint and took them to Chicago overnight against their will. One of the girls said that Albert told her that "if she didn't 'work' for him she would become 'like that 14-year-old girl; ashes to ashes, dust to dust."[1157]

* * *

In late January, Judge Michael Fisher dismissed first-degree murder charges against Albert Gooch for insufficient evidence in the death of Candy Lee Jones. Nathaniel Johnson, on the other hand, was bound over to circuit court and was held on a $100,000 bond.

* * *

At about the same time, Archie "Tito" Gooch pled not guilty of first-degree sexual assault, aiding, and abetting first degree sexual assault, and two counts of false imprisonment regarding the encounter with the young Racine girls.[1158]

On April 13, 1978, the Gooch brothers changed their pleas to guilty of second-degree sexual assault, aiding and abetting sexual assault, and two counts of false imprisonment. The judge sent them to the Central State Hospital at Waupun for a 60-day mental exam.

Nathaniel "Hollywood" Johnson

In early May, Nathaniel "Hollywood" Johnson stood trial for shooting Candy Lee Jones. Timothy Green, the key witness, testified to what he saw but also reported that Tito Gooch had threatened his wife if "she did not 'go to the corner' for him." He said that "one of Hollywood's ladies" tried to persuade her at gunpoint.[1159] Timothy Green had it in for both Nathaniel Johnson and Tito Gooch.

As the trial continued, more shocking evidence was offered. Twelve-year-old Chevette Carr was led into court in handcuffs. She was held as a material witness because she had attempted to flee rather than testify. Reluctantly, she told the jury that she and Candy Jones were best friends, and that Johnson could not have shot her because at the time of the shooting she and Johnson were in bed together in his apartment. The prosecutor introduced several more witnesses challenging Green's testimony including his stepfather – a minister – who denied that Green told him anything about the shooting. The jury remained sequestered.[1160]

On the last day of the trial, Johnson admitted that five women worked for him and said that "he expected loyalty from his girls and, in return, saw to it that they were "taken care of." He testified that neither "Candy or Chevette worked as prostitutes for him" and he denied killing Candy.[1161]

Knowing that the verdict depended on Green's story, the defense attorney meticulously unraveled his testimony. On May 10, 1978, the effort paid off when the jury found Nathaniel "Hollywood" Johnson not guilty.[1162] If Johnson was not guilty of the shooting, then his partner, Albert Gooch, must have been the shooter. However, he was never tried for this murder.

* * *

Nathaniel Johnson was never far from trouble. In August 1980, rival groups raged against each other in separate vehicles along Sheridan Road in Kenosha. Eventually, they stopped, and a brawl ensued. After the fight, the groups left in opposite directions. The police stopped one of the vehicles at 68th and 15th, and found Johnson, now 29, with a broken jaw. They sent him to the hospital.[1163]

* * *

On September 4, 1980, Johnson stood in the doorway of J. and B. Coins on Roosevelt Road. His accomplice, John Bartlett, 37, went into the store with a sawed-off shotgun and demanded money from the owner, Jerome Binsfeld. When Binsfeld denied the order, Bartlett shot him in the stomach. The Police found their car along with the shotgun and a derringer. They arrested Johnson and Bartlett for attempted first-degree murder and armed robbery and the judge set bond at $150,000 each.[1164] In December, Johnson pled guilty to attempted armed robbery and attempted second degree murder.[1165] On January 21, 1981, the judge sentenced him to two concurrent six-year terms in the Green Bay reformatory. The judge was lenient because Johnson was outside when Bartlett shot the operator. However, the judge wasn't lenient enough to allow Johnson's request to be married before beginning his sentence.[1166]

* * *

Prison did nothing to reform Nathaniel Johnson. In March 2000, police charged him with possession of heroin with intent to deliver. However, somehow the authorities mistakenly destroyed the evidence and despite facing additional penalties for bail jumping, he was exonerated.[1167] At this point, 50-year-old Nathaniel "Hollywood" Johnson, fades from the record, just like the heroin.

John Bartlett

In January 1981, John Bartlett, the shooter in the coin shop robbery, awaited trial. Because of overcrowding at the Kenosha County jail, Bartlett was sent to the Milwaukee House of Corrections. Along with three other prisoners Bartlett beat a 62-year-old guard, broke a window, and scaled a fence to escape. The bitter cold prohibited the escape and within a day, the police nabbed all the frozen inmates except Bartlett. Within a couple of days, police apprehended Bartlett after a truck repair foreman noticed the letter "HC" (House of Corrections) stenciled on Barlett's jacket.[1168] Medical staff treated him for frostbite. On February 19, 1981, Judge William Zievers sentenced John Bartlett to 30 years at the state prison in Waupun.[1169] He is never heard from again.

Timothy Green

Timothy Green, the eyewitness to the shooting of Candy Lee Jones had been relocated to Seattle because of threats from Nathaniel Johnson. However, Green returned to Kenosha after a couple of years. Realizing that all of his old rivals were either gone or in prison, he assembled a new crew. In

December 1979, police arrested him in connection to burglaries that occurred over a period of two months. They found 40 of the past 60 house burglaries attributable to the same gang and suspected Green as the "ringleader." When the police raided Green's home, they not only found the recently stolen property but also property reported stolen in Seattle.[1170] On February 22, 1980, Green pled not guilty to two burglary counts but faced a $10,000 bond.[1171] In April, he changed his plea to no contest and on May 22, 1980, the judge sentenced Timothy Green to two years at the Green Bay reformatory.[1172]

Albert "Lee" Gooch

On June 15, 1978, Judge Earl D. Morton, sentenced Albert Gooch to 11 years at Waupun state prison for sexually assaulting the two Racine girls." [1173]

Archie "Tito" Gooch

On June 15, 1978, Judge Morton sentenced younger brother Archie "Tito" Gooch to eight years at the Green Bay reformatory on sexual assault and false imprisonment charges.[1174] Gooch's defense attorney petitioned the court saying that his client's only previous offense was a weapons violation in Memphis in 1974 for which he served nine days in jail. Koos told the judge that "Gooch is 20 years old and 'is sincerely interested in improving himself and becoming a useful member of society.'" [1175] After the appeal by Gooch's attorney, the judge reduced his sentence to six years which would turn out to be a mistake.

* * *

On October 16, 1984, Archie Gooch, now 27, was traveling on Sheridan Road with 21-year-old Debra Douglas and 17-year-old Josette Powell. Gooch was drunk, driving exceptionally fast, and hopelessly reckless. He lost control and struck a tree, severing the car in half. Debra Douglas died instantly, and Josette Powell was seriously injured. Gooch had a back injury and cuts. The sheriff charged Gooch with operating a vehicle while intoxicated and vehicular homicide.[1176]

A jury found Gooch guilty on May 16, 1985. On June 21, 1985, the judge sentenced Gooch to six years in prison plus six years of probation for homicide by the intoxicated use of a motor vehicle.[1177]

* * *

In March 1989, Kim Dobner, 24, appeared in Kenosha County Court for harboring a felon – one Archie Gooch – now 32. Dobner was accused of transporting Gooch to her home despite knowing that he was a known felon and wanted for violating parole. Police arrested Gooch at her home. She was held on a $10,000 cash bail bond.[1178] Within a short period, police arrested Gooch on two charges of delivering cocaine as a repeat offender.

* * *

Oddly, abruptly, and fortuitously, Archie "Tito" Gooch falls from the record in 1989 along with this reign of terror.

1979

Hurley: Trouble at the French Casino

J AMES VITICH CLOSED THE French Casino while he served a prison term for interstate transportation for prostitution. The club reopened in December 1978 when the city issued a liquor license to James Wilson.

At the end of March 1979, a 16-year-old girl fled an adolescent center in Milwaukee. Milwaukee police asked the Wisconsin Department of Justice to investigate a rumor that she was hiding at the French Casino in Hurley. The DOJ dispatched two agents to Hurley on the first weekend of April.

Hurley Police Chief Ted Erspamer closed the tavern while the agents looked for evidence of wrongdoing. Erspamer delivered the findings within a few days to the Iron County District Attorney Paul Sturgul. After review, Sturgul pressed charges in Iron County Court.[1179]

On April 4, Hurley Police arrested James Vitich, 53, and James Wilson, 38. Sturgul charged Vitich with soliciting a prostitute and Wilson for keeping a house of prostitution. After Judge Alex Raineri signed warrants for their arrests, he ordered the building shuttered.[1180] On April 27, Wilson was bound over for trial in Iron County Court.[1181]

Despite the DOJ investigation, the police arrests, the preliminary exam, the pre-trial hearing, the arraignment, and the setting of trial dates, the case went cold. It is likely that this case, while substantive, failed to gain traction because of what happened to Iron County Judge Alex Raineri in early 1980.

Hurley: The Show Bar Goes Up in Flames

A FTER THE FIRE IN 1971, Jack Gasbarri repaired the building. When he died in 1975, his wife, Cira, operated the nightclub. On the morning of April 20, 1979, Gasbarri reported a possible fire in the tavern. A police officer checked the building, found no sign of fire, and thought that Gasbarri mistook the lights behind the bar as flames. Nonetheless, Gasbarri kept her eye on the building, and, at mid-afternoon, she saw smoke coming from the roof. When Hurley firefighters arrived, the building was engulfed in smoke and the roof exploded in flames.

The Hurley fire chief suspected that someone might have been in the building when the fire began and asked the state fire marshal to investigate. On April 24, the fire marshal, the Iron County sheriff, and the Hurley fire chief investigated the remains of the Show Bar but nothing suspicious was found.[1182] This fire left another empty lot on Silver Street and Cira Gasbarri was out of a job.

1980

Hurley: The Case of Alex Raineri

ALEX RAINERI, NOW 61, SERVED as Iron County District Attorney from 1960 to 1978 before becoming Iron County judge. In early 1980, the Wisconsin Judicial Commission received a complaint from Cira Gasbarri about Raineri's behavior. They passed the information on to the Wausau office of the FBI. A subsequent grand jury convened, and on Friday, June 6, 1980, federal attorney Frank Tuerkheimer shocked Iron County when he announced that a federal grand jury in Madison indicted Iron County Judge Alex Raineri on five charges.

The first charge was that Raineri committed perjury when he denied traveling to Reno, Nevada, for a judicial seminar in the fall of 1978 accompanied by Cira Gasbarri, the operator of Ritz Bar Inc., doing business as the Show Bar, on Silver Street. Raineri claimed that Gasbarri and her family were in Nevada on a hunting trip when they met.

The second charge alleged that Raineri was involved in interstate transportation for prostitution because of a check he wrote via an Ironwood bank to Yvonne Spears, a prostitute at the Show Bar.

The third charge was that Raineri was involved in interstate transportation for prostitution because of a check from the Ritz Bar to Lake Superior District Power Company on September 19, 1978.

The fourth charge alleged that Raineri was involved in interstate transportation for prostitution because he wrote a check to a business in Hibbing, Minnesota, for cleaning the linen for the Show Bar.

The fifth charge claimed Raineri "conspired to impede justice" by threatening a witness, Patricia Colassaco, of the Hurley-Ironwood taxi service. [1183]

* * *

In early June, Raineri was suspended from the bench without pay after the Wisconsin Judicial Commission filed a formal complaint with the Wisconsin Supreme Court. The complaint, however, had nothing to do with the grand jury charges. Instead, the Commission alleged that Raineri violated the Code of Judicial Ethics by hearing a close relative's drunken driving case involving his brother-in-law in December 1978. [1184]

* * *

In June 1980, two Milwaukee, Sandra Fay Spears, 23, and Jacola Eaton, 27, stayed in an Ironwood motel but danced in Hurley. Near the end of the month, Hurley police collared them for prostitution. The women appeared in Iron County Court in front of Judge Ronald Keberle of Marathon County, who was sitting in for Raineri. [1185] On June 23, both pled guilty and paid fines. The arrest of Sandra Spears would be important in the case against Raineri.

* * *

Raineri, recognizing the seriousness of the federal charges, hired brothers Gene and Daniel Linehan as his attorneys. They estimated that the trial would take about three to four weeks with up to 50 defense witnesses, whereas Tuerkheimer said the government would call 25 to 30 witnesses. The first thing that the Linehan brothers did was file a dozen motions. They wanted to move the trial from Madison to Hurley or Ashland, change it to October, and dismiss eight of the motions for legal reasons. The Linehan's asked for handwriting examples from six people and for a prosecution witness to undergo a psychiatric examination. In addition, they claimed that the government withheld evidence. Wary of delay tactics, the judge set the trial date for August 29.[1186]

In response to the "evidence" allegation, Tuerkheimer presented flight coupons, personal check stubs, and other evidence to support the government's claim. The evidence for obstruction was the testimony of the bartender from the Show Bar who "complained to Raineri that a female dancer and male customers were going upstairs to bedrooms above the bar." She said Raineri assured her that "she could not get into any trouble as a consequence of the activities."

The government claimed that Raineri talked to the brother of the bartender the next day. He told him to tell his sister he could "get a couple of guys to talk to her and get her to stop telling lies and keep her mouth shut." This put Raineri in a pinch because he had testified to the grand jury that he "was never informed" about prostitution at the bar.

It got worse. Tuerkheimer said Cira Gasbarri told the grand jury that Raineri hired dancers, handled bookwork, and collected money from prostitution. She said, "Whatever the girls got paid, well, we got half of it." Another bartender testified that "she saw Raineri counting proceeds from prostitution which were kept in an envelope in a cash register."[1187]

* * *

In late July, defense Attorney Daniel Linehan requested the trial be moved to Hurley with local jurors. He also wanted "Judge Barbara Crabb disqualified because Raineri served in her district. Cira Gasbarri was the prosecution's main witness, and Linehan wanted the case dismissed because of her alleged emotional instability. Linehan pushed to dismiss the charge of "interstate banking," arguing that it was only because of geography and not "any nefarious scheme to outwit local law enforcement through complex use of interstate commerce."[1188]

* * *

In early August, the Wisconsin Judicial Commission filed a second charge against Raineri. They said that after Raineri got a traffic ticket in Michigan, he tried negotiating with a prosecutor to get the citation dismissed. The incident occurred on December 24, 1978, in Gogebic County, Michigan. The incident took up three columns of ink in the newspaper laying out the blow-by-blow events. It was clear that Tuerkheimer was digging deep and using all sources to make the case against Raineri.[1189] The traffic case drew more ink on August 5, and it became apparent that it was a distraction fueled by legal minutia rather than genuine evidence of wrongdoing.[1190] Raineri's lawyer admitted that "the misconduct charges are minor compared to the federal charges."[1191]

* * *

Because of the traffic incident, Raineri was suspended from the bench along with his salary. In mid-July, Linehan petitioned the Supreme Court to pay Raineri during his suspension, claiming that withholding his pay "violated due process of law."[1192] He argued, "Judge Raineri is in a position where he can't go out now and earn a living practicing law because he is a judge. Under these facts and circumstances, it is not fair. There is an allegation, but there is a presumption of innocence."

* * *

On August 11, the Supreme Court ruled against Raineri receiving pay during the suspension.[1193] Later, Raineri said, "That decision hurt. I was surprised by it because it was almost a determination of guilt at a time when I am only charged. I am not guilty of anything until proven guilty. I felt it was kind of drastic."[1194]

*   *   *

Raineri's path was replete with obstacles. On October 7, 1980, U.S. Court Commissioner William Gansner denied ordering a psychiatric examination of Cira Gasbarri. Commissioner Gansner said, "Raineri's attorneys can open the examination issue with Raineri's trial judge instead, as the 'appropriate means of inquiry' into the competence of a witness."[1195] A couple of weeks later, Ganser denied the change of venue, saying Raineri "Had no constitutional or statutory right to a trial in northern Wisconsin instead of Madison." At the same time, Commissioner Gansner refused to disqualify Judge Barbara Crabb.[1196] Finally, on October 30, Ganser denied motions to dismiss prostitution-related charges against Raineri.[1197] All efforts to stall or sidestep the charges were exhausted. Raineri was stuck and was going to have to face a jury in federal court in Madison.

*   *   *

In an interview, a reporter wrote about Raineri, "The mental pressure of awaiting trial has been so difficult he has not had time to consider how he will recover financially from deep legal debts or what he will do if he is acquitted." Raineri said, "There is a lot of embarrassment, you know, because in 35 years of professional life I've never had this before. And there is pressure, the charges and the penalties involved. It's tough, it's all you've got, all that pressure on you. It's nerve-wracking. I think it probably has affected my health, yeah. I'm not a doctor so what affect it has had, I don't know, but I don't think it has done any good."[1198] Given the posture of the Wisconsin Judicial Commission and the aggressiveness of U.S. Attorney Tuerkheimer, Raineri had good reason to worry.[1199]

*   *   *

Cira Gasbarri, now 45, was born in Cuba on August 3, 1935, and still carried a heavy accent. She arrived in Hurley in 1962 to dance at the Club Carnival, and in 1968, she married Jack Gasbarri, the owner of the club. At trial, she told a lengthy story about her relationship with Alex Raineri and a compelling tale of corruption. Being the prosecution's main witness, Linehan needed to discredit her. In his opening argument, he would try to "show that Mrs. Gasbarri suffered from mental illness, that she was delusional, paranoid, and not in touch with reality."

*   *   *

As the trial opened, she testified that after she married Jack Gasbarri, she and Jack became good friends with Raineri and his wife, Doris. She told the jury that after her husband Jack died in 1975, she moved to California, "but at Raineri's urging, she returned to Hurley to reopen the Show Bar." Gasbarri told the jury that she and Raineri became lovers after her husband died. She said that "prostitution had been a fixture at the Show Bar when Jack owned it, but when she attempted to limit the activity to nude dancing, Raineri changed her mind." She said that Raineri told her, "Don't worry about any law enforcement coming to town because they have to come to me first." She said Raineri dismissed a court case for an unpaid construction bill for the Show Bar, placed ads in the newspaper for a new bartender, put the liquor license in the janitor's name, took her on trips, bought her clothes, and gave her money. To back up the claims, Tuerkheimer presented canceled checks for $2,000 for a car, $1,000 for cash, and $500 "to pay bills at the bar."

Raineri faced a perjury charge relating to a trip to Reno. Gasbarri said Raineri "Asked her to go with him, bought her plane ticket, and was with her for the entire three weeks except when she visited her family in California." She said, "When they returned to Hurley, they were not satisfied with the conduct of the man who had been in charge of the show bar while they were gone, James Vitich." She said she fired him and operated the tavern until the fire. In his opening argument, Linehan used this testimony to disconnect Raineri from the prostitution charge. He told the jury, "Vitich was running a whorehouse in Hurley, but Raineri and Mrs. Gasbarri were not in town."

The prosecutor pressed the witness and it paid dividends. Gasbarri testified that Raineri came to the Show Bar every night to count the money after which he would pay her $50 and keep the rest. She told the jury that she removed the booths where prostitutes performed sex acts but Raineri "Told me to put the booths back in there and let the girls mingle with the customers."

The story evoked an accusation of mayhem. Gasbarri said after they "had become lovers, the relationship soured, and she believed that Raineri was trying to kill her. She said that while in Reno, he arranged to have a "man named Jerry from Iron River," to "get rid of her."

Gene Linehan, a member of Raineri's defense team, grilled Gasbarri during cross-examination. He presented a pistol and asked her if she used it to fire a shot at Raineri in his chambers the day after the Show Bar fire in 1979. Linehan followed up by asking if she intentionally rammed Raineri's car. Linehan wanted to degrade Gasbarri's testimony by showing that she was hostile toward Raineri and would do anything to see him punished for being scorned. He argued that Gasbarri intended to implicate Raineri in the operation of the Show Bar and that "she was out to get him." He said, "She didn't get him with that shot (in the chambers). Evidence will show she's back to get him with another shot with her testimony here."[1200]

On November 26, Barney Hinch, the Show Bar's accountant, testified that Raineri called him in March 1980, a few days before the grand jury investigation. Hinch said that Raineri enquired about his wife and children and then said that if he was called to testify, he should tell the jury that he "had no business activity in the show bar." Hinch said that he was "rather stunned" by Raineri's instruction.

That same day, Gasbarri's niece, Angel Acebal, 21, testified that "she often saw Raineri and her aunt counting cash receipts from both the bar and from prostitution." Acebal was from Hollywood, California, and visited her aunt periodically. She told the jury that when she worked as a bartender at the Show Bar in mid-1978, her aunt told her "To give the key" to the upstairs dancers when asked. She said that the dancers returned the key with an envelope when they came downstairs and that this happened "about 10 to 15 times a night." She said that while she was in Hurley, she saw Raineri at her aunt's house "nearly every day."

On cross-examination, Acebal told the jury that her aunt "has been in at least two mental hospitals in the past year" and that after her aunt attacked her with scissors in November 1979, she was committed to a California mental hospital. She said that during a visit with her in December 1979, her aunt was drinking heavily. Acebal said that she "Just wasn't herself and thought that she was being followed and that 'everybody was out to kill her.'" Acebal said that her aunt "told her that she had been to her own funeral several times."[1201]

The fourth day of the trial was devastating for Raineri. Albert Stella held the liquor license because Cira Gasbarri was not a U.S. citizen. Stella, a former Hurley chief of police, was now the Show Bar janitor, and Tuerkheimer suspected Raineri posed as Stella when needed.

In March 1979, state agents James Boatman and Ted Seefeldt inspected the Show Bar. They testified that the records were "a mess" and that they "could not find invoices for liquor purchases and were suspicious that a bottle marked Seagram's actually contained an inferior liquor." When the agents said they were going to confiscate the liquor, Gasbarri made a phone call. She handed the phone to agent Boatman, telling him that the license holder, Albert Stella, was on the line.

However, rather than Stella, it was Raineri. Impersonating Stella, he told the agent that he was "depriving Mrs. Gasbarri of her constitutional rights by seizing the bottle of liquor." Raineri continued, "Look, you're going to have to appear before Judge Raineri, and you won't get very far."[1202] He said that he would call their boss to straighten out the situation. The next day, the agents learned that an FBI wiretap captured the call, and they pegged Raineri as impersonating Stella. This happened again a month later, and this time, the agent recognized Raineri's voice. It would be unfair to refer to Stella as a shill since he was unknowingly being used.

Albert Stella served as a Hurley police officer for 21 years, four of which as chief. After retiring from the police department, he spent four years working as a janitor at the Show Bar. He testified that when he was police chief, he confiscated the liquor license of the Show Bar when he suspected prostitution. Stella said he discouraged hiring James Vitich, who he suspected was connected to prostitution. Citing differences with Gasbarri, Stella quit in April 1979.[1203]

* * *

On the fifth day of the trial, U.S. Attorney Tuerkheimer called Raineri's daughter from New York to the stand to question her about a joint checking account she shared with her father. When asked about withdrawals, she said she was unaware of her father's withdrawals of $95,000 between December 1976 and December 1979.

* * *

On January 3, 1980, Tuerkheimer called Yvonne Spears, 21, from Milwaukee. She raised a lot of eyebrows when she told the jury that while working at the Show Bar in 1978, her "dates" included police officers, a Northern Wisconsin mayor, a Northern Michigan district attorney, a prominent Milwaukee County judge, and police officers from Green Bay and Bessemer. Tuerkheimer granted Spears immunity from prosecution at the federal and county levels for her activities in Hurley. She told the jury that she worked as a prostitute and bartender for eight months in 1978.

During that time, police arrested her for stealing jewelry and jailed her. She called Gasbarri and told her to post bail or else she would expose the prostitution at the Show Bar. Gasbarri took the threat seriously but wanted to protect herself. So, before giving her the bail money, she took her to an Ironwood bank and had her sign an affidavit in the presence of a bank official swearing that "no prostitution took place at the bar." This event twisted in a most unpredictable way. Tuerkheimer asked Spears if the banker knew she was telling the truth. She said, "Yes, because he was a date of mine." I am sure this surprised Gasbarri, Raineri, and the defense counsel.

She said eventually, all the girls needed to sign similar affidavits. On cross-examination,

Linehan argued that she only cooperated in "exchange for lenient treatment" because of Milwaukee drug charges for selling heroin. In customary fashion, Judge Crabb wouldn't let Linehan question the prostitute about her customers' names. That didn't prevent Spears from quipping that she may have mistaken the identity of the Milwaukee judge as "At the time I had seen him he had covers over his head."

Spears testified that she met Gasbarri at the Jack O'Lantern Bar in Iron River, Michigan. Gasbarri invited her to work in Hurley at the Show Bar and put her up at the White Way Motel on Silver Street. When the owner of the White Way wanted a cut of her prostitution fees, she moved to the second floor of the Show Bar. She said that in 1978 there were "4 or 5 other prostitutes working at the bar" under the management of both Gasbarri and Vitich.[1204]

*   *   *

On day six, Raineri's testimony at the 1978 grand jury was recalled. At that time, he testified that he traveled alone on a trip to Reno. He said that while in Reno, he met Gasbarri, her brother and her sister. Then, he returned to Wisconsin alone. His testimony was shattered when a Western Airlines official testified that Raineri purchased two tickets to Reno in September 1978 and that Raineri and Gasbarri were on the same flight from Minneapolis to Reno.[1205]

Tuerkheimer called Jack Erspamer, who owned the new grocery store on the second block of Silver Street. Prostitutes cashed their payroll checks at the store and he identified a check cashed by Yvonne Spears.[1206] The evidence mounted against Raineri as Tuerkheimer methodically built his case.

*   *   *

Patricia Colassaco was a bartender at the Show Bar and a taxi driver, and she was talkative on day seven of the trial. Cira Gasbarri hired her to tend bar at the Show Bar from the summer of 1977 through June 1978. She told the jury that she "frequently saw Raineri at the bar and he called Mrs. Gasbarri 'just about every night,'" She said that she knew that prostitution was ongoing, "both upstairs and in booths." Expressing concern, both Gasbarri and Raineri reassured her that she would not get into trouble for prostitution. Not long afterward, Raineri warned her that she "could get into trouble for driving prostitutes and their customers in her taxi from Hurley to motels across the state line in Ironwood, Michigan."

Colassaco said that, on one occasion, the dancers wanted to get paid early but didn't want to wait for the bookkeeper, so Gasbarri called Raineri at 3 a.m. on a Sunday. She said Raineri and Gasbarri retreated to the office and "about 15 minutes later" asked her to distribute the checks. The defense argued that Colassaco sought retribution for how Raineri handled a paternity case in which she had been involved several years before. Tuerkheimer leveraged Patricia Colassaco and, by so doing, she implicated her brother Ken.

Kenneth Colassaco was a Hurley police officer and the Iron County Coroner. When he took the stand, he said that when the news of the grand jury came out, Raineri called him to his chambers to talk about his sister, Patricia. Raineri told him, "Pat was down there (Madison), doing some talking, telling some lies about him." Raineri instructed Colassaco to have his sister "keep her nose out of that business, to keep her mouth shut and quit telling those lies." The next day, Colassaco relayed the message to his sister but added that if she didn't comply, "someone else would talk to her." The threat was moot as she had already testified before the grand jury in April.

Things got more tangled. When Ken Colassaco received a summons to testify to the grand jury in June, he consulted with Hurley Police Chief Ted Erspamer. Erspamer, in turn, called Raineri "to find out what the summons was about" and learned it involved the obstruction charge stemming from Colassaco's conversation with his sister. Raineri then instructed Ken Colassaco to "say I didn't hear anything from him (Raineri), that it was just street talk, I picked it up in the coffee shop and talked to my sister."

Gene Linehan tried to mitigate the damage. He asked Colassaco, "Ken, did you threaten your sister?" Colassaco responded, "I told her to keep her mouth shut." Linehan leaned in, "Did you intend to threaten her?" Colassaco said, "I wanted her to keep her nose out of this," For a final time, Linehan probed for an answer, "Ken, you didn't threaten her, did you?" Colassaco relinquished his position and said, "I guess I did. I told her to keep her nose out of there or somebody else would talk to her." He acknowledged that Raineri did not ask him to "lean on her." Patricia, his sister, took the phone call as a threat and testified that "she later wore a body microphone when she met Ken for coffee. She said she attempted to get him to repeat the message from the telephone call, but he did not."[1207]

*   *   *

On December 6, 1980, after the testimony from 33 witnesses and the introduction of 50 pieces of evidence, the government rested its case. It would take a week for the defense to introduce its evidence.[1208]

*   *   *

On December 8, defense attorneys Gene and Danial Linehan tried to introduce Cira Gasbarri's mental health records as evidence that she was not a reliable witness, but Federal Judge Barbara Crabb denied the motion.[1209]

*   *   *

On the first day of the defense case, Bernice DiGiorgio, Cira Gasbarri's long-time friend and employee, was called to the stand. DiGiorgio said she had known Gasbarri since she came from Cuba in 1962. She told the jury that Gasbarri had "done all kinds of crazy things that I couldn't understand." DiGiorgio said, "prostitution sometimes took place after the bar closed but that Mrs. Gasbarri repeatedly fired dancers who were taking men to their rooms." She said that when she was a bartender, she would only occasionally see Raineri but that "he was not part of the operation."

Tuerkheimer pressed DiGiorgio, and she admitted spending three years in 1972 in prison for manslaughter for a stabbing death in Wakefield. DiGiorgio testified that she worked at the Show Bar "almost every day it was open from 1976 through 1979." She testified that Gasbarri "was a lesbian because she saw her and female bartenders 'making love' in front of customers." She said that they were both opposed to prostitution and that they fired women for prostitution and "threw the dancer's clothes into the street." DiGiorgio said that Gasbarri often rehired the women because "she was afraid that they would burn down her house or bar." She said that "in late 1978 and 1979, Gasbarri was "completely loco" and that she "tore the electrical outlets and thermostats out of her house because she thought FBI agents were inside."

DiGiorgio said that she had no idea how much money she earned because it was always cash and that "she never filled out a tax return." Tuerkheimer's ears piqued at this comment, and he enquired, "You've never filled out a tax return?" She responded, "I was paid cash every day I

293

worked. I never knew you had to pay income tax on cash. Income tax never entered my mind."

Gasbarri's mental health was wobbly, and nearly everyone who knew her well was aware of it. Despite his efforts, Linehan could not get Gasbarri's medical history into the record but promised to subpoena her doctors.[1210]

*   *   *

On December 10, the tenth day of testimony, three bartenders testified that for them to get paid, they needed to get their checks from Raineri. Gasbarri employed three sisters as bartenders: Nancy Gross, Paulette Osmak, and Patricia Colassaco along with Rose Carli and Eleanore Fochinelli. Gross testified that "she had heard dancers making dates and heard them mention a $100 price." Osmak testified that she heard the girls talking about turning tricks and making dates. Carli and Fochinelli said that Pat's brother, Ken, "once warned them not to cooperate with federal investigators."

Rose Carli testified that "on several occasions," Gasbarri locked dancers upstairs "for more than a day without food or heat or a way to escape in case of fire." Eleanore Fochinelli said that she believed Gasbarri was so angry with Raineri that she rammed her car into his, but the judge struck this testimony.[1211]

*   *   *

On December 11, Reverend Joseph Polakowski testified that Raineri and Gasbarri came to his church in mid-1979, wanting counsel, because Gasbarri shot at him in his office. When he asked what happened, Gasbarri admitted shooting at the judge. The priest was able to testify because he said it was "strictly confidential, but not a confessional matter." Reverend Polakowski said that Gasbarri said she shot at Raineri because "he had stolen precious objects from her apartment." The priest said that Gasbarri also accused Raineri of burning her bar. When Polakowski "asked the woman again why she shot at Raineri." She said, "Because I love him," to which Raineri responded, "I love you too." Polakowski said that Gasbarri told him, "Father, you don't understand what love means. If you truly love, you can kill somebody."

Gasbarri testified that Jerome Tarnowski, a student from Marquette, was the person who tried to kill her in Reno. Tarnowski testified that he had never been to Reno and never threatened Gasbarri. He said he once had sex with a prostitute above the Show Bar, and after he left the building, he discovered that his wallet was missing $800.[1212]

*   *   *

On December 12, 1980, the 12th day of the trial, Alex Raineri took the stand. He pled not guilty to all the charges against him and proceeded to itemize the denials. He denied helping Gasbarri, hiring or firing dancers, and managing the operation. He said that the handwriting on the check stubs was not his. He denied having an affair, saying they were just "very good friends." He said he didn't recall seeing Gasbarri on the plane trip to Reno and denied threatening a grand jury witness.

Under cross-examination, he told Tuerkheimer that the priest's testimony was in error. Raineri admitted purchasing two airplane tickets, one for him to travel to Reno and the other for Gasbarri so she could continue to California to see her mother. He said he purchased the ticket for her because of her "difficulty with the language." He said that Gasbarri had returned to Reno so they could visit over dinner. Tuerkheimer reminded him that he told the grand jury they spent the day together. Raineri said that the grand jury testimony was in error. He said he never threatened

294

Patricia Colassaco and only talked to her brother to find out if his sister was going to testify.

Raineri explained the shooting in his chamber. He said that Gasbarri wanted help on the insurance claim from the fire at the Show Bar. He told her that as a judge, he couldn't practice law and she became "quite distressed" and wouldn't leave. When he tried phoning the police, she pulled a gun from her purse and fired a shot at him. He said, "I saw the orange flame and smoke come out of the gun. I thought she hit me because she was aiming right at me." He said he took her to see the priest after the shooting.[1213]

*   *   *

On December 15, Judge Crabb allowed Dr. George Paz, a physician, and Connie Williams, a social worker, to testify about Gasbarri's mental well-being. Both were flown in from California for the trial. Crabb said the doctor's duty to answer questions should "override the reluctance he felt because of his code of ethics."[1214] Dr. Paz told the jury that Gasbarri had been "hospitalized voluntarily for 15 days for treatment of 'psychotic depressive reaction.'"

*   *   *

During a recess on the 14th day of the trial, with the jury sequestered, Tuerkheimer declared that he had a witness who would testify that on the morning of the Show Bar fire, she saw Raineri holding the door of a red van while "men loaded cases of beer and a cash register." When Tuerkheimer made this statement, Raineri's wife, Doris, told reporters that he was in Milwaukee that day, and then she reminded her husband of the same thing. Linehan told Judge Crabb the woman who wanted to testify was "a disgruntled former client of Raineri." Raineri's attorneys called the statement "totally prejudicial," worrying jurors might have heard the remark. He told Judge Crabb, "My God, it's just totally damnable." Tuerkheimer dropped the issue.[1215]

*   *   *

Judge Crabb recalled the eight-man, four-woman jury back into the courtroom on December 16, 1980. Then Lenehan delivered his final argument telling them that it was "a case with more than 100 exhibits, 50 witnesses, and 'a million inferences.'"[1216]

*   *   *

On December 18, 1980, after deliberating for seven hours, the jury found Raineri guilty of all five counts. Tuerkheimer called the verdict "bittersweet." He said, "I think it is tragic when a person who is intimately involved with the administration of justice breaks the law." He said the prostitutes would not be prosecuted, and Kenneth Colassaco would not face charges for threatening remarks.[1217]

*   *   *

On December 31, Attorney Gene Linehan asked Judge Crabb to stay the execution of sentencing because of an intended appeal. Linehan cited Judge Crabb's refusal to allow him to use Cira Gasbarri as a defense witness, her refusal to allow the jury to see her mental health records from California, and the denial to move the trial venue.[1218] On January 20, 1981, Linehan filed a motion in U.S. District Court for a new trial.[1219] The motion rested with Judge Crabb while she set the sentencing date for March 6.[1220] On February 25, Judge Crabb rejected all of the arguments presented by Linehan.[1221]

1981

Madison: The Judge Gets Sentenced

ON MARCH 7, 1981, U.S. Judge Barbara Crabb sentenced former Iron County Judge Alex Raineri to three years in prison and fined him $15,000. Raineri stood mute at sentencing as the judge said that Raineri "lacks any recognition of the seriousness of his activities" and "his actions reveal to others a shameless disregard for the laws he was elected to uphold. She said his "refusal to reveal much of himself to federal probation officials makes it more difficult for her to understand him or his offense." She specifically took umbrage with Linehan's characterization of Hurley as "a unique society."[1222]

Raineri's entire life on Silver Street was encapsulated in the moment. His thoughts must have traversed the years like pages of an old manuscript being blown by the rusty winds of the iron range. He was alone and had to bear the consequences of bad judgement. These were not nefarious acts of violence such as murder, extortion, or rape. They were crimes involving paper checks, linen, and passion. Raineri got caught up in what seemed a normal operating business, as that is what it was on Silver Street.

Ironwood: The Source of an Unlikely Exposition

THE *IRONWOOD DAILY GLOBE* REPORTER Dennis McCann was criticized for exaggerating parts of the trial and minimizing others. McCann made up for any shortcomings on March 25, 1981, in a front-page, honest, and stinging rebuke of Madison's double standard. He wrote that after a long day in court, Raineri walked around the capital square and through the capitol rotunda, a shortcut from his attorneys office to the courthouse. But when Raineri walked in other directions, for lunch or to unwind after a day in court, the scenery was not so stately or impressive. Two blocks to the south of the courthouse was the Rising Sun, one of Madison's notorious massage parlors. To the north was Cheri's Massage Parlor, with its offer of "encounters." If court recessed late, Raineri's fellow walkers might be state employees on their way home from work, or perhaps women on corners looking for customers. The irony of walking past evidence of prostitution in Madison while being tried for prostitution-connected offenses in Hurley was not lost on Raineri or Iron County residents who witnessed the trial."

When challenged about a double standard, U.S. Attorney Frank Tuerkheimer said, "That's ludicrous. We didn't pick on Hurley.[1223] Depending on the context and the time frame, the claim was debatable.

Langlade County: Wisconsin's So-Called Last Known Brothel

MEANWHILE, ON APRIL 25, 1981, the *Wausau Daily Herald* proclaimed "Wisconsin's last known brothel" was being sold at auction, and the bill of sale would be a collector's item. It was Ella "Bev" Blechschmidt's White House tavern. The brothel's demise coincided with Blechschmidt's death in February at 78. The auction bill included a warning system, an intercom, assorted mirrors, and a large number of sheets, towels, and pillowcases. In addition to the White

House, the Red Star was for sale. The Red Star was Blechschmidt's temporary facility used when agents closed the White House after multiple raids.

Blechschmidt's attorney said, "The death of Bev has ended an era which had long outlasted its competitors." And this was true. Blechschmidt, an intelligent operator, skirted turmoil as she watched agents focus on Hurley.[1224]

Hurley: Choices

ALTHOUGH TUERKHEIMER PROMISED not to file charges against Hurley police officer Kenneth Colassaco for threatening his sister, the Iron County District Attorney was not so generous. In November 1981, after reviewing the court record, Iron County District Attorney Paul Sturgul gave Colassaco the choice of being subject to criminal proceedings or resignation. Colassaco resigned, but on December 1, he withdrew his resignation, and the police commission reinstated him. Eventually, Sturgul dropped the charges.[1225]

1982

Hurley: The Judge Goes to Prison

ALEX RAINERI REPORTED TO THE federal correction institution at Lexington, Kentucky, on April 21, 1982, to serve a term of three years.[1226] Presented with a contempt order, he paid a $15,000 fine in early October 1983.[1227] Alex Raineri died in Utah on October 17, 1994, at 76.

* * *

After this exhausting event, Hurley, Madison, and the rest of Wisconsin returned to their customary behavior of creating stories for future writers.

Silver Street from old Chicago & Northwestern Trestle
2024
~Photo courtesy of Gary Jackson

~ FINITO ~

Epilogue

THE PRECEDING STORIES HAVE BEEN plucked from newsprint and placed in somewhat chronological order. They are not metaphorical representations of society as most people went about everyday life filled with events such as football, scholarly activities, and church services.

This narrative is crowded with crime stories, as was the intent. There are several notable characters and, in each case, the energy of the infamous encircled others: some accomplices, some witnesses, and some victims.

Although every journalist in the state used Hurley to get headlines, they often cast their own municipalities as morally superior. There were many reports of vice around the state, but Hurley was the most poignant because of geography, distance from authority, tenacity, and because of familial relationships. Silver Street was home to a tribe of like-minded people trying to make a living based on fundamental human desires. They were often cooperative and sometimes competitive. Fortitude was the glue that held the tribe together and John Roach nailed it when he said, "Hurley never quits."

The down note is that prostitution is a nefarious operation and people suffer. Women suffer at the hands of pimps and johns alike. The business is often based on violence and the use of drugs as motivators. It is different than gambling or liquor which are individual decisions. The stories in this narrative are replete with the silent agony of mothers and fathers of girls who changed their names and painted their faces to trade their bodies for money. There are no words to express the sadness of the death of young women such as Marie Sukup, Carrol Purpora, Marcia Jean Jester, or Candy Lee Jones. The unsolved murders are particularly haunting.

Some of the stories are genuinely humorous as when the 69-year-old madam wanted to barter groceries for services or when Misty Hayes directed traffic in nothing by high black boots or when the former Democratic National spokesperson use the word "prostitution" instead of "prosecution" in a speech.

Some stories strain belief such as when the prostitute swam on a layer of beer across the bar, or when the guy threw a pistol out of the second floor window of Frenchy's narrowly missing a city employee on the street below, or when the guys tried to shove a bunch of slot machine up the stairway in the women's bathroom at the Congress Bar, or when the cop bribed a prostitute to dance at his colleagues stag party.

Taken as a collection, I trust that this accumulation will serve to document this slice of Wisconsin vice from 1942 – 1982. ~gjl.

Addenda

Tavern Operator Records

The following tables show liquor license holders for the properties on the lower two blocks of Silver Street from 1942 to 1982. The annual license period began on July 1 and ended on June 30. A date such as 1946 means that the license was effective on July 1 of that year. Dates other than that mean that the license expired or was surrendered. The license was issued to an individual. In many cases, the name of the establishment was not identified when the license was issued. The information was organized using information from the City of Hurley Clerks office.[1228]

Address	From	To	License Holder	Name
7 Silver Street	1946	1952	Idele Bowers	The Dells
	1952	Oct 1956	Josie Marins	Jodie's Bar
	1957	Feb 1958	Edward L Jansen	No Name Listed
	Feb 1958	Jul 1958	Andrew A. Holappa	Kay's Bar
	1958	1959	William Soucie	Lucky 7
	1959	1962	Anton Lysczyk	Kay's Bar
	1962	1965	Marcia (Kay) Lyon	Kay's Bar

Address	From	To	License Holder	Name
9 Silver Street	1946	1946	John W. Korpela	Alice & Johnny's Bar
	1947	1947	Ervin N. Edmark	Alice & Johnny's Bar
	1948	1948	Frank Boho & Mary Madgziak	No Name Listed
	1949	1949	Frank Boho	Frank's Bar
	1950	1950	Francis Boho	Do
	1951	1954	John Kalasardo	Band Box
	1954	1956	John Vincent Saura	Riverside Bar
	1956	1960	Andrew V. Rodigheiro	Smokey's Bar
	1960	1962	Anton Lysczyk	Four Aces
	1962	1966	Charles Chandler	Hotel Bar
	1966	1972	Marcia Lyon	Hotel Bar

Address	From	To	License Holder	Name
10 Silver Street	1946	1947	Remigio Lerza	Wine Cellar
	1947	1951	Fred Lerza	Wine Cellar
	1951	1952	Melio L. Lerza	Wine Cellar
	1952	1955	Mary Lerza	Wine Cellar
	1955	1956	Fred Lerza	Wine Cellar
	1960	1961	Melio L. Lerza	Wine Cellar
	1970	1971	Robert J. Smith	Smitty's
	1972	1973	Robert J. Smith	Smitty's
	1976	1980	Robert J. Smith	Pier 10
	1980	1982	Pier 10, Inc.	Pier 10 Supper Club

Address	From	To	License Holder	Name
12 Silver Street	1946	1967	Joe Iafolla	Allie's Inn
	1967	1978	Anthony F. Iafolla	Tony's Tap

Address	From	To	License Holder	Name
13 Silver Street	1946	1954	Joseph McRainels, Sr	Lucky 13
	1954	1959	James B. Quigley	No Name Given
	1959	1961	Agnes Perlberg	Aggie's
	1961	1964	Anton DeGeorgio	Club 13
	1964	1966	Henry B. Kimball	Club 13
	1967	1969	William L. DeSautel	Club 13
	1969	1970	Marvin Bruneau	Club 13
	1971	1973	Three Dee, Inc Ed Rovelsky	Beer Barrel
	1981	1982	Elar Corporation	Beer Barrel

Address	From	To	License Holder	Name
14 Silver Street	1946	1950	Earl G. Maki	Carl's Place and Avel's
	1950	1951	Jonas Biller	No Name Listed
	1951	1952	John Rajkovich	No Name Listed
	1953	1954	Jack Gasbarri	No Name Listed
	1955	1956	Gilbert Boatz	No Name Listed
	1956	1965	Richard Matrella	Club Carnival
	1965	1965	John J. Ravanelli	Club Carnival
	1965	1971	Louis P. Gasbarri	Club Carnival

Address	From	To	License Holder	Name
15 Silver Street	1946	1953	Mrs. Louis Gasbarri	Jackpot's Flame
	1953	1955	James Gasbarri	Jackpot's Flame
	1955	1956	Hjalmer Harris	No Name Listed
	1956	1959	Josie B. Harrop	Jody's Bar
	1959	1966	Bertha Jokipii	Bertha's
	1966	1967	Margaret Jenkins	Pink Poodle

Address	From	To	License Holder	Name
16 Silver Street	1946	1947	John J. Fontecchio	The Royal Palms
	1947	1947	Lulu M. Koski	Club Chateau
	1948	1948	Loise Baratono	Club Chateau
	1949	1950	William Matrella	Club Chateau
	1950	Oct 1950	Joseph Howell	Club Chateau
	Oct 1950	1951	Julius Mattei	Club Chateau
	1951	1952	William Matrella	Black Hawk

Address	From	To	License Holder	Name
17 Silver Street	1946	1952	Agatino J. DiGiorgio	Ritz Bar
	1952	1953	Shirley Feerick	Ritz Bar
	1953	1956	Pearl DiGiorgio[1229]	Ritz Bar
	1956	Nov 1960	Agatino J. DiGiorgio	Ritz Bar
	Nov 1960	1963	John Carli	Ritz Bar
	1963	1964	John C. Briskie	Briskie's

Address	From	To	License Holder	Name
18 Silver Street	1946	1952	Sam Galka	White Front
	1953	1953	Mrs. Sam Galka	White Front
	1953	1954	Blanche Briski	White Front
	1954	1961	Margaret Prickett	Margaret's Bar

Address	From	To	License Holder	Name
19 Silver Street	1946	Feb 1947	Edmund G. La Pointe	Welcome Bar
	Feb 1947	Feb 1947	Gaetano Del Boni	Welcome Bar
	Mar 1947	Jun 1953	Andrew Rodigheiro	Welcome Bar
	Jul 1953	Sep 1956	Andrew Rodigheiro	Smokey's bar
	Oct 1956	1957	James Vitich	The Chateau
	1957	1961	Joan A. Jakubiak	No Name Listed
	1961	1963	Josie Harrop	No Name Listed
	1963	1964	Margaret Prickett	Margaret's Bar
	1964	1965	Joan Howell	Joan's
	1965	1970	Ellen Vitich	French Casino
	1970	1972	Nineteen Silver, Inc	French Casino
	1972	1978	Vacant	Vacant
	Dec 1978	1979	James E. Wilson	French Casino

Address	From	To	License Holder	Name
20 Silver Street	1946	1951	Regina Dary	The Shamrock
	1951	1953	Jack Gasbarri	No Name Listed
	1953	1954	Adele Petri	Blackhawk Tavern
	1954	1955	James Gasbarri	Blackhawk Tavern
	1955	1956	Andrew Holappa	No Name Listed
	1956	1958	Josie Marins	Shamrock
	1958	1961	Adina Gasbarri	Red Feather
	1961	1961	Louis Gasbarri	Red Feather
	1962	1963	Margaret Pickett	No Name Listed
	1963	1964	John C. Briskie	No Name Listed

Address	From	To	License Holder	Name
21 Silver Street	1946	1947	Loise Pictor	Hi-Ho Bar
	1947	1948	Domenic Fontecchio	Hi-Ho Bar
	1948	1952	Joseph Vita	Hi-Ho Bar
	1952	1953	Ann Montonati	Hi-Ho Bar
	1953	1955	Joseph Vita	Hi-Ho Bar
	1955	1961	Ann Montonati	Hi-Ho Bar
	1961	1965	Joseph Vita	Hi-Ho Bar
	1965	1974	Vacant	Hi-Ho Bar
	Oct 1974	1977	Michael E. Montonati	Crossroads Bar
	1977	1982	El Cantina, Inc.	El Cantina
	1982	1983	Patricia E. Wood	El Cantina

Address	From	To	License Holder	Name
22 Silver Street	1946	1946	Dan P. Angelo	Pastime Tavern
	1947	1949	Dan P. Angelo	Mickey's Rendezvous
	1949	1950	Madeline Kozup	Mickey's Rendezvous
	1950	1951	Frank Reardon	Mickey's Rendezvous
	1951	1952	Erma Patritto	Mickey's Rendezvous
	1952	1953	Richard Matrella	Mickey's Rendezvous
	1953	1954	John Kalasardo	Mickey's Rendezvous
	1954	1955	Theresa Kalasardo	Band Box
	1955	1961	John Kalasardo	Band Box
	1961	1973	Theresa Kalasardo	Band Box

Address	From	To	License Holder	Name
23 Silver Street	1946	1954	Louis Gasbarri	Red Feather
	1954	May 1958	Adina Gasbarri	Red Feather
	May 1958	Jun 1958	Jack Romanowski	Club 23
	Oct 1958	Jun 1959	Richard Matrella	No Name Listed
	1959	1961	James B. Quigley	Hi-Hat Bar
	Aug 1961	1962	Thomas Chiolino	Club 23
	1962	1971	J. K. Soffa	Shorty & Mary's
	1971	1975	Mary B. Soffa	Shorty & Mary's
	Jul 1978	Aug 1978	B & K Associates, Inc.	Silver Dollar Bar
	Aug 1978	1980	David Dietscher	Silver Dollar Bar
	1980	1982	B & k Associates, Inc.	Silver Dollar Bar
	1982	1983	Paul Novak, Inc	Silver Dollar Saloon

Address	From	To	License Holder	Name
24 Silver Street	1947	1947	Virgil DaPra	No Name Listed
	Jul 1947	Aug 1947	John DaPra	No Name Listed
	Sep 1947	May 1948	Mattie Bertolini	Mattie's bar
	1948	1953	Andrew Carli	The Bowery
	1953	1954	Verna Carli	The Bowery
	1955	1956	Steve Trochim	The Bowery
	1956	Apr 1961	Virgil DaPra	Ace of Clubs
	1961	1963	Frank Boho	Boho's Tavern
	1964	1970	Victoria Lipske	Vickie's Bar
	1970	1973	Terrence D. Boho	Out House Inn

Address	From	To	License Holder	Name
25 Silver Street	1946	1948	John K. Soffa	Shorty's Bar
	1948	1951	John K. Soffa & Mary Colassaco	Shorty's & Mary's
	1951	1955	John K. Soffa	Shorty's Bar
	1955	1956	Mary Soffa	Shorty's Bar
	1956	1963	John K. Soffa	Shorty's Bar
	1967	1962	Marie A. Richardson	Blue Bird
	1974	1976	Frank Hanousek	Idle Hour
	1976	1980	Mrs. Frank (Joann) Hanousek	Idle Hour
	1980	1988	Frank Hanousek	Idle Hour

Address	From	To	License Holder	Name
26 Silver Street	1946	1947	John F. Califano	Black Hawk
	Jan 1948	Jan 1948	John F. Califano & Daisy E. Wilds	Black Hawk
	Feb 1948	Jun 1948	James A. Francis	Club Francis
	1948	1949	Mattie Bertolini	Black Hawk
	Jul 1949	Nov 1949	Matt Bertolini	Black Hawk
	Dec 1949	Jun 1950	James Quigley	Black Hawk
	1950	1951	William Matrella	Black Hawk
	1952	1953	Frank Companese	Black Hawk
	1953	1954	J. K. Soffa	No Name Listed
	Jul 1954	Dec 1954	Bernard F. Patritto	No Name Listed
	Dec 1954	1955	Matt Bertolini	Holiday Inn
	1955	Mar 1956	Lois Gasbarri	Holiday Inn
	Mar 1956	Jun 1956	John Rajkovich	No Name Listed
	Jul 1956	Sep 1956	Mathew Bertolini	No Name Listed
	Sep 1956	Mar 1957	Anton DeGeorgio	French Casino
	Mar 1957	Jun 1957	Mrs. William Matrella	No Name Listed
	Aug 1958	1962	Adele J. Petri	Club 26
	1962	1963	Josie Harrop	Club 26
	1967	1970	Helen J. Niemi	Cactus Bar
	1970	1971	John S. Carli, Jr.	Cactus Bar

Address	From	To	License Holder	Name
28 Silver Street	1946	1947	Daniel P. Angelo	Mickey's Tavern
	1947	1948	Dominic F. Napoli	No Name Listed
	1948	1949	Fred Fontecchio, Jr.	Club Francis
	Jul 1949	Oct 1949	Thomas Baribeau	Club Francis
	Oct 1949	1950	Pasco Pezzetti	Club Francis
	1950	1951	James Francis & Pasco Pezzetti	Club Francis
	1951	1952	Eugene DeCarlo	Club Francis
	1952	1953	Richard Matrella	Sown Bar
	1953	1955	Belle Pappas	Club Francis
	Jul 1955	Dec 1955	Guido Fontecchio	Club Francis
	Dec 1955	1956	Hjalmer Harris	Show Bar
	1956	1957	Jack Gasbarri	Club Francis
	1957	1963	Adele Petri	Club Francis
	1963	1969	Jack Gasbarri	Club Francis
	1969	1971	Ritz Bar, Inc. Agent Edith Rudolphi	No Name Listed
	1971	1973	Louis Gasbarri	Show Bar
	1973	1974	Adina Gasbarri	Show Bar
	1974	1979	Ritz Bar, Inc, Agent Adina Gasbarri	Show Bar

Address	From	To	License Holder	Name
29 Silver Street	1946	1954	Nunzio Santini	Santini's Hotel
	1954	1955	Ruby Santini	Santini's Hotel
	1975	1976	Leon Anderson	Santini's Hotel
	1976	1988	Ann D. Anderson	Santini's Hotel

Address	From	To	License Holder	Name
100 Silver Street	Jul 1945	Sep 1945	Matt Bertolini	Showboat
	Oct 1945	1948	Richard Matrella	Showboat
	1948	Nov 1948	Nicholas Casanova	Showboat
	Nov 1948	1949	Richard Matrella	Showboat
	1949	1950	Doris Grant	Showboat
	1950	1951	Richard Matrella	Showboat

Address	From	To	License Holder	Name
101 Silver Street	1946	1952	Ben Mark	Kentucky Club Bar
	Aug 1952	1953	Louise Doll	Kentucky Club Bar
	1954	Mar 1955	Mrs. Andrew Carli Xfr from 24	Kentucky Club Bar
	Apr 1955	Jun 1955	Bernardino Fontecchio Xfr from 507 Granite	Freddie's Bowery
	1955	1956	Fred Fontecchio, Jr.	No Name Listed

Address	From	To	License Holder	Name
102 Silver Street	1945	1946	Sam Galka	No Name Listed
	1946	1947	Domenic J. Santini	No Name Listed
	1947	May 1948	Orazio Caruso	Sonata Bar
	May 1948	1950	John Califano	Magic Bar
	1950	1951	William Aijala	Magic Bar

Address	From	To	License Holder	Name
104 Silver Street	1946	1947	Fred Fontecchio, Jr.	Club Fiesta
	Jul 1947	Jan 1948	Dominic F. Napoli	Club Fiesta
	Jan 1948	Jun 1948	James A. Francis	Club Fiesta
	1948	1949	Fred Fontecchio, Jr.	Club Fiesta
	1949	Oct 1949	Eugene DeCarlo (surrendered)	Club Fiesta
	Oct 1949	Jun 1950	Ray H. Anderson	Club Fiesta
	1950	1951	Bernardino J. Fontecchio	Club Fiesta

Address	From	To	License Holder	Name
105 Silver Street	1945	Mar 1950	George DiBucci	Round Up Bar
	Mar 1950	1951	Jonas Biller	Round Up bar
	1951	1952	Margaret Prickett	No Name Listed
	1952	Nov 1954	John Rajkovich	French Casino
	Nov 1954	Nov 1954	James Francis	French Casino
	1955	Nov 1959	Xfr from 321 to 105 Elsie K. Ring	Elsie's Bar
	Nov 1959	1960	Xfr from 117 to 105 Don Davis	No Name Listed
	1960	1961	Nora Davis	No Name Listed
	1961	1962	Don Davis	No Name Listed

Address	From	To	License Holder	Name
106 Silver Street	1946	Sep 1957	Elizabeth Hiiro	Town Tavern
	Sep 1958	1959	Xfr from 121 to 108 Fred Jenkins	Holiday Inn
	1959	1960	Arnold F Overby	Brass Rail

Address	From	To	License Holder	Name
107 Silver Street	1945	1949	Theodore Albasini	Charlie's Tavern
	1949	1950	Lawrence Trochim	The Spa
	1950	1952	Josie Marins	The Spa
	1952	1953	Virgil DaPra	The Spa
	1953	Mar 1956	Emil Erickson	The Spa
	1956	Oct 1959	Then Xfr to 15 Bertha Jokipii	Berthas Bar

Address	From	To	License Holder	Name
109 Silver Street	Dec 1946	1947	Andrew Johnson	No Name Listed
	1947	1948	Esa Salmi & August Ilminen	Salmi's Tavern
	1948	Feb 1949	John Kaukonen	No Name Listed
	Feb 1949	1965	Mrs. Matt Ritmanich	L & M Bar
	1966	1982	Ray, Herman, John Erspamer	Erspamer's Grocery

Address	From	To	License Holder	Name
110 Silver Street	1945	1951	Andrew Abrahamson	North Star
	1951	1958	Frank Boho	Boho's
	1958	1960	John Schnoor	Boho's
	1960	1964	Frank Boho	Boho's

Address	From	To	License Holder	Name
111 Silver Street	1946	1951	Otto Salmi	Otto's Tavern
	1951	1959	Lydia Salmi	Salmi's Tavern

Address	From	To	License Holder	Name
112 Silver Street	1945	1952	Florian A. Friola	Flory's
	1952	1953	Frank Kolesar	Flory's

Address	From	To	License Holder	Name
114 Silver Street	1946	1948	Rudolph P. Santini	Golden Bell
	1948	1952	Rudolph P. Santini	Rudy's Bar
	1952	1955	Filomena Santini	Rudy's Bar
	1955	Oct 1975	Rudolph P. Santini	Rudy's Bar & Grill
	Oct 1975	1977	Pogo's Inc. Jack E. Hunter	Pogo's
	1977	Mar 1981	Jack E. Hunter	Pogo's Bar & Grill
	1981	1982	Shirley L. Jones	Pogo's

Address	From	To	License Holder	Name
115 Silver Street	1945	1953	Onni Kangas	Kangas Tavern
	1953	1954	Allie Lambert	Kangas Tavern
	1954	1956	James F. Vallino	No Name Listed
	1956	Apr 1957	Geno R. Priante	Clinker's
	May 1957	1958	Floyd P. Calligaro	Medo's Speedway
	Oct 1958	1960	Robert A. Kostopolus	Bob's Bar
	1964	1965	Xfr from 115 to 26 Helen Niemi	Helen's Tap
	1965	1967	Helen Niemi	Cactus Bar

Address	From	To	License Holder	Name
116 Silver Street	1945	1955	James C. Shields	TryAngle Inn
	1955	1960	Mildred Lutz	TryAngle Inn
	1960	1965	James C. Shields	TryAngle Inn
	1965	1966	Bertha G. Lowe	TryAngle Inn

Address	From	To	License Holder	Name
117 Silver Street	1945	1947	William Aijala	Victory Bar
	1947	1948	William Aijala & Elsie Stulac	Victory Bar
	1948	1949	William Aijala	Victory Bar
	1949	1951	Mary Magdiak	No Name Listed
	Sep 1951	1952	Robert Vioski	No Name Listed
	Dec 1953	Mar 1954	Frank Verbos	No Name Listed
	Apr 1954	Jun 1954	Tony Ogrenc	No Name Listed
	1954	1955	Xfr from 105 to 117 John S. Rajkovich	French Casino
	Mar 1958	Jun 1958	Albert Allen	Tiny's Flame Bar
	1959	1961	Xfr to 105 then 18 to 117 Don Davis	The Hut

Address	From	To	License Holder	Name
118 Silver Street	1946	1950	Nora Abraham	Smokey's Bar
	1950	Oct 1952	Arthur Abraham	Nora's
	Oct 1952	1953	Andrew Abraham	Nora's Bar
	1953	1954	Nora Abraham	Nora's Golden Nugget
	1954	1955	Arthur Abraham	Nora's Golden Nugget
	1955	1963	Nora Abraham	Nora's Bar
	1963	1966	Andrew Abraham	Nora's Bar
	1967	1970	Nora Juntunen	Nora's Bar
	1970	1992	Nora Juntunen	Nora's Red Carpet Lounge

Address	From	To	License Holder	Name
119 Silver Street	1945	1952	Peter DeFranco	Montreal House
	1952	1953	Xfr from 118 Lois Gasbarri	Frenchy's
	1953	1954	William S. Hart	Frenchy's
	1954	1965	Sigrid Aho	Sigs

Address	From	To	License Holder	Name
120 Silver Street	1946	1962	Gabriel Stella	Norther Tavern
	1962	1964	Anthony Trolla	Jim's Bar
	1964	1965	Robert J. Ferkovich	Ferkie's Bar
	1965	1968	Amelia Vernetti	Big John's Bar
	1968	1972	John J. Vernetti	Big John's Bar
	1972	Nov 1972	Amelia Vernetti	Big John's
	Nov 1972	Nov 1974	Helen M. Beckstron	Dry House
	Nov 1974	Jun 1975	Hugh Charles Holz	Dry Haus
	1975	1977	Dianne M. O'Leary	Dry Haus
	1977	1981	Lynn Marie Peterson	Dry Haus
	Sep 1981	Apr 1982	Dennis Kellerman	Dry Haus

Address	From	To	License Holder	Name
121 Silver Street	1945	1946	Henry Lauri Niemi	No Name Listed
	1946	1947	Raymond Dudra	Down Beat Club
	1947	1948	Joseph C Moselle	Down Beat Club
	1948	1949	Ann Moselle	Down Beat Club
	1949	1950	Joseph Moselle	Down Beat Club
	1950	1951	Marie Nygaard	No Name Listed
	1951	Apr 1952	William Aijala	No Name Listed
	Apr 1952	Mar 1953	Xfr from 16 to 121 Julius Mattei	Club Chateau
	Mar 1953	Jun 1953	Name Change	Blue Note
	1953	1954	Bernard Patritto	No Name Listed
	1954	1955	John W. Carli	No Name Listed
	1955	1957	Xfr from 26 to 121 Lois Gasbarri	Frenchy's
	1957	1958	Fred Jenkins	Holiday Inn
	Oct 1958	1959	John Finnegan	Finnegan's Bar
	1959	1960	John Finnegan	Finnegan's Rainbow Bar

Address	From	To	License Holder	Name
123 Silver Street	1945	1946	Ray Anderson	No Name Listed
	1946	1949	Jim Richard Lawless	Congress Bar
	1949	1954	Blanche Lawless	Congress Bar
	1954	1955	James Lawless	Congress Bar
	1960	1963	Blanch M Lawless	Congress Bar
	1963	1965	Jim Lawless	Congress Bar

Address	From	To	License Holder	Name
507 Granite	1945	1950	Domenic C. Vita	Swing Club
	1950	1951	Mrs. Domenic Vita	Swing Club
	1951	1953	Domenic C. Vita	Swing Club
	Mar 1954	May 1954	Roderick G. Lamarche	Swing Club
	May 1954	1955	Berardino Fontecchio	Swing Club

Endnotes

[1] My Grandmother, on my mother's side, was Rosaria Fontecchio (Alleva). She was Fred Fontecchio Senior's sister. She was born on June 5, 1887, in Capestrano, L'Aquila, Abruzzo, Italy and emigrated to the Unites States in 1908. She died in 1947. Fred and Carmella Fontecchio opened a tavern/restaurant on 5th Avenue in Hurley. They had three children: Fred Jr., Elizabeth, and Patrick.

[2] Susan Sontag, *On Photography*, Farrar, Straus, and Giroux, 1977.

[3] Sevgi O. Aral, John M. Douglas, Behavioral Interventions for Prevention and Control of Sexually Transmitted Diseases, Springer Science & Business Media, Dec 3, 2008.

[4] "Nation Warned of Air Attacks, Germ Warfare," *The Eau Claire Leader-Telegram*," January 13, 1942.

[5] "Claims Venereal Diseases Still Scourges of Army," *The Capital Times*, February 6, 1942.

[6] International Convention for the Suppression of the "White Slave Traffic," May 4, 1910, 211 Consol. T.S. 45, 1912 GR. Brit. T.S. No. 20, as amended by Protocol Amending the International Agreement for the Suppression of the White Slave Traffic and Amending the International Convention for the Suppression of the White Slave Traffic, May 4, 1949, 2 U.S.T. 1999, 30 U.N.T.S. 23, entered into force June 21, 1951. http://hrlibrary.umn.edu/instree/whiteslavetraffic1910.html

[7] Classification 18 (May Act) Headquarters and Field Office Case Files, Index, and Microfilm, 1942-1949, National Archives.

[8] "May, Garsson Brothers Given 8 Months to Two Years for War Frauds," *The Capital Times*, July 25, 1947.

[9] Public Health Service Act, 1944, https://www.ncbi.nlm.nih.gov/pmc/articles/PMC1403520/

[10] "53 in Court in Vice Raid," *Montreal River Miner*, August 7, 1942.

[11] Cedric Parker, "Arrest 54 in Vice Cleanup at Hurley: 36 Women, 18 Men Held After Sensational Raid by State Agents," *The Capital Times*, August 5, 1942.

[12] In Wisconsin, the duties of the district attorney are described in s. 978.05 Wis. Stats. The statute states the district attorney shall, (1) prosecute all criminal actions, (2) prosecute all state forfeiture actions, participate in investigatory John Doe proceedings, (3) attend a grand jury for the purpose of examining witnesses in their presence, (4) give the grand jury advice in any legal matter; draw bills of indictment; and issue subpoenas and other processes to compel the attendance of witnesses, (5) Cooperate with the departments of children and families and health services regarding the fraud investigation, (6) Upon the request and under the supervision and direction of the attorney general, brief and argue all criminal cases brought by appeal or writ of error or certified from a county within his or her prosecutorial unit to the court of appeals or supreme court, (7) represent the state in criminal appeals in the prosecutional unit, (8) Institute, commence or appear in all civil actions or special proceedings as the judge may request to represent the interests of the public, (9) Enforce the provisions of all general orders of the department of commerce relating to the sale, transportation and storage of explosives, and (10) prosecute or defend actions transferred to another county.

[13] "Announce Appointment of Tire Rationing Board: Applications Must Get Approved of Inspector; No Tires for Pleasure Cars," *Iron River Miner*, January 8, 1942.

[14] Robert H. Fleming, "Forces of Vice to Use Tricky Methods to Gain Foothold in Area, Fear: Taxis, Movable Cabins and Trailers Utilized in Some Defense Areas," *The Capital Times*, February 26, 1942.

[15] "Ban on Prostitution in Merrimac Area is Urged: Dr. Harper, Health Officer, Writes to Officials of Communities," *The Capital Times*, February 3, 1942.

[16] Wis. Stats 944.30(1), (2), and (3).

[17] Taxation Department's *Enforcement Manual*

[18] Jerry Freeman, "Put Harlots in 'Army', State Official Urges" *The Wisconsin State Journal*, October 28, 1942.

[19] "State Treasurer Smith Urges Forced Military Life for Prostitutes Under Women Officers to Stamp Out Vice," *The Eau Claire Leader-Telegram*, October 29, 1942.

[20] "National Crime Syndicate," The Kefauver Hearings, October 10, 2019,

[21] The law reads in part, "SEC. 2. That any person who shall knowingly transport or cause to be transported, or aid or assist in obtaining transportation for, or in transporting, in interstate or foreign commerce, or in any Territory or in the District of Columbia, any woman or girl for the purpose of prostitution or debauchery, or for any other immoral purpose, or with the intent and purpose to induce, entice, or compel such women or girl to become a prostitute or to give herself up to debauchery or to engage in any other immoral practice;..." The Mann Act (1910), 36 Stats., Vol. I, p. 825 (1910), https://archive.org/stream/283075-the-mann-act-1910/283075-the-mann-act-1910_djvu.txt

[22] "17 Departments of State Spent $897,109 for Traveling in Year: Conservation Body's Costs are Highest; Roach is Most-Traveled Employe, with Mart a Close Second." *The Capital Times*, January 25, 1942.

[23] "Hurley's Quota 78, Declares Roach," *Montreal River Miner*, May 22, 1942.

[24] "Tavern Officials Meet with State Officials," *The Rhinelander Daily News*, May 19, 1942.

[25] "Little Bohemia Lodge: The Gun Battle, *Wikipedia*, https://en.wikipedia.org/wiki/Little_Bohemia_Lodge

[26] "Hurley Has One Tavern for Every 40 Residents; Officials May Face Suit: Licenses Exceed Legal Quota, Roach Says, Warned City," *The Capital Times*, August 6, 1942.

[27] "Taverns are to be Limited," *Iron River Miner*, May 1, 1942.

[28] In Wisconsin, the duties of the attorney general are described in s.165.015, Wis. Stats. as follows: (1) Give his or her opinion in writing, when required, without fee, upon all questions of law submitted to him or her by the legislature, either house thereof or the senate or assembly committee on organization, or by the head of any department of state government. (2) Protect trust funds. Examine all applications for loans from any of the trust funds, and furnish to the commissioners of public lands his or her opinion in writing as to the regularity of each such application, and also of the validity of any bonds or other securities purchased for the benefit of such funds. (3) Certify bonds. Examine a certified copy of all proceedings preliminary to any issue of state bonds or notes, and, if found regular and valid, endorse on each bond or note his or her certificate of such examination and validity. (4) Keep statement of fees. Keep a detailed statement of all fees, including his or her fees as commissioner of public lands, received by him or her during the preceding year, and file such statement with the department of administration on or before June 30 in each year. (5) Report to legislature. Upon request of the legislature or either house thereof, submit a report upon any matters pertaining to the duties of his or her office to the chief clerk of each house of the legislature, for distribution to the legislature.

There are two annotations in Wisconsin Statutes. First, the attorney general, absent a specific legislative grant of power, is devoid of the inherent power to initiate and prosecute litigation intended to protect or promote the interests of the state or its citizens and cannot act for the state as parens patriae. Second, the attorney general does not have authority to challenge the constitutionality of statutes. Any authority the attorney general has is found in the statutes. The attorney general's constitutional powers and statutory powers are one and the same.

[29] "City council Wrestles with Tavern Licenses," *Iron River Miner*, June 26, 1942.

[30] "Two Counties Tell Roach Disorderly Houses Closed," *The Capital Times*, June 16, 1948.

[31] "Bulk of Tavern Houses of Prostitution Cleaned Out Now, Roach Reports," *The Capital Times*, June 30, 1942.

[32] William T. Evjue, "Hello Wisconsin," *The Capital Times*, July 20, 1942.

[33] "Arrest Tavern Man on Disorderly House Charge," *The Capital Times*, July 13, 1942.

[34] Side Note: John Roach and Clyde Tutton lived in the same neighborhood on the near west side of Madison. Roach lived at 2115 Van Hise Street and Tutton at 2525 Gregory Street. (For 22 years, but at a different time, I lived half way between them at 2300 Rugby Row.)

[35] "Raineri Now Practicing Law in Arizona," *Iron County Miner*, May 8, 1953.

[36] "A. Raineri Succeeds Ahonen as Undersheriff," *Iron County News*, May 22, 1942.

[37] "Doris Bertagnoli is Wed to Alex Raineri," *Montreal River Miner*, April 30, 1943.

[38] "Law Firm of Raineri & Raineri Established," *Iron County News*, May 26, 1944.

[39] "Margaret P. Varda, *Wikipedia*, https://en.wikipedia.org/wiki/Margaret_P._Varda

[40] "Hurley Attorney Gets Eisenhower Award," *Iron River Miner*, August 6, 1954.

[41] Obituaries, *Iron County Miner*, May 31, 1963.

[42] "Mrs. Gasbarri Passes," *Iron County Miner,* November 29, 1957.

[43] "Obituaries," James Gasbarri, *Iron County Miner*, May 31, 1963.

[44] "Locals," Mr. and Mrs. C. Vita Observe 50th Anniversary. *Iron River Miner,* May 17, 1963.

[45] Ad, *Iron River Miner,* May 24, 1940.

[46] The 1910-1940 U.S. Census show number Carli's in the Ironwood area. In the same year that Andrew Carli is shown as a beer distributor in Ironwood, two other Carli's are listed. The May 11, 1933, *Ironwood Daily Globe* shows a John A. Carli at 111 East Bonnie Street, and a John B. Carli at 107 South West Street. The relationship between the John A. and John B. is not clear. However, the 1910 census shows John Carli, 30, as owning a saloon.

[47] "Claims No Court Will Oppose NRA," *Ironwood Daily Globe,* August 28, 1933.

[48] The Social Security Index shows a John A. Carli born to Modesto Carli and Mary Rodeghiero in 1904. His relationship to Chink is unclear. Perhaps he was a cousin.

[49] "36 Applicants for Licenses," *Ironwood Daily Globe,* April 11, 1936.

[50] "Proceedings of the City Commission," *Ironwood Daily Globe,* December 5, 1939.

[51] "Proceedings of the City Commission," *Ironwood Daily Globe,* December 20, 1939.

[52] "Council Proceedings," *Iron River Miner*, October 4, 1940.

[53] "Council Proceedings," *Iron River Miner*, October 11, 1940.

[54] For a short period, he was associated with the Chink-Kuba tavern in Carey.

[55] Current location of the Hurley post office.

[56] "Council Grants 13 Operator's Licenses," *Montreal River Miner*, September 10, 1943.

[57] "Pick Carli, Morzenti for Deputy Jobs," *Ironwood Daily Globe,* January 31, 1967.

[58] John Carli sometimes used the name John Stephen Bohrmann.

[59] Ancestry.com. U.S., Social Security Applications and Claims Index, 1936-2007, Provo, UT, USA: Ancestry.com Operations, Inc., 2015.

[60] "Kietho" is how the name is spelled in the census record. There are no other references with this spelling; it may be in error.

[61] Obituaries, *Iron River Miner*, July 12, 1935.

[62] William DeLong, "Why Frank Capone Was Even More Bloodthirsty Than His Brother Al," *ATI*, January 30, 2019.

[63] Carmella (D'Andrea) Fontecchio claimed that her father, Frank D'Andrea and brother Tony D'Andrea

were the first Capistranese to arrive in the area in 1900. "At 85, Tony Trolla is Still 'Boss,'" *Ironwood Daily Globe,* March 30, 1973.

[64] Daniel Peter Angelo was born in Italy in 1899. He immigrated in 1914. In 1937, he married Marie Hakka and lived at 100 First Avenue North in Hurley, next to Gus and Irene Giancola. Dan was educated through eighth grade and worked as a bartender in 1940. Angelo was later married to a woman named Anna, and then in June 1936, he married Madeline Kozup from Mellen. Mickey's Place, Mickey's Bar and Café, later known as Mickey's Rondevoo (Rendezvous), located at 22 Silver Street. On April 12, 1949, Daniel P. Angelo, 51, died at home. His wife would declare a suspicious death and demand an exhumation.

[65] In 2011, Madeline Capone Morichetti, via Christie's Auction house, sold a Colt .38 revolver that was previously owned by Al Capone at auction for $110,000. *The Times,* June 23, 2011.

[66] Serafino Anthony "Suds" Morichetti was born in 1918 in Hurley. He was an actor in "A Beautiful Summer Weekend Raid" in 1954, "1955 Raid #1," and "Warrants for Revocations" in 1957. He married Naomi Lucille Willard in 1955. In 1977, he married Madeleine M. Capone (Kozup), to whom he was married for 23 years. Suds Morichetti died in 2000 in Alaska at age 82 and was buried in Hurley.

[67] "Descendants of Baxter Lyon, Tampico Historical Society, July 7, 2020.

[68] Year: 1900; Census Place: Montreal, Iron, Wisconsin; Page: 5; Enumeration District: 0043; FHL microfilm: 1241791

[69] "Married at Duluth," *Iron County News*, February 16, 1918.

[70] Year: 1920; Census Place: Hurley, Iron, Wisconsin; Roll: T625_1988; Page: 6B; Enumeration District: 98

[71] The National Archives in St. Louis, Missouri; St. Louis, Missouri; Draft Registration Cards for Wisconsin, 10/16/1940-03/31/1947; Record Group: Records of the Selective Service System, 147; Box: 739

[72] Holmes, Fred L. (ed.) / *The Wisconsin Blue Book*, 1927

[73] "Obituaries: R. C. Trembath, *Ironwood Daily Globe,* March 17, 1964.

[74] Wisconsin did not have a dedicated FBI field office in 1942. Instead, the state fell under the jurisdiction of two neighboring field offices in Chicago and St. Paul. The St. Paul office covered the western portion of Wisconsin and half of the Upper Peninsula of Michigan. By December 1942, the FBI established a resident agency in Milwaukee which became a field office in 1951. Later, the St. Paul office moved to Minneapolis and a resident agency was opened in Duluth.

[75] "Badger State Athletes Go to Outside Colleges and Become Pigskin Luminaries," *The Eau Claire Leader Telegram*, December 5, 1925.

[76] "Inspectors Arrest Five Tavern Men," *The Sheboygan Press*, May 23, 1934.

[77] "Treasury Agent Killed in Raid: Matt Schumacher, 33, of State Department, Shot to Death at Kenosha" *The La Crosse Tribune*, September 22, 1934.

[78] "Roundy Says," *The Wisconsin State Journal*, November 17, 1934.

[79] "Duester Loses State Beverage Division Post," *The Capital Times*, June 15, 1939.

[80] "Age Limitations Part of the Spoils Technique," *The Capital Times,* June 20, 1939.

[81] "Progressives in Nap, Patronage Plan Succeeds: Senate Acts to Put Beverage Tax Jobs on New Basis," *The Capital Times,* August 9, 1939.

[82] "August Frey is So Alone; Can't Find Office Space," *The Capital Times,* December 27, 1940.

[83] "State Goes After Liquor Violators," *The Capital Times*, October 9, 1940.

[84] "Tavern Men Hear Press Attacked as 'Buzzards' for Printing 'Dry Lies.'," *The Capital Times*, January 22, 1941.

[85] "Tavernkeepers Laud Roach in Resolution," *Wisconsin State Journal*, March 18, 1941.

[86] "With the State Press," *The Sheboygan Press*, April 2, 1941.

[87] "North Ignores Tavern Code, Roach Says," *Wisconsin State Journal*, July 9, 1941.

[88] "Roach Bares Secret List of Slot Machines," *The Capital Times*, October 1, 1941.

[89] John "Johnny" Mario Califano was born in Naples, Italy, in 1880. He emigrated to the U.S. in 1905. In 1928 John lived at the Burton Hotel. In 1940, he lived at 118 North First Avenue, and his occupation was a saloon keeper. He died in 1966 in St. Paul, Minnesota.

[90] "Hurley Has One Tavern for Every 40 Residents; Officials May Face Suit," *The Capital Times*, August 6, 1942.

[91] Harry Ferguson, "Ladies are Eight Times as Law Abiding as Men: The American Woman – No. 3," *The Capital Times,* February 13, 1963.

[92] "Raided Hurley Tavern Owners Fight Charges of Prostitution," *The Capital Times*, August 6, 1942.

[93] Edna was married to James. She was born in Indiana in 1908. They lived at 108 First Avenue North and operated the TryAngle Inn at 116 Silver Street. After a recent divorce, Edna Shields died by suicide at the Club Chateau in 1945 at age 38.

[94] State Promises to War on Taverns Linked with Vice: Roach Announces Clean-Up Policy to Be Continued," *The Wisconsin State Journal*, June 12, 1942.

[95] "Officials to Free Defense Areas from Prostitution," *Wisconsin State Journal*, June 16, 1942.

[96] Rod Van Every, "State Raids Hurley Vice Dens: Roundup Follows U.S. Plea to Purge War-Effort Areas," *Wisconsin State Journal*, August 5, 1942,

[97] Ibid.

[98] Ibid.

[99] Ibid.

[100] Ibid.

[101] "A Housecleaning," *Wisconsin State Journal*, August 6, 1942.

[102] "Arrest 54 In Vice Cleanup at Hurley: 36 Women, 18 Men Held After Sensational Raid by State Agents," *The Capital Times*, August 5, 1942.

[103] The Sixth Service Command was responsible for providing logistical support, including administrative, operational, and supply services, to the Army.

[104] "Raids Surprise Hurleyites: Roach Has His Revenge," *Montreal River Miner*, August 7, 1942

[105] "Grant Two Tavern Licenses," *Montreal River Miner*, September 4, 1942

[106] James Andrea Francis was born in December 1909. In 1930, he lived at 103 North First Avenue, a few doors north of Silver Street. He died in 1986, in Bessemer, Michigan, at 76.

[107] "Vice Offenders Pay $250 Fine," *Iron River Miner*, October 2, 1942.

[108] "Clean Out 110 Disorderly Houses in State, Edict," *The Capital Times*, June 12, 1942.

[109] "Six Arrested in Vice Raids," *Wisconsin State Journal*, July 28, 1942.

[110] No relation to the Hi-Ho in Hurley.

[111] "Eight Arraigned After Vice Raid," *Green Bay Press Gazette*, August 22, 1942.

[112] "State Anti-Vice Drive Continues," *Wisconsin State Journal*, September 3, 1942.

[113] "Arrest Six More on Vice Counts in Tavern Raids," *The Capital Times*, September 3, 1942.

[114] "81 Prostitutes Under Arrest, Roach Declares," *Wisconsin State Journal*, September 6, 1942.

[115] "White Slaver Suspect Held," *The Minneapolis Star*, March 4, 1943.

[116] "Girl Held as Slave in Kankakee, Claim," *Wisconsin State Journal*, December 29,1935.

[117] "Inmates of Disorderly House Pay Heavy Fines," *Marshfield News-Herald*, January 13, 1942.

[118] "'Al' Legato Nabbed for White Slavery," *Deadwood Pioneer-Times*," March 5, 1943.

[119] "J. Gasbarri Faces Mann Act Charge," *Iron River Miner*, May 7, 1943.

[120] "J. Gasbarri Gets 2 ½ Year Sentence; Fine," *Iron River Miner*, May 14, 1943.

[121] "Deaths," *Star Tribune*, November 22, 1969.

[122] "Argue Over License Transfer," *Iron County Miner*, October 9, 1942.

[123] James Ceylon Shields was born in Pennsylvania in 1903. The 1940 Census shows James being married to Edna, born in Indiana in 1908. They lived at 108 First Avenue North and operated the TryAngle Inn at 116 Silver Street.

[124] "John Roach Makes Another Visit; Five Taverns Raided," *Iron County Miner*, December 18, 1942.

[125] "F.B.I. Offers Clerical Positions to Woman," *Iron River Miner*, January 1, 1943.

[126] "Tavern Keepers Given Hearings," I*ron County Miner*, January 22, 1943.

[127] "John Roach Enters the Army as a Captain,' *Iron River Miner*, January 22, 1943.

[128] "Tavern Owners Warned by Tutton," *Iron River Miner*, January 29, 1943.

[129] Stephen "Steve" Joseph Trochim Jr. was born in Hurley in 1909. His father was born in 1868 and married Mary "Raskowski" "Trochim" Janiszewski, born in 1868, about the turn of the century. Mary had three children with Trochim, and Stephen Jr. was born in 1909 in Hurley. Steve lived in Reno, Nevada, when he filed his WWII draft registration in 1940. He listed his notification person as his wife, Letitia Frances Trochim, and his employer's name as Jack Sullivan of the Bank Club. He moved to Reno and worked as a dealer at the Horseshoe Club for many years. Steve Trochim died in Reno, Nevada, in 1965 at 55.

[130] As much as this work dabbles in a modicum of creative fiction, it would be uncharitable to say that the shot was "spot on."

[131] "Tries William Tell Act; Steve Trochim Wounded in Left Hand," *Montreal River Miner*, May 22, 1936.

[132] "Drunk Drivers Enrich County Court Treasury," *Montreal River Miner*, September 24, 1937.

[133] "Intoxicated Driver Sentenced to Jail: Reinold Maki Unable to Pay Fine of $50 and Costs," *Ironwood Daily Globe*," November 22, 1937.

[134] "Announcements: Personals," *Ironwood Daily Globe*, December 22, 1938.

[135] "Legals: Legal Notices," *Ironwood Daily Globe*, February 7, 1939.

[136] "Two are Fined for Fighting at Hurley," *Ironwood Daily Globe*, August 3, 1939.

[137] "Common Council Proceedings: Regular Meeting August 1, 1939," *Iron County News*, August 18, 1939.

[138] "Council," *Ironwood Daily Globe*, August 2, 1939.

[139] Ruth Shimondle, "Montreal News Notes: Stanley Serbin in the Toils Again; Was Ordered Out of Town," *Montreal River Miner*, December 15, 1939.

[140] "Takes Serbin to Waupun," *Montreal River Miner*, December 29, 1939.

[141] Steve, the father's namesake, was born in 1935 and stayed on the "other side of the bar." He was a Hurley policeman for 14 years. Steve died in 1946 at 55. Steve Rajkovich's son, John, appears later and is associated with the French Casino.

[142] "Court News: Prison Term for Serbin," *Montreal River Miner*, February 12, 1943.

[143] "Dec. 20 Hearing Set in Stabbing Case," *Wisconsin State Journal*, December 16, 1949.

[144] "Stanley Serbin, Ex-Cab Driver, Dies Here at 48," *Ironwood Daily Globe*, January 31, 1955.

[145] "Tavern Industry Future Depends on Legal Compliance," *Iron River Miner*, April 9, 1943.

[146] "Taverns Must Close from 1 A.M. to 8 A.M.," *Iron River Miner*, July 16, 1943.

[147] "Dist. Atty. Raineri in the Naval Reserve," *Iron River Miner*, September 3, 1943.

[148] "15 Tavernkeepers Nabbed: State Beverage Tax Men Get Evidence in Advance and Make Raid," *Iron*

River Miner, October 22, 1943.

[149] "Ironwood Cop Runs Amuck Here: Shots at a Customer in the Gus Lewis Café," *Iron River Miner*, November12, 1943.

[150] "Shortage of Whiskey to Grow, Says Tutton," *Iron River Miner*, November 19, 1943.

[151] "Allows Music in His Tavern; Pays $25 Fine," *Iron River Miner*, December 24, 1943.

[152] "The Real Hurley," *Iron River Miner*, December 24, 1943.

[153] The 1940 U.S. Census reports a John Carollo born in Peshtigo in 1908 with a residence in Florence in 1935. The surname has been spelled in the press as Carollo, Carolla, Caroola, and Caroolo. https://www.ancestryheritagequest.com/search/collections

[154] William T. Evjue, "Hello Wisconsin," *The Capital Times*, February 22, 1943.

[155] "Dismisses Grand Jury," *Ironwood Daily Globe,* January 10, 1936.

[156] Ray Derham was member of Michigan state senate 31st District, 1933-34. He was defeated in primary, 1934; candidate for circuit judge in Michigan 25th Circuit, 1947. Died in Iron Mountain, Dickinson County, Mich., November 27, 1957: The Political Graveyard.

[157] "Derham Disbarred in Federal Court: Judge Raymond Admonishes All Other Attorneys in Peninsula," *Ironwood Daily Globe,* October 10, 1936.

[158] "Padlock 3 Places in Florence Co." *Montreal River Miner*, July 21, 1939.

[159] "Council Proceeding," *Montreal River Miner*, July 21, 1939.

[160] "Seven More Liquor Licenses," *Montreal River Miner*, July 14, 1939.

[161] Ibid.

[162] "Padlock 3 Places in Florence Co.," *Montreal River Miner*, July 21, 1939.

[163] "Hurley City Council," *Ironwood Daily Globe,* August 2, 1939.

[164] "Flannery Gets Tavern License," *Montreal River Miner*, August 4, 1939.

[165] "Fontecchio and Flannery Pay UP," *Montreal River Miner*, August 11, 1939.

[166] "Green Bay Man Held for Mann Act Charge," *The La Crosse Tribune*, August 21, 1942.

[167] "White Slaver is Sentenced: Given Two Years in Federal Prison," *Manitowoc Herald Times*, February 8, 1943.

[168] "Spread Eagle Man Faces 2nd Charge: Appeal Pending, He is Arrested Second Time," *Ironwood Daily Globe*, March 30, 1943.

[169] "Arraign Two Men at Manitowoc," *The Sheboygan Press*, May 28, 1942.

[170] "Plea for Clemency Denied by Goodland," *The Sheboygan Press*, October 12, 1943.

[171] "Keeping House of Ill Fame Charged at Spread Eagle," *Green Bay Press-Gazette*, February 24, 2963.

[172] "Kennedy Files Motion in Two Florence Cases," *Rhinelander Daily News*, March 30, 1965.

[173] "Women Fined on Vice Charges in Florence County," *The Rhinelander Daily News*, March 16, 1966.

[174] "Three Persons Face Vice Charges," *Green Bay Press-Gazette*, September 15, 1968.

[175] "Spread Eagle Man Is Fined in Vice Case," *Green Bay Press-Gazette*, September 20, 1968

[176] Hazel Meihan Bond was born in 1914 in Pennsylvania. Her mother was Violet Francesco, and her father was James W. Meihan. Hazel married John B. Calligaro in 1937 and lived at 23 Silver Street in 1940, where she worked as a "lodging housekeeper." There is no public record of her death.

[177] "Around the Town," *The Minneapolis Star, "* June 24, 1944.

[178] "Mann Act Case to Jury Monday, *The Austin Daily Herald*, May 6, 1944.

[179] "Nine Facing White Slave Sentences," *Minneapolis Daily Times*, May 17, 1944.

[180] "Nine Handed Mann Terms," *The Minneapolis Star*, May 19, 1944.

[181] "City council proceedings," *Iron County News*, June 20, 1947.

[182] "Slot Machines Must Move Out: Governor Sends Word to Sheriff, District Attorney," *Iron River Miner*, June 9, 1944.

[183] "Raineri Brothers Form Law Firm," *Iron River Miner*, August 4, 1944.

[184] Robert L. Roemer would eventually serve as the mayor of Appleton from 1946 through 1957.

[185] "51 Tavernmen in Hurley Area Arrested," *The Wisconsin State Journal*, September 20, 1944.

[186] "Seek Brother of Al Capone in This Area," *Iron River Miner*, March 28, 1944.

[187] Al Capone had contracted syphilis during his time as a bouncer in Chicago in about 1920. This is one of the reasons he was released from prison. https://www.pbs.org/newshour/health/infectious-disease-sprung-al-capone-alcatraz, January 25, 2017.

[188] Henry J. McCormick, "Upstate Show No Capone Fear," *The Wisconsin State Journal*, December 14, 1944.

[189] Henry J. McCormick, "Capones Become Retiring, Benevolent: It's Better Business," *Wisconsin State Journal*, December 15, 1944.

[190] Henry J. McCormick, "Scarface Al Retires, a Mental Wreck," *The Wisconsin State Journal*, December 17, 1944.

[191] From a personal interview with John Roach Jr., the son of John Roach.

[192] Henry J. McCormick, "Not Capones but 'Outsiders' Worry State Resort Owners," *The Wisconsin State Journal*, December 18, 1944.

[193] "Alex J. Raineri, Wikipedia, https://en.wikipedia.org/wiki/Alex_J._Raineri

[194] Matt-Moore Taylor, "Assembly Acts to Shorten Tavern House," *The Wisconsin State Journal*, February 15, 1945.

[195] "Anti-gambling Bill is Offered," *Iron River Miner*, February 5, 1945.

[196] Aldric Revell, "Gives Strong Message to Solons Today," *The Capital Times*, January 10, 1945.

[197] "Slot Machines are Out in City, County," *Iron River Miner*, February 23, 1945.

[198] The author was the beneficiary of one nickel and one dime machine that had been buried in hay and forgotten about. One was a nickel machine, the other a dime. They found new homes many years ago.

[199] Matt-Moore Taylor, "Tavern – Gambling Forces Get 56-38 Setback in Assembly," *The Wisconsin State Journal*, February 21, 1945.

[200] "War Bond Meeting at Saxon H. S. Friday Ev'g," *Montreal River Miner*, June 22, 1945.

[201] "Slot Machines May Have to Go," *Montreal River Miner*, March 9, 1945.

[202] "City Grants 57 Tavern Licenses: Council Has Special Meeting Friday Evening," *Iron River Miner*, June 22, 1945.

[203] "Provisions of State's Anti-Gambling Law," *Iron River Miner*, June 29, 1945.

[204] E. E. Roberts, "Hurley, Hayward and Hell," *Esquire Magazine*, June 1, 1945.

[205] Aldric Revell, "Pass Anti-Gambling, Building Bills: Progressives Hit GOP as Solons Quit," *The Capital Times*, June 20, 1945.

[206] "Gambling and Building Bills Signed Today," *The Capital Times*, June 27, 1945.

[207] "Subpoenas for 33 Senators are Issued: All-Day Sessions of Investigation Set." *The Capital Times*, June 27, 1945.

[208] John Wyngaard, "The Legislative Probe," *The La Crosse Tribune*, July 7, 1945.

[209] "Evjue Among Those Called to Appear Before Grand Jury," *Chippewa Herald-Telegram,* July 9, 1945.

[210] William T. Evjue, San Francisco is Start…Goodland Fools 'Em…Another Defalcation", *The Capital Times*, July 2, 1945.

[211] "Anti-gaming Law Effective," *The Eau Claire Leader-Telegram*, July 1, 1945.

[212] Wyngaard was the Madison bureau chief for the *Appleton Post-Crescent* and *Green Bay Press-Gazette*

[213] Wyngaard, "Under the Capitol Dome: Head of Tax Beverage Division Takes Enforcement Job in Stride," *The Eau Claire Leader*-Telegram, July 15, 1945.

[214] 'Slots' Seized by State: 50 Machines are Confiscated by Beverage Agents." *The Waukesha Daily Freeman*, July 6, 1945.

[215] "State Agents Make First Raids on Gamblers; 'Slots' Seized'": Places in Nine Counties Visited by Raiders," *The Rhinelander Daily News*, July 6, 1945.

[216] "Six Gambling Charges Filed: Cases Will be Heard by Judge Risjord August 7," *Iron River Miner*, July 20, 1945.

[217] Ibid

[218] "Anti-Gambling Law Explained: Enforcement to be Strict, Says Tutton," *The La Crosse Tribune*, July 17, 1945.

[219] "Pages I and II," The Wisconsin State Journal, August 5, 1945.

[220] "33 Gambling Devices Seized at 12 Placed in Five Counties," *Wisconsin State Journal*, August 6, 1945.

[221] "Wow! 21,000 Cigarettes Stolen," *Iron River Miner*, August 10, 1945.

[222] "Seize 36 Gambling Devices in Raids," *The La Crosse Tribune*, August 13, 1945.

"[223] Gambling Cases Just Fizzle Out: Only One Tavern May Have License Revoked," *Iron River Miner*, August 10, 1945.

[224] "Two Tavernkeepers Fined $50 and Costs," *Iron River Miner*, August 17, 1945.

[225] "Celebrate V-J Day in Hurley: Crowds Gathered on Silver Street Tuesday Evening," *Iron River Miner*, August 17, 1945.

[226] "Gambling Law to be Enforced: Ruling by Chippewa Co. Judge to be Appealed," *Iron River Miner*, August 28, 1945.

[227] Rex Karney, "Supreme Court Reverses Verdict Invalidating Act: Unanimous Opinion Strongly Defends State Thomson Law," *Wisconsin State Journal*, January 11, 1946.

[228] "Slot Machines Gone, Tutton Says: Devices Found in Only One Place in 3 Weeks," *Iron River Miner*, September 21, 1945.

[229] "Youth Digs Way Out of St. Paul Jail with Spoon: Uses Bed Sheet Rope to Lower Shelf 65 Feet," *Albert Lea Evening Tribune*, September 2, 1938.

[230] Kahl was unaware that Dahl had received an annulment.

[231] "Kahl Faces Four Possible Charges: Poses as Doctor During One Man Crime Wave," *Moorhead Daily News*, September 10, 1945.

[232] U.S. Penitentiary, Prisoner Index, 1934-1963, Ancestry.com,

[233] Jennifer Chen, "Dawn Shields Legacy: I Am Not 12 Anymore," *Rangefinder Magazine*, May 2010.

[234] Aldric Revel, *The Capital Times*, August 29, 1945.

[235] "Roach Cracked One of the Toughest Murder Cases in Pacific Theater," *The Capital Times*, October 26, 1945.

[236] "Tutton Will Quit as Beverage Tax Head," *Iron River Miner*, October 12, 1945.

[237] "Tutton Quits State Post to be Manager of Liquor Company," *The La Crosse Tribune*, September 24, 1945.

[238] "Roach Resumes Post as Beverage Tax Head," *Iron River Miner*, November 2, 1945.

[239] "Mr. Tutton Takes A New Position," *The Capital Times*, September 25, 1945.

[240] John Wyngaard, "Under the Capitol Dome: Seems Like Everyone Has a Lobbyist," *The Waukesha Freeman*, January 17, 1949.

[241] "Question of "Tavern" is Cleared Up at Meeting," *Montreal River Miner*, January 11, 1946

[242] Rex Karney, "State Agents Raid Hurley, Arrest 19: Roach Makes Haul on Order of Governor," The *Wisconsin State Journal*, January 18, 1946.

[243] The reporters were from *The Wisconsin State Journal* and *The Capital Times*.

[244] Armas Hill was born in Finland in 1890. He primarily worked the gambling games around the Club Fiesta. He died in Ironwood in 1958 and is buried in Hurley.

[245] Aldric Revell, "State Agents Swoop on Hurley in New Cleanup Ordered by Goodland: 28 Nabbed as Roach Leads Drive After Vets are Reported Fleeced," *The Capital Times*, January 18, 1946.

[246] Aldric Revell, "Hurley in New Cleanup Ordered by Goodland: 28 Nabbed as Roach Leads Drive After Bets are Reported Fleeced," *The Capital Times*, January 18, 1946.

[247] "Did Not Order Raid," *Iron River Miner*, January 25, 1946.

[248] Ella Reid Cone and Margaret Pricket were sisters originally from Prattville, Alabama. After moving to Atlanta, the sisters moved to Hurley in 1943.[248] They must have had a penchant for the tavern business as Cone operated the White Front tavern at 20 Silver Street, and Pricket eventually ran Margaret's at 415 Silver Street and 18 Silver Street.

[249] "The Law Comes to Hurley Again; Raid by State Agents," *Iron River Miner*, January 25, 1946.

[250] "The Law Comes to Hurley Again; Raid by State Agents," *Iron River Miner*, January 25, 1946.

[251] Aldric Revell, *The Capital Times*, January 23, 1946.

[252] "Cleanup in Hurley Asked: Goodland Offers State Aid to County," *The La Crosse Tribune*, January 23, 1946.

[253] "Enforce Liquor Law in Hurley, is Ultimatum: Prosecutor and Sheriff Given Orders in Letter from Gov. Goodland," *The Capital Times*, January 25, 1946.

[254] "A Lawmaker Learns Some Law," *The Wisconsin State Journal*, January 21, 1946.

[255] "Tavern Trials Held at Hurley," *Ironwood Daily Globe*, January 29, 1946.

[256] "Only 8 Out of 33 Pled Guilty After Cleanup Raid on Hurley," *The Capital Times*, January 19, 1946.

[257] Iron County Court Record, Iron County Court House, January 29, 1946.

[258] "The Law Comes to Hurley Again; Raid by State Agents," *Iron River Miner*, January 25, 1946

[259] Ibid

[260] Ibid

[261] Ibid

[262] "Honor State Official," *The La Crosse Tribune*, March 7, 1946.

[263] "Bonacci Wins by Slim Margin; 5 New Councilmen," *Montreal River Miner*, April 5, 1946

[264] "Council Grants 72 Licenses; Table 12 Until Next Meeting," *Montreal River Miner*, June 14, 1946.

[265] "Hurley Council Proceedings," *Montreal River Miner*, June 21, 1946

[266] "All Settled: Amicable Solution to Liquor License Wrangle Reached at Tuesday's Council Meet," *Iron County Miner,* July 5, 1946.

[267] "State Agents Raid Houses of Ill Fame," *Wisconsin State Journal*," July 13, 1946.

[268] "Local Officials Crack Down on Gambling," *Iron County News*, September 27, 1946.

[269] "This or That," *The Eau Claire Leader*, August 10, 1946.

[270] Rex Karney, "Gov. Goodland's Opponents Gain in Close-Paced Republican Race," *The Wisconsin State Journal*, August 1, 1946.

[271] "No Syndicate Gambling in State: Roach," *The Capital Times*, September 10, 1946.

[272] "Roach Writes for Detective Magazine," *The Wisconsin State Journal*, December 10, 1946.

[273] "Wisconsin News Briefs: State A-C Sympathy Strike Urged," *Waukesha Daily Freeman*, December 12, 1946.

[274] "Seven Get $524 in Fines After Hurley Raids," *The Capital Times*, June 16, 1947.

[275] "Raid Three Hurley Taverns," *Iron County News*, January 16, 1947.

[276] "Three Fined for Gambling," *Ironwood Daily Globe*, January 9, 1947.

[277] "8 Tavernkeepers Fined for After-hours Selling of Liquor," *Montreal River Miner*, February 7, 1947.

[278] "Historic Burton is No More; Old Landmark Levelled by Fire, *Montreal River Miner*, February 7, 1947

[279] My older brother Virgil was born in 1934. We would often talk about Hurley, and he would tell me stories about of how he shined shoes on the veranda of the Burton. He passed away on May 15, 2020.

[280] "Roach Will Not Run for Congress," *The Capital Times*, February 20, 1947.

[281] "Goodland Dies," *Iron River Miner*, March 14, 1947.

[282] "Alex Raineri Heads County Republicans," *Montreal River Miner*, April 25, 1947.

[283] "Mayor Rules Tavern Decrease a Dead Issue; Ademino Quits," *Montreal River Miner*, May 16, 1947.

[284] "Tavern Operators are Fined $35," *Montreal River Miner*, June 6, 1947.

[285] "Seize 10 in Raid on Hurley Spots," *Waukesha Daily Freeman*, June 16, 1947.

[286] "Knifing Victim 'Satisfactory: Hurley Carpenter Held for Inquiry," *Ironwood Daily Globe*, July 28, 19947.

[287] "Stella is Held to Stand Trial: Hurley Man Bound Over After Hearing," *Ironwood Daily Globe*, September 27, 1947.

[288] "Stella Hearing Delayed Again as Dudra Suffers Relapse," *Montreal River Miner*, August 22, 1947.

[289] "Stella Sentenced to Nine Months: Jury Finds Him Guilty of Simple assault; Sentenced Carries Hard Labor," *Iron County News*, December 5, 1947.

[290] "GOP 'Get Roach' Plot is Charged: Bill Advanced to Put Division Under Tax Unit," *Ironwood Daily Globe*, July 16, 1947.

[291] "Roach Wins Support of Kiwanis Club," *The Rhinelander Daily News*, July 25, 1947.

[292] "State Agents Raid 3 Hurley Nightspots," *The Capital Times*, Aug 11, 1949.

[293] "Rennebohm Names One of His Employes as Acting State Treasurer: John M. Sonderegger to Hold Position Pending Permanent Appointment," *The Capital Times*, August 19, 1947.

[294] "Under the Capital Dome: Reports of Gambling in Northern Wisconsin to be Investigate," *The Eau Claire Leader*, August 30, 1947.

[295] "No Complaints on Gambling Here, O'Melia Reports, *The Rhinelander Daily News*, August 20, 1947.

[296] "Gambling Flourishing in State's Norther Resort area, Survey Discloses," *The Capital Times*, August 21, 1947.

[297] "State Press: Where's Roach?" *The Rhinelander Daily News*, August 23, 1947.

[298] "What Others Think: Report Gambling Rackets Area Back," *The Oshkosh Northwestern*, August 25, 1947.

[299] "State Men Raid 2 Hurley Clubs: John Roach Directs Latest Investigation," *Ironwood Daily Globe*, August 27, 1947.

[300] "No Action Slated on Club Permits: Raineri's Decision Based on June Case," *Ironwood Daily Globe*, September 3, 1947.

[301] "Club Operator Pays Fine," *Montreal River Miner*, September 12, 1947.

[302] Mathew Comilo Bertolini was Born in Hurley in 1905, the son of Mathew Bertolini and Celesta Bott. He died at age 50 in 1956 in Hurley.

[303] "Fined on Assault Charge," *Montreal River Miner*, September 26, 1947.

[304] "Fined on Assault Charge," *Montreal River Miner*, September 26, 1947.

[305] "'The Heat's on Gambling,' Says Hurley Chief," *Iron River Miner*, November 7, 1947.

[306] "Liquor Dealer's Suit to Test Validity of Vets Housing Law: Hits State Law Which Doubled Tax on Liquor," *Waukesha Daily Freeman*, November 4, 1947.

[307] "Roach Renews Raids on Hurley," *Waukesha Daily Freeman*, November 3, 1947.

[308] "Oshkosh Man Goes to Hospital in Shooting Affray," *The Oshkosh Northwestern*, November 7, 1947.

[309] "Prison Term For Keeper Of Illegal House," *Green Bay Press Gazette*, November 20, 1947.

[310] "Hunters Let Down As 'Bear Case' Is Scheduled for Dec. 10," *Green Bay Press Gazette*, December 3 3, 1947.

[311] "Moonshining at Its Lowest Ebb," *Janesville Daily Gazette*, December 9, 1947.

[312] John Wyngaard was the Madison bureau chief for the *Appleton Post-Crescent* and *Green Bay Press-Gazette*. According to an article in the *Superior Telegram*, he wrote 650,000 words in his column over the period of 55 years. He wrote his last essay at age 78 in 2016.

[313] "John Wyngaard: The Pay in Public Office," *The La Crosse Tribune*, December 31, 1947.

[314] "Roach is Expected to Keep State Position, *The Daily Tribune*, January 7, 1948.

[315] John Wyngaard, "Some of Top State Republicans Are Cordial to Harold Stassen," Marshfield News-Herald, January 13, 1948.

[316] "State Questions Two Liquor Licenses," *Iron County News*, January 9, 1948.

[317] https://www2.census.gov/library/publications/decennial/1950/pc-02/pc-2-38.pdf

[318] "State Tax Agents Raid 13 Taverns, *Leader-Telegram*, February 4, 1948.

[319] "Some Wisconsin Highlights," *The Capital Times*, March 22, 1948.

[320] "Lawyers Hit Roach After Tavern Raids," *The La Crosse Tribune*, March 16, 1948.

[321] "To Ask Probe of Disorderly House Action," *The Capital Times*, March 16, 1948.

[322] "Roach Hurls 'Hypocrite' Charge at Solons Who Hinder Law Enforcement," *The Capital Times*, April 5, 1948.

[323] "Seek Better Examination of Tavern Operator Applicants," *The La Crosse Tribune*, April 16, 1948.

[324] "Fatal Accident at Montreal Mine: Thomas Belanger Killed; Dante Barnabo Injured," *Iron River Miner, September 8, 1944.*

[325] "Buys North Side Confectionery Store," *Iron River Miner*, March 30, 1945.

[326] "New City Officers Take Over: Mayor Barnabo and Other City Officials Assume Their Duties Tomorrow," *Iron County News*, April 30, 1948.

[327] John I. Patritto was born in 1878. He and his wife had seven children, including Bernard, born in Bessemer, Michigan, in 1904, and Felix John, born in 1909. Felix died in 1974 at 65.

[328] "About People You Know: Youths Arrested for Robbery," *Iron River Miner*, February 13, 1925.

[329] "About People You Know: Arrest Young Patritto in Duluth," *Iron River Miner*, February 25, 1925.

[330] "Hoskins Gets One to Seven Years: Man Who Robbed Cash Register at Marble Hall Sentenced; One to Five for Check Forger," *Iron County News*, October 17, 1925.

[331] "Two are Sentenced by Judge Risjord: Felix Patritto to Reformatory; Joe Masemski is Given 60 days," *Ironwood Daily Globe*, January 12, 1926.

[332] "Dr. Bonacci Wins Election for Mayor: Has Majority of 440 Over Dominic Rubatt – Several New

Faces on City Council" *Iron River Miner*, April 8, 1938.

[333] "Dr. Bonacci Wins Again for Mayor: Has Majority of 28 Over DeRubeis and Williams – 5 New Face on City council," *Iron River Miner*, April 5, 1940.

[334] "City council Has Lengthy Meeting; Votes Funds for Water Drilling Project; Rejects Purchase of New Grader," *Montreal River Miner*, August 5, 1940.

[335] "Council Proceedings," *Iron River Miner*, July 11, 1941.

[336] "License Committee OK's 29 Bartenders' Licenses," *Iron River Miner*, July 25, 1941.

[337] "Mayor Bonacci for 5th Term: Hurley Mayor Defeats DeRubeis; Third Ward Race Close," *Ironwood Daily Globe*, April 8, 1942.

[338] "Appoint Firemen," *Iron River Miner*, May 8, 1942.

[339] "State Officers Make Raid on Hurley Vice Dens; 51 Arrested," *Iron River Miner*, August 7, 1942.

[340] "City Employes Get Increases: Hurley Council Approves Pay Recommendations at Meeting," *Ironwood Daily Globe*, May 5, 1943.

[341] "Trio Given Prison Terms," *Iron County News*, October 6, 1944.

[342] "New Administration Moves in At Hurley City Hall May 1," *Montreal River Miner*, April 30, 1948.

[343] "Comment on Sports," Sir Riley, *Montreal River Miner*, July 2, 1948.

[344] "Social," *Iron County News*, April 22, 1949.

[345] "Proceedings of Joint School District No. 1," *Iron County Miner*, July 24, 1953

[346] "Four Candidates for Board Chairman," *Iron County Miner*, April 13, 1956.

[347] "Recreation Program Meeting," *Iron County Miner*, June 1, 1956.

[348] "Bill Zell is Hurley Recreation Leader," *Iron County Miner*, June 8, 1956.

[349] "City Authorizes Buying of Gov. Bonds," *Iron County Miner*, July 27, 1956.

[350] "Patritto Names as Scout Drive Head," *Iron County Miner,* November 13, 1964.

[351] "Hurley Council Proceedings," *Montreal River Miner*, May 21, 1948

[352] James R. Lawless, born in 1907, lived in Winchester. He was married to Blanche, born in 1909 to Thomas and Swea LaBlonde. Together, they operated the Congress Bar on the corner of Silver Street and U.S. 51. James died in 1989 in Wakefield, and Blanche died in 1997.

[353] "State Agents Raid Gambling Dens at Hurley, Arrest Six," *The Wisconsin State Journal*, May 3, 1948.

[354] "State Agents Raid; "Not Guilty," is Tavernkeepers' Plea," *Iron River Miner*, May 7, 1948.

[355] "License Revocation Hearings Monday," *Montreal River Miner*, June 4, 1949.

[356] "Council Argues Loud and Long Over Liquor Licenses," *Montreal River Miner*, July 2, 1949.

[357] "Roach Denies Report He Will Quit," *Sheboygan Press*, August 10, 1948.

[358] "Roach to Take Calverts Public Relations Post," *The Capital Times*, August 14, 1948.

[359] Roach would continue to reside at 2115 Van Hise Street, in Madison.

[360] "Report Roach Will Take Job with Distillery," *The Capital Times*, August 8, 1948.

[361] "Pay Fines on Gambling Counts: Six Seized in Raids Saturday Night Turn over $1,375 in Court," *Iron County News*, August 27, 1948.

[362] "State Raids Hurley Area," *Waukesha Daily Freeman*, August 23, 1948.

[363] "Pay Fines on Gambling Counts: Six Seized in Raids Saturday Night Turn over $1,375 in Court," *Iron County News*, August 27, 1948.

[364] "State Press: in Hurley, *The Rhinelander Daily News*," September 8, 1948.

[365] "Other Editors Say: Incorrigible Hurley," *Waukesha Daily Freeman*, September 11, 1948.

[366] "New Office Holders: State Capital Letter," *Waunakee Tribune*, October 7, 1948.

[367] "Roach Quits Beverage Tax Division Today: to Join Calvert Corp.; David Prichard is Named Acting

Director," *The Capital Times*, August 23, 1948.

[368] *Montreal River Miner*, November 5, 1948.

[369] Ibid.

[370] Paul and Antonette Cestkowski emigrated from Poland. They had two daughters, one being Agnes, born in 1910. Agnes married Edward Perlberg in 1929 but divorced in 1944. Agnes lived in Ironwood and died in 1976.

[371] Buddy Howell fails to appear in any official record. His real name has likely been lost. There are many "Buddy Howells" in ancestry records, but none match up with any events in Iron County.

[372] "Nab 6 in Game Raid at Hurley; One at Wausau," *The Capital Times*, December 13, 1948.

[373] Cedric Parker, "Hurley Gamblers Get 'Tip-off' on Raid, But Games Still Run: Knew 12 Days in Advance That State's Agents Had Been in City," *The Capital Times*, December 26, 1948.

[374] The *Iron County Miner* was, and still is, located at 216 Copper Street, three blocks west and one block south of the "lower block,' far enough away to be considered in the sanctimonious area.

[375] AFC, "Disappointed in Hurley Saga: Hurleyites Regret Expenditures of 15 Cents to Purchase the Alleged 'Stirring Story'; Tale is Only Reasonably Accurate, But Pretty Dull!," *Iron River Miner*, December 17, 1948.

[376] Panucci's were the name for an Italian bread, cooked in rolls about the same dimension as a dinner roll. The name is not common, but I think it could be loosely interpreted as a "little bread."

[377] "Brazen Robbery Takes Place at Rodeghiero Bakery; Loot $27," *Montreal River Miner*, January 7, 1949.

[378] "Find Body of Montreal Man," *Montreal River Miner*, January 14, 1949.

[379] "Forecasts," *Ironwood Daily Globe*, January 6, 1949.

[380] "Obituaries: Julius Barto," *Iron County News*, January 14, 1949.

[381] "Speed Cops Grab Drunken Drivers," *Iron County News*, May 7, 1926.

[382] "Rennebohm Signs Bill Transferring Beverage Cigarette Tax Bureaus," *The La Crosse Tribune*, March 17, 1949.

[383] "Hurley Never Quits – Roach Knows," *The Rhinelander Daily News*, April 7, 1949.

[384] "Trio Involved in Shooting Sentenced," *Montreal River Miner*, May 27, 1949.

[385] In one account, Burgoyne said that he brought the gun just to frighten Bertolini. When he pulled it, Bertolini threw a bottle at him and that is why he shot him in the arm. Also, Burgoyne argued that he carried the gun because he was afraid of Bertolini. Despite the bullet hole in the wall, he denied he shot at Mrs. Bertolini. He also said that Bertolini placed the money on the bar rather than taking from the till. Apparently, the judge didn't buy his story.

[386] "Hurley Tavern Operator Shot Twice in Holdup Early Today," *Ironwood Daily Globe*, May 12, 1949.

[387] "Two Arrested After Shooting, Matt Bertolini is Gun Victim," *Montreal River Miner*, May 13, 1949.

[388] "Nab Pair in Shooting of Hurley Tavernkeeper," *The Capital Times*, May 12, 1949.

[389] "Burgoyne Held to Circuit Court," *Iron County News*, May 20, 1949.

[390] Armand Cirilli, "About Things and People...," *Montreal River Miner*, May 20, 1949.

[391] "Marguerite Cole to Serve Longer Term," *Ironwood Daily Globe*, January 12, 1950.

[392] "Man in Hurley Shooting Affair Given Freedom," *Iron County Miner*, February 8, 1952

[393] "Thirsty, Try to Break Down Tavern Door After 1 a.m.," *Iron County News*, May 20, 1949.

[394] "Five Tavern Operators Fined: Officer Make Arrests for Keeping Open After Closing Hours, *Iron County News*, May 20, 1949.

[395] "State Agents Visit Hurley; Three Taverns Pay $1,400 Fines," *Montreal River Miner*, May 27, 1949.

[396] "Licenses to be Revoked Will Expire on June 30," *Montreal River Miner*, June 17, 1949.

[397] "Ban on Gambling to Stick, Pledge," *The Capital Times*, June 4, 1949.

[398] "Raid 9 Night Clubs in Vilas, Iron Counties: Mattingly Leads 21 Agents in Crack-Down on Gambling, Prostitutions," *The Capital Times*, July 12, 1949.

[399] "Gambling, Vice Raid by Agents," *The Montreal River Miner*, July 15, 1949.

[400] "State Agents Raid 3 Hurley Nightspots," *The Capital Times*, August 11, 1949.

[401] "State Agents Here Again," *The Montreal River Miner*, August 12, 1949.

[402] Phil Drotning, "State Journal Reporter Learns First Hand – Gambling Still Flourishes at Hurley," *Wisconsin State Journal*, August 22, 1949.

[403] "Still at the Head of the List is Hurley," *Waukesha Daily Freeman*, August 23, 1949.

[404] Phil Drotning, "Hurley Gamblers Bide Their Time: Residents Cite Tradition, Wait for Lid to Lift," *Wisconsin State Journal*, August 23, 1949.

[405] "Under the Dome: Reform? Hurley Never Heard of It!," *The Wisconsin State Journal*, August 23, 1949.

[406] John Wyngaard, "Drotning Most Successful Young State Politico in Recent Years, *Marshfield News Herald*, June 26, 1951

[407] https://prabook.com/web/phillip_thomas.drotning/566840

[408] "About People and Things," *Montreal River Miner*, September 2, 1949.

[409] "We Help Hurley Make a Vow," *Wisconsin State Journal*," September 13, 1949.

[410] Armand F. Cirilli, "About People and Things…, *Montreal River Miner*, September 23, 1949.

[411] Mark Schorer, "Wisconsin," *Holiday Magazine*, July 1949.

[412] Armand F. Cirilli, "Gets Ink…on Slick Paper: Holiday Magazine Revives Old Stuff in Wisconsin Article; Rowdy, Roaring Town of 2,000 Souls, 80 Taverns, Says Tale," *Iron River Miner*, June 17, 1949.

[413] "Gambling 'Down and Will Stay Down,' Says Hurley Chief," *Montreal River Miner*, September 2, 1949.

[414] "State Asks 3 License Revocations," *Montreal River Miner*, September 9, 1949.

[415] "State Agents Raid County; 32 Arrested," *Montreal River Miner*, October 7, 1949.

[416] "Licenses are 'Revoked' Amid Confusion," *Montreal River Miner*, October 21, 1949.

[417] "State Men Make Calls on Taverns," *Montreal River Miner*, December 16, 1949.

[418] Armand F. Cirilli, "About People and Things," *Montreal River Miner*, January 20, 1950.

[419] "Legality Stalls 11 Tavern License Suspensions Here," *Montreal River Miner*, January 20, 1950.

[420] "12 Taverns Now Have License Suspensions From 5 to 90 Days, *Montreal River Miner*, January 27, 1950.

[421] "Minor 'Mystery' Develops from Christmas Eve Fight," *Montreal River Miner*, December 30, 1949.

[422] "Tavern Trials Stir Up Talk," *Montreal River Miner*, January 13, 1950

[423] "Judge Trembath to Rule on Tavern Suspension Proceedings Sunday," *Montreal River Miner*, January 20, 1950

[424] "12 Taverns Now Have License Suspensions form 5 to 90 Days." *Montreal River Miner,* January 27, 1950

[425] James Bernard Quigley was born in 1894 in Gile, Wisconsin, to Barney and Johanna Marcallo. His father was born in Ireland, and his mother in Italy. His WWI draft registration card showed that he was a miner at the Odanah Iron Company in Hurley. His WWII draft registration showed that he worked for Frank Stella at 321 Silver Street. He listed his younger sister, Mary Fossati, as next of kin. James Quigley died in 1961 at 67 in Iron Mountain, Michigan.

[426] "Vice Raid," *Montreal River Miner*, March 10, 1950.

[427] Armand F. Cirilli, "About People and Things…," *Montreal River Miner*, March 10, 1950.

[428] "DeRubeis is Mayor-Elect," *Montreal River Miner*, April 7, 1950.

[429] "New Newspaper to be Known as 'Iron County Miner,'" *Iron County Miner*, April 7, 1950.

[430] "State Agents Arrest 27 Tavernkeepers, *Iron County Miner*, June 9, 1950.

[431] "Tavernkeepers Pay Fines," *Iron County Miner*, June 16, 1950.

[432] "Pays Fine," *Iron County Miner*, June 23, 1950.

[433] The Hurley City Clerk's office shows that Boho also operated a tavern at 110 Silver Street.

[434] "Intoxicating Liquor License Applications," *Iron County Miner*, June 9, 1950.

[435] "D. A. Raineri Recommends Refusal of Tavern Permit to Boho." *Iron County Miner*, June 9, 1959.

[436] "Hurley Tavernkeepers Seek Licenses," *Iron County Miner*, June 8, 1950.

[437] "Hurley Council Proceedings," *Iron County Miner*, July 7, 1950.

[438] "State Official Promises Law Enforcement, *Iron County Miner*, June 16, 1950.

[439] "Nab Four in Raid at Cary," *Montreal River Miner*, August 31, 1928.

[440] "Home News," *Montreal River Miner*, May 19, 1922.

[441] "Found Guilty of Resisting an Officer," *Iron County News*, May 14, 1927.

[442] "Starts Suit Against Sheriff and Deputy," *Iron County News*, May 21, 1927.

[443] "About People You Know," *Montreal River Miner*, January 13, 1928.

[444] "Obituaries," *Montreal River Miner*, July 12, 1935.

[445] "Mayor Rubatt Re-elected; Enters on Fourth Term, *Iron County News*, April 9, 1932.

[446] "Council Proceedings," *Montreal River Miner*, May 14, 1937.

[447] Hyman M. Mark was born in Minnesota in 1891. In 1950, he operated the Kentucky Liquor House on Silver Street and the Mark Distributing Company. He served two terms in the Wisconsin Assembly in 1920 and 1924.

[448] "Words, Charges Hurled at City council Meeting," *Iron County Miner*, June 16, 1950.

[449] "Council Defeats Mayor's Veto," *Iron County Miner*, June 23, 1950.

[450] Armand Cirilli, "About People and Things," *Iron County Miner*, June 23, 1950.

[451] "Hunt Continues for Assailant," *Ironwood Daily Globe*, July 21, 1950.

[452] "Stabbing Here," *Iron County Miner*, July 21, 1950.

[453] "Hill Pleads Innocent in Stabbing Affair," *Iron County Miner*, August 18, 1950.

[454] "Hill Sentenced to Prison Term," *Ironwood Daily Globe*, September 19, 1950.

[455] As told to me by the owner of 314 John Street. Many years after these raids, a realtor listed the 2,500-square-foot "residence" at 314 John Street as a 14-bedroom house.

[456] "Keeper of Disorderly House, Inmates Arrested," *The Evening Telegraph*, August 4, 1950.

[457] "Nine Arrested in Raid on Gambling House," *The Evening Telegraph*, September 11, 1950.

[458] "Drury Killed by Shotgun Slugs," *Decatur Herald*, September 27, 1950.

[459] "Politico Mysteriously Murdered in Chicago," *The News-Review*, September 26, 1950.

[460] "Capone Given Summons in Crime Probe," *Ironwood Daily Globe,* September 21, 1950.

[461] "Senate Probers to Check on Chicago Crime, Says Wiley," *Ironwood Daily Globe,* September 28, 1950.

[462] Robert T. Loughran, "Ralph Capone, Once Overshadowed by Al, Now 'Syndicate' Director, *The Terre Haute Star*, July 27, 1950.

[463] M Woodiwiss. "Capone to Kefauver: Organized Crime in America." *History Today*, June 1987.

[464] A couple of different versions of this story came out at the meeting of the city council. The story

related seems to be the most accurate.

[465] "Tavern Brawl Sets Off Furore," *Iron County Miner*, October 14, 1950.

[466] "'Exotic Dancer' Arraigned Here." *Iron County Miner,* October 20, 1950.

[467] Ibid.

[468] "Hurley Building Destroyed by Fire: Damage of More Than $150,000 Caused by Blaze," *Ironwood Daily Globe,* November 24, 1950.

[469] "Fires Take Almost Million Dollar Toll," *Iron County Miner*, December 1, 1950.

[470] Ibid.

[471] "Fire at Hurley Breaks Out Anew: Damage Estimated at About $13,000. *Ironwood Daily Globe,* December 2, 1950.

[472] "Epidemic of Fires Continues," *Iron County Miner*, December 8, 1950.

[473] "7 Fined After Raid on Lincoln County House of Ill Repute," *Wisconsin State Journal*, October 25, 1949.

[474] "'Blondie's Place' Closed by Court," *The Rhinelander Daily News*, January 3, 1951.

[475] Wikipedia Contributors, "Walter J. Kohler Jr.," *Wikipedia, The Free Encyclopedia*, April 15, 2020.

[476] "The Planned Community of Greendale, Wisconsin-Image Gallery Essay, undated, https://www.wisconsinhistory.org/Records/Article/CS370

[477] "6 Disorderly Houses' Raided in East County," *The La Crosse Tribune*, January 28, 1951.

[478] "Fine Five Women After Vice Raid," *The Capital Times*, February 15, 1951.

[479] DA Starts Crackdown on Prostitution," *The La Crosse Tribune*, March 30, 1951,

[480] Armand F. Cirilli, "About People and Things…," *Iron County Miner*, March 23, 1951.

[481] "Dismiss Hurley Assault Cases," *Ironwood Daily Globe,* April 18, 1951.

[482] "Hurley Tavern Keepers Fined," *Ironwood Daily Globe,* April 25, 1951.

[483] "Tavern Operator, Girl Involved in a Brawl." *Iron County Miner*, May 25, 1951.

[484] "Trials of Two Hurley Persons Postponed," Iron County Miner, Mune 8, 1951.

[485] "1951 Convention Fourth on Range, "*Ironwood Daily Globe*, June 21, 1951.

[486] Steven J. Rajkovich was born in 1891 in Austria, and Agnes Punice in 1896 in Yugoslavia. They married in 1920 in Bessemer, Michigan. By 1940, they had nine children: five girls and four boys. John Steven, the middle son, was born in 1923 when the family lived at 802 Division Street in Hurley. His 1942 WWII draft registration showed that he lived in Cicero, Illinois, and worked for Trop-Aire, Inc.

[487] "9 Arrested in Hurley Raids Go to Court," *The Capital Times*, June 26, 1951.

[488] Agatino Joe DiGiorgio was born in 1915 in Hurley. His father was Dominic DiGiorgio, and his mother was Josephine Franco. In 1940, they lived on First Avenue South in Hurley, and in 1945, he married Pearl Mattson. He died in 1980 in Iron Mountain, Michigan.

[489] Jerome "Julius" Mattei (pronounced Ma-Tay') was born in 1902 in Corsica. He emigrated to the United States and worked as a miner. He married Pauline, and they lived in Pence. The 1940 census shows they had five children: Angeline, 14; Julius, 11; Carl, 9; Frank, 5; and Phillip Anthony, 1. Julius Mattei was born on September 27, 1928, in the small mining town of Pence, five miles west of Hurley. His mother was the former Pauline Alfonsi and his father, a French immigrant named Jerome Mattei. He had three younger brothers: Karl, Frank, and Phillip and one older sister, Angeline.

[490] Lois Gasbarri "Frenchy", (Jack Gasbarri's first wife) *was* born on September 5, 1913, in McKenzie County, North Dakota. Her parents were Lawrence Bannon and Sadie Cartwright. She grew up in St. Paul, Minnesota. After her second year of high school, at 16, she traveled to Hurley in 1929. She became known as "Frenchy." The 1940 Census[490] shows her living at 9 Silver Street. She listed that she had been born in

Florida and that she was married. She was, in fact, at that time married to Jack. Lois and Jack spit sometime before 1968. Lois continued to work the Silver Street taverns until she retired in 1975. Lois L. "Frenchy" Gasbarri died at 80 on March 12, 1994.

[491] "Trouble Continues on Lower End; Revocation is Threatened as Charges Fly Thick and Fast," *Iron County Miner*, July 20, 1951.

[492] "Slot Machines Whirl in County Court – Fail to Pay Off," *Iron County Miner*, July 20, 1951.

[493] "'Not Guilty,' Say Seven in Vice Case," *The Rhinelander Daily News,* September 15, 1951.

[494] "Federal Jury Opens Capone Income Probe: U.S. Revenue Bureau in Claim All Assets Not Listed by Mercer Man." *The Capital Times*, September 10, 1951

[495] "Ralph Capone Now at New Lodge at Mercer," *The Capital Times*, June 13, 1942.

[496] R. K. DeArment, "'Two-Gun' Hart: The Prohibition Cowboy," undated. Note: on HistoryNet, DeArment tells a brief but compelling story about James Vincenzo Capone aka Two-Gun Hart https://www.historynet.com/two-gun-hart-the-prohibition-cowboy.htm

[497] "Capone's Wisconsin family on TV," *The Journal Times*, September 9, 1990.

[498] "The Last Capone," Dir. John Gray, Turner Network Television, 1990.

[499] Cedric Parker, "Now Manager of Mercer Bar is Son of Capones' 'Lost Brother,'" *The Capital Times*, September 20, 1951.

[500] "Capone's Brother to Testify Friday," *The Capital Times*, September 20, 1951.

[501] Cedric Parker, "Ralph Capone Blames Family Name for Probe by Federal Grand Jury," *The Capital Times*, September 21, 1951

[502] Billy's Bar was then purchased by Mr. and Mrs. Leonard Maes of Chicago in June of 1953.

[503] Cedric Parker, "Grand Jury Witness to Testify Ralph Capone is 'Honest, Hard-working," *The Capital Times*, September 24, 1951.

[504] Cedric Parker, "Ralph Capone is Trying to Make Good, Mercer Priest, Residents Agree," *The Capital Times*, September 25, 1951.

[505] "County Residents Appear in Ralph Capone Tax Investigation Case," *Iron County Miner*, September 21, 1951.

[506] "Ralph Capone Tax Charges are Dropped," *The Capital Times*, November 21, 1952.

[507] "New Tax Move Against Capone," *The Capital Times*, March 22, 1955.

[508] "Ralph Capone Pays Tax Bill; Another Waits," *Janesville Daily Gazette*, February 13, 1958.

[509] "Ralph Capone Asks Police for Privacy," *The Eau Claire Daily Telegram*," July 3, 1958.

[510] G. Milton Kelly, "Probe Can't Find 'Missing' Gang Barons." *The Capital Times*, February 25, 1959.

[511] Bruce Staser, "U.S. Marshall Has Little Need for a 6-Shooter Today," *The Capital Times*, May 20, 1959.

[512] "Editorially Speaking: Hurley Maligned Again," *Iron County Miner*, September 11, 1959

[513] Cedric Parker, "Now Manager of Mercer Bar is Son of Capones' 'Lost Brother,'" *The Capital Times*, September 20, 1951.

[514] "U.S. Sells Property of Capone," *The Capital Times,* March 16, 1963.

[515] "Blast Rocks Neighborhood of 123rd And Western Ave." *Blue Island Sun-Standard*, March 21, 1963.

[516] "Call on FBI to Investigate Latest Chicago Area Bombing," *Streator Times-Press*, March 19, 1963.

[517] "U.S. Still Trying to Collect Taxes from Ralph Capone," *Janesville Daily Gazette*, November 22, 1965.

[518] "Got Evidence as Kohler Warned Sheriffs," *The Capital Times*, December 14, 1951.

[519] "Kohler Orders 4 Sheboygan 'House' Raids, *The Eau Claire Leader-Telegram*, December 15, 1951.

[520] "State Vice Raid," *The La Crosse Tribune*," December 15, 1951.

[521] "Four Sheboygan Joints Raided," *Janesville Daily Gazette*, December 14, 1951.

[522] "Fine Five Women After Raid," *The Capital Times*, February 15, 1951.

[523] "Sheboygan Woman Faces Tax Lien," *Kenosha Evening News*, March 22, 1952.

[524] Armand Cirilli, "About People and Things…", Iron County Miner, February 1, 1952

[525] "Large Scale 'Shoplifting' Uncovered." January 4, 1952.

[526] "State Men Make Arrests Here," *Iron County Miner*, January 18, 1952.

[527] "Vice Cases Set for Trial Next Week," *Iron County Miner*, February 1, 1952.

[528] "$2,000 in Fines Levied in 5 Cases: State agents Hint 'Padlocking,'" *Iron County Miner*, February 8, 1952.

[529] The spelling of Julies Mattei's surname is in question. The 1930 U.S. Federal Census Records clearly shows the surname spelled "Mattie." However, the 1940 is less clear and throughout the record, it is spelled at Mattei and pronounced "Matt-tay'." My sense is that the census taker misspelled it from the pronunciation received.

[530] 'Fire Destroys Two Local Taverns," *Iron County Miner*, April 4, 1952.

[531] "$30,000 Loss in Fire at Hurley Early Today: Blaze Destroys Two Taverns on Silver Street," *Ironwood Daily Globe,* March 28, 1952.

[532] 'Fire Destroys Two Local Taverns," *Iron County Miner*, April 4, 1952.

[533] "County Officers Testify at Madison," *Iron County Miner*, May 16, 1952.

[534] "Grand Jury Puts Finger on Hurley." *Iron County Miner*, May 16, 1952.

[535] "Postpone Hurley Tavern Cases Again," *Iron County Miner*, May 9, 1952.

[536] "W. Matrella Being Held on Serious Charge," *Iron County Miner,* July 30, 1954.

[537] "Hurley Tavern Keeper Sentenced on Mann Act," *Leader-Telegram*, January 27, 1955.

[538] "Hurley Taverns Hit a New Low," *Iron County Miner*, June 27, 1952.

[539] "Three Taverns Padlocked Here," *Iron County Miner*, July 18, 1952.

[540] "Taverns to Post Bonds to Avert Padlocking," *Iron County Miner*, August 1, 1952.

[541] John Rocco Kalasardo was born in 1913 in Melrose Park, Illinois, to Jim Kalasardo and Mary Scabone. He was married to Teresa nee Julseth from Minnesota. Together, they ran the Band Box at 9 Silver Street. John died in 1980 at the age of 67, and Teresa died in 1985 at 73.

[542] "Pandering" is acting as a go-between a prostitute and a customer.

[543] "Vice Raids," *Iron County Miner*, August 15, 1952.

[544] "Open After-hours: Three are Arrested," *Iron County Miner*, October 3, 1952.

[545] Mickey's "Rendezvous" was often spelled as "Rondevoo."

[546] "State Men in Red Nab 5 Taverns," *Iron County Miner*, November 28, 1952.

[547] "Mattei Convicted on Gambling Charge," *Iron County Miner*, December 19, 1952.

[548] "Mattei Found Guilty: Will Appeal Case," *Iron County Miner*, December 26, 1952.

[549] "Woman Tavern Owner Pays a $400 Fine," *Iron County Miner*, February 6, 1953.

[550] Thomas James Chiolino was born on September 29, 1934. His father was James, and his mother was Angela Gentile. He lived in Ironwood and later in Minocqua. He died on May 8, 1994, at 59 years of age.

[551] "Tavernkeeper is Freed at a Jury Trial," *Iron County Miner*, September 26, 1952.

[552] "Two Jailed on Dope Count," *Iron County Miner*, September 5, 1952

[553] "3 Pled Guilty; One Pays Fine of $400," *Iron County Miner*, October 3, 1952.

[554] "Arrest Woman in Tavern Shooting Affray," *Iron County Miner*, October 31, 1952.

[555] "Woman Tavern Owner Held for Trial," *Iron County Miner*, December 5, 1952.

[556] "'Hung Jury' in Shooting Case," *Iron County Miner*, February 27, 1953.

[557] "Mrs. Lois Gasbarri Gets Jail Sentence and Fine," *Iron County Miner*, May 29, 1953.

[558] "Two Girls Face Narcotic Charge," *El Paso Times*, September 7, 1952.

[559] "Dope Case to Begin In Court Here Today," *Wisconsin State Journal*, June 9, 1953.

[560] "Charges Dropped by Jury: Evidence Lacking on Postal Job 'Pressure'," *The Capital Times*, January 21, 1953.

[561] "Testify on Heroin," *The Capital Times*, June 9, 1952.

[562] "Five Testify in Dope Case at Madison," *Iron County Miner*, June 12, 1953.

[563] "Testify on Heroin," *The Capital Times*, June 9, 1953.

[564] "2 Ex-Hurley Dancing Girls Testify at Dope Trial Here," *Wisconsin State Journal*, June 10, 1953.

[565] "Is Found Guilty In Heroin Sale," *The Capital Times*, June 10, 1953.

[566] "Man Sent to Prison for Heroin Sale," *The Capital Times*, August 24, 1953.

[567] Aldric Revell, "State Tax Agents No Longer to Raid Disorderly Houses: No Workmen's Compensation," *The Capital Times,* January 8, 1953.

[568] "Jury Eyes St. Paul White Slave Ring," *Eau Claire Leader-Telegram*, January 23, 1953.

[569] "Indict 3 for White Slavery," *The La Crosse Tribune*, January 27, 1953.

[570] "Policeman Being Tried," *Kenosha Evening News*, September 30, 1953.

[571] "John Carli to Face 4 Charges on Friday," *Iron County Miner*, February 13, 1953.

[572] "Bulletin!," *Iron County Miner,* February 20, 1953.

[573] "3 Slot Machines Found Here," *Iron County Miner*, February 27, 1953.

[574] "Two Hurley Tavernkeepers are Fined," *Iron County Miner*, March 13, 1953.

[575] "Allow Transfer of J. Mattei's License," *Iron County Miner*, March 13, 1953.

[576] Frank Orsonne (Orsoni) was born in 1886 on the French island of Corsica, where he married Jeromine Giacomoni. They emigrated to Montreal, Wisconsin, and Jeromine had three daughters and five sons. One of the boys was Andrew Ambrose Frank Orsoni, born in 1914. Andrew died in 1995 in Ashland, Wisconsin.

[577] "Tavernkeepers Pay Fine for 'After-hours' Charge." *Iron County Miner*, May 1, 1953.

[578] "Open After-hours; Pays $35 Fine Again," *Iron County Miner*, May 15, 1953.

[579] "State Agents Raid Again," *Iron County Miner*, May 29, 1953.

[580] "State Agents Nab Tavern Men Again," *Iron County Miner*, June 26, 1953.

[581] "State Agents Nab 25 Innkeepers in County," *Iron County Miner,* August 7, 1953.

[582] Adele Josephine Petri was born in 1919 in St Paul, Minnesota, to Charles Petri and Catherine White. Charles was Italian, and White was born in England. Adele married Roy Smith in 1935 in Northwood, Iowa, but the marriage broke up within ten years, and she reverted to her original surname. Adele Petri died in 1990, in Pence, at 71.

[583] "State Raids Hurley Again," *Iron County Miner*, November 27, 1953.

[584] A "disorderly roadhouse' carried a lesser charge than a "house of ill repute" when sentencing. However, in common use, these terms are often used synonymously.

[585] "$1,400 Levied in Fines in Seven Tavern Cases," *Iron County Miner*, December 18, 1953.

[586] "Vita's Tavern License Suspended for 90 Days," *Iron County Miner,* January 15, 1954.

[587] Same as bingo.

[588] "Of Beano game Pays $100 Fine." *Iron County Miner*, December 18, 1953.

[589] "Woman Jumps from Window of Tavern," *Iron County Miner*, April 10, 1953.

[590] "Man Arrested on Morals Count," *Iron County Miner*, April 10, 1953.

[591] "Morals Case to Circuit Court," *Iron County Miner*, April 17, 1953.

[592] "Judge Denies Habeas Corpus Petition," *Iron County Miner*, May 15, 1953.

[593] "Transfer Morals Case," *Iron County Miner*, May 22, 1953.

[594] There is no record of a marriage license, and it is presumed that Patrick Judge and June Judge were married. There is an obituary in the October 7, 1960, Wisconsin Rapids Daily Tribune for 32-year-old Patrick Judge. His age matches that of the Patrick Judge in Hurley. Further, the obituary states that he had been living in Milwaukee before he died in an Oconomowoc hospital. The obituary says that he married the former Beverly Hamm. So, to a large extent, marriage of June and Patrick Judge is conjecture.

[595] "Mattei and Mrs. Judge Each Fined $250," *Iron County Miner*, July 3, 1953.

[596] "To Appeal Case," *Iron County Miner*, July 17, 1953

[597] "Morals Trial Set for Next Tuesday at Superior, *Iron County Miner*, September 4, 1953.

[598] "Judge Found Guilty at Superior," *Iron County Miner*, September 11, 1953.

[599] The fact that Delores Nelson, Mrs. Patrick Judge, and June Judge are the same person is derived by the sequence of events in the newspaper stories.

[600] "Circuit Court Starts Monday," *Iron County Miner*, December 4, 1953.

[601] "Circuit Court Trials Over," *Iron County Miner*, December 18, 1953.

[602] "Patrick Judge Begins Serving Prison Term," *Ironwood Daily Globe*, October 8, 1954.

[603] This issue raises a lot of questions. A wouldn't be difficult for a good fiction writer to describe the circumstances whereby Dolores Nelson would be highly motivated to abandon her circumstances. Perhaps someone was chasing or threatening her, and her only option was the window. What sort of motivation would be required from someone to leap from a second story? Could she have been in a lover's triangle and have threatened do spill the beans on certain circumstances? We will never know but a good fiction writer could fill in the blanks.

[604] "Hurley Clean as A 'Hound's Tooth,'" *Iron County Miner*, April 24, 1953.

[605] "Hearing Set on Revocation Action: Mayor Asks for 'Repeal' of two Tavern Permits," *Iron County Miner*, April 17, 1953.

[606] Could those "three or four days" that Patrick Judge stayed at Frenchy's have been coincidental with the leaper?

[607] "Two Tavern Licenses Revoked Here," *Iron County Miner*, April 24, 1953.

[608] "Appeal Made on Revocations: State Man will represent City, Says DeRubeis," *Iron County Miner*, May 1, 1953.

[609] "Court Acts in Mattei Tavern Case," *Iron County Miner*, June 5, 1953.

[610] "Writ is Dismissed in Hurley Tavern Case, *Iron County Miner*, June 26, 1953.

[611] Armand Cirilli. "About People and Things," *Iron County Miner*, April 24, 1953.

[612] Arne Wickland was born in Gile, Wisconsin, and while attending Lincoln High School in Hurley, he was a reporter for the Iron County Miner newspaper. He earned a bachelor's degree from University of Wisconsin–Madison and a law degree from University of Wisconsin Law School. He practiced in Hurley and served in the Wisconsin State Assembly from 1951-1953. He then was a right-of-way attorney for the state of Wisconsin and a Wisconsin Highway Supervisor. From 1964 to 1972, he served as Iron County judge. Arne H. Wicklund. (2024, January 16). In *Wikipedia*. https://en.wikipedia.org/wiki/Arne_H._Wicklund

[613] "Another Boom in Prostitution in Wisconsin," *The Capital Times*, April 30, 1953.

[614] "Local Officials Testify at Hearing on Bill Permitting Vice Raids," *Iron County Miner*, May 1, 1953.

[615] "Council Reject Tavern License Application," *Iron County Miner*, May 15, 1953.

[616] Armand F. Cirilli, "About People and Things," *Iron County Miner*, May 22, 1953.

[617] "Prichard Talks to Tavernkeepers," *Iron County Miner*, May 29, 1953.

618 "Suspended Cop Denies Aiding Street Girls," *Albert Lea Evening Tribune*, October 2, 1953.

619 "White Slaver Gets Term in Prison," *Albert Lea Evening Tribune*, December 22, 1953.

620 "Montreal Man Fined $115." *Iron County Miner*, June 19, 1953.

621 "18 Hurley Tavern Licenses are Granted," *Iron County Miner*, July 3, 1953.

622 "61 Taverns are Licensed Here." *Iron County Miner*, July 3, 1953.

623 "Gov. Kohler Signs anti-Vice, Other Bills," *Iron County Miner*, July 10, 1953

624 Alton L. Blakeslee, "Find Women Have Longer Sex Life: Roaring '20s Brought New Wave of 'Freedom.'" *The Capital Times*, August 20, 1953.

625 John Hunter, "Says Local Authorities Give Little or No Help in Vice, Liquor Raids," *The Capital Times,* August 26, 1953.

626 Dan Satran, "One O'clock Closing is Unpopular and Unjust," *Iron County Miner*, August 21, 1953.

627 Armand F. Cirilli, "About People and Things," *Iron County Miner*, August 21, 1953.

628 "Lawlessness in the North; are Laws That Interfere with Profits to be Ignored," *The Capital Times*, August 28, 1953.

629 Armand F. Cirilli, "About People and Things," *Iron County Miner*, September 4, 1953.

630 "'Suspicious" Fire Here Wednesday," *Iron County Miner*, September 11, 1953.

631 "Club Fire Being Investigated," *Iron County Miner*, September 18, 1953.

632 Armand F. Cirilli, "About People and Things," *Iron County Miner*, September 25, 1953.

633 "This or That," *The Eau Claire Leader-Telegram*," September 27, 1953.

634 Armand F. Cirilli, "About People and Things," *Iron County Miner*, September 25, 1953.

635 Armand F. Cirilli, "About People and Things," *Iron County Miner*, October 2, 1953.

636 "Those Downstate 'Holy' Cities," *Iron County Miner*, October 2, 1953.

637 Armand F. Cirilli, "About People and Things," *Iron County Miner*, October 16, 1953.

638 "Piano Player Arrested," *Iron County Miner*, October 2, 1953.

639 "Entertainer Being Held on Dope Charge," *Iron County Miner*, October 9, 1953.

640 "10 Tavernkeepers Face Revocation of Licenses." *Iron County Miner*, October 23, 1953.

641 George Lawrence Reardon was born on December 5, 1907, in Hurley, Wisconsin, to Isadore (Helen) Scott, from Rochester, New York, and John Francis Reardon, from Ontario, Canada. George married Leona Haus, who died in 1949 at 43. George Reardon died in 1999 at 91.

642 "8 Tavern Licenses are Suspended," *Iron County Miner*, December 11, 1953.

643 "Two Hurley Tavern Cases Postponed," *Iron County Miner*, December 11, 1953.

644 "Four Appeal Revocation Order," *Iron County Miner*, December 18, 1953.

645 Armand F. Cirilli, "About People and Things," *Iron County Miner*, October 23, 1953.

646 Havens Wilber, "Hurley's Mayor Says His City is 'Pushed Around,'" *The Capital Times*, October 15, 1953.

647 "Tavernkeeper to be Charged with Assault," *Iron County Miner*, October 23, 1953.

648 "Matrella Assault Case is Dismissed; John Carli Arraigned," *Iron County Miner*, October 30, 1953.

649 "Carli Found Guilty on Three Counts," *Iron County Miner*, November 6, 1953.

650 "Circuit Judge Denies Motion," *Iron County Miner,* November 26, 1954.

651 "Circuit Court Cases Settled," *Iron County Miner,* December 17, 1954.

652 Ibid.

653 Armand F. Cirilli, "About People and Things," *Iron County Miner*, November 6, 1953.

654 Armand F. Cirilli, "About People and Things," *Iron County Miner*, December 4, 1953.

655 "Trembath Head Masons," *Iron County Miner*, December 11, 1953.

[656] "Hurley Taverns Hit Most in State," *The Rhinelander Daily News*, December 21, 1953.

[657] "State Agents Raid Beano Game Tues. Night," *Iron County Miner*, January 8, 1954.

[658] Armand F. Cirilli, "About People and Things," *Iron County Miner*, January 8, 1954.

[659] "Woman Brandishes Gun; Gets Jail Sentence," *Iron County Miner*, January 29, 1954.

[660] "Bulkowski Bound Over to Circuit Court," *Iron County Miner*, February 19, 1954.

[661] "Circuit Court Will Try Four Cases," *Iron County Miner*, May 21, 1954.

[662] Armand F. Cirilli, "About People and Things," *Iron County Miner*, March 12, 1954.

[663] "Council Grants Tavern Licenses to 61," *Iron County Miner*, July 2, 1954.

[664] Bernard was born in Bessemer, Michigan, in 1904.

[665] "State Men Raid Here; Arrest 17," *Iron County Miner*, April 9, 1954; *Iron County Miner*, June 11, 1954; "State Agents Nab 22," *Iron County Miner*, May 7, 1954; '4 Tavernmen Pay Fines." *Iron County Miner*, May 28, 1954; "State Men Make Another Big Raid Saturday," *Iron County Miner*, August 6, 1954.

[666] "Entertainers Pled Guilty," *Iron County Miner*, July 9, 1954.

[667] "Pay Fines on State Charges," *Iron County Miner*, August 13, 1954.

[668] Armand F. Cirilli, "About People and Things," *Iron County Miner*, August 13, 1954.

[669] "Morals Case Goes to Jury," *Wausau Daily Herald*, April 26, 1955.

[670] "U.S. Grand Jury Convenes Here," *Wisconsin State Journal*, December 7, 1954.

[671] "Grand Jury Questions Some Hurleyites," *Iron County Miner*, December 10, 1954.

[672] Calumet City straddles the Illinois/Indiana border and references to both either are accurate.

[673] "Hurley Men Held on Mann Act Charges," *Iron County Miner*, December 17, 1954.

[674] "Trial Set on Charge of Transporting Woman," *Manitowoc Herald Times*, February 17, 1955.

[675] "Dismiss Mann Act Count in Hurley Case," *Iron County Miner*, April 29, 1955.

[676] "Receives 2 ½ Years, *Wisconsin State Journal*," June 28, 1955.

[677] "Gets Prison Term for 'White Slavery,'" *Iron County Miner*, June 24, 1955.

[678] "'Guilty on Two Count's White-Slave Ruling," *Iron County Miner*, October 21, 1955.

[679] "Gary Man Sentenced for 'White Slavery,'" *Wisconsin State Journal*, November 2, 1955.

[680] Ken McCormick, "'The FBI Puts the Heat on Hurley,'" *Detroit Free Press*, July 11, 1954.

[681] Armand F. Cirilli, "About People and Things," *Iron County Miner*, July 30, 1954.

[682] "Two Ironwood Lads 'Purloin' Squad Car," *Iron County Miner*, September 10, 1954.

[683] "Ironwood Young Man Gets Probation," *Iron County Miner*, September 17, 1954.

[684] Armand F. Cirilli, "About People and Things," *Iron County Miner*, November 19, 1954.

[685] Lewis C. Reimann, "Letters to the Editor," *Iron County Miner*, February 4, 1955.

[686] Armand F. Cirilli, "About People and Things," *Iron County Miner*, February 4, 1955.

[687] Armand F. Cirilli, "About People and Things," *Iron County Miner*, May 27, 1955.

[688] "Thee Hurley Boys Admit Burglary," *Iron County Miner*, November 19, 1954.

[689] "Slate Hearing in Burglary Case," *Iron County Miner*, November 26, 1954.

[690] "Fracas at the Bowery Bar," *Iron County Miner*, December 24, 1954.

[691] "3 Face Trials for Assault," *Ironwood Daily Globe*, December 20, 1954.

[692] "A. Carli Faces Assault Trial," *Ironwood Daily Globe*, January 5, 1955.

[693] "Alfred Carli is Bound Over to Circuit Court, *Iron County Miner*, January 7, 1955.

[694] "Garber Sues Carli for $161,000," *Iron County Miner*, February 11, 1955.

[695] "Grand Jury Threat is Ended," *Iron County Miner*, February 4, 1955.

[696] "Carli Suing J. Garber for $456,000," *Iron County Miner*, March 11, 1955.

[697] "New, More Serious Charges Placed Against Carlis," *Iron County Miner*, May 20, 1955.

[698] Judge Trembath defined the use of the term "privy." He said that "when the term is used as an adjective it has been held to mean 'admitted to the participation of knowledge with another of a secret transaction,' private knowing, and secretly cognizant' and also that it has been held that privy means that it 'conveys the idea of a special or particular knowledge, or of such cognizance as implies active consent or concurrence.'" *Rhinelander Daily News*, June 24, 1954.

[699] "Mayhem Case Hearings Held," *Iron County Miner*, June 2, 1955.

[700] "John Carli Faces Trial on Mayhem Charge in Hurley," *The Rhinelander Daily News*, June 24, 1955.

[701] "Carli Trial Opens Today," *Ironwood Daily Globe*, March 14, 1956.

[702] "Mayhem Trial Ends at Hurley, *Ironwood Daily Globe*, March 16, 1956.

[703] "Carli Given Stay in Prison Term." *Ironwood Daily Globe*, June 27, 1956.

[704] "Judge Considers Newest Appeal in Carli Case," *Iron County Miner*, July 27, 1956.

[705] "Judge Denies Motions Made in Carli Case," *Ironwood Daily Globe*, August 7, 1956.

[706] "Carli to Appeal to State Court," *Ironwood Daily Globe*, May 2, 1957.

[707] "J. Carli Appeals Prison Sentence." *Ironwood Daily Globe*, October 8, 1957.

[708] "Justices Study J. Carli Case," *Ironwood Daily Globe*, November 11, 1957.

[709] "Must Serve 1 year for Biting Ear," *The Capital Times*, December 3, 1957.

[710] "J. Carli Asks for Rehearing," *Ironwood Daily Globe*, December 26, 1957.

[711] "Carli Starts Serving Sentence at Waupun." *Ironwood Daily Globe*, June 26, 1958.

[712] "Time for Action!," *Iron County Miner*, December 24, 1954.

[713] The Bowery moved from 24 to 101 Silver Street (previously occupied by the Kentucky Club tavern in June 1954.

[714] "Hurley Mayor Calls Meeting of Council," *Ironwood Daily Globe*, December 22, 1954.

[715] "Hearing to Revoke Bowery License Friday," *Iron County Miner*, December 31, 1954.

[716] "Hurley Council Acts to Revoke Tavern License," *Ironwood Daily Globe*, December 27, 1954.

[717] "Hurley Council Votes to Revoke Tavern License," *Ironwood Daily Globe*, December 31, 1954.

[718] "Order Prevents City from Taking Tavern License," *Ironwood Daily Globe*, January 3, 1955.

[719] "Judge Upholds Council Action," *Ironwood Daily Globe*, January 11, 1955.

[720] "Tavern License Action is Dismissed by State Supreme Court," *Iron County Miner*, March 18, 1955.

[721] "Supreme Court Order Revocation is Received," *Iron County Miner*, March 25, 1955.

[722] "License is Rejected," *Iron County Miner*, April 15, 1955.

[723] "License Request is Denied," *Iron County Miner*, March 11, 1955.

[724] "Mayor Vetoes Bartender Permits," *Iron County Miner*, June 17, 1955.

[725] "Hurley Council Grants License by & to 3 Vote," *Ironwood Daily Globe*, March 14, 1956.

[726] "License Matters Occupy Council," *Iron County Miner*, March 16, 1956.

[727] "D. A., Sheriff Make 'After-hours' Arrests," *Iron County Miner*, February 25, 1955.

[728] "Three Tavern Men Arrested; Deny Charges," *Iron County Miner*, July 1, 1955. P.6

[729] "State Agents in Vice Raid Here," *Iron County Miner*, March 18, 1955; "State Agents 'Park' in Hurley; More Arrests," *Iron County Miner*, July 22, 1955; On March 12, 1955, agents arrested Matt Bertolini of Frenchys, James Gasbarri of Jackpot's Flame, James Francis of the Doll House, Joe Vita of the Hi-Ho, John Rajkovich of the French Casino, and John Sauro of the Riverside. Then, on July 7, the state agents arrested Lois Gasbarri of Frenchy's Holiday Inn, Guido Fontecchio of Freddy's Bowery, Hjalmer Harris of Jackpot's Flame, and John Rajkovich at the French Casino. In the final state raid for 1955, agents arrested Andrew Rodeghiero of Smokeys and the only double offender, Lois Gasbarri of Frenchy's Holiday Inn. Lois Gasbarri was the only keeper arrested twice for the same offense in 1955.

[730] The lower two blocks of Silver Street were in the first ward.

[731] Armand F. Cirilli, "About People and Things," *Iron County Miner*, August 4, 1955.

[732] The worst offenders from the August 26, 1955, raid included John Sauro, of the Riverside, Hjalmer Harris, of the Flame, John Rajkovich from the French Casino, Steve Trochim at the Hi-Ho, Fred Fontecchio, Jr. of the Bowery Club, Guido Fontecchio of the Club Francis, Margaret Prickett of Margaret's, Lois Gasbarri from the Holiday Inn, Naomi Willard, of Connie's Drumstick, Gilbert Boatz of the Club Carnival, Teresa Kalasardo from the Band Box, and Andrew Holappa, of the Blackhawk.

[733] "Hurley Tavernkeepers are Arraigned in Court," *Iron County Miner,* September 2, 1955.

[734] "Jury Clears Mattrella in $102,000 Assault Suit," *Iron County Miner*, June 10, 1955.

[735] "$300 Fine Levied in Liquor Case," *Ironwood Daily Globe*, November 23, 1956.

[736] "Two More Actions in Tavern Fracas," *Iron County Miner*, April 22, 1955.

[737] "Jury Clears Mattrella in $102,000 Assault Suit," *Iron County Miner*, June 10, 1955.

[738] "Sulo Hellen Signs Complaints Against 5 Hurley Tavernkeepers," *Iron County Miner*, June 10, 1955.

[739] "Deny Motion for New Trial in Hellen Case," Iron County Miner, August 12, 1955.

[740] *The Father – Luigi Brunello*
Luigi Louis P. Brunello was born in 1864 in San Giacomo, Treviso, Italy. He had seven sons and four daughters with Katarina Covello between 1894 and 1914. Two of the sons were Arthur, born in 1912, and August Joseph, born in 1914. Luigi died in 1936 at the age of 72.

The Oldest Son – Arthur Brunello
Arthur Brunello married and lived in the Town of Kimball, west, and north of the city of Hurley. He was a farmer and bootlegger who lived in the Town of Kimball, and the story is told in "The Arthur Brunello Incident" in 1995. He died in Carey at the time of his death in 1976 at the age of 64.

The Younger Son – August Brunello
He was involved in the "Mayday Raid in the Lady's Room" in 1948 at the Bank Club at 220 Silver Street, the "The 6th Raid of 1949 Comes to Trial and Things Get Complicated" road in 1950, and "Raids as a Way of Life" in 1953. August died in 2006 at the age of 92.

[741] This is the name of the road according to the official entry in the 1950 census. It is now Valley Road.

[742] "Still Found in Hurley." *Wisconsin State Journal*, May 8, 1955.

[743] "A. Brunello Gets Probation," *Iron County Miner*, May 20, 1953.

[744] "State Starts Action to Close Seven Taverns," *Iron County Miner*, July 1, 1955.

[745] "Four Hurley Taverns Named in Injunctions," *Iron County Miner,* August 19, 1955

[746] "Tavernkeepers, Others Pay $8,000 in Fines in '54 and to June, '55," *Iron County Miner*, July 22, 1955.

[747] Armand Cirilli, "About People and Things," *Iron County Miner,* September 9, 1955.

[748] Armand Cirilli, "About People and Things," *Iron County Miner,* October 28, 1955.

[749] "Woman Bound Over for Murder Trial," *La Crosse Tribune*, December 22, 1955.

[750] "Woman Guilty in Antigo Killing," *The Capital Times*, April 18, 1956.

[751] "20% of Hurley Taverns Face Closing," *Iron County Miner,* November 4, 1955.

[752] "Padlocks Fixed on 2 Taverns; License Suspensions in Effect," *Iron County Miner,* November 11, 1955.

[753] "Fines Paid by Two Tavernkeepers," *Iron County Miner,* November 25, 1955.

[754] Andrew A. Holappa was born in 1901 and died in 1971 at 69 in Hurley.

[755] Hjalmer Harris Harju was the only son of Minnie Wainionpaa and Aukusti Harris Harju "Charles Harris." He was born in 1907 and lived in Montreal and Carey, Wisconsin. Harris died in Bessemer in 1971

at 64.

[756] "Tavernkeepers Pay Fines of $500," *Iron County Miner,* December 2, 1955.

[757] "Two Hurley Bars Ask Court for Stay," *Iron County Miner,* December 9, 1955.

[758] "Council Votes to Transfer License," *Iron County Miner,* December 16, 1955.

[759] "Band Box and Club Carnival Submit to License Suspension, *Iron County Miner,* January 6, 1956.

[760] "State Men Make Arrests on Liquor, Gambling Counts," *Iron County Miner,* February 3, 1956; "3 Tavernkeepers Pay Total of $575 in Fines," *Iron County Miner,* March 2, 1956; "State Agents Make Arrests in Hurley Taverns," *Iron County Miner,* March 30, 1956; "Police to Enforce Tavern Laws," *Iron County Miner,* May 11, 1956; "8 Tavernkeepers Pay After-Hours Fines," *Iron County Miner,* May 25,1956; "Police Still Cracking Down on Hurley Taverns, *Iron County Miner,* June 8, 1956; "4 Tavern Operators Fined," *Iron County Miner,* June 22, 1956; "Three Hurley Tavern Operators Pay $50 Fines," *Iron County Miner,* July 6, 1956; "Tavernkeeper Fined $50," *Iron County Miner,* July 13, 1956; "Tavernkeeper Fined $70," *Iron County Miner,* August 3, 1956; "Tavern Man Pays $75 Fine," *Iron County Miner,* September 7, 1956; Matt Bertolini was reported to be despondent because of ill health and on September 26, the 50-year-old took his life; "Jury Trials on Vice Charges," *Iron County Miner,* October 12, 1956; "Two Women Change Plea and are Fined," *Iron County Miner,* October 19, 1956; "Women Change Pleas and are Fined," *Iron County Miner,* November 2, 1956; "Tavernkeeper Fined," *Iron County Miner,* October 26, 1956.

[761] "Two Tavern Keepers Pay $50 Fine." *Iron County Miner*, July 20, 1956.

[762] Rick Kogan, "A Chicago Tavern: A Goat, a Curse, and the American Dream," Lake Claremont Press, Chicago.

[763] "Enforcement of Tavern Laws Draws Protest," *Eau Claire Leader-Telegram*, March 28, 1956.

[764] Armand Cirilli, "About People and Things," *Iron County Miner,* May 11, 1956.

[765] "Tavern Licensing After Convictions Hit by Prichard," *The Capital Times*, June 21, 1956.

[766] "Council Grants 54 Tavern Licenses," *Iron County Miner,* June 29, 1956.

[767] Armand Cirilli, "About People and Things," *Iron County Miner,* June 29, 1956.

[768] Complete lists of those receiving licenses have previously been omitted from the text as they had less relevance for the period. The lists are provided here so the reader can appreciate the interrelated ownerships of the tavern owners and bartenders during this time in Hurley.

[769] "Refuse License to Violators, Plea to Hurley: State Says the City Has Necessary Power," *Ironwood Daily Globe,* September 19, 1956.

[770] "Estes Kefauver 'Comes to Town,'" *Iron County Miner,* September 28, 1956.

[771] "State Tax Department Seeking Investigators," *The Eau Claire Leader-Telegram,* October 21, 1956.

[772] $51,000/year today.

[773] Armand Cirilli, "About People and Things," *Iron County Miner,* September 28, 1956.

[774] Tryge M. Ager and Robert T. Smith, *Minneapolis Star Tribune,*" November 12, 1956.

[775] Armand F. Cirilli, "Newest Yard on Hurley Has Something Old, Something New," *Iron County Miner,* November 16, 1956.

[776] "Milwaukee Man Arrested on Misconduct Charge," *Iron County Miner,* November 30, 1965.

[777] "Milwaukee Man Pays $40 Fine," *Ironwood Daily Globe*, November 30, 1956.

[778] "Man Drops Dead on Silver Street," *Iron County Miner,* December 28, 1956.

[779] "State Agents Make 9 Arrests," *Iron County Miner,* March 15, 1957; "Tavern Man Pays $125 Fine," *Iron County Miner,* April 5, 1957; "Hurley Operators Enter Pleas," *The Rhinelander Daily News,* March 30, 1957; "State Men Make Arrests in County," *Iron County Miner,* July 26, 1957.

[780] "Change Plea; Tavern Men Fined," *Iron County Miner,* August 2, 1957.

[781] "Hurley Man Acquitted on Gambling Charge," *Iron County Miner,* August 16, 1957.

[782] "Prickett Vice Case to Circuit Court," *Iron County Miner,* August 23, 1957; "Tavernkeeper Fined," *Iron County Miner,* July 26, 1957.

[783] "Tavernkeeper Fined $250; Beer Sale to Minor," *Iron County Miner,* September 27, 1957; "Tavernkeeper Fined $250," *Iron County Miner,* October 18, 1957.

[784] "Ask Revocation of 4 Licenses," *Iron County Miner,* April 19, 1957.

[785] "Council Grants License for Club Carnival." *Iron County Miner,* June 21, 1975.

[786] "Tavern Man Pays $125 Fine," *Iron County Miner,* July 12, 1975.

[787] "Tavern Licenses are Suspended," *Iron County Miner,* May 31, 1975.

[788] "Tavern Keeper Fined $125," *Iron Count Miner*, September 20, 19057.

[789] "Sheriff Concedes Langlade County Has Prostitution," *The Capital Times,* January 28, 1957.

[790] Wikipedia contributors, "Fred R. Zimmerman," Wikipedia, The Free Encyclopedia, https://en.wikipedia.org/w/index.php?title=Fred_R._Zimmerman&oldid=951012509 (accessed June 6, 2020).

[791] Bailey was also known as Margaret or Marguerite M. Koerner.

[792] "Oneida County Prosecutor Warns 'Houses' to Close," *Iron County Miner*, August 13, 1943.

[793] "'Ma' Bailey Fined $600 as 'Keeper,'" *The Rhinelander Daily News,* August 22, 1944.

[794] "'Ma' Bailey Fined $800 as Of Disorderly House." *The Rhinelander Daily News*, August 30, 1951.

[795] "State Secretary Accused of Interfering with Court Action," *The Eau Claire Leader-Telegram,* September 1, 1951.

[796] "Top State Official 'Interceding' in Ma Bailey Case, Claim," *The Rhinelander Daily News*, August 30, 1951.

[797] "'Ma' Baily Action, 'Highly Improper.'" *The Rhinelander Daily News*, August 31, 1951.

[798] "'Ma' Bailey Has Defenders Among Woodruff Neighbors," *The Rhinelander Daily News*, September 1, 1951.

[799] "'Ma' Bailey Says She's Known State Official for Years," *The Rhinelander Daily News*, September 1, 1951.

[800] "'Ma' Bailey Must Face Trial, Edict of Judge Boileau," *Janesville Daily Gazette*, September 17, 1951.

[801] Harland Carl played football for the University of Wisconsin Badgers in 1950. He was exceptionally quick.

[802] Miles McMillin, "'Ma Bailey Outburst a Bit Delayed,'" *The Capital Times*, October 6, 1951.

[803] "'Ma' Bailey, Two Others Bound Over to Circuit Court," *The Rhinelander Daily News*, June 12, 1957.

[804] "'Ma' Bailey Fined, Given Probation in Morals Case," *The Rhinelander Daily News*, December 3, 1957.

[805] "Winona Murphy Fined $100." *Green Bay Press Gazette*, June 27, 1950.

[806] "Two Arraigned After Vice Raaid at Bellevue Bar," *Green Bay Press Gazette*, March 18, 1957.

[807] "Two fined $650 Each on Two Vice Charges,' *Green Bay Press Gazette*, June 17, 1957.

[808] "Oneida Indian New Brown Co. Sheriff," *Wausau Daily Herald*, November 8, 1956.

[809] "Sheriff Wants Single Trial on State Counts," *The Eau Claire Leader-Telegram*, January 20, 1956; "Retiring Sheriff Will Ask County Government Probe," *Janesville Daily Gazette*, November 1, 1956; "Brown Co. Elects Indian Sheriff," *La Crosse Tribune*, November 8, 1956; "Two Arraigned After Vice Raid At Bellevue Bar," *Green Bay Press-Gazette*," March 18, 1957; "Two Fined $650 Each on Two Vice Charges," *Green Bay Press-Gazette*," June 17, 1957; "Brown County Sheriff Denies All Charges of Illicit House Operator," *Leader-Telegram*, March 1, 1958; 'Sheriff Cleared by Thomson's Decision: Governor Can Fine No Evidence of Wrong-Doing by Brown Co. Officer," *Appleton Post Crescent,* April 21, 1958; Elliott

Maraniss, "Paid Skenandore for 'Protection,' Ex-Madam Asserts, *The Capital Times,* July 16, 1958; "Former Sheriff Testifies Against Skenandore: Reuben Lasee Tells of Brown County Official's Long Visits to Clipper Inn," *Appleton Post Crescent*, July 17, 1958; "Thomson Mulls Sheriff Hearing," *Racine Journal Times*, August 7, 1958; "Check Transcript on Sheriff Hearing," *Racine Journal Times*, August 27, 1958; John Wyngaard, "Thomson Moves to Clear Skenandore: Sheriff was 'Extremely Indiscreet' in Actions, Judge tells Governor," *Appleton Post Crescent*, October 20, 1958.

[810] "Miner Editor to Take Welfare Director Job, *Iron County Miner,* December 20, 1957.

[811] "Fined for Selling Beer to Minors," *Iron County Miner,* March 14, 1958; "Two Tavern Men Pay $390 in Fines and Costs," *Iron County Miner,* April 18, 1958; "Charges Filed Against Three Tavernkeepers," *Iron County Miner,* May 9, 1958; "Tavern Operator Fined," *Iron County Miner,* August 1, 1958; "Tavernkeepers Fined," *Iron County Miner,* October 3, 1958; "Tavern Operators Pay Fines on Vice," *Iron County Miner,* December 19, 1958; "18 arraignments Pleas Innocent as State Men Make Hurley Invasion," *Iron County Miner,* November 21, 1958; "Four Charges Costly to Tavernkeeper," *Iron County Miner,* January 9, 1959; "'Girls' Pay Fines," *Iron County Miner,* December 5, 1958; "Tavern Operators Pay Fines on Vice," *Iron County Miner,* December 19, 1958; "Agents Hit Hurley Two Weeks in Row," *Iron County Miner,* November 28, 1958.

[812] "Gets 5 Years Probation," *Iron County Miner,* June 6, 1958.

[813] "Fadness, State Agent, Dies During Raid," *Iron County Miner,* September 5, 1958.

[814] "Youth to Stand Trial for Window Smashing," *Iron County Miner,* October 24, 1958.

[815] "Window Breakers are Sentenced on Tuesday," *Iron County Miner,* October 31, 1958.

[816] "John Carli Freed from Prison," *Iron County Miner,* January 9, 1959.

[817] "Carli Files Second Suit for $50,000 Damages at Hurley, *The Rhinelander Daily News*, September 3, 1959.

[818] "Hurley Rejects Carli's Claim," *Ironwood Daily Globe,* May 13, 1959.

[819] "Hurley, Officers Named in Case." *Ironwood Daily Globe,* May 25, 1959.

[820] "Hurley Employs Merrill Lawyers," *The Rhinelander Daily News*, June 12, 1959.

[821] "Dismiss Suit," *The Capital Times,* August 12, 1959.

[822] "Carli Case Trial Set for Monday," *The Rhinelander Daily News*, June 24, 1960.

[823] "Carli's $50,000 Suit Dismissed," *Ironwood Daily Globe,* June 27, 1960.

[824] "Commission to Study Testimony," *Ironwood Daily Globe,* September 16, 1960.

[825] "Carli's Charges Are Dismissed, *Ironwood Daily Globe*, November 8, 1960.

[826] "Hurley Council Proceedings," *Iron County Miner,* December 9, 1960.

[827] "Hurley Council Proceedings," *Iron County Miner*, July 7, 1961.

[828] "Hurley Council Proceedings," *Iron County Miner*, July 20, 1962.

[829] "Eight Arraigned on Vice Charges by State," *Iron County Miner,* November 27, 1949.

[830] "Four Tavernkeepers Pay $1,150 in Fines," *Iron County Miner,* December 4, 1959; "Six Fined on tavern Law Violations," *Iron County Miner,* August 12, 1960.

[831] "Judge Disqualifies Himself in Theft Case," *Iron County Miner,* July 17, 1959.

[832] Ancestry.com. Global, Find A Grave Index for Burials at Sea and other Select Burial Locations, 1300s-Current [database on-line]. Provo, UT, USA: Ancestry.com Operations, Inc., 2012.

[833] on February 11, 1980, the Slipper Club would be the site of a murder where Sheila Martin shot Ronald Fortune. The judge sentenced Martin to 20-years.

[834] "Floyd Calligaro Cleared in Case: Ref-Face Suspect Hunted in Slaying," *Ironwood Daily Globe,* December 23, 1959.

[835] "Entertainer's Death Probed," *The Decatur Daily Review*, December 22, 1959.

[836] "Wife of Ironwood Man Found Slain: Floyd Calligaro Given Lie Tests," *Ironwood Daily Globe*, December 22, 1959.

[837] Tony Holloway, "Homicide Verdict Returned in Death of Peoria Dancer: Police Still Hunt Man with Red Face," *The Pantagraph*, January 21, 1960.

[838] "George Sullivan Appointed Judge by Gov. Nelson," *Iron County Miner*, January 29, 1960.

[839] Anton "Tony" Lysczyk was born in Bessemer in 1921. His parents, Michael and Amelia, emigrated to Michigan from Poland in 1907 and had six children, with Anton being the youngest. Michael Lysczyk was a carpenter and worked for a local mine. Tony Lysczyk died in 2015 in Hurley. Marcia Lyon and Tony Lysczyk were partners in business and life for many years.

[840] "Hurley Council Grants Licenses for 51 Taverns," *Iron County Miner*, June 15, 1960.

[841] "Deny Vice Charges," *Iron County Miner*, July 22, 1960.

[842] "Six Fined on Tavern Law Violations," *Iron County Miner*, August 12, 1960.

[843] "Tavern Operator Turns in License," *Iron County Miner*, September 23, 1960.

[844] "Tavernkeepers Fined $1,500." *Iron County Miner*, September 30, 1960.

[845] "Woman is Fined, Put on Probation," *Ironwood Daily Globe*, December 22, 1960.

[846] "Tavern Operator Pleads Guilty," *Iron County Miner*, October 13, 1961.

[847] "2 Tavern Keepers Pay Court Fines," *Ironwood Daily Globe*, March 14, 1961.

[848] "Hurley Men at Work in Hurley Again," *Iron County Miner*, September 1, 1961.

[849] "A. J. Raineri to Run for County Judgeship," *Iron County Miner*, February 3, 1961.

[850] "Licenses of Two Bars Suspended," *Ironwood Daily Globe*, February 18, 1961.

[851] "Taverns Ordered to Close at 1 O'clock," *Iron County Miner*, March 17, 1961.

[852] "Sullivan Wins Race for County Judge," *Iron County Miner*, April 7, 1961.

[853] "Federal Agents Close Hurley Nightclub," *Iron County Miner*, May 26, 1961.

[854] "Hurley Council Proceedings," *Iron County Miner*, July 7, 1961.

[855] "Barmaid is Bound Over in Shooting," *Ironwood Daily Globe*, June 12, 1961.

[856] "Gets 5 to 25 Years for Murder Here," *Iron County Miner*, November 10, 1961.

[857] "Hurley Man's Killer Escapes," *Ironwood Daily Globe*, May 28, 1962.

[858] "Trial in East is Scheduled for Inmate," *Fond Du Lac Commonwealth Reporter*, January 31, 1966.

[859] "Mystery Shrouds Shooting of Man," *The Kentucky Post and Times-Star*, October 15, 1948.

[860] "Newport Pair Held in Gun 'Accident;' Victim to Hospital," *The Cincinnati Enquirer*, October 16, 1948.

[861] "Suitor Charged with Shooting At Girl In 19 Club Building," *The Cincinnati Enquirer*, November 18, 1949.

[862] "Gun Wielder Asks Release to Obtain Gaming Warrants." *The Cincinnati Enquirer*, November 23, 1949.

[863] "Led Banker to Card Game, Got $1,640, Drive Admits," *The Cincinnati Enquirer*, May 20, 1950.

[864] "Wilders Club May Be Padlocked," *The Kentucky Post*, May 20, 1950.

[865] "Smithson Declines to Aid Grand Jurors," *The Kentucky Post and Times-Star*, October 5, 1950.

[866] "New Plea Is Filed for James Harris," *The Kentucky Post and Times-Star*, February 22, 1956.

[867] "James Harris To Quit Prison," *The Kentucky Post and Times-Star*, May 15, 1958.

[868] "Doom Sealed for Stardust?" *The Kentucky Post and Times-Star*, January 10, 1959.

[869] A layoff bet is a type of bet made by a bookmaker to balance the amount of money placed on each

side of a wager. This helps the bookmaker avoid losing too much money and ensures that the total amount of bets is equal on both sides. Source: LSD.Law, February 23, 2024.

[870] "Campbell Vice Probe Ends Today," *The Paducah Sun*, September 12, 1961.

[871] "Jury Will Work on William Wise Case," *The Advocate-Messenger*, November 16, 1961.

[872] "Arrest Hurley Man on Grand Jury Contempt," *The La Crosse Tribune*, November 19, 1961.

[873] "Found Guilty on Contempt Charge," *Iron County Miner*, December 1, 1961.

[874] http://www.preservinggaminghistory.com/other/WHENVICEWASKING.pdf

[875] "Hurley Man to Face Tax Charge," *The Daily Telegram*, July 8, 1964.

[876] "Hurley Bar Operator Guilty on Tax Charge," *Iron County Miner,* September 4, 1964.

[877] "Newport Police Arrest Six Operators of Night Spots," *The Cincinnati Enquirer*, July 7, 1972.

[878] Michael L. Williams, "Sin City Kentucky: Newport, Kentucky's Vice Heritage and Its Legal Extinction, 1920-1991." University of Louisville. https://ir.library.louisville.edu/cgi/viewcontent.cgi?article=2573&context=etd

[879] "State Agents Charge Vice Offenses in City," *Iron County Miner*, August 14, 1959.

[880] "Tavern Keeper is Sentenced," Ironwood Daily Globe, November 1, 1960.

[881] "Fire Destroys Silver St. Bar," *Iron County Miner*, March 2, 1962.

[882] "City Council Takes Action on Licenses," *Ironwood Daily Globe*, June 14, 1966.

[883] Philip Warden, "AGVA Linked to Traffic in White Slavery: Agencies Sent Canada, Cuban Girls to U.S." *Chicago Daily Tribune*, June 20, 1962.

[884] G. Milton Kelly, "Prostitution Encouraged B-Girls Say," *The Capital Times*, June 14, 1962.

[885] "Hurley D. A. Says Girls' Charge of Imprisonment 'Probably True,'" *Leader-Telegram*, June 20, 1962.

[886] "Crackdown on Hurley Promised," *Janesville Daily Gazette*, June 21, 1962.

[887] "Hurley Has Been There – Where Has the Attorney General Been?, *The Capital Times*, June 22, 1962.

[888] "Three Hurley Arrests Precede State Warning," *Leader-Telegram*, June 22, 1962.

[889] "State and Local Officials to Cooperate on Silver St. Clean-Up," *Iron County Miner*, July 6, 1962.

[890] "City council Rejects Ordinance Suggested by State Tax Head," *Iron County Miner*, July 13, 1962

[891] "State Maps Hurley Drive," *The Capital Times*, July 16, 1962.

[892] "Hurley Officials Lay Plans for 'Crackdown,'" *Iron County Miner*, July 20, 1962.

[893] "Standing Up for Sin," *Iron County Miner*, July 20, 1962. This was a copy of an editorial in *Chicago's American* newspaper that was sent to Police Chief Geach.

[894] "Court Asked to Close Taverns," *Iron County Miner*, August 10, 1962.

[895] "Suspend License in Four Taverns," *Iron County Miner*, November 23, 1962.

[896] "Grand Jury Checks on White Slavery," *Iron County Miner*, September 14, 1962.

[897] "Two Convicted on Moral's Charges," *The Minneapolis Star*, Oct 23, 1962.

[898] "White Slaver Sentenced to Five-Year Term," *The Minneapolis Star*, November 20, 1963.

[899] "Price County Judge Dismissed Court Case," *Iron County Miner,* January 25, 1963.

[900] "Vice Charges," *Waukesha Daily Freeman*, January 27, 1954.

[901] *The Daily Telegram*, December 21, 1963.

[902] "Chief of Police Geach Resigns," *Iron County Miner*, January 4, 1963.

[903] "Fire Here Tues. Claims One Life," *Iron County Miner,* March 22, 1963.

[904] "Fireman John Gentile Gets Commendation," *Iron County Miner,* April 22, 1963.

[905] "Three Women Face Vice Charges Here." *Iron County Miner*, April 5, 1963.

[906] "State Agents Charge Eight in Co. Court," *Iron County Miner,* June 21, 1963.

[907] "At Last – The 'Hurley of The South' Gets Cleaned Up," *The Capital Times,* August 21, 1963. P52.

[908] "Gambling Raid in Ironwood," *Iron County Miner,* September 13, 1963.

[909] "Last Ore Shipped Out of Montreal," *Iron County Miner,* October 25, 1963.

[910] "Bessemer Man Pulls Gun in Local Club," *Iron County Miner,* October 25, 1963.

[911] Michael J. Barron. (2023, August 23). In *Wikipedia.* https://en.wikipedia.org/wiki/Michael_J._Barron

[912] "Hello Wisconsin: Who is Behind Drive to Make Wisconsin Part of the $22 Billion Dollar Gambling Industry?", *The Capital Times*, April 20, 1964.

[913] "State Lawmakers Tell of Offer to Help Campaigns for Gambling Law," *Green Bay Press-Gazette,* December 16, 1964.

[914] "Old Bowery Building Destroyed by Fire Here Thursday Morning," *Iron County Miner,* May 22, 1964.

[915] "Tax Chief Reports Old Habits Back at Hurley," *Stevens Point Journal,* May 29, 1964.

[916] Harvey Breuscher, Hurley Bad Spots Back in Business," *The Capital Times,* May 30, 1964.

[917] There were several significant legislative changes and court decisions in the 1980s that addressed these issues. Section 125.04(13) Wis. Stats.

[918] "Hurley Bar Operator Pays Fine Plus Taxes," *Iron County Miner,* June 19, 1964.

[919] "State and Local Backgrounders: Alcohol Taxes," The Urban Institute.

[920] https://www.salestaxhandbook.com/wisconsin/alcohol

[921] Sarah Hauer, "Wisconsin residents bought a lot of alcohol last year, causing the largest increase in alcohol taxes since 1972." *The Milwaukee Journal Sentinel*, September 8, 2021.

[922] "Hurley Women Gets Fine and Probation," *Iron County Miner,* June 26, 1964.

[923] "Council Grants More Licenses," *Iron County Miner*, July 24, 1964.

[924] "Attempted Arson in Early Fire Wed." *Iron County Miner,* July 24, 1964.

[925] "12 Arrested by State Agents," *Iron County Miner,* August 7, 1964.

[926] "Council Revues Recent Arrests," *Iron County Miner,* August 14, 1964.

[927] "3 More Charged by State Men," *Iron County Miner,* September 18, 1964.

[928] "Two Charges Are Dismissed," *Ironwood Daily Globe*, November 10, 1964.

[929] "Police at Hurley to Enforce Law," *The Daily Telegram*, November 27, 1964.

[930] "3 Hurley Strip Joints Ordered Shut: Write is Issued by Judge," *The Capital Times,* November 25, 1964.

[931] "State Tax Dept. Takes Steps," *Iron County Miner,* September 4, 1964.

[932] "County Judge G. Sullivan Dies," *Iron County Miner,* October 30, 1964.

[933] "Arne Wicklund is County Judge," *Iron County Miner,* November 13, 1964.

[934] "Seeks to Void Hurley Bar License, *The Capital Times*, September 1, 1964.

[935] "Hurley Tavern's License Revoked," *The Capital Times*, September 25, 1964.

[936] "Second Hurley License Revocation," *Janesville Daily Gazette*, October 21, 1964.

[937] "Tavern Licenses are Revoked," *Ironwood Daily Globe,* November 23, 1964,

[938] "The Time is Now," *Iron County Miner,* November 27, 1964.

[939] "Let's Follow the Rules," *Iron County Miner,* December 4, 1964.

[940] "Man Dies After Bar-Room Brawl," *Iron County Miner,* March 5, 1965.

[941] "Kivi Pleads Not Guilty," *Ironwood Daily Globe,* March 12, 1965.

[942] "Charge Against Kivi Dismissed," *Ironwood Daily Globe,* March 18, 1965.

[943] Ralph Ansami, "Hurley Murder Solved When Witness Confesses," *Ironwood Daily Globe*, February 21, 1981.

944 Paul Kending, "State Agents Raid in Our City Sunday," *Iron County Miner,* April 2, 1965.

945 "Bartender Fined $100 in Vice Case," *Ironwood Daily Globe*, June 5, 1965.

946 "Silver Street Site of New Erspamer Market," *Iron County Miner,* May 28, 1965.

947 "Council Grants Tavern Licenses to 40 Applicants, *Ironwood Daily Globe,* June 23, 1965.

948 "Gaming Equipment Seized in Milwaukee," *The Appleton Post Crescent*, August 28, 1965.

949 This was an eye-witness account told to me by Anton Lysczyk who was watching the event unfold from the second story window of Kay's at 7 Silver Street.

950 "Of Hurley Tavern is Killed: Henry Kimball, 25, is Shot on Silver Street," *Ironwood Daily Globe,* October 15, 1965.

951 "Murder Case Trial Begins," *Ironwood Daily Globe,* December 14, 1965.

952 "Trial Set in Murder Case," *Ironwood Daily Globe,* November 5, 1965.

953 "Trial Changed to Ashland," *Ironwood Daily Globe,* December 7, 1965.

954 "Murder Case Trial Begins," *Ironwood Daily Globe,* December 14, 1965.

955 "Hurley Man Gets 10-Year Prison Term," *Ironwood Daily Globe,* December 16, 1965.

956 "Last of Mines Will Close in February," *Iron County Miner,* November 26, 1965.

957 "Release Woman on Own Signature in Hurley Case," *The Capital Times*, December 10, 1965.

958 Frank Custer, "Two More Tell of Roles in Vice Spot at Hurley," *The Capital Times*, November 29, 1966.

959 1961 Travel Act, 18 U.S.C. § 1952.

960 "Investigation is on at Madison," *Iron County Miner,* December 3, 1965.

961 "U.S. Jury to Probe Hurley Rackets: Secret Sessions Set Here," *The Capital Times,* November 24, 1965

962 Armand F. Cirilli, "Pot Pourri," *Iron County Miner,* December 17, 1965.

963 Robert Meloon, "Hurley Action is Near," *The Capital Times,* December 2, 1965.

964 "Release Woman on Own Signature in Hurley Case," *The Capital Times,* December 10, 1965.

965 Robert Meloon, "Three Deny Vice Roles in Hurley," *The Capital Times,* December 16, 1965.

966 "Hurley Pair Convicted on Prostitution Count," *Waukesha Daily Freeman*, December 2, 1966.

967 Dennis Cassano, "Hurley Police Rapped in Prostitution Case," *Madison State Journal*, June 20, 1967.

968 Doug Moe, "Lawyer redefined rambunctious," *The Capital Times*, November 8, 2003.

969 The Wisconsin Bar Association suspended his law license on June 28, 1967, and wanted to disbar him. However, while the Supreme Court felt that MacIntyre's conduct was unprofessional, they suspended his license for two years instead of the lifetime ban. The Court reinstated MacIntyre's license on June 28, 1969; Robert Melloon, "MacIntyre's Law License Reinstated by State Court," *The Capital Times*, February 4, 1969.

970 "Nix to Enforce Law in Hurley," *Eau Claire Leader*, November 5, 1968.

971 Wikipedia contributors, "Billie Sol Estes," Wikipedia, The Free Encyclopedia, https://en.wikipedia.org/w/index.php?title=Billie_Sol_Estes&oldid=961808186 (as of July 13, 2020).

972 "Hurley Woman's Conviction Upset," *The Capital Times,* June 29, 1968.

973 "Charges State Officials Ignore Vice in Hurley," *The Capital Times,* March 8, 1969.

974 Alderson is same prison that housed TV personality Martha Stuart in October 2004. From personal interview with Marcia Lyon, September 5, 2007.

975 Reported to me in an interview.

976 On September 5, 2007, I interviewed Marcia and Anton that their place on Silver Street. The facility had two entrances, but they only used one. The entrance and interior of the 9 Silver Street was closed. At this

point they had both retired and lived a modest life. When I told them what I was doing, they invited me in for coffee in the back kitchen and treated me nicely. Marcia became most animated when talking about Edmund Nix, as one might imagine.

[977] "Club Carnival is Now Supper Club." *Iron County Miner,* December 17, 1965.

[978] "Editorially Speaking - - 'Grand Jury' Over, What Now?" *Iron County Miner,* December 10, 1965.

[979] "Shawano Man is Boosting Gambling in Northern Resorts," *The Capital Times*, Jan 31, 1966.

[980] Dan Satran, "Open Gambling Proposal Meeting with Resistance," *The Capital Times*, February 7, 1966.

[981] "The Department of Revenue's auditors and Alcohol and Tobacco Enforcement agents ("A&T") are working together to ensure compliance with Wisconsin laws as they apply to video gambling machines. Auditors routinely verify whether the correct amounts of Wisconsin income, franchise, sales and use taxes are reported and remitted with respect to income and gross receipts from the operation of such machines. Auditors may request assistance from A&T for purposes of determining the gross receipts from video gambling machines and whether violations of Wisconsin video gambling laws have occurred." Wisconsin TAX BULLETIN www.dor.state.wi.us Number 140, October 2004.

[982] "The Evolution of Legalized Gambling in Wisconsin, State of Wisconsin Legislative Reference Bureau, Information Bulletin 12-2, November 2012.

[983] https://wilottery.com/

[984] "Playing the Odds: State Variations in Lottery Revenues and Impacts," The Pew Charitable Trusts, 2017

[985] "State Asks for Revocations of Four Licenses," *Iron County Miner,* February 18, 1966.

[986] "Four Hurley Taverns Face Loss of License," *The Daily Telegram*, February 14, 1966.

[987] "Extent of Crime in State Causes Dispute," *The Daily Telegram*, May 9, 1967.

[988] "1969 Senate Bill 280," Chapter 141, Laws of 1969, August 15, 1969.

[989] Wis. Stats., Chapter 75, Laws of 1967

[990] "Bender Indicted for Aiding in Edgerton Embezzlement," *The Capital Times,* August 15, 1967.

[991] "Gets 18 Months for Hurley Trip with Woman," *The Capital Times,* March 7, 1968.

[992] "Don't Nix This Record," *The Capital Times,* March 11, 1968.

[993] "Jobs of Interest Male: Investigators," *Wisconsin State Journal*, January 21, 1968.

[994] "Dalton Bares State Probe of Vice," *The Capital Times*, January 19, 1968.

[995] "Window on Wisconsin," *The Capital Times*, October 7, 1968.

[996] Not to be confused with the 1963 *Warren Commission Report* headed by Chief Justice Earl Warren regarding the assassination of President John Kennedy.

[997] Omnibus Crime Control and Safe Streets Act of 1968

[998] James D. Selk, "Mafia's 'Mob' Said Operating in State," *Wisconsin State Journal*, May 22, 1969.

[999] "Stag Case Judge Was There Also," *The Capital Times,* February 11, 1969.

[1000] "Drop First Stag Party Bet Charge," *The Capital Times*, March 3, 1969.

[1001] Robert Meloon, Irvin Kreisman, Dave Zweifel, "Released Stag Figure Has Long Crime Record: Vice and Tax Violations," *The Capital Times,* March 5, 1969.

[1002] Irvin Kreisman, "Julius Mattei Gets 6-Day Term for Tax Filing Failure," *The Capital Times,* July 25, 1969.

[1003] "9 Accused for Failing to report for Draft," *Waukesha Daily Freeman*," July 2, 1969.

[1004] "Anti-Vice Drive Sought in Hurley," *Janesville Daily Gazette*, November 21, 1969.

[1005] "Hurley Witness Granted Immunity," *Wisconsin Rapids Daily Tribune*, July 16, 1970.

[1006] "Vitich Trial Resumed," *Ironwood Daily Globe*, July 16, 1970.

[1007] "Mrs. Vitich Acquitted," *Ironwood Daily Globe*, July 18, 1970.

[1008] "Three Indicted by Grand Jury," *Ironwood Daily Globe*, July 2, 1969.

[1009] "69-Year-Old Arrested for Prostitution." *Greenville Daily Advocate*, September 25, 1969.

[1010] "For the Record," *Janesville Gazette*, January 31, 1970.

[1011] "Rock Springs Stag Party---Julius Mattei---A Correction," *The Capital Times*, January 29, 1970.

[1012] "Files Libel Suit Against Local Stations," *The Daily Tribune*, April 8, 1971.

[1013] "Janesville Paper in Million Dollar Suit," *Monroe Evening News*, April 9, 1971.

[1014] Jim Hougan, "Lake Delton Chief Swears to Mattei Good Character," *The Capital Times*, August 27, 1971.

[1015] "Defamation Suit Against WKTY Radio Dismissed." *La Crosse Tribune*, May 30, 1973.

[1016] "Mattei Drops Suit Against Capital Times," *The Capital Times*, June 18, 1973.

[1017] "Housewives in Winnipeg Help Budgets with Prostitution," *The Racine-Times Sunday Bulletin*, February 8, 1970.

[1018] "Hurley Nightspot Burns to Ground," *Kenosha News*, March 9, 1971.

[1019] "Fire Destroys Hurley Taverns," *Stevens Point Daily Journal*, May 15, 1971

[1020] Reginald Stuart, "Investigators Seek Cause of Club Fire," *The New York Times*, June 1, 1977.

[1021] "Band Box Club Burns in Hurley," *Ironwood Daily Globe*, February 26, 1973.

[1022] U.S. Probes Prostitution at Hurley," *The Capital Times*, November 19, 1971,

[1023] Irvin Kreisman, "Feds Found Bugging Devices in Bedrooms at Hurley, *The Capital Times*, August 18, 1972.

[1024] "5 Women Charged in Hurley Probe," *The Capital Times*, February 24, 1972.

[1025] "D. A. is Subpoenaed to Testify on Prostitution," *The Capital Times*, July 12, 1972.

[1026] "Capsules in the News: Judge was a Cheapskate," *Waukesha Freeman*, August 3, 1972.

[1027] "Hooker from Hurley Fired for Refusing to Cut Rate for Judge," *The Capital Times*, August 2, 1972.

[1028] Irvin Kreisman, "Says Hurley Inmate Told of Being Struck by Judge," *The Capital Times*, August 3, 1972.

[1029] Irvin Kreisman, "D.A. at Hurley Did Work for Alleged Vice Houses," *The Capital Times*, August 3, 1972

[1030] "Perjury Defendant is Charged Again," *Wisconsin State Journal*, August 11, 1972.

[1031] "Women on Probation on Perjury Counts," *Manitowoc Herald Times*, August 16, 1972.

[1032] Irwin Kreisman, "'No Discount' Prostitute Get 3 Years Probation, "*The Capital Times*, August 16, 1972

[1033] Irvin Kreisman, "Feds Found Bugging Devices in Bedrooms at Hurley, *The Capital Times*, August 18, 1972.

[1034] "Hurley Bar Operators in Not Guilty Pleas," *The Capital Times*, August 25, 1972.

[1035] "Grand Jury Calls Hurley Police Chiefs," *Janesville Gazette*, October 2, 1972.

[1036] "Hurley Officers Testify in Vice Hearing," *Ironwood Daily Globe*, November 2, 1972.

[1037] Irvin Kreisman, "Jury Selection Begins in Hurley Prosecution," *The Capital Times*, November 7, 1972.

[1038] Irvin Kreisman, "'Practiced Answers' Prostitution Probe," *The Capital Times*, November 8, 1972.

[1039] Irvin Kreisman, "2 Found Guilty in Perjury Trial on Hurley Jury Probe," *The Capital Times*, November 10, 1972.

[1040] "Subpoena 12 in Vice Case," *Ironwood Daily Globe*, December 4, 1972.

[1041] Irvin Kreisman, "Hurley Operator City in Contempt," *The Capital Times,* May 5, 1973.

[1042] Irvin Kreisman, "Hurley Houses' Laundry Makes a Federal Offence," *The Capital Times,* April 14, 1973.

[1043] Irvin Kreisman, "Hurley Operator City in Contempt," *The Capital Times,* May 5, 1973.

[1044] "Fire Damages 2 Hurley Taverns," *Ironwood Daily Globe*, May 5, 1973.

[1045] "Vitich Changes Prostitution Plea," *Wisconsin State Journal,* May 18, 1973.

[1046] "Woman Guilty in Prostitute Case," *Wisconsin State Journal,* May 19, 1973.

[1047] Irvin Kreisman, "2 From Hurley Get Prison Terms; Doyle Rejects 'Condoning' Plea," *The Capital Times,* July 12, 1973.

[1048] Irvin Kreisman, *"Minocqua Club Owner Gets 6-Months Prison Sentence,"* *The Capital Times,* July 31, 1973.

[1049] "Prostitution Case Figure Charged with Perjury." *The Capital Times,* July 17, 1973.

[1050] "Prostitution Case Figure Charged with Perjury." *The Capital Times,* July 17, 1973.

[1051] "Hurley Woman Gets Probation," *Wisconsin State Journal*, August 2, 1974.

[1052] "Hurley Vice Trial Figure Found Dead," *The Capital Times,* March 5, 1973.

[1053] "Page of Opinion; Beyond Crime Stories; Still, a Good Capital City," *Wisconsin State Journal*, January 19, 1972.

[1054] "1978 Madison Police Department Annual Report," https://www.ojp.gov/pdffiles1/Digitization/69194NCJRS.pdf1978.

[1055] Patricia Simms, "Jury Here Charges 'White Slavery' Ring," *Wisconsin State Journal,* January 18, 1972.

[1056] Frank Custer, "3 Jailed Here After Forced-Vice Charges," *The Capital Times,* January 19, 1972.

[1057] Bruce Swan, "U.S. Equity Pay Action," *The Capital Times,* January 21, 1972.

[1058] Irvin Kreisman, "Sauna Quiz Resumed; Expect More Charges," *The Capital Times,* January 27, 1972.

[1059] "Sauna Defendant Artez is Freed on $20,000 Bail," *Wisconsin State Journal,* March 22, 1972.

[1060] "Artez Finally Shows Up; Jailed on $1,000 Bail on Battery Count," *Wisconsin State Journal,* March 29, 1972.

[1061] Patricia Simms, "Artez Sought for Assault in Slave Suit," *Wisconsin State Journal,* March 25, 1972.

[1062] "Court Ends Freedom for Artez," *Wisconsin State Journal,* March 31, 1972.

[1063] Patricia Simms, "Judge Boosts Bail for Artez, Notes 'More Serious Crimes,'" *Wisconsin State Journal,* April 1, 1972.

[1064] Irvin Kreisman, "Sauna Girl Drops Plea of Innocent; To Testify," *The Capital Times,* April 7, 1972.

[1065] Patricia Simms, "96 Grand Jury Indictments No Small Thing," *Wisconsin State Journal,* April 30, 1972.

[1066] "Bizarre, Sad Story Predicted as White Slavery Trial Opens," *Wisconsin State Journal,* June 6, 1972.

[1067] "Sauna Girl Claims Torture," *Portage Daily Register*, June 7, 1972.

[1068] Patricia Simms, "Sauna Employe Says Artez Tortured Her." *Wisconsin State Journal,* June 7, 1972.

[1069] Patricia Simms, "Jury Told of White Slavery Service," *Wisconsin State Journal,* June 8, 1972.

[1070] Patricia Simms, "Sauna Witness Tells of Suicide Try," *Wisconsin State Journal,* June 9, 1972.

[1071] Patricia Simms, "Artez Is Cleared of Two Charges," *Wisconsin State Journal,* June 10, 1972.

[1072] Maureen Santini, "Artez Gets 10 Years, $3,000 Fine," *Wisconsin State Journal,* June 23, 1972.

[1073] Rosemary Kendrick, "Ald. Parks Sees Hypocrisy In Nude Dancing Reaction Here." *The Capital Times,* June 24, 1972.

[1074] Irvin Kreisman, "Bardwell Sees Clear Path To Closing of Nude Joints." *The Capital Times,* June 24,

1972.

[1075] Irvin Kreisman, "Ex-Sauna Operator Pleads Guilty In Federal Court on Morals Count," *The Capital Times,* October 30, 1972.

[1076] Irvin Kreisman, "'Chico' Artez Gets 5 Years On Federal Sauna Charge," *The Capital Times,* November 1, 1972.

[1077] Irvin Kreisman, "Kathi Testifies 'Tex' Boasted of Torturing Girls at Sauna." *The Capital Times,* November 9, 1972.

[1078] "Sauna Case Witness Testifies of 'Prison,'" *Wisconsin State Journal,* November 10, 1972.

[1079] Tom Hubbard, "Simpson Stuns Courtroom with Cruel and Puritanical Tangle of His Life," *The Capital Times,* November 11, 1972.

[1080] Patricia Simms, "Simpson Convicted of Sauna Offenses," *Wisconsin State Journal,* November 11, 1972.

[1081] Irvin Kreisman, "'Tex' to Spend More Time in Dane Jail." *The Capital Times*, November 17, 1972.

[1082] Patricia Simms, "Probation Granted, and Refused," *Wisconsin State Journal,* November 29, 1972.

[1083] Irvin Kreisman, "Kathi, Of the Sauna, Gets Change to Go to School." *The Capital Times,* November 30, 1972.

[1084] Irvin Kreisman, "Tex Begs for Full Sentence, Gets Just 9 Years in Jail." *The Capital Times,* December 19, 1972.

[1085] "Diamond Don Makes God His Boss," *Wisconsin State Journal*, Aug 16, 1987.

[1086] Mike Miller, "He Was Kathi's 'Enforcer,'" *The Capital Times,* March 26, 1982.

[1087] Anita Clark, "Protesters Tour Book Store," *Wisconsin State Journal,* February 9, 1986.

[1088] "The Judge Gets An Invitation to Chico's Wedding," *The Capital Times,* November 20, 1975.

[1089] Bardwell Cuts Artez' Term," *The Capital Times,* March 25, 1976.

[1090] Anita Clark, "White-slaver Artez Charged With Transporting Teen-age Prostitutes," *Wisconsin State Journal,* November 18, 1978.

[1091] "Artez Waives Extradition to Madison on U.S. Charge," *Wisconsin State Journal,* November 30, 1978.

[1092] "Metro Digest: Artez Released On Surety Bond, "*Wisconsin State Journal,* December 1, 1978.

[1093] "Prostitution Ring Indictment Returned," *Eau Claire Leader Telegram*, December 9, 1978.

[1094] "City Briefs: Change in Artez Charge Sought," *The Capital Times,* January 3, 1979.

[1095] "Teen Alleges Beating by Artez," *The Capital Times,* March 16, 1979.

[1096] "Member of Artez's Alleged Prostitution Ring Pleads Guilty," *Wisconsin State Journal,* March 23, 1979.

[1097] "Artez Guilty On 8 Counts of Interstate Prostitution," *The Capital Times,* March 31, 1979.

[1098] "Artez Gets 15 Years for Prostitution Ring," *The Capital Times,* June 2, 1979.

[1099] "Sex Offended Moves to City's West Side," *Green Bay Press-Gazette*, December 12, 2003.

[1100] "Sex Offender Faces New Felony Charges," Green Bay Press-Gazette, December 20, 2003.

[1101] "Artez Case Likely to Go to Trial," *Green Bay Press-Gazette*, June 15, 2004.

[1102] Andy Nelesen, "Time with Teen Girls Gets Offender Prison Term," *Green Bay Press-Gazette*, August 14, 2004.

[1103] "Take Action on Buildings," *Ironwood Daily Globe*, May 17, 1973.

[1104] "Lawyer Arraigned as Pimp," *Ironwood Daily Globe,* February 17, 1976.

[1105] "Lawyer Give Up License in Scandal," *Ironwood Daily Globe,* August 3, 1976.

[1106] "FBI Asked to Probe Witness' Death," *Waukesha Daily Freeman*, October 4, 1973.

[1107] United States of America V. Jewel. United States: United States Court of Appeals for the Seventh Circuit, 1974. Page 2.

[1108] Milwaukee District Atty. Edward Michael McCann served as the DA in Milwaukee from 1968 to 2006 and in 1991, he prosecuted cannibal serial killer Jeffrey Dahlmer.

[1109] STATE v. WHITE, Supreme Court of Wisconsin, Jun 3, 1975,68 Wis. 2d 628 (Wis. 1975), 229 N.W.2d 676

[1110] Frank Custer. "Pleads Not Guilty of Murder," *The Capital Times,* June 29, 1970.

[1111] Off-Duty Officer Tells of Seeing Fatal Shot Fired on Commercial Ave." *The Capital Times,* July 8, 1970.

[1112] Robert Pfefferkorn, "Found Guilty, Odell White Gets Life Term for Murder," *Wisconsin State Journal*, November 13, 1970.

[1113] United States of America V. Jewel. United States: United States Court of Appeals for the Seventh Circuit, 1974; Ferris Jewel died in 2013 at 79.

[1114] James A. Rousmaniere, Jr., "Streaking Case to Test Whether Justice is Blind," *The Baltimore Sun*, March 22, 1974.

[1115] "Men to Face Morals Court," *Ironwood Daily Globe*, November 2, 1973.

[1116] Irvin Kreisman. "Hurley's $55 Champagne Includes Sexual Favors," *The Capital Times,* April 2, 1974.

[1117] "Man Guilty in Vice Trial," *Ironwood Daily Globe*, April 4, 1974.

[1118] "2nd Man Guilty of Vice Charge," *Ironwood Daily Globe*, April 10, 1974.

[1119] "Pair with Hurley Ties Sentenced," *The Capital Times,* June 22, 1974.

[1120] "Gets Probation in Hurley Case," *Kenosha News*, August 3, 1974.

[1121] "Judge Comments on Hurley," *Leader-Telegram*, July 30, 1974.

[1122] Irvin Kreisman. "Hurley Night Life Too Much for Visiting Judge to Take." *The Capital Times,* July 26, 1974.

[1123] "Hurley's Prostitution," *The Capital Times,* July 30, 1974.

[1124] Miles McMillin. "Hello Wisconsin," *The Capital Times,* July 31, 1974.

[1125] Armand Cirilli, "Voice of the People: Hurley Resident: Judge Less Charitable Than Lord," *The Capital Times,* August 7, 1974.

[1126] "Dancer Faces Trio of Charges After Incident," *The Rhinelander Daily News*, January 20, 1973.

[1127] "Newbold Eyes Nudity Ban," *Rhinelander Daily News*," January 14, 1975.

[1128] "Brothers' Cases Transferred," *The Rhinelander Daily News*, March 23, 1976.

[1129] "Women Dancing Nude, But Who's Complaining," *The Rhinelander Daily News*, July 22, 1986.

[1130] "Stripper Bar Attacks Hinted," *Marshfield News-Herald*, July 4, 1994,

[1131] "Woman Intimate with Cops" *Wisconsin Rapids Tribune*, February 15, 1975.

[1132] "Milwaukee Cop Fined for Stag Party Role." *The Capital Times,* March 12, 1975.

[1133] "Stag Party Probe Finished by Judge," *Stevens Point Daily*, July 17, 1975.

[1134] "Lucey Hep on Hurley," *Wisconsin State Journal,* February 18, 1975.

[1135] "'Escort Services' Offering Massages, Maybe Prostitutes," *Waukesha Daily Freeman*, April 24, 1976.

[1136] "Madison Called 'New" Hurley," *Wisconsin State Journal,* November 10, 1975.

[1137] "8 Charged in State Vice Probe," *Sheboygan Press*, October 25, 1975.

[1138] "Sid Caesar Prime Witness in State Prostitution Case," *Janesville Gazette*, January 9, 1976.

[1139] "Found Guilty of Soliciting a Prostitute," *Sheboygan Press*, January 16, 1976.

[1140] Tom Butler, "Roach Made His Life Interesting," *Wisconsin State Journal*, May 30, 1976.

[1141] "Six Seeking Three City Council Seats Including Two Incumbents," *Leader-Telegram*, March 26, 1976.

[1142] "Jail Term Ordered in Pandering Case," *Leader-Telegram*, April 13, 1976.

[1143] "Five Charged with Prostitution," *Neenah Menasha Northwestern*, March 27, 1976.

[1144] "Tart Sues for Fee Lost to Policeman," *Ironwood Daily Globe*, September 4, 1976.

[1145] Anita Clark, "Madison Vice Squad Keeps Lid on Illegal Sex," *Wisconsin State Journal*, May 22, 1977.

[1146] "Women Arrested for Prostitution," *Wisconsin State Journal*, February 24, 1977.

[1147] "Couple Charged with Pandering, Prostitution," *Wisconsin State Journal*, June 16, 1977.

[1148] "Escort Operator is Charged with Soliciting Prostitute." *Wisconsin State Journal*, April 1, 1977.

[1149] "3 Women Arrested for Prostitution." *Wisconsin State Journal*, April 15, 1977.

[1150] "Man Innocent of Soliciting Prostitutes," *Wisconsin State Journal*, May 19, 1977.

[1151] "Prostitution Termed an 'Addiction," *Waukesha Daily Freeman*, May 4, 1977.

[1152] In 1970, the Dangle "lost its liquor license because of the bottomless dancing there. The club got its license back in July 1971, after promising to eliminate nudity. The club became a jazz club and a burlesque club in the early 1970's, before nude dancing entertainment returned," *Wisconsin State Journal*, May 25, 1977.

[1153] Paul Feldman, "Soglin Suggests Push on Courts to Act on Sex Law Prosecution," *Wisconsin State Journal*, May 25, 1977.

[1154] Anita Clark, "Madison Vice Squad Keeps Lid on Illegal Sex," *Wisconsin State Journal*, May 22, 1977.

[1155] "8 Arrested in Raid on Massage Parlors," *The La Crosse Tribune*," January 18, 1978.

[1156] "Prostitution Charge, Woman to Have Trial," The *Oshkosh Northwestern*, January 4, 1978.

[1157] "Charge Two in Death of Girl, 14," *Kenosha News*, January 5, 1978.

[1158] "Denies Sex Raps," *Kenosha News*, January 31, 1978.

[1159] "Witness Tells Jury: Heard 2 Shots," *Kenosha News*, May 4, 1978.

[1160] "Murder Trial Continues: Ex-Girlfriend Alibis for Johnson," *Kenosha News*, May 6, 1978.

[1161] "Murder Trial Nearly Over: 'Hollywood' Testifies, *Kenosha News*, May 9, 1978.

[1162] "Don Jensen, "Not Guilty: Murder Trial Verdict Delivers a Real 'Hollywood' Ending, *Kenosha News*, May 10, 1978.

[1163] "Police Investigating Assault," *Kenosha News*, August 19, 1980.

[1164] "Charges for Two," *Kenosha News*, September 4, 1980.

[1165] "Court Report," *Kenosha News*, December 30, 1980.

[1166] Don Jenson, "Johnson Receives Six-Year Sentence'" *Kenosha News*, January 21, 1981.

[1167] "Court Report," *Kenosha News*, September 13, 2000.

[1168] "Bartlett Recaptured Near Jail," *Kenosha News*, January 13, 1981.

[1169] "Coin Shop Robber Draws 30 Years," *Kenosha News*, February 19, 1981.

[1170] "Burglary Suspect Held After Chase," *Kenosha News*, December 22, 2979.

[1171] "Court Report," *Kenosha News*, February 22, 1980.

[1172] "Court Report," *Kenosha News*, May 22, 1980.

[1173] "Judge OK's Reduced Tito Gooch's Sentence," *Kenosha News*, June 27, 1978.

[1174] "Younger Gooch Sentenced," *Kenosha News*, June 16, 1978.

[1175] "Judge OK's Reduced Tito Gooch's Sentence," *Kenosha News*, June 27, 1978.

[1176] "Car Slams Tree, Passenger Killed," *Kenosha News*, October 16, 1984.

[1177] "Court Report," *Kenosha News*, June 21, 1985.

[1178] "Court Report, *Kenosha News,* March 1989.

[1179] "Tavern Closed, Charges Pending," *Ironwood Daily Globe*, April 3, 1979.

[1180] "2 Hurley Men are Arrested," *Ironwood Daily Globe,* April 5, 1979.

[1181] "Wilson Bound Over on Prostitution Charge, *Ironwood Daily Globe*, April 27, 1979.

[1182] "Fire Guts Hurley Landmark Show Bar," *Ironwood Daily Globe,* April 21, 1979.

[1183] "Raineri Indicted by Grand Jury," *Ironwood Daily Globe,* June 6, 1980.

[1184] "Raineri Denies Allegations," *Ironwood Daily Globe,* June 7, 1980.

[1185] "Hold Two for Prostitution," *Ironwood Daily Globe,* June 23, 1980.

[1186] "Raineri Pleads Innocent, Trial Date August 29." *Ironwood Daily Globe,* June 25, 1980.

[1187] Dennis McCann, "Federal Evidence in Raineri Case Disclosed," *Ironwood Daily Globe,* July 23, 1980.

[1188] Dennis McCann, "Requests Moving Raineri Trial to Hurley." *Ironwood Daily Globe,* July 30, 1980.

[1189] Dennis McCann, "File 2nd Charge Against Raineri," *Ironwood Daily Globe,* August 2, 1980.

[1190] "Raineri Requests Hearing on Commission Charge," *Ironwood Daily Globe,* August 5, 1980.

[1191] Dennis McCann, "Raineri: Strange to be on Other Side of Fence," *Ironwood Daily Globe,* November 25, 1980.

[1192] Dennis McCann, "Decision Pens on Raineri Bid for Return of Pay," *Ironwood Daily Globe,* August 11, 1980.

[1193] "Raineri Denied Pay," *Ironwood Daily Globe,* August 12, 1980.

[1194] Dennis McCann, "Raineri: Strange to be on Other Side of Fence," *Ironwood Daily Globe,* November 25, 1980.

[1195] "Exam Denied in Raineri Case,' *Ironwood Daily Globe,* October 8, 1980.

[1196] Dennis McCann, "3 Raineri Motions Denied by Magistrate," *Ironwood Daily Globe,* October 24, 1980.

[1197] Dennis McCann, "Motions Dismissed in Raineri Case," *Ironwood Daily Globe,* October 31, 1980.

[1198] Dennis McCann, "Raineri: Strange to be on Other Side of Fence," *Ironwood Daily Globe,* November 25, 1980.

[1199] Dennis McCann, "Raineri: Strange to be on the Other Side of the Fence," *Ironwood Daily Globe,* November 25, 1980.

[1200] Dennis McCann, "Ex-Club Owner Takes Stand in Raineri Case," *Ironwood Daily Globe,* November 25, 1980.

[1201] Dennis McCann, "Owner's Niece, Accountant Testify at Raineri Trial," *Ironwood Daily Globe,* November 26, 1980

[1202] Dennis McCann, "Raineri Trial in 4th Day," *Ironwood Daily Globe,* December 1, 1980.

[1203] Dennis McCann, "Agent Testifies at Raineri Trial," *Ironwood Daily Globe,* December 2, 1980.

[1204] Dennis McCann, "Ex-Prostitute Testifies," *Ironwood Daily Globe,* December 3, 1980.

[1205] "Judge's Flight Testimony Disputed," *Wisconsin State Journal*, December 4, 1980.

[1206] Dennis McCann, "Say Raineri Bought Tickets," *Ironwood Daily Globe,* December 4, 1980.

[1207] Dennis McCann, "Hurley Police Officer Testifies." *Ironwood Daily Globe,* December 5, 1980.

[1208] Dennis McCann, "Government Rests in Raineri Case," *Ironwood Daily Globe,* December 6, 1980.

[1209] Dennis McCann, "Denies Mental Health Records as Evidence," *Ironwood Daily Globe,* December 8, 1980.

[1210] Dennis McCann, "Raineri Defense Case Opens," *Ironwood Daily Globe,* December 9, 1980.

[1211] Dennis McCann, "Bartenders Testify at Raineri Trial," *Ironwood Daily Globe,* December 10, 1980.

[1212] Dennis McCann, "Priest Testifies in Raineri Case," *Ironwood Daily Globe,* December 11, 1980.

[1213] Dennis McCann, "Raineri Denies Charges," *Ironwood Daily Globe,* December 12, 1980.

[1214] Dennis McCann, "Psychiatrist Must Testify," *Ironwood Daily Globe,* December 15, 1980.

[1215] Dennis McCann, "Raineri Jury Sequestered," *Ironwood Daily Globe,* December 16, 1980.

[1216] Clair Simmons, "Raineri Jury Is Sequestered," *Wisconsin State Journal,* December 16, 1980.

[1217] Dennis McCann, "Raineri Convicted on 5 Counts," *Ironwood Daily Globe,* December 18, 1980.

[1218] "Raineri Will Appeal," *Ironwood Daily Globe,* December 31, 1980.

[1219] "New Raineri Trial Sought," *Ironwood Daily Globe,* January 20, 1981.

[1220] "Sentence Date Set for Raineri," *Ironwood Daily Globe,* February 18, 1981.

[1221] Dennis McCann, "No New Raineri Trial," *Ironwood Daily Globe,* February 25, 1981.

[1222] Dennis McCann, "Raineri Gets 3 Years, $15,000 Fine," *Ironwood Daily Globe,* March 7, 1981.

[1223] Dennis McCann, "Double Standard for Hurley and Madison?" *Ironwood Daily Globe,* March 25, 1981.

[1224] Dewey Pfister, "Antigo Auction Marks End of an Era," *Wausau Daily Herald*, April 25, 1981.

[1225] "Faced with Charge, Hurley Police Officer Resigns," *Ironwood Daily Globe,* November 17, 1981.

[1226] Dennis McCann, "Raineri Report to Federal Prison," *Ironwood Daily Globe,* April 6, 1982.

[1227] "Raineri Pays Court Fine," *Ironwood Daily Globe,* October 10, 1983.

[1228] This information was collected by Kathleen Byrns, Hurley City Clerk's Office.

[1229] Pearl S. DiGiorgio nee Mattson was born in 1909 in Superior. She was the daughter of John Mattson and Sophie Abrahamson. She married Agatino DiGiorgio in 1945. Pearl S. DiGiorgio died in 1962 in Hurley.

Made in United States
Cleveland, OH
04 July 2025

18252220R00197